Historical
Archaeology
and the Study of
American Culture

Historical Archaeology and the Study of American Culture

EDITED BY

Lu Ann De Cunzo
Bernard L. Herman

The Henry Francis du Pont Winterthur Museum, Inc.
WINTERTHUR, DELAWARE

Distributed by University of Tennessee Press
KNOXVILLE, TENNESSEE

Copy Editors: Patricia Rice and Teresa Vivolo
Production Manager: Susan Randolph

Library of Congress Cataloging-in-Publication Data

Historical archaeology and the study of American culture / edited by Lu Ann
    De Cunzo, Bernard L. Herman.
        Papers from the 1991 Winterthur Conference.
        Includes bibliographical references.
        ISBN 0–912724–36–6
        1. Archaeology and history—United States. 2. Material culture—United
    States. 3. United States—antiquities. I. De Cunzo, Lu Ann. II. Herman,
    Bernard L., 1951– . III. Winterthur Conference (1991)
    E159.5.H55 1996
    930.1—dc20   96–2463
                                                                    CIP

Contents

Preface   ix
  Lu Ann De Cunzo and Bernard L. Herman

*Introduction: People, Material Culture, Context, and
  Culture in Historical Archaeology*   1
  Lu Ann De Cunzo
  Assistant Professor
  Department of Anthropology
  University of Delaware

*Introduction: Historical Archaeology and the Search for
  Context*   19
  Bernard L. Herman
  Associate Professor, Department of Art History
  Associate Director, Center for Historic Architecture
    and Engineering
  University of Delaware

CONSTRUCTION OF CONTEXT: NEGOTIATING
CONSUMER CULTURE

Archaeology from the Ground Up   35
  John Worrell
  Director Emeritus
  Research and Collections
  Old Sturbridge Village
  David M. Simmons
  Senior Archaeologist
  Old Sturbridge Village
  Myron O. Stachiw
  Director
  Research, Interpretation, and Education
  Society for the Preservation of New England
    Antiquities

Frontier Boys and Country Cousins: The Context for Choice
in Eighteenth-Century Consumerism   71
     Ann Smart Martin
     Historian
     Colonial Williamsburg Foundation

Form, Fabric, and Social Factors in Nineteenth-Century
Ceramics Usage: A Case Study in Rockingham Ware   103
     Jane Perkins Claney
     Ph.D. candidate, American Civilization
     University of Pennsylvania

Negotiating Industrial Capitalism: Mechanisms of Change
among Agrarian Potters   151
     Paul R. Mullins
     Anthropology Program
     George Mason University

European Textiles from Seventeenth-Century New England
Indian Cemeteries   193
     Linda Welters, Professor and Chair
     Margaret T. Ordoñez, Associate Professor
     Kathryn Tartleton, M.S Graduate
     Joyce Smith, Research Associate
     Department of Textiles, Fashion Merchandising, and
        Design
     University of Rhode Island

Artifacts, Networks, and Plantations: Toward a Further
Understanding of the Social Aspects of Material Culture   233
     Charles E. Orser Jr.
     Professor
     Anthropology Program
     Illinois State University

"IN THE ACTIVE VOICE": REMAKING THE AMERICAN LANDSCAPE

Pollen Analysis in Urban Historical Landscape Research   259
    Gerald K. Kelso
    Archaeologist
    Plumas National Forest, California

The Urban Landscape, the Work Yard, and Archaeological Site Formation Processes in Charleston, South Carolina   285
    Martha A. Zierden
    Curator of Historical Archaeology
    The Charleston Museum

Mind Reading the Urban Landscape: An Approach to the History of American Cities   319
    Eric Sandweiss
    Director of Research
    Missouri Historical Society

Remaking the Barnyard: The Archaeology of Farm Outbuildings in the Connecticut River Valley of Massachusetts, 1770–1870   359
    J. Ritchie Garrison
    Associate Director, Museum Studies Program
    Associate Professor of History, University of Delaware
    Associate Professor, Office of Advanced Studies
    Winterthur Museum, Garden & Library

WORKING TOWARD MEANING: THE SCOPE OF HISTORICAL ARCHAEOLOGY

Feminist Historical Archaeology and the Transformation of American Culture by Domestic Reform Movements, 1840–1925   397
    Suzanne M. Spencer-Wood
    Associate
    Peabody Museum of Archaeology and Ethnology, Harvard University

Nature, Society, and Culture: Theoretical Considerations in Historical Archaeology   447
   Stephen A. Mrozowski
   Associate Professor
   University of Massachusetts, Boston

Reinventing Historical Archaeology   473
   Mary C. Beaudry
   Associate Professor of Archaeology and
      Anthropology
   Department of Archaeology
   Boston University

Preface

Lu Ann De Cunzo
Bernard L. Herman

This volume grew out of the 1991 Winterthur Conference: Historical Archaeology and the Study of American Culture. Scott T. Swank, formerly of Winterthur Museum, first proposed that the museum devote an annual conference to historical archaeology. Without his vision of historical archaeology's contributions to American cultural studies, the conference would likely never have happened. In his conference proposal, Swank wrote that the "field appears to be at a particularly fruitful and promising juncture, . . . [with new] archaeological publications . . . altering perceptions and understandings of American history, and providing significant case studies of material culture research." Our aim in implementing his vision has been to produce a conference and a publication that would indeed alter understandings of American history and culture.

The conference, held in October 1991, explored historical archaeology with a particular emphasis on the field's unique methodological, theoretical, and interpretive contributions to historical and cultural inquiry. The interdisciplinary conference continued the Winterthur tradition of bringing together scholars from diverse fields to exchange and challenge ideas about how to make the material expressions of America's past cultures yield ever clearer insights into those cultures.

At the conference and in this volume, historical archaeology emerges as a field in which material culture stands at once at the center and at the periphery of our inquiries. Material culture occupies the center in that it is *what* historical archaeologists study and the periphery in that it is *means* to interpretation and not *end*. Material culture provides historical archaeologists with access to what the field really centers on—*culture*. This volume attests to the many ways scholars have devised to think about what culture is and how it works and the many ways to study material culture in context in order to illuminate the shadows of culture. This historical archaeology practiced in this volume emphasizes the interactive relationships among material culture, culture, and people. Material culture is understood to facilitate, reproduce, and produce social action and to produce and reproduce cultural ideas and values through the multivalent meanings it encodes in multiple contexts. Herein lies the power of material culture, and, as the study of culture through material culture, herein lies the power, potential, and challenge of historical archaeology.

Responding to ideas and perspectives exchanged at the conference and in subsequent discussions, the authors have rethought and reshaped their original presented papers, transforming them into the essays composing this volume. We present them in three sections: "Construction of Context: Negotiating Consumer Culture," " 'In the Active Voice': Remaking the American Landscape," and "Working toward Meaning: The Scope of Historical Archaeology." Each essay, however, bridges the essential themes of all three sections. The authors' searches for past meanings have required them to construct and reconstruct contexts. To be meaningful, contexts must incorporate the many, sometimes discordant voices of the people actively contributing to the unique cultures of their historical times and places. Interaction among individuals and groups led to a constant, culturally mediated negotiation of social order; in the process the material world was remade. The same attention to context and voice infuses the essays that make up this volume.

We are indebted to many people for their efforts on behalf of this volume. Scott T. Swank provided the vision, and many of his colleagues at Winterthur offered technical and intellectual assistance: Katharine Martinez, then chair of the conference committee, and committee members James Curtis, Catherine E. Hutchins, Ian M. G. Quimby, and Philip D. Zimmerman helped us move from vision to reality; research assistant Sheryl Hack aided Swank in his original planning; Patricia Elliott, office of Advanced Studies, directed the conference arrangements as only she can; and Catherine Hutchins, Gary

Kulik, Susan Randolph, Teresa Vivolo, and the Publications Division staff shepherded the volume through production. We thank the authors not only for their commitment to the highest quality scholarship but also for their patience, collegiality, and attention to endless detail. We are grateful also to the conference audience, who engaged us all in spirited and challenging discussions and sent us back to the field invigorated and thoughtful. Finally, we thank our families for the understanding and support that sustained us throughout this project.

Introduction
People, Material Culture, Context, and Culture in Historical Archaeology

Lu Ann De Cunzo

Historical Archaeology and the Study of American Culture explores historical archaeology as a means to interpret, understand, deconstruct, and reconstruct American culture both past and present. In this process of coming to know culture and cultural actors, archaeologists engage material culture. This volume's authors offer historical archaeologists and other material culture scholars creative, insightful, and powerful approaches to material culture as cultural expression. Emphases on material culture's communicative qualities, its active roles in facilitating social performance, constructing sociocultural identity, and mediating individual and group interaction and its meaninglessness outside of context transcend and link the authors' diverse perspectives and techniques.

As the reader will see, concern with context and with the cultural situatedness of scholarship resonates throughout this volume as, indeed, it does throughout cultural studies today. Archaeologists and material culture scholars must attend to the historical context of the objects, people, and places we study and to the historical context of our own scholarly traditions. It is thus appropriate if not essential to open this

The author wishes to thank her co-editor, Bernard L. Herman, and all the volume's authors for their hard work, stimulating discussions, and fine scholarship. They have influenced her thinking immeasurably.

volume with a brief foray into the historical context of historical archaeology.

The process of intellectual inquiry proceeds as each new generation of critics questions, revises, and sometimes replaces the disciplinary
canon. "Argument has raged for at least the past twenty years as to
what archaeology should be," and Eric R. Wolf has written, "In anthropology we are continuously slaying paradigms. . . . As each successive
approach carries the ax to its predecessors, anthropology comes to re-
semble a project in intellectual deforestation." In fields that transcend
the boundaries of the traditional disciplines, this process of definition,
of constructing an identity, of carving intellectual, methodological, and
substantive niches in the structure of scholarship often virtually dominate the discourse. "American Studies," Linda K. Kerber claims, "has
been a field in crisis . . . ; a field in permanent redefinition of its
subject and itself."[1]

Such self-reflexivity, which historical archaeologists inauspiciously
claim has produced "a split personality," "a serious crisis in the field,"
and "schizophrenia," has characterized the field since its emergence,
as the following quotations attest:

No one supposes that the archaeologist working around Independence Hall
will prove that the Declaration of Independence was signed in some year other
than 1776. Archaeology may be able to verify or confirm a questionable or
uncertain historical fact, . . . [but] it is unrealistic to expect much more.

— J. C. Harrington, 1955

[1] Michael Shanks and Christopher Tilley, *Re-Constructing Archaeology: Theory and
Practice* (Cambridge, Eng.: Cambridge University Press, 1987), p. 8; Eric R. Wolf,
"Distinguished Lecture: Facing Power—Old Insights, New Questions," *American Anthropologist* 92, no. 3 (September 1990): 588; Linda K. Kerber, "Diversity and the
Transformation of American Studies," *American Quarterly* 41, no. 3 (September 1989):
419. For additional perspectives on the "crisis of representation" in American studies
and related disciplines, see George Lipsitz, "Listening to Learn and Learning to Listen:
Popular Culture, Cultural Theory, and American Studies," *American Quarterly* 42, no.
4 (December 1990): 615–36; Steven Watts, "The Idiocy of American Studies: Poststruc-
turalism, Language, and Politics in the Age of Self-Fulfillment," *American Quarterly*
43, no. 4 (December 1991): 625–60. For one model of the intellectual inquiry process,
see Thomas Kuhn, *The Structure of Scientific Revolutions* (2d ed.; Chicago: University
of Chicago Press, 1970). For a critique of Kuhn's paradigms' applicability in the social
sciences, see Marilyn Strathern, "An Awkward Relationship: The Case of Feminism and
Anthropology," *Signs: Journal of Women in Culture and Society* 12, no. 2 (1987):
276–92.

The archeologist is concerned with understanding past lifeways, culture history, and culture process by examining the material remains of culture. . . . Once pattern is abstracted [from the archaeological record], . . . these demonstrated regularities are often expressed as empirical laws. The explanation of why these lawlike regularities exist is the goal of archeology.

— Stanley South, 1977

Historical archaeologists are combining sophisticated ethnographic analysis of documentary and oral historical data with their anthropologically sensitive excavation and material culture research to produce highly contextualized and nuanced studies of historical sites, neighborhoods, and communities.

— Mary C. Beaudry, 1996[2]

The discourse has centered on the questions, What is historical archaeology? and What can it contribute to the scholarly enterprise? Essentially, the debate has turned on a few key issues: historical archaeology's rightful place in history and the humanities or in anthropology and the sciences, our sources of evidence and approaches to analyzing and interpreting them, and the theoretical paradigms driving our investigations with their associated conceptions of culture and its relationship to material culture.

The debate between archaeologists trained in the anthropological tradition—most often as prehistorians—and those schooled as historians raged loudly and vehemently for more than three decades. "Anthropologists . . . ask questions of archaeological data never dreamed of by academically trained historians," Bernard L. Fontana claimed definitively. Robert L. Schuyler agreed, calling in 1970 for an anthropological historical archaeology to make "major contributions to our understanding of the expansion of Europe and the world wide impact of that expansion, rather than adding marginal footnotes to historical re-

---

[2]J. C. Harrington, "Archaeology as an Auxiliary Science to American History," *American Anthropologist* 57, no. 6 (December 1955): 1129; Stanley South, *Method and Theory in Historical Archeology* (New York: Academic Press, 1977), p. xiii; Mary C. Beaudry, "Reinventing Historical Archaeology," elsewhere in this volume. James F. Deetz, "Scientific Humanism and Humanistic Science: A Plea for Paradigmatic Pluralism in Historical Archaeology," *Geoscience and Man* 22 (1983): 27; Charles E. Orser, Jr., "Toward a Theory of Power for Historical Archaeology: Plantations and Space," in Mark P. Leone and Parker B. Potter, Jr., eds., *The Recovery of Meaning: Historical Archaeology in the Eastern United States* (Washington, D.C.: Smithsonian Institution Press, 1988), p. 314; Barbara J. Little and Paul A. Shackel, "Scales of Historical Anthropology: An Archaeology of Colonial Anglo-America," *Antiquity* 63 (1989): 495.

search." Almost twenty years and many marginal footnotes later, Schuyler admonished his colleagues at the twentieth annual meeting of the Society for Historical Archaeology to "stop trying to kiss the derriere of historians."[3]

Advocates of history as historical archaeology's proper home responded in kind. "History," Iain Walker explained impatiently, "is the interpretation of whole series of interrelated events, their causes, and their effects. . . . We are studying people, and anything else is a waste of time." Others accused historical archaeologists of mystification, of presenting their research in a form comprehensible only to other archaeologists; still others have decried archaeologists' woeful ignorance of the relevant historical literature. Most limiting to interdisciplinary dialogue, however, has been some historians' privileging of documents over material culture and oral history as historical evidence.[4]

Indeed, historical archaeologists have intimately linked the issue of sources of evidence with the question of disciplinary association. As early as the 1950s, a few historical archaeologists sought to resolve the debate or at least found it irrelevant. They envisioned archaeology as merely a body of techniques available to both historians and anthropologists. Rather than offer a resolution, however, this position added another facet to the discourse. Responding to historians' privileging of language and written text, some historical archaeologists argued that "the archaeologist *must dig* for his data." Many have continued to place material culture and documents in mutually exclusive ethnosemantic domains. Archaeologists study material culture; historians study documents. James F. Deetz and others recognized the constraints of this

---

[3]Bernard L. Fontana, "On the Meaning of Historic Sites Archaeology," *American Antiquity* 31, no. 1 (1965): 64; Robert L. Schuyler, "Historical and Historic Sites Archaeology as Anthropology: Basic Definitions and Relationships," *Historical Archaeology* 4 (1970): 88; Robert L. Schuyler, "Archaeological Remains, Documents, and Anthropology: A Call for a New Culture History," *Historical Archaeology* 22, no. 1 (1988): 36.

[4]Iain C. Walker, "Binford, Science, and History: The Probabilistic Variability of Explicated Epistemology and Nomothetic Paradigms in Historical Archaeology," *Conference on Historic Site Archaeology Papers* 7, pt. 3 (1972): 184. For a discussion of historians' responses to the archaeology of slavery, see Theresa A. Singleton, "An Archaeological Framework for Slavery and Emancipation, 1740–1880," in Leone and Potter, *Recovery of Meaning*, esp. p. 363. Others arguing for historical archaeology as history include Harrington, "Archaeology as an Auxiliary Science," pp. 1121–30 and Ivor Noël Hume, *Historical Archaeology* (New York: W. W. Norton, 1968).

position. While not abandoning the notion of excavation's central place in the historical archaeologist's repertoire, Deetz appealed to historical archaeologists to draw into their purview a culture's entire material culture vocabulary—from foods to performances to the cultural landscape. He, Schuyler, and others advocated historical archaeology built on archaeological data, documents, oral history, ethnographic observations, and other "above-ground" material culture—"the spoken word, the written word, observed behavior, and preserved behavior." Their vision represented a watershed in the "reinventing" of historical archaeology.[5] It lifted the myopic veil that had so limited the vision of archaeologists whose eyes and minds never left their sites' dirt and discarded bits of ceramics, glass, and bones.

Even so, the written word's role in historical archaeology remains central to the field's discourse today, a metaphor of the larger process

[5]Vincent P. Foley, "On the Meaning of Industrial Archaeology," *Historical Archaeology* 2 (1968): 67; Robert L. Schuyler, "The Spoken Word, the Written Word, Observed Behavior, and Preserved Behavior: The Contexts Available to the Archaeologist," *Conference on Historic Site Archaeology Papers* 10, pt. 2 (1977): 99–120. Those arguing for archaeology as technique have included John W. Griffin, "End Products of Historic Sites Archaeology," and John L. Cotter, "Symposium on Role of Archaeology in Historical Research, Summary and Analysis," in John L. Cotter, ed., *Symposium on Role of Archaeology in Historical Research* (1958; reprinted in Robert L. Schuyler, ed., *Historical Archaeology: A Guide to Substantive and Theoretical Contributions* [Farmingdale, N.Y.: Baywood Publishing Co., 1978], pp. 20–22, 18–20); and Albert C. Spaulding, "Distinguished Lecture: Archeology and Anthropology," *American Anthropologist* 90, no. 2 (June 1988): 263–71. For Deetz's definition of material culture and a discussion of the relationship between historical archaeology and material culture, see James Deetz, "Material Culture and Archaeology—What's the Difference?" in Leland Ferguson, ed., *Historical Archaeology and the Importance of Material Things* (Lansing, Mich.: Society for Historical Archaeology, 1977), pp. 10–11. For a more extensive treatment, see James Deetz, *In Small Things Forgotten: The Archaeology of Early American Life* (Garden City, N.Y.: Anchor Books, 1977). Deetz's position grew out of his adherence to the structuralist paradigm. For brief discussions and critiques of structuralism in American historical archaeology, see Stephen A. Mrozowski, "Nature, Society, and Culture: Theoretical Considerations in Historical Archaeology," elsewhere in this volume. More recently, the call for a historical archaeology based on multiple lines of evidence is reiterated and restated by Kathleen A. Deagan, "Neither History nor Prehistory: The Questions That Count in Historical Archaeology," *Historical Archaeology* 22, no. 1 (1988): 9–10; Schuyler, "Archaeological Remains," p. 40; Mary C. Beaudry, ed., *Documentary Archaeology in the New World* (Cambridge, Eng.: Cambridge University Press, 1988); Mary C. Beaudry, "Introduction," in Mary C. Beaudry and Stephen A. Mrozowski, eds., *Interdisciplinary Investigations of the Boott Mills, Lowell, Massachusetts, vol. III: The Lowell Boarding House System as a Way of Life* (Boston: National Park Service, 1989), p. 2; and Beaudry, "Reinventing Historical Archaeology."

of self-definition. If viewed as epistemologically separate and tested against each other, some argue, the ambiguity discernible between documents and the archaeological, material culture record becomes the focus of explanation. Others claim this merely recasts slightly the worn old debate, and worse, the method "fails to treat either the documentary or archaeological record with . . . analytical thoroughness." Historical archaeology as historical anthropology or anthropological history must instead consider documents and other material culture as complex "storehouse[s] of ethnographic evidence" that our methods must allow us to "blend and merge" in sophisticated ways.[6] Although not deconstructing the old document/material culture dichotomy, this approach nevertheless moves toward evidential and disciplinary synthesis—toward a truly interdisciplinary historical archaeology.

The debates surrounding the field's definition also forced historical archaeologists to position themselves in the sciences or humanities and to engage in theoretical discourse. Most recently, the posturing and struggles over empowerment have been played out with virulence on this latter discursive plane. It is in terms of conceptions of culture, human agency, material culture, and their interrelationships that historical archaeologists today are redefining and "reinventing" the field.[7]

Each paradigm's proponents—the scientific, processual, cultural materialists of the "New Archaeology"; the structural, cognitive, and symbolic "mentalists"; the Marxian historical materialists; the critical theorists; the interpretive contextualists; the feminists; the eclectics—have both offered and sustained critique. Despite venomous attacks

[6]Mary C. Beaudry, review of Mark P. Leone and Parker B. Potter, Jr., eds., *The Recovery of Meaning: Historical Archaeology in the Eastern United States* (Washington, D.C.: Smithsonian Institution Press, 1988), in *Historical Archaeology* 24, no. 3 (1990): 116; Anne Yentsch, "Access and Space, Symbolic and Material, in Historical Archaeology," in Dale Walde and Noreen D. Willows, eds., *The Archaeology of Gender: Proceedings of the 22nd Annual Chacmool Conference* (Calgary, Alba.: Archaeological Association of the University of Calgary, 1990), p. 259. For the view that historical archaeologists must consider documents and material culture epistemologically separate, see Mark P. Leone and Constance A. Crosby, "Epilogue: Middle-Range Theory in Historical Archaeology," in Suzanne M. Spencer-Wood, ed., *Consumer Choice in Historical Archaeology* (New York: Plenum Press, 1987), pp. 401–2.

[7]Many historical archaeologists have envisioned historical archaeology as scientific humanism or humanistic science, thus resolving the field's crisis of identity. I will discuss this briefly in the context of resolutions. For a summary of the major theoretical paradigms in historical archaeology, see Beaudry, "Reinventing Historical Archaeology."

and counterattacks, the most thoughtful historical archaeologists have forged ahead to demonstrate their position's potential rather than retreat into mere unproductive rhetoric.

Prehistoric and historical archaeologists alike have deconstructed the search for archaeological pattern-logical positivist-materialism of the "New Archaeology." It oversimplified and misinterpreted the philosophy of science; it explained change virtually exclusively in technological-environmental (or external) terms; it masked the cultural situatedness of the practitioner; it elevated system over people, thereby relegating human agency, social relations, and the role of sociocultural constructions such as gender to the status of epiphenomena; it minimized *context*; it ignored the *meanings* in cultural symbol systems and their expression and thus accessibility in material culture; and it privileged material culture over the particularity of historical documents.[8]

The structural-cognitive-mentalists, the positivist-materialists responded, conceived of culture as shared symbolic systems, the cumulative creation of human minds. In seeking to discover the mental principles that generate cultural forms and structure cultural domains, these anthropologists and archaeologists engaged not in objective analysis but in creative storytelling. Marxian scholars in turn point to flaws in both

---

[8] Innumerable critiques have appeared over the past two decades; the discourse is of course much more complex than merely enumerating the basic issues of contention can explicate. For the most recent overviews and bibliographic guides, see especially Ian Hodder, *Reading the Past: Current Approaches to Theory in Archaeology* (2d ed.; Cambridge, Eng.: Cambridge University Press, 1991); Bruce G. Trigger, *A History of Archaeological Thought* (Cambridge, Eng.: Cambridge University Press, 1989); C. C. Lamberg-Karlofsky, ed., *Archaeological Thought in America* (Cambridge, Eng.: Cambridge University Press, 1989); Joan M. Gero and Margaret W. Conkey, eds., *Engendering Archaeology: Women and Prehistory* (Oxford: Basil Blackwell, 1990); Shanks and Tilley, *Re-Constructing Archaeology*; Patty Jo Watson, "The Razor's Edge: Symbolic-Structuralist Archeology and the Expansion of Archeological Inference," *American Anthropologist* 92, no. 3 (September 1990): 613–21; Elizabeth M. Brumfiel, "Distinguished Lecture in Archaeology: Breaking and Entering the Ecosystem—Gender, Class, and Faction Steal the Show," *American Anthropologist* 94, no. 3 (September 1992): 551–67; Mary C. Beaudry, Lauren J. Cook, and Stephen A. Mrozowski, "Artifacts and Active Voices: Material Culture as Social Discourse," in Randall H. McGuire and Robert Paynter, eds., *The Archaeology of Inequality* (Cambridge, Eng.: Basil Blackwell, 1991), pp. 150–91. See also Beaudry, "Reinventing Historical Archaeology," Suzanne M. Spencer-Wood, "Feminist Historical Archaeology and Domestic Reform," and Charles E. Orser, Jr., "Artifacts, Networks, and Plantations: Toward a Further Understanding of the Social Aspects of Material Culture," elsewhere in this volume.

conceptualizations of culture. Created through historical processes of individual and group social interaction with the "material conditions of life," individuals share differentially in culture based on their social interests. Internally contradictory and inconsistent as a result, culture is a social process that masks and mystifies difference and inequality. Feminist scholars, however, have revealed the sexist bias in Marxians' virtual equation of social relations with class conflict. Other historical archaeologists have found critical Marxian discourse even more specious, promoting a partisan, sociopolitical agenda that seeks to dominate the field through exclusion, appropriation, mystification, and dismissal.[9]

The resolution to historical archaeology's conflicted identity offered in this volume's chapters—historical archaeology "reinvented" —draws on a rich legacy of what some have denigrated as disciplinary, theoretical, and epistemological eclecticism. Thirty-eight years ago, in a 1958 symposium on the role of archaeology in historical research, John W. Griffin challenged historical archaeologists to undertake descriptive and interpretive culture history, cultural anthropology, social history, and historical ethnography. He knew that the approach and

[9]See Stanley South, "Santa Elena: Threshold of Conquest," in Leone and Potter, *Recovery of Meaning*, p. 34; Charles E. Cleland, "Questions of Substance, Questions That Count," *Historical Archaeology* 22, no. 1 (1988): 15. For cultural paradigms in anthropology that have influenced theoretical discourse in historical archaeology and especially for culture conceived as symbolic system, see Roger M. Keesing, "Theories of Culture," *Annual Review of Anthropology* 3 (1974): 73–97, esp. 77–79. See also Mark P. Leone, "Symbolic, Structural, and Critical Archaeology," in David Meltzer, Don Fowler, and Jeremy Sabloff, eds., *American Archaeology: Past and Future* (Washington, D.C.: Smithsonian Institution Press, 1986), pp. 415–38. Randall H. McGuire, "Dialogues with the Dead: Ideology and the Cemetery," in Leone and Potter, *Recovery of Meaning*, p. 471. For Marxian perspectives in historical archaeology, see also Randall H. McGuire, *A Marxist Archaeology* (San Diego: Academic Press, 1992); Leone and Potter, *Recovery of Meaning*; Charles E. Orser, Jr., "On Plantations and Patterns," *Historical Archaeology* 23, no. 2 (1989): 28–40; Charles E. Orser, Jr., "The Continued Pattern of Dominance: Landlord and Tenant on the Postbellum Cotton Plantation," in McGuire and Paynter, *Archaeology of Inequality*, pp. 40–54; Terrence W. Epperson, "Race and the Disciplines of the Plantation," *Historical Archaeology* 24, no. 4 (1990): 29–36; Jean E. Howson, "Social Relations and Material Culture: A Critique of the Archaeology of Plantation Slavery," *Historical Archaeology* 24, no. 4 (1990): 78–91; Orser, "Artifacts," and Paul R. Mullins, "Negotiating Industrial Capitalism: Mechanisms of Change among Agrarian Potters," elsewhere in this volume. The feminist critique in historical archaeology is reviewed in Spencer-Wood, "Feminist Historical Archaeology." See also Beaudry's critique in review of Leone and Potter, *Recovery of Meaning*.

the results counted, not the academic label. John L. Cotter, too, realized the counterproductive nature of the history versus anthropology debate: "There is a point at which one eye gazing at history and the other eye at culture manages to focus on a remarkably enlightening, three-dimensional image of the past."[10]

Elegantly stated and piercingly insightful, Cotter's vision, nevertheless, proved deceptively simple, as few historical archaeologists have truly achieved that enlightening focus. As some clung tenaciously to one side or the other of the chimerical dichotomies—history/anthropology, humanism/science, mentalist/materialist—others saw our practice falling short. Calls for resolution and synthesis punctuated the discourse each decade. In 1967 Walker sought to collapse the distance that historical archaeologists perceived as separating history and science. He argued that in all disciplines, knowledge accrues through the "continuous process of interaction between the . . . [scholar] and his facts and the unending dialogue between the present and the past." Ten years later, Henry Glassie asked us to situate historical archaeology "directly over the fault on the academic landscape that separates the social sciences from the humanities." Such historical archaeology could attend to both "the humanist's concern for meaning, intention, and being, and to the scientist's concern for form, behavior, and conditions," and avoid, James Fitting wrote the same year, the "blindness" of any single approach. In the past decade, Deetz's writings, too, have resonated with the plea that historical archaeologists make room at the table for the "particularism of those who labor long and hard to relate objects to individuals and to instill an honest respect for the complexities of the historical record, the scientific archaeologists who rightly insist on the importance of controlled quantification, and the humanists who know that numbers can at times burden the soul."[11]

[10] Griffin, "End Products," p. 22; Cotter, "Symposium on Role of Archaeology," p. 18. On eclecticism, see Orser, "Toward a Theory of Power," p. 315.

[11] Iain Walker, "Historic Archaeology—Methods and Principles," *Historical Archaeology* 1 (1967): 27; Henry Glassie, "Archaeology and Folklore: Common Anxieties, Common Hopes," in Ferguson, *Historical Archaeology*, p. 24; James E. Fitting, "The Structure of Historical Archaeology and the Importance of Material Things," in Ferguson, *Historical Archaeology*, p. 67; James F. Deetz, "Material Culture and Worldview in Colonial Anglo-America," in Leone and Potter, *Recovery of Meaning*, p. 232. Among numerous other synthetic statements in historical archaeology, see also William H. Adams, "Historical Archaeology: Science and Humanism," *North American Archaeolo-*

Constructing a self-identity for historical archaeology has involved not only situating the field on the academic landscape but also defining its territory and marking its boundaries. What is historical archaeology, and what is it not? The decades-long struggle for a legitimate place in the scholarly world has led historical archaeologists to conceive of their research domain broadly. In this era of multiculturalism, historical archaeology as the study of the emergence of the modern world has great promise. Drawing on all available evidence of people's actions and their consequences, historical archaeologists seek the stories of European expansion worldwide, of the resulting interactions among and displacement of millions of people, and of cultural continuity, contest, and change.[12]

This definition provides a starting point, and this volume's authors show us how such historical archaeology works, and what it can do. Historically constituted and actively constructed in the present by its practitioners, historical archaeology today has much to contribute to American cultural studies.[13] It has transcended the crippling history/

---

gist 1, no. 1 (1979–80): 85–96; Deetz, "Scientific Humanism," pp. 27–34; James Deetz, "History and Archaeological Theory: Walter Taylor Revisited," *American Antiquity* 53, no. 1 (1988): 13–22. Prehistorians and anthropologists, too, are seeking resolutions to the intellectual discord sundering their fields. Recent contributions to the debate include Ian Hodder, "Interpretive Archaeology and Its Role," *American Antiquity* 56, no. 1 (1991): 7–18; Charles L. Redman, "Distinguished Lecture in Archaeology: In Defense of the Seventies," *American Anthropologist* 93, no. 2 (1991): 295–307; Bruce G. Trigger, "Distinguished Lecture in Archaeology: Constraint and Freedom," *American Anthropologist* 93, no. 3 (1991): 551–69; Wolf, "Distinguished Lecture," pp. 586–96.

[12] Several historical archaeologists have defined the field similarly. See Schuyler, "Historical and Historic Sites Archaeology," p. 83; Deetz, *In Small Things Forgotten,* p. 5; Deagan, "Neither History nor Prehistory," p. 8; Stanley South, "Whither Pattern?" *Historical Archaeology* 22, no. 1 (1988): 25; James Deetz, "Introduction: Archaeological Evidence of Sixteenth- and Seventeenth-Century Encounters," in Lisa Falk, ed., *Historical Archaeology in Global Perspective* (Washington, D.C.: Smithsonian Institution Press, 1991), p. 1; Orser, "Artifacts"; John Worrell, Myron O. Stachiw, and David M. Simmons, "Archaeology from the Ground Up," elsewhere in this volume.

[13] In many ways the historical archaeology I describe corresponds to "postprocessual," "contextual," "interpretive" archaeology as constituted by Hodder and others. See especially Hodder, *Reading the Past*; Ian Hodder, "This Is Not an Article about Material Culture as Text," *Journal of Anthropological Archaeology* 8 (1989): 250–69; Hodder, "Interpretive Archaeology"; Paul A. Shackel and Barbara J. Little, "Post-Processual Approaches to Meanings and Uses of Material Culture in Historical Archaeology," *Historical Archaeology* 26, no. 3, Meanings and Uses of Material Culture, ed. Barbara J. Little and Paul A. Shackel (Fall 1992): 5–11; and Beaudry, "Reinventing Historical Archaeology." Nevertheless, I prefer to avoid such labels, which have proliferated lately, as they both constrain and confuse.

anthropology and humanism/science debate. Truly an interdisciplinary endeavor, historical archaeology brings innovative approaches and perspectives from a constellation of disciplines to bear on the study of the past.

An interdisciplinary historical archaeology requires neither denying nor abandoning the field's historical connections principally to anthropology and history but rather building from their cores. Thus, at the center of historical archaeological inquiry stand both people and culture. People think and act in cultural terms, intentionally and unconsciously. People devise, interpret, manipulate, and recreate symbols to communicate, to act, and to define themselves, giving meaning to their and others' actions and lives and to their world. From the environment, people draw life through a process of perceiving, making, and doing. They thereby create, participate in, act on, and are influenced by cultural systems comprised of complexly interrelated biological, environmental, technological, economic, social, political, ideological, and historical forces and phenomena.[14]

This centering on people and culture has three significant implications for the practice of historical archaeology. First, the past we seek to recover lacks unity, even when we narrow our focus to one place, one time, one event. The unity dissolves into a multiplicity of individuals thinking, feeling, speaking, and acting. Each cultural persona—an identity woven from strands of gender, age, family, community, ethnicity, education, religion, occupation, wealth, and numerous other influences—was thus at once both unique (an individual) and social (a member of many groups). We aspire to hear this multiplicity of voices, to know their many pasts, to privilege no single perspective.[15]

[14] The massive anthropological literature on culture theory is succinctly summarized by Keesing, "Theories of Culture," pp. 73–97; and Sherry B. Ortner, "Theory in Anthropology since the Sixties," *Comparative Studies in Society and History* 26 (1984): 126–66. Ortner also discusses the recent emphasis on human agency, practice, praxis, and performance in anthropological analyses. That American studies scholars need to attend more to issues of human agency as well is argued by Watts, "Idiocy of American Studies," pp. 625–60, esp. pp. 655–56. A concern for people's intentions, choice, agency, and action also pervades the essays in this volume.

[15] The goal of writing a multivocal past today pervades all scholarly disciplines concerned with the human past. Perspectives in historical anthropology and prehistoric archaeology have especially influenced historical archaeology. See, for example, Shanks and Tilley, *Re-Constructing Archaeology*; Jonathon D. Hill, "Overview of 'Contested Pasts and the Practice of Anthropology, Contemporary Issues Forum,'" *American Anthropologist* 94, no. 4 (December 1992): 809–15. In historical archaeology, see Beaudry,

Second, context is everything. At the sites we excavate, we interpret each artifact, soil stratum, feature, faunal element, and ethnobotanical specimen in its archaeological context. We study material culture's contexts, too, from conceptualization through production to
acquisition, use, and ultimately disposal. Indeed, material culture,
events, people, and their beliefs and actions have meaning only in their
multicomponent, cultural, systemic contexts. Moreover, each context
incorporates many scales, from minutes to millennia, from the individual to the global. Recovering the past can proceed only from constructing and reconstructing this multitude of contexts.[16]

Third, human social action and cultural logic embody incredible
complexity and confusing ambiguity. In addressing this complexity and
ambiguity, we are becoming increasingly dissatisfied with reducing social action to relationships of power or ways of thinking and hence
doing (cultural logic) to universal structures. Historical archaeologists
have only recently "discovered" power as an organizing principle of
social order and relations. Now, to avoid reductionist, determinist interpretations, we also are seeking the other principles on which people
built their societies. Similarly, structuralist interpretations of mind
served historical archaeology well, teaching us to see all material culture as interrelated cultural expressions, as a means to access culture.
Recognizing the complexity and ambiguity inherent in culture understood as both historically and contextually constituted, this volume's

---

"Reinventing Historical Archaeology"; Mrozowski, "Nature, Society, and Culture";
Orser, "Artifacts"; Spencer-Wood, "Feminist Historical Archaeology"; and the literature
that these scholars cite.

[16] All the authors in this volume share a concern with context. Indeed, it forms a
central characteristic of historical archaeology as Beaudry "reinvents" it ("Reinventing
Historical Archaeology"); see also Bernard L. Herman, "Introduction: Historical Archaeology and the Search for Context." For other statements of the roles of contextual analysis
and interpretation in archaeology, see Cleland, "Questions of Substance," pp. 13–17;
Schuyler, "Archaeological Remains," pp. 36–43; Mark P. Leone, "The Georgian Order
as the Order of Merchant Capitalism in Annapolis, Maryland," in Leone and Potter,
Recovery of Meaning, pp. 235–62; Beaudry, Cook, and Mrozowski, "Artifacts and Active
Voices," pp. 150–91; Little and Shackel, "Meanings and Uses"; John C. Barrett, "Contextual Archaeology," *Antiquity* 61 (1987): 468–73; Ian Hodder, ed., *The Archaeology
of Contextual Meanings* (Cambridge, Eng.: Cambridge University Press, 1987); Ian Hodder, ed., *The Meanings of Things: Material Culture and Symbolic Expression* (London:
Unwin Hyman, 1989); Shanks and Tilley, *Re-Constructing Archaeology*.

authors and others know that they need to attend to the smallest details of people, place, and time.[17]

Historical archaeologists interpret past peoples, cultures, and contexts. This does not make our undertaking "antiscientific." Rather, it acknowledges that all scholarly inquiry, even science, proceeds from ongoing dialogues between researchers and data, between present and past. We can divorce ourselves neither from our cultural situatedness in the present nor from the research process. We pose the questions, we devise the methods to answer them, we define and generate the data, and we interpret the data in light of our original questions and new ones suggested along the way. The authors in this volume demonstrate that accepting these principles does not lead to unconstrained storytelling about the past or the present. These historical archaeologists do not deny the existence of the past nor the materiality of its remains in the present. These material remains and people's memories of their pasts ground our stories and our interpretations. We define material culture broadly, to include everything people have made, every material consequence of people's actions, and every way people have altered

[17]On power, see especially Leone and Potter, *Recovery of Meaning*; McGuire and Paynter, *Archaeology of Inequality*; Little and Shackel, "Meanings and Uses." Not all the studies in these volumes see power in negative terms or as the sole basis of social relations; see, for example, David Hurst Thomas, "Saints and Soldiers at Santa Catalina: Hispanic Designs for Colonial America," in Leone and Potter, *Recovery of Meaning*, pp. 73–140; Singleton, "Archaeological Framework," pp. 345–70; Leland Ferguson, "Struggling with Pots in Colonial South Carolina," in McGuire and Paynter, *Archaeology of Inequality*, pp. 28–39; Beaudry, Cook, and Mrozowski, "Artifacts and Active Voices," pp. 150–91; Steven R. Pendery, "Consumer Behavior in Colonial Charlestown, Massachusetts, 1630–1730," *Historical Archaeology* 26, no. 3, Meanings and Uses of Material Culture, ed. Barbara J. Little and Paul A. Shackel (Fall 1992): 57–72; Margaret Purser, "Consumption as Communication in Nineteenth-Century Paradise Valley, Nevada," *Historical Archaeology* 26, no. 3, Meanings and Uses of Material Culture, ed. Barbara J. Little and Paul A. Shackel (Fall 1992): 105–16. Deetz is virtually synonymous with structuralism in historical archaeology; see, for example, Deetz, *In Small Things Forgotten*. Deetz's students Beaudry, Anne E. Yentsch, and Leslie Stewart-Abernathy rank among the leaders of this generation of historical archaeologists moving beyond structuralism. For their work and that of others "reinventing" historical archaeology, see Anne E. Yentsch and Mary C. Beaudry, eds., *The Art and Mystery of Historical Archaeology: Essays in Honor of James Deetz* (Boca Raton, Fla.: CRC Press, 1992). See also Anne E. Yentsch, "Farming, Fishing, Whaling, Trading: Land and Sea as Resource on Eighteenth-Century Cape Cod," in Beaudry, *Documentary Archaeology*, pp. 138–60; Mary C. Beaudry and Stephen A. Mrozowski, eds., *Interdisciplinary Investigations of the Boott Mills, Lowell, Massachusetts*, vols. 1–3 (Boston: National Park Service, 1987–89).

their physical world and their bodies. Only integrating all the material and oral evidence brings us as close as we can come to regaining the past from its many actors' perspectives.[18]

Because historical archaeologists write culture history from material culture, we center material culture methodologically. Of necessity, we think continually of how and why we study material culture. The reasons are many and compelling. People "make and use" material culture, "express their lives" in material culture, "create and recreate themselves" in material culture. Performance produces material culture, and material culture in turn makes action possible, recursively shaping and, in some cases, controlling it. A culturally constituted, symbolic, physical manifestation of social and ideological discourse, material culture also communicates. People create, interpret, and value it at once both consciously and subconsciously. People actively employ

---

[18] Most recently, South has condemned what he describes as an "antiscience groundswell" in historical archaeology, one that he equates with "a personal, subjective, internally creative, artistically oriented, non-archaeological, interpretive" storytelling (Stanley South, "Strange Fruit: Historical Archaeology, 1972–1977," *Historical Archaeology* 27, no. 1 [1993]: 17–18). Walker, however, reminded us more than 25 years ago that all scholarship is interpretation, as South admits ("Strange Fruit," p. 18); see Walker, "Historic Archaeology," p. 27. Equally elegantly, Cleland wrote a half decade later: "the events of the past can only be examined through the prism of current experience. . . . Just as our culture is a product of our history, so is our history a product of our culture! . . . If we are to develop a more thoughtful and balanced interpretation of history, it will be because we understand the kind of history that we make" (Charles Cleland, "On Making History," *Historical Archaeology* 7 [1973]: 1–2). More recently, historical archaeologists embracing critical theory to varying degrees have argued both the potential and the limitations presented by researchers' social and cultural context. See Mark P. Leone and Parker B. Potter, Jr., "Introduction: Issues in Historical Archaeology," in Leone and Potter, *Recovery of Meaning*, pp. 7–9, 19; and Parker B. Potter, Jr., "Critical Archaeology: In the Ground and on the Street," *Historical Archaeology* 26, no. 3, Meanings and Uses of Material Culture, ed. Barbara J. Little and Paul A. Shackel (Fall 1992): 117–29. For explicit discussions of historical archaeology as interpretation and of the situatedness of the archaeologist in this volume, see especially Beaudry, "Reinventing Historical Archaeology," and Mrozowski, "Nature, Society, and Culture." This definition of material culture follows Deetz; see Deetz, "Material Culture and Archaeology," pp. 10–11; Deetz, *In Small Things Forgotten*, pp. 23–25. In this volume, the necessity of integrating all available lines of evidence is stressed by Beaudry, "Reinventing Historical Archaeology"; J. Ritchie Garrison, "Remaking the Barnyard: The Archaeology of Farm Outbuildings in the Connecticut River Valley of Massachusetts, 1770–1870"; Gerald K. Kelso, "Pollen Analysis in Urban Historical Landscape Research"; Ann Smart Martin, "Frontier Boys and Country Cousins: The Context for Choice in Eighteenth-Century Consumerism"; Spencer-Wood, "Feminist Historical Archaeology"; and Worrell, Stachiw, and Simmons, "Archaeology from the Ground Up."

material culture to express and shape individual and group interrelationships of all sorts—physical, moral, social, economic, political. Thus, as both individuals and groups use material culture to define themselves and to negotiate or cooperate with, distance, or embrace others, the components of the material world acquire multiple meanings. Beyond human relationships, material culture also offers insights into people's ways of classifying, ordering, and assigning meaning to "the universe as they imagine it." Material culture, then, allows historical archaeologists and other scholars to understand people in their cultural context and culture in its human context.[19]

The archaeological site has always been the essential building block of historical archaeology. This attentive focus on place—house lot, blacksmith shop, farm, plantation, slave quarter, pottery, cemetery, school—remains one of historical archaeology's greatest strengths.

[19]Martin, "Context for Choice"; Leone, "Georgian Order," p. 237; Martin Hall, "Small Things and the Mobile, Conflictual Fusion of Power, Fear, and Desire," in Yentsch and Beaudry, *Art and Mystery*, p. 396; Rhys Isaac, "Imagination and Material Culture: The Enlightenment on a Mid Eighteenth-Century Virginia Plantation," in Yentsch and Beaudry, *Art and Mystery*, p. 401. For more in-depth discussions of these views of material culture by historical archaeologists, see Beaudry, "Reinventing Historical Archaeology"; Beaudry, Cook, and Mrozowski, "Artifacts and Active Voices," p. 150; Mark P. Leone, "Epilogue: The Productive Nature of Material Culture and Archaeology," *Historical Archaeology* 26, no. 3, Meanings and Uses of Material Culture, ed. Barbara J. Little and Paul A. Shackel (Fall 1992): 131; Barbara J. Little, "Craft and Culture Change in the Eighteenth-Century Chesapeake," in Leone and Potter, *Recovery of Meaning*, p. 287; Barbara J. Little, "Explicit and Implicit Meanings in Material Culture and Print Culture," *Historical Archaeology* 26, no. 3, Meanings and Uses of Material Culture, ed. Barbara J. Little and Paul A. Shackel (Fall 1992): 86; Barbara J. Little, "Texts, Images, Material Culture," in Barbara J. Little, ed., *Text-Aided Archaeology* (Boca Raton, Fla.: CRC Press, 1992), p. 219; Potter, "Critical Archaeology," p. 117. In this volume, see especially Martin, "Context for Choice"; Beaudry, "Reinventing Historical Archaeology"; Jane Perkins Claney, "Form, Fabric, and Social Factors in Nineteenth-Century Ceramics Usage: A Case Study in Rockingham Ware"; Orser, "Artifacts"; Eric Sandweiss, "Mind Reading the Urban Landscape: An Approach to the History of American Cities"; Spencer-Wood, "Feminist Historical Archaeology." A coterie of British archaeologists have influenced historical archaeologists' views on material culture in recent years; see especially Ian Hodder, "The Contextual Analysis of Symbolic Meanings," in Hodder, *Archaeology of Contextual Meanings*, pp. 1, 8; Hodder, "This Is Not an Article about Material Culture," p. 257; Keith Ray, "Material Metaphor, Social Interaction, and Historical Reconstructions: Exploring Patterns of Association and Symbolism in the Igbo-Ukwu Corpus," in Hodder, *Archaeology of Contextual Meanings*, p. 67; and Christopher Tilley, "Interpreting Material Culture," in Hodder, *Meanings of Things*, pp. 185–94.

Richly textured historical ethnographies of individual sites will continue to anchor the field. Beginning with all the details that surviving buildings, landscapes, documents, the archaeological record, and surviving and recovered material culture offer, archaeologists and their colleagues can reconstruct a site's material world at discrete moments in time and document continuity and change across time. Then decentering material culture, we refocus on the people, placing them into the material world they inherited and recreated. We begin to perceive the choices they made in their lives, always in material contexts and with material consequences. Finally, beyond the people themselves, we seek the culture that informed their choices and that in turn their actions altered, inevitably if almost imperceptibly.[20]

But site ethnographies are not enough. Alone, they cannot provide all the contexts that historical archaeology requires to recover the past. Studies of the "material systems" in which all material culture is embedded also contribute to the construction of context. Material system studies begin with an item of material culture (or a class of items) and move outward to the constellation of associated objects, people, places, processes, performances, and ideas. They push far beyond the comparison across archaeological sites of disembodied artifact counts. They teach us about material culture's multiple meanings and active roles. When we encounter the items again in the context of our sites, the material system we now comprehend enriches and extends our interpretation of the people and their culture.[21]

[20] This volume's authors focus on these examples of site types: for house lots, see Kelso, "Pollen Analysis"; Worrell, Stachiw, and Simmons, "Archaeology from the Ground Up"; Zierden, "The Urban Landscape, the Work Yard, and Archaeological Site Formation Processes in Charleston, South Carolina"; for the blacksmith shop, see Worrell, Stachiw, and Simmons, "Archaeology from the Ground Up"; for the farm, see Garrison, "Archaeology of Farm Outbuildings"; for plantations and slave quarters, see Orser, "Artifacts"; for potteries, see Mullins, "Negotiating Industrial Capitalism"; for cemeteries, see Linda Welters, Margaret Ordoñez, Kathryn Tarleton, and Joyce Smith, "European Textiles from Seventeenth-Century New England Indian Cemeteries"; and for schools (among other domestic reform property types), see Spencer-Wood, "Feminist Historical Archaeology." For a model example of such a site biography, see Worrell, Stachiw, and Simmons, "Archaeology from the Ground Up." Kelso, "Pollen Analysis," writes of one technical study that contributed much to the Boott Mills site biographies.

[21] Barrie Reynolds, "Material Systems: An Approach to the Study of Kwandu Material Culture," in Barrie Reynolds and Margaret A. Stott, eds., *Material Anthropology: Contemporary Approaches to Material Culture* (Lanham, Md.: University Press of America, 1987), pp. 155–87. "Material system" studies in this volume represent a range

Still other studies must center on particular aspects of context; the possibilities are endless. In this volume, for example, scholars explore consumerism, industrial capitalism, urban as process, and the cultural construction of gender.[22] Like the material system studies, context studies both build on and enhance site ethnographies. Moreover, they illuminate American culture in ways that individual site ethnographies and material system studies alone cannot.

These three complementary scholarly genres, each exemplified in this volume, comprise the forms of contemporary historical archaeological inquiry. With a firm groundwork laid in individual studies in these genres, we can approach syntheses. Historical ethnographies of sites can become community studies and be interwoven with material systems and contexts into ever more complex and global constructs.

Simultaneously, we will—we must—continue to reinvent historical archaeology through discourse and practice. As we do, we will invariably rethink and reinterpret what has always constituted its core—people, culture, and context. To their credit, this volume's authors have done so. Now it is your turn.

---

of approaches to the genre: Claney, on Rockingham ware; Garrison, on Massachusetts farm outbuildings; Orser, on the social aspects of material systems; Welters et al., on European trade textiles in seventeenth-century New England; Zierden, on Charleston house lot work yards.

[22] Martin, "Context for Choice"; Mullins, "Negotiating Industrial Capitalism"; Sandweiss, "Mind Reading"; and Spencer-Wood, "Feminist Historical Archaeology."

Introduction
Historical Archaeology and the Search for Context

Bernard L. Herman

We are, in some sense, all archaeologists.

Dedicated to the interpretation of American culture in context, we seek to comprehend the past based on the systematic recovery and reading of evidence—material, documentary, and oral. Always fragmentary and always ambiguous in content, the materials we depend on to craft our understandings demand the reconstruction and evocation of context. The search for context, particularly through the exploration of material culture, stands at the very core of historical archaeology.

What is context? As historical archaeology demonstrates and the essays in this volume amplify, context is multilayered and complex. Ian Hodder has pushed the critical reassessment of context to the forefront of archaeological debate. "Archaeologists," writes Hodder, "use the term 'context' in a variety of ways which have in common the connecting or interweaving of things in a particular situation or group of situations." Hodder emphasizes two types of contextual meaning. First, he identifies "the structured system of functional interrelationships" where "we give the object meaning by seeing how it functions in relation to . . . other factors and processes and in relation to eco-

Both this volume and my essay have benefited immeasurably from the advice and insights of many people, including all of the authors. Particular thanks are extended to Lu Ann De Cunzo, David Orr, Scott Swank, and Henry Glassie.

nomic and social structures." Second, Hodder describes "the structured content of ideas and symbols. Archaeologists," he continues, "need to make abstractions from the symbolic functions of the objects they excavate in order to identify the meaning content behind them, and this involves examining how the ideas denoted by material symbols themselves play a part in structuring society." Hodder's formulation of context is hardly unique. Henry Glassie, for example, states, "all objects are simultaneously sets and parts of sets" and "as parts of sets, all objects exist in context." Context, then, "is all of that, visible or not, which goes with the text—the one woven together by the other to make it meaningful." Both of these formulations conjure up Lewis Binford's functional model identifying the utilitarian, social, and symbolic or ideological functions of expressive culture and springs from the premise "that 'material culture' can and does represent the structure of the total cultural system." As Binford recognized, and as other writers have elaborated, function represented in objects suggests: there is a level of textuality; singular objects may possess multiple functional attributes; and the discovery of function is a search for content, context, and voice. More recently the roles of "speakers" and "hearers" have led to speculation by historical archaeologists and others on the rhetorical aspects of material culture where the purpose of rhetoric is one of personal and social persuasion. Thus, archaeologist Anne Yentsch's work on folk and courtly foodways examines the concept of recursive relationships evidenced in the archaeological record and from that evidence suggests how the material culture of the table represents a cognitive map that describes social territory and hierarchy.[1]

Hodder's definition of context stresses the "excavated" character

---

[1] Ian Hodder, *Reading the Past: Current Approaches to Interpretation in Archaeology* (Cambridge, Eng.: Cambridge University Press, 1986), pp. 120, 121; Henry Glassie, "Studying Material Culture Today," in Gerald L. Pocius, ed., *Living in a Material World: Canadian and American Approaches to Material Culture* (St. John: Memorial University of Newfoundland Institute for Social and Economic Research, 1991), pp. 256, 258; Lewis Binford, *An Archaeological Perspective* (New York: Seminar Press, 1972), pp. 20–32. Aspects of Binford's formative concepts have been made more accessible in James Deetz, *In Small Things Forgotten: The Archaeology of Early American Life* (New York: Anchor Press/Doubleday, 1977), pp. 50–51. Terry Eagleton, *Literary Theory: An Introduction* (Minneapolis: University of Minnesota Press, 1983), pp. 204–17; Anne Yentsch, "Minimum Vessel Lists as Evidence of Change in Folk and Courtly Traditions of Food Use," *Historical Archaeology* 24, no. 3 (1990): 24–53.

of archaeological evidence. Archaeologists, however, are increasingly engaged in the examination of nonexcavated materials. "Documentary archaeology," as defined by Mary Beaudry, proceeds from a materialist perspective. "Archaeologists," Beaudry observes, "necessarily tend to focus upon material culture—in the ground as well as in documents." Thus, archaeologists, as well as those of us who would benefit from an archaeological approach, "come to the documents with new notions of what could be gleaned from them, notions arising from a materialistic perspective on the past dictated by the value of archaeological evidence."[2] Similarly, students of American culture have engaged in other archaeologies, such as industrial archaeology or commercial archaeology. What seems to define archaeology—documentary, industrial, commercial, or architectural—is not where and how the evidence is found but rather the intellectual and analytical means of discovery. There is an archaeological way of thinking, but what defines that mode of thought? To find an answer, we return to the organizing concept of context.

At its most basic physical level, archaeology records and recovers the artifacts of the past with assiduous attention to time and space measured through how and where things lay in the earth or, more generally, in relation to space, time, and other artifacts ranging from pollen to foundations. The science of stratigraphy and site formation provides the rigorous means to determine these physical relationships. Archaeology also evaluates context in other dimensions. For example, the comparative analysis of ceramics links the findings from one site to others in an effort to reconstruct broader patterns of acquisitions and use. The assessment of physical associations are, in turn, broadened through the analysis of documentary evidence ranging from estate lists of personal property to the prescriptive literature of etiquette manuals. Beyond physical associations, historical archaeology seeks the cognitive and experiential contexts of how objects functioned in social and symbolic settings. The simple questions that historical archaeology poses for all of us ask: What are the significances of material culture? and How and what do we learn from the material world?

The perspectives, strategies, and methodologies afforded by histori-

---

[2] Mary C. Beaudry, ed., *Documentary Archaeology in the New World* (New York: Cambridge University Press, 1988), pp. 1–2.

cal archaeology and reflected in the essays that follow are of use to all who quest for sense and sensibility in the material world. An archaeological perspective is one that will benefit historians, folklorists, geographers, art historians, and all of those who dedicate themselves to the recovery of meanings encoiled in the remains of the past. Central to all the essays that follow is what Beaudry describes in her far-reaching concluding chapter as a process of "reinventing historical archaeology."

A reinvented historical archaeology moves freely across disciplinary boundaries, but it does not reject the old positivist, cultural materialist approach in its entirety; in fact, the emphasis placed on *context* in all its manifestations necessarily fosters a grounded empiricism and an openness to scientific procedures and technical analyses. An interpretive, contextual archaeology is not reductionist or formulaic but rather inclusive, open-ended, and self-critical. Historical archaeology in this mode stresses internal cultural logic through "active voice"—indeed, multiple voice—interpretation of artifacts, features, sites, and landscapes; is attentive to nuance, ambiguity, and variability; and acknowledges and welcomes complexity—cultural complexity as well as complexity in the archaeological record.

Beaudry's statement of reinvention coupled with her affirmation of the complexity and centrality of context for historical archaeology is a mandate for all areas of historical inquiry. Her call for a reinvented historical archaeology is not just a challenge for historical archaeologists; it challenges us all.

The essays published in this volume are neither exclusively by nor exclusively for archaeologists—they are, in fact, for all of us who seek to interpret the past through a lens ground not just from what people wrote but also from what they made, used, and valued. Historical archaeology offers the potential for us to gaze both minutely and expansively into a broader field of historical discourse oriented to a materialist perspective on the past. A materialist perspective goes beyond the straightforward description and analysis of objects in and of themselves or the simple use of objects as illustration (not as evidence) for social and cultural histories. Our goal is nothing less than an enterprise based on the possibilities inherent in learning to ask questions about how people lived, interacted, and considered themselves and the world around them. The basis for those considerations springs from the things with which they furnished and embellished their lives. Those things might be as obvious as houses, furniture, and ceramics, but as Stephen A. Mrozowski and Gerald K. Kelso demonstrate in their essays, they also were as small as pollen and microorganisms.

Our ability to ask meaningful questions of material things stems directly from the sense that the environments that humans perceive, occupy, or affect are somehow "touched" in a lasting way that incorporates cultural attitudes and social relationships. We also realize now that our questions depend on the persona and human textures that we seek in historic artifacts. Historical archaeology has been instrumental in broadening the sense of just whose archaeology we study. Just as literary theory has opened up the consideration of authorship to include the idea that reading represents a kind of writing, historical archaeology has moved the analysis of artifacts from a limited sense of object as thing to an expanded notion of object as action. Not only do the contextual concerns of historical archaeology describe time and place, they also seek the intimate social and symbolic details of human agency in all its diversity.

The kinds of questions we can ask of objects are fundamentally different from those found in documents and oral tradition. In the world of expressive culture in context, we can agree that all forms of human conduct share the quality of expression. We also realize that varying modes of expression entail often conflicting perceptions. The idea of coexistent, conflicted expressive systems between material genres is just one facet of the larger interpretive problem. Objects evaluated in context possess dramatically different situational meanings for the individuals who effect and are affected by every circumstance. Difference may be rooted in class, race, gender, wealth, age, or any number of other variables. Thus, divergent circumstances in single situations represents myriad contextual possibilities. Simply stated, context is defined by multiple, competing, individually held contextual readings. Writings on teaware and tea rituals in early America, for example, have increasingly focused on the equipage of taking tea.[3] From the array of

---

[3] The material culture and the ritual of tea ceremonies is discussed in Ann Smart Martin, "Frontier Boys and Country Cousins: The Context for Choice in Eighteenth-Century Consumerism," elsewhere in this volume. An expanded perspective on the gendered cosmopolitan context for tea drinking in colonial America can be found in David S. Shields, "From Tea Table to Salon" (Paper presented at the Delaware Seminar on History, Art History, and Material Culture, Newark, Autumn 1992).

tea bowls, saucers, and pots recovered from archaeological sites throughout the eastern United States, we have constructed a myth of a normative culture where the mysteries and artifacts of a particular social ritual are so widespread that we assume they enjoy equal social currency wherever they appear. That focus narrows our vision to the top of the tea table. Even in a single eighteenth-century urban setting, the tea service held widely differing senses of place and identity for the African American servant waiting to the side, the mistress deftly manipulating the artifacts of the table, the female visitor schooled in the niceties of polite society, the merchant husband in his dockside counting house toting up sales of Bohea, his commercial clients equally engaged in the competitive sphere of trade, and so on. But, if we think about the tabletop as a landscape of social relationships and of individuals' actions in and around that rarified countryside, then we move toward a richer archaeological conception of historic behaviors based on conversation instead of soliloquy, movement instead of stasis. The conjunction of the study of historic settings and societies with the ethnographic investigation of complex behavior is where historical archaeology bridges history and anthropology through a materialist orientation.

Historical Archaeology and the Study of American Culture is about the utility of material culture as evidence and about the efficacy of materialist perspectives to generate new kinds of questions and interpretive paths. For those of us who strive to recover the multivalent American past through objects, historical archaeology offers a tantalizing array of theoretical tools—all of which are designed to measure, assess, and describe some aspect of the contexts in which objects were acquired, used (in all the multiple ways that a concept of use entails), and discarded.

What distinguishes historical archaeology in the broader field of material culture studies is its unswerving orientation to the discovery and recovery of context. To honor that commitment, historical archaeologists have developed a wide array of analytical methods and concepts that enable them to situate objects in place, time, and their relationship to human agency. Archaeological concepts of seriation, stratigraphy, intrasite/intersite analysis, and horizon, for example, all begin with the realization of comparative relationship. If we turn, for example, to the idea of an archaeology of architecture, we can readily identify some of the most basic archaeological tools and strategies that possess utility for all of those who seek to recover and interpret past lives through material culture.

The goals of historical archaeology converge with those of architectural history, history, folklore, cultural geography, and anthropology at the point where each discipline seeks to explicate and then make sense of patterns of past behavior. Each field of study employs methods particularly suited to the types of data investigated, and each enjoys (and suffers from) its own inherent biases and theoretical perspectives. Historical archaeology and the branch of architectural history exploring buildings as indexes to social and cultural change also share similar methodologies for reading the narratives contained in the material histories of specific sites. Some of the "excavation" principals for aboveground sites are what I will address in the following discussion on an archaeology of historic architecture.

As an urban row house, plantation mansion, barn, mill, or any other building passes through time, it is subject to change at the hands of its owners, users, and occupants. Alterations worked on existing architectural fabric may be as subtle as a single coat of paint or as radical as a total remodeling extending to plan, ornament, and construction. Our immediate task, given a basic knowledge of historic building materials coupled with an emerging sense of regional pattern in American architecture, is twofold: identifying sequences of change and reconstructing histories of appearance, use, and significance.

We achieve these ends by conceptually breaking a building down to its constituent elements of form (space), fabric (construction), and fashion (ornament). Students of American vernacular architecture have found that of the three components, form is the least susceptible to radical transformations and that overlays of fashion are often manipulated to suggest stylishness within familiar domestic and working spaces.[4] Form, fabric, and fashion are unified in the process of expression and made meaningful within parameters of social and cultural circumstance.

In our attempt to realize the principles of an archaeology of archi-

---

[4]Henry Glassie, "Eighteenth-Century Cultural Process in Delaware Valley Folk Building," in Ian M. G. Quimby, ed., *Winterthur Portfolio* 7 (Charlottesville: University Press of Virginia, 1972), pp. 42–43.

tecture, we can begin by outlining some of the basic rules of historical archaeological inquiry. Ivor Noël Hume introduced basic concepts of particular utility to students of American architecture in his classic guide, *Historical Archaeology*.[5] The two central ideas, as Noël Hume has pointed out, are embarrassingly simple. First, the last changes made are the first ones we perceive. Second, each layer of change can date no earlier than the invention of the technology with which it was accomplished. Combined, these two principles designate the rules of chronologically defined stratigraphy or layered-site occupation. Buildings admittedly do not evince patterns of stratification in the same way as found in subsurface sites, but layers of occupation and alteration are no less discernible.

Properly reading the layers of architectural change in a building is contingent on three additional concepts borrowed from archaeology: clarity, horizon, and seriation. Clarity denotes the level of readability in a given site.[6] If human behavior were orderly, if nature were a rational construct, if accidents did not happen, then we could expect the layering contained in archaeological deposits to be neatly stratified and easily read. Unfortunately for students of architecture and archaeology, the preceding *ifs* are more often *buts*. Historic layers of occupation and change, both above and below ground, would be easily discerned and read except that most folk are given to secret bouts of disorderliness, nature is unpredictable, and accidents happen with depressing and confounding frequency. The result is that some sites and structures offer up their histories more readily than others. The house built in the early colonial period and never altered in its ensuing history is the grail of early Americanists studying architecture. Like the museum concept of the period room furnished in a single shopping spree and never updated, the quest for the unaltered building denies the reality and vitality of human endeavor. People are constantly at work on their environment, shaping and reshaping its contours, furnishings, and meanings. A building's physical history may or may not possess clarity, but the evidence of a structure's historic progress is always present.

---

[5] Ivor Noël Hume, *Historical Archaeology: A Comprehensive Guide for Both Amateurs and Professionals to the Techniques and Methods of Excavating Historical Sites* (New York: Alfred A. Knopf, 1972); see esp. the chap. "Beginning to Dig."

[6] The issue of clarity in terms of archaeological visibility and focus is addressed in Deetz, *In Small Things Forgotten*, pp. 94–95.

The notion of horizon may be simply defined as the geographically broad and chronologically rapid spread of complex cultural traits lasting a relatively short period of time. In material culture studies including historical archaeology and architectural history, we can recognize horizon through seriated patterns in the advent, acquisition, and discarding of specific types of material goods and technological innovations. Through the close dating of technological innovation and change, we can establish a reasonably precise series of construction materials and techniques that enable us to place a building in time. The principles of seriation extend beyond technological change to encompass chronologies of building types, ornament, room use, and siting strategies. The widespread distribution of machine-cut nails in the early nineteenth century is an example of the applicability of the horizon concept for architectural analysis. Cut nails possess a well-defined historical technological inception, a rapid rise in general use, and a decline with the advent of wire-cut nails. We know that their presence in historic building fabric provides clues for determining dates of construction and alteration. Similarly, we can turn to the evidence of brick bonds, cast-iron storefronts, roofing materials, and any of the other things from which buildings are assembled. More than providing the means to dating a building, the horizon concept enables us to address specific sites in the larger contexts of the flow of goods and the acceptance of technological innovation. From a materialist point of view, we generate further questions about the introduction of technology and skill and their relationship to the economics and sociology of building.[7] Thus, we can determine not only calendric time but also times of cultural stasis and change.

The horizon concept has a utility much greater than the straightforward dating of building activity. In the spread of architectural fea-

---

[7] Deetz, *In Small Things Forgotten*, pp. 40–43. An often-cited model for the application of the horizon thesis is found in Stanley South, "Evolution and Horizon as Revealed in Ceramic Analysis in Historical Archaeology," as reprinted in Robert L. Schuyler, ed., *Historical Archaeology: A Guide to Substantive and Theoretical Contributions* (Farmingdale, N.Y.: Baywood Publishing Co., 1978), pp. 68–82. Deetz, *In Small Things Forgotten*, pp. 67–69. See Michael J. Chiarappa, "The Social Context of Eighteenth-Century West New Jersey Brick Artisanry," in Thomas Carter and Bernard L. Herman, eds., *Perspectives in Vernacular Architecture IV* (Columbia: University of Missouri Press, 1991), pp. 31–43.

tures, we also discern patterns of artifact consumption. The popular dissemination of Greek revival detailing from Alabama to upstate New York illustrates how rapidly and how broadly a "style" can circulate. We can date these buildings, and we can map their occurrence. A Greek revival plantation house sited on the banks of the lower Mississippi does not convey the same values as a dwelling using parallel design elements in the Hudson River valley. To make sense of those sorts of connections, we turn to the use of intersite or comparative analysis.

Historical archaeologists, like field-oriented architectural historians, encounter their sites one at a time. The process of examination is necessarily *intrasite*—that is, description and analysis begin by establishing the relationships between the historical phases contained within the site being scrutinized. *Intersite* analysis seeks to establish broader sets of relationships by looking at the relationships established between whole sites and the discrete historical periods identified within those sites.[8] Greek revival architectural elements may exhibit a tight horizon, but it would be odd to argue that matters of metope meant the same for a southern slave holder and a northern farmer. Still, though not here, we must attempt to explain the singular popularity of the style across such diverse social and cultural horizons.

Turning away from horizon, we encounter a final theoretical perspective of particular utility for the archaeology of architecture. As articulated by Lewis Binford, there are three (often overlapping) functional dimensions to any object: technomic (utilitarian), sociotechnic (social), and ideotechnic (symbolic). Objects are utilitarian in the sense of "coping directly with the physical environment," the signification of social relationships, and the codification of cultural ideology. More to the point, however, is the implication that objects exist in multiple, simultaneous functional contexts—that the purely utilitarian always enjoys some measure of the symbolic. A presenter at a Canadian conference on material culture neatly summarized this possibility in a discussion on fireplace tools. "When is a poker not a poker?" he asked; "When it is something else," he answered. The something else is de-

---

[8]William Turnbaugh and Sarah Peabody Turnbaugh, "Alternative Applications of the Mean Ceramic Date Concept for Interpreting Human Behavior," *Historical Archaeology* 11 (1977): 90–104.

fined by the perception of the object beyond its purpose as a tool to stir the ashes and by the ability of those who see that object to assign it other occasional meanings. What Binford sets out is the framework for distinguishing between the processes of historical description and interpretation. This is important to the present discussion for several reasons. First, the act of describing anything cultural from the fabric and form of a tobacco barn to the rituals of the courtroom is in and of itself a form of analysis.[9] Second, the intimate comprehension of the building as text is indispensable to drawing inferences about historical process and meaning. Third, whether we seek to understand architectural fabric for purposes pragmatic or theoretical, we share a commitment to reading the text in context.

The distinguishing commitment to contextual concerns at the heart of the historical archaeological enterprise is reflected in all the contributions that compose the following collection of essays. The last forty years have witnessed a dramatic rise in the desire by archaeologists, geographers, folklorists, art historians, and historians to use objects ranging from landscapes to teacups as evidence about the organization and values of historical societies. The belief that objects possess evidential potential resides in the complementary sense that objects function on a variety of expressive levels and that their functions can be understood only in context. Objects, then, are a medium of communication. Moreover, the social values historically and circumstantially encoded into artifacts are deemed to be recoverable. The proposition emerges that if our methods are sound and our readings of the artifact penetrat-

[9] Binford, *Archaeological Perspective*, pp. 23–25. Jean-Claude Dupont, "The Meaning of Objects: The Poker," in Pocius, *Living in a Material World*, pp. 1–18. The tripartite distinction between technomic, sociotechnic, and ideotechnic artifacts has been applied in material culture studies to a variety of objects. For example, see Bernard L. Herman, "Multiple Materials/Multiple Meanings: The Fortunes of Thomas Mendenhall," *Winterthur Portfolio* 10, no. 1 (Spring 1984): 67–86. Clifford Geertz, "Thick Description: Toward an Interpretative Theory of Culture," in Clifford Geertz, *The Interpretation of Cultures* (New York: Basic Books, 1973), pp. 3–30. Historical studies employing an ethnographic approach include Rhys Isaac, "A Discourse on the Method: Action, Structure, and Meaning," in Rhys Isaac, *The Transformation of Virginia, 1740–1790* (Chapel Hill: University of North Carolina Press, 1982), pp. 324–57; Robert Darnton, *The Great Cat Massacre and Other Episodes in French Cultural History* (New York: Basic Books, 1984); Dell Upton, *Holy Things and Profane: Anglican Parish Churches in Colonial Virginia* (Cambridge: MIT Press/Architectural History Fndn., 1986); Bernard L. Herman, *The Stolen House* (Charlottesville: University Press of Virginia, 1992).

ing and sensitive, we can rescue the perishing meanings of the past. Thus, in the study of American culture through material culture, we find ourselves increasingly dedicated to a shift away from the study of objects in and of themselves and toward the study of artifacts as defining and defined by the situations and settings in which they historically operated. The shift in attention, however, has been a long time in coming. The distinction between language and speech, for example, has been at the center of linguistic debate for much of the twentieth century. More recently the textuality of speech—the said—has come to the forefront as the object of interpretation. For late twentieth-century students of material culture, linguistic theory has provided a powerful and seductive explanatory model. Although material culture is not language and speech, it is analogous to language and speech in key ways— chiefly composition, transformation, and performance—that have been advanced by Henry Glassie, Dell Upton, James Deetz, and others.[10] Material culture, and its relationship to the exploration of American culture, stands in a metaphorical relationship to linguistics and socio-linguistics. While we are all generally in agreement that material culture shares generative and communicative elements with language and speech, we also are increasingly aware that material culture as discourse

[10] For a summary of Ferdinand de Saussure's distinction between *language* and *parole* in his 1916 *Course in General Linguistics*, see Rulon S. Wells, "De Saussure's System of Linguistics," in *Introduction to Structuralism*, comp. Michael Lane (New York: Basic Books, 1970), pp. 102–7; Dell Hymes, *Foundations in Sociolinguistics: An Ethnographic Approach* (Philadelphia: University of Pennsylvania Press, 1974); Basil B. Bernstein, *Class, Codes, and Control: Theoretical Studies toward a Sociology of Language*, vol. 1 (London: Routledge and Kegan Paul, 1971–75), pp. 170–89. For a critique of linguistic approaches to material culture, see Grant McCracken, "Clothing as Language: An Object Lesson in the Study of the Expressive Properties of Material Culture," in Grant McCracken, *Culture and Consumption: New Approaches to the Symbolic Character of Consumer Goods and Activities* (Bloomington: Indiana University Press, 1988), pp. 57–70. For a superbly argued counterpoint, see Gerald L. Pocius, "Gossip, Rhetoric, and Objects: A Sociolinguistic Approach to Newfoundland Furniture," in Gerald W. R. Ward, ed., *Perspectives on American Furniture* (New York: W. W. Norton, 1988), pp. 303–45. Henry Glassie, *Folk Housing in Middle Virginia: A Structural Analysis of Historic Artifacts* (Knoxville: University of Tennessee Press, 1975); Dell Upton, "Toward a Performance Theory of Vernacular Architecture: Early Tidewater Virginia as a Case Study," *Folklore Forum* 12, nos. 2/3 (1979): 173–96; Jay Edwards, "The Evolution of a Vernacular Tradition," in Carter and Herman, *Perspectives in Vernacular Architecture IV*, pp. 75–86; James Deetz, *Invitation to Archaeology* (Garden City, N.Y.: Natural History Press, 1967), pp. 83–101.

operates in very different ways from the spoken culture. Similarly, the more recent equation of material culture with issues of textuality have enabled us to enrich the ways in which we read objects as texts. Historical archaeology, with its emphasis on materialist perspectives and the recovery and assessment of physical contexts, provides us with the means to carry our investigations of material culture forward through strategies predicated on the material substance as well as the semiotic content of context. It is on this point that the essays in this collection and historical archaeology in general offer exciting potential for the expanded study of American culture.

Historical archaeology offers us a concrete set of approaches to the social and symbolic consideration of the material world, but is there an archaeological way of thinking that those of us who are not archaeologists by training can adopt? The short answer is yes. The orientation to material culture as viable, substantive evidence and not just as the stuff of incidental illustration is one distinguishing characteristic of archaeological thought. The devotion to the recovery of context— beginning with the physical and proceeding to the symbolic—is a second. Historical archaeology also provides the means to deny the evanescence of past everyday life. Material culture anchors forms of usage and encodes values and meaning. The difficulty comes in learning how to read objects as evidence. The essays in this volume provide ample demonstration of archaeological thinking in a forum that extends beyond an archaeological audience. Taken as a whole, the essays published here stand as a collective invitation for the uses of historical archaeology in the study of American culture.

Construction of Context: Negotiating Consumer Culture

Archaeology from the Ground Up

John Worrell, Myron O. Stachiw, and David M. Simmons

Kurt Vonnegut recounts that during a brief and unrewarding student career as an archaeologist he only "learned something [he] already knew: that man had been a maker and smasher of crockery since the dawn of time."[1] Unfortunately, he was not the only student to encounter archaeology as a discipline whose theories and methods were so narrowly developed that even the most meticulous effort was guaranteed a trivial result.

The study reported here broadens the definition and the investigative strategy of archaeology considerably beyond that which so disillusioned Vonnegut. We agree with Colin McEvedy that "the recovery of the human past is after all the only reason for digging up pots."[2] We understand "archaeology" in its broadest classical sense: the study of the remains of the past, including all direct and indirect residues of human activity.

---

[1] Kurt Vonnegut, "Address to the National Institute of Arts and Letters, 1971," pp. 173–81, reprinted in Kurt Vonnegut, *Wampeters, Foma, and Granfalloons* (New York: Dell Publishing Co., 1976), p. 176.

[2] Colin McEvedy, *The Penguin Atlas of Ancient History* (London: Penguin Books, n.d.), p. 9.

Historical archaeology does not move away from material culture as its primary research medium nor does it diminish the strategic importance of stratigraphic excavation and recording. Rather, it permits the powerful advantage of integrating documentary and aboveground material artifacts into the core research design. Bringing together the fullest possible complement of historical resources and disciplinary methodologies produces the essential synergism that illuminates both larger patterns and ephemeral details that would remain undetected if the independent researches were to be conducted in isolation.[3] Where patterns that have been independently derived from discrete and diverse sets of resources overlap, the degree of probability of an interpretation increases exponentially. Such investigation must be conducted interactively on various levels.

This study centered on the lifeways and economics of farmer/blacksmith Emerson Bixby and his family, especially during the pivotal second quarter of the nineteenth century. The next larger level of concentration was on the agricultural/crafts neighborhood historically known as "Four Corners" in the northernmost tip of Barre, Massachusetts. Its settlement, initial diversity, and sufficiency and its conspicuous decline spanned the relatively brief period extending from the end of the eighteenth century through the mid nineteenth century. By determining the neighborhood's composition and functional relationships through time, we fixed the context in which to understand the Bixby activities while simultaneously setting this case study into the larger complex of forces that were transforming the cultural and material life of all rural central New England.[4]

---

[3] James Deetz, "American Historical Archaeology: Methods and Results," *Science* 239 (January 22, 1988): 362–67; John Worrell, "Toward the Holistic Investigation of the Connecticut River Valley," in Robert Paynter, ed., *Ecological Anthropology of the Middle Connecticut River Valley* (Amherst: University of Massachusetts Press, 1979), pp. 152–61; John Worrell, "Scars upon the Earth: Physical Evidences of Dramatic Social Change at the Stratton Tavern," in James A. Moore, ed., *Proceedings of the Conference on Northeastern Archaeology* (Amherst: University of Massachusetts Press, 1980), pp. 133–45; John Worrell, Linda Ammons, James Blackaby, and William Gates, "The Cultural Resources of Historic Phoenixville" (Connecticut Historical Commission, Hartford, 1980, monograph).

[4] This research was conducted as one component of the project "Tradition and Transformation: Rural Economic Life in Central New England, 1790–1850," undertaken by the Research Department of Old Sturbridge Village with partial funding by the National Endowment for the Humanities. Research in public and private documentary

At the turn of the nineteenth century, a primary trafficway ran from the center of Barre northward to Phillipston and Templeton. Another connected the town centers of Hubbardston to the east and Petersham to the west. The two intersected in the northern tip of Barre, forming a crossroads so prominent that the neighborhood was commonly referred to as "Four Corners," without the necessity of further qualification (fig. 1). Today the eastern leg of that crossroad can be ascertained only by careful inspection of the overgrown landscape, and the seldom-used northern leg is scarcely improved beyond its eighteenth-century condition. The southern and western legs remain to form a right-angle turn in a very rural road carrying little other than local resident traffic. Material evidences of the once-bustling neighborhood—its several shops, mills, barns, outbuildings, and even the majority of its houses—are now informative only through archaeological investigation. Even most people living nearby have never heard of a community named Barre Four Corners.

The anonymity of Barre Four Corners on modern maps and memory provides us with a reasonable metaphor for the problems confronting any researcher who attempts to reconstruct the life of such a vanished community. Several kinds of obstruction hinder our investigation from this temporal distance. One is, inevitably, that we are unwilling victims to the caprice of preservation. Our thoughtfully crafted research designs are never rewarded with wholly preserved sets of resources, and even those minimally necessary for multidimensional investigation are seldom without omissions and problems of comparability. Worse yet, the material and documentary evidences that bear the highest potential

---

sources was conducted in the Old Sturbridge Village Research Library and Research Department files as well as in the records and archives of the Town of Barre, the Barre Historical Society, and the holdings of other local and state institutions. The account books of Emerson Bixby covering the years 1824–55 are in the collections of the American Antiquarian Society, Worcester, Mass. Citations for other primary sources have been omitted in this work, for the most part, but are readily available in other works by the authors cited throughout the text and in the Research Department files at Old Sturbridge Village. The authors acknowledge the contributions of the following individuals: Jack Larkin, Jeanne Whitney, Marcia Jordan, Jane and Charles Pelletier, Greg Hill, Nora Pat Small, Thomas Paske, Caroline Sloat, Andrew Baker, Martha Lance, Linda Ammons, Larry Ingalls, Dorothy Ingalls, and Walter Fullam and Dorothy Fullam. We especially thank the respective staffs and students of the Old Sturbridge Village Field Schools in Historical Archaeology and in Architectural History.

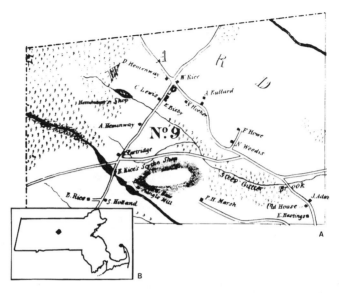

Fig. 1. Detail, Map of Barre, Massachusetts, 1835, published by Samuel F. Ainsworth. (Old Sturbridge Village; Photo, Thomas Neill.) The Barre Four Corners neighborhood was located in School District Number 9, situated in the extreme northern corner of the town of Barre.

for detailing ordinary lives of families and communities are those least likely to have been recorded or preserved without ambiguity. But the largest barrier of all is cognitive: both by experience and by conceptual framework, we stand at a considerable cultural distance from Barre Four Corners of the early nineteenth century. The Bixbys and their community were, in a real sense, a contact community living, functioning, and reacting at the intersection of agrarian and industrial/commercial societies. Their marks were made largely on the other side of a transformation in the fundamental meanings and values that we impute to the basic categories of our experience. It was that separation that was most difficult for us to transcend. It was likewise the object of our most intense research interest.[5]

[5] See, for example, the discussion in David Lowenthal, *The Past Is a Foreign Country* (New York: Cambridge University Press, 1985).

The human mind requires system and order. It is therefore a universal tendency to collapse the unsettling complexities of reality into simplistic formulas, to imprint valued abstractions onto historic persons or events, and to turn case studies into covering laws. Archaeologists and historians have scarcely shown less susceptibility than other disciplines to what Henry Glassie refers to as the modern superstition of pure science. *Space* and *time* are two human constructs that have served historical archaeologists so well as we attempt to classify our imperfect and ambiguous data that we have been tempted to treat them as axial constants of natural law. That has led us too often to regard our task as the collection and quantification of objective bits of pure data whose sum corresponds to historical reality. This is, to our discipline, the same fallacy that Stephen Jay Gould has criticized in his field as "the usual mythology about scientific practice."[6]

The urge to turn a single case study into an "Everyman" archetype is frequently reinforced beyond recall by the absence of comparative and corrective data. A broadly based research design that makes deep incursions at selected points, however, can hold both individual cases and cultural generalizations in focus. This provides the antidote to what geographers have called the "genetic fallacy" of confusing sequence with consequence. In our case, that fallacy takes the form of assuming that the diverse array of rural New England's cultural components changed simultaneously in all localities—or even in a regular, universally applicable sequence in each. From our historical distance, we recognized that this radical cultural transformation was the summary of a nearly infinite complement of somewhat related individual reactions to a diverse but interacting set of motivations, occurring irregularly over an extended period.[7]

[6] Henry Glassie, "Archaeology and Folklore: Common Anxieties, Common Hopes," in Leland Ferguson, ed., *Historical Archaeology and the Importance of Material Things* (Society for Historical Archaeology, 1977), p. 26. Stephen Jay Gould, "Piltdown Revisited," *Natural History* (March 1979): 94. Alan Watts discusses the "scanning process that observes the world bit by bit [that] soon persuades its user that the world is a great collection of bits, and these he calls separate things or events." This forced separation of causal nexus blinds us to integral relationships. "The problem would never have arisen if we had been aware that it was just our way of looking at the world which chopped it up into separate bits, events, causes, and effects" (Alan Watts, *The Book: On the Taboo against Knowing Who You Are* [Westminster, Md.: Random House, 1972], p. 28).

[7] David Harvey, *Explanation in Geography* (London: E. Arnold, 1973), pp. 409–16. Paul Coones observes: "The tendency to confuse sequence with consequence (*post hoc ergo propter hoc*), and to employ temporal explanations carelessly is unfortunately none

Both social historians and historical archaeologists have come to recognize that broadly based, multidimensional investigation of the commonplace elements of cultural history is the essential corrective for the biases produced by a longstanding fascination with things famous, urban, sensational, or stereotyped.[8] Unfortunately, it is far easier to derive both material and descriptive evidence about the sensational exceptions than it is about the pervasive rule. But it is the evasive residues of everyday life that provide the essential elements for reconstructing the extensive processes that have produced our modern culture. Because the larger questions of cultural process will not reliably yield to a monodirectional analysis, the "archaeology of everyday life" employs a far broader complement of investigative methods and resources than has traditionally been found in the archaeologist's tool kit.

The synergistic research strategy designed for our investigation of the Bixbys in Barre Four Corners applied a common idiom to all stages of acquisition, formulation, and processing of the different lines of data. We examined the architectural fabric; the interior configuration,

---

too rare, and is especially inappropriate to the pre-industrial period where change was not always the most apparent element and in any case was not synonymous with growth" (Paul Coones, "Manufacture in Pre-Industrial England: A Bibliography," *Journal of Historical Geography* 5, no. 2 [1979]: 131). As important as each is in our history and as much truth as is symbolized in their respective clichés, both the American Revolution and the industrial revolution have often been misunderstood to signify cataclysmicly what was in actuality the cumulative coalescence of innumerable cultural processes spanning several generations. James Deetz, *In Small Things Forgotten: The Archaeology of Early American Life* (Garden City, N.Y.: Anchor/Doubleday, 1977), does a remarkable job of tracing the stages of transformation epochally through various material and social lines while avoiding overcaricaturing pivotal events.

[8] John Worrell, "Research and Resource Management Priorities for Northeast Historical Archaeology: A Plea for the Common Man," in James A. Moore, ed., *Proceedings of the Conference on Northeastern Historical Archaeology* (Amherst: University of Massachusetts Press, 1980), pp. 173–78. For recent trends in this direction in architectural studies, see Dell Upton, "Ordinary Buildings: A Bibliographical Essay on American Vernacular Architecture," *American Studies International* 19 (Winter 1981): 57–75; Dell Upton and John Michael Vlach, eds., *Common Places: Readings in American Vernacular Architecture* (Athens: University of Georgia Press, 1986); Camille Wells, ed., *Perspectives in Vernacular Architecture* (Annapolis, Md.: Vernacular Architecture Forum, 1982); Camille Wells, ed., *Perspectives in Vernacular Architecture II* (Columbia: University of Missouri Press for Vernacular Architecture Forum, 1986); Thomas Carter and Bernard L. Herman, *Perspectives on Vernacular Architecture III* (Columbia: University of Missouri Press for Vernacular Architecture Forum, 1988); Thomas Carter and Bernard L. Herman, *Perspectives on Vernacular Architecture IV* (Columbia: University of Missouri Press for Vernacular Architecture Forum, 1991).

embellishments, furnishings, and functional areas related to both the house and the blacksmith shop; the structuring, functions, and alterations of exterior spaces; the subsurficial stratigraphy; and the documentary record, all according to an interactive research design. Because it was organized according to our elaborate archaeological recording system, we dubbed this integrated method "archaeology from the ground up." The reciprocity between the diverse resources moved the investigation well beyond description of physical and functional changes to produce a revealing biography that chronicles the complex interaction between elements of family structure, household economy, technical innovations and choices, patterns of exchange and preferences in selection, and utilization and disposal of material culture.

Early nineteenth-century New England was a primary arena for this dramatic socioeconomic change. But there is no simple model by which a historian may predict the precise moment at which new styles, technologies, products, or concepts will appear at any given point on the rural landscape. To understand how and why specific responses took the forms and timing that we have identified, we developed a strategy of nested research units. Each had its own appropriate set of questions organized to intersect with those of the next levels, larger and smaller. The concentric circles of investigation expanded from the individual case study to its neighborhood, cultural region, and on to national or international social and economic trends. By filling in as many empirical pieces as possible at each level, we developed a consistent chain of interpretation that plotted trajectories across the boundaries between levels of investigation. This strategy was equipped to deal with inevitable idiosyncracies while removing the too-usual "leap of faith" across the disjunction between "site-specific" and "cultural generalization."[9]

In Barre Four Corners we located a neighborhood that was sufficiently cohesive, documented, and materially preserved to afford such comprehensive analysis, and the Emerson Bixby site was ideally provisioned for exhaustive focal study. Bixby's account books survive, and

[9] John Worrell, "Getting from Here to Barre Four Corners; or, Plotting Trajectories through Space and Time" (Paper presented to the annual meeting of the Northeastern Anthropological Association, 1988; Research Department, Old Sturbridge Village, manuscript on file).

his house and site had scarcely been altered for more than a century when we began our investigation.

A rich complement of public and private documents proved instrumental in our attempt to place people and events accurately in spatial and temporal perspective. Tax, census, evaluation, probate, property, school district, church, and town clerk records were supplemented by a diary, individual reminiscences, Bixby's records, old maps and photographs, and oral history.[10]

Computer-assisted analysis of a wide range of individual, family, institutional, town, state, and federal documents was directed at identifying, defining, and evaluating the members of Emerson Bixby's economic network. Bixby and his family, neighbors, and trading partners have been located geographically and economically. His account book began with his arrival in Four Corners in 1824 and continued to record exchanges through a peak in the 1830s and a decline that extends until the record ends in 1855. All accounts for twenty-two years were coded, providing more than 12,000 entries for the 164 trading partners. The nature, range, and extent of their relationships were defined, yielding patterns of seasonality in Bixby's work, a profile of the changing nature of his craft and of his economic structure. Kinship research identified family composition and marriage ties within the neighborhood and trade network. These were ranked and analyzed within the trading area, town, and region over a thirty-year period. Analysis of Barre tax records provided the context for determining localized economic trends as well as the wealth profiles of the Four Corners neighborhood and its respective individuals. Household composition, age/sex ratios, wealth ranges, occupational status, nativity, and other factors were determined via computer analysis of United States census returns. Analysis of more than fifty probate inventories taken between 1815 and 1855 provided information on the nature of the neighborhood's material culture and wealth. The diary of Jane Brigham, the young daughter of one of Bixby's trading partners, provided direct information on local social

---

[10] The extensive documentary research undertaken for this project has been reported in Myron Stachiw, "Social and Economic Change in a Rural Neighborhood: The Documentary Record from Barre Four Corners, Barre, Massachusetts, in the Early Nineteenth Century" (Research Department, Old Sturbridge Village, 1987, manuscript). It is summarized here to reference its reciprocity with the material investigations that are focal for this paper.

activity and relationships, work patterns of respective individuals and categories of persons, evidence of changes in buildings and furnishings, and the subjective implications of those changes—all made more tangible by the architectural survey and analysis of the Brigham house.[11]

This documentary analysis rendered an extensive framework of names, motives, and explanatory connections into which the more traditional activities of archaeology dovetailed with apt complementarity. The specificity in spatial, functional, technical, and aesthetic details that the documents lacked was precisely that which meticulous stratigraphic excavation, recording, and analysis conclusively provided. Together they described the preferences and specified the activities by which choices were rendered economically and technically possible and became reality. The combined evidence furnished a graphic picture of what was happening in the lives of actual people, supplementing theory with biography.

Three major lines of physical investigation framed the neighborhood reconstruction. The first was archaeological survey and mapping. A neighborhood map was drafted to scale, depicting existing features with all evidences of foundations, trafficways, stone walls, hydrological features, and every trace of intentional spatial organization or alteration. These were located from maps and property records, conversations with local informants, and walkover and instrument survey. The neighborhood map and larger-scale measured drawings of all important features within it provided the spatial matrix in which to understand and reference all cultural elements.[12]

A second line of inquiry was architectural survey. Thirteen dwellings in the locality having histories relevant to the Bixby study were carefully investigated and recorded and were keyed to measured draw-

[11] Myron O. Stachiw and Nora Pat Small, "Tradition and Transformation: Rural Society and Architectural Change in Nineteenth-Century Central Massachusetts," in Carter and Herman, *Perspectives in Vernacular Architecture III*, pp. 135–48. The diary of Jane Brigham begins in her thirteenth year (1847) and ends in 1863, 3 years after her marriage. It is in the holdings of the Petersham Historical Society, Petersham, Mass. Karin Nelson's analysis of the diary is on file in the Research Department, Old Sturbridge Village.

[12] David Simmons, "The Emerson Bixby Project: Family, Work and Community of an Early Nineteenth-Century Blacksmith" (Paper presented to the annual meeting of the Society for Historical Archaeology, 1987; Research Department, Old Sturbridge Village, manuscript on file). Worrell, "Getting from Here to Barre Four Corners."

ings indicating their components and alterations. Paint sequences and decorative embellishments, technical structural details, and site history were among the factors thoroughly annotated for each house and evaluated comparatively. This revealed an extensive set of standards of vernacular conventions and taste through which to understand the basic features and specific alterations of each structure, especially those structures exhaustively documented at the Bixby site.[13]

Our most comprehensive examination of the material evidences came in the intensive archaeological investigation of the Bixby house and dooryard, farm lot, and shop and those of farmer/shoemaker Cheney Lewis directly across the road. The Lewises and the Bixbys, each newly married, moved into the neighborhood within a year of each other to begin farming and plying their respective artisanry. The Bixbys located in an existing structure, while the Lewises built anew, with Bixby making their architectural hardware.[14] Comparison of the features, arrangement, materials scatter, functional areas, and other appointments on the two sites was therefore especially significant. The following brief description of the techniques employed is intended to provide an explanatory framework for evaluating the interpretations that follow.

Initially, the sites were gridded by transit into five-meter units, each subdivided into one-meter squares. A contour map was drawn from instrument survey and served as the base upon which all information discovered during any stage of the investigation was referenced. All surficially observable information was recorded for each five-meter square. Surficial anomalies, features, and suspected activity areas were selectively sampled and stratigraphically recorded in half-meter–square test probes. Ten major block excavations on the Bixby home lot recovered successive stratigraphic data to sterile soil. The smithy site was similarly block excavated, and four block excavations were conducted at the Lewis site. All archaeological data was recorded stratigraphically by one-meter lateral increments, providing detailed fine-tuning of arti-

---

[13] Nora Pat Small, "Recording of the Bixby House, 1986: Final Report" (Research Department, Old Sturbridge Village, manuscript on file); Stachiw and Small, "Tradition and Transformation."

[14] Account with Cheney Lewis, 1825–26, Emerson Bixby account book, ledger, American Antiquarian Society, Worcester, Mass.

fact distribution and soil data. Several hundred measured plans and recording forms contained the field data. More than three thousand total excavation subunits formed the matrix in which hundreds of thousands of bits of data—material and technical—were organized in three major computer databases. Each database broke down its respective coverage into specific subunits of provenience. One summarized the relative frequency of material culture by category and further according to several typological distinctions. A second database similarly sorted the ceramic assemblages, recording information about sixteen attributes for each excavated sherd. Although it is far less visible than artifacts, the physical and chemical composition of the soils, properly analyzed and plotted, frequently contains functional information that is even more valuable for interpreting the use of space. The third database, therefore, applied six categories of analytical variables for the soils stratigraphically sampled in each of the excavated subunits. Sorting within these databases arealy by locus, phase, and feature, we defined specific functional areas, traffic patterns, and use changes at the site as the fabric of structures was altered, features were moved, and occupants changed.[15]

These techniques were designed to disclose functional details and evidences of activity that were unrecorded or, at best, ambiguous. Our investigation of the Bixby smithy illustrated their efficacy especially well. Technical details of the apprenticed crafts were never specified in descriptive or prescriptive literature. They are recoverable only by this type of archaeology. To address this problem directly, we sampled soils stratigraphically at quarter-meter intervals throughout the shop interior and the suspected work space in front. The samples were analyzed for relative iron content, and the results were mapped. Combined with the rest of the archaeological record, this provided a plan of the

---

[15]The procedural and technical details for this and all other techniques here discussed are explained in John Worrell, David Simmons, and Will Gates, *Small Things Considered: Guidelines for Field Recording in Archaeological Excavation* (Sturbridge, Mass.: Old Sturbridge Village, 1992). David Simmons, "Computers and a Blacksmith: Sorting out the World of Emerson Bixby" (Paper presented at the Microcomputer Applications in Archaeology Symposium, Princeton University, 1986; Research Department, Old Sturbridge Village, manuscript on file); David Simmons, "Dirt, Documents, and Databases" (Paper presented to the annual meeting of the Council for Northeast Historical Archaeology, 1986; Research Department, Old Sturbridge Village, manuscript on file).

probable layout of the shop, including the placement of such functional furniture as the hearth, anvil, and workbench. Such fine-grained information enabled us to combine spatial arrangement, kinetifacts, and artifacts in reconstructing the dynamics of this vanished artisanry.[16]

What should be self-evident—but what appears to be frequently ignored by archaeologists, architectural historians, and preservationists, among others—is that the architecture and the home lot *together* make up a functional site. Therefore, to understand the spatial dimensions of the story, we applied the principles of stratigraphic excavation to the Bixby house as it was being partially dismantled in preparation for its removal to Old Sturbridge Village, recording all clues bearing on its construction, decoration sequences, alterations, and functional/spatial organization in a specifically revised version of the elaborate archaeological field recording system. The phased architectural data therefore integrated readily with that produced by four seasons of archaeological excavation, revealing three major phases of site reorganization. This "total site matrix" was then merged with exhaustive documentary information to produce a comprehensive and persuasive site biography that specified stages in the lives of identifiable persons in the two families— the Hemenways and the Bixbys—who left their material marks there for us to interpret in the context of neighborhood, town, and regional developments.[17]

Any less comprehensive approach could not have allowed us to piece together the personal and cultural significances of an important

[16] We are deeply grateful to John Light of Parks Canada for assisting us in developing this investigative strategy and interpreting the results. Light and materials analyst Henry Unglik had pioneered this approach on Canadian smithy sites; see John D. Light and Henry Unglik, *A Frontier Trade Blacksmith Shop, 1795–1812* (Ottawa: Environment, Parks Canada, 1987). For a technical report on Light and Unglik's analytical work in our project, see Henry Unglik, "Observations on the Structures and Formation of Microscopic Smithing Residues from the Bixby Blacksmith Shop at Barre Four Corners, Massachusetts, 1824–55," *Historical Metallurgy* 25, no. 2 (1991): 92–98. This basic strategy and its results as applied to the similar rural craft of earthenware production are reported in John Worrell, "Recreating Ceramic Production and Tradition in a Living History Laboratory," in Sarah Peabody Turnbaugh, ed., *Domestic Pottery of the Northeastern United States, 1625–1850* (Orlando, Fla.: Academic Press, 1985), pp. 81–97.

[17] David Simmons, Myron Stachiw, and John Worrell, "The Total Site Matrix: Strata and Structure at the Bixby Site," in Edward Harris, Marley Brown, and Gregory Brown, eds., *Practices of Archaeological Stratigraphy* (London: Academic Press, 1992); Small, "Recording of the Bixby House"; Worrell, Simmons, and Gates, *Small Things Considered.*

transformation in the history of the Bixby family and site. It involved the physical manifestation of a striking major shift in lifestyle for which there had been no substantial direct evidence in the documentary record. It encompassed a comprehensive restructuring of the house and yard spaces that occurred at a pivotal moment in the family's life cycle—a situation that has recurred frequently in our comprehensive case studies. For the Bixbys, a motive force was the "coming of age" of the daughters, who had attained a level of maturity sufficient to exert influence over stylistic preferences that they could affect with economic input of their own. The neighborhood and trading network had for some time been exhibiting various responses to regional currents of transformation in consumption patterns as well as in the conceptions and conventions of propriety and style. When they reshaped their personal world, the Bixbys were participating in a general pattern of social change that involved local, regional, and national reorganization of economic power and cultural priorities. They were personally involved in the pervasive cultural conversion epitomized by historians with grandiose terms such as "capitalist transformation" and "industrial revolution." But the timing and effective details of their unpretentious participation therein was more directly determined by personal factors that we could come to understand only through the *reciprocity* of material and documentary researches whose respective data within their confines presented conflicting conclusions.

Remote and diffused agricultural neighborhoods like Barre Four Corners do not fit comfortably on any pat schedule of transformation. For the residents of the scattered farms and the tiny agricultural crafts and mill neighborhoods, the social distance was even more pronounced than was the spatial distance from the centers of change. The concerns of countryside dwellers were more immediate and pragmatic than were those of residents of the center villages, and they were less consciously provoked or constrained by the neighborhood gaze of those who set social standards or monitored the norms of propriety. Therefore, elements of both social and material culture in the scattered countryside responded less predictably to the winds of change that blew generally through traditional New England agrarian culture in the early decades of the nineteenth century.[18]

---

[18] For distinctions between rural and urban and countryside and village life and their residents' responses to changes in social, cultural, and material life, see especially Jack

The town of Barre, which has generally good agricultural soils for upland New England, became an important cattle and dairying area before the end of the eighteenth century. A major in-migration between 1765 and 1775 doubled the town's population and settled the first families in what became the Four Corners neighborhood.[19]

Preparation of the trafficways that accompanied this influx of settlement left the earliest archaeological evidences found at the site. Typical of early roads in most rural New England neighborhoods, the two thoroughfares that cross at Four Corners have few initial records. The north–south road improved an ancient Indian trail and was officially laid out by the town in 1771. The origin is obscure for the road on which the Bixby lot fronts, but it was officially laid out in 1772 and was a major east–west route across the county and state during the late eighteenth and early nineteenth centuries. The crossroads attracted a tavern and a district school before the end of the eighteenth century, and a series of agricultural craft shops and mills were added by the farmer neighbors nearby during the next few decades (see fig. 1).[20]

Larkin, *The Reshaping of Everyday Life* (New York: Harper and Row, 1988); Jack Larkin, "From 'Country Mediocrity' to 'Rural Improvement': Transforming the Slovenly Countryside in Central Massachusetts, 1775–1840," in Catherine E. Hutchins, ed., *Everyday Life in the Early Republic* (Winterthur, Del.: Henry Francis du Pont Winterthur Museum, 1995), pp. 175–200; Stachiw and Small, "Tradition and Transformation"; William J. Gilmore, *Reading Becomes a Necessity of Life: Material and Cultural Life in Rural New England, 1780–1835* (Knoxville: University of Tennessee Press, 1989), esp. part 1, chaps. 2–4; Richard D. Brown, "The Emergence of Urban Society in Rural Massachusetts, 1760–1820," *Journal of American History* 61 (1974): 29–51; Francis Underwood, *Quabbin: The Story of a Small Town with Outlooks on Puritan Life* (1893; reprint, Boston: Northeastern University Press, 1986); Richard L. Bushman, *The Refinement of America: Persons, Houses, Cities* (New York: Knopf, 1992), chap. 11, esp. pp. 379–82.

[19] "Barre Town Report" (Massachusetts Historical Commission, Boston, 1982, manuscript). Synthesized information was published in Michael Steinitz, Claire Dempsey, Myron Stachiw, and Charlotte Worsham, *Historical and Archaeological Resources of Central Massachusetts* (Boston: Massachusetts Historical Commission, 1985). Barre was part of a larger tract purchased from Native Americans in 1686 and incorporated as Rutland in 1714. A 6-mile square, having its corners rather than its sides oriented roughly toward the cardinal compass directions, was set off as a separate district in 1753, incorporated as Hutchinson in 1774, and renamed Barre in 1776.

[20] Stachiw, "Social and Economic Change," p. 5. Property records are in the Worcester County Courthouse, Worcester, Mass. (microfilm, Old Sturbridge Village Research Library). Barre Town Records are largely complete in the Town Clerk's Office, Barre Town Hall.

Probing and excavation provided details about the original natural topography, giving us a basis for assessing human alteration of the landscape. Experience at previous sites prepared us to expect that considerable earth and stone moving might have been done to bring the house and barn lots into conformity with pragmatic and even aesthetic objectives of the occupants. But we were surprised to discover the prodigious recontouring that occurred well before any indication of significant occupation of the site.[21]

A huge granite outcropping that formed a natural watershed had been quarried to ground level during preparation for the road right-of-way. This may phase with the official assumption of the road by the town in 1772, while a later improvement evident in our excavations may relate to that mentioned in 1802 town records. Sometime between those two phases of road improvement, the entire site was burned off, leaving residues of ash, char, and heat-altered soil throughout.[22]

Soon after the burn off, an agricultural outbuilding was erected near the road in what would later become the front yard of the house. While the structure was in place, the area around it was tilled or

---

[21] John Worrell, "Landscape as Artifact: Archaeological Evidences of Artificial Site Formation" (Paper presented to the annual meeting of the Conference on New England Archaeology, 1991; Research Department, Old Sturbridge Village, manuscript on file).

[22] Much of the quarrying debitage, along with a chisel, cascaded down its quarried faces where we discovered them beneath considerable later fill. Nearly identical evidences were found in our archaeological investigations of the Pliny Freeman site in Sturbridge, where quarrying had initially phased with road construction. In both cases this made the sites much more favorable for domestic development. John Worrell, "The Pliny Freeman Site: A Preliminary Report" (Research Department, Old Sturbridge Village, manuscript); Worrell, "Landscape as Artifact." The original roadbed fronting the Bixby site remained as an extremely hard-packed cobbled surface sloping down westward to a low natural water catchment. There the road builders constructed a ford of boulders—including some very angular, newly broken ones, which may have come from the quarrying on the site—that allowed the water to pass through while providing a firm base for traffic above. Subsequently, but also before the site received a house, the roadbed was raised even more by adding a curbing of boulders and hauling in fill. Burn evidence stratigraphically preceded the quarrying and earliest road building but appeared not to have preceded the second phase of improvement by very long, as char and heat-altered soils remained intact immediately beneath that fill. Consistent deposits of char and ash persisted only where some deposition shortly after the conflagration sealed them against erosion and biodegradation. We found evidence of site burning in preparation for occupation at every rural domestic site in central New England that we have investigated archaeologically. See Worrell, "Landscape as Artifact"; and Worrell, "Scars upon the Earth."

harrowed, leaving a rich, evenly mixed soil thinly preserved where it was protected subsequently by ejecta from the cellar or well.[23]

A four-bay English-style barn with slightly ramped front entry was in place before construction of the house and remained in place during the early part of the first domestic phase. The small triangular parcel on which it was situated had been purchased by neighborhood farmer Daniel Hemenway from his son Amos in 1807. The deed does not mention any buildings. In 1809 he sold the lot "with dwelling house thereon" to another son, Rufus. Each man was listed as "housewright."[24] The documentary record therefore presented a good case for the phase one dwelling on the site having been built by one or both of the father and son builders between 1807 and 1809 (fig. 2). The archaeology of the soil and of the building, however, suggested that the story may have been somewhat more complicated.

The initials "NH" etched into integral timbers may indicate that an older brother Nathan actually erected the original structure. Nathan was married in 1802 but had moved out of town before the 1810 census, when he appears in the nearby town of Athol, listed as a "carpenter." Analysis of the archaeological and architectural evidence in the dooryard indicated that the house was in place and in use for a time before it was "finished" according to usual conventions of architectural completeness. The outside sheathing showed considerable weathering before being clapboarded, and ceiling joists in the kitchen, discolored

---

[23] The preservation of the char residues inside the structure's "footprint" indicated that it was built soon after the burn off and that it was floored. Foundation stones and "ghosts" of others along with traces of collapsed structural timbers, all sealed beneath the ejecta from the house cellar, confirmed that the building was not in existence by the time the house was built. The well preceded the house stratigraphically, but it was not clear whether it was dug initially to service the agricultural phase of the site or in preparation for domestic use. Similarly phased beneath the apron of ejecta, we found an enigmatic series of stacked stones and postmolds that apparently defined the boundary between the lot and the road right-of-way. The posts themselves had not penetrated the subsoil, apparently having been supported by the stacked stones. Some had been partially disturbed when the ejecta was deposited, but the posts themselves were not pulled out until the house had been in use for some time. Their purpose is still unknown.

[24] Worcester County Manuscript Property Records, vol. 184, p. 322, Worcester County Courthouse, Worcester, Mass. The road crossed the original border between Great Farms One and Two at an acute angle, giving the lot its asymmetrical, truncated-triangle shape, its eastern line being 6½ rods along the common boundary between Amos and Daniel. Two years later Daniel completed the triangle, adding from his original farm the point where the road and southern line met.

Fig. 2. Arrangement of the house and shop lots and buildings at the Bixby site, ca. 1809–ca. 1815. (Old Sturbridge Village: Drawing, Melanie Shook; Photo, Henry E. Peach.)

by hearth smoke, demonstrated that it was lived in while both unplastered and unceiled. Stratified materials in the rear dooryard also disclosed changing patterns of domestic activity and refuse scatter during phase one, with residues from plastering and other construction activities found at the juncture of change.

Nathan may have erected the shell of the structure and lived in it with his wife before it was finished—perhaps soon after his marriage, while the property still belonged to his brother Amos. The absence of any reference to a dwelling in the 1807 intrafamily transaction may reflect only that it was not finished nor being lived in at the time of sale, with Daniel and Rufus making it more livable and calling it a dwelling by the time of their transaction two years later.

The original house was about twenty-seven feet on a side, with the ridge line paralleling the road that passed on the northern side of the house lot (see fig. 2). The house was surrounded by a terrace built up primarily of the mixed glacial till that was excavated for its cellar. Because cellars were primarily intended for food storage, reasonable dryness and protection from freezing were essential. The terracing provided insulation and diverted surface drainage away from the dry-laid foundations and cellar. Traces of hewing and masonry activities immediately beneath the apron of cellar ejecta confirmed that the chimney stack was erected and that some of the framing took place before the cellar was fully excavated—a construction sequence that we have documented archaeologically at other sites as well.[25]

The frame rested on long, nicely faced granite sill stones that had been surface quarried in the immediate neighborhood. Apart from its relatively equal exterior dimensions, virtually everything else about the single-story structure was asymmetrical, displaying characteristics that stood in contrast to the standards of neoclassical architectural form that were issuing from the cultural centers of the period. Its kitchen extended across the northern side, two unevenly sized rooms made up the southern side, and the chimney stack and fireplaces were built off center. The interior of the house was decorated sparingly in ocher, dark red, brown, and blue colors in the wallpaper and painted surfaces; some of the walls remained unpainted horizontal sheathing.[26]

[25] This is a characteristic that we have found to be nearly universal for rural central New England domestic construction of the period; see Worrell, "Landscape as Artifact"; Worrell, "Scars upon the Earth," pp. 138, 140–41. A well-executed fieldstone drain from the cellar, installed after a brief period of occupancy, answered a problem that was unanticipated when the house was sited on the highest part of the lot. Excavation found that the large stone in the front yard, which had been quarried much earlier, defined a subsurficial watershed that was not evident to the builders. The drain employed a structural technique prescribed in period literature for field drainage, but we have not found it described in architectural or archaeological literature. For reports on additional documented sites, see Worrell, "Pliny Freeman Site"; and Worrell, "Landscape as Artifact."

[26] A rough, unimproved lot bordering the Bixby lot on the southwest belonged to tavernkeeper Moses Smith. It has many glacial erratics and bedrock outcroppings that show evidence of quarrying, including one granite boulder displaying the contours of removed sillstones and tool marks of the process. Still in place are some feathers and wedges locked tight at points where the stone proved intractable. Sill stones similar to those supporting the Bixby house have been found in all the early house foundations in the area. The diagnostic, heavily framed, three-room plan was common in this neighborhood. Stachiw and Small, "Tradition and Transformation"; Myron O. Stachiw, "The Color of Change: The Bixby House and the Social and Economic Transformation of the Household, 1807–1850," in Sarah Chase and Patricia Weslowski, eds., *Paint in America* (Washington, D.C.: Preservation Press, forthcoming 1996). The roof line in these houses invariably paralleled the road, regardless of direction, while the interior of each was consistent in relation to compass orientation. In effect, the interior and exterior responded independently—demonstrating a grammar of local folk culture that accommodated some stylistic innovation while generally adhering to traditional functional norms.

Three doors provided access to this small structure: a southern door into the best room and northern and western entries to the kitchen. All were subsequently removed or enclosed, but their use histories have been described by archaeology. The publicly visible door facing the road had been fitted only with a simple wooden step structure, and the surrounding area showed very little evidence of use. The door at the rear, or southern, facade of the house was clearly the formal entry, having had a large stone doorstep founded on a substantial stone pad, and witnessed moderate traffic. This door also opened into the most formal interior space of the house, the best room.[27] The western door, opening from the kitchen toward the barn and well, also had a simple wooden step, but its vicinity revealed strikingly heavy use. Refuse disposal, compacted pathways, and prepared trafficway features all described it as the family door. Unlike most residences erected during the period, this house type had no vestibule or entry hall to mediate between the outside world and the intimate family spaces.

The dooryard and unretained terrace around the house had little vegetation and must have presented a much more barren look than modern tastes would approve. The terrace was composed essentially of a gravelly mix with little humic soils to support vegetation or to consolidate sufficiently to allow its growth. The front yard beyond the terrace was largely a similar material that had been deposited during the road improvement. None of this was enriched by topsoil, and it appears to have been several decades before anything approaching a lawn developed.

Compacted pathways led from the rear (western) door of the kitchen to the well and diagonally to the southern end of the terrace wall, indicating the usual access to the livestock quartering area of

---

[27]The south-facing orientation of the principal room and formal facade was a traditional form usually associated with an earlier era. For discussions of building orientation see Abbott Lowell Cummings, *The Framed Houses of Massachusetts Bay, 1625–1725* (Cambridge: Harvard University Press, 1979), p. 38; Thomas C. Hubka, *Big House, Little House, Back House, Barn* (Hanover, N.H.: University Press of New England, 1984), esp. chap. 5; Henry Glassie, "Eighteenth-Century Cultural Process in the Delaware Valley," in Ian M. G. Quimby, ed., *Winterthur Portfolio* 7 (Charlottesville: University Press of Virginia, 1972), pp. 50–57; Robert Blair St. George, " 'Set Thine House in Order': The Domestication of the Yeomanry in Seventeenth-Century New England," in Jonathan L. Fairbanks and Robert F. Trent, eds., *New England Begins*, vol. 2 (Boston: Museum of Fine Arts, 1982), pp. 162–63, 189.

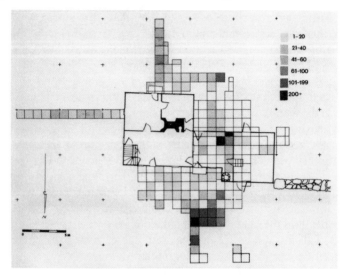

Fig. 3. Distribution of ceramic sherds within 1-meter-square archaeological excavation units; phase one occupation, ca. 1802–ca. 1815. (Old Sturbridge Village: Drawing, Charles Pelletier; Photo, Thomas Neill.)

the barn (see fig. 2). Chickens and other livestock were active near the western door, and a woodpile may have been located there. The buildup of domestic rubbish (including ceramics, glass, and bones) was extensive here, and many layers of ashy refuse suggest that hearth cleanings were regularly deposited to improve traction underfoot (fig. 3). This very tight and cluttered space was organized for optimal utility, largely devoid of considerations of privacy or fashion.[28] At some point

[28] Several traffic-related improvements were made throughout this first phase, especially where the path descended the terrace toward the barn. Structural foundation arrangement and a rectangular socket cut into a boulder inside the northeastern corner, probably for a manger support, combined with soil chemistry and stratigraphy to place the milking stall in the bay nearest the house. A large posthole between the barn and the well probably supported a well sweep before the shed and the well house were built. Ceramics from the earliest phase were found in any appreciable scatter only in this area of the western terrace and just off of it in the front yard near the well and in the rear yard along the path to the barn. Because a phase two structure was built there, integrity of materials and soils, including fragile biota, was extraordinary on the western terrace.

early in this phase the well was enclosed and a shed was attached to the barn, reducing the heavily used kitchen dooryard space even further. This yard space was the only part of the site to demonstrate extensive activity during phase one.

Coincident with these exterior site changes, the interior and exterior of the house were "finished." It was ceiled and trimmed, the best room was plastered and papered, and clapboards and trim were applied to the exterior. This improvement may be what prompted an increased tax evaluation in 1813, two years before Rufus Hemenway's marriage. The physical history of the total site, written in the rhythms of material distribution and change, is an essential part of the biography of its inhabitants.[29]

The second phase of domestic development featured modest expansion of the house and an extensive reorganization of the home lot (fig. 4). The barn was moved back into the lot, and areas devoted to livestock and refuse disposal were taken farther from the road. In an illuminating example of the interrelationship of material culture with stratigraphy, we used sherds from a single, very distinctive earthenware vessel to unify stratigraphically three important sequences of change undertaken during this phase. Sherds from this vessel were found in three discontinuous excavation areas: exposed immediately beneath the stones of a wall that accompanied a major shift in the traffic pattern from the house to the barn; mixed with residues from constructing an extension to the terrace retaining wall and a new set of steps leading to the rear of the lot; and mingled with structural materials from changes related to the addition of a new shed. It was clear from this serendipitous ceramics event that all these diverse landscape transformations occurred as parts of a single site restructuring.

Analysis of the structures and stratified artifacts sealed beneath them, with the initials "RH" etched into a framing member, attest that Rufus Hemenway gave the house its new wing and connected large

[29] John Worrell, "People Lived in Those Houses, and They Recorded Their Personalities in the Dirt" (Paper presented to the Conference on New England Archaeology, 1983; Research Department, Old Sturbridge Village, manuscript on file); Worrell, "Scars upon the Earth," pp. 137–42. David Simmons, "The Archaeology of Rural New England Craftsmen and Their Households" (Paper presented to the annual meeting of the Society for Historical Archaeology, 1989; Research Department, Old Sturbridge Village, manuscript on file). Stachiw and Small, "Tradition and Transformation."

Fig. 4. Arrangement of the house and shop lots and buildings at the Bixby site, ca. 1815–38. (Old Sturbridge Village: Drawing, Melanie Shook; Photo, Henry E. Peach.)

shed. The framing pattern and spacing in the new addition suggest that he intended it to have a kitchen hearth. But that intention was never realized, and neither the addition nor the unusual, large shed attached to it were ever provided with ceiling or interior finish (see fig. 4).[30]

The Four Corners neighborhood reached the height of its size and activity about the time that newly married Emerson Bixby opened his account book in 1824 with a debit entry to Alanson Green, the carriagemaker who that year purchased Hemenway's property. Two years later, when Green divided the lot, the house and barn are mentioned on the one acre sold to Bixby, while carriagemaking and blacksmith shops are listed on the half acre sold to Ethan Hemenway, Rufus's nephew, for whom Bixby continued "ironing wagon bodies."[31]

[30] Simmons, Stachiw, and Worrell, "Total Site Matrix"; Stachiw and Small, "Tradition and Transformation."

[31] Bixby accounts, American Antiquarian Society, Worcester, Mass. Emerson was the third generation of Bixbys to live in Barre, his grandfather settling about a mile southwest of Four Corners in 1758. Samuel, Emerson's father, purchased a farm a ½-mile east of Four Corners where Emerson was born in 1797. In 1807 Samuel moved

The previous year, 1825, Bixby had purchased a tiny parcel on which he erected his blacksmith shop directly across the road from the carriagemaker's shop. Perhaps he was already living in the house at that time, renting it from Green. As we have been unable to locate a residence elsewhere for either Bixby or Green, it is possible that the two young families shared this small house for those two years.

Despite Rufus's modest emendations, the house and lot into which Emerson and Laura Bixby moved with their infant daughter in 1826 differed little, conceptually or functionally, from the clustered configuration described for phase one, and it became even more crowded as two additional daughters were born during their first decade there. The single-room addition received only a few purely utilitarian changes, but its interior was never ceiled or fully sheathed. Likewise, the interior of the large shed was never ceiled, floored, or sheathed. Floorboards discovered during excavation in the shed were only loosely laid on the leveled earth surface. Although its height indicates the intention of a loft, none was ever installed. Its exterior was clapboarded on the front from the beginning, with the rear and gable end showing planed, match-board sheathing. It also was originally outfitted with opposing oversize doors on the front and rear. A slight earthen ramp had originally accessed it from the road, and a large stone step feature accompanied the rear. All of this seems to indicate a grander intention than the woodshed function it served for the Bixbys.

When the barn was moved back into the lot, a stone wall was built from the shed westward. That caused traffic to enter the lot through a barway farther west and made the entire barn and shed complex less open to the road and the public. The livestock quartering area also was enclosed at this time, removing it somewhat from the public road, although it remained quite proximate to the living quarters.[32]

with his wife and 6 children to Vermont, accompanying other family members and Barre residents. Emerson probably learned blacksmithing in Vermont before he and Samuel returned to Barre in 1820. He married in 1823, and 3 months later his wife, Laura, delivered the first of their 3 daughters. Archaeology at the site of the carriage shop revealed it to have been a long, relatively shallow structure having a wide door near one end. The blacksmith shop was probably an adjacent building right at the road, which excavations showed to have burned at some undetermined time.

[32] Previously, direct access from the road to the barn had been provided by a central, graded ramp that was later covered by a substantial stone wall. Excavation revealed an old fence line running from the rear of the new barn placement to the southern wall of

The interior arrangement of the living space remained much as it had been in phase one. The best room was the only one with plastered walls and ceiling and surely was the place of entertaining. It also appeared to have served as the parental bedroom and the family dining and dishwashing area; it came to be used for sewing and palm-leaf–hat making as well. The small daughters no doubt slept for most of the year in the unfinished garrett, moving their bedding down, probably into the kitchen, in the hottest weather.[33] Material evidence showed the sitting room and especially the kitchen to have been the most active domestic work spaces, while sewing, braiding, and shoe stitching also were conducted in the unfinished ell and in the rear dooryard.

During the early part of this phase, refuse was swept out of the best-room door or thrown into the heavily used but secluded area bounded by the house, shed, and barn. But later, as access to the house was rearranged, most nonfood refuse was deposited through a hole in the foundation, removing it entirely from view (fig. 5; see also fig. 3).

The net effect of the changes made during phase two was somewhat to expand and privatize the frequently used space. But the domestic and agricultural activities stayed tightly clustered in the lot. It remained for the Bixbys during the next phase to initiate a pattern of spatial reorganization that responded more to concerns of style than utility.

When farmer/craftsmen Bixby and Lewis made their purchases of property and developed their living and work spaces in the 1824–26 period, they had cause for optimism. The neighborhood was at the height of its growth and activity, sharing in a period of regional and national prosperity that lasted through the middle of the next decade. Agriculture and artisanry were burgeoning, cash was entering the local

---

the property. The western end of the lot had been plowed, while east of the fence line the deep, irregular disturbance with high-organic soil was diagnostic of a livestock yard. The other side of this barnyard was at the eastern line of Bixby's property. When Bixby and Hemenway purchased the divided lot from Green, their property division continued that barn-lot line northward to the road, running only a few feet east of the house.

[33] This disparate array of activities was demonstrated by materials excavated from beneath and within its floors and walls and from a distinctive scatter pattern beyond its door. It meshed with documentary sources from elsewhere that described living practices in the traditional mode. Larkin, *Reshaping of Everyday Life*, pp. 105–48; Larkin, "Country Mediocrity." This practice has local documentation as well; see Jane Brigham diary, Petersham Historical Society, Petersham, Mass.

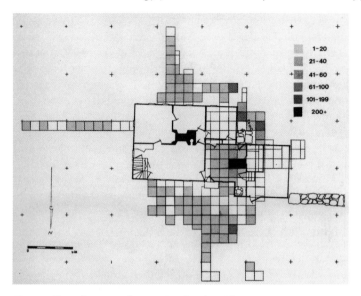

	1-20
	21-40
	41-60
	61-100
	101-199
	200+

Fig. 5. Distribution of ceramic sherds within 1-meter-square archaeological excavation units; phase three occupation, after ca. 1838. (Old Sturbridge Village: Drawing, Charles Pelletier; Photo, Thomas Neill.)

economic mix, and credit and consumerism were dramatically on the rise.

Bixby's tiny parcel with its modest smithy began immediately fulfilling his intentions, which were clearly rooted in a traditional agricultural/craft economy. Archaeological investigation of the blacksmith shop found that his technical procedures, equipment, and materials remained traditional. Debitage from metalworking and animal shoeing supported the account data indicating a predominance of agriculturally related work. His hearth structure and the analysis of slag from working at it gave no indication that Bixby made the shift from charcoal to coal or from wrought iron to mild steel—the changes that characterized the primary transformation to specialized smithing that occurred elsewhere during the middle decades of the century. But the large amount of work he did for vehicle manufacturers demonstrated that he also participated in the intermediate level of protoindustrial market production, which became an important agent in the economic transformation of the remote countryside.

The town of Barre shared strongly in the general economic upsurge. Its population steadily increased through the first three decades of the nineteenth century, and it became a major participant in the groundswell of household outwork industries and dairy production. In addition to the shoe trade, in which Lewis participated, Barre became a regional leader in the production of palm-leaf hats. By 1832 five dealers in the town supplied raw materials to hundreds of local women and girls, including the Bixbys. Simultaneously, new industrial clusters were formed, roads were built and improved, and a major newspaper was begun. All this provided sufficient variety and vitality for the town to withstand the panic of 1837 and the extensive recession that followed with only a temporary economic setback.

Although Barre continued to be an economic center through midcentury, a different fate struck its remote Four Corners neighborhood. The new town roads constructed during that period led elsewhere, two of the primary ones diverting most through-traffic around the crossroads neighborhood. Textile and tool manufacturing burgeoned farther south in Barre, while the immediately surrounding towns, which provided some economic interaction with the neighborhood, also began industries in textile and furniture manufacture. The *Barre Gazette* began publishing in 1834 and continues today. But as the regionwide crest of vitality for small-scale, decentralized rural production was rendered terminally obsolete by the radical changes of the late 1830s, this neighborhood joined many similar rural crafts neighborhoods in a sharp and conclusive transformation.

During the 1830s at least three shops run by farmer/artisans who also were Bixby trading partners closed their doors, removing scythemaking, carriagemaking, and woodturning from the neighborhood complement. The aging of the population and decline in craft production were accompanied by a steady decline in the volume and value of blacksmithing work recorded in Bixby's account book from the late 1830s onward.

Our focal site bears the contrasting evidence of two diverse fortunes that, combined, typify the story of the neighborhood during the period of dramatic economic transition. The two rural artisans who divided Green's property and began their careers promisingly during their first decade there had experienced radically different fates by the end of the second. Ethan Hemenway's material and documentary clues suggest that a paradigm of the agrarian economic structure had become obsolete. In contrast, Bixby's evidence of continuation and adaptation represents an equally pervasive story of survival that has frequently been obscured by the vastness of the general transformation.

The material remains of Hemenway's 1830/31 expansion reflect the marginality of his enterprise. His hydrological system had neither the structure nor the flowage to compete with the impressive water-powered industries on the Prince River or with those in Williamsville, each a scant half mile away; and his vehicle shop foundations are quite meager compared with those erected nearby by a nephew a few years later. After increasing business through the early 1830s, Hemenway's accounts with Bixby declined rapidly, their final settlement taking place in 1837. That year the tax list for Hemenway showed no stock in trade, and his property was foreclosed in 1839.

Hemenway's real-estate valuation declined each year from 1838 to 1841, but Bixby's remained steady, as did that of many of the long-term partners in his exchange network. Their story is dissimilar to that of Hemenway and the numerous others whose cumulative misfortunes caused School District 9—which encompassed this neighborhood—to go into long-term decline.[34]

Surprisingly the Bixbys made an extensive set of improvements to their physical domestic environment during this period of apparent economic decline. They acquired a horse and an additional cow; dramatically improved the house, barn, and lot; purchased sizable parcels of farmland; lent money at interest; and saw one daughter marry. Some of the changes (the site and house reorganization, for example) strongly

---

[34] The divergence in the Bixby and Hemenway fortunes was not the result of differing demands for their respective crafts. Early nineteenth-century turnpike connections to Albany, N.Y.; Keene, N.H.; Brattleboro, Vt.; and Worcester, Mass. and beyond contributed to Barre's becoming an important center for wheeled-vehicle manufacturing, with at least 4 shops continuing well through midcentury. Within a decade and a half of Ethan Hemenway's departure, his nephew, Willard, established a larger and successful vehicle shop only a few rods away. The degree to which fortune and even survival is occasioned by personal "luck" continually haunts us as we conduct such personalized research. Hemenway's wife died during this time, and he may have suffered some other reversals that were not simply economic. Every case study is, to an appreciable degree, idiosyncratic.

suggest accommodation to the elements of innovation; others square nicely with retention of traditional agrarian economics (for example, livestock and land in supplement to his craft). Together they add up to a neat story of one family's variegated economic strategy for easing into society's transformation while avoiding the trauma of radical divorce from traditional culture. It is a story that could be learned only from the combined resources that were implemented in this investigation. Indeed, it would have been severely *mis*understood by analysis of any set in isolation.

In 1834 and 1837 Bixby purchased two parcels of land, totaling thirty-two acres, about a quarter mile up the road into Hubbardston, and in 1841 he purchased a small piece abutting his house and barn lot that formerly held Ethan Hemenway's carriagemaking shop. Those transactions symbolize the economic transition that was taking place, as two former protoindustrial features that had played an important role in his craft were restructured into Bixby's agricultural program. Charcoal for his smithing had been made on one of the Hubbardston parcels, which Bixby now used for pasture and hay, and Hemenway's carriage shop became the site of the new Bixby barn.[35]

Within a few years a dairy room was added in the ell/shed complex, and a new sink was purchased and installed nearby. Although dairying was clearly expanded, livestock evidences were no longer found around the house nor anywhere on the lot, except for the immediate vicinity of a new barn on the carriage-shop lot. A garden was placed where the old barn had been, and fruit trees were planted in the former barnyard. The smithy also was renovated, and flooring was installed— certainly in keeping with the overall program of tidying up the functional areas.

Changes in intrasite traffic patterns further demonstrated the diversification and segregation of functional spaces (fig. 6). After the barn was removed, traffic in the western dooryard, toward the garden, be-

[35]The Hubbardston property belonged to James Newton, a trading partner whom Bixby had credited for sizable quantities of charcoal. Our survey and shovel probing located the charcoal-making area but no evidence of subsequent intensive tillage. During the year following Bixby's acquisition of the Hemenway shop, accounts referred to "work on the barn." There was clear archaeological evidence that the barn west of the house was removed about this time. The conversion of Hemenway's shop to Bixby's barn was a signal act in a major transformation of function and fashion at their home lot.

Fig. 6. Arrangement of the house and shop lots and buildings at the Bixby site, ca. 1838–55. (Old Sturbridge Village: Drawing, Melanie Shook; Photo, Henry E. Peach.)

came far less intensive, and a privy was installed west of the shed.[36] Domestic refuse ceased to be scattered in the dooryards, now being found only in the most remote peripheral areas (see fig. 5). Even the archaeological corpus of ceramics indicated that Laura Bixby was refurnishing with an eye to style and color.

The Bixbys' intention to clean up and open out their personal world was most conspicuously realized in their transformation of the house between 1838 and 1845 (see fig. 6). For its first three decades the interior was painted in dark hues, and the exterior was notably asymmetrical and unpainted except for the doors and their casings. Plastering the ceilings began a comprehensive brightening and modernizing of the dwelling that took several years to complete.

A large closet was built into a corner of the kitchen, presumably

[36] We found no earlier privy location elsewhere on the site, and it is possible that there was no earlier privy, the convenient barn having served that purpose. The Lewises, in contrast, appear to have had an appropriately situated privy from the beginning. Worrell, "Landscape as Artifact."

to accommodate clothing and other previously conspicuous personal items. It represented the first move in a sweeping practical and cognitive change in the Bixbys' material environment that defined phase three (fig. 7). Stratigraphically phased with the closet was replacement of the original front and rear doors with windows. This arrangement inserted a distance between the private and the public spaces that had not been implicit in the previous arrangement. All outside access to the primary domestic spaces was now indirect—buffered by the unfinished ell.

A major addition constructed in 1844/45 made the boldest contribution to their overall objective of modernization and expansion. The two new chambers provided appropriately private sleeping quarters, more in keeping with contemporary norms. The parents moved out of the public best room into the most secluded area downstairs, while the daughters now had a modern, finished chamber instead of an open, unfinished attic. Both rooms were plastered, trimmed, and decorated in progressive patterns and light, neutral colors that contrasted starkly with the archaisms of the original house. Outdated sash and trim were replaced, and the entire exterior was clapboarded anew and painted white. The Bixbys joined a conscious and uniform phenomenon that has been termed "the whitening of New England."[37]

The combined evidence that produced this surprising story fit a pattern that is persuasive and enlightening, on both the individual and the larger levels of significance. We believe that the decline in Bixby's account-book work entries was a specific instance, and in a sense a paradigm, of the economic transformation of the culture at large. Account books recorded the exchanges of goods and services for settlement sometime in the future. The new order replaced future exchange obligations with discrete cash payments, settled on the spot with no extending web of indebtedness.[38]

[37] For travelers' impressions of New England village buildings painted white, see Timothy Dwight, *Travels in New England and New York* (New Haven, Conn.: S. Converse, 1821), p. 184; Patrick Shirreff, *A Tour through North America* (Edinburgh: Oliver and Boyd, 1835), pp. 38, 40; Larkin, *Reshaping of Everyday Life*, p. 130; Jack Larkin, "Interim Center Village Report" (Research Department, Old Sturbridge Village, 1978, manuscript).

[38] Jack Larkin, "Accounting for Change: Exchange and Debt in the Rural New England Economy, 1790–1850" (Paper presented at the annual meeting of the Society for Historians of the Early American Republic, 1988; Research Department, Old Sturbridge Village, manuscript on file).

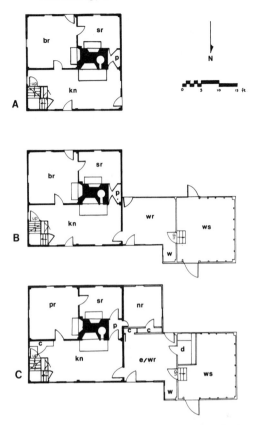

Fig. 7. Phases of construction, the Bixby house: (A) phase one, the initial form as erected, ca. 1802–09; (B) phase two, connecting wing between the house and woodshed added, ca. 1815–24; (C) phase three, a new room in the southwest corner of the house, a plastered room in the garret, and a dairy added, ca. 1838–45. Key: (br) best room; (c) closet; (d) dairy; (e/wr) entry/work room; (kn) kitchen; (nr) new room (bedroom); (p) passage; (pr) parlor; (sr) sitting room; (w) well; (wr) workroom; (ws) woodshed. (Old Sturbridge Village: Drawing, Myron O. Stachiw; Photo, Henry E. Peach.)

The durability of the old order, however, was demonstrated by undiminished account-book trading with a small nucleus of long-term partners in the neighborhood trading network. This continued until 1855, abated primarily only by death or aging of those involved. Several years earlier, a neighbor, Willard Hemenway, built a large carpentry and vehicle manufacturing shop immediately adjacent to Bixby's smithy. Archaeology revealed that the two structures were connected. Within a few years, Bixby's account book–keeping ceased altogether. All this promoted the tantalizing interpretation that the aging Bixby, at that point, replaced his rapidly shrinking traditional economic involvements with cash labor for the vehicle shop.[39]

Yet another factor loomed large in the story of the economic and material transformation of the Bixbys' world: the domestic labor of the women of the household. Such organized "outwork" provided an avenue for female participation in the economic revolution, and it did not involve the radical upheaval of traditional agrarian lifeways required by new mechanized industrial and urban innovations.[40] Significantly, the

[39] The evidence that Bixby was converting a portion of his smithing to cash payment was inconclusive but probable. Recording of transactions with the 10 close neighbors who remained longest in the exchange network varied little over the entire period, supporting the conclusion that his blacksmithing activities did not decline dramatically. These exchanges were predominantly for agricultural goods and labor or for agriculturally related blacksmithing such as shoeing oxen and horses and demonstrated the continuing viability of the traditional exchange system. However, the records of transactions with others took a precipitous decline from the mid 1830s onward. It is tempting to see this as the conversion of that portion of his work to cash. If this was the case, Bixby was operating in a dual economic system for about 2 decades. He continued traditional account-book exchanges with his long-term partners in the agricultural neighborhood, while increasingly entering the emerging cash exchange structure with others. The transition appears to have become complete when he began working in Willard Hemenway's new vehicle manufacturing enterprise for cash wages. Willard's father was one of the 10, long-trading account-book partners; Bixby's book did not even contain an entry for Willard. The generational gap between Bixby and the younger Hemenway was clearly an important factor in the way they chose to conduct their economic exchanges. Myron Stachiw, "Emerson Bixby and the Social, Material, and Cultural World of Barre Four Corners" (Paper presented to the Society for Historians of the Early American Republic, 1988; Research Department, Old Sturbridge Village, manuscript on file).

[40] Thomas Dublin, "Rural Putting-Out Work in Early Nineteenth-Century New England: Women and the Transition to Capitalism in the Countryside," *New England Quarterly* 64, no. 4 (December 1991): 531–73; Thomas Dublin, "Women and Outwork in a Nineteenth-Century New England Town: Fitzwilliam, New Hampshire, 1830–1850," in Steven Hahn and Jonathan Prude, eds., *The Countryside in the Age of Capitalist Transformation* (Chapel Hill: University of North Carolina Press, 1985), pp. 51–69;

transition in Emerson's accounting and neighborhood exchange took place simultaneously with the increasing involvement in market activities by his daughters and wife, and it concurred with the general loss of vitality in the surrounding neighborhood.

The abundant physical and documentary evidence for increased cheese and butter production demonstrated that this staple activity of domestic agriculture was expanded beyond the traditional exchange system to become a cash-market activity. The several material evidences for straw braiding and palm-leaf–hat making indicated a different kind of cash source beyond traditional agricultural household economics. Archaeologically recovered leather cuttings and equipment and a single account entry debited to Cheney Lewis "to bind 91 pare of shoes" in 1826 add a further outwork dimension. Cordwainer Lewis probably became a source of cash into the neighborhood and especially into the economics of his closest neighbor.[41]

The types of household production practiced at the Bixby site are those that were increasingly evident in the aggregate data for the towns of the region. What was most interesting was that *all* of them were found in the Bixby economic complement, partially answering the discrepancy between the blacksmith's decreasing accounts and the costly improvements in his holdings.

The increasing importance of the maturing daughters in this story seems assured. Income added by their outwork and dairying and their growing social awareness as they reached courting age may well have been the key elements in the profound changes that brought the appear-

---

"Women's Work and the Family Economy: Textiles and Palm Leaf Hatmaking in New England, 1830–1850," *Tocqueville Review* 5 (1983): 297–313; Caroline F. Sloat, " 'A Great Help to Many Families': Strawbraiding in Massachusetts before 1825," in Peter Benes and Jane Montague Benes, eds., *House and Home* (Boston: Boston University Press, 1990), pp. 89–100; Gail Fowler Mohanty, "Putting Up with Putting Out: Power Loom Diffusion and Outwork for Rhode Island Mills, 1821–1829," *Journal of the Early Republic* 9 (Summer 1989): 191–216.

[41] Sally McMurry, "Women and the Expansion of Dairying: The Cheesemaking Industry in Oneida County, New York, 1830–1860" (Paper presented at the Seventh Berkshire Conference on the History of Women, 1987); Andrew H. Baker and Holly Izard Paterson, "Farmers' Adaptations to Markets in Early Nineteenth-Century Massachusetts," in Peter Benes and Jane Montague Benes, eds., *The Farm* (Boston: Boston University Press, 1988), p. 106; Mary Blewett, "Women Shoeworkers and Domestic Ideology: Rural Outwork in Early Nineteenth-Century Essex County," *New England Quarterly* 60, no. 3 (September 1987): 403–28.

ance and spatial organization of the house and lot more into line with a new generation's priorities. Analysis of other houses and families in the neighborhood has strikingly confirmed the hypothesis that the timing of architectural change regularly coincided with changes in family structure and household economy.[42]

Tidying up the house and lot did not bring the Bixbys into the avant-garde of the elegant lifestyles, to be sure. But it was a clear, concerted, and conscious response to the persuasive cultural transformation occurring at large. Some of the changes in attitude and accoutrements that often have been ambiguously used to distinguish between eighteenth- and nineteenth-century material life may now be tangibly fixed in this specific biography.[43]

The significance of the transformation in the material and social lifeways of the Bixbys in Barre Four Corners—and the economic strategy by which it was effected—lies neither in its uniqueness nor its typicality but in the specific linkage that it makes between a detailed biography and a major transformation in traditional agrarian culture. The clues that came from the pages, the structures, and the ground combined to tell a fascinating story of a real family, at an identifiable stage in its life, responding to recognizable social and economic influences in which it was enmeshed.

Perhaps the most important contributions of this study are methodological. The story that we discerned could be brought into focus only through the reciprocity of specific data, meticulously derived from all available material and documentary resources, analyzed according to the respective disciplinary rigors of archaeology, vernacular architecture studies, and social and economic history. A less complete investigative strategy could never have ascertained the data and made the connections that enabled us to understand both what went on and what it demonstrates about the personal and larger contexts. Indeed, any monodimensional study would have inevitably led to error at some of the most crucial points of interpretation.

---

[42] Stachiw and Small, "Tradition and Transformation," pp. 140–41, 144–48. Another example of generational change illustrated in architecture and archaeology is reported in Worrell, "Scars upon the Earth," pp. 133–45.

[43] Many conceptual and practical elements of this overall transition argued for increased control of the house and lot by the women of the household, a conscious

We have traced a single thread through the vast tapestry that depicts the economics of a turbulent era. At the site level, it provides a specific and intriguing biography. At the neighborhood level, the personalities and actions become less descript, but the basic pattern and many of its parts are still discernable. As we move outward to the town, the region, and the society as a whole, the details become progressively less specific, but the implications of status, gender, class, and social structure remain connected and retain their interpretive value and color.

We do not pretend that this one story suffices to explain, or even to symbolize, the vast cultural transformation that irrevocably altered the traditional New England social and economic structure. We have, however, tied the specific stage and circumstance of one family's history and the transition of their household dynamics to the entire constellation of social, material, and economic changes that occurred in New England and the nation between 1790 and 1850. Most important, this study shows the depth and complexity of the transformation, and it demonstrates the indispensable role played by material evidence—architectural, archaeological, and documentary—in understanding the nature and meaning of these changes.

We have identified many of the personal choices and motives and the physical and kinetic details of human life that would otherwise have been averaged into indistinguishable summaries within the massive cultural shift. It *is* possible to continue recognizing individual faces without losing track of the moving crowd.

"feminization" of the domestic spaces; see Simmons, "Archaeology of Rural New England."

Frontier Boys and Country Cousins

The Context for Choice in Eighteenth-Century Consumerism

Ann Smart Martin

A satire appeared in a Virginia newspaper in 1815. It told the sad tale of a country cousin trying desperately to behave correctly at a city tea table. The poor soul struggled while the young folks "twittered like blackbirds," in one hand holding a teacup "hot as a warming pan" and in the other "a great hunk of bread and butter." He did not know "which way to go to eat the one or drink the other." Sweat pouring down his face in vexation, he spilled his tea, broke his cup, and finally ran home, his wife furious that he had disgraced the family.[1]

A similar traumatic experience was reported by a six-year-old boy around the time of the American Revolution. Raised on the frontier, he saw his first cup and saucer while visiting distant relatives.

Long-term research always engenders too many debts to briefly acknowledge. But special thanks are due: for local research materials, Warren Moorman and Anne Carter Lee; for illustrations, Kimberly Wagner, Hans Lorenz, and Carl Lounsbury, from the departments of Archaeological Research, Collections, and Architectural Research at the Colonial Williamsburg Foundation, respectively; and for editing and suggestions, James P. Whittenburg, Lu Ann De Cunzo, and Bernard L. Herman.

[1] *Norfolk Gazette and Publick Ledger*, June 21, 1815.

Fig. 1. A new consumer world: objects increasingly found
in middling households of the eighteenth century. (Courtesy, Colonial Williamsburg Foundation: Photo, Hans
Lorenz.)

He had no idea what to do with the "little cup [that] stood in a big-
ger one with some brownish looking stuff in it," so he mimicked
the actions of the grown-ups carefully. To his horror, the cups contained a brew of coffee "nauseous beyond anything" he had ever
known, and even though tears streamed down his face, his cup was
continually refilled. It was not until he finally saw another give the

proper "sign," an overturned cup with a spoon across it, that his night-mare was over.[2]

Both these scenes are comical. Perhaps they were not uncommon. They are merely encounters between people and unfamiliar things, commodities, and behaviors. They occurred when average people were faced with a remarkable new range of choices in how they filled their domestic environments. For it was in the eighteenth century that greater prosperity, improvements in manufacturing and distribution, and a new willingness to spend somehow combined to bring a greater quantity, quality, and variety of objects into the lives of the Anglo-American middling ranks. While not all these objects were new prod-ucts, many were novel to the people of the middling ranks of colonial Virginia society (fig. 1).

The origins and trajectory of these changes are currently under heated debate by economic and cultural historians. According to Neil McKendrick, John Brewer, and J. H. Plumb, new methods of market-ing, techniques of manufacture, and attitudes toward leisure combined in a revolutionary level of consumerism and fashion interest in the eighteenth century. The catalyst to set the fashion wheel in motion, they claimed, was social emulation. They cite a litany of complaints from elites horrified by what they saw as the desire by social inferiors to live and dress above their station. Yet other modern historians such as Carole Shammas, Lorna Wetherill, Grant McCracken, and Cary Carson have recently begun to argue about the timing and scope of any such changes and even to reject social emulation as the probable mainspring. Historians seem to be left with a Gordian knot: a list of variables but little way to untangle the questions of supply and demand, dropping prices and rising incomes, symbolic power and economic value that resulted in an industrial—and consumer—revolution.[3]

[2] Joseph Doddridge, *Notes on the Settlement and Indian Wars* (Pittsburgh: John S. Ritenour and William T. Lindsay, 1912), p. 88.

[3] Neil McKendrick, John Brewer, and J. H. Plumb, *The Birth of a Consumer Society: The Commercialization of Eighteenth-Century England* (Bloomington: Indiana Univer-sity Press, 1982). The literature of the consumer revolution seems to grow exponentially and is scattered through the works of social and economic historians and material culture specialists. Scholars are currently arguing about the cause, scope, and timing of this transformation. Only the most recent works will be included here. For England, see Lorna Wetherill, *Consumer Behavior and Material Culture in Britain, 1660–1760* (London: Routledge and Paul, 1988). On this side of the Atlantic, see Grant McCracken,

Perhaps one way the knot can be loosened is by turning from the study of products to the story of artifacts. This acknowledges that objects do not emerge mysteriously from economic institutions; they are made and used by people. A material culture approach privileges the host of new household goods themselves to have a voice in the story. It turns our eye inward to question what these common objects were as well as their quality, decoration, and utility. It asks what functions they performed and what behaviors they enabled. But already the eye is creeping outward to people, behaviors, and cultures. For it is here that a material culture approach also helps to untangle the knot of consumerism by focusing on the context of objects and the discourse in which they functioned. It allows us to ask what meanings objects may have had to those who made, purchased, used, and witnessed them.[4]

Historical archaeologists have long struggled with ways to read the artifact patterns they recover. Much of the larger archaeological debate of the 1970s, particularly, attempted to posit cultural laws and models and test them with independent data from the archaeological record.

Culture and Consumption: New Approaches to the Symbolic Character of Consumer Goods and Activities (Bloomington: Indiana University Press, 1988); and Colin Campbell, *The Romantic Ethic and the Spirit of Modern Consumerism* (London: Basil Blackwell, 1987). For the colonies, see Cary Carson, "The Consumer Revolution in Colonial America: Why Demand?" in Cary Carson, Ronald Hoffman, and Peter J. Albert, eds., *Of Consuming Interests: The Style of Life in the Eighteenth Century* (Charlottesville: University Press of Virginia, 1994). A critical evaluation of McKendrick, Brewer, and Plumb's work is found in Ben Fine and Ellen Leopold, "Consumerism and the Industrial Revolution," *Social History* 15 (May 1990): 151–79. A recent call for more precise measures of consumer changes is found in Carole Shammas, "Explaining Past Changes in Consumption and Consumer Behavior," *Historical Methods* 22, no. 2 (Spring 1989): 61–67. Shammas has written one of the few works comparing England and America in *The Pre-industrial Consumer in England and America* (Oxford: Clarendon Press, 1990). A specific view of changes in the Chesapeake standard of living can be seen in the works of Lois Carr and Lorena Walsh, whose most recently expanded work is "Changing Lifestyles and Consumer Behavior in the Colonial Chesapeake," in Carson, Hoffman, and Albert, *Of Consuming Interests*. A much abbreviated version is found in "Forum: Toward a History of the Standard of Living in Colonial America," *William and Mary Quarterly*, 3d ser., 45, no. 1 (January 1988): 116–70.

[4]Historical archaeologists have embraced the problem of consumerism by looking at these very questions. Susan Henry has attempted to construct a model for consumer behavior in "Consumers, Commodities, and Choices: A General Model of Consumer Behavior," *Historical Archaeology* 25, no. 2 (Summer 1991): 3–14. Other essays in that volume consider similar themes and contexts. See also Suzanne M. Spencer-Wood, *Consumer Choice in Historical Archaeology* (New York: Plenum Press, 1987).

It became increasingly clear, however, that there are no independent data, no Rosetta stone that tells us unambiguously of the direct connection of culture and its material correlates. The failure of law-seeking archaeology can be seen on three levels. First, there is no mode of analysis that is independent of the larger culture in which scholars work. Second, such universal laws and models deny social and individual agency. For example, archaeologists might demonstrate that adaptation occurred, but there is little sense that people—behaving in a highly socialized context—did the adapting. Finally, within such a framework, there was little room for change; a structuralist analysis, for instance, describes pattern but provides little mechanism for historical progression.[5]

Historical archaeologists today are more often concerned with context, defined by Ian Hodder as "the totality of the relevant environment" for any given object—*relevant* in this case meaning all the "relationships necessary for discerning the object's meaning." No longer must archaeologists wait for their data to speak to some larger theory; everything that has a relationship with that object is necessary to arrive at its larger meaning. It is the layering of particular precise historical circumstances with larger cultural systems that allows the material world to have a voice. It also is the juxtaposition of varying kinds of material culture and documentary data that leads to new questions. Second, historical archaeologists have turned to the recursive nature of material culture. Material culture is not just the product or reflection of culture, it is imbedded in culture; it is symbolic, active, and communicative and carries its own meaning.[6]

Both of these larger ideas have informed this study. If one is searching for the context of artifacts, one must understand the larger society that produced, marketed, valued, used, and discarded them and

---

[5] For one recent critique, see Paul A. Shackel and Barbara J. Little, "Post-processual Approaches to Meanings and Uses of Material Culture in Historical Archaeology," *Historical Archaeology* 26, no. 3, Meanings and Uses of Material Culture, ed. Barbara J. Little and Paul A. Shackel (Fall 1992): 5–11.

[6] Ian Hodder, *Reading the Past: Current Approaches to Interpretation in Archaeology* (Cambridge, Eng.: Cambridge University Press, 1986). For an elegant summary of these ideas, see Christopher Tilley, "Interpreting Material Culture," in Ian Hodder, ed., *The Meanings of Things: Material Culture and Symbolic Expression* (London: Unwin Hyman, 1989), pp. 185–94.

what factors might have affected any of those processes. Moreover, this paper examines acquisition, a critical point in the life cycle of domestic artifacts. It begins with the premise that any consumer good is chosen for a host of reasons, and careful examination of those choices will help elucidate the meaning those objects may have had. It goes to a particular place and time (backcountry Virginia just before the American Revolution) and examines different kinds of evidence (probate evidence, architecture, and store records) to create multiple portraits of the material world and the choices that residents made. It will demonstrate that it is the counterposing, and in this case disjunction, of these differing kinds of evidence that can lead us more closely to understanding our texts as well as any truth of meaning.

When theories of material culture are brought to the study of consumerism, it is easier to see that the dynamic relationship between new objects and a host of new social rules for their use was a major aspect of any new consumer world of the eighteenth century. As more of the population obtained access to the material objects of social prestige, the wealthy were able to change the rules. One must now not only own a proper set of accoutrements for smart living but also know a complex package of behaviors to use them. These social rules were part of a complex group of ideas about gentility that were gaining currency in the early modern era as more of the English gentry invested time and money in proper education, manners, and leisure. Many Chesapeake elites, anxious to be considered up-to-date, modeled their behavior and lifestyles on those of their English peers. Genteel and sociable behavior became the hallmark of the well bred and wealthy, including accomplished conversation, dancing, games of skill, tea drinking, and elaborate dining. But behavioral knowledge (socialization) was also buttressed with cultivation knowledge (cultural capital) in the form of the pursuit of taste, often expressed in fashion and furnishings. Knowing how to act was reinforced by knowing what to buy or use.[7]

---

[7] The most elegant summary of notions of gentility is Richard Bushman, *The Refinement of America: Persons, Houses, Cities* (New York: Alfred A. Knopf, 1992). For the Chesapeake, see Richard D. Brown, "William Byrd II and the Challenge of Rusticity among the Tidewater Gentry," in *Knowledge Is Power: The Diffusion of Information in Early America, 1700–1865* (Oxford: Oxford University Press, 1989), pp. 42–64. Mary

Even as we attempt to describe this remarkable intersection of material culture and social relations in the eighteenth century, however, our understanding is in many ways impossible. We are separated by our own postmodern explosion in the world of goods. But the story of eighteenth-century consumerism is not merely one of new things or different things or better things. It is a tale of how material objects became important strategies of social mediation, how frontier boys and country cousins were increasingly excluded by a material world that left them socially inept when transplanted from their settings. Society was no longer merely divided into the haves and the have-nots but, increasingly, the knows and the know-nots.

Perhaps none of these changing social contexts had more daily impact than sweeping differences in how people consumed their meals. Words of contemporaries tell the tale. The wealthy Alexander Hamilton was shocked when visiting a poor ferryman and his family at "vittles," eating from "one deep, dirty bowl," and marveled that "they used neither knife, fork, spoon, plate or napkin." Hamilton recorded this Susquehanna River scene in his diary in 1744 because it struck him as "primitive simplicity practiced by our forefathers." Those basic eating implements—individual tableware, cutlery, and linens—that Hamilton so took for granted would have been considered luxuries even among the wealthy only a few generations before.[8]

Yet sometime around the middle of the eighteenth century, those everyday items of comfort and convenience became common for much of free Virginia society. By the end of the eighteenth century, the dinner table for many had been transformed from the "vittles" enjoyed from a common pot to one with multiple dishes. Benjamin Latrobe's first impression of Virginia cooking came when he landed at Norfolk in 1796. He described a bountiful table with "Hog and Greens" at one end balanced by "roast lamb at the other end of the table; four dishes of salted chads at each corner, a dish of peas and one of asparagus on each side . . . and sallad in the middle." While Latrobe was impressed

---

Douglas and Baron Isherwood, *The World of Goods: Toward an Anthropology of Consumption* (New York: W. W. Norton, 1979), pp. 176–84.

[8] Carl Bridenbaugh, ed., *Gentleman's Progress: The Itenerarium of Dr. Alexander Hamilton, 1744* (Chapel Hill: University of North Carolina Press for the Institute of Early American Culture, 1948), p. 8.

with the abundance and the multiple dishes of food, he had no compliments for Virginia cooking, noting, "if there is a morality in cooking, this must be culinary adultery."[9]

The foods on Virginia tables were no longer tossed in a simple bowl. Barbara Carson has recently vividly demonstrated how America slowly evolved from a society that hunkered on chests or sat in doorways, eating from spoons or with hands, to one that sat at tables, used linens, and transferred food from plate to mouth with knife and fork. The social elite further transformed mealtimes by creating a complex pattern of foods, courses, and material objects that demonstrated wealth, abundance, and decorum. This group also mimicked their peers in England by a new fascination with the whirling dervish of fashion, changing their tablewares frequently to match new styles in ceramics, glass, and silver.[10]

A parallel trend was the introduction of tea. Virtually unknown beyond the very wealthy in the seventeenth-century colonies, tea drinking spread across social ranks so rapidly that most household inventories in eastern Virginia contained some apparatus for its consumption by the American Revolution. While for many the drinking of tea was no more than a gathering of friends and family, again, among the wealthiest, new forms, styles, and intricate formal behaviors proliferated.[11]

[9] Edward C. Carter, ed., *The Virginia Journals of Benjamin Latrobe, 1795–1798*, vol. 1 (New Haven: Yale University Press, 1977), p. 79.

[10] Barbara G. Carson, *Ambitious Appetites: Dining, Behavior, and Patterns of Consumption in Federal Washington* (Washington, D.C.: American Institute of Architects Press, 1990). Louise Belden, *The Festive Tradition* (New York: W. W. Norton, 1983), pp. 3–40.

[11] The spread of tewares has been documented through the analysis of probate inventories in many different locations in Maryland and Virginia. See, for example, Carr and Walsh, "Changing Lifestyles"; Stacia M. Gregory, "The Elements of Consumption: Tea and Tableware in Baltimore County, Maryland, before and after the Revolution" (Master's thesis, University of Delaware, 1987); Gary Wheeler Stone, "Artifacts Are Not Enough," *Conference on Historic Sites Archaeology Papers* 11 (August 1987): 43–63. The formal behaviors and equipments of tea drinking are described in Rodris Roth, *Tea Drinking in Eighteenth-Century America: Its Etiquette and Equipage*, United States Museum Bulletin 225, Contributions from the Museum of History and Technology, paper 14 (Washington, D.C.: Smithsonian Institution, 1961), pp. 1–30. Much recent work has demonstrated, however, that drinking took on many forms among differing social groups and contexts. For example, how meanings of tea consumption were extensified to become a working-class staple of the industrial revolution was brilliantly demonstrated by Sidney Mintz, *Sweetness and Power: The Place of Sugar in Modern History* (New York: Viking Penguin, 1985).

Contemporary glimpses into changing behaviors are rare. But the historical evidence of material culture can help us to understand how quickly such changes may have spread. To begin, we can see the introduction of new kinds of objects. In one way, the introduction and popularity of new items such as teawares is merely the rational movement of the market to fulfill such needs. In a perfectly constructed market, well-designed products that best meet certain functions offered at a competitive price win out and gain popularity. While no economy is theoretically perfect—to the chagrin of economists and their models—the introduction and popularity of certain categories of objects often can stand as proxy for the changing needs themselves. At the same time, from a user's point of view, the spread of such goods across the landscape helps to identify a cultural horizon.[12]

Yet, tea could easily have been brewed in a saucepan, poured into mugs, and served on the doorstep. In many households this may have been the case. But when tea drinkers or diners perform their roles successfully in particular social contexts, objects take on essential functions as social and behavioral props. To understand that function, we can turn to recent studies as disparate as how identities are formed or cognition occurs and briefly extrapolate a few key themes. First, goods take on a heightened resonance in particular contexts. Scholars of modern society have recently pointed out that at least until the passage of middle age, the most important reason cited for acquisition of any object was that it made possible some activity or provided some enjoyment. There are other times, however, when the role of object in behavior is not so obvious. This is particularly true when activities are socially charged, when they represent a complex pattern of activity that demonstrates a competence of social knowledge and require use of particular objects. Of course, some cultural knowledge is necessary for use of any artifact. It is indeed that vast lexicon of tiny, unconscious, socially prescribed customs that prevents the strain of continual and unlimited choice of options at every moment. But if some components

---

[12] For definitions, see James Deetz, *Invitation to Archaeology* (Garden City, N.Y.: Natural History Press, 1967), p. 79. This theme is used in the broader material culture context by Kenneth L. Ames, "Material Culture as Non-Verbal Communication: A Historical Study," in Edith Mayo, *American Material Culture: The Shape of Things around Us* (Bowling Green, Ohio: Bowling Green State University Popular Press, 1984), pp. 25–47.

of behavior were the casual, everyday knowledge shared by all, other parts built upon cultural capital in complex, explicit ways.[13]

That is why we might think of such patterns as scripts, certain sequences of events that are expected by participants or observers. Set against this backdrop can be put the concept of role, a "set of related meanings that directs the individual's behavior in a social setting." Drinking tea demands knowledge of the script: not only of how to brew the bitter foreign commodity but the proper form of banter and table talk, of pouring and eating, even knowing when to go home. At the same time, different roles can be played out: drinking tea could be relaxing by the fireside with family, gossiping with friends as a break from a hurried workday, or participating in elite social conventions. All required different actions, dress, and speech.[14]

Material objects also take on a heightened role when the player is uncertain or uncomfortable with the social script. Goods actually can then serve as stimuli, helping the player to "fake it through the muffed lines." The need for these social stimuli varies with one's comfort with the role one is performing. Michael Solomon points to the contemporary importance of colognes and fast cars to adolescent males not yet comfortable with their masculinity. "Looking the part" is a component of the mirror view of self; it reinforces one's belief in an ability to play the role. Products are important in how others see us; they thus have

[13] Lita Furby, "Possessions: Toward a Theory of Their Meaning and Function throughout the Life Cycle," in *Life-span Development and Behavior*, vol. 1, ed. Paul B. Baltes (New York: Academic Press, 1978), p. 312. Similar conclusions are found in Mihaly Csikszentmihalyi and Eugene Rochberg-Halton, *The Meaning of Things: Domestic Symbols and the Self* (Cambridge, Eng.: Cambridge University Press, 1981); and Douglas and Isherwood, *World of Goods*. In George Simmel's terms, forms of socialization—such as the stylized conversation of the tea table—are not trivial conventions but play-forms of society itself; see *The Sociology of George Simmel*, trans. and ed. Kurt Wolff (London: Free Press of Glencoe, 1950).

[14] Sidney J. Levy, "Interpreting Consumer Mythology: A Structural Approach to Consumer Behavior," *Journal of Marketing* 45 (Summer 1981): 49–61; Michael R. Solomon, "The Role of Products as Social Stimuli: A Symbolic Interactionism Perspective," *Journal of Consumer Research* 10 (December 1983): 319–39; Erving Goffman, *The Presentation of Self in Everyday Life* (Garden City, N.Y.: Doubleday, 1959). Another view of this notion of changing frames of time and behavior, drawing more explicitly on the work of Victor Turner, can be found in Joseph R. Gusfield, "Passage to Play: Rituals of Drinking Time in American Society," in Mary Douglas, ed., *Constructive Drinking: Perspectives on Drink from Anthropology* (Cambridge, Eng.: Cambridge University Press, 1987), pp. 73–91.

a heightened part in how we see ourselves. Moreover, merely having the correct props informs the observer that one knows the script. Having sugar tongs, for instance, signals that you know it is improper to touch food with your fingers. The neoclassical ornamentation on a creamware teapot drew upon an appreciation of Greek temples and Roman villas that was one part of elite notions of the development of taste. Thus, with the appearance of script knowledge, the stage has been set for the proper action, and the observer now expects socially prescribed behavior. Paradoxically, the greater the comfort with role and familiarity with script, the less reliance on material objects is necessary. It is any nouveau riche that may most conspicuously overspend to obtain the material symbols of wealth and prestige. Reliance on material objects can be a compensatory measure for missing confidence.[15]

In summary, an object can not only properly fulfill a function, but it also can fulfill it best. First, this occurs when a number of social and cultural criteria about behaviors are met, when it has become encoded as proper and necessary for that script to be correctly performed. Second, goods do not just reflect needs, they also can create them. The use of goods as behavioral props, for instance, is necessary to convince not only the audience but often oneself as well. But material objects are more than just props for social scenarios. Human behavior is more than speaking the proper lines. If this were the case, cultural change would never occur, and new products would never be accepted. People, behaviors, and objects did intersect in particular formal, readable ways in the eighteenth century, but they also could be quickly recast with a different context, audience, and time. The meanings and uses of objects are no less complex; they serve as badges of class and rank, symbols of cultural meaning, conduits of emotion, and elements of art, style, or fashion. Here, too, the roles of goods can shift or gain

---

[15] Solomon, "Role of Products," p. 6. Joanne Finkelstein, *The Fashioned Self* (Philadelphia: Temple University Press, 1991). The design of household objects often contain references to much larger systems outside themselves, such as modern teapots expressing art deco aesthetics described in Sharon Zukin, "Socio-spatial Prototypes of a New Organization of Consumption: The Role of Real Cultural Capital," *Sociology* 4, no. 1 (February 1990): 46. Pierre Bourdieu, *Distinction: A Social Critique of the Judgement of Taste*, trans. Richard Nice (Cambridge, Eng.: Cambridge University Press, 1984). Some of these class notions are parodied by Paul Fussell in *Class: A Guide through the American Status System* (New York: Summit Books, 1983).

importance in differing cultural contexts and are mediated or differentiated when among varying groups based on social position or ethnic,
age, or gender group affiliations.

Material objects matter because they are complex symbolic bundles of social, cultural, and individual meaning fused into something
we can see, touch, and own. That very quality is the reason that social
values and meaning can so quickly penetrate into and evaporate out of
common objects. It also is why they are so immensely important in
times of social and cultural transformation. One such period of intense
social pressure was eighteenth-century Anglo-America, as traditional
notions of rank and place began to be challenged by new ideas about
social mobility and new measures of human worth. It also was then
that the term *class* glided into the language, first coexisting with old
terminology but slowly emerging into something approximating upper,
middle, and lower groups of society by the 1740s. Even the beginning
of such ideas demonstrate the extraordinary challenge against old ideas
about a human's fixed place in a social hierarchy.[16]

Scripted behaviors were carried out in many forms in the eighteenth century. The tiny ways in which proper attention to ritual excluded those not in the know is nicely demonstrated in the remarks of
Philip Fithian, a schoolteacher in the home of Robert Carter in the
1770s. He described with disdain the tobacco inspector who joined the
family table and made clear his unfamiliarity with such company by
timid and awkward toasts. Fithian snorted that the man gave away his
station even in how he held his glass. What is important is that objects
give us a window to these behaviors and the desires of their owners to
participate in new social standards and behaviors.[17] They attest to a

---

[16] P. J. Corfield, "Class by Name and Number in Eighteenth-Century Britain,"
History 72, no. 234 (February 1987): 38–61. Similar themes of the complex transitions
in the way eighteenth-century men and women *themselves* envisioned a social hierarchy—this time in France—are found in Robert Darnton, *The Great Cat Massacre and
Other Episodes in French Cultural History* (New York: Vintage Books, 1985), see esp.
pp. 107–45.

[17] Hunter Dickinson Farish, *Journal and Letters of Philip Vickers Fithian: A Plantation Tutor of the Old Dominion, 1773–1774* (Charlottesville: University Press of Virginia,
1968), p. 138. A brilliant example of the role of everyday ritual in early American life
is Gerald W. R. Ward, " 'Avarice and Conviviality': Card-Playing in Federal America,"
in Benjamin A. Hewitt, Patricia E. Kane, and Gerald W. R. Ward, eds., *The Work of
Many Hands: Card Tables in Federal America, 1790–1820* (New Haven: Yale University

tuning in to broader cultural patterns of urban Anglo-America, changes that began in the cultural core of London and were disseminated across the miles and across classes. But these broad trends of refinement of manners and relations did not come prepackaged; the most important question may be, what did colonial Virginians adopt as important, enjoyable, or useful, and in what ways did they reformulate these behaviors for their particular needs? Specifically, we might ask, what kinds of choices were made in the acquisition of objects that were related to these genteel behaviors, and why? How can we use these broader theoretical concepts to build an appropriate context for any given artifact?

The rest of this essay examines a community that in some ways seems to have stood outside that new interest in fashion, domestic comfort, ritual, and refinement. Located some 150 miles from the fall line of the James River, rural Bedford County around New London, Virginia, just before the American Revolution was not a new frontier—the true line of settlement had already passed far over the mountains—but it was still a relatively new society (figs. 2, 3). County elites established there for a generation already monopolized power and land. James Callaway, for one, had moved with his parents in the 1750s to what would become Bedford County, served as an officer in the French and Indian War, and at the age of thirty was elected as the representative to the House of Burgesses. His multiple business enterprises included partnership in a mercantile business and an important ironworks. He also sired twenty-two children and acquired more than seventeen thousand acres of land.[18]

Few were so fortunately situated as Callaway to profit from the new waves of settlers after the French and Indian War quieted frontier violence. The mere choice of the name New London reflected the optimism and vision of early Bedford County residents for the new

Press, 1982), pp. 15–28. For more discussion of objects as "props for the drama of life," see Kenneth L. Ames, "Meaning in Artifacts: Hall Furnishings in Victorian America," in Thomas J. Schlereth, comp. and ed., *Material Culture Studies in America* (Nashville: American Association for State and Local History, 1982), pp. 206–21.

[18] Lula Jeters Parker, *Parker's History of Bedford County, Virginia*, ed. Peter Viemeister (Bedford, Va.: Hamiltons, 1988), p. 7. Land information was culled from land tax lists and deed books from Bedford, Campbell, and Franklin counties from the early 1780s.

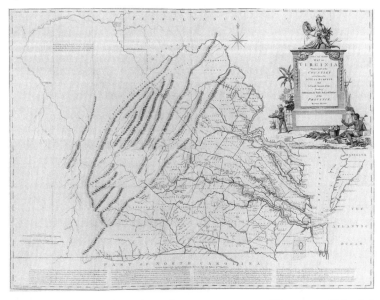

Fig. 2. John Henry, *Map of Virginia*, 1772. (Courtesy, Colonial Williamsburg Foundation.) Bedford County is in the lower left quadrant, east of the Blue Ridge Mountains.

county seat, which they established seven years after the county was formed in 1754. The court ordered a plan of half-acre lots and mandated that a 16-by-20-foot frame house had to be built within one year of the lot's purchase. They further added that a brick chimney must be built within four years. By the late 1770s, New London was described as a "pretty considerable town, [of] at least 70 or 80 houses" and home to four or five merchants. While we know little about the appearance of this town in the eighteenth century, here in 1771 and 1772 John Hook constructed his two-story frame 28-by-30-foot house for his new bride (fig. 4).[19] Hook's house was more than two-and-a-half times the

[19] Warren L. Moorman, "John Hook, New London Merchant," *Journal of the Roanoke Valley Historical Society* 11 (1980): 47. The "Plan of New London Town" is found in Bedford County Deed Book A, Virginia State Library, Richmond [hereafter VSL], p. 434. For more discussion of the layout and development of this town, see Christopher Hendricks, "Town Development in the Colonial Backcountry: Virginia and North Carolina" (Ph.D. diss., College of William and Mary, 1992). Original house

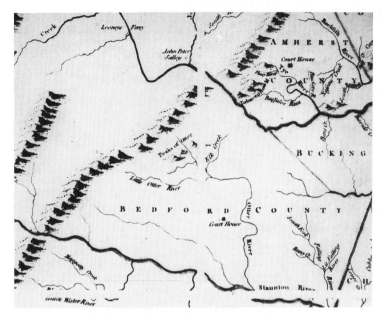

Fig. 3. Detail of figure 2. (Courtesy, Colonial Williamsburg Foundation.) New London is marked "Court House."

size of those dictated by law and represented a modish plan in a world of one- or two-room houses.

While the commercial economy of the town was flourishing, the majority of the rural population seemed little concerned with the polite behaviors of elite hegemony found in eastern society. A peddler visiting the area in 1809 was disappointed upon finding a "very poor Court, no fighting or Gouging, very few Drunken people." A local resident remembered fighting as being the "prevalent vice in the community" in his early nineteenth-century childhood there, beginning as "furious quarreling," leading to "revolting profanity, [and] ending in a regular game of fisticuffs." Rough-and-tumble eye-poking may have been as

---

plan, undated John Hook papers, Special Collections, Duke University, Durham, N.C. Copies are in the Hook Papers, Business Records Collection, VSL. Hook also discusses this house in a letter to David Ross on October 26, 1771, Hook papers. Bills for building supplies are found in Hook's memorandum book, Duke University.

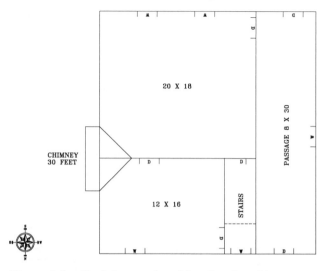

Fig. 4. John Hook house plan, New London, Va., 1772.
(John Hook papers, Special Collections, Duke University;
Drawing, Kim Wagner.)

much of a hallmark of backcountry life as elite horseracing in the
Tidewater.[20]

Nor does it seem that the material trappings of elite life were
immediately sought after. For example, a 1785 tax list for a rural county
to the southwest demonstrates that nearly all the population there lived
in log houses. In addition, not all who owned slaves had quarters,
suggesting that even some who had the capital to acquire bound labor

[20] Richard R. Beeman, ed., "Trade and Travel in Post-Revolutionary Virginia: A
Diary of an Itinerant Peddlar, 1807–1808," *Virginia Magazine of History and Biography*
84, no. 2 (April 1976): 174–88. William Eldridge Hatcher, *The Life of J. B. Jeter*
(Baltimore: H. M. Wharton, 1887), p. 24; Elliot J. Gorn, " 'Gouge and Bite, Pull Hair
and Scratch': The Social Significance of Fighting in the Southern Backcountry," *American Historical Review* 90 (1985): 18–43. For Tidewater gambling, see T. H. Breen,
"Horses and Gentlemen: The Cultural Significance of Gambling among the Gentry of
Virginia," *William and Mary Quarterly*, 3d ser., 34, no. 2 (1977): 239–59.

lived side by side with them. Like other Piedmont and southside places, the earliest gentry brick houses still standing in Bedford County were built after the Revolution.[21]

The snapshot of county life gained from the Bedford County probate record for 1768–77 seems to indicate a society that did not place a high premium on creating the interior environment for correct elite behavior. To enable precise comparison, these probate inventories were analyzed using categories and boundaries of wealth devised by Lois Carr and Lorena Walsh for contemporary Chesapeake communities. For this method the scholar assigns a proxy for economic position based on total inventoried property and selects particular catgories for analysis from the total items listed.[22] Turning to Bedford County, bound labor and livestock accounted for an average of about three-fourths of inventoried wealth, although that number varied across economic level. For instance, in the lowest rung, no slaves were owned, but livestock made up nearly half of the probate estate. In the wealthiest households, three-fourths of inventoried wealth was in the form of bound labor (table 1). This meant that all forms of consumer goods were a smaller and smaller part of the richest household's wealth.

Probate records also demonstrate that most households were simply furnished. Only a third of the poorest part of society had tables and chairs from which to eat in the new "civilized" manner (fig. 5). Moving into the middling ranks, only about half were so equipped. Looking at the problem differently, those who had estate inventory values between £50 and £94 owned an average of only two chairs. At the same time, comparable households in eastern York County, Virginia, contained almost a dozen chairs for friends and family. Those who were relatively well off—in the upper middling and upper economic ranks—invested

[21] "A List of Whit[e] People and Buildings in the Bounds of Capt. Rubles Company," Henry County Courthouse, Martinsville, Va., cited and discussed in John S. Salmon and Emily J. Salmon, *Franklin County, Virginia, 1786–1986: A Bicentennial History* (Rocky Mount, Va.: Franklin County Bicentennial Commission, 1993). Anne Carter Lee provided me with the manuscript copy of this tax list. My heartfelt thanks to John Salmon for graciously sharing his manuscript and to Anne Carter Lee for this and other original research materials from Franklin County. Richard R. Beeman, *The Evolution of the Southern Backcountry: A Case Study of Lunenburg County, Virginia, 1746–1832* (Philadelphia: University of Pennsylvania Press, 1982).

[22] Will Book 1, Bedford County, VSL. Carr and Walsh, "Changing Lifestyles."

Table 1. Total Wealth in Bedford County Inventories, 1768–77

	£0–49 28	£50–94 18	£95–224 18	£225–490 12	£491 + 4
Slaves	0.0	11.4	31.6	63.2	75.7
Livestock	44.4	46.6	33.6	20.8	12.1
Furniture	17.7	10.7	12.3	7.0	5.5
Linen: Bed/table	0.1	0.3	0.7	0.2	0.0
Literacy	0.4	0.9	1.0	0.2	0.2
Cloth production	2.4	1.5	1.6	0.4	0.1
Foodways	5.4	3.7	2.8	1.9	1.0
Grocery	0.3	0.2	0.3	0.2	0.5

Source: Bedford County Will Book 1, 1763–87, Virginia State Library, Richmond, Va.

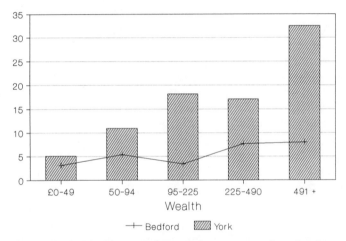

Fig. 5. Household ownership of chairs, in rural and urban Virginia and Maryland, 1768–77. From Will Book 1, Bedford Co., Va., 1763–87, Virginia State Library and from Lois Green Carr and Lorena S. Walsh, "Changing Lifestyles and Consumer Behaviour in the Colonial Chesapeake," in Cary Carson, Ronald Hoffman, and Peter J. Albert, eds., *Of Consuming Interests: The Style of Life in the Eighteenth Century* (Charlottesville: University Press of Virginia, 1994), table 11.

Table 2. Consumer Wealth in Bedford County Inventories, 1768–77

	£0–49 28	£50–94 18	£95–224 18	£225–490 12	£491 + 4
Furniture	31.9	25.5	35.2	41.1	44.9
Linens: Bed/tables	0.1	0.7	1.9	1.5	0.0
Literacy	1.6	2.2	1.0	1.1	1.3
Cloth production	4.2	3.6	4.6	2.4	1.1
Foodways	9.7	8.9	8.0	11.1	8.6
Cooking	3.6	3.2	2.9	3.7	3.2
Dining	5.6	4.3	4.8	6.4	4.6
Tea drinking	0.1	0.7	0.1	0.5	0.6
Utilitarian	0.4	0.5	0.3	0.5	0.2
Grocery	0.5	3.0	0.8	1.2	4.4
Foodstuffs	0.3	0.5	0.6	1.2	4.0

Source: Bedford County Will Book 1, 1763–87, Virginia State Library, Richmond, Va.

in a few chairs and tables but again lagged far behind their eastern counterparts. At the top of the Bedford social hierarchy, no inventoried household had the overall package necessary for the correct elite environment. While wealthy York County residents assorted an average of eight tables and thirty chairs for multiple social functions, Bedford elite households contained less than a fourth of these furnishings. Only a handful of the wealthiest residents had a desk to keep accounts or complete correspondence; none had prints on the walls or silver plate on their tables.

What about less expensive items to grace those tables? Overall, about two percent of the personal wealth of all households was invested in foodways objects. Factoring out slaves and livestock to examine consumer wealth alone, that percentage remained relatively constant even as wealth increased (table 2). This remained true after separating these items into categories of cooking, dining, tea drinking, and utilitarian storage. Those with greater consumer wealth acquired more furniture and a great deal more bedding and table linens, but expenditure on ceramics and related items was relatively inelastic. That is, while the *amount* invested in such items increased, the *proportion* of one's estate value did not. Moreover, pewter was overwhelmingly the tableware of choice, with the addition of wooden wares and fine ceramics in some households.

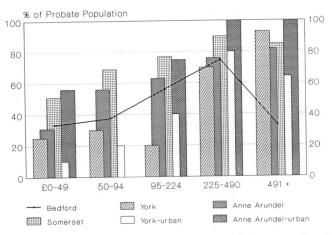

Fig. 6. Household ownership of knives and forks in rural and urban Virginia and Maryland, 1768–77. From Will Book 1, Bedford County, Va., 1763–87, Virginia State Library and from Lois Green Carr and Lorena S. Walsh, "Changing Lifestyles and Consumer Behaviour in the Colonial Chesapeake," in Cary Carson, Ronald Hoffman, and Peter J. Albert, eds., *Of Consuming Interests: The Style of Life in the Eighteenth Century* (Charlottesville: University Press of Virginia, 1994), tables 1, 3, 4, 5, 6.

Yet, these backcountry folk compared favorably to their eastern cousins in other ways. For instance, high incidence of owning knives and forks suggests—albeit tentatively—that new manners of eating had gained a foothold (fig. 6). Even if old-fashioned pewter had not been replaced by ceramic items, and even if not all could gather around a table, old methods of scooping, pushing, fingering, and spooning one's food were passing away.[23] These households also contained a number of books, including bibles and religious texts, comparable to their peers

[23] The high incidence of knives and forks in Bedford County may be measured in another way. Just over half the Bedford probates did not contain knives and forks in the approximate decade before the Revolution. Yet Barbara Carson's study of probate inventories from Washington, D.C., dating a half century later found that about 40 percent of the decedents still did not own knives and forks; see Carson, *Ambitious Appetites*, p. 31.

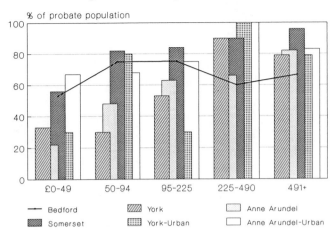

Fig. 7. Household ownership of books in rural and urban Virginia and Maryland, 1768–77. From Will Book 1, Bedford County, Va., 1763–87, Virginia State Library and from Lois Green Carr and Lorena S. Walsh, "Changing Lifestyles and Consumer Behaviour in the Colonial Chesapeake," in Cary Carson, Ronald Hoffman, and Peter J. Albert, eds., *Of Consuming Interests: The Style of Life in the Eighteenth Century* (Charlottesville: University Press of Virginia, 1994), tables 1, 3, 4, 5, 6.

in eastern society, suggesting a priority placed on literacy and religion (fig. 7).

One more surprise remained. Teawares were virtually absent in these probate inventories (fig. 8). The presence of a few teakettles indicates that water was being heated and that tea was probably being consumed, and a few teawares were listed in the inventories of the wealthy; but a comparison to other counties demonstrates a shocking rejection of tea drinking in the ritualized way recorded in more eastern society. Bedford County residents did indeed seem to select—and reject—new social patterns.

The snapshot we gain from the probate record gives us only one more angle of view. Inventories of estates are weighted heavily toward the wealthy and the elderly, representing a sum of past consumer be-

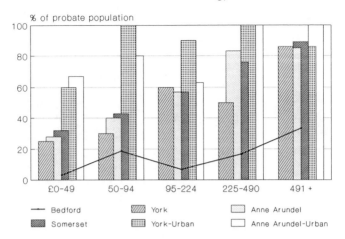

Fig. 8. Household ownership of teawares in rural and urban Virginia and Maryland, 1768–77. From Will Book 1, Bedford County, Va., 1763–87, Virginia State Library and from Lois Green Carr and Lorena S. Walsh, "Changing Lifestyles and Consumer Behaviour in the Colonial Chesapeake," in Cary Carson, Ronald Hoffman, and Peter J. Albert, eds., *Of Consuming Interests: The Style of Life in the Eighteenth Century* (Charlottesville: University Press of Virginia, 1994), tables 1, 3, 4, 5, 6.

havior, rather than a moving picture of current behavior.[24] The means to understand consumer choice lies in determining the kaleidoscope of options confronting any individual at any given time. Only by under-

[24] For discussion of the problems of probate inventories and the potential for correction of these biases, see Lois Green Carr and Lorena S. Walsh, "Inventories and the Analysis of Wealth and Consumption Patterns in St. Mary's County, Maryland, 1658–1777," *Historical Methods* 13 (1980): 96–100; Harold B. Gill, Jr., and George M. Curtis III, "Virginia's Colonial Probate Policies and the Preconditions for Economic History," *Virginia Magazine of History and Biography* 87, no. 1 (January 1979): 1–73; Gloria L. Main, "Probate Records as a Source for Early American History," *William and Mary Quarterly*, 3d ser., 32, no. 1 (January 1975): 89–99. Daniel S. Smith, "Underregistration and the Bias in Probate Records: An Analysis of Data from Eighteenth-Century Hingham, Massachusetts," *William and Mary Quarterly*, 3d ser., 32, no. 1 (January 1975): 100–110. Margaret Spufford, "The Limitations of the Probate Inventory," in John Chartres and David Hey, eds., *English Rural Society, 1500–1800* (Cambridge, Eng.: Cambridge University Press, 1990), pp. 139–74. Books by Shammas and Wetherill also contain measures for correcting biases.

standing the prerequisites of availability and affordability can we then focus on consumer desire, the vast and complex host of variables that encompasses cultural, economic, and social value of any given object. Indeed, all three conditions—affordability, availability, and desirability—must be met before any object can move into any particular household. Studying the consumer choices of the backcountry in these terms thus allows the study of what kinds of items moved most quickly into backcountry life and why one item might be preferred over another.

The means to examine the countless consumer choices of average men and women is through the records of the single most important avenue to manufactured goods in eighteenth-century America—the local store. While wealthy planters continued to ship their crops and order on their accounts from England, local merchants bought crops and supplied goods to most Virginians. This business drew particularly on smaller planters who could not afford the risks of consignment and who sold their crops and were granted credit by local agents, often of Scottish or British firms, to purchase goods in a local store. These middling planters were thought by at least one merchant to be the preferred customers; the supervisor of factors for one of the colony's largest merchant chains advised one storekeeper, "People who have only one or two hogsheads [of tobacco] to dispose of and who want all goods" are the "best customers a store can have." The innovation of Scottish chains of year-round stores across Virginia and into the backcountry were a particularly well-organized, competitive, and modernizing development in the store trade and set the pace for other merchants from the 1730s.[25]

---

[25] James Robinson to Bennet Price, October 7, 1767, as published in T. M. Devine, ed., *A Scottish Firm in Virginia, 1767–1777* (London: Clark Constable, 1982), p. 2. The study of the tobacco trade in the historical literature is immense, although few concentrate on the items for sale as an important part of the story. The most significant work on the retail side of the tobacco trade is Calvin B. Coulter, "The Import Trade of Colonial Virginia," *William and Mary Quarterly*, 3d ser., 2, no. 3 (July 1945): 296–314. Two unpublished works that are particularly useful are Harold B. Gill, "The Retail Business in Colonial Virginia" (Colonial Williamsburg Fndn., typescript); and Mary R. W. Goodwin, "The Colonial Store" (Colonial Williamsburg Research Study, 1966, typescript). Few stores have been studied archaeologically, and hence synthesis is problematic. One Virginia store from the early eighteenth century has been studied in Patricia Samford, "Archaeological Investigations of the Bates Site, 44Yo205" (Colonial Williamsburg Fndn., Department of Archaeological Research, report on file). An excellent study of a late eighteenth-century Delaware store is Wade P. Catts, Jay Hodny, and Jay

While the organizational details of these businesses differed by the American Revolution, there were so many merchants that competition was fierce. Indeed, one historian has estimated that by 1773 one-fourth of all tithables may have been merchants. To gain customers, a merchant had to offer ever higher prices for tobacco and an ever-improving selection of attractive, affordable goods. For instance, Falmouth merchant William Allason stocked silver and gold lace even though he barely had managed to sell a tenth of it in two years. With such small demand, this may seem surprising. But Allason pointed out that he needed a good assortment to prevent his customers from going to his competitors for "trifles." As population moved westward in the eighteenth century, stores quickly followed. Local merchants channeled agricultural produce eastward and supplied farmers with manufactured and semiprocessed goods. But the role of local merchant was not just to follow demand but also to help shape it. William Eddis described stores moving in "to supply the real and imaginary necessities" of farmers and their wives in the western Maryland backcountry just before the Revolution. He also saw, however, that as "wealth and population increased, wants were created, and many considerable demands, in consequence, took place for the various elegancies as well as necessaries of life." [26]

One such merchant was John Hook, in business in New London from 1766 until the county seat moved in 1783. Hook first arrived in Virginia from his native Scotland in 1758 as an indentured apprentice clerk and shopkeeper for a Glasgow merchant. [27] At the end of his

F. Custer, " 'The Place at Christeen': Final Archaeological Investigations of the Patterson Lane Site Complex Christiana, New Castle County, Delaware" (Delaware Department of Transportation Archaeological Series 74, 1989).

[26] Peter Victor Bergstrom, "Markets and Merchants: Economic Diversification in Colonial Virginia, 1700–1775" (Ph.D. diss., University of New Hampshire, 1980), p. 219. William Allason to unknown, June 15, 1761; Allason to James Mitchell, Falmouth, August 19, 1760; Allason letterbook, 1757–1770, Business Records Collection, VSL. William Eddis, *Letters from America*, ed. Aubrey C. Land (Cambridge: Harvard University Press, Belknap Press, 1969), pp. 51–52.

[27] Hook later commemorated this momentous beginning in his new career by embossing the date and colony on an expensive leather pocketbook that still survives locally in the Franklin County Public Library, Rocky Mount, Va. My thanks to Anne Carter Lee for this find. The survival of such an artifact should come as no surprise as Hook may be one of the best documented—and least known—merchants in eighteenth-century Virginia. His extant papers include 7,289 items and 103 account volumes in Special

indenture he took a position with James and Robert Donald, serving as their storekeeper in Warwick (near Richmond on the James River) and was able to become partners with them in a store in New London in September 1766. By 1771 their contract had expired and Hook parted bitterly from the Donalds. But he had already been campaigning to find another partner and by September had an agreement with David Ross, who operated a Petersburg warehouse and had an extensive network of stores in the backcountry, landholdings in Bedford, and interest in local ironworks. Ross and Hook signed a co-partnership in September 1771 for Hook to run a store in New London and a smaller one at Falling River in the southern part of the county (fig. 9).

Because of intense local competition, Hook continually stressed to Ross the importance of having quality goods at attractive prices at the proper time of the year. He pointed out that the other merchants were well stocked, writing that he had "difficulties enough to get [his] best friends to [his] self." He wished that he could exceed his rivals in the qualities of his goods, asking always to be sent the best of their kind. Indeed, Hook advised his partners that the success of their business in Bedford County was absolutely dependent on the "dispatch, exactness, and judgement in the choise of the goods, respecting the quallity, collours, patterns and fashions." His frustration turned to sarcasm as he warned, "for me to make money without Goods is as absurd as to suppose a Taylor to make a Coat without cloth by the needle and Shears alone."[28]

Hook's business philosophy must have been heeded, for the qual-

---

Collections, Duke University. Most, however, relate to a later period than that studied here. Scratch copies of letterbooks and other miscellaneous items are found in the John Hook Papers, Business Records Collection, VSL. Parts of these collections are on microfilm at Colonial Williamsburg. Dr. Warren Moorman has allowed my access to Hook's store, which was built in the early 1780s at Hale's Ford in Franklin County and still stands on family property. My thanks to Carl Lounsbury, Department of Architectural Research, Colonial Williamsburg, for accompanying me to study the building, a rare example of a standing eighteenth-century Virginia store. Only two studies of John Hook have been completed; see Willard Pierson, Jr., "John Hook: A Merchant of Colonial Virginia" (History honors thesis, Duke University, 1962); and Warren Moorman, "John Hook: New London Merchant," *Journal of the Roanoke Valley Historical Society* 11 (1980): 40–54.

[28] John Hook to David Ross, November 7, 1771, John Hook papers, VSL (microfilm, Colonial Williamsburg Fndn.). Hook to Walter Chambre, December 28, 1773, John Hook letterbook, 1772–1774, John Hook papers, VSL.

Fig. 9. John Hook store, Hale's Ford, Va., 1991. (Courtesy, Colonial Williamsburg Foundation: Photo, Carl Lounsbury.) After the courthouse was moved out of New London in 1781, John Hook moved his business to a main thoroughfare on a turnpike southward in what is now Franklin Co., Va.

ity, variety, and fashionability of the items carried when his store was stocked in 1771 hardly fit the picture of a rugged and sparse life gained from the probate record. For example, Hook's customers could thumb through the *Spectator* or *Johnson's Dictionary* or handle backgammon boards, china teacups, and feather plumes. His competition also carried fine goods. A customer at James Callaway's store could go home with a cream-colored teapot, the new novel *Tom Jones*, or *Allan Ramsay's Teatable Miscellany*, a book of popular songs.[29] Good businessmen stock what sells. Callaway and Hook knew that they had to be ready

[29] Invoice of goods shipped by Walter Chambre on the *Milham* for Norfolk and James River, Va., by order of Eilbeck, Ross, and Co., John Hook papers, Duke University. Invoice of goods, fall 1772, by Messrs. Dobson, Daltera, and Walker, Merchants in Liverpool, to Messrs. Trent and Callaway, Bedford, James River, Va. Callaway vs. Dobson, U.S. Circuit Court, Virginia District, 1811, VSL.

Table 3. Expenditures
at John Hook's Store,
September–December 1771

Type of expenditure	%
Textiles	35.1
Clothing	10.5
Alcohol	11.0
Grocery	6.6
Saddlery	5.7
Foodways	4.0
Hunt/fish	3.2
Sewing	3.0
Building	1.5
Literacy	0.2
Miscellaneous	19.2

Source: John Hook Daybook, 1771–72, Special Collections, Duke University Library, Durham, N.C.

for whatever anyone might want or risk losing their business to another merchant.

Clearly, well-chosen, attractive, and fashionable items were available to Bedford County residents. But were they affordable? A printed teapot in 1774 cost much less than the four yards of fabric necessary for a fine linen shirt or the same amount of osnaburg for a slave shirt. A pewter dish or Hook's best quality shoe buckles also cost more.

But a teapot was just one of hundreds of items available when a customer crossed the threshold of these stores. Hook recorded about 3,000 transactions of some 390 customers from September to December 1771, a period of expanded mercantile credit and busy trade. The top four categories of expenditures were textiles, clothing, bedding, and alcohol, which accounted for more than 60 percent of these customers' expenditures, although none has left a large mark on the archaeological record (table 3). Grocery items were the next most popular category, with sugar representing about 50 percent of these purchases. Material objects related to foodways accounted for only about 5 percent of the money spent; 3 percent can be linked to the serving of food and drink.

Only 0.3 percent of all consumer wealth was made up of objects related to tea drinking.[30]

What kind of objects were these? Most popular were tin drinking vessels in pint, half-pint, and quart sizes. The importance of drinking was further indicated by the number of bottles sold, either empty or containing rum. Pewter dishes, basins, and plates were the next most common items, followed by knives and forks. Several tin sugar and pepper boxes also were sold. Finally, the only ceramics purchased were two water jugs, three bowls, and one cracked earthenware basin.

What is immediately most noticeable is that the most popular dining wares were not breakable. We might speculate that the mere fragility of ceramics—not their fashion—may have been the most salient characteristic to a still mobile society like Bedford County. Thinking about material objects in terms of their physical properties also helps us to understand the infrequency of purchases of items related to cooking and dining. These kinds of goods are what economists call consumer durables—durable in this sense being an expected use life of three years or more. Unlike clothing that wore out or food that was consumed, a new cooking pot could last five years, pewter at least seven, new furniture perhaps ten to fifteen years. The "superfine hard metal spoons" purchased by William Buford at John Hook's store in 1771 could well be the same recorded in his appraisal some twenty-eight years later.[31]

Ceramics and glass also are consumer durables, but durability is, of course, relative. Breakage rates of ceramics could vary widely from

---

[30] Daybook, September 21, 1771, to April 1772, John Hook papers, Duke University. Purchases of goods totaled £429, although credits for payments and cash loans represented financial activity of more than £1,000. The late 1760s and early 1770s was a time of expanded credit from British merchants, a boom that would soon end with the credit crisis of 1772 and the later political and economic dislocation of the Revolution. This question of the archaeological visibility of store inventories has been discussed only in one significant study. A late nineteenth-century Mississippi store ledger is studied and compared to archaeological remains of customers in William Hampton Adams and Steven D. Smith, "Historical Perspectives on Black Tenant Farmer Material Culture: The Henry C. Long General Store Ledger at Waverley Plantation, Mississippi," in Theresa A. Singleton, *The Archaeology of Slavery and Plantation Life* (New York: Academic Press, 1985), pp. 309–34.

[31] Lorna Weatherill, *Consumer Behaviour and Material Culture in Britain, 1660–1760* (London: Routledge, 1988), p. 136. Appraisal, William Buford, June 26, 1797, Bedford County Will Book 2, 1787–1803, p. 195, VSL.

household to household, and they also were likely to be replaced for whim or fashion. Probates do not tell us what was broken; archaeology does not tell us what survived. Only records of acquisition will enable us to see the ceramics and other items that made their way into the lives of average men and women over the life cycle of any particular household.

One example may suffice. The wealthy Mrs. George Callaway purchased a number of items at Hook's store on June 24, 1772, including one glass tumbler, a half-pint pocket bottle, a butter boat and stand, a pint bowl, a milk pot, and a half dozen china cups and saucers. After a week, she returned for one coffee can. Three weeks later she took home a queen's ware bowl and a new half-pint pocket bottle. The following winter she purchased a printed teapot. Mrs. Callaway either was replacing ceramic vessels as they rapidly were broken or perhaps was browsing and shopping at whim. But even she purchased her items one at a time as necessity and desire came together.[32]

This pattern is replicated in the accounts of the purchases of another local planter's wife. John Smith, Jr., owned about one thousand acres in Halifax County and had a running account with Hook's main competitor in New London. In the year from September 1769 to 1770, Mrs. Smith purchased on her personal account a half dozen blue-and-white china coffee cups, two pottle jugs, a fine printed quart bowl, a fine quart mug of queen's china, a two-and-one-half gallon jug, a pint tumbler, and two pewter dishes. Both Mrs. Smith and Mrs. Callaway had the financial means to buy ceramics in quantity, yet both most often purchased vessels one at a time, each with the exception of a half dozen china coffee cups or teacups. These women did not seem to purchase ceramics in huge quantities as did wealthy eastern elite who ordered from London. Such behavior has been taken as evidence of a heightened concern for matching wares. Various contextual factors may explain backcountry women's apparent lack of preference for large sets. Perhaps it was western culture; perhaps it was women buying. But we also could ask how the *methods* of acquisition may have impacted the choices of the elite. Large Virginia planters, such as Thomas Jefferson and George Washington, ordered dozens upon dozens of ceramic table-

[32] John Hook petty ledger, Duke University.

wares from agents in England. But these orders were made in anticipa-
tion of having to wait as much as a year to receive one's purchases
from abroad. Perhaps long-term plan-ahead purchasing led to such
large orders and a concern for matching items. Those who shopped at
local stores did not have to plan ahead so carefully, although there was
always the risk that stock would be depleted or fashion would change
after breakage occurred.[33] If our picture from the probate record is
confirmed in the sale of pewter and knives and forks, what about those
missing teawares? None of the customers at Hook's store in these two
months chose such items. But expensive copper teakettles were purchased, as were tin coffeepots. Six purchases of tea and seven of coffee
also remind us that the real cost of drinking these beverages was not
the teacups but the tea to put in them. One pound of good bohea cost
more than four times the same quantity of refined sugar or coffee (both
luxuries). A customer at Hook's store would have had to trade fifteen
pounds of butter or forty-seven pounds of fresh beef to obtain a pound
of good bohea tea. Adding in a full equipage of teawares, including
silver teaspoons, and a tea table, as well as servants, food, and the
leisure for such hospitality, raises the cost quite high. Tea drinking was
indeed beginning to make inroads into Bedford society but not necessarily in the same manner as in the East.

The customers at John Hook's store did not simply reject new
behaviors and values. By choosing knives and forks, they made the first
step in the revision of eating behaviors, adopting new cultural standards
that touching food with the hands was inappropriate—a cultural taboo
that was slowly spreading from the courts of Europe in the early modern
era.[34] Through the choice of tea, some Bedford residents linked themselves to a broader cultural enjoyment of a new beverage. But only
slowly would the proper accoutrements of sociability and leisure make
their way into the workaday world of the agricultural economy—even
among the elite. Like rural people everywhere, only those behaviors

[33] Invoices, Pocket Family Plantation papers, Alderman Library, University of Virginia, Charlottesville (microfilm, "Records of Antebellum Southern Plantations: From
the Revolution to the Civil War," Series E: Part 1, Reels 11, 12, 13). Susan Detweiler,
George Washington's Chinaware (New York: Harry N. Abrams, 1982).

[34] See, for example, Norbert Elias, *The History of Manners*, vol. 1, *The Civilizing
Process*, trans. Edmund Jephart (New York: Pantheon Books, 1978).

that could fit into the sun-up to sun-down tasks of the agricultural world were accepted.

But the early rejection of tea by the backcountry may have been far more complex. The frontier boy who suffered so in his first encounter with cups and saucers also reminisced that true backwoods men thought tea only for people of quality, those who do not labor, or the sick. Teacups were fine for women and children, he declared, but too delicate for men. Tea drinking was rejected as the symbol of the very eastern society they chose to leave behind.[35]

Changes in the way food was consumed or sociability performed were not trivial. Remember that Alexander Hamilton experienced shock and revulsion at the old ways of eating with the hands from a common pot, and tea would in only a few years help to divide an empire. At the end of the eighteenth century, one English social critic noted with pride that even the peasants could now sit together at a table for their meals. He declared this act to be "the strongest characteristic of civilization and refinement."[36] The relative infrequency of purchases of ceramics and like items does not make them insignificant. Their acquisition demonstrates a conscious choice made amid an explosion of manufactured and processed items at the end of the eighteenth century. The popularity of specific artifacts tells us that these things indeed mattered and that they played vital roles in buttressing and shaping correct performance of social scripts.

At the same time, artifacts like ceramics were not then, and are not now, merely static symbols of social position. Meanings can simply be adopted in a trickle-down fashion, but they also can be reworked to reflect standards of community, gender, race, or economic position. Choosing one ceramic over another is an index of an ability to buy. But that is only one factor of consumer choice, the complex black box in the human mind that processes information about economic, social, and symbolic values and crafts, ways to solve problems and gain pleasure. It is that protean quality of meaning in any object that makes our task so difficult and exciting. It is also the reason that small things can soar from the prosaic to the profound.

The archaeological record contains countless clues to values and

[35] Doddridge, *Notes on the Settlement*, p. 88.
[36] Cited in Shammas, *Pre-industrial Consumer*, p. 188.

behaviors in worlds we have lost. But ceramic shards or bones must be added to the multidimensional and complex lexicon of material culture—documents or objects or houses or landscapes—for cultural meaning to be teased out. Bernard Herman has most recently likened this larger process to cross-mending artifacts from the archaeological record into a larger whole, with each shard carrying its own stratigraphic and other contextual information. It is that larger culture that is the goal. Christopher Tilley simply says, "In order to understand material culture we have to think in terms that go entirely beyond it, to go beneath the surface appearances to an underlying reality."[37] One reality is that institutions of distribution and industrial production were being transformed at the same time that objects, commodities, and people were entering into new relationships in the eighteenth century. These two larger patterns are tightly intertwined in stubborn knots of cause and effect. What is clear, however, is that the study of changing patterns of consumerism cannot be complete without understanding the multiple levels of those relationships—and the country cousins and frontier boys who dropped their teacups.

[37] Bernard L. Herman, *The Stolen House* (Charlottesville: University Press of Virginia, 1992), p. 14; Tilley, "Interpreting Material Culture," p. 188.

Form, Fabric, and Social Factors in Nineteenth-Century Ceramics Usage
A Case Study in Rockingham Ware

Jane Perkins Claney

In his keynote address to the 1972 Winterthur conference, Ceramics in America, Bernard L. Fontana demanded a change in the direction of American ceramics studies: "As important and as interesting as studies of potters, potting, potteries, and nomenclature may be, it is a knowledge of the final utilization of fired-clay objects that will enable

The author is grateful to the more than 100 historical archaeologists, curators, and archivists who provided her with information or access to collections and without whom there would be no database. Only a few of these contributors are specifically cited. The author also thanks: Karin Calvert and Susan Dawson Thomas, who read critically an earlier version of the paper, making suggestions for clarification; Lu Ann De Cunzo and Bernard L. Herman, whose comments and suggestions for changing the emphasis of the study from descriptive to interpretive were exceedingly helpful; Jonathan Holt Claney, Jr., for helping with the statistical analysis; Ruth Irwin Weidner for sharing her paper on hunt imagery before publication; Arlene Palmer Schwind for providing the nineteenth-century material on spittoons; Robert L. Edwards for providing the twentieth-century decorator's advice about the Rebekah-at-the-Well teapot; J. Garrison Stradling for information about the Oddfellows Degree of Rebekah; Diana Stradling for suggestions relating to the history of Rockingham-ware production, and Kenneth L. Ames, Susan H. Myers, and the Ulster County Historical Society for help with the photographs.

us best to write human history." Construing "utilization" to include the use of objects as culture symbols, this paper heeds Fontana's call.[1]

In studying ceramics, historians have traditionally consulted the same sources that are used for studying other domestic artifacts: documents that consumers themselves have generated or conserved such as letters, diaries, bills, and household inventories; material from production and marketing such as price lists and advertisements; and other sources such as probate inventories, contemporary descriptions, and pictorial images. Artifacts mentioned or illustrated in literature and art are especially potent communicators of social behavior and attitudes. In such works, artifacts are specifically chosen for their ability to convey meaning. For example, in eighteenth- and early nineteenth-century portraits, women are often shown holding porcelain teacups. At that time, tea was expensive, and serving tea was a socially prestigious activity. Porcelain also was expensive, being made from ingredients not readily obtainable and through a manufacturing process difficult to control. Thus, until about the middle of the nineteenth century, serving tea in porcelain teaware was an expression of the elite mode, as Dell Upton defines "mode": ownership of goods that "set one off from one's neighbors, and intentionally so."[2] At the opposite extreme of the price scale, red earthenware was made from locally obtained clays in numerous small potteries throughout the country. By the early nineteenth century, when inexpensive fine earthenware tablewares, mostly from England, were widely available in America, the appearance of redware tablewares in art symbolized low economic status. In *Old Pat, the Independent Beggar*, for example, the sitter is shown eating from a redware porringer (fig. 1).

Ironically, many of the traditional sources of information listed above become less useful as we investigate ceramics consumption closer to our time. As the quantity and variety of industrially produced household goods, including ceramics, increased during the nineteenth century, ownership of all but the most expensive varieties became com-

---

[1] Bernard L. Fontana, "The Cultural Dimensions of Pottery: Ceramics as Social Documents," in Ian M. G. Quimby, ed., *Ceramics in America* (Charlottesville: University Press of Virginia, 1973), p. 11.

[2] Dell Upton, *Holy Things and Profane: Anglican Parish Churches in Colonial Virginia* (New York: Architectural History Fndn., 1986), p. 102.

Fig. 1. Samuel Lovett Waldo, *Old Pat, the Independent Beggar*, New York, 1819. Oil on panel; H. 33″, W. 25″. (Boston Athenaeum.)

mon, thus unremarkable and less frequently recorded. Even in inventories and other household records, descriptive itemization became less common. It is true that more supply-oriented material, price lists, advertising, and the like survive from this period, but these sources address only the availability of ceramics, not their ownership and usage. Even discussions of ceramics in the household advice literature that proliferated in the late nineteenth and early twentieth centuries identify only a hypothetical market. Many photographs of late nineteenth-century interiors display ceramics in situ, but a disproportionate number of these are images of elite interiors. Photographs of nonelite interiors are less common. All these factors contribute to the phenomenon Edgar Martin observed in *The Standard of Living in 1860*: "What is commonplace at one time is likely to be the most difficult thing to find out about at a later time."[3]

If the usage of some types of ceramics in nineteenth-century America is difficult to track through documents and images, it is a subject ideally suited for archaeological research. For, unlike artifacts made of wood, textiles, or metals, which disintegrate when buried in the earth, ceramics remain intact. In the field of historical archaeology, which combines systematic excavation of discarded or abandoned material with documentary investigation of excavation sites, scholars over the past several decades have done a great deal of work with nineteenth-century American sites using ceramics deposits as part of their analyses. Thus, they have linked a vast number of ceramics assemblages with their historic owners, enabling them to correlate patterns of consumption with a variety of social factors, paramount among which has been socioeconomic status. In two publications, "Classification and Economic Scaling of Nineteenth-Century Ceramics" and "A Revised Set of CC Index Values for Classification and Economic Scaling of English Ceramics from 1787 to 1880," George L. Miller has facilitated these studies by providing a means of comparing ceramics expenditures. He has devised a scale for determining the relative cost of the white and cream-colored English ceramics such as creamware, transfer-printed earthenware, and plain whiteware that constituted the bulk of the American market for ceramics during the nineteenth century.[4]

Almost all the work historical archaeologists have done on correlating ceramics usage with socioeconomic status in the nineteenth and early twentieth centuries has been with the Staffordshire whitewares that Miller classified, not only because of the classification, but, more

[3] Edgar Martin, *The Standard of Living in 1860* (Chicago: University of Chicago Press, 1942), p. 45.

[4] George L. Miller, "Classification and Economic Scaling of Nineteenth-Century Ceramics," *Historical Archaeology* 14 (1980): 1–41; George L. Miller, "A Revised Set of CC Index Values for Classification and Economic Scaling of English Ceramics from 1787 to 1880," *Historical Archaeology* 25, no. 1 (1991): 1–25.

importantly, also because they account for at least three quarters of typical nineteenth-century domestic ceramics assemblages, often more. Five, six, or more other varieties of ware, one of these being porcelain, usually make up the rest of the assemblage. Despite their relative unimportance statistically, some of these other minor wares may become cultural markers equal in importance to porcelain once their social context is understood.

Testing this assumption, I have studied the nineteenth- and early twentieth-century ceramic Rockingham ware, a brown-glazed buff-bodied ceramic, usually earthenware, sometimes stoneware, that was mass produced in America and other countries from the 1830s into the 1930s or later. Sometimes the ware was thrown; more often it was press molded, often with embossed decoration. Rockingham ware, a variety that cannot be adequately researched through documents or images, generally accounted for only a small percentage of the domestic ceramics assemblages in which it occurred, one or two percent at most, but its use was widespread in America. Daniel G. Roberts and Betty J. Cosans noted in a 1980 archaeological site report: "At least some pottery of this type [Rockingham ware] is usually recovered from mid-19th-Century proveniences."[5] In fact, it is found so frequently in archaeological sites dating from the mid nineteenth century to the early twentieth, that the mere presence of Rockingham ware per se is of little interpretive value. The key to discovering the cultural meaning of Rockingham ware lies in linking its historic consumers to the vessel forms, shapes, and decorative motifs they chose. This approach might be useful with other types of ceramics as well. With knowledge of what groups of

---

[5] Daniel G. Roberts and Betty J. Cosans, *The Archeology of the Nineteenth Century in the Ninth Ward, Philadelphia, Pennsylvania* (West Chester, Pa.: John Milner Associates, 1980), p. 119. Embossed ceramic decoration is achieved in one of three ways: separate decorative elements can be applied to each piece (sprigging); liquified clay can be poured into molds and allowed to dry until a vessel wall of desired thickness has formed inside the mold (slip casting), or firm but moist, malleable (plastic) clay can be pressed into molds. (In both the latter methods, molds are usually made of two or more parts bound together while the vessel is being formed.) Press-molded wares are then smoothed inside with a sponge, allowed to dry, then removed from the mold and smoothed on the outside before firing. Molded American Rockingham ware was almost always press molded. Much of it was made from a highly refractory clay called "fireclay," which rendered Rockingham-ware vessels resistant to damage from heat but was not suitable for liquefying into slip.

consumers used a particular variety of ceramics and what vessel forms and designs they favored, explanations as to why they made these choices become possible.

The archaeological approach did indeed disclose patterns of Rockingham-ware consumption unrecoverable through other sources of information. It showed that in terms of vessel form preference, patterns of use differed between Rockingham and Staffordshire whiteware and between Rockingham and the other nineteenth-century minor wares. In addition, socioeconomic status, geographic region, and residence in rural or urban communities all produced distinct variation in Rockingham-ware vessel form preference. Finally, the archaeological approach revealed why Rockingham ware was seldom found in large quantities on any one site. The reason was not marginal popularity but specialized consumer acceptance. Early in its production especially, Rockingham ware was offered in every conceivable form for household use, but it was not popular in the most numerous household vessel forms, those for individual use such as plates and cups. Rather, it was favored in forms for corporate use, such as pitchers, teapots, spittoons, and cooking ware. It is not surprising that Rockingham ware failed to catch the public's fancy in plates and cups. When white tablewares became available—porcelain, tin-glazed earthenware, eighteenth-century creamware and salt-glazed stoneware, and several types of nineteenth-century whiteware—Europeans and Euroamericans preferred to eat from them. Reasons for the success of the Rockingham-ware forms that did catch on vary according to the form. Spittoons were practical; their color acted as camouflage, as a late nineteenth-century housewares catalogue explained: "These are a strong, durable article, of good size, at a very reasonable price, and as they are of a bright Brown color, they do not show the contents like white ones." Rockingham ware for cooking vessels also was discussed in practical terms: it was "capable of standing the fire, and resisting changes of temperature," according to *An Encyclopaedia of Domestic Economy*. In their book of household advice, Catharine E. Beecher and Harriet Beecher Stowe noted that "brown earthen pans" were "said to be best for milk and cooking. Tin pans are lighter, and more convenient, but are too cold for many purposes."[6] Reasons for the popularity of teapots and pitchers, however,

---

[6]Catalogue of Progressive Manufacturing Co., Trenton, N.J., ca. 1895, Hagley Museum, Wilmington, Del. Thomas Webster, *An Encyclopaedia of Domestic Economy*

went far beyond issues of practicality. I will argue in this paper that Americans used particular examples of these Rockingham-ware vessel forms to express and to mediate deeply held cultural values.

Several decades' worth of historical archaeologists' site reports, artifact inventories, field notes, and artifact collections provided the data for the study. Historical archaeologists do not always incorporate Rockingham ware and other minor ceramics in their site analyses, but they do catalogue and store the artifacts. Before starting on the project, it was necessary to determine whether Rockingham ware was used by enough nineteenth-century Americans to have had significant cultural meaning and whether there was enough archaeological data available to assess that meaning. In addition to relevant documents, historical archaeologists often use thousands of artifacts in interpreting each site. Turning the process around, using the sites to interpret one type of artifact, the historian must have access to many sites to discern usage patterns.[7]

The site sample for this study includes 132 consumer sites with a total of 291 Rockingham-ware vessels. They are located in seven regions of the United States: the Middle Atlantic (52 sites), Southeast

---

(New York: Harper and Bros., 1845), p. 320. Catharine E. Beecher and Harriet Beecher Stowe, *The American Woman's Home* (New York: J. B. Ford, 1869), p. 374. It is clear that Beecher and Stowe were not referring to brown-glazed redware, because redware is mentioned elsewhere in the same paragraph.

[7] I answered both preliminary questions by first finding sites from the period when Rockingham ware might have been deposited (the mid nineteenth to the mid twentieth century) and then reading site reports or asking the historical archaeologists in charge of the projects whether they had recovered Rockingham ware. Among the best sources to start finding sites from the right time are the reports on excavations completed or in progress published in *Society for Historical Archaeology Newsletter* and in newsletters from regional associations such as the Council for Northeastern Historical Archaeology. Having ascertained that plenty of data was available, I extracted information about context from site reports or from census records, city directories, property deeds, and other documents and then, whenever possible, examined the artifacts, which are usually stored in sherd form in archaeological laboratories. I used a few sites for which I was unable to examine the artifacts but for which the site reports contain information about vessel forms and occasionally decoration. For sites for which they were available, I also included minimum vessel counts of selected vessel forms in ware types other than Rockingham. Minimum vessel counts refer to the number of distinct vessels recognizable from ceramic fragments. One thing that I was unable to learn through this research strategy was what percentage of Americans used Rockingham ware. A way to accomplish that would be to examine *all* artifact inventories from sites formed during the appropriate time period to see what percentage of them contained Rockingham ware, but until all or most such inventories are included in a computerized database, such a project is not practical.

(27), Midwest (22), Northeast (15), Gulf states (2), Southwest (2), and West Coast (12). Ninety-two sites are urban, twenty-five are rural, and fifteen are located in villages.[8] Ninety-four sites were either wholly residential or primarily residential with some commercial activity also occurring on the site; eleven sites were hotels or boardinghouses; seven were restaurants or taverns; twelve were used for public or semipublic activities. These included a school, an abbey, a clubhouse, business offices, government buildings, and military installations. The historic use of eight sites could not be determined. Table 1 shows Rockingham-ware vessel distribution among these sites.

Before describing and attempting to interpret the consumption patterns these data reveal, I will briefly outline the history of Rocking-ham ware. Originating in England, the term *Rockingham ware* first referred to a white-bodied earthenware with brilliant brown glaze and smooth, unembossed surface on which there was often gilded or colored enamel decoration. Introduced in the late eighteenth century, it was produced, mostly in teapot and coffeepot or pitcher forms, by a pottery located in Swinton, Yorkshire, on the estate of the Marquis of Rocking-ham. Perhaps stimulated by the popularity of Rockingham ware in high places—the Prince of Wales was an early customer—other En-glish potteries such as Wedgwood and Spode copied the Swinton prod-uct, marking with the name "Rockingham" as well as their own factory marks. Many other potteries jumped on the brownware bandwagon but with wares of a different type: buff-bodied instead of white and relief-decorated instead of gilded or enameled. Some of these also were marked "Rockingham." Thus the term became generic for a broad range of brown-glazed wares.[9]

Ware of the smooth gilded or enameled type does not seem to have been much used in nineteenth-century America. Rarely do surviv-als fitting the description appear in ceramics collections, and there was

[8] A discussion of small communities that are neither urban nor rural may be found in Timothy A. Thompson and D. Katharine Beidleman, "Nineteenth-Century Bridgeboro, New Jersey: Urban or Rural?" (Paper delivered at the meeting of the Society for Historical Archaeology, Williamsburg, Va., 1984).

[9] Alwyn Cox and Angela Cox, *Rockingham Pottery and Porcelain, 1745–1842* (Lon-don: Faber and Faber, 1983), pp. 34, 60, 108–10; Llewellynn Jewitt, *The Ceramic Art of Great Britain* (2d ed., 1883; reprint, Poole, Eng.: New Orchard Editions, 1985), p. 281.

Table 1. Distribution of Rockingham-ware Vessel Forms by Historic
Use of Site

	Type and Number of Sites					
Vessel form	Residence (94)	Hotel or boarding-house (11)	Restaurant or tavern (7)	Public or semipublic (12)	Historic use unknown (8)	Total
Teapot	65	15	3	2	1	86
Spittoon	30	9	10	10	6	65
Pitcher	41	4	10	0	4	59
Mixing bowl	31	4	1	0	0	36
Baking vessel*	14	0	1	0	0	15
Serving dish	6	0	0	0	0	6
Mug	3	0	0	2	1	6
Flower pot	2	0	0	0	0	2
Jar	0	1	1	1	0	3
Marble	1	1	0	0	0	2
Tobacco jar	2	0	0	0	0	2
Box	1	0	0	0	0	1
Bottle	1	0	0	0	0	1
Canning jar	1	0	0	0	0	1
Chamber pot	1	0	0	0	0	1
Crock	0	0	1	0	0	1
Figurine	1	0	0	0	0	1
Milk pan	1	0	0	0	0	1
Soap dish	0	0	0	0	1	1
Tumbler	1	0	0	0	0	1
Total vessels by site	202	34	27	15	13	291

* Includes nappies, baking dishes, and pie plates.

Sources: Rockingham-ware fragments and documentary data from archaeological sites in 7
regions of the United States: Middle Atlantic, Southeast, Midwest, Northeast, Gulf States, Southwest,
West Coast.

only one such vessel among the excavated artifacts in this study: a
gilded teapot from the site of a late nineteenth-century Pittsburgh
home-furnishings store. (Since the store was not a consumer site, it is
not included in the site or vessel analyses.) From both archaeological
evidence and aboveground survivals, it is clear that Americans preferred
Rockingham ware with embossed decoration. Glazes were all shades
of brown from amber through rust to dark chocolate and were translucent or opaque, solid colored, streaked, or mottled. Bodies were cream

or buff colored. The majority of American Rockingham ware was made of the same earthenware body as yellowware, a buff-bodied yellow- or clear-glazed ceramic. Indeed, from the 1840s many potters specialized in yellowware and Rockingham ware only. A substantial minority of Rockingham ware, however, was produced by stoneware potters. Although some writers on American ceramics consider only the former to be Rockingham ware, often defining it as "Rockingham-glazed yellow ware," the stoneware versions were sold as "Rockingham ware" and, presumably, so perceived by the historic consumers who are the subjects of this paper.[10]

Although the earliest known advertisement for American-made Rockingham ware appeared in 1846—Bennett and Brothers' Pennsylvania Pottery advertised "Fancy Rockingham Ware"—at least one pottery was producing it fifteen years before that. Eleazer Orcutt and Charles W. Thompson of Poughkeepsie, New York, whose standard product was salt-glazed stoneware with cobalt blue decoration, also produced a handsome relief-decorated Rockingham-ware pitcher in several sizes. Pride in their achievement was evident, for the legends AMERICAN/MANUFACTURE and ORCUTT & THOMPSON/POKEEPSIE are emblazoned on the sides (figs. 2, 3). The partnership existed from sometime in 1830 until August 1, 1831.[11] No documents survive to indicate what Orcutt and Thompson called their Rockingham ware.

[10] Verna L. Cowin, Pittsburgh Plate Glass Site report, forthcoming; see also Verna L. Cowin, *Pittsburgh Archaeological Resources and National Register Survey* (Pittsburgh: Carnegie Museum of Natural History, 1985). For writers who include only yellow-bodied earthenware, see, for example, Edwin AtLee Barber, *The Pottery and Porcelain of the United States* (3d ed., 1909; reprint, New York: Feingold and Lewis, [1976]), p. 18; Joan Leibowitz, *Yellow Ware: The Transitional Ceramic* (Exton, Pa.: Schiffer Publishing, 1985), p. 14; Ellen Denker and Bert Denker, *The Warner Collector's Guide to North American Pottery and Porcelain* (Clinton, N.J.: Main Street Press, 1982); William C. Ketchum, Jr., *Potters and Potteries of New York State, 1650–1900*, 2d ed. (Syracuse, N.Y.: Syracuse University Press, 1987), pp. 15–16. Ketchum revised his opinion saying that an accurate definition of Rockingham ware should include "the extremely common nineteenth-century 'Rockingham,' which consisted of a stoneware body dipped completely in a brown manganese slip" (William C. Ketchum, Jr., *American Country Pottery: Yellowware and Spongeware* [New York: Alfred A. Knopf, 1987], p. 10). Stoneware potters occasionally called their Rockingham "fancy pressed ware"; more often they called it "Rockingham ware." See price lists from "Nichols & Boynton, Manufacturers and Wholesale Dealers in Stone and Fancy Pressed Ware," 1854, and "Hudson River Stone Ware Pottery, Fort Edward, N.Y.," 1876, Winterthur Museum, Winterthur, Del.

[11] The advertisement appeared in the *Mercantile Register* and was reprinted in *Antiques* 28, no. 4 (October 1935): 168–69. An announcement of dissolution of the Orcutt-Thompson partnership appeared in *Poughkeepsie Telegraph*, August 1, 1831; as cited in

Fig. 2. Orcutt and Thompson, pitcher, Poughkeepsie, New York, 1830–31. Buff earthenware
with translucent brown glaze; H. 11″. (Ex. collection of John P. Remensnyder: Photo, Robert Edwards.)

From the 1830s until at least the second third of the twentieth
century, a vast quantity of relief-decorated Rockingham ware was made
in America. The shapes and designs were frequently derived from a
popular English ceramic called "drabware," a molded, usually un-
glazed, refined stoneware, characteristically decorated in relief. American potters who made this type of ware in the 1830s, calling it "flint
ware" on their price lists, also produced brown-glazed versions from

Ketchum, *Potters and Potteries*, pp. 115, 191. John F. Remensnyder, "The Potters of
Poughkeepsie," in Diana Stradling and J. Garrison Stradling, eds., *The Art of the Potter:
Redware and Stoneware* (New York: Main Street/Universe Books, 1977), pp. 125–26.

Fig. 3. Detail of figure 2, opposite side.
(Photo, Robert Edwards.)

the same molds in both stone- and earthenware bodies. Starting in the 1840s, this kind of ware was known as "Rockingham ware," but the term has not yet turned up on American documents from the 1830s. Rockingham ware dating from the 1830s or 1840s often exhibited classical motifs and was frequently glazed a solid brown. When the rococo revival style came into fashion during the 1840s, Rockingham-ware manufacturers kept pace, producing ware with a streaked or mottled glaze that resembled the mid eighteenth-century creamware that had a brown, mottled, lead glaze known as "tortoiseshell." A variant of Rockingham ware known as flint enamel or variegated ware had splashes of green and/or blue, yellow, and gray similar to eighteenth-century versions. Sometimes, in teaware and coffee ware particularly, there were direct references to the eighteenth-century rococo in the form of tilted flower finials, rustic handles, and naturalistic motifs. Comparison of the Orcutt and Thompson pitcher with a pitcher made by E. and W. Bennett, Baltimore, in the 1850s, aptly illustrates the shift from the neoclassical to the rococo style in Rockingham ware (fig. 4; see fig. 2). Classical anthemia decorate the neck of the 1830 pitcher. The Bennett pitcher, with handle in the form of a tree branch, is decorated at the neck with a realistically rendered trailing grapevine. Transition from the neoclassical to the rococo also is suggested in the

Fig. 4. E. and W. Bennett, pitcher, Baltimore, ca. 1850–55. Impressed on base: E. & W. BENNETT/ CANTON AVE./BALTIMORE, MD. Buff earthenware with translucent mottled brown glaze; H. 8¾". (Private collection: Photo, Robert Edwards.)

nomenclature that Christopher Webber Fenton of Bennington, Vermont, employed. He called the Rockingham ware he produced around 1848 "dark lustre" or "dark finish." A later invoice dating from the 1850s, after the company had reorganized as the United States Pottery Company, called it "mottled." Through shape rather than glaze, a Zanesville, Ohio, potter's transition into the exuberantly curvilinear rococo style is noted in a letter that his wife, Sarah Tunnicliffe, wrote to England in 1848: "You would say that we had got Rockingham to perfection. Our last kiln was better than ever. We are just bringing out a kind of scroll ware which is likely to gain great credit."[12] In the

[12] Drabware occasionally had an almost imperceptible, thin, colorless glaze called a "smear glaze," which may have been formed, like salt glaze, by volatile substances in the kiln (George Savage and Harold Newman, *An Illustrated Dictionary of Ceramics* [London: Thames and Hudson, 1985], p. 266); "List of Prices of Fine Flint Ware, Embossed and Plain, Manufactured by D. and J. Henderson, Jersey City, N.J. . . . 1830," reprinted in *Antiques* 26, no. 3 (September 1934): 109. In 1833 the firm incorporated as the American Pottery Manufacturing Company; price list from "Salamander Works, 62 Cannon St., New York. Flint and Fire Proof Ware Manufactory. . . . April,

late nineteenth-century neoclassical revivals, Rockingham ware again appeared appropriately classicized, with egg-and-dart borders, palmettes, and portrait medallions of Roman warriors decorating teapots, pitchers, and spittoons. Often, but not always, it was again a solid brown as it had been earlier in the nineteenth century.

1837," Bella Landauer Collection, New-York Historical Society. Numerous marked examples of American Pottery Company and Salamander Works Rockingham ware exist. A Salamander pitcher in the collection of the Henry Ford Museum is datable to the 1830s by its inscription, "KIDD'S TROY HOUSE." Archibald Kidd was keeper of the Troy House, Troy, New York, from 1834 to 1838. For Rockingham-ware decoration and glazes, see, for example, Lura Woodside Watkins, *Early New England Potters and Their Wares* (1950; reprint, Hamden, Conn.: Archon Books, 1968), p. 96; Richard Carter Barret, *Bennington Pottery and Porcelain* (New York: Crown Publishers, 1958), pp. 24–25. There are no ceramics histories that deal with American Rockingham ware exclusively, but discussions of or references to the ware also are included in: Barber, *Pottery and Porcelain; Bennington Pottery: The Robert B. and Marie P. Condon Collection* (Hyannis, Mass.: Richard A. Bourne Co., 1988); M. Lelyn Branin, *The Early Makers of Handcrafted Earthenware and Stoneware in Central and Southern New Jersey* (Rutherford, N.J.: Fairleigh Dickinson University Press, 1988); M. Lelyn Branin, *The Early Potters and Potteries of Maine* (Augusta: Maine State Museum, 1978); Arthur W. Clement, *Our Pioneer Potters* (New York: Arthur W. Clement, 1947); Elizabeth Collard, *Nineteenth-Century Pottery and Porcelain in Canada* (Kingston and Montreal: McGill-Queen's Universal Press, 1984); Denker and Denker, *Warner Collector's Guide*; Arthur E. James, *The Potters and Potteries of Chester County, Pennsylvania* (Exton, Pa.: Schiffer Publishing, 1978); Ketchum, *American Country Pottery*; Ketchum, *Potters and Potteries*; William C. Ketchum, Jr., *Pottery and Porcelain* (New York: Alfred A. Knopf, 1983); Jeannette Lasansky, "Lancaster County, Pennsylvania, Pottery," *Antiques* 122, no. 3 (September 1982): 538–47; Leibowitz, *Yellow Ware*; Susan H. Myers, *Handcraft to Industry: Philadelphia Ceramics in the First Half of the Nineteenth Century* (Washington, D.C.: Smithsonian Institution Press, 1980); *The Pottery and Porcelain of New Jersey, 1688–1900* (Newark, N.J.: Newark Museum, 1947); John Ramsay, *American Potters and Pottery* (New York: Tudor Publishing Co., 1947); Marvin D. Schwartz, *Collectors' Guide to Antique American Ceramics* (Garden City, N.Y.: Doubleday, 1969); John Spargo, *Early American Pottery and China* (1926; reprint, Rutland, Vt.: Charles E. Tuttle Co., 1974); Stradling and Stradling, *Art of the Potter*; and [Stradling and Stradling], *The Jacqueline D. Hodgson Collection of Important American Ceramics* (New York: Sotheby Parke-Bernet, 1974). Tortoiseshell ware is defined in Savage and Newman, *Illustrated Dictionary*, p. 295. An example is in the 1773 probate inventory of William Bourn of Marblehead, Mass., which lists "2 Turtle Shell Tea Pots," as quoted in Vernon G. Baker, *Historical Archaeology at Black Lucy's Garden, Andover, Massachusetts: Ceramics from the Site of a Nineteenth-Century Afro-American* (Andover, Mass.: Robert S. Peabody Fndn. for Archaeology, 1978), pp. 15–16. Christopher Webber Fenton is discussed in Ruth Howe Wood, "Memories of the Fentons," *Antiques* 8, no. 3 (September 1925): 153; United States Pottery Company invoice from the Warshaw Collection of Business Americana, National Museum of American History, Washington, D.C. Tunnicliffe quoted in Norris F. Schneider, "Staffordshire Potters," *Zanes Times Signal* (Zanesville, Ohio), November 17, 1957.

English immigrant potters constituted almost the entire first generation of American Rockingham-ware makers. Since they brought with them designs and sometimes molds, it is not surprising that much American Rockingham ware is identical in shape to English relief-molded wares. Other designs mirror English ware except for the addition of American symbols. A Rockingham-ware spittoon, probably made in New Jersey, exhibits seven scenes and motifs from Robert Burns's poem "Tam O'Shanter," taken directly from an English stoneware pitcher made by William Ridgway in 1835; on the eighth panel there is an American eagle.[13] Americanization is evident in the imagery of another pitcher bearing figures of two huntsmen taken from Staffordshire figure groups. On the Rockingham-ware pitcher, the huntsmen stand improbably amid Indian corn, an American plant and an American symbol. In another version, the bearded English huntsmen are transformed into American Indians, having shed their beards, boots, cloth coats, and cockaded hats in favor of buckskins, feathers, and warbonnets.

By far the most brilliant adaptation of an English design for the American market—so successful that it became the best- and longest-selling Rockingham-ware pattern in history—involved no change in the English image. Edwin and William Bennett, of Baltimore, simply transferred the design from an English embossed stoneware pitcher with the exotic title "Arabic" to a Rockingham-ware teapot, which they entitled "Rebekah at the Well" (fig. 5).[14] The pitcher, probably by Samuel Alcock and Company, and the Minton figure on which it was based were executed in the mid 1840s; the title "Arabic" was printed on the pitcher base. The title "Rebekah at the Well" was inscribed on a raised rectangle on both sides of the Bennett teapot, an unusually emphatic manner of identifying the subject inasmuch as imagery on Rockingham ware was rarely titled, even on the base of the piece. The Bennetts knew their market. As this paper will demonstrate, they

[13] Edwin AtLee Barber, "Early Ceramic Printing and Modeling in the United States," *Old China* 3, no. 2 (December 1903): 51. The Ridgway pitcher is illustrated and discussed in R. K. Henrywood, *Relief-Moulded Jugs, 1820–1900* (Woodbridge, Eng., 1984), pp. 65–68.

[14] Barber, *Pottery and Porcelain*, pp. 196–97; Henrywood, *Relief-Moulded Jugs*, pp. 233–34; Susan H. Myers, "Edwin Bennett: An English Potter in Baltimore," *Ars Ceramica*, no. 4 (1987): 31–35.

touched the very core of mid nineteenth-century domestic values simply by renaming an old image and placing it on a teapot instead of a pitcher.

More than eighty different vessel forms in a variety of sizes and embossed decorations were made in Rockingham ware. The list of forms, compiled from survivals, archaeological recoveries, and potters' price lists or other documents, includes:

ale jugs	hanging baskets
architectural elements	icewater pitchers
*baking pans	inhalators
banks	inkwells
basins	*jars
batter jugs	lamp bases
bedpans	*milk pans
birdbaths and cups	*marbles
*bottles	molds
*bowls	*mugs
*boxes	nameplates
bread boxes	*nappies (round dishes)
butter dishes	paperweights
butter tubs	pickle dishes
cake plates	picture frames
candlesticks	*pie plates
*canning jars	pipkins
*chamber pots	*pitchers
chicken waterers	plates
coffeepots	plug basins (sinks)
coffee urns	salad dishes
coin covers	sauce dishes
cookie jars	shakers
covered dishes	shaving mugs
creamers	shovel plates
*crocks	slop jars
cups	snuffboxes
curtain tiebacks	*soap dishes
desk sets	spill holders
*dishes	*spittoons
doorknobs	stove supports
ewers	sugar bowls
*figurines	*teapots

flasks	*tobacco jars
*flowerpots	toby jugs
footbaths	toothbrush holders
foot warmers	toys
furniture knobs	*tumblers
garden seats	wafer pots
goblets	washboards
hall dogs	water coolers

* Denotes vessels found on archaeological sites in this study.

Only twenty-two of these forms turned up on the sites included in this study, and at that, most were in minuscule quantities. As table 1 shows, only four or five forms appear to have really caught on: teapots, which accounted for 30 percent of the total; spittoons, 22 percent; pitchers, 20 percent; mixing bowls, 12 percent; and nappies, other baking dishes, and pie plates, which together accounted for 5 percent. (Nappies were flat-bottomed slant-sided vessels for baking, offered in six or eight different sizes.) Chronological comparison of Rockingham-ware potters' price lists reveals that the variety of forms offered decreased after the 1850s, probably reflecting the potters' awareness of market preferences. In 1852 the United States Pottery Company, Bennington, Vermont, offered sixty-two different forms including: picture frames; pocket flasks; mantel ornaments, such as reclining cows and a poodle carrying a basket in its mouth; and "architectural work made to order." Rockingham-ware objects and the few other price lists that survive from the period indicate that while the United States Pottery's scope was probably the most ambitious, other potteries were also offering a variety of forms such as "figured" candlesticks, fancy cake plates, toby flasks, and "Octagon" or "Turk" inkstands. These forms did not appear on price lists of the later nineteenth or early twentieth centuries. Most potters continued to produce food-preparation vessels and a few other forms such as soap dishes, mugs, and a Rockingham-ware specialty called a "hall dog" (a large figurine, usually a seated spaniel), and it appears that all continued to produce teapots, pitchers, and spittoons.[15]

[15] "Fenton's Patent Flint Enamel Ware, Manufactured in Benington, Vermont," price list/invoice dated July 20, 1852, Warshaw Collection of Business Americana, National Museum of American History, Washington, D.C. "Figured" candlesticks and "octagon" and "turk" inkstands quoted from "Mansion Pottery, Wm. G. Smith & Co.,"

Comparing vessel form usage between Rockingham ware and the white, transfer-printed, painted, edged, or dipped Staffordshire wares that dominated the American market emphasizes the specialty status of Rockingham ware. George L. Miller describes an equally limited acceptance of most Staffordshire vessel forms; out of more than ninety forms produced, fifteen made up 95 percent of the market.[16] Miller's figures disclose an important difference, however, between the Staffordshire- and Rockingham-ware forms that were popular. Analyzing only the periods when Rockingham ware was also in production, individual food consumption forms—cups, saucers, and dinner plates, which were rare in Rockingham—constituted more than 80 percent of imported Staffordshire ware, while teapots and pitchers accounted for no more than 3 and 6 percent respectively. Spittoons did not figure at all or were subsumed under "other vessels." Even if cups, saucers, and dinner plates are left out of the white-ceramics analysis, Rockingham-ware teapots, pitchers, and certainly spittoons still accounted for far greater shares of the Rockingham-ware market than the same forms in Staffordshire ware.

Rockingham ware demonstrates a pattern of vessel-form usage different not only from Staffordshire wares but also from any other variety of ceramics that nineteenth-century Americans used. Whiteware and transfer-printed earthenware were used across the entire utility spectrum from food-preparation forms used in production areas of the house to ornaments for the parlor and teawares. (Teawares were generally the ceramic vessels most important for validation of social status, and households typically spent more for them than for vessels in other functional groups.)[17] Porcelain was used in tea- and tablewares, and

East Liverpool, Ohio, price list ca. 1855, Ohio Historical Society, East Liverpool. My observation about changing Rockingham-ware production patterns is based on examination of 36 price lists dating from 1837 to ca. 1935; Ohio Historical Society, East Liverpool, Ohio; Winterthur Museum, Wilmington, Del.; Warshaw Collection of Business Americana, National Museum of American History, Washington, D.C.; photocopies of other price lists in author's collection. Some price lists are published in Barret, *Bennington Pottery*; and Leibowitz, *Yellow Ware*.

[16] George L. Miller, "The 'Market Basket' of Ceramics Available in Country Stores from 1780 to 1880" (Paper delivered at the meeting of the Society for Historical Archaeology, Tucson, January 1990).

[17] Diana Di Zerega Wall, "Sacred Dinners and Secular Teas: Constructing Domesticity in Mid Nineteenth-Century New York," *Historical Archaeology* 25, no. 4 (1991): 79; Miller, "Classification and Economic Scaling," p. 14.

porcelain chamber sets were not uncommon; but porcelain food preparation forms were. Other ceramic varieties such as yellowware and a
cheap cream-colored ware called C.C. in the pottery trade were used
primarily for food preparation and chamber forms. Still others such as
copper luster and black refined stoneware were used mostly for teawares. Rockingham ware, however, cannot be classed as either fancy or
utilitarian ware, nor was it a general line, as the white-bodied Staffordshire wares were. In this study, the most numerous vessel form from
residential sites, which constituted almost one-third of the entire assemblage, was the teapot. The second most numerous functional group
was the category of food preparation and storage vessels. These constituted nearly one-fourth of all vessels from residential sites and included
mixing bowls, nappies, baking dishes, pie plates, a bottle, a canning
jar, and a milk pan (see table 1).

Representing opposite poles on a hypothetical continuum of potential for symbolic meaning are Rockingham-ware teapots, which, in
addition to the symbolic significance of the form, were often elaborately
decorated, and food preparation forms, which were minimally decorated at most. This is not to suggest that any artifact may not be endowed
with meaning beyond its strictly utilitarian function—a Rockingham-
ware nappy, for example, occupies a central decorative position in
the home of Alvin Rackliff, a seventy-five-year-old Maine lobsterman,
because it was the "bowl" his grandfather used for the ritual Saturday-
night baked-bean supper—but going beyond personal associations,
some artifacts are more likely to have meaning for the culture at large.
They may symbolize cultural values and help to maintain or alter
them, as Ian Hodder explains: "Each use of an artefact, through its
previous associations and usage, has a significance and meaning within
society so that the artefact is an active force in social change." Teapots,
in the nineteenth century, were notably charged with meaning and,
according to Annie Trumbull Slosson, power to transform: "A woman
may be expected to retain and increase the womanly characteristics of
gentleness, kindness, and all kinds of loveliness, who has a pretty tea-
service to preside over every day, . . . and men under the influence of
such women, and such cheerful home associations, are always better
citizens."[18]

<hr />

[18] Information about Rockingham-ware nappy from Alvin Rackliff, Spruce Head,
Maine, August 1993; Ian Hodder, "Theoretical Archaeology: A Reactionary View," in

Given the centrality of the teapot in the enactment of woman's role, it is no wonder that the Bennett Pottery's Rebekah-at-the-Well teapot met with such success. The Old Testament story, in which Abraham's servant recognized the woman whom God had chosen to be Isaac's wife by her offer to carry water from the well until all his thirsty camels were satiated, resonated with a dominant theme in American discourse at the time: the equation of women's role in maintaining the home with her responsibility for maintaining and perpetuating the sacred aspects of home and family life. The theme was sounded from the pulpit, the influential Protestant theologian Horace Bushnell declaring in 1847: "Religion never thoroughly penetrates life, till it becomes domestic." Moreover, with Rebekah as symbol, the theme was turned to potent political use. In 1851 the International Order of Oddfellows, a men's secret social and benevolent society, established a "Degree of Rebekah" to be conferred on members and their wives for the purpose of defusing "the prejudice felt against the Order by many of the fairer sex in various portions of the Union." The wives, however, were not entitled to membership because, the manual explained, "while man is called upon to go forth into the world and fight its battles, woman's place is at the home-altar, as the high-priestess of that sacred spot; and her business—one which she well understands—is to cheer *him* in his rough journey, and to nerve him to proceed in it with faith and patience."[19]

By converting "Arabic" into "Rebekah at the Well" and placing it on a domestic artifact in 1851, the same year the Oddfellows established the Degree of Rebekah, the Bennetts were able to place both a reminder of her highest duty and a means through which to effect it in every woman's home. For, in the prevailing belief in the power of

---

Ian Hodder, ed., *Symbolic and Structural Archaeology* (Cambridge, Eng.: Cambridge University Press, 1982), p. 10; Slosson quoted in Elizabeth Stillinger, *The Antiquers* (New York: Alfred A. Knopf, 1980), p. 64.

[19] See Barbara Welter, "The Cult of True Womanhood: 1820–1860," *American Quarterly* 18, no. 2, pt. 1 (Summer 1966): 151–74. Bushnell quoted in Colleen McDannell, *The Christian Home in Victorian America, 1840–1900* (Bloomington: Indiana University Press), p. 19. Paschal Donaldson, *The Odd-Fellows' Text-Book; An Elucidation of the Theory of Odd-Fellowship: Embracing a Detail of the System, in All Its Branches, with Forms, Ceremonies, and Odes with Music, for Important Occasions, and a Manual of Practice for the Guidance of Officers and Lodges* (Philadelphia: Moss and Bro., 1852), pp. 214, 217–18.

house design and home furnishings to influence character and moral stance, it was thought that household furnishings incorporating religious symbolism contributed to the religious well-being of the family. In addition to the overt iconography of the biblical story on the Rebekah-at-the-Well teapot, the designer went to the trouble of placing the embossed image against a paneled background instead of the plain background of the English pitcher. This type of paneling, known as "gothic" during the period, was one of many gothic motifs in domestic furnishings, which, flourishing with Gothic revival domestic architecture from the 1840s until after the Civil War, graphically associated religious edifices of the past with the home.[20]

After E. and W. Bennett introduced the Rebekah-at-the-Well teapot, nearly all the potteries in the United States copied it, and it was in production intermittently at the Bennett pottery until the factory burned down in 1936. More than a third of the sixty-five Rockingham-ware teapots on domestic sites in this study were definitely Rebekah at the Well, and five fragmentary examples appeared to be. The subject matter of twenty could not be determined, but it is probably fair to assume that more than a third of these were also Rebekah at the Well. Thus, at a conservative estimate, teapots of this design made up more than half the Rockingham-ware teapots on residential sites. Only one other decoration, a trailing rose motif, also by the Bennett pottery, appeared as many as three times. By the century's end, Rebekah-at-the-Well teapots had become such a standard that they were advertised in four sizes in the 1897 Sears Roebuck catalogue.[21]

In 1907 an article in the *Baltimore Sunday Sun* stated that "Rebekah drawing water at the well continues to draw womankind unto her with such irresistible attraction that 100 specimens of this teapot are sold at the [Bennett] manufactory to one of any other design." But what was the nature of the attraction? Was Rebekah still a symbol of the "true woman"? For some, perhaps, but for others she appears to

---

[20]McDannell, *Christian Home*, pp. 16–51; Susan Williams, *Savory Suppers and Fashionable Feasts: Dining in Victorian America* (New York: Pantheon Books, 1985), pp. 65–67; Wall, "Sacred Dinners," pp. 78–79.

[21]Barber, *Pottery and Porcelain*, pp. 196–97; J. F. Gates Clarke, "Rebekah-at-the-Well Teapots," *Spinning Wheel* 34, no. 6 (July/August 1978): 20; Fred L. Israel, ed., *1897 Sears Roebuck Catalogue* (New York: Chelsea House, 1968), p. 686. Although there is a picture of a Chinese motif teapot, the caption reads "Rebecca Tea Pot."

have become simply a means of introducing an appealing touch of nostalgia into home decor. Edwin Bennett's grandson reported that because the teapot had become "an antique," the pottery had begun making and marketing it again, and an early twentieth-century decorator advised putting a Rebekah-at-the-Well teapot on the mantel to achieve an "old timey look." What had happened during the final decades of the nineteenth century and the beginning of the twentieth to transform this symbol of ideal womanhood into a mere icon of nostalgia? One answer, of course, is that through long familiarity, the meaning of an image can loose impact and specificity. In *Disorderly Conduct: Visions of Gender in Victorian America*, however, Carroll Smith-Rosenberg provides an alternative answer as she describes the development during this period of the "new woman," who, in seeking gender equality and challenging gender conventions, repudiated the cultural norms inherent in the cult of true womanhood.[22] As these changes were occurring, consumers were mediating them perhaps with such familiar and well-understood iconographic messages as the Rebekah-at-the-Well teapot. Although not necessarily with fully articulated intention, they may have been casting an affectionate (or disdainful) glance backward at the old cultural values or, perhaps, symbolically preserving them.

After teapots, pitchers were the most numerous Rockingham-ware vessels recovered from residential sites in this study, forty-one pitchers accounting for 20 percent of the aggregate residential assemblage (see table 1). At least thirty were decorated in relief, supporting ceramics historian Hugh Wakefield's assertion that "the jug [pitcher] was considered preeminently the subject for relief decoration" during "early and middle Victorian times." The reason offered was that the pitcher was "constantly in view," an observation born out by the frequent appear-

---

[22] *Baltimore Sunday Sun* quoted in Myers, "Edwin Bennett," p. 33. George Bennett Filbert to B. Floyd Bennett, January 29, 1962. Filbert referred to the Edwin Bennett Pottery Company, a reorganization of the Bennett Pottery that took place in 1890. I do not have the citation for the interior decorator's advice. Robert L. Edwards, editor and publisher of *Tiller*, read the quotation to me from an early twentieth-century home decorating book or magazine about ten years ago. I wrote down the quotation but neglected to record the citation. Mr. Edwards has been unable to find it again. Carroll Smith-Rosenberg, *Disorderly Conduct: Visions of Gender in Victorian America* (New York: Oxford University Press, 1985), pp. 173–78.

Fig. 5. E. and W. Bennett, "Rebekah-at-the-Well" teapot, Baltimore, ca. 1850–55. Buff earthenware with translucent mottled brown glaze; H. 9". (Smithsonian Institution.)

ance of pitchers in nineteenth-century paintings and prints of domestic interiors. Often they were shown on the mantel, a virtually sacred domestic space. Of eleven subjects appearing in the imagery of the archaeologically excavated Rockingham-ware pitchers in this study, two predominated: floral designs (ten examples) and hunting themes (nine examples). Hunting themes also occurred on Rockingham-ware pitchers excavated from restaurant and tavern sites. In addition to the archaeological data, I examined a group of Rockingham-ware presentation pitchers—pitchers were the prime vessel form for inscribed presentation pieces during the nineteenth century—and found that hunting motifs vastly outnumbered all other subjects; thirty of thirty-seven presentation pitchers bore embossed scenes of stag hunts (see fig. 4). Some of these depicted on the opposite side boar hunts, hunters, or examples of their prey—often a dead game bird. As presentation pieces, pitchers depicting hunt scenes had historical precedent, especially in England, as part of the hunt ritual. They served as trophies in which a fox hunter might receive the brush (fox tail) from the master of the hunt. In another way also, Rockingham-ware presentation pitchers connected to formulaic gift-giving. Almost half the inscribed hunt pitchers had large green ceramic frogs in their interior. Frog mugs (or toad mugs) were tavernware that had evolved from the age-old practical joke of slipping a live toad into a fellow drinker's beer. According to D. S. Skinner, frogs, which were fertility cult objects in some ancient cultures and good-luck symbols in more recent times, came to predominate as the hidden ceramic surprise over toads, which had darker associations. As the nineteenth century progressed, painted, gilded, and inscribed presentation frog mugs were produced. "It is evident that frogs were moving into the parlour . . . their status changed, so that they began to be considered pleasant additions to showy presentation pottery: an accepted symbol of good luck expressed to the recipient by his friends and well-wishers."[23]

If highly decorated objects frequently displayed by a large segment of the population are presumably culturally expressive, personalized gifts, especially ones rooted in tradition, are unequivocally so, informing about the attitudes and values inherent in the culture within which both the giver and the recipient operated. The question is then, what did the popular Rockingham-ware hunt pitchers signify, and for whom were they meaningful? Evidence suggests that they filled gender-specific roles analogous to Rebekah-at-the-Well teapots; they were male accouterments that expressed and reinforced the prevailing image of masculinity. Scholars who have written about images of hunting in nineteenth-century art and artifacts have stressed the symbolic relationship between hunting and the nineteenth-century concept of masculinity. "In the nineteenth century," Kenneth L. Ames writes, "man as hunter was considered as inseparable from certain conceptions of 'natu-

---

[23] Hugh Wakefield, *Victorian Pottery* (London: Herbert Jenkins, 1962), p. 37. See examples of inscribed pitchers in David Battie and Michael Turner, *The Price Guide to Nineteenth and Twentieth Century British Pottery* (1979; reprint, Woodbridge, Eng.: Antique Collector's Club, 1982), p. 69; and Alice Cooney Frelinghuysen, *American Porcelain, 1770–1920* (New York: Metropolitan Museum of Art, 1989). For Rockingham-ware examples, see Stradling, *Hodgson Collection*; *Pottery and Porcelain of New Jersey*; Rockingham-ware presentation pitchers also are included in the collections of the Brooklyn Museum, Newark Museum, New Jersey State Museum, and Philadelphia Museum of Art. D. S. Skinner, *Hops and Venom; or, Looking into Frog Mugs* (Stoke-on-Trent, Eng.: Stoke-on-Trent City Museum and Art Gallery, 1988), p. 2.

ral' masculinity as it is today. Men are supposed to hunt. Men are supposed to kill." Elizabeth Johns also mentions the emphasis on violence in the male-as-hunter construct. Discussing genre paintings of Western trappers and hunters, she argues that the "representations preserve the illusion of masculine independence, and they construct male power as attained through violence."[24]

The context of Ames's comments on hunt imagery is discussion of the subject matter found in mid nineteenth-century dining-room decoration, concentrated especially in the relief decoration on sideboards produced between the 1840s and 1870s. The "iconography of dining" included fruits; vegetables; attributes of the hunt, harvest, and vintage; and representations of "dead rabbits, deer and other mammals, fish, and fowl." Dead game suspended by the hind legs from a branch was often the centerpiece of sideboards and also constituted a genre of Rockingham-ware pitchers called "game pitchers" (figs. 6 and 7). These were included on Rockingham-ware manufacturers' price lists from the 1850s to the 1880s. Among the hunt images occurring on archaeological sites in this study, game pitchers were found on one residential site, one restaurant or tavern site, and one other site, the historic use of which is unknown. Ames interprets these images of hanging dead game as elements of the violence that was "a prime ingredient of the Romanticism of the last century," but a subdued form, "the violence occurring offstage, so to speak." He sees the images as a complex of meanings, among which were statements perhaps about "the relationship of humankind to the natural world, expressing and endorsing a highly human-centered vision," or about predation, natural and also national predation, as explicitly suggested by the overarching presence of the American eagle at the top of the sideboard illustrated in figure 6. (The Rockingham-ware pitcher [fig. 7] bears the same messages, the Ameri-

---

[24] Kenneth L. Ames, *Death in the Dining Room and Other Tales of Victorian Culture* (Philadelphia: Temple University Press, 1992), pp. 73–74. For sources on nineteenth-century perceptions of masculinity, Ames cites John D'Emilio and Estelle B. Freedman, *Intimate Matters: A History of Sexuality in America* (New York: Harper and Row, 1988); Shere Hite, *The Hite Report on Male Sexuality* (New York: Ballantine Books, 1981); and Michael S. Kimmel, ed., *Changing Men: New Directions in Research on Man and Masculinity* (Newbury Park, Calif.: Sage, 1987). Elizabeth Johns, *American Genre Painting: The Politics of Everyday Life* (New Haven: Yale University Press, 1991), pp. 77–78.

Fig. 6. Sideboard, probably New York, ca. 1855. Black walnut, marble, with tulip and white pine secondary woods; H. 106″. (Museum of Fine Arts, Houston; museum purchase with funds provided by Anaruth and Aron S. Gordon: Photo, Peter Hill, Inc.)

Fig. 7. Pitcher, attributed to Taylor and Speeler, Trenton, N.J., 1852–ca. 1856. Buff earthenware with translucent streaked brown glaze and blue-green splashes (flint enamel); H. 8″. (Private collection: Photo, Robert Edwards.)

can eagle under the spout being in a position of honor analogous to that of the eagle at the top of the sideboard.) Ames continues: "It is difficult . . . to speak of predation without also speaking of gender, of conventional Victorian understandings of what masculinity was all about." Ruth Irwin Weidner also discusses the gendered aspects of images of dead game in art, specifically the hunter "returning with a gift of game to a waiting woman. . . . It is at the time of the hunters' return that the archetypal gender duality between the male prowess of the hunters and the domestic sphere of the waiting females is most accentuated."[25]

[25] Ames, *Death in the Dining Room*, pp. 44, 63, 68–73; Ruth Irwin Weidner, "Gifts of Wild Game: Masculine and Feminine in Nineteenth-Century Hunting Imagery" (Paper presented at the Winterthur Conference: The Gender of Material Culture/The Material Culture of Gender, October 1989).

Although the gender of the owners could not be established for any of the archaeologically excavated Rockingham-ware hunt pitchers, the names on the presentation pieces indicated, not surprisingly, that most of the recipients were men. But (perhaps surprisingly) four were women. Another woman, a piano teacher and church organist, owned a Rockingham-ware hunt pitcher with a frog. Three of these women, however, were related to owners of or workmen at the Swan Hill Pottery, South Amboy, New Jersey, which produced a popular version of the "frog" hunt pitcher from the 1850s into the 1890s; and Miss Lizzie, the organist, lived near the pottery.[26] Personal associations rather than gender appropriateness were undoubtedly the operative factors in these examples.

Rockingham-ware hunt pitchers, then, were symbols of masculinity. As such, they defined the man's sphere of action as far from hearth and home, underscoring the separateness of male and female roles. In her discussion of the popularity of hunt-scene genre painting, Johns examines the male sense of autonomy that hunt images reinforced. Her emphasis is on male identification with Western hunters, but I would argue that her explanation can be extended to other hunting imagery:

As the popularity of images of Western trappers and hunters would suggest, white American males' assumption of their absolute autonomy as *males* bolstered the justification of separate spheres for the sexes. And as a counter to the worrisome implications of class stratification in the democracy, men's devotion to the exploration of economic and political autonomy was in many ways a commitment to a self-sufficient masculinity that underlay class. Fascinated by this phenomenon, Tocqueville wrote that American men rarely enjoyed the communal sympathy with their wives typical of gender relations in Europe, in which men and women shared the circumstances of class. If American men felt any common identity, he observed, it was with other (white) men, with whom they shared the opportunity—more accurately, the fierce drive—to go for the main chance.[27]

---

[26]Ruth Justice Nebus, interview, 1987; granddaughter of Samuel Locker (superintendent of the Swan Hill Pottery, South Amboy, N.J., during the 1880s) provided information about Miss Lizzie. Interview with the author, 1987. *Pottery and Porcelain of New Jersey*, p. 53; Branin, *Early Makers*, pp. 201, 205.
[27]Johns, *American Genre Painting*, pp. 141–42.

Fig. 8. Spittoon, probably American, nineteenth century. Buff earthenware with translucent brown glaze; H. 4¼″, L. 8⅛″. (Private collection: Photo, Robert Edwards.)

The third Rockingham-ware vessel form found on residential sites in significant numbers was the spittoon; thirty spittoons accounted for 15 percent of the assemblage (see table 1). Spittoons seem to have been the functional and culturally expressive equivalents in the nineteenth century of ashtrays in the twentieth. Supporting this observation, "china parlor spittoons" were deemed "suitable for presents," and early Rockingham-ware potters listed spittoons with vases and mantel ornaments. Embossed decorative motifs on spittoons drew from much of the natural world, shells, flowers, and birds being especially prevalent. Geometric designs were popular, and religious themes were not neglected. They included various examples of gothic paneling and ornament, and one model seems to represent a gothic edifice with elaborately leaded windows (fig. 8). It is unusual for the commonplace equipage of daily life to figure much in contemporary discussion, but spittoons were an exception because foreign visitors to the United States, being repelled by the American habit of chewing tobacco, discussed them at length. "Spittoons should replace the eagle as the American national emblem," a British commentator unkindly quipped, and Eyre Crowe, who traveled through America with William Thackeray in 1852–53, described them as if they were an exotic genus. He complained about their exclusion from dictionaries: "For example, they [lexicographers] allude to pipes, they dilate upon tobacco, but the useful receptacles for the moistening results, popularly known as 'spittoons,' or 'expectorators,' or 'expectaroons,' are terms jealously excluded from their vocabularies; yet they are palpable enough to the senses. The courtyard of the Charleston Hotel was piled with these in the morning, when the wholesome water-hose was turned upon them vigorously, a sight quite unique in its way." In noting the blasé attitude of his fellow passengers toward their opulent surroundings, a Russian passenger traveling in 1857 on one of the numerous elegantly appointed American steamships described "the cool, eternally busy American [who] had already dragged out the newspaper just in from California, had put his feet on the marble fireplace or on its bronze grille, had pulled out some chewing tobacco from the front pocket of his waistcoat and had managed to savor its taste, spitting into spittoons placed for this noble purpose by every table, couch, and armchair."[28]

Usually men people the nineteenth-century images in which spittoons appear—typically barrooms, newsstands, or hotel lobbies—and one might easily think of spittoons as exclusively male accouterments were it not for the report of Isabella Lucy Bird, an Englishwoman traveling in America in 1854. Among the places she described were an inn in Chicago that she considered beneath her standards and the saloon of the *Mayflower*, a luxurious steamship that "impressed me much more than anything I have seen in the palaces of England." At the inn, on ascending the stairs to "the so-called 'ladies' parlour, I found a large, meanly-furnished apartment, garnished with six spittoons, which, however, to my disgust, did not prevent the floor from receiving a large quantity of tobacco-juice." In the *Mayflower* saloon, "porcelain spittoons in considerable numbers garnished the floor, and their office was by no means a sinecure one, even in the saloon exclusively devoted to ladies."[29]

[28]Catalogue of the Progressive Manufacturing Co., of Trenton, N.J., ca. 1895, in the collection of Hagley Museum, Wilmington, Del.; Phoenix Pottery Works advertisement in *Wellsville Patriot* (Wellsville, Ohio), July 29, 1851, p. 3. The anonymous British commentator was quoted in a display label; Museum of Ceramics, East Liverpool, Ohio; Eyre Crowe, *With Thackeray in America* (New York: Charles Scribner's Sons, 1893), pp. 32–33; Arnold Schrier and Joyce Story, eds. and trans., *A Russian Looks at America: The Journey of Aleksandr Borisovich Lakier in 1857* (Chicago: University of Chicago Press, 1979), p. 60.

[29]Isabella Lucy Bird, *The Englishwoman in America* (Madison: University of Wisconsin Press, 1966), pp. 147–48, 170.

Unlike teapots and pitchers, spittoons do not seem to appear in images of nineteenth-century domestic interiors, but, thanks to archaeology, we know that they were there. Their noninclusion could mean that they were relatively unfreighted with cultural meaning, or it could mean that the homeowners were not proud of the cultural meaning the spittoons carried. The latter interpretation would not be surprising considering that Europeans were vocal in their dislike of tobacco chewing, and nineteenth-century Americans typically looked to Europe for cultural validation. It is supported, moreover, by the testimony of such offerings as "Kilian's Patent Spittoon-Footbench," a footstool with pedal-operated hinged top that opened to reveal a spittoon inside (fig. 9).[30]

The specialization that Rockingham ware demonstrates bears theoretical implications for material culture studies. An often expressed theory in this field is that the range of domestic artifacts actually used historically is not accurately represented by surviving objects. The theory holds that family sentiment and aesthetic selectivity tend to favor decorated and fashion-bearing objects for survival as well as objects used in status-conferring activities or those with significant monetary value or that hold other important cultural meanings for their owners. Thus, one would anticipate that ornamented pitchers and teapots would have been preserved in greater numbers than butter tubs or chamber pots and that the archaeological record would reveal more plain utilitarian forms. Evidence from this project refutes the hypothesis. In Rockingham ware, at least, artifact survival reflects not selective survival, but actual usage patterns. Relief-decorated teapots, pitchers, and spittoons predominate in the body of Rockingham ware that survives aboveground to be seen in antiques and museum collections, but they also are the most numerous vessel forms in the archaeological record.[31]

As the distribution of vessels in this study makes clear, from the

[30] Advertisement in *The American Cabinet-Maker, Upholsterer and Carpet Reporter* 13, no. 23 (October 21, 1876): xxiv. Five different spittoon footstools, all with upholstered tops, are illustrated in *Maine Antique Digest* (January 1992): 42-F.

[31] Sources for this assessment include the collections of the Bennington Museum, Brooklyn Museum, Henry Ford Museum, Landis Valley Farm Museum, Metropolitan Museum of Art, New Jersey State Museum, Newark Museum, Ohio Historical Society at East Liverpool and Columbus, Philadelphia Museum of Art, Staten Island Historical Society; private collections comprising in aggregate more than 1,000 pieces of Rockingham ware; antiques shops and shows; and collectors' books on antiques and auction catalogues.

Fig. 9. Kilian Brothers advertisement, New York, 1876. From *American Cabinet-Maker, Upholsterer and Carpet Reporter* 13, no. 23 (October 1876): xxiv. (Strong Museum: Photo, Robert Edwards.)

mid nineteenth century into the twentieth, Rockingham ware could be found in all types of American settings: in rural locations, villages, towns, and cities; in households representing all socioeconomic levels; and in all kinds of public establishments such as restaurants, taverns, and hotels. At government facilities from the Army fort at Apache Pass, Arizona, to Independence Hall in Philadelphia, a Rockingham-ware spittoon seems to have been de rigueur. Deep in tobacco country, the Kentucky state legislature went through at least 477 Rockingham-ware spittoons, for that many were discarded on the site. Even not counting that extraordinary accumulation, spittoons accounted for nearly 40 percent of the Rockingham ware on nonresidential sites (see table 1). Rockingham-ware pitchers with gothic paneling were used at the hotel that Mormon prophet Joseph Smith built to accommodate visitors to his settlement at Nauvoo, Illinois, and the tip of a teapot spout indicates that a Rockingham-ware teapot was in the slave quarters of Andrew Jackson's Hermitage.[32] However, to say simply that everyone used Rockingham ware, while true, is misleading, for everyone did not use the same vessel forms and decorative motifs. Gender as a factor in consumer choice has been discussed. The region of the country that the consumer lived in, rural or urban residence, and socioeconomic status were also factors. I will confine my discussion of these primarily to socioeconomic status.

To identify the socioeconomic status of site occupants in this study, I have chosen occupation, verified by documentary evidence, as the best single indicator and have grouped occupations, following Theodore Hershberg and Robert Dockhorn's classification of nineteenth-century work nomenclature into the categories "professional and high white collar," "proprietary and low white collar," "skilled craftsman," "unskilled occupations, specified as to the type of labor," and "unskilled, unspecified" (table 2). Additional categories are owner-

[32] Robert M. Herskovitz, *Fort Bowie Material Culture* (Tucson: University of Arizona Press, 1978). Information on Independence Hall from Steven Patrick, May 18, 1987; Ronald W. Deiss, *Archaeological Investigations at Kentucky's Old State Capitol* (Frankfort: Kentucky Historical Society, 1988), p. 170; Paul DeBarthe, *The Smith Mansion Hotel Latrine and Other Discoveries of the 1978 Archaeological Project* (Columbia: University of Missouri, 1979). Background information for the Hermitage site from Samuel D. Smith, *An Archaeological and Historical Assessment of the First Hermitage* (Nashville: Division of Archaeology, Tennessee Department of Conservation, 1976).

Table 2. Distribution of Rockingham-ware Vessel Forms by Occupational Level

Vessel form	Occupational Level and Number of Sites									
	Professional/ high white collar (5)	Proprietary/ low white collar (14)	Owner-operator farmer (10)	Craftsman/ proprietary (3)	Craftsman (7)	Unskilled, specified (10)	Unskilled, mixed (3)	Tenant farmer (4)	Slave (3)	Total (59)
Teapot	0	4	2	0	4	11	1	3	6	31
Pitcher	1	13	3	3	6	2	1	0	0	29
Spittoon	0	6	6	1	2	3	3	1	0	22
Mixing bowl	1	1	10	2	1	6	0	0	1	22
Baking vessel*	4	3	2	0	0	1	0	2	0	12
Serving dish	0	0	1	0	0	0	0	1	2	4
Mug	0	0	1	0	0	0	0	0	0	1
Flower pot	0	0	0	2	0	0	0	0	0	2
Tobacco jar	0	1	0	1	0	0	0	0	0	2
Box	0	0	1	0	0	0	0	0	0	1
Bottle	0	0	0	0	0	0	1	0	0	1
Chamber pot	0	0	0	1	0	0	0	0	0	1
Figurine	0	1	0	0	0	0	0	0	0	1
Milk pan	1	0	0	0	0	0	0	0	0	1
Total vessels by occupation	7	29	26	10	13	23	6	7	9	130

* Includes nappies, baking dishes, and pie plates.

Sources: Rockingham-ware fragments and documentary data from archaeological sites in 7 regions of the United States: Middle Atlantic, Southeast, Midwest, Northeast, Gulf States, Southwest, West Coast.

operator farmer, tenant farmer, and slave. (Slaves could have performed either skilled or unskilled labor; the category is based solely on their unfree social and economic status.) Suzanne M. Spencer-Wood summarizes precedent for using occupational category as a measure of socioeconomic status in *Consumer Choice in Historical Archaeology*, and, discussing work as the primary determinant of class structure in nineteenth-century America, Stuart M. Blumin maintains that social identities "arose from, and were most generally framed in terms of, economic activity." [33] (Although the term *class* is broader than *socioeconomic status*, including cultural as well as social and economic characteristics, it will not be ambiguous to use the terms interchangeably in this paper, and I will do so in order to accommodate discussion of sources that use both.)

In grouping occupations into larger hierarchical categories for use as the defining variable of class, Blumin argues that the pursuit of nonmanual versus manual labor separated the middle from the lower class, thus placing skilled craftsmen in the lower class. In "Late Nineteenth-Century American Working-Class Living Standards," however, John F. McClymer finds a small but significant number of skilled workers (18.7 percent of a sample of 385) able to go beyond adequate housing and nourishment to meet consumption standards deemed necessary for middle-class status—the ability to afford presentable clothes and furnish a parlor for entertaining guests, for example. Other studies of nineteenth-century earnings and living standards tend to support this finding. Moreover, in the area of perception and consciousness of class, Blumin acknowledges (although he finds evidence to the contrary more compelling) that "the tendency to perceive mechanics as members of the middle class may have been widespread." Richard P. Horwitz offers corroborative evidence in his study of a nineteenth-century Maine town. [34]

[33] Theodore Hershberg and Robert Dockhorn, "Occupational Classification," in *Historical Methods Newsletter* 9, nos. 2/3 (March/June 1976): 59–77. Suzanne M. Spencer-Wood, "Miller's Indices and Consumer-Choice Profiles: Status-Related Behaviors and White Ceramics," in Suzanne M. Spencer-Wood, ed., *Consumer Choice in Historical Archaeology* (New York: Plenum Press, 1987), p. 324; Stuart M. Blumin, *The Emergence of the Middle Class: Social Experience in the American City, 1760–1900* (Cambridge, Eng.: Cambridge University Press, 1989), p. 11.

[34] John F. McClymer, "Late Nineteenth-Century American Working Class Living Standards," in *Journal of Interdisciplinary History* 17, no. 2 (Autumn 1986):

Blumin does not introduce the category of lower middle class into his discussion, and I would be inclined to classify skilled craftsmen as such were it not for an overriding complication that Blumin discusses throughout his work and that has become apparent in the data for my study: the ambiguity of artisan-level occupational terminology in nineteenth-century directories and census data. Blumin wrote: "Many of the wealthier manual workers . . . were in reality manufacturers, retailers, and other nonmanual businessmen who retained artisanal occupational labels." Documents for several workers in the Rockingham-ware study identify such a pattern: the 1860 census, for example, lists John S. Ginn, forty-eight, of 818 Callowhill Street, Philadelphia, and his eighteen-year-old son Jacob as shoemakers. The business directory for that year lists "John L. Gill boot & shoemaker ladies." The 1870 census lists John Gill, 58, and Jasper, 28, as shoemakers, while the business directory for that year adds "also manuf" to the Gill listing. In 1880 the census lists John Gill as "shoemaker," and "Casper" as "works shoemaking"; the business directory has "Aspar J. Gill, boot & shoemaker plus stores." The Gills, then, were proprietors, but there were seven "skilled craftsman" level sites in the Rockingham-ware study that remain ambiguous. These sites potentially cross the boundary between Blumin's lower and middle class and my lower middle and middle class. In addition, there were three sites occupied mostly by residents falling into the above category; but on these sites there also lived residents from the proprietary/low white-collar level either because there were multiple households on the same site or because the occupation level of households on the site changed during the period of artifact deposition. I have listed "craftsman" and "craftsman/proprietary" as separate entities in table 2 and combined them in table 3, where occupational categories are consolidated into three socioeconomic status

---

379–98. See Martin, *Standard of Living*; William J. Rorabaugh, "Beer, Lemonade, and Propriety in the Gilded Age," in Kathryn Grover, ed., *Dining in America, 1850–1900* (Amherst: University of Massachusetts Press, 1987), pp. 25–26. For an extensive discussion of what were and were not considered decent standards of living, see Ruth Schwartz Cowan, *More Work for Mother: The Ironies of Household Technology from the Open Hearth to the Microwave* (New York: Basic Books, 1983), pp. 152–73. Blumin, *Emergence of the Middle Class*, p. 247. Richard P. Horwitz, *Anthropology toward History: Culture and Work in a Nineteenth-Century Maine Town* (Middletown, Conn.: Wesleyan University Press, 1978).

Table 3. Distribution of Rockingham-ware Forms by
Socioeconomic Level

	Socioeconomic Level and Number of Sites			
	Middle (29)	Craftsman/ proprietor (10)	Lower (20)	Total (59)
Vessel form				
Teapot	6	4	21	31
Pitcher	17	9	3	29
Spittoon	12	3	7	22
Mixing bowl	12	3	7	22
Baking vessel*	9	0	3	12
Serving dish	2	0	2	4
Mug	0	0	1	1
Flower pot	0	2	0	2
Tobacco jar	1	1	0	2
Box	0	0	1	1
Bottle	1	0	0	1
Chamber pot	0	1	0	1
Figurine	1	0	0	1
Milk pan	1	0	0	1
Total vessels by socioeconomic level	62	23	45	130

* Includes nappies, baking dishes, and pie plates.

Sources: Rockingham-ware fragments and documentary data from archaeological
sites in 7 regions of the United States: Middle Atlantic, Southeast, Midwest, Northeast,
Gulf States, Southwest, West Coast.

levels. For rural domestic sites, I placed owner-operators of farms and
plantations in the top level and tenant farmers, from wage laborers and
sharecroppers to cash renters, in the lower.[35]

[35] Blumin, *Emergence of the Middle Class*, p. 119. For Gill family, see Daniel G.
Roberts, Michael Parrington, Betty Cosans-Zebooker, and David Barrett, *Archeological
Investigations in Association with the Center City Commuter Rail Connector: A Study
of Nineteenth Century Urban Development in Philadelphia and Spring Garden* (West
Chester, Pa.: John Milner Assoc., 1985). Census and directory data are from the Commuter Tunnel project files, John Milner Associates, Philadelphia. For rural class divisions, see Blumin, *Emergence of the Middle Class*, p. 308; Claudia C. Holland, "Tenant

Not all sites in this study could be classified socioeconomically. Thirty were primarily nonresidential, and the historic use of eight is unknown (see table 1). Nor were all the residential sites homogeneous as to class either synchronically or over time, but approximately two-thirds were. The figures in table 3 show that the lower-class category averaged slightly more Rockingham-ware vessels per site than the middle class (2.3 to 2.1), but the difference is not statistically significant. Markedly significant, however, is the distribution of the two most popular Rockingham-ware vessel forms on residential sites, teapots and pitchers. Three-fourths of all lower-class sites had at least one teapot. As table 3 shows, teapots accounted for almost half of all vessels occurring on lower-class sites, where pitchers accounted for less than one-tenth. Pitchers were the most popular form on middle class sites, however, representing 27 percent of the total. Teapots represented less than one-tenth. The contrast becomes more striking when it is learned that of the six middle-class sites that had teapots, five are known to have been occupied by households with servants or slaves, suggesting the possibility that the teapot was for their use. Class-related differences in Rockingham-ware consumption are further underscored by the fact that only ten residential assemblages contained both pitchers and teapots. Not surprisingly, five of these came from sites that were heterogeneous in socioeconomic status. Two of the others came from middle-class sites that had slaves or servants; one was from a craftsman's household, and two were recovered from lower-class sites in Alexandria, Virginia. All three Rockingham-ware pitchers found on lower-class sites were from three sites in Alexandria within the same residential block. Two were from both sides of a duplex; the third belonged to Charles McKinny, a mariner living at the opposite end of the block from the duplex on a parallel street where real-estate values were rising and shopkeepers and white-collar workers were taking over properties formerly occupied by unskilled workers like McKinny. Possibly propinquity to higher-status neighbors impelled McKinny to social emulation. British archaeologist Danny Miller discusses the strategy wherein people wishing to improve their relative position within the social hierarchy

Farms of the Past, Present, and Future: An Ethnoarchaeological View," *Historical Archaeology* 24, no. 4, Historical Archaeology on Southern Plantations and Farms, ed. Charles E. Orser, Jr. (1990): 61–62, 66.

"may seek to emulate the group above . . . by adopting certain of the products or styles associated with the higher group."[36] Following this line of thought, it should be noted that in table 3 the craftsman/proprietor status level more closely resembles the middle than the lower class in teapot and pitcher usage.

For about half the sites that were socioeconomically classifiable, minimum vessel counts for ware types other than Rockingham were available. Only one lower-class site with Rockingham-ware teapots also contained teapots of other ware types: a Michigan iron worker's household had one in majolica and one in pearl- or whiteware. Minimum vessel counts were available for only one of the five lower-class sites that did not contain Rockingham-ware teapots; that site did not have teapots of any kind but did have teacups and saucers, suggesting that teapots simply were not discarded. By contrast, there were many teapots in wares other than Rockingham on middle-class sites, notably that of Joseph Smith's summer kitchen at Nauvoo. Required to entertain many visitors to the Mormon settlement, the Smith household had discarded four transfer-printed white earthenware teapots, two of porcelain and one in the fashionable black refined stoneware. One middle-class householder's probate inventory included a metal teapot, and undoubtedly other householders in the middle-class sample also owned them. These would not have appeared in the archaeological record, however, because they were rarely discarded and, if they were, would not have lasted in the soil as long as ceramics.[37] Both classes owned pitchers in

[36]The difference between the lower-class mean (2.25) and the middle-class mean (2.14) is .11, which is smaller than the sigmas for either mean: lower-class sigma is 1.87, middle-class sigma is 1.27. On the majority of craftsman/proprietor and lower-class sites, it could not be determined whether servants were present. Where it could, there were none. Archaeological investigation found that artifact disposal across the boundary between the contiguous yards of the duplexes was possible but unlikely: Pamela J. Cressey, "The Alexandria, Virginia, City-Site: Archaeology in an Afro-American Neighborhood, 1830–1910" (Ph.D. diss., University of Iowa, 1985), pp. 148–49; John F. Stephens, "Vertical Integration Study by Year and Occupation Rank," City Survey Socioeconomic Data, Alexandria Archaeology, Alexandria, Va.; "Alexandria Archaeology Street Profile," Alexandria Urban Archaeology Program, City of Alexandria, 1983; T. B. McCord, Jr., *Across the Fence, but a World Apart: The Coleman Site, 1796–1907* (Alexandria, Va.: Alexandria Urban Archaeology Program, 1985), pp. 46–48. Danny Miller, "Structures and Strategies: An Aspect of the Relationship between Social Hierarchy and Cultural Change," in Hodder, *Symbolic and Structural Archaeology*, p. 89.

[37]Patrick E. Martin, *Archaeological Investigation at Fayette State Park* (Lansing: Michigan Historical Museum, 1986), pp. 25–26, 29. Gregory Waselkov, Robert T. Bray,

other types of ware: yellowware and a range of white earthenware varieties occurring on lower-class sites; these varieties, plus redware, stoneware, and porcelain occurring on middle-class sites.

Many explanations are possible for the class-differentiated pattern evident in Rockingham-ware consumption, but relative cost of the vessel forms is not one of them; Rockingham-ware teapots cost almost twice as much as same-size Rockingham-ware pitchers. Cost was undoubtedly a factor, however, in the number of Rockingham-ware teapots appearing on lower-class sites, for Rockingham ware was among the least expensive ceramics of the day, but not *the* least. Teapots also were available in the cheaper yellowware, usually made by the same manufacturers who made Rockingham. Why then did people who bought inexpensive teapots not buy the cheapest? Since at least the beginning of the eighteenth century, teapots in dark colors had been popular. Dark teapots were not necessarily expensive, but they were directly employed in the display of social status. For white hands were a sign that a woman had servants and did not have to work, and pouring tea from a dark teapot in the parlor was an ideal means of showing them off. Thus the great entrepreneur Josiah Wedgwood wrote to his partner Thomas Bentley in 1772: "Thanks for your discovery in favor of the black Teapots. I hope *white hands* will continue in fashion & then we may continue to make *black Teapots* 'til you can find us better employment." In the century following Wedgwood's comment, contrasting teaware continued in fashion. When Annie Trumbull Slosson discussed the transforming power of "a pretty tea-service . . . however cheap and homely it may seem to the more wealthy," she was contrasting teaware to white ware: "There cannot be any force exerted on a man's or a woman's mind by a lot of white crockery set out to eat from."[38]

and Linda Waselkov, *Archaeological Investigations of the Hyrum Smith Site* (Columbia: University of Missouri, 1974). Middle-class inventory is in Lu Ann De Cunzo, "Economics and Ethnicity: An Archaeological Perspective on Nineteenth-Century Paterson, New Jersey" (Ph.D. diss., University of Pennsylvania, 1983), p. 507; Ann Smart Martin, "The Role of Pewter as Missing Artifact: Consumer Attitudes toward Tablewares in Late Eighteenth-Century Virginia," *Historical Archaeology* 23, no. 2 (1989): 1.

[38] David Buten with Jane Perkins Claney, *Eighteenth-Century Wedgwood: A Guide for Collectors and Connoisseurs* (New York: Methuen, 1980), p. 90; Gaye Blake-Roberts, lecture, Hagley Museum, October 30, 1989. Slosson quoted in Stillinger, *Antiquers*, p. 64.

Slosson was a member of the middle class. Indeed the "cult of true womanhood" or "women's sphere" as discussed by such scholars as Barbara Welter and Mary P. Ryan, has been specifically identified with the middle class. Blumin, however, summarizes evidence from several scholars that "the domestic ideal influenced life within working-class homes," and certainly the Oddfellows, who, as mentioned earlier, incorporated "woman's place at the home-altar" into the very text of their operating principles, exemplify this. The organization was founded as a working-class club and retained that association even though some businessmen subsequently joined. Pamela J. Cressey found the distinction Slosson made between tea and dining vessels to have been operative among low economic-status residents of a nineteenth-century African American neighborhood in Alexandria, Virginia. Vessels for serving tea and coffee were generally of refined redware or Rockingham ware; dining forms were of whiteware. In interviewing elderly members of the African American community in their homes, Cressey saw Rockingham-ware teapots, sometimes containing plastic flowers or the like, on mantels or windowsills. Informants would say that the teapots belonged to their mothers or grandmothers, which suggests, if only unconsciously, the symbolic transfer of women's role from one generation to the next.[39]

If, then, Rockingham-ware teapots were associated with lower-class status, and the predominant image on Rockingham-ware teapots was Rebekah at the Well, one must ask why turn-of-the-century prescriptive literature proposed decorating with Rebekah-at-the-Well teapots. For examination of these works convinces that they were addressing readers with a more than comfortable income: those of middle-class or elite status. Why was the Rebekah-at-the-Well teapot recommended as a reminder of the past to those who would not previously have been using it, and was this new market actually buying the teapot? The answer to the first question is that the decorating advice

[39] Welter derives her evidence for the most part from fiction and prescriptive literature that was written for the middle class. See especially Welter, "Cult of True Womanhood," p. 168; Mary P. Ryan, *Cradle of the Middle Class: The Family in Oneida County, New York, 1790–1865* (Cambridge, Eng.: Cambridge University Press, 1981). Blumin, *Emergence of the Middle Class,* pp. 188–89; see esp. pp. 221–29 for the Oddfellows information. Cressey, "Alexandria City-Site," pp. 245–47. Pamela J. Cressey, conversation with author, March 31, 1989.

falls into the category that Pierre Bourdieu calls "the 'rehabilitation' of 'vulgar' objects." Reversing Miller's emulation process described above, wherein a lower-status group copies the consumption patterns of those who rank higher, Bourdieu discusses the phenomenon of the higher group appropriating the lower group's artifact, investing it with new meaning in the process to perform a new social function. A familiar example is the practice of dining by candlelight. Photographs of middle-class or elite Victorian dining rooms never show candles on the table, for those who could do so acquired the lighting innovations of the day: gas, then electricity. When these were no longer innovations, and the avant-garde were ready to move on to a new mode, only those who could never be mistaken for members of social groups who still had to use more primitive forms of lighting could risk using candlelight. Candlelight dining was one of a congeries of behaviors and attitudes that constituted the colonial revival—that turn to an American past the Establishment perceived as simple and wholesome compared to the urbanizing, industrializing, ethnically diversifying present. Decorating the home to achieve an "old timey look" with artifacts such as the Rebekah-at-the-Well teapot was an integral part of the colonial revival impulse. (The concept of "colonial" was vague enough chronologically to include almost anything perceived as from the past.) It is my contention, however, that the Rebekah-at-the-Well teapot would not have been put forth as one of these artifacts if there had not been several ranks in the social hierarchy between the group to whom it was recommended and the group with whom it was formerly associated. In addition, enough time had to have elapsed since the object was introduced not only to make it seem quaint but also to make it "sufficiently dated to cease to be 'compromising,'" for, as Bourdieu observes, "the 'rehabilitation' of 'vulgar' objects is more risky . . . the smaller the distance in social space or time."[40]

Evidence of middle-class or elite ownership of the Rebekah-at-the-Well teapot is scanty but does exist. An example in my database be-

---

[40] Pierre Bourdieu, *Distinction: A Social Critique of the Judgement of Taste*, trans. Richard Nice (Cambridge: Harvard University Press, 1984), p. 61. For table lighting, see, for example, Kathryn Grover, ed., *Dining in America, 1850–1900* (Rochester, N.Y.: Margaret Woodbury Strong Museum, 1987); and Williams, *Savory Suppers*. Bourdieu, *Distinction*, pp. 61–62.

longed to a plantation owner of elite status and could have been discarded around the turn of the century, but since there were servants in the household, the status of those who used the teapot cannot be identified. There is anecdotal evidence, however, that is clear. Mary Lucy Macon Michaux Harvie, born in 1855 on her father's plantation, Beaumont, in Powhatan County, Virginia, lived there until about 1890 when, with her husband and children, she moved to Richmond. My informant, Mary Harvie's granddaughter, born in Richmond in 1904, remembers as a child having tea with her grandmother every afternoon "up in her room." There was a Rebekah-at-the-Well teapot in the house, but they did not use it for tea, nor did she ever remember seeing it in use. There were servants, a cook, a housemaid, and a chauffeur or horse driver, but the teapot was not for their use either; "it belonged to the family." The teapot remained in Mary Harvie's possession until she died in 1945, when her granddaughter incorporated it into her own household, where it remained on a shelf in the kitchen cabinet—a beloved inutility.[41]

The author of a review of the Bennington, Vermont, United States Pottery Company's exhibit of Rockingham ware at the New York Crystal Palace exhibition in 1853 might have been surprised to learn that Rockingham-ware pitchers were popular with the middle class. Mentioning "candlesticks, pitchers, spittoons, picture-frames, teapots, etc.," the reviewer said: "This ware has become a favorite article in New England, and deserves much merit as cottage furniture." The term *cottage* at that time in the United States meant specifically working-class housing.[42] The class-related prediction proved to be accurate for teapots, as we have seen, but wrong for pitchers. As shown in table 3, pitchers outnumbered all other vessel forms on middle-class sites, and there were more pitchers on middle-class sites than on craftsman/proprietor and lower-class sites put together. It is necessary, however, to establish that in households occupied by members of more than one

---

[41] Mary Michaux Graves Danzoll, interview with author, December 27, 1987.

[42] "Specimen of Flint Ware," *Gleason's Pictorial* 5, no. 17 (October 22, 1853): 1. The reviewer uses the terms *enamel ware* or *flint ware* or *enamel flint wares*, but the ten-foot-high centerpiece of the exhibit, now housed in the Bennington Museum, is of plain Rockingham ware. For "cottage," see A. J. Downing, *The Architecture of Country Houses, including Designs for Cottages, and Farm-Houses, and Villas* (1850; reprint, New York: Dover Publications, 1969), esp. p. 40.

class, such as middle-class households with servants, the heads of the household were the ones using the Rockingham-ware pitchers. (Households from two of the fourteen middle-class sites that had pitchers are known to have had servants.) For this purpose, we have the evidence of presentation pieces whose owner's occupation and, in many instances, degree of affluence are a matter of documentary record. Research on the thirty-seven Rockingham-ware presentation pitchers in this study turned up information about occupation, wealth level, or both for the recipients of twenty of the pitchers. All were of the middle class, and more than half belonged to the professional/high white-collar or wealthy landowner group.

Considering the generally held belief that there is a positive correlation between the cost of a commodity and its role in status establishment or maintenance, one must ask how it is possible that Rockingham ware, cheaper by half than the white ceramics that filled the needs of most middle-class householders, fitted into the middle-class menage without upsetting what Grant McCracken has intriguingly named the "Diderot unity"—the manner in which "consumer goods in any complement are linked by some commonality or unity." (In an essay entitled "Regrets on Parting with My Old Dressing Gown," Diderot recounts how the gift of a sumptuous red dressing gown had compelled him to redecorate his shabby and comfortable old study to match the elegance of the gown.) I maintain that the presence of Rockingham-ware pitchers in middle-class houses illustrates the role that fashion, fundamentally capricious, had begun to play in consumer choice after the middle of the eighteenth century, when, Upton observes, "status was no longer a stable condition, but had to be maintained constantly by a quick grasp and speedy adoption of the newest material goods." The outstanding eighteenth-century parallel to the use of Rockingham ware by the middle class was the social position of creamware. Through obtaining royal patronage, Wedgwood had managed to attain such cachet for the relatively cheap product he brand-named "Queensware," that a customer wrote to him in 1789 asking for a dessert service that, she said, was "designed to be used after China, therefore I[d] wish to have it elegant." The parallel is not exact; I know of no evidence that American Rockingham-ware manufacturers tried for high-status patronage. In fact, the Crystal Palace review suggests otherwise. However, if, unlike Queensware, Rockingham-ware pitchers had come into the market at the cottage level, it is doubtful that the middle class would have taken to them, at least during their first "generation" of usage. Both Miller and Bourdieu stress the perceived need of upper-status groups to maintain the contrast in consumer choices between themselves and lower status groups.[43]

What then was the appeal of Rockingham-ware pitchers to middle-class consumers? Color and theme coordination with fashionable interiors may have contributed. Brown harmonized with the rustic decor that was a component of the rococo revival, and branch handles, flowers, and trailing vines were stock elements in Rockingham-ware pitcher decoration. Rockingham ware subsequently blended with the brown interiors that, as Lewis Mumford pointed out, dominated the American scene for thirty years following the Civil War. But the striking prevalence of hunt subjects, especially in pitchers that were presents for middle-class recipients, suggests that there may have been a more specifically class-related meaning. In all variations of the Rockingham-ware hunt pitcher, there was an image of the stag hunt. Ames points out that stag-hunt references carry class allusions, referring to royal game preserves of the Middle Ages and, later, to deer parks of the wealthy. "Throughout, the possession of deer and the right to hunt them were identified with royalty, power, status," and during the nineteenth century, for "much of white, urbane Western society, the vision of the good life was derived largely from European monarchical and aristocratic lifestyles of the past." Having established that hunting was a key ingredient in the nineteenth-century concept of masculinity, Johns links hunt images to the middle class by explaining how the concept of masculinity served middle-class requirements: "This ideology of masculinity—and with it the ideology of the domestic sphere—was particularly useful to men of the new urban middle classes, who wished to be at once essentially male (independent and strong) and successful in the social world of the city. To assume this identity, they needed the 'natural' arrangements of urban middle-class gender

[43] Grant McCracken, *Culture and Consumption: New Approaches to the Symbolic Character of Consumer Goods and Activities* (Bloomington: Indiana University Press, 1988), pp. 118–19. Upton, *Holy Things*, p. 229. Customer quoted in Buten, *Eighteenth-Century Wedgwood*, pp. 19–20. Miller, "Structures and Strategies," pp. 89–90; Bourdieu, *Distinction*, pp. 58–60.

definitions." ("Urban" and "middle-class" because, John points out, exercising "sweet domestic influence in the parlor" was not an option for women doing half the outdoor farm work or working in industry or as domestics.) Many of the "new urban merchants, professionals, bankers, clerks, and publishers" were "new to the social requirements of middle-class status," and needed the tempering influence of women who "through natural expertise in the finer points of arts and social relations, [could] give them respectability by Old World genteel standards." As Johns was specifically discussing the urban middle class, it should be noted that all but one of the hunt pitchers in the archaeological database for this study occurred on urban sites; the other was in the DuPont powder plant's industrial village near Wilmington, Delaware.[44] The presentation hunt pitchers were owned by people who lived in cities or towns near large metropolitan areas, mostly in northern New Jersey.

The data from this study has clearly revealed that Rockingham ware as an entity did not fit neatly into a ceramics social hierarchy. The fabric of which it was made, brown glaze on a buff earthenware or stoneware body, was evidently deemed particularly appropriate for certain cultural expressions, the Rebekah-at-the-Well teapot and the hunt pitcher for example, and these appealed to different social groups. Manufacturers tried to branch out. I have seen one example of a game image, familiar in Rockingham ware, on a heavy porcelain pitcher, and Rebekah at the Well has turned up in whiteware with polychrome glaze and even on a polychrome vase topped with crenellation. These are rare examples, however, proving only that manufacturers tried to expand the market for these popular images but did not meet with success. These favorites were evidently considered suitable only for certain vessel forms and only for one fabric, Rockingham ware.

I have argued that the Rebekah-at-the-Well teapot—unquestionably the most popular Rockingham-ware vessel ever produced—symbolized and helped to perpetuate the cult of domesticity in nine-

[44] Lewis Mumford, *The Brown Decades: A Study of the Arts in America, 1865–1895* (1931; reprint, New York: Dover Publications, 1971), pp. 2–3. Ames, *Death in the Dining Room*, pp. 74–75. Johns, *American Genre Painting*, p. 142. Samuel W. Shogren, "Lifeways of the Industrial Worker: The Archaeological Record (a summary of three field seasons at Blacksmith Hill)," (Hagley Museum and Library, Wilmington, Del., 1986, research files).

teenth-century America and that a new clientele, composed of the chiefly middle-class "new woman" that Smith-Rosenberg describes, adopted the old symbol, packed with its familiar associations and usage, as one small means, perhaps, of negotiating a profound change in the traditional role of women. Rockingham-ware hunt pitchers seem to have performed an analogous function in the lives of middle-class men, symbolizing their role as the male provider and identifying the locus of their activity as the "wilderness" outside the domestic sphere. The pervasiveness and insistence of such symbols embodied in the minor artifacts of daily life—their messages delivered each time the objects were seen or used—are compelling evidence of the depth of these concerns in the lives of those who experienced them.

Negotiating Industrial Capitalism

Mechanisms of Change among Agrarian Potters

Paul R. Mullins

This essay examines how archaeologists can illuminate the material world of one community of ceramics producers and consumers to interpret how agrarian craftspeople experienced and shaped industrial society. This study of industrial change builds on archaeological interpretations of pots, kilns, ledgers, and regional ceramics stylistics in Rockingham County, Virginia, to argue that production technologies, vessel decoration, and workplace organization were active social and material strategies with communally comparable yet individually di-

Critical ideas on the intellectual substance and form of this paper were provided by Marlys Pearson and Bob Paynter. Mary Corbin Sies, Paul Shackel, Barbara Little, Stan Kaufman, Janice Bailey Goldschmidt, Lu Ann De Cunzo, and Bernard Herman commented on various drafts. The research that this paper builds on was initiated by the Massanuten Chapter of the Archeology Society of Virginia; Janice Biller and Eleanor Parslow's insights have been essential. The Emanuel and Elizabeth Suter Collection and the Virginia Mennonite Conference Archives are in Eastern Mennonite College's Menno Simons Library; access to the Suter Collection was graciously bestowed by Grace Grove and the late Mary Suter. Thanks to the librarians, Lois Bowman and Harold Huber, for guiding me through their resources. Kurt Russ and Stan Kaufman have provided me with their own research, considerable intellectual support, and abundant good advice; much of this work would not have been possible without their insights and counsel. Any misinterpretations or shortcomings in this paper are entirely my responsibility.

verse forms. The focus on one community's many material strategies for negotiating and shaping industrial change offers one of archaeology's most important insights into the diverse forms taken by industrial capitalism.

In American ceramics production, industrialization has had among its material forms the texts, social identities, craft techniques, kilns, and pottery that constitute the archaeological record. Yet archaeologists often have avoided confronting decorative preferences, functional variation, and production techniques as strategies used to negotiate social change. Archaeologists instead have examined the diverse decorative, technical, and organizational expressions of craftspeople as though they primarily reflected aesthetic inclinations and industry's seemingly overwhelming technological and economic capacity to transform agrarian communities.

Archaeological interpretations of ceramics industrialization often have assumed their subject to be contrasting, internally coherent "craft" and "industrial" modes of production and consumption. Typical characterizations of shifting production/consumption relations have centered on technological forms (machinery changes), economic and labor organizations (division of labor), and product transformations (standardized material forms), which changed in various regions from the mid eighteenth century (in the urban Northeast) to the early twentieth century (in the rural South).[1]

---

[1] Examples of research that contrast craft and industrial organizations in ceramics production and consumption include Samuel D. Smith and Stephen T. Rogers, *A Survey of Historic Pottery Making in Tennessee* (Nashville: Tennessee Department of Conservation, 1979), pp. 7–8; Susan H. Myers, *Handcraft to Industry: Philadelphia Ceramics in the First Half of the Nineteenth Century* (Washington, D.C.: Smithsonian Institution Press, 1980); Susan H. Myers, "A Survey of Traditional Pottery Manufacture in the Mid-Atlantic and Northeastern United States," *Northeast Historical Archaeology* 6 (1977): 1–13; Charles H. Faulkner, "The Weaver Pottery: A Late Nineteenth-Century Family Industry in a Southeastern Urban Setting," in Roy S. Dickens, Jr., ed., *Archaeology of Urban America: The Search for Pattern and Process* (New York: Academic Press, 1982); and Richard Hunter, "The Demise of Traditional Pottery Manufacture on Sourland Mountain, New Jersey, during the Industrial Revolution," in Sarah Peabody Turnbaugh, ed., *Domestic Pottery of the Northeastern United States, 1625–1850* (Orlando, Fla.: Academic Press, 1985). The terms *folk, craft, family,* and *traditional* pottery often are used interchangeably; see John A. Burrison, *The Meaders Family of Mossy Creek: Eighty Years of North Georgia Folk Pottery* (Atlanta: Georgia State University Art Gallery, 1976), p. 3; Smith and Rogers, *Survey of Historic Pottery Making,* p. 8. For the Northeast, see Myers, *Handcraft to Industry.* For the South, see John Burrison, *Brothers in*

The dominant material changes associated with industrialization have been thoroughly described and analyzed, but the most persuasive interpretations emphasize the dynamism and subtleties of the industrialization process. The most compelling archaeological interpretations of industrialization firmly link diverse local processes of change to the dominant material forms of ceramics industrialization (labor reorganizations, technological change, and new pottery forms).[2] A failure to probe the relationship between local socioeconomic processes and dominant changes implies that industrial technologies and economic strategies possessed an overwhelming capacity to transform agrarian ceramics production and social relations.

I will examine how agrarian producers and consumers in Rockingham County attempted to define what industrialization meant in their community (fig. 1). At least twenty-three potteries operated in Rockingham County between about 1800 and 1920, with a total of fifty-nine individuals documented as potters and pottery laborers in the county (see Appendix). Besides these individuals, an untold number of potters' family members and neighbors occasionally worked in the pottery shop on various semiskilled tasks, such as hauling clay, selling ware, and

---

Clay: The Story of Georgia Folk Pottery (Athens: University of Georgia Press, 1983); Charles G. Zug III, *Turners and Burners: The Folk Potters of North Carolina* (Chapel Hill: University of North Carolina Press, 1986).

[2] Examples of persuasive research include Bruce Laurie, *Artisans into Workers: Labor in Nineteenth-Century America* (New York: Hill and Wang, 1989); Steven Hahn, *The Roots of Southern Populism: Yeomen Farmers and the Transformation of the Georgia Upcountry, 1850–1890* (New York: Oxford University Press, 1983); Daniel T. Rodgers, *The Work Ethic in Industrial America, 1850–1920* (Chicago: University of Chicago Press, 1978); E. P. Thompson, *The Making of the English Working Class* (New York: Vintage Books, 1967); Christopher Clark, "Household Economy, Market Exchange, and the Rise of Capitalism in the Connecticut Valley, 1800–1860," *Journal of Social History* 13 (1979): 169–89; James Henretta, "Families and Farms: *Mentalité* in Pre-Industrial America," *William and Mary Quarterly*, 3d ser., 35 (1978): 3–32; Michael Merrill, "Cash Is Good to Eat: Self-Sufficiency and Exchange in the Rural Economy of the United States," *Radical History Review* 4 (1977): 42–71; Gregory Nobles, "Capitalism in the Countryside: The Transformation of Rural Society in the United States," *Radical History Review* 41 (1988): 163–76; Robert Blair St. George, "Maintenance Relations and the Erotics of Property in Historical Thought" (Paper delivered at American Historical Association meeting, San Francisco, 1983). Examples linking processes to forms include John Worrell, Myron O. Stachiw, and David M. Simmons, "Archaeology from the Ground Up," elsewhere in this volume; and John Worrell, "Ceramic Production in the Exchange Network of an Agricultural Neighborhood," in Turnbaugh, *Domestic Pottery*.

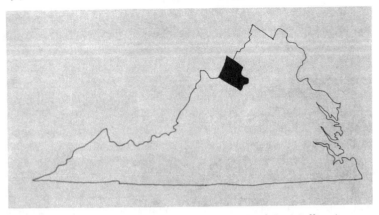

Fig. 1. Rockingham County, Va. (Drawing, Paul R. Mullins.)

setting (loading) the kiln. Six of the twenty-three county operations were pottery factories, and these factories employed many laborers who have not been identified individually. None of the individuals identified in the survey were female, but women certainly worked in the farm potteries quite extensively, despite their documentary invisibility.[3]

Of the twenty-three potteries for which there is physical or textual documentation, seven have yielded substantial material remains including pottery waster deposits, shop equipment (kiln components),

---

[3]This number of 59 persons includes both potters (individuals who worked at the wheel and administered a shop) and individuals who worked in a pottery in other capacities (for example, digging clay, selling ware, burning kilns). Extensive biographical information on all individuals is included in Paul R. Mullins, "Historic Pottery-Making in Rockingham County, Virginia" (Paper presented at Archeology Society of Virginia Spring Symposium, Charlottesville, 1988). Emanuel Suter's 1864–1902 diaries, account books, and papers mention 18 people who worked on tasks besides turning (working at the potter's wheel), the most specialized potterymaking skill; see Emanuel and Elizabeth Suter Collection, Virginia Mennonite Conference Archives, Eastern Mennonite College Menno Simons Library, Harrisonburg) (hereafter cited as EESC). The many undocumented family members and neighbors who had some role in pottery production are emphasized in Zug, *Turners and Burners*, pp. 238–41. The factories were Virginia Pottery Co.; Broadway Porcelain Manufacturing Co.; Harrisonburg Steam Pottery; two Adamant Porcelain Co. potteries in Rockingham County, one of which operated in Broadway and the other in Harrisonburg; and Broadway Pottery. That it was very uncommon for women to work at the potter's wheel is noted in Burrison, *Brothers in Clay*, pp. 6, 47–49. Examples of some of the work done by women at potteries are documented in Zug, *Turners and Burners*, pp. 258–60.

surviving pottery shop buildings, and even one partially surviving up-draft kiln (at the Morris pottery). For eleven other operations there are no undisturbed kiln remains (beyond light scatters of vessel wasters) or an identifiable kiln site, but marked vessels from these shops have been identified and examined in contemporary private collections. For the remaining five operations, only textual references without marked wares or kiln remains have been used to identify the shop.[4]

[4]The 7 sites are the William C. Coffman shop, the Heatwole shop, the Morris pottery, the Suter pottery at Mt. Clinton, Harrisonburg Steam Pottery, the William S. Coffman pottery, and Virginia Pottery Co. The extent and method of survey among these sites varies. Because of the very large amounts of pottery from all these sites, only large vessel fragments identifiable by form and capacity and marked and decorated wares were collected from 6 of these sites (except the Morris pottery). The Harrisonburg Steam Pottery site and the neighboring Virginia Pottery Co. were disturbed by extensive construction in 1978; Stanley A. Kaufman, *Heatwole and Suter Pottery* (Harrisonburg, Va.: Good Printers, 1978), p. 12. Work directed by Stanley Kaufman salvaged a large sample of ceramics from each pottery that has not been systematically catalogued. Kaufman also directed surface collections in artifact concentrations at Suter's Mt. Clinton site and excavated 3 5-by-5-foot units at that site and the Heatwole shop; Kaufman, interview with author, January 1988. Decorated shards, identifiable forms, and samples of kiln furniture were surface collected by Kaufman at the two Coffman sites. At the seventh site, a standing kiln operated by the Morris family, the Massanuten Chapter of the Archeology Society of Virginia conducted a systematic surface survey in which all vessel wasters (total of 1,047 shards) and kiln furniture (for example, coils, props, saggers, and draw trials; 1,507 shards) were collected and quantified; see Mullins, "Historic Pottery-Making," p. 9; unpublished catalogue sheets on file with author and Massanuten Chapter, Archeology Society of Virginia. Marked vessels were examined from the following potteries with textual references but without physical, kiln-site remains: Andrew Coffman pottery; Zigler pottery; Silber pottery; Ireland, Duey, and Shinnick pottery; Shinnick pottery; Good pottery; Adamant Porcelain Co.'s two potteries; and Broadway Porcelain Manufacturing Co. George M. Woods potted with Silber ca. 1870, and a marked "Woods" vessel exists (Kaufman, interview with author, January 1988), but it is unknown if Woods operated his own kiln and shop. A shard marked "William and J. Ricketts / Harrisonburg" was recovered at the Suter farm (collection of Mary Nell Rhodes, Harrisonburg, Va.), but no references to Ricketts are in the Suter records or county censuses. The amount of attributable wares surviving from these shops varied because some of these potteries were short-lived and others rarely marked vessels. Of the potteries for which there are no marked wares or kiln site remains, 5 have convincing documentation. They are the Conrad, the Kline/Cline, the Kite, the Broadway, and the Logan potteries. Two other Rockingham County potters cannot be conclusively associated with a known pottery shop. Mathias Bright's only identification as a potter is in the 1850 Census; see Manuscript Population Schedule, Plains Township, Rockingham County, 7th U.S. Census (1850). Branson O'Roark was a potter living in northern Rockingham County in 1860 and 1870, and his son was a potter in New Market after ca. 1880, but the elder O'Roark probably potted for his father-in-law, John C. Coffman, in neighboring Shenandoah County; see Manuscript Population Schedule, Plains Township, 8th and

Among Rockingham County potters and their Shenandoah Valley consumers, the ability to define industrialization involved selectively incorporating particular industrial organizations into their existing sociolabor structure. Ceramics producers and consumers in Rockingham County integrated or modified certain industrial strategies, which they did not perceive as antagonistic to their unique social identities. In exercising such agency over some of the forms that industrialization took in their lives, these potters probably were not at all unlike craftspeople in most other regions.[5] Distinctive communities negotiated industrialization through far-reaching processes that continually contested, embraced, and rejected industrialization's emerging labor and social relations. The process of active negotiation within regions and among particular social groups gave industrialization very distinct local impacts, despite broad, heuristic similarities among regions. Ultimately archaeology can forcefully demonstrate that both the communal effects of industrialization and its broader domestic consequences reflect local agency as well as the influences of the industrial elite.

Craft Exchange and Industrial Capitalism in the Shenandoah Valley

During the late eighteenth and nineteenth centuries, almost every family in the Shenandoah Valley was involved in farming as its primary economic activity, but families supplemented their farm output by exchanging labor or other specialized craft services, such as blacksmithing, carpentry, or potterymaking. These family units formed networks of part-time tradespeople who bartered specialized craft products, services, and labor. These exchanges often involved several individuals, and "debt" typically would be negotiated in future transactions and could be settled in a variety of forms (for example, goods, labor, or cash). In 1879, for instance, potter Emanuel Suter settled a standing debt to William Minnick with "Boots half soled by J M Vint . 50." Vint,

---

9th U.S. Censuses (1860, 1870); Charles Fahs Kauffman, *A Genealogy of the Kauffman-Coffman Families of North America, 1584 to 1937* (Scottsdale, Pa.: Mennonite Publishing House, 1960), p. 286.

[5] Compelling arguments that potters were much like other agrarian craftspeople appear in Burrison, *Brothers in Clay,* pp. 3–14.

a shoemaker who occasionally worked in the Suter pottery, received in return for his boot work "goods bought at H Shacklett" by Suter.[6] This typical transaction involved four people (Suter, Vint, Minnick, and Shacklett), exchanged a variety of goods and services (cobbling skill, repaired boots, imported goods, and probably some cash), and was settled over an unspecified, extended period.

A predominantly barter economy oriented to household consumption and a diverse mode of production (multiple craft and farm resources) is relatively typical of agrarian craft communities. In the Shenandoah Valley, like much of republican America, surface egalitarianism masked a network of contested social relationships. Between 1775 and 1800, the valley's population doubled, and by 1800, when the first potters appeared in Rockingham County, half the population did not own land. Geographer Robert D. Mitchell has observed that during the same period the valley also emerged as a decentralized producer of a diverse range of raw goods, such as leather, cloth, and hemp. Substantial profits from this production were made by the minority controlling distribution rather than the numerous household producers. To compound material inequality, extremely few valley craftspeople and landless farmers were upwardly mobile as the result of their labor, creating what Mitchell has called "a growing rural proletariat by the end of the [eighteenth] century."[7] Social relations clearly must have been significantly influenced by these inequalities in land ownership, control of distribution, and the socioeconomic immobility of tenant farmers.

The land and distribution hierarchies described by Mitchell promoted thriving craft exchange networks. Farmers with large landholdings supported these trade networks because they relied on local laborers

---

[6] Suter account book, April 17, 1879, EESC. Shacklett was a county merchant, so the goods were probably imported. Robert D. Mitchell, *Commercialism and Frontier: Perspectives on the Early Shenandoah Valley* (Charlottesville: University Press of Virginia, 1977), pp. 135–40. The same strategies among nineteenth-century rural Massachusetts craftspeople, including potters, are identified in Worrell, "Ceramic Production," p. 159. Such extended, flexible exchange practices are called a common, if not the predominant, form of transaction among North Carolina potters by Zug, *Turners and Burners*, p. 264.

[7] Burrison, *Brothers in Clay*, pp. 3–6; Zug, *Turners and Burners*, pp. 263–66; Worrell, "Ceramic Production," pp. 164–65. Mitchell, *Commercialism and Frontier*, pp. 238, 161–88, 203, 155, 199–200, 237, 127. That potterymaking provided at best a beneficial yet supplementary income to farming is demonstrated in Zug, *Turners and Burners*, p. 237.

to maintain their farms and multiple commercial activities. John Conrad, for example, owned a vast tract in eastern Rockingham County, which his family claimed during the eighteenth century. On this tract Conrad farmed and operated a tannery, a still, a pottery, and possibly a mill, which would have required the labor of neighbors. These operations exchanged goods for other goods, labor, and land, as is illustrated in his 1807 purchase of one thousand acres in return for "potter's ware, whisky, and flour."[8]

This strategy of diversified production with multiple means of craft manufacture and farm subsistence was recreated throughout the region. For instance, during the 1830s the Zigler family owned a pottery in Broadway, in northern Rockingham County. At that location the family farmed and operated a tannery and a hemp mill. After 1855, Emanuel Suter and his family farmed, potted, and operated a smithy, and Lindsey Morris's family reportedly made brooms as well as ceramics at his post-1872 Dry River pottery.[9]

Exchange networks among craftspeople such as potters created interdependent relationships that bound groups together. However, since they were fostered by social inequalities (primarily interdependence between tenants and small landholders and a landed class), the craft networks also reproduced social relations between those groups.[10]

[8] Floyd Wilmer Coffman, *The Conrad Clan: The Family of John Stephen Conrad and Allied Lines* (Harrisonburg, Va.: Charles F. McClung, 1959), p. 107. Such cross-class interdependence between craftspeople and influential landowners is called "maintenance relationships" in St. George, "Maintenance Relations." The first record of land purchase in Rockingham County by the Conrads is April 20, 1770; see Coffman, *Conrad Clan*, p. 97.

[9] Mitchell, *Commercialism and Frontier*, pp. 189, 237; Manuscript Population Schedules, Timberville, Rockingham County, 4th, 5th, and 6th U.S. Censuses (1820, 1830, 1840); Elmer L. Smith, *Pottery: A Utilitarian Folk Craft* (Lebanon, Pa.: Applied Arts Publishers, 1972), p. 31; Kurt C. Russ and John McDaniel, "The Traditional Pottery Manufacturing Industry in Virginia: Examples from Botetourt and Rockbridge Counties, 1775–1894" (Paper presented at meeting of the Rockbridge Historical Society, Lexington, Va., February 1987), p. 10; Paul G. Kline, *The Cline-Kline Family* (Dayton, Va.: Shenandoah Press, 1971), p. 3; John Wayland, *History of Rockingham County* (Strasburg, Va.: Shenandoah Publishing, 1967), p. 378; Kaufman, *Heatwole and Suter Pottery*, p. 9; Sybil Coakley and Marion Coakley, interview with author, June 1987; Manuscript Population Schedule, Ashby District, Rockingham County, 10th U.S. Census (1880).

[10] Similar conclusions are drawn in other regions by Clark, "Household Economy"; Merrill, "Cash Is Good to Eat"; Henretta, "Families and Farms"; St. George, "Maintenance Relations."

The exchange networks provided reliable subsistence, but they paradox-ically promoted the socioeconomic immobility of craftspeople because they restricted opportunities for profit accumulation and promoted the dependence of craftspeople on the region's landed farmers.

The exchange networks restricted the purely local opportunities for socioeconomic mobility, but they did not wholly obstruct potters' efforts to improve their socioeconomic standing. For instance, at least a few potters are known to have exchanged ware outside the county (and it is likely that many more did). Emanuel Suter exchanged wares throughout the Shenandoah Valley and into West Virginia after 1864, sometimes as small lots of crocks exchanged with households scattered throughout the mountains. In May 1881, for example, Suter recorded driving a herd of cattle to Pendleton County, West Virginia, where he "sold a Load of crocks" he had with him. However, there is no evidence that such expeditions made any Rockingham County potters signifi-cantly wealthier than other people in the community. Even after 1880, when Suter began to ship ceramics by rail, the vast majority of his ware still was marketed within Rockingham or to neighboring Augusta County. For instance, of thirty-eight "loads" of ware Suter shipped in 1881, twenty-seven were to destinations in Rockingham or Augusta counties, and the remaining eleven went to unspecified locations.[11]

Agrarian exchange networks were structured by kin relations. Con-siderable analysis has focused on the kinship dimension of craft net-works. Indeed, Rockingham County potters, like most traditional crafts-people, shared close kin ties. There are sound functional reasons for these close relations among craft potters: potterymaking demanded mul-tiple skills that required a lengthy training period, the equipment and

[11] Suter diaries, May 31, 1881, EESC; Suter account book, EESC; Paul R. Mullins, "Defining the Boundaries of Change: The Records of an Industrializing Potter," in Barbara J. Little, ed., *Text-Aided Archaeology* (Boca Raton, Fla.: CRC Press, 1992), pp. 187–88. The exact makeup of a "load" varied between orders. That Georgia and North Carolina folk potters' markets also were not wholly local is noted in Burrison, *Brothers in Clay*, p. 36; and Zug, *Turners and Burners*, pp. 278, 284. Joseph Silber, for instance, lived just a short wagon ride from the West Virginia border, where the Morrises and John Heatwole exchanged wares, so it is likely that Silber also marketed his pottery in West Virginia; see D. J. Lake and Co., *An Atlas of Rockingham County, Virginia* (1885; reprint, Harrisonburg, Va.: Harrisonburg-Rockingham Historical Society, 1982), p. 19. The Suter pottery eventually even sold wares as far away as New Jersey (Suter diaries, April 6, 1894, EESC) and New York (Suter to family, April 10, 1894, EESC).

resources for the craft were usually owned by a family group, and operating a pottery required a dependable labor base.[12]

Kinship also represented a self-empowering mechanism that craftspeople employed to define their identity. To the valley's potters, like most craft producers, kinship committed social labor by embedding it in affinal and extended kin relations. Neighbors as well as immediate family were part of extended kin groups whose prestige had less to do with the economic gain of exchange than with the symbolic value of reproducing socioeconomic interdependence within the community.

This strategy of situating socioeconomic production in the kin unit is well illustrated by the Coffmans. Andrew Coffman moved to eastern Rockingham County in about 1819, and four generations of his family maintained an operation in three neighboring locations for eighty years. Andrew had five sons, all of whom potted in their family shops, and two of his three daughters married Coffman-trained potters. The family also trained a series of neighbors and kin who went on to establish shops in Rockingham, Augusta, Roanoke, and Rockbridge counties.[13] These potters established an extensive network that exchanged pottery

[12] Zug, *Turners and Burners*, pp. 237–48; Burrison, *Brothers in Clay*, pp. 43–52.

[13] Coffman, *Conrad Clan*, p. 106; Kauffman, *Kauffman-Coffman Families*, p. 205; Manuscript Population Schedules, Elk Run, Stonewall District, Rockingham County, 5th, 6th, 7th, 9th, and 10th U.S. Censuses (1830, 1840, 1850, 1870, 1880); Smith, *Pottery*, p. 27; Mullins, "Historic Pottery-Making," p. 2. Lindsey Morris married Andrew Coffman's daughter Nancy in 1846. John Heatwole married Coffman's daughter Elizabeth in 1848. Coffman's daughter Mary married John Southard in 1849. Southard cannot be documented as a potter, but he was closely associated with potters all his life; see Kauffman, *Kauffman-Coffman Families*, pp. 210–11. Isaac Lamb appeared in the 1850 Rockingham County census as a potter in the household of William C. Coffman and in 1860 with Coffman's brother-in-law and neighbor, John Southard; see Manuscript Population Schedule, Elkton, Rockingham County, 7th and 8th U.S. Censuses (1850 and 1860). Lamb established the Rockbridge Baths Pottery in Rockbridge County by 1870; see Kurt C. Russ, "Historic Pottery Making in Virginia," in Michael B. Barber, ed., *Upland Archeology in the East* (Atlanta: Forest Service Southern Region, 1984), p. 10. Lindsey Morris potted in North River District, Augusta County, ca. 1860, before moving back to Rockingham County after the war; see Jim Hanger, "Pots, Potteries, and Potting in Augusta County, 1800–1870," *Augusta Historical Bulletin* 9 (Spring 1973): 4–15. John Heatwole trained in the Coffman shops and later established a shop in Rockingham County near the Morrises; see Kaufman, *Heatwole and Suter Pottery*, p. 6. Andrew Coffman's nephew David was a potter living in Andrew's household in 1850; see Manuscript Population Schedule, Elkton, Rockingham County, 7th U.S. Census 1850. David married and moved to Roanoke County in 1869, where he continued to pot; see Kauffman, *Kauffman-Coffman Families*, p. 237.

for goods throughout the region and then redistributed those goods within the neighborhood.

The wares produced by the Coffmans and other Rockingham potters before the Civil War were uniform. Earthenware fruit storage vessels and small, multifunctional vessels composed the majority of the forms being produced. Decoration was sparse, marked wares were relatively uncommon, and potters personally bartered most wares with members of the community.

Uniformity in wares, aesthetic similarity, and dominance of barter exchange is very much like traditional craft production in other regions.[14] Craftspeople negotiated communally specific decorative, production, and consumption styles that reproduced the values of kin networks. The social significance of craft goods was in their culturally "visible" reference to the craftsperson and the communal context of labor, exchange, and use. These values were "visible" in the sense that a Rockingham County consumer would readily recognize local ceramic forms (for example, small-mouthed crocks used as preserve jars), decoration (for example, sparse cobalt floral designs on gray-bodied stoneware), and other aesthetic features (for example, squat-profiled, one-half to one-gallon redware crocks glazed only on the vessel interior). During barter exchange, the producer of a pot (or one of his kin) usually also was present at the transaction, so the relationship between regional style and local craft producers would have been clear and tangible.

Civil War Social Change and Ceramics Transformation in Rockingham County

In Rockingham County the clearest historical effect of industrialization was its ability to fragment and transform the social relations of craft communities. Before extensive industrialization, craft producers and consumers were characterized by internally well-defined associations with distinct community identities. These communal identities were

---

[14] For example, craft regionalism in Georgia ceramic forms and decorative types is examined in Burrison, *Brothers in Clay*, pp. 63–77, 120–21. Regional ceramics trends in Tennessee are identified in Smith and Rogers, *Survey of Historic Pottery Making*, pp. 9–25.

complex associations of kinship, regional, and neighborhood affiliations (such as the Coffman potters); labor alliances (such as neighbors with complementary craft skills); religion (for example, associated Mennonite potters, such as Suter, John Heatwole, and Isaac Good); or any other category of experienced social identity (for example, ethnicity).

Communal identities were reproduced through material exchange. Craft exchange was a crucial, constantly enacted social interaction that defined the roles of transactors via the give-and-take of barter between producers. In Rockingham County, a post–Civil War transformation of the relationship between local producers and consumers took material form in new networks of pottery consumers and laborers, the manner in which production and sales were organized, and in the vessels themselves.

Like much of the South, the Shenandoah Valley confronted social instability after the middle of the nineteenth century. In the wake of the Civil War, the valley was economically impoverished and materially devastated. Social networks had been transformed by migration, group animosities, and death.[15] This social instability prompted extensive changes in local craft production and consumption.

The upheaval of the Civil War compelled a dramatic change in Emanuel Suter's social identity and production strategies. Suter was trained in 1851 by his cousin John Heatwole, who was Andrew Coffman's son-in-law. After his marriage in 1855, Suter established a barnyard shop at his new farm west of Harrisonburg (fig. 2).[16] From this location, Suter bartered small amounts of redware and stoneware throughout the immediate neighborhood in a production/consumption organization like that of the majority of his neighbors.

Suter and Heatwole were Mennonites, and the church's conscientious objector doctrine was unique in the Confederacy. Their nonresistance doctrine alienated Mennonites to many of the South's social mores, and within the Mennonite community there was disagreement over appropriate methods of resisting the Confederate draft. Most Men-

---

[15] Eric Foner, *Reconstruction* (New York: Harper and Row, 1988), pp. 11–18; the war's impact in the South and the Shenandoah Valley is noted on pp. 124–28. The war's impact on the valley's Mennonite community is examined in Harry Anthony Brunk, *History of Mennonites in Virginia, 1727–1900* (Staunton, Va.: McClure Printing Co., 1959), pp. 167–69.

[16] Kaufman, *Heatwole and Suter Pottery*, p. 9.

Fig. 2. Agrarian production unit: Emanuel and Elizabeth Suter and their children, August 1, 1896. Front row, *left to right,* C. Charles, Virginia, Emanuel, Elizabeth, Lillie, Reuben, P. Swope. Back row, *left to right,* John, David, Emanuel J., Eugene, Perry, and Laura. (Emanuel and Elizabeth Suter Collection, Virginia Mennonite Conference Archives, Eastern Mennonite College and Seminary, Harrisonburg, Va.)

nonites served, simply refusing to fire at enemy troops. Confederate general Thomas "Stonewall" Jackson even wrote of these drafted Mennonites, "There lives a people in the Valley of Virginia, that are not hard to bring to the army. . . . Nor is it difficult to have them take aim, but it is impossible to get them to take correct aim."[17]

Heatwole, like many Mennonites, served an imposed one-year term in the Confederate army. At the end of his year's service, Heatwole returned to his farm, but he was reenlisted. Ninety-four county residents signed and submitted a petition to the Confederate War De-

---

[17] Brunk, *History of Mennonites,* pp. 157–69; Jackson is quoted on pp. 158–59.

partment, arguing that Heatwole's potting skills were needed in the community. A pardon from service, however, was refused in April 1863. Faced with extended service, Heatwole went into hiding in West Virginia, as did many other Mennonites. His pursuit by Confederate bounty hunters and his wartime work for the Mennonite church in West Virginia are today well known in the community.[18]

In June 1860 Suter contributed to a local Confederate military group, the Valley Guard, to secure a year's exemption. Eventually, in March 1862, he "furnished a substitute for the war in the person of Ebenezer Nicely," paying Nicely to assume Suter's place in the Confederate military. Suter continued to pot until late 1864, when Union troops began a destructive valley campaign and the desperate Confederacy rescinded its exemptions from service. Threatened by advancing Union troops, Suter and his immediate family fled to Harrisburg, Pennsylvania. While in Pennsylvania, Suter glazed and decorated vessels in the Cowden and Wilcox Pottery factory from February to April 1865. He and his family returned to Harrisonburg in June 1865.[19]

The potters who most rapidly adopted industrial organizations following the war were distinguished by similar alienation from the larger community. Some of these producers migrated to the valley, and others, like Suter, maintained social values that distanced them from the community. This alienation promoted distinctive production strategies that often differed significantly from those of kin-based craft networks. Joseph Silber, for example, came to Rockingham County from Pennsylvania in 1865. Silber, who was born in Germany, apparently had worked in the Cowden and Wilcox factory, where he met Suter. In 1865 he established a partnership with Heatwole. Silber and Heatwole produced a range of vessels standardized by capacity and function and marked with the potters' names, techniques that Heatwole's shop had never adopted. These were common factory procedures, but they yielded vessels that looked unlike the region's typical wares.[20]

---

[18] Minnie R. Carr, " 'Potter' John Heatwole," *Valley Mennonite Messenger* 5, no. 27 (May 1967): 1, 4; no. 28 (May 1967): 3, 5; no. 29 (May 1967): 3; Kaufman, *Heatwole and Suter Pottery*, p. 6; Brunk, *History of Mennonites*, p. 158.

[19] Manuscripts, June 14, 1860, March 21, 1862, EESC; Suter diaries, February 27–April 15, 1864, EESC; Kaufman, *Heatwole and Suter Pottery*, p. 11.

[20] Manuscript Population Schedule, Franklin Township, Rockingham County, 9th U.S. Census (1870); Manuscript Population Schedule, Central Township, Rockingham

In a few months Silber established his shop and initiated an aggressive advertising campaign. Advertisements were by no means alien to the valley's consumers, but locally produced goods were typically exchanged by word of mouth or a consumer's familiarity with the producer. During the course of several months in 1866, Silber advertised five thousand gallons of his stoneware in the Harrisonburg newspaper. Stoneware was rapidly replacing earthenware in the region, but some local potters clung to earthenware production, including Suter and a network of German potters in the northern Shenandoah Valley. Silber's advertisements, though, openly maligned lead-glazed redware, observing that his stoneware was priced at "a small advance above that of Earthenware, to which it is so greatly superior in beauty, finish and utility, besides being warranted perfectly free from all those noxious and poisonous mineral compounds necessarily used in the manufacturing of Earthenware, rendering it not only deleterious and pernicious to health, but in many cases known fatal to human life itself."[21]

Such new strategies of representing the producer and product were not limited to the few potters who migrated to the area. When he returned to Virginia in 1865, Suter changed his barnyard pottery considerably. Many of these changes were functional improvements probably prompted by Suter's exposure to the Cowden and Wilcox operation. For example, Suter's November 9, 1868, diary entry notes that he "commenced makeing moalds" (vessel molds). Suter continued to turn

---

County, 10th U.S. Census (1880); Kaufman, *Heatwole and Suter Pottery*, p. 6. Silber's Harrisburg address is included in the inside cover of Suter's 1864 diary, EESC. Silber may have met Suter in Harrisburg, probably at Cowden and Wilcox. Kaufman, *Heatwole and Suter Pottery*, p. 7. That more thoroughly agrarian regional ceramics producers marked wares less often than those in regions with intense competition is demonstrated in Burrison, *Brothers in Clay*, pp. 122–275.

[21] *Rockingham Register* (Harrisonburg, Va.), July 1866. Preservation of pre–Civil War newspapers in the region is very poor. Single issues of the *Rockingham Register* survive from 1822 and 1837, but few papers exist from before 1861 (Rockingham County Public Library, Harrisonburg, Va.). At least a few advertisements for coarsewares appeared in local papers, but they do not identify those wares as local. For example, in 1861 the *Rockingham Register* published this ad: "Crocks, Crocks! 300 assorted sizes in store and for sale by Isaac Paul" (August 30, September 18, 20, 27, 1861). That newspaper advertisements by Georgia potters were rare well into the twentieth century is indicated in Burrison, *Brothers in Clay*, p. 36. The persistence of earthenware production is detailed in A. H. Rice and John Baer Stoudt, *The Shenandoah Pottery* (Berryville, Va.: Virginia Book Co., 1929); and William E. Wiltshire III, *Folk Pottery of the Shenandoah Valley* (New York: E. P. Dutton, 1975).

ware on the potter's wheel, but molds produced larger quantities of ware and could be operated by semiskilled laborers. The February 12, 1866, entry records, "This forenoon I was making arrangements for making a glazing machine," and the February 21 entry observes, "This forenoon myself and father finished my glazing machine." Rather than buy a professionally made glazing machine (which used air pressure to blow glaze onto vessels), Suter apparently built one himself, perhaps as a duplicate of the large glazing equipment he had seen and used in the Cowden and Wilcox factory. Suter also dismantled the standing kiln beginning September 15, 1866, and burned (fired) the first load of ware in the new kiln on November 14.[22] Such technical changes increased the pottery's production and soon were accompanied by a range of new exchange strategies.

Ceramics Industrialization Strategies

Suter was not alone in incorporating elements of industrial ceramics production. Indeed, he was one of a diverse group of Rockingham County potters who embraced factory technologies and production techniques in the decade after the war. Those technologies included vessel molds, glazing equipment, kiln modifications, and increasing reliance on technological specialists, such as kiln designers. The new production strategies included manufacture of previously uncommon ceramic goods (such as tile and flowerpots), standardization of vessels by capacity and form, increasing reliance on professionally prepared clays and glaze materials, adoption of new sales tactics (for example, increased cash exchange in stores and standardized prices for ware), and pervasive production of stoneware.

The adoption of such technologies and organizational tactics by several post–Civil War shops argues that some county potters saw no break with tradition in the shift to "industrial" machinery and production strategies in "craft" potteries. In the period 1870–75, eight potteries are known to have been operating in Rockingham County. Various technological and sales strategies typical of factory potteries were

[22] Suter diaries, November 9, 1868, February 12, 21, September 15, November 14, 1866, EESC.

adopted by Suter (vessel molds, price lists, cash exchange); Heatwole (merchant contracts, marked vessels); Silber (advertising, marked vessels, elaborate decoration); Ireland, Duey, and Shinnick (administration of pottery by nonpotter—namely, Ireland); and J. H. Kite. The October 11, 1866, *Rockingham Register* reported that Kite's shop had "just finished and opened an experimental kiln which has proved to be a complete success." The paper called Kite's product "Rockingham ware . . . moulded into shape and beauty . . . comparable with the first English 'Rockingham ware.' "[23]

Most potters did not simply abandon prewar community relations; rather, they incorporated industrial technologies into preexisting pottery organizations. Suter, for instance, changed the products and machinery of his shop dramatically, yet he did not relinquish the family's control of the pottery's everyday administration. Until the pottery was moved to Harrisonburg in 1891, production was wholly controlled by Suter or his sons.[24] This organization integrated kin-based administration, which was typical of craft production, with the technological improvements being used by factory potters.

Charles Zug has called a three-phase pattern of pottery training (in which a potter trained in the pottery of his family or a neighbor, then worked as a journeyman for regional potters, and finally established his own operation) the most common form of traditional pottery "apprenticeship." The Ireland, Duey, and Shinnick pottery in Mt. Crawford modified this craft production strategy by having a journeyman workforce overseen by a nonpotter. The Ireland, Duey, and Shinnick shop was administered by Mathew Ireland, a chairmaker with no apparent experience as a potter. After the Civil War, Ireland recruited two skilled potters, George Duey and James Shinnick, as partners. The Ireland, Duey, and Shinnick trio probably hired Reuben Coffman,

[23] The Suter; Heatwole; Silber; Kite; Morris; Logan; William C. Coffman; and Ireland, Duey, and Shinnick potteries were all operating between 1870 and 1875. *Rockingham Register*, October 11, 1866, p. 3. Some stoneware attributed to Kite's shop remains with the Kite descendants; Kaufman, interview with author, January 1988. Of the three other 1870 shops, the Morrises exchanged some ware directly with merchants, albeit in mixed barter, which was probably common before the war. No ware has been identified from the Logan pottery, and there is no evidence of "industrial" techniques being used at the William C. Coffman shop.

[24] Kaufman, *Heatwole and Suter Pottery*, p. 12.

Lindsey Morris and his son Erasmus, Silber, or George M. Woods, potters who neighbored Ireland, Duey, and Shinnick but possessed no shop of their own. Ireland, Duey, and Shinnick may have hired these potters to turn ware in return for use of the Ireland, Duey, and Shinnick shop and kiln. Trading skilled labor for kiln use was relatively common among journeyman craft potters, including Silber and Isaac Good, who each "barrowed" Suter's shop and kiln and turned ware for Suter in return.[25] The work of Morris and Coffman for Ireland, Duey, and Shinnick, and Good for Suter corresponds well to a journeyman stage like that described by Zug. The administration of the Ireland, Duey, and Shinnick shop by a nonpotter, however, was unique among Rockingham potteries before 1890.

An organization analogous to the relationship between a master craftsperson and apprentice had precursors before the war. For instance, Thomas Logan and his two sons operated a pottery in Harrisonburg from the 1830s until the early 1870s. The Logans employed free African Americans from a nearby neighborhood and trained at least one during the 1850s, Abraham Spencer, to work on the wheel.[26] Before the late nineteenth century, many other neighborhood potters also clearly trained their neighbors in return for labor.

Many Rockingham craftspeople apparently felt that improved technologies and profit accumulation could be accommodated to craft production without creating labor or consumer alienation.[27] The result was a community of thoroughly industrialized producers and consum-

[25] Zug, *Turners and Burners*, p. 261; Manuscript Population Schedules, Mt. Crawford, Rockingham County, 7th and 8th U.S. Censuses (1850, 1860) (Ireland's father also was a chairmaker); Franklin Township, Rockingham County, 9th U.S. Census (1870). Isaac Good was working for Suter in return for goods and ware by 1872; Suter account books, EESC. Good's account books begin in 1873 and record various pottery production until March 4, 1877, when Good first records Suter as an employer; Isaac Good account books, collection of Stanley A. Kaufman. The first ware burned in Suter's new post–Civil War kiln was a load of Silber's ware; Suter diaries, November 14, 1866, EESC.

[26] Manuscript Population Schedules, Harrisonburg, Va., Rockingham County, 6th, 7th, 8th, and 9th U.S. Censuses (1840, 1850, 1860, 1870); John W. Wayland, *Historic Harrisonburg* (Staunton, Va.: McClure Printing Co., 1949), pp. 5–8. Spencer later worked in the Bell Pottery in Strasburg; see Rice and Stoudt, *Shenandoah Pottery*, pp. 62–65.

[27] This argument is made in Leo Marx, *The Machine in the Garden* (New York: Oxford University Press, 1964), p. 146.

ers; but industrialization took various forms in different potteries. The introduction of machines and new organizational techniques was certainly essential to the shape that ceramics industrialization took in Rockingham County, but that change was given a diverse, regionally distinct form by the way potters chose to integrate specific technologies and organizations.

The changes Suter made in his operation were particularly dramatic. Suter had returned to an internally divided Mennonite community, and his family confronted significant social and material rebuilding in the midst of an extensive, regional socioeconomic depression: Faced with such circumstances, Suter made some of the most striking changes of any potter in the county. Perhaps his most dramatic shift was the adoption of text-based records. Before 1865, only one other county potter (John Zigler) is known to have kept any form of textual record. In a community in which transactions were person to person, exchange values were negotiable, and illiteracy was high, a person's word was a more tangible form of record keeping than any written text.[28]

Nevertheless, on his flight to Pennsylvania, Suter began to keep a daily diary, which he maintained until his death in 1902. He meticulously recorded each day's activity, stressing his social visits, church and family activities, and the operation of his farm and potteries. Each day also contained a record of the day's weather and an original prayer. Divine authority and weather were not simply matters of central interest to a Mennonite farmer but also two factors over which he had no control. The diaries offered him a forum to organize his consciousness of both in the same way that they organized his perceptions of his destabilized community.[29]

In addition to the diaries, Suter began to keep an account book, which followed the form of contemporary business manuals. The account book and Suter's other business papers are of interest for their

[28] The postwar Mennonite community is examined in Brunk, *History of Mennonites*, pp. 158–59. The condition of the Suters's farm following the war is unknown. The Zigler records, which were not available for examination during this research, are in the Ronald Carrier Library, James Madison University, Harrisonburg, Va. An 1873–91 account book also survives for Isaac Good, who worked for Suter (collection of Stanley A. Kaufman). Zug draws a similar conclusion in *Turners and Burners*, p. 264.

[29] Suter diaries, 1864–1902, EESC; Mullins, "Defining the Boundaries," p. 185.

form as well as their content. The systematic ledger format reflected part of Suter's broad effort to standardize all aspects of his pottery operation from record keeping to production to the vessels themselves. In barter, a tangible surplus product—a manufactured craft good, a farm product, labor, or the promise of any of these—was received in an exchange, which usually was validated by a verbal agreement. Such informal verbal agreements probably continued after the Civil War, but following his return to Virginia, Suter systematically began to record such everyday transactions in his account book. In 1867, for example, he wrote, neighbor "Mrs Ann Layman helped me to plant corn . . . on the 2, 3, & 4 days of May 1867. . . . To be paid in wheat after harvest." Suter carried debt in his ledgers for varying amounts of time, typically settling outstanding debts at year's end. For example, Suter noted in an 1872 written note, "This Evening Jeremiah Falls & myself settled in full of our accounts this the 5th day of January 1872." These debts also could be carried over for longer periods. In 1866, for instance, Suter's ledger noted an "Amt of Ware Bought by John weaver Oct 17th 1866 $1.80." Below that debt, Suter subsequently wrote "settled this 7th of November 1871."[30] Suter previously had reached oral exchange agreements with the neighbors now recorded in his written ledgers, suggesting that their relationship had begun to change. However, his written records do not include debts or agreements made within Suter's immediate family, arguing that labor roles for the family were defined and valued through agreements more typical of kin-based craft production.

The texts also provide a strong indication of the shift in his conceptions of "value" as Suter engaged in increased cash exchange. In cash exchange, in contrast to barter, surplus or debt was intangible in the sense that a monetary value did not have the material substance of a bartered object with some obvious utility; that is, cash's material form was paper, and its associated value was abstract. As Suter used increasingly more cash in exchange and began to pay some of his laborers with currency, the written account books gave that cash value a material form.

[30] Suter account book and papers, EESC; Suter diaries, undated memoranda section, 1867, EESC; manuscript, January 5, 1872, EESC; Suter account book, October 17, 1866, November 7, 1871, EESC.

Just as vessels were assigned standardized cash prices, Suter's laborers also were contracted and recorded in the ledger. For example, in 1874 he wrote, "David A Heatwole set in to work for me one month in the potter shop at thirteen Dollars." This strategy of paying individuals for their labor wholly in cash stood in contrast to Suter's earlier practice of compensating laborers with negotiable combinations of material goods, services, and cash. An example of such a negotiated accord was Suter's 1870 agreement: "Joseph Ganes set in to work for me another year at nine Dollars per month & is to Board himself for which I am to furnish him two hundred weight of Bacon & three Barrels of flour."[31] Beginning during the early 1870s, the general trend in the account book appears to be a shift from material good compensation to payment combining goods and cash and finally to standardized cash settlements.

Standardization was perhaps clearest in the product itself. Suter's 1865 diary included a list of vessel heights, diameters, and clay weights used to manufacture vessels marketed by form and capacity, and Suter's diaries and ledgers mention what he identified as more than seventy-five vessel forms.[32] In the case of all these vessels, Suter used a consistent terminology to distinguish wares by distinct vessel forms intended for specific uses. The ubiquitous, multipurpose half-gallon crock began to be produced alongside increasingly larger amounts of forms such as tile, chambers, guttering, pie plates, and cream pitchers. Capacity also began to be increasingly standardized and included in the presentation of the product by stamping vessels with capacity impressions. Despite the functional adaptability of some forms and the variation between individual vessels, Suter understood every vessel type as having a specific identity. This would appear to stand in contrast to the pre–Civil War strategy of producing multifunctional nonstandard capacity vessels that could be adapted to a very wide range of purposes.

Although Suter's operation was perhaps more thoroughly transformed than any other in the region, different forms of price, product, and business standardization appeared in other county potteries in the ten years following the war. Such standardization took a very wide

---

[31] Suter account book, April 6, 1874, December 5, 1870, EESC.
[32] Karen Steiner, "A Study of the Business Letters Written to Emanuel Suter" (collection of Paul R. Mullins, manuscript), p. 6.

range of forms and was never universal. John Heatwole, for example, was closely associated with Suter throughout his life, yet Heatwole represented perhaps the opposite end of the spectrum of county responses to ceramics industrialization. Heatwole produced a wide range of idiosyncratic vessels throughout his career. He lavishly decorated vessels with busy painted motifs, an uncommon practice in the region, and he produced unusual forms, including ornate crocks, ceramic banks, and even slab gravestones (fig. 3). Heatwole's workforce was limited to his immediate family and a few neighbors, and his shop apparently rejected permanent adoption of vessel molds or other industrial technologies. However, Heatwole at least occasionally sold or bartered ware to merchants, in addition to individual barter exchange. One Suter merchant even complained to Suter in 1871 that "Mr. Heatwool is around Retailing Gallon Crocks a[t] 10 c. He has been here at my *Door* selling at that price. I want to know if he can sell Gallon crocks at Retail without License. . . . He has hurt the sale of your crocks."[33]

The Coffmans rejected Heatwole's decorative eccentricity and produced a uniform, unelaborate range of wares over four generations of potters. Like potters in virtually all the county's craft potteries, the Coffman potters were trained in all phases of production from clay digging to turning to exchange. Operations such as Suter's, in contrast, eventually employed wage laborers to perform semiskilled tasks such as preparing clay, setting and burning the kiln, hauling vessels to general stores, and selling wares to farmers throughout the county. Like Heatwole, the Coffmans resisted much of the ceramics industrialization adopted by Suter. Coffman potters almost never marked their wares or decorated vessels, their shops remained in the same area for eighty years, and family and neighbors always managed the operation.

[33] F. M. Stinespring to Emanuel Suter, August 16, 1871, EESC. Comments on Heatwole's unusual decorative style appear in Kaufman, *Heatwole and Suter Pottery*, p. 6. Decoration is an uncommon practice among southern potters. In the Deep South, alkaline-glazed stonewares predominate, and traditional ceramics decoration in the form of cobalt painted motifs is rare; see Burrison, *Brothers in Clay*, pp. 68–77. Although sparse, painted decorations are relatively common in Rockingham County, elaborate decoration is uncommon in rural Virginia; see Smith, *Pottery*, p. 3. Virtually no molded Heatwole vessels survive in private collections. Given their distinctiveness and the numerous marked examples of Heatwole's wares, these surviving vessels seem to be good evidence that vessel molds were not used extensively in Heatwole's shop.

Fig. 3. John Heatwole, salt-glazed stoneware gravestone from Bank Mennonite Church, Rockingham County, Va., 1853. (Virginia Mennonite Conference Archives, Eastern Mennonite College and Seminary, Harrisonburg, Va.) (Photo, Stanley Kaufman.)

An indication of increasing social distance between potters and consumers is a shift in vessel decoration. In the instability of the postwar valley, potters began to develop what might appear to be mundane decorative ways of distinguishing their wares to identify their products and the potter's place in the community. After the war, for example, Suter began impressing and stenciling vessel capacities and his name and pottery location on many of his wares. One Suter merchant even commented that he was "much pleased with them the way they [were] numbered." Heatwole also often impressed, painted, stenciled, and inscribed unusual impressions on vessels and decorated wares idiosyncratically. Those potters who most aggressively resisted industrial techniques, though, such as the Coffmans and Morrises, virtually never marked or decorated their wares. Of 1,047 vessel waster shards surface collected at the Morris kiln, for example, only ten shards had any decoration.[34] Aesthetic options were not simply innocuous decorative whims, rather they were strategies that communicated the producer's identity and relation to consumers and the community.

Strategies such as Heatwole's use of traditional technologies or the Coffmans' aesthetic conservatism focused on their identities as farm producers. Indeed, virtually no agrarian potter wanted to be considered an "artisan." John Worrell has observed that the status of "farmer" implied land ownership, the fundamental source of prestige in an agrarian community. Worrell points out that the concept of the "artisan" really only emerged during industrialization, in the midst of an increasingly larger population of landless farmers. Even those who consciously made potting a business perceived it as having less social prestige than farming. By the 1870s, for instance, Suter had adopted many of the organizational elements of industrial potteries and was clearly quite prosperous as a potter. Yet in the 1870 and 1880 censuses, he still

[34] A sample of such vessels is illustrated in Kaufman, *Heatwole and Suter Pottery*, p. 14. J. H. Plecker to Suter, September 30, 1878, EESC. A Heatwole vessel rim stamped "IXL," which cannot be read as a roman numeral, is illustrated in Kaufman, *Heatwole and Suter Pottery*, p. 17. Kaufman has suggested that it stands for "I excel," which he has noted on a knife handle; Kaufman, interview with author, January 1988. Other examples are illustrated in Kaufman, *Heatwole and Suter Pottery*, pp. 14–17. Only 2 marked Coffman vessels are known (collection of Stanley A. Kaufman; private collection). Kaufman indicates that a single marked Morris vessel survives in a private collection; Kaufman, interview with author, January 1988. Mullins, "Historic Pottery-Making," p. 12. The only decorative technique in the Morris assemblage was brushed cobalt painting on gray-bodied stoneware.

Fig. 4. The Suters' New Erection Pottery, Mt. Clinton, ca. 1885. By this time the Suter operation was larger than most county potteries, which had considerably smaller kilns and shops than this one. (Emanuel and Elizabeth Suter Collection, Virginia Mennonite Conference Archives, Eastern Mennonite College and Seminary, Harrisonburg, Va.)

considered himself a "farmer and potter," refusing to relinquish the title of farmer (fig. 4). After Suter's death in 1902, a review of his life was included in the *Mennonite Year-Book and Directory*, but in two full pages it was only mentioned in passing that "he was, also for many years, engaged in operating on an extensive scale the pottery plant established on his farm." Worrell indicates that Hervey Brooks, one of the most thoroughly researched potters in New England, considered himself a farmer, much as Suter did. Yet Brooks was not even noted as a potter in a community history published twenty-three years after his death.[35] These examples argue strongly that potters and their com-

[35] Worrell, "Ceramic Production," p. 163; Manuscript Population Schedules, Central Township, Rockingham County, 9th and 10th U.S. Censuses (1870, 1880); L. J. Heatwole, "A Sketch of the Life and Work of Emanuel Suter," in J. S. Shoemaker,

munities considered their identity as potters to be subordinate to their
identity as farmers.

Potters and Merchants: The Business of Industrializing Craft Potteries

Much like their neighbor John Heatwole, Lindsey Morris and his sons
Erasmus and Andrew maintained a modest operation that was peripheral to their farming. The Morrises dug clay from the nearby riverbed,
turned ware in their barnyard, and burned ware in a modest updraft
kiln a hundred yards from their house. While potters such as Suter
were increasing the scale of their operation and introducing a wider
range of new technologies, neighboring producers such as Morris and
Heatwole resisted extensive technical modifications and economic reorganization. For instance, Morris and Heatwole exchanged their ware
for negotiable combinations of goods and cash. In 1878 a Suter merchant even warned Suter, "Morris from Dry River has sold good stoneware here at 10 cts. per gal. half payable in goods." Morris and Heatwole clearly did not reinvest significantly in their pottery operations,
which remained modest. Potters such as Morris and Heatwole attempted to remain viable by diversifying their exchange strategies, flex-
ibly bartering with merchants for goods and cash. Suter, in contrast,
continually increased the scale of his operation, and the cash for that
reinvestment probably came from his sales to merchants.[36]

Since the late eighteenth century, Shenandoah Valley craftspeople
occasionally had bartered their wares to local merchants for goods, just
as they would with any other member of the exchange networks. After
the Civil War, though, a few potters such as Suter and Silber began
to sell their ware to merchants for cash alone. These alliances between
local potters and merchants typically were codified through some form
of explicit "contract." Although the verbal agreement between barter

---

ed., *Mennonite Year-Book and Directory* (Scottsdale, Pa.: Mennonite Board of Charitable
Homes and Missions, 1906), pp. 31–32; Worrell, "Ceramic Production," pp. 162–63.

[36] J. H. Plecker to Emanuel Suter, July 8, 1878, EESC. Suter's records make it
difficult to establish exactly how all his "profit" from pottery exchange (cash as well as
bartered goods) was distributed, but they document continual cash purchase of specialized
equipment and materials.

transactors also was a form of "contract," the agreements between post–Civil War potters and merchants were very explicit and specific, detailing the exact form and quantity of ware, cash, or both to be exchanged; they allowed for little flexibility in negotiation; they typically included only two transactors, the potter and the merchant; and they generally were settled immediately or in a short period. Suter's 1886 price list even specified, "Goods will be shipped C.O.D., where contracts have not been made, as the low prices at which these goods are sold will justify no other course."[37]

For Suter, these contracts were agreements to deliver a precise quantity of ware and vessel forms specified by the merchant. Suter recorded these agreements and itemized the orders in his account book (that is, he priced each individual vessel form and specified the number of those forms delivered). Some merchants itemized their orders, and others simply agreed to take a general "load" of wares. For example, H. M. Baker wrote in 1879 requesting, "dont send any pitchers and but few larger sized jars or crocks milk crocks & pans and jars . . . in fact send me a saleable Bill as you know more about such things than I do."[38]

Local general stores, however, were still bartering goods with their customers and wished to continue trading goods with county potters as well. For instance, in an 1876 letter to Suter, a local merchant indicated, "I want to trade you some goods, Boots, shoes, woolen goods, etc" for a half dozen stoneware chambers. Suter's insistence on currency exchange apparently alienated some valley merchants. In 1869 a merchant demanded that Suter accept at least $1,000 in goods in exchange for a 275-gallon load of ware, arguing, "I represent two stores and the quantity of crocks we will buy certainly ought to induce you to take some goods or I will try to make arrangements with some other kiln." In 1878 the same merchant complained to Suter about the refusal to accept goods, noting that Lindsey Morris "sold good stoneware

[37] Mitchell, *Commercialism and Frontier*, pp. 210–11; New Erection Steam Pottery price list, 1886, EESC.

[38] For example, "49 1 gallon pots earthen 12½ cents $6.12½" corresponds to 49 one-gallon earthenware crocks at 12.5 cents each, for a total purchase of $6.12 ("Bill of ware taken to D. Siber and Sink," June 12, 1867, Emanuel Suter account book, EESC). A full order included each vessel type itemized in this format. H. M. Baker to Emanuel Suter, August 1, 1879, EESC.

here . . . half payable in goods." In 1877 merchant J. W. Minnick complained to Suter about the refusal to exchange pottery for goods, asserting that he had never dealt with another potter, "though we have been frequently urged to do so by other manufacturers."[39]

Suter introduced price lists some time after 1866 and turned his production and sales emphasis to local merchants, who in turn marked up and sold Suter's ware. Other potters also made forms of "contractual" agreements to market their wares in general stores regularly during the 1870s. The practice was probably not unknown before the war, but merchants' letters to Suter indicate that there was considerable postwar competition among potters to secure the exclusive business of various general stores. There are no indications of comparable competition among potters before the war. For example, merchant J. H. Plecker counseled Suter in 1879 to "let Mr. Hiram Huffman have 75 crocks. . . . I think you can get 8 cts per gal for them as he has been paying Watson 12½ cts for them." In 1879 F. M. Stinespring notified Suter, "I will need more Crocks Soon. If you can furnish them as low as Mr. Sylberts [Silber's] 1 Gal = 8 cents you may bring me 100 Gal crocks 50 ½ Gal." Suter's correspondence also indicates that Heatwole and Morris were visiting area merchants in an effort to secure orders.[40]

Affiliations with merchants would have decreased interpersonal contact between potters and consumers and promoted cash exchange between merchant and consumer where once potter and consumer had bartered goods and services. Perhaps most significantly, consumers experienced less tangible social commitment to craft producers, since two known transactors no longer interpersonally negotiated exchanges of one person's products and skills for those of the other transactor. This distance between potter and consumer increased the attraction of mass-produced goods such as glass jars, which were functionally equivalent to locally produced crocks.

[39] Joseph Mitchell to Suter, August 7, 1876, EESC. Plecker to Suter, September 27, 1869, July 8, 1878, EESC; J. W. Minnick to Suter, June 7, 1877, EESC. General stores may have reserved cash to purchase goods from the valley's large importers in Winchester and Staunton. This practice became common in the late eighteenth century; see Mitchell, *Commercialism and Frontier*, p. 237.

[40] Plecker to Suter, September 11, 1879, EESC. J. W. Watson was a potter in Augusta County; Hanger, "Pots, Potteries and Potting," p. 14. Stinespring to Suter, May 26, 1878, August 16, 1871, EESC; Plecker to Suter, July 8, 1878, EESC.

Rockingham County Pottery Factories

In 1890 land grant companies were formed to promote economic growth in the Shenandoah Valley. These companies attempted to coax industries to the area by purchasing farmland at the edge of towns and offering it to industrial investors free of charge. Three factory potteries were established on land grant properties. The New Jersey–owned Virginia Pottery Company, which produced Rockingham-glazed ware and ironstone, was established in Harrisonburg in 1890. Broadway Porcelain Manufacturing Company was established in 1891.[41] Formed by Albert Radford, a potter who had previously worked in factories in New Jersey and Baltimore, the Broadway pottery produced refined white earthenware and art pottery.

Suter obtained a Harrisonburg tract neighboring Virginia Pottery Company in 1890. Now called Harrisonburg Steam Pottery, Suter's new operation and its products expanded many of the industrial organizations Suter had used at his farm pottery. In the Harrisonburg factory, the individual as a multiskilled laborer was no longer prominent in the operation. Instead, a few potters administered semiskilled laborers who were paid by their time on a task, such as setting the kiln or molding vessels. Unlike the family and neighbors who administered a farm pottery as part of a neighborhood's broader agrarian production, these laborers were from throughout the region, many probably did not personally know the Suters, and the pottery's administrators and stockholders were not always present at the shop and active in everyday decisionmaking.[42]

---

[41] Kaufman, *Heatwole and Suter Pottery*, p. 12; *Rockingham Register*, August 29, 1890, p. 3; *Clay Record*, September 15, 1902, p. 26; Wayland, *Historic Harrisonburg*, p. 170; *Broadway Enterprise*, January 29, 1892; Frederick W. Radford, *Family History* (n.p.: By the author, n.d.).

[42] The Harrisonburg Steam Pottery charter was granted May 31, 1890. The firm was licensed "to manufacture and sell all kinds of pottery" and to issue 100 shares of stock to a total capital between $2,500 and $10,000. The charter was amended May 31, 1892, to increase that capital stock to an amount not exceeding $20,000; see Kaufman, *Heatwole and Suter Pottery*, p. 12; Mary E. Suter, *Memories of Yesteryear* (Waynesboro, Va.: Charles F. McClung Printing Co., 1959), pp. 49–53. Oliver Roller, who was Suter's partner in the new business, had no known experience as a potter. Emanuel Suter's diaries, EESC, indicate that he worked in the pottery on an irregular schedule, and Roller and his sons apparently spent little time in the shop.

Labor on a farm pottery and the flexibility of interpersonal barter represented a social commitment between individuals in an agrarian network, but the social relationship between laborer and administrator was different in the new Suter pottery. The semiskilled laborers who performed the factory's everyday operations were bound by contractual obligations, emphasizing their subordinate position in production. Most of these workers were unfamiliar with or strangers to Suter and their job skills were relatively useless outside a highly mechanized pottery, so they probably had less invested in their labor identities than the extended kin who worked on the Suter farm pottery. This decreased commitment between Suter and his laborers was reflected in decreased reliability of employees. For example, Suter hired Adam Linhoss to build a new shop building in February 1891, but he wrote, "I had expected that A Linhoss would be [at the pottery] with his hands to commence work on our shop but for Some Cause failed to be there I came home this evening I confess not very well pleased."[43]

The Harrisonburg operation was funded by stockholdings and administered by a five-person board of directors, which included two businessmen not trained as craft or industrial potters. Much of the technological foundation for the operation came from outside the community. Suter hired several turners from Pennsylvania on the recommendation of F. H. Cowden, who owned the Pennsylvania pottery factory at which Suter had worked in 1865. Cowden provided Suter with a considerable amount of supplies and technical advice. Cowden sold Suter prepared Albany slip, and he counseled Suter on wage rates ("1½ cts per gal for turning"), clay preparation, and appropriate equipment such as iron bands for the kiln and vessel molds. In April 1891 Suter went to Pennsylvania and New Jersey and established suppliers of machinery and materials, and he toured potteries in Ohio, New Jersey, West Virginia, and Maryland to inspect contemporary technologies. Suter's understanding of state-of-the-art technologies in ceramics is indicated by his comments about the A. P. Donagho and Sons Pottery in Parkersburg, West Virginia. Suter was surprised to find that they were still "grinding clay with horse useing the common pug mill, turning ware with kicking wheel, useing updraft kiln, Set ware in old

---

[43] Suter diaries, February 11, 1891, EESC.

Style." He was more impressed with the Zanesville Stoneware Pottery, which had a twenty-seven-foot diameter downdraft kiln and used "the latest improved machinery." After this trip, Suter paid a professional kiln engineer to construct downdraft rather than updraft kilns in the new pottery, and he eliminated production of earthenware in vessel forms other than flowerpots, stove flues, and molded Rockingham ware.[44]

Some of the technical modifications at the Harrisonburg pottery produced considerable difficulties. The shift to coal as kiln fuel, for example, was standard in industrial potteries, but for Suter it proved far less predictable than wood fuel. For instance, when the first kiln load was burned at the pottery in June 1891, Suter noted, "to day we drawed the first kiln out of our new kiln it was an earthen ware kiln it turned out pretty well burned most too hard."[45]

In the short run, the operation was apparently very profitable. By September 1891, Suter already noted that "great many came after ware," and two days later he "had quite a time Selling crocks [and]

[44]The charter-named board of directors consisted of Suter (president), Reuben Suter (treasurer), Oliver Roller (secretary), John R. Suter, and John Roller; see Kaufman, *Heatwole and Suter Pottery*, p. 12. For example, a Suter diary entry notes "a turner of Harrisburg, Pa, came to day he will turn for us" (Suter diaries, June 15, 1891, EESC). F. H. Cowden to Suter, March 4, 1887, September 29, 1890, EESC. Cowden wrote: "I hardly know what to advise you in regardd to Rose & sons clay but think it would be safer to use Ernst & Formans [?] mixed with Woodbridge to start with. You have a new enterprise and should take no more risks than is absolutely necessary at the start" (Cowden to Suter, April 8, 1891, EESC). Cowden to Suter, March 23, 1895, EESC. Again Cowden wrote: "If you want these molds I can send them to you at any time . . . they will be cheaper than to make them" (Cowden to Suter, September 29, 1890, EESC). Suter diaries, April 3, 1891, EESC; Suter to family, n.d., EESC. Suter notes that he toured A. P. Donagho and Sons Pottery in Parkersburg, W.Va., June 18, 1890, dating the letter to late June 1890. John Hawthorn, a New Jersey kiln designer who had built the Virginia Pottery Company kilns (*Rockingham Register*, August 29, 1890, p. 3), was paid $400 by Harrisonburg Steam Pottery to build their kiln; Suter diaries, February 5, 1891, EESC. Downdraft kilns are favored for large-capacity burning because they have more consistent temperature control and economic fuel consumption than updraft kilns; see Frederick Olsen, *The Kiln Book* (Bassett, Calif.: Keramos Books, 1973), p. 54. Suter's diaries do not systematically record the types of ware produced at the Harrisonburg pottery, and he did not administer the pottery's account books (which have been lost) or keep his own copies. The vast majority of the ware recovered from the kiln site in 1978 is undecorated stoneware with Albany slip, with extremely few earthenware vessels recovered; see Kaufman, *Heatwole and Suter Pottery*, p. 12.

[45]Faulkner, "Weaver Pottery," p. 231; Suter diaries, June 29, 1891, EESC.

came home late." The capital stock in the company rose to $20,000 in 1892. However, the fifty-eight-year-old Suter apparently became burdened by the time and energy necessary to manage the more highly structured operation. Suter dramatically decreased his role in the operation, and he relinquished most of the pottery's day-to-day management to his sons. An indication of his increasing distance from the operation is the number of diary entries that discuss pottery activities. In 1891 Suter mentioned the pottery in 223 of his 365 entries, but in 1892 that number sharply decreased to ninety. Suter continued to contribute to the pottery's management until 1897, but his daily participation was restricted to occasional technical advising, sales, and highly specialized turning.[46]

In January 1897 the Suters went to Harrisonburg to balance the pottery's books and found suspicious inconsistencies with their ledgers and those balanced by the company's secretary, O. B. Roller. Exhausted with the technical challenges of maintaining the pottery and troubled by his inability to manage the factory's business administration, Suter sold his share of the operation to Roller for $2,000, simply commenting in his diary, "This releves me of further trouble whit that works."[47]

By the turn of the century only the last generation of Coffmans was still potting using traditional techniques and vessel styles, and their operation closed around 1905. Roller and his brother John apparently gave up the Harrisonburg Steam Pottery by 1900 and purchased the closed factories of both Broadway Porcelain Manufacturing Company and Virginia Pottery Company. The Rollers adapted these factories to produce "sanitary porcelains" (electric fixtures and insulators), employing about thirty-five individuals in each plant. The firm closed within ten years. A final Rockingham County pottery was opened in Broadway in 1918, probably in one of the town's already closed potteries, but it closed by the early 1920s.[48]

---

[46] Suter diaries, September 5, 7, 1891, EESC; Kaufman, *Heatwole and Suter Pottery*, p. 12; Mullins, "Defining the Boundaries," p. 190. In one of his increasingly less frequent references to his work at the pottery, Suter notes: "went to the Pottery turned 5 gallon jugs" (Suter diaries, May 2–4, 1894, EESC).

[47] Suter diaries, April 10, 1897, EESC.

[48] The last operation was the William S. Coffman shop; see Russ and McDaniel, "Traditional Pottery Manufacturing Industry," p. 9; Mullins, "Historic Pottery-Making,"

Conclusion

In the wake of the Civil War, individuals as different as Suter and the Coffmans actively renegotiated their roles as subordinated laborers, producers, and consumers. However, these producers responded with a diversity of changes. These diversified, highly individualized responses to postwar instability were intended to improve upon craft producers' socioeconomic standing yet restore certain elements of agrarian social structure. Suter, for instance, worked very hard to maintain kin-based control of production, despite the introduction of profitable industrial machinery and sales techniques. The Coffmans, at the other extreme, apparently rejected the vast majority of the trappings of ceramics industrialization and remained a predominately local operation run by and for neighborhood producers.

Despite pervasive industrial change in Rockingham County pottery production, the agrarian identities of the county's potters were never discarded. Heatwole, the Morrises, and the Coffmans were farm families throughout the nineteenth century, and while Suter may have become perhaps the most "industrialized" potter in Rockingham County, he, too, clung to his identity as a farmer. Even as industrializing producers, many craftspeople retained aspects of traditional craft production and consumption, and many distinctive elements of traditional social interdependence survive in the rural valley today.

Rockingham County's craft community perceived industrialization as the improved production of industrial technologies, the lower cost of mass-produced goods, and the flexibility to exchange their products for both goods and cash. The region's potters, like many agrarian producers, examined such mechanisms of industrial society in relation to the interests of their communities and families. In Rockingham County, factors such as increased quantities of craft and mass-produced

---

p. 21. *Rockingham Register*, May 16, 1905. Massaneta Art Pottery Co. apparently purchased Virginia Pottery Co. in 1902 (*Clay Record*, September 15, 1902), and advertisements were circulated in East Liverpool, Ohio, for laborers (*Illustrated Glass and Pottery World*, November 1902). Roller purchased the factory from Massaneta Art Pottery Co. in 1904 (*Rockingham Register*, January 10, 1905); it is unknown if Massaneta Art Pottery ever produced any ware at the Harrisonburg factory. *Rockingham Register*, May 16, 1905; Stanley Kaufman, interview with author, January 1988; *Daily News Record*, March 20, 1918, March 25, 1918, November 20, 1918.

goods seemed beneficial, particularly in relation to the destabilized post–Civil War communal structure and the long-standing socioeconomic subordination of craftspeople. Rather than perceive mass-produced goods and market exchange as the surface of a dominating socioeconomic system, many local producers and consumers clearly embraced much of industrial society.

The diverse experiences of production and consumption within this community emphasize that the dichotomy between craft and industrial production is useful, but it remains purely heuristic. The community that emerged in the valley was the product of a subtle yet dynamic interaction among factory elite, agrarian craftspeople, and local consumers who had many different interests. The experience of ceramics industrialization in Rockingham County is simply one example of a process in which local producers and consumers negotiated new identities that would preserve the social continuity of their communities yet improve the socioeconomic standing of farmer-potters. Rockingham County's experience of industrialization is socially, regionally, and temporally distinct, but it is by no means unique to the world of craft producers and consumers. Indeed, the experience of industrialization in Rockingham County was simply one of many locally directed transformations of a distinctive community social structure throughout the United States.

Appendix

Rockingham County, Virginia,
Potters and Potteries: A Chronological List

(Potteries ordered from earliest to most recent date of operation)

Principal potter: John Stephen Conrad, Jr. (1749–1822)
Pottery location: Elkton
Dates of operation: 1800–1822
Associated potter: Andrew Coffman
References: Floyd Wilmer Coffman, *The Conrad Clan: The Family of John Stephen Conrad and Allied Lines* (Harrisonburg, Va.: Charles F. McClung, 1959), pp. 106–7; Paul R. Mullins, "Historic Pottery-Making in Rockingham County, Virginia" (Paper presented at Archeology Society of Virginia Spring Symposium, Charlottesville, 1988), p. 14.

Principal potter: Andrew Coffman (1795–1853)
Pottery location: Elkton
Dates of operation: 1820–53
Associated potters: William C. Coffman (son), John Coffman (son; 1824–99), Andrew C. Coffman (son; b. 1832), Reuben S. Coffman (son; 1836–1900), David Coffman (nephew; b. 1829), Isaac Lamb (1832–82), Lindsey Morris (son-in-law), John Heatwole (son-in-law), John Stephen Conrad, Jr., possibly Joseph H. Kite, possibly John Southard (son-in-law; b. 1824)
References: Charles Fahs Kauffman, A *Genealogy of the Kauffman-Coffman Families of North America, 1584 to 1937* (Scottsdale, Pa.: Mennonite Publishing House, 1960), p. 205; Elmer L. Smith, *Pottery: A Utilitarian Folk Craft* (Lebanon, Pa.: Applied Arts Publishers, 1972), p. 27; Floyd Wilmer Coffman, *The Conrad Clan: The Family of John Stephen Conrad and Allied Lines* (Harrisonburg, Va.: Charles F. McClung, 1959), p. 106; Manuscript Population Schedules, Stonewall

District, Rockingham County, Va., 5th, 6th, and 7th U.S. Censuses (1830, 1840, and 1850).

Principal potter: George Kline/Cline (b. 1770)
Pottery location: Harrisonburg (Black's Run and German St.)
Dates of operation: ca. 1826
Associated potters: unknown
References: Paul G. Kline, *The Cline-Kline Family* (Dayton, Va.: Shenandoah Press, 1971), pp. 2–3; John W. Wayland, *Historic Harrisonburg* (Staunton, Va.: McClure Printing Co., 1949), p. 338; *Rockingham Register* (October 5, 1876).

Principal potter: John Zigler (b. 1809)
Pottery location: Timberville
Dates of operation: 1830–40
Associated potters: unknown
References: Elmer L. Smith, *Pottery: A Utilitarian Folk Craft* (Lebanon, Pa.: Applied Arts Publishers, 1972), p. 31; John Wayland, *History of Rockingham County* (Strasburg, Va.: Shenandoah Publishing, 1967), p. 378; Paul G. Kline, *The Cline-Kline Family* (Dayton, Va.: Shenandoah Press, 1971), p. 3; Manuscript Population Schedules, Timberville, Rockingham County, Va., 4th, 5th, and 6th U.S. Censuses (1820, 1830, and 1840).

Principal potter: Thomas Logan (b. 1791, Ireland)
Pottery location: Harrisonburg
Dates of operation: 1840–70
Associated potters: Thomas G. Logan (son; b. 1819), Neville Logan (son; b. 1824); Abraham Spencer (b. 1812)
References: John W. Wayland, *Historic Harrisonburg* (Staunton, Va.: McClure Printing Co., 1949), pp. 5–8; Manuscript Population Schedules, Harrisonburg, Rockingham County, Va., 6th, 7th, 8th, and 9th U.S. Censuses (1840, 1850, 1860, and 1870).

Principal potter: William C. Coffman (1822–96)
Pottery location: Elkton
Dates of operation: 1850–90
Associated potters: Edwin E. Coffman (son), William S. Coffman (son), Robert A. Coffman (son), possibly Joseph H. Kite, possibly John Southard (brother-in-law)

References: Charles Fahs Kauffman, A *Genealogy of the Kauffman-Coffman Families of North America, 1584 to 1937* (Scottsdale, Pa.: Mennonite Publishing House, 1960), p. 205; Kurt C. Russ and John McDaniel, "The Traditional Pottery Manufacturing Industry in Virginia: Examples from Botetourt and Rockbridge Counties, 1775–1894" (Paper presented at meeting of the Rockbridge Historical Society, Lexington, Va., February 1987), p. 9; Manuscript Population Schedules, Elk Run, Stonewall District, Rockingham County, Va., 7th, 9th, and 10th U.S. Censuses (1850, 1870, and 1880).

Principal potter: John Heatwole (1826–1907)
Pottery location: Dry River
Dates of operation: 1850–61, 1865–ca. 1890
Associated potters: Alfred N. Powell (b. 1834), Lindsey Morris, Reuben S. Coffman (brother-in-law), Daniel A. Coffman (brother-in-law; b. 1839), Joseph Silber, John W. Ford (son-in-law; 1850–1925), Andrew Heatwole (son; b. 1853), Emanuel Suter
References: Stanley A. Kaufman, *Heatwole and Suter Pottery* (Harrisonburg, Va.: Good Printers, 1978), pp. 5–8; Manuscript Population Schedules, Central Township, Ashby District, Rockingham County, Va., 7th, 8th, 9th, and 10th U.S. Censuses (1850, 1860, 1870, and 1880).

Principal potter: Emanuel Suter (1833–1902)
Pottery location: Mt. Clinton
Dates of operation: 1854–64, November 1866–90
Associated potters: sons Reuben (b. 1858), John R. (b. 1863), Emanuel J. (b. 1868), and Peter S. (b. 1871); John Heatwole; Isaac Good; John P. Good; John W. Ford; Joseph Silber; Andrew Heatwole; James Keister; Jeremiah Falls; Peter Layman; Fred Cline; Jacob Fultz; Samuel Lineweaver; Newton Burkholder; Joseph Gaines; Bill Hopkins; James M. Vint; Joseph Breeding; Jacob Bensfeld; Charles Bensfeld; John Rhodes; Abraham Weaver; John Roller; Oliver B. Roller; possibly William and J. Ricketts
References: Mary E. Suter, *Memories of Yesteryear* (Waynesboro, Va.: Charles F. McClung Printing Co., 1959), pp. 49–53; Stanley A. Kaufman, *Heatwole and Suter Pottery* (Harrisonburg, Va.: Good Printers, 1978), pp. 9–13; Manuscript Population Schedules, Central Township, Rockingham County, Va., 9th and 10th U.S. Censuses (1870,

1880); 1864–1902 Emanuel Suter diaries, account book, and papers, Emanuel and Elizabeth Suter Collection, Virginia Mennonite Conference Archives, Eastern Mennonite College Menno Simons Library, Harrisonburg, Va. (hereafter EESC).

Principal potter: Joseph H. Kite (1828–89)
Pottery location: Riverton (Elkton)
Dates of operation: 1866–89
Associated potters: possibly William C. Coffman and William S. Coffman
References: Elmer L. Smith, *Pottery: A Utilitarian Folk Craft* (Lebanon, Pa.: Applied Arts Publishers, 1972), p. 31; *Rockingham Register* (September 11, 1866), p. 3; Manuscript Population Schedules, Elk Run, Stonewall Township, Rockingham County, Va., 9th and 10th U.S. Censuses (1870, 1880).

Principal potter: Mathew/Matthias Ireland (b. 1828), George Duey (b. 1832, Pennsylvania), and James Shinnick (b. 1813, Maryland)
Pottery location: Mt. Crawford
Dates of operation: 1870–75
Associated potters: possibly Reuben Coffman, Joseph Silber, George M. Woods, Lindsey Morris, and Erasmus Morris
References: A. H. Rice and John Baer Stoudt, *The Shenandoah Pottery* (Berryville: Virginia Book Co., 1929), p. 79; Elmer L. Smith, *Pottery: A Utilitarian Folk Craft* (Lebanon, Pa.: Applied Arts Publishers, 1972), p. 24; Manuscript Population Schedules, Mt. Crawford, Franklin Township, Rockingham County, Va., 7th, 9th, and 10th U.S. Censuses (1850, 1870, 1880).

Principal potter: George M. Woods (b. 1822)
Pottery location: Mt. Crawford
Dates of operation: ca. 1870
Associated potters: Joseph Silber

Principal potter: Lindsey Morris (1820–1902)
Pottery location: Dry River
Dates of operation: 1872–90
Associated potters: sons Erasmus (b. 1846) and Andrew J. (1853–88); Reuben S. Coffman; possibly John Southard
References: Jim Hanger, "Pots, Potteries, and Potting in Augusta

County, 1800–1870," *Augusta Historical Bulletin* 9 (Spring 1973): 15; Stanley A. Kaufman, *Heatwole and Suter Pottery* (Harrisonburg, Va.: Good Printers, 1978), p. 6; Manuscript Population Schedule, Stonewall Township, Rockingham County, Va., 7th U.S. Census (1850); Manuscript Population Schedule, North River District, Augusta County, Va., 8th U.S. Census (1860); Manuscript Population Schedule, Franklin Township, Rockingham County, Va., 9th U.S. Census (1870); Manuscript Population Schedule, Ashby District, Rockingham County, Va., 10th U.S. Census (1880).

Principal potter: Isaac Good (1851–1907)
Pottery location: Mt. Clinton (?)
Dates of operation: 1873–77
Associated potters: Emanuel Suter

Principal potter: Joseph Silber (1830 [Prussia]–1890)
Pottery location: Rawley Springs
Dates of operation: 1875–90
Associated potters: John Heatwole, Emanuel Suter, possibly George M. Woods
References: Stanley A. Kaufman, *Heatwole and Suter Pottery* (Harrisonburg, Va.: Good Printers, 1978), p. 6; Manuscript Population Schedule, Franklin Township, Rockingham County, Va., 9th U.S. Census (1870); Manuscript Population Schedule, Central Township, Rockingham County, Va., 10th U.S. Census (1880).

Principal potter: James Shinnick (b. 1813, Maryland)
Pottery location: Mt. Crawford (?)
Dates of operation: 1875–80
Associated potters: possibly sons William C. (b. 1852) and George T. (b. 1855)
References: Elmer L. Smith, *Pottery: A Utilitarian Folk Craft* (Lebanon, Pa.: Applied Arts Publishers, 1972), p. 24; Kurt C. Russ, "Historic Pottery Making in Virginia," in Michael B. Barber, ed., *Upland Archeology in the East* (Atlanta: Forest Service Southern Region, 1984), p. 261.

Principal potter: William S. Coffman (1846–1912), Robert A. Coffman (1855–1921), and Edward E. Coffman (1853–1919)
Pottery location: Elkton

Dates of operation: 1882–1900
Associated potter: Clinton Coffman (son of William S.; b. 1874)
References: Elmer L. Smith, *Pottery: A Utilitarian Folk Craft* (Lebanon, Pa.: Applied Arts Publishers, 1972), p. 27; Kurt C. Russ and John McDaniel, "The Traditional Pottery Manufacturing Industry in Virginia: Examples from Botetourt and Rockbridge Counties, 1775–1894" (Paper presented at meeting of the Rockbridge Historical Society, Lexington, Va., February 1987), p. 9; Manuscript Population Schedule, North River District, Augusta County, Va., 10th U.S. Census (1880).

Principal potter: Virginia Pottery Company
Pottery location: Harrisonburg
Dates of operation: October 1890–ca. 1900
References: *Rockingham Register* (August 29, 1890), p. 3; *Clay Record* (September 15, 1902), p. 26; John W. Wayland, *Historic Harrisonburg* (Staunton, Va.: McClure Printing Co., 1949), p. 170.

Principal potter: Broadway Porcelain Manufacturing Company
Pottery location: Broadway
Dates of operation: March 1891–ca. 1895
Associated potters: Albert Radford (1862 [England]–1904)
References: *Broadway Enterprise* (January 29, 1892); Frederick W. Radford, *Family History* (n.p.: By the author, n.d.).

Principal potters: Harrisonburg Steam Pottery; Emanuel Suter
Pottery location: Harrisonburg
Dates of operation: June 1891–ca. 1898
Associated potters: John and Oliver Roller
References: Mary E. Suter, *Memories of Yesteryear* (Waynesboro, Va.: Charles F. McClung Printing Co., 1959), pp. 49–53; Stanley A. Kaufman, *Heatwole and Suter Pottery* (Harrisonburg, Va.: Good Printers, 1978), pp. 9–13; 1864–1902 Emanuel Suter diaries, account book, and papers, EESC.

Principal potter: Adamant Porcelain Company
Pottery location: Broadway
Dates of operation: October 1900–ca. 1909
Associated potter: John Roller (owner)
References: *Evening News* (October 9, 1900), p. 1.

Principal potter: Adamant Porcelain Company
Pottery location: Harrisonburg
Dates of operation: May 1905–ca. 1909
Associated potter: John Roller (owner)
References: *Rockingham Register* (May 16, 1905), p. 1.

Principal potter: Broadway Pottery
Pottery location: Broadway
Dates of operation: ca. 1918
References: *Daily News Record* (March 20, 1918), p. 4; *Daily News Record* (March 25, 1918), p. 5; *Daily News Record* (November 20, 1918), p. 4.

Principal potter: William and J. Ricketts
Pottery location: unknown
Dates of operation: unknown
Associated potter: possibly Emanuel Suter
References: Marked sherd found at Suter farm (Collection of Mary Nell Rhodes).

Principal potter: Mathias Bright (b. 1798, Prussia)
Pottery location: unknown
Dates of operation: ca. 1850
Associated potters: unknown
References: Manuscript Population Schedule, Plains Township, Rockingham County, Va., 7th U.S. Census (1850).

Principal potter: Branson O'Roark (b. 1812)
Pottery location: unknown
Dates of operation: 1860–70
Associated potters: possibly John C. Coffman (New Market)

European Textiles from Seventeenth-Century New England Indian Cemeteries

Linda Welters, Margaret T. Ordoñez, Kathryn Tarleton, and Joyce Smith

Analysis of European-made textiles from two seventeenth-century southeastern New England Indian cemeteries provides new insights for textile history. Combined with other primary sources, these small textile fragments provide evidence for international trade patterns, the physical properties of cloth exchanged with Indians, and the use of cloth in Indian mortuary practice.

European-made textiles can be distinguished from native-made textiles in seventeenth-century burials by both material and construc-

Textile analysis for the RI-1000 project was funded through a grant from the Rhode Island Historic Preservation Commission and a University of Rhode Island Grant-in-Aid. Funding for the Long Pond project was provided by a grant from the Mashantucket Pequot Tribal Council. Both the RI-1000 and Long Pond projects were carried out as joint ventures with the tribes whose ancestral burial grounds were being affected by development. Tribal authorities determined the extent of the excavations and the terms of reburial.

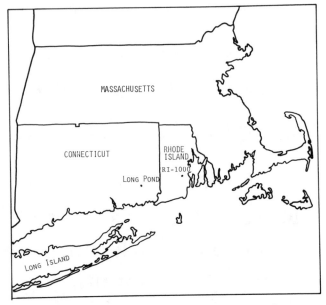

Fig. 1. Map of lower New England indicating site location.
(Map, Linda Welters.)

tion. European textiles were made from fibers, such as wool, silk,
flax, hemp, and cotton, produced specifically for textile usage. Yarns
made with precious metals sometimes were incorporated into prestigious cloth. Most European textiles were made of woven constructions
(yarns interlaced at right angles on a loom). Knits and fabrics of other
nonwoven constructions, such as lace, were less common than they
are today.

Algonkian Indians in the Northeast made textiles from locally
available plant materials such as bulrushes, bent grass, maize husks,
flag leaves, the inner bark of basswood and linden trees, and Indian
hemp (*Apocynum cannabenum*), also known as dogbane. Animal sinew
was sometimes used as thread or string. Textiles were constructed using
off-loom techniques like plaiting, twining, and sewing. During the
seventeenth century, Indians combined European and native technologies by using European materials in native constructions (wool in a

twined bag) or native materials added to European constructions (sinew to attach hoops to European cloth).[1]

Eighty European textile fragments were excavated from a Narragansett Indian cemetery called RI-1000 located in North Kingstown, Rhode Island (fig. 1). A bulldozer disturbed at least nine graves in an unmarked cemetery in 1982. Since the land was slated for development, the remaining graves were systematically excavated the following summer by a team of archaeologists under the direction of the Rhode Island Historical Preservation Commission and Brown University and by members of the Narragansett Tribe. The site, which was used between 1650 and 1670, consisted of the graves of fifty-six individuals. An interdisciplinary approach was used to analyze skeletal remains and associated grave goods. In addition to European textile fragments, native-made textiles, such as mats and cordage, were present along with numerous grave offerings including spoons, hoops, hoes, and beads.[2]

In 1990, 122 European textiles were excavated from a Mashan-

---

[1]Catherine Marten, *The Wampanoags in the Seventeenth Century* (Plymouth, Mass.: Plimoth Plantation, 1970), pp. 9–10; William S. Simmons, "Narragansett," in Bruce Trigger, ed., *Northeast*, vol. 15 of *Handbook of North American Indians* (Washington, D.C.: Smithsonian Institution, 1978), p. 192.

[2]Counting the number of textile fragments excavated from archaeological sites is an arbitrary process. Textiles bagged and numbered as a single specimen in the field may separate into multiple textile types in the laboratory. Likewise, separately bagged and numbered specimens from the same grave may be 1 textile type. The European textiles from RI-1000 were counted by the number assigned at the site. Initially, 74 European textiles were studied. During analysis of other grave goods, 6 additional textiles of European origin were identified (adhering to the back of a spoon; lying under a section of wampum headband). The European material culture of RI-1000 includes brass kettles, spoons, rings, and bells; iron axes, knives, scissors, hoes, and nails; clay pipes; glass beads; and glass bottles, ceramics, and gun-related items in addition to textiles. These objects are typical of trade goods produced in many western European countries between about 1650 and 1670; most are datable to the decade 1650–60. William A. Turnbaugh, *The Material Culture of RI-1000, a Mid-Seventeenth-Century Narragansett Indian Burial Site in North Kingstown, Rhode Island* (Kingston, R.I.: Department of Sociology and Anthropology, University of Rhode Island, 1984), pp. 7–8. Paul A. Robinson, Marc A. Kelley, and Patricia E. Rubertone, "Preliminary Biocultural Interpretations from a Seventeenth-Century Narragansett Indian Cemetery in Rhode Island," in William W. Fitzhugh, ed., *Cultures in Contact: The Impact of European Contacts on Native American Cultural Institutions A.D. 1000–1800* (Washington, D.C.: Smithsonian Institution Press, 1985), pp. 107–30; Linda M. Welters, "Narragansett Bay Survey: Conservation and Analysis of European Textiles from RI-1000" (Rhode Island Historic Preservation Commission, Providence, 1985, report).

tucket Pequot cemetery in Ledyard, Connecticut. This cemetery, tentatively dated 1670–1720, is named Long Pond for the lake above which it was located and was part of the Pequot reservation established in 1667. The Long Pond cemetery was discovered when a house foundation was being dug on private land. Approximately twenty graves were bulldozed before the Public Archaeology Survey Team at the University of Connecticut and the Mashantucket Pequot Tribe were notified. The Tribal Council made the decision to excavate only those graves that would be disturbed by the house construction, leaving the remainder of the cemetery intact. Ten of the twenty-one excavated graves yielded European textiles including a variety of wool textiles and ferrous oxide casts of textiles. Native-made necklaces, bracelets, and wampum headbands of bast fiber (either dogbane or flax) and sinew were recovered from this site.[3]

As textile specialists, we focus on the characteristics of the cloth (fiber content, yarn structure, fabric structure, finish, and coloration) and the possible end use for the cloth (clothing, shroud, wrapping for grave goods, or grave linings). Our methods combine scientific examination of the objects with the study of relevant historical documents. We study textile fragments with the aid of stereo, polarizing, and scanning electron microscopes to determine physical characteristics. We perform diagnostic tests to determine features such as fiber content and coloring agent. We use studies based on seventeenth-century documents such as merchants' records and travelers' accounts for names and descriptions of textiles, as well as studies providing the context in which the textiles were used. Since we are neither archaeologists nor anthropologists, our work is not meant to extrapolate on tribal religious beliefs or, more broadly, on tribal culture and the changes native cultures underwent as a result of contact with Europeans. Yet answers to some of the questions raised by archaeologists, textile historians, and Native Americans are evident through careful technical analyses of textiles present in the graves.

To date, European textiles have been recovered from only a few archaeological excavations of seventeenth-century Indian cemeteries in

[3] Margaret T. Ordoñez, Linda Welters, and Kathryn Tarleton, "Analysis of Textiles from Long Pond Site" (Public Archaeology Survey Team, University of Connecticut, Storrs, 1991, report).

New England. Burr's Hill, a Wampanoag cemetery dated 1650–75 in Warren, Rhode Island, contained seventy-three fragments of European textiles. The Burr's Hill examples are almost all fragments of various woven-wool fabrics, except for a piece of linen holland and a length of silk-and-silver galloon trim. Other seventeenth-century sites where European textiles were recovered include the Whitford site in North Kingstown, which contained several fragments of coarse wool plus an iron-encrusted fragment of fine wool, and the West Ferry site in Jamestown from which a single silver-colored cloth was excavated.[4]

Since the textiles from the RI-1000 site were not slated for reburial, their preanalysis treatment was more involved than if the intention was for them to be reinterred like the Long Pond textiles. The RI-1000 textiles are housed at the Rhode Island Historical Preservation Commission and may be studied with the permission of the Narragansett Tribe. These textiles might be reburied in the future. The Long Pond textiles were reinterred with the skeletal remains and other funerary offerings on November 25, 1991. They were cleaned only enough to facilitate analysis of surface characteristics.

Given that cloth was one of the chief commodities exchanged with Indians in the seventeenth century, it is unfortunate that European textiles have received so little attention in comparison to other archaeological finds. The work done by Phyllis Dillon for the catalogue on the Burr's Hill site is virtually the only substantial written information on the subject. Dillon was the first to publish descriptions of European textiles from seventeenth-century Indian cemeteries as distinct cultural objects, separate from aboriginal textiles and other trade goods. Robert Trent's essay on the coastal Algonkian culture in *New England Begins*,

---

[4]Beth Bower, "Aboriginal Textiles," in Susan G. Gibson, ed., *Burr's Hill: A Seventeenth-Century Wampanoag Burial Ground in Warren, Rhode Island* (Providence: Brown University and the Haffenreffer Museum of Anthropology, 1980), pp. 89–91; Phyllis Dillon, "Trade Fabrics," in Gibson, *Burr's Hill*, pp. 100–107. Well-preserved fragments from a particularly colorful woolen blanket have been exhibited and published; see Florence M. Montgomery, *Textiles in America: 1650–1870* (New York: W. W. Norton, 1984), pl. D-21; Robert F. Trent, "Blanket Fragment," catalogue entry in Jonathan L. Fairbanks and Robert F. Trent, eds., *New England Begins: The Seventeenth Century* (Boston: Museum of Fine Arts, 1982), p. 74. William Turnbaugh to Linda Welters, April 2, 1985; William Scranton Simmons, *Cautantowwit's House* (Providence: Brown University Press, 1970), pp. 45, 87. The textiles from the Whitford site have not been published.

Fig. 2. Woolen textile with copper sulfate deposit in spoon impression, Long Pond cemetery, Ledyard, Conn., cat. no. 14–2-13 (3 of 3). (Photo, Linda Welters.)

the catalogue for the landmark exhibition at the Museum of Fine Arts, Boston, included European textiles in the analysis, presenting them as replacements for equivalent forms in native culture.[5]

Part of the reason for this dearth of information is that textiles are fragile by nature, and climatic conditions in New England are not conducive to preservation of textiles in burials. Most European textiles recovered from the sites mentioned previously were preserved through their contact with metal and were fragmentary at best (fig. 2). Sometimes the only evidence for the existence of a textile was a short length of yarn. Another reason for the lack of information is that archaeologists might be unfamiliar with conservation and analytical tech-

[5]Robert F. Trent, "Coastal Algonkian Culture, 1500–1680: Conquest and Resistance," in Fairbanks and Trent, *New England Begins*, pp. 66–71, 74.

niques for textiles from wet terrestrial sites. The excavation and on-site treatment of organic material such as textiles is a subject in need of much study.[6]

Besides the paucity of archaeological textiles and the relatively recent development of conservation and analytical techniques for textiles, a more pervasive problem exists. Evident in the literature at least through the 1970s is a preference by North American archaeologists for the study of aboriginal textiles over trade textiles. Native-made baskets, mats, and twined bags intrigued material culturists as indigenous art forms, whereas European textiles were largely ignored. Perhaps field archaeologists did not take the extra precautions necessary to excavate and conserve the rotting cloth found in burials properly because little scholarly interest in trade textiles existed. For example, one wonders if the "dark, feltlike, decomposed matting" from burial 4 at the West Ferry site might have been a European textile.[7] The Burr's Hill site appears to be the exception among the New England sites excavated in the decades before the 1980s.

Documentary sources for the study of textiles used in New England during this period are much more plentiful than the textiles themselves. Most helpful is written evidence such as probate records, journals, and merchants' records. George Francis Dow's work on life in the Massachusetts Bay Colony contains a glossary of "fabrics used in the early days." Working from fabric names appearing in probate inventories, court records, and newspaper advertisements, he listed 151 fabrics known to have been imported or manufactured in the Massachusetts Bay Colony. Dow provided definitions for most fabric names. For example, the entry for *camlet* defines the fabric as "originally made of silk and camel's hair, hence the name, but later of silk and wool." Dow listed seven examples of camlet located in documentary sources, including "camlet breeches" (1625) and "a watered camlet gown" (1719).[8]

---

[6] Methods of stabilizing archaeological textiles from wet terrestrial sites is the subject of a thesis completed by an author of this essay: Kathryn Tarleton, "Analysis of Post-Excavation Stabilization Methods for Wet Site Archaeological Textiles" (Master's thesis, University of Rhode Island, 1992).

[7] Simmons, *Cautantowwit's House*, p. 81.

[8] George Francis Dow, *Every Day Life in the Massachusetts Bay Colony* (Boston: Society for the Preservation of New England Antiquities, 1935), pp. 70–83.

Linda R. Baumgarten's study of eighty-three Boston merchants' inventories from the second half of the seventeenth century builds on Dow's work. Although Baumgarten's goal was to provide more accurate data for furnishing period rooms, the study informs textile historians as well. One appendix lists and defines fabric names encountered in the Boston inventories, while another ranks the twenty-four most important fabrics in the merchant records. For example, citing six sources, Baumgarten defined *camlet* as "a worsted fabric, sometimes calendered [pressed with revolving cylinders to increase sheen], mixed with silk or hair."[9] *Camlet* appeared twenty times in the inventories; thus, it was included in the list of the twenty-four most important fabrics.

Important to the RI-1000 study are the records of William and John Pynchon, who traded with the Squakheags in Springfield, Massachusetts. These documents date from 1635, when William Pynchon founded Springfield, and provide detailed evidence of the textile trade with Native Americans in one New England community. Peter Thomas used the Pynchon records in his study of the Indian trade in the middle Connecticut River valley. Thomas noted that cloth goods dominated the Pynchon inventories in a variety of forms ranging from piece goods to finished articles of clothing. Paradoxically, excavation of the Squakheag site of Fort Hill (1663–64) in Hinsdale, New Hampshire, recovered no cloth. A button mold, two garters, and a bone button are the only archaeological evidence that European-style clothing was in use among the Squakheags.[10]

Other useful documentary accounts are those that describe Indian appearance, customs, and trading practices in the seventeenth century. Accounts with passages relevant to the study of European textiles acquired by Indians begin with John Brereton's account of Bartholomew Gosnold's exploration of the New England coastline in 1602 during which six Indians came out to the English ship, one of them "appar-

[9]Linda R. Baumgarten, "The Textile Trade in Boston, 1650–1700," in Ian M. G. Quimby, ed., *Arts of the Anglo-American Community in the Seventeenth Century* (Charlottesville: University Press of Virginia, 1975), pp. 219–73.

[10]*The Pynchon Papers: Selections from the Account Books of John Pynchon*, ed. Carl Bridenbaugh (Charlottesville: University Press of Virginia, 1985); Peter Allen Thomas, "In the Maelstrom of Change: The Indian Trade and Cultural Process in the Middle Connecticut River Valley, 1635–1665" (Ph.D. diss., University of Massachusetts, 1979), p. 379.

elled with a waistcoat and breeches of black serdge made after our sea-fashions, hose and shoes on his feet."[11]

Additional descriptions of Indian manners and apparel reveal the subtle differences in appearance among Indians in the seventeenth century and the precise ways in which Indians acquired and used European cloth and clothing. Some of these writers mention how the apparel of the Indians had changed from the time "before the *English* came amongst them." Daniel Gookin's description is particularly insightful:

The Indians' clothing in former times was of the same matter as Adam's was, viz. skins of beasts, as deer, moose, beaver, otters, rackoons, foxes, and other wild creatures. Also some had mantles of the feathers of birds, quilled artificially; and sundry of them continue to this day their old kind of clothing. But, for the most part, they sell the skins and furs to the English, Dutch and French, and buy of them for clothing a kind of cloth, called duffils, or trucking cloth, about a yard and a half wide, and for matter, made of coarse wool, in that form as our ordinary bed blackets are made, only it is put into colours, as blue, red, purple, and some use them white. Of this sort of cloth two yards make a mantle, or coat, for men and women, and less for children. This is all the garment they generally use, with this addition of some little piece of the same, or of ordinary cotton, to cover their secret parts.[12]

Few pictorial images survive to help us visualize the appearance of southern New England's Native Americans in the seventeenth century. The most relevant image to this study is *Portrait of Ninigret II, Son of Ninigret I, Chief of the Niantic Indians* (fig. 3). Niantic tribal lands abutted both Narragansett and Pequot territories. After the massacre of the Narragansetts in the Great Swamp Fight of 1675, Narra-

[11] John Brereton, *Discoverie of the North Part of Virginia* (1602; Ann Arbor, Mich.: University Microfilms, 1966), p. 4.

[12] G. Mourt, *A Journal of the Pilgrims at Plymouth, Mourt's Relation*, ed. Dwight B. Heath (1622; reprint, New York: Corinth Books, 1963), pp. 54, 60, 65; William Wood, *New England's Prospect*, ed. Alden T. Vaughn (1635; reprint, Amherst: University of Massachusetts Press, 1977), pp. 84–85, 115; Thomas Morton, *New English Canaan, or New Canaan* (1637; Ann Arbor: University Microfilms, 1972), pp. 28–31; Roger Williams, *A Key into the Language of America* (1643; 5th ed.; Providence: Rhode Island and Providence Plantations Tercentenary Commission, 1936), pp. 118–22; Paul J. Lindholdt, ed., *John Josselyn, Colonial Traveler* (Hanover, N.H.: University Press of New England, 1988), pp. 92–93; Daniel Gookin, *Historical Collections of the Indians in New England* (Boston: Massachusetts Historical Society, 1792), p. 152.

Fig. 3. *Portrait of Ninigret II, Son of Ninigret I, Chief of the Niantic Indians*, ca. 1681. Oil on canvas; L. 33", H. 30". (Museum of Art, Rhode Island School of Design.)

gansett survivors mingled with the Niantics.[13] Ninigret's portrait illustrates use of European cloth for both the mantle and the breechcloth. The headband, jewelry, moccasins, and leggings are of native manufacture.

Other helpful documentary sources are colonial records, which show evidence of official visits and exchanges between colonists and native populations. Recorded are the amounts colonists paid for Indian land. Sometimes payment to Indians was made with European textiles

[13] Simmons, "Narragansett," p. 195.

and ready-to-wear apparel. Roger Williams and Gov. John Winthrop of Massachusetts, for example, purchased Prudence Island, located just off the Rhode Island coast in Narragansett Bay, "for 20 fathom wampum, and two coats" in 1638.[14]

Accounts written by settlers who survived capture by Indians also reveal information about acquisition and use of European textiles and apparel. Mary Rowlandson made more than two dozen references to clothing production, cloth acquisition, and Indian appearance in her captivity account, including that trading cloth and two coats were part of her ransom.[15]

Few actual textiles and apparel items from seventeenth-century America have survived, and those that have are almost always of the type afforded by the gentry. Rare examples of clothing worn by early colonists in New England include Gov. John Leverett's gauntlets (gloves with extended cuffs) at the Essex Institute, Penelope Winslow's silk wedding shoes at Pilgrim Hall, and Richard Smith, Jr.'s, camlet cloak at the Rhode Island Historical Society (fig. 4). To our knowledge, no swatch books prepared by British agents acting for American merchants are extant from this early date, although they must have existed considering the structure of the transatlantic textile trade. Montgomery's work on textiles in America, partially based on pattern books with original swatches of cloth, includes swatch cards from the eighteenth century but not the seventeenth century.[16] A limited number of portraits and broadsides of colonists provide visual evidence.

Native American graves of the seventeenth century are among the few sites where European-made textiles of such early manufacture intended for ordinary use might be found in the United States; therefore, these textiles have much to tell us. These small fragments, after nearly three hundred years of burial in wet soil, provide tangible evidence of international textile trade, physical properties of textiles traded to New England Indians, and use of European cloth in Indian mortuary practice.

---

[14]Christina B. Johannsen, "European Trade Goods and Wampanoag Culture in the Seventeenth Century," in Gibson, *Burr's Hill*, p. 31; Elisha R. Potter, *The Early History of Narragansett*, vol. 3 (Providence: Marshall, Brown, 1835), p. 29.

[15]Mary Rowlandson, "The Sovereignty and Goodness of God," in Alden T. Vaughan and Edward W. Clark, eds., *Puritans among the Indians* (Cambridge: Harvard University Press, Belknap Press, 1981), pp. 31–75.

[16]Montgomery, *Textiles in America*.

Fig. 4. Camlet cloak worn by Richard Smith, Jr. (1630–92), of Cocumscussoc, R.I. L. 44 ½", W. 48". (Rhode Island Historical Society.)

Cloth was an important trade commodity during the early modern period. As popular consumerism arose in the later 1600s, the range and diversity of textile products increased. The types of fibers and fabrics found in New England Indian cemeteries reflect the complexities of the textile marketplace.

Many countries were involved in the expanding world of textile production and consumption in the second half of the seventeenth century. Fabrics made from short staple wool were manufactured in several European countries where textile industries were well established, especially England and Holland. The silk industry was still centered in the Mediterranean, particularly Italy, although drawloom silk weaving had begun in Lyons, France, in the sixteenth century. Germany, the Low Countries, and the Baltics excelled at linen production. India was the source for cotton fabrics.[17]

Often fibers that originated in one country were exported to another country for manufacture into cloth, then exported again to destinations throughout the known world. One example of this phenomenon is "Spanish cloth." Spain, the only seventeenth-century source for the fine long-staple wool from the merino breed of sheep, sold the wool fiber on European markets from which Spanish cloth and other fine wools were made. Spanish cloth was a west-of-England specialty in the seventeenth and eighteenth centuries. It was imported into Boston as early as 1650.[18]

England dominated the woolen cloth industry in the seventeenth century. Woolen manufacture extended throughout the realm with sections of the country specializing in specific types of cloth for different end uses. England did not yet have big textile factories, a development of the industrial revolution in the second half of the eighteenth century. In the seventeenth century the various woolen textile processes of shearing, spinning, weaving, and finishing were carried out by specialists in a well-organized industry. Some of the processes, such as spinning and weaving, were cottage industries, while others, like fulling and dyeing, required special facilities termed "mills" or "manufactories." Finished textiles were collected by middlemen and sold throughout the world. Historian Eric Kerridge estimated that a third of the textiles produced in England at this time were exported. By the end of the seventeenth century, textiles made up four-fifths of the country's total exports.[19]

England's main rivals in the wool industry were Germany, France, and Holland. English wool had been exported to the continent for centuries, particularly to medieval Flanders, where it was manufactured into cloth superior to that woven in the British Isles. English weaving

---

[17] Eric Kerridge, *Textile Manufactures in Early Modern England* (Manchester, Eng.: Manchester University Press, 1985), pp. 1–4, 214–25; Kax Wilson, *A History of Textiles* (Boulder, Colo.: Westview Press, 1979), p. 207.

[18] Montgomery, *Textiles in America*, p. 350; Baumgarten, *Textile Trade in Boston*, p. 250.

[19] Kerridge, *Textile Manufactures*, p. 220.

and finishing expertise had increased by 1600, and new varieties of wool fabrics were developed for consumption both in and out of England, including the "new draperies" made with Spanish merino wool. Lancashire and Norwich specialized in these fabrics, which were softer, lighter, and more pliable than the older, stiffer woolens, making them suitable for wear in warm weather.[20]

In the 1500s the Portuguese initiated the sea trade that brought large quantities of all-cotton fabrics to Europe from India. After the founding of the Dutch and English East India companies around 1600, exotic printed cotton cloths and utilitarian cotton fabrics became widely available in Europe. European merchants also sent such fabrics to America. Between 1650 and 1699, Boston merchants imported calicoes variously described as "flowered," "glazed," "painted," "printed," or "speckled." Although cotton weaving existed in medieval Europe, the resultant fabric, known as "fustian," had a linen warp and a cotton weft. Only in India were weavers successful at making fabrics with cotton in both warp and weft direction. All-cotton fabrics were made in England starting in the eighteenth century as an important new product of the industrial revolution.[21]

The American colonies represented a vital market for the European textile industry, particularly for English cloth merchants who recognized the potential profits in exporting finished cloth to a vast land that had no organized textile industry. New England imported almost all its textiles from abroad despite legislative incentives by colonial governments for colonists to raise sheep, grow flax, spin yarn, and weave cloth. Both piece goods and ready-to-wear clothing arrived in New England harbors aboard English ships and then were transported to inland settlements via middlemen. Dutch ships also plied the coast along Long Island Sound, ready to trade liquor, firearms, hardware, and cloth to colonists and Indians alike. The French were more active in northern New England, although evidence also exists for their trading presence in southern New England.[22]

---

[20] Wilson, *History of Textiles*, pp. 197–98.

[21] Baumgarten, *Textile Trade in Boston*, p. 249; Wilson, *History of Textiles*, pp. 18–19.

[22] Bernard Bailyn, *The New England Merchants in the Seventeenth Century* (Cambridge: Harvard University Press, 1955), pp. 58–61, 71–72; Simmons, *Cautantowwit's House*, p. 40.

The Native American market was important to the textile industry as cloth was a principal item of exchange in the fur trade. Beaver pelts were traded for European-made goods long before the Pilgrims landed in 1620. Soon after settlement, entrepreneurs established trading posts where Indians exchanged furs, corn, and venison for European goods, and subtraders obtained items to trade among the Indians in more remote regions. The fur trade was so successful in southern New England that the fur-bearing animal population was nearly depleted by the 1660s. This necessitated expansion of Indian trade networks, and Indian middlemen traveled farther inland to acquire furs to exchange for European products.[23]

Typical of goods exchanged with Indians were ready-made coats, stockings, caps, and coarse woolen cloth. The stockings traded to Indians in the seventeenth century were probably knitted from wool or cotton and shaped to cover the leg to mid thigh. The caps resembled twentieth-century wool stocking caps; such caps were sometimes called Monmouth caps after their place of manufacture in England. The word *coat* had several meanings in the seventeenth century but most often refers to a tailored upper-body garment. Until 1660 *coat* referred to a close-fitting jacket or jerkin with sleeves, known to costume historians as a *doublet*. Length varied from waist to hip. It buttoned or tied in the front. Gradually after 1666 the doublet was replaced by the coat, a sleeved outer garment fitted at the shoulders and worn loosely to just below the knees; such coats were fastened down the front with a single row of buttons, points (ties), or hooks and eyes.[24]

The desirability of coats by Native Americans is especially interesting in light of some contemporary observations about Indian adaptability to tailored English clothing. Roger Williams observed, "while they [the Narragansetts] are among the *English* they keep on the *English* apparell, but pull of all, as soone as they come againe into their owne Houses, and Company." Only the Christian Indians of New England

---

[23] Bailyn, *New England Merchants*, pp. 58–61.

[24] For costume terminology, see Patricia Trautman, "Dress in Seventeenth-Century Cambridge, Massachusetts: An Inventory-Based Reconstruction," in Peter Benes, ed., *Early American Probate Inventories* (Boston: Boston University Press, 1989), pp. 56–57, 70–71. In ethnohistorical accounts, the term *coat* is used more broadly (that is, a cape made of native materials such as skin, fur, or feathers); see Williams, *Key into the Language*, p. 119.

wore coats daily to distinguish themselves from non-Christian Indians by their English-style clothes. Coats, it would seem, were desirable as status items to wear when conducting official business with the English and to give away to others. Peter Thomas, in his research on the Indian trade in the Connecticut River valley, was puzzled by Pynchon's heavy trade in wool coats and cloth compared to the limited mention of European-style cloth and clothing in contemporary English accounts of Indian appearance. He postulated that the purchase of trade cloth by Indians was a form of social prestige. Acquisition of European cloth by an Indian might have signified status as a good hunter and adept trader.[25]

Thomas recognized the monetary value of cloth to the Indian trade when he observed that in the Pynchon merchant records "the consumption of cloth goods was more than twenty-three times that of glass, iron, brass or copper articles combined." Cloth was Pynchon's most successful commodity after wampum. Pynchon's records indicate that from 1652 to 1663 he provided known fur traders with more than thirty different varieties of cloth, including flannel, calico, and trading cloth; eight types of trims, such as gimp lace, silk lace, and tape; and nine different kinds of ready-to-wear clothing items, including caps, coats, stockings, and petticoats.[26]

The actual process of trading with Indians is revealed in the ethnohistorical accounts. William Wood, writing in 1635, stated: "If their fancie drive them to trade, they choose rather a good coarse blanket, through which they cannot see, interposing it between the sun and them; or a piece of broad cloth, which they use for a double end, making it a coat by day, and a covering by night." Williams included a chapter entitled "Of Buying and Selling" in A Key into the Language of America based on his experience in trading with the Narragansetts. He listed separate Narragansett words for different types and colors of cloth, such as Koppócki for thick cloth, Etouwawâyi, meaning "Wollie on both sides," and Mishquinuit for red cloth. Williams's chapter re-

---

[25] Williams, Key into the Language, p. 121; Thomas, "In the Maelstrom of Change," pp. 184, 309.

[26] Peter A. Thomas, "Cultural Change on the Southern New England Frontier, 1630–1665," in Fitzhugh, Cultures in Contact, p. 146; Thomas, "In the Maelstrom of Change," pp. 457–70.

vealed additional information about the process of selling to the Indian consumer. The condition of the cloth (for example, "It is torne," "It is Old," and "There is no Wool on it") was part of the negotiations. Fabric was measured from the bolt or longer piece in "spans," then "torn off." Payment could be made in furs ("I will pay you Beaver") or in the shell currency known as wampum ("I will give you Money").[27]

These accounts reveal that the Indians recognized variations in cloth types and demanded those that best suited their desires. Trading cloth, the thick woolen variety described by Williams, closely approximated traditional skin garments when used in one- or two-yard lengths; therefore, it was more readily incorporated into everyday wear than fine cloth or tailored coats. Williams observed, "They all generally prize a Mantle of *English* or *Dutch* Cloth before their owne wearing of Skins and Furres, because they are warme enough and Lighter."[28]

By 1677 some English towns had become known for the manufacture of textiles made expressly for the Indian trade. According to Robert Plot's account of production in the town of Witney in Oxfordshire, woolen fabrics called "Duffields" (also spelled duffel, duffil, or duffle), "shags," or "trucking-cloth" were made to please "the Indians of Virginia and New England, with whom the Merchants truck them for Bever, and other Furrs of several Beasts, &c." A woolen cloth called "stroud," woven and dyed on the River Stroud in Gloucestershire, also was popular among North American Indians.[29]

Identifying the country of origin is almost impossible for the fragments found at the RI-1000 and Long Pond sites. As noted earlier, English, French, and Dutch middlemen all traded with the Indians. English traders did not sell only English cloth, nor the Dutch trade only fabrics made in Holland. John Pynchon stocked a wide variety of European textiles at the Springfield trading post, including a fabric he listed as "Dutch cloth." To complicate matters further, textiles such as the aforementioned "Duffields" sometimes were woven in England but

---

[27] Wood, *New England's Prospect*, p. 84; Williams, *Key into the Language*, pp. 160, 161, 163–65.

[28] Williams, *Key into the Language*, p. 160.

[29] Robert Plot, *The Natural History of Oxfordshire: Being an Essay toward the Natural History of England* (Oxford: Printed at the theatre, 1677); Montgomery, *Textiles in America*, pp. 228, 353.

dyed and finished in Holland.[30] Analysis of the fibers themselves is not definitive in determining a fabric's country of origin since both English short wools and Spanish merino wools were available to weavers throughout Europe.

Some of these fragments could have been colonial-manufactured fabrics retraded to Native Americans, since early settlers offered merchants woolen and linen textiles of their own manufacture in exchange for other commodities. This is unlikely, however, since seventeenth-century textile production in New England was so meager that it could not begin to satisfy the colonists' textile needs. Bernard Bailyn, in his study of New England merchants of the seventeenth century, estimated that one Boston merchant's shipload in 1650 contained more than all the cloth woven by the most productive weaver in Rowley, Massachusetts, between 1673 and 1682. Spinning and weaving were only the "occasional occupation[s] of a population of farmers and petty artisans who bought almost all their textiles from the port town importers or from middlemen."[31]

The RI-1000 site was located only a few miles from the trading post founded by Williams in Wickford, Rhode Island, in 1636. The next year Richard Smith set up a rival trading post, finally buying out Williams's interest in 1651. Williams mentioned English and Dutch cloth in association with the Narragansetts; this might be interpreted to mean that Williams stocked English and Dutch cloth at this trading post.[32] The Narragansetts also might have obtained their cloth from the Dutch and French traders who plied the Rhode Island coast to trade with the Indians until midcentury. The numerous European textile fragments, which survived due to well-drained sandy soil and proximity to metal objects, indicate that the Narragansetts made use of a variety of European textiles.

The Long Pond site provides evidence that the Mashantucket Pequots also made use of a variety of European-made cloth similar to the types found in RI-1000. However, the manner in which these

---

[30] Thomas, "In the Maelstrom of Change," p. 463; Montgomery, *Textiles in America*, p. 228.

[31] Bailyn, *New England Merchants*, p. 74.

[32] Bailyn, *New England Merchants*, pp. 58–59; Williams, *Key into the Language*, p. 160.

textiles were acquired is unclear since no trading post existed in the vicinity. The Mashantucket Pequots were living on a reservation established for them in 1667. Settled colonial towns, such as Norwich, Mystic, and Stonington, were within ten miles of the reservation. Since trading skins and furs for textiles was no longer feasible due to overtrapping, the Mashantucket Pequots might have sold fruit from the reservation's orchards, rented land to colonial farmers, or perhaps worked as day laborers for colonists.[33]

Most of the European textiles present in the burials were typical of export fabrics manufactured in England during the period 1650–1720. Studying the surviving fragments allows us to place these textiles into broad classes of fabric types that confirm, fine-tune, and correct the information in the documentary sources. These textile fragments assist historians in reconstructing a more inclusive view of how Native Americans in southern New England incorporated European-made goods into their culture than do documents alone.

By far the largest number of surviving fabrics in both cemeteries were made from wool fibers. This is consistent with the archaeological evidence for textiles from other sites in southern New England (table 1). Numerous wool fragments survived at four of the five sites, while only a few fragments of linen, cotton, or silk were found. One explanation for this occurrence is that protein fibers, like wool and silk, have been preserved better than cellulosic fibers, such as linen or cotton, in acidic New England soil. Another explanation is that the Indians acquired and used more wool fabrics than linen, cotton, or silk fabrics. The presence of native textiles made from cellulosic materials in each of the five sites contradicts the notion that only protein fibers can survive in acidic soil and supports the explanation that wool usage was more prevalent among Native Americans, as does the frequent mention of wool fabrics in the ethnohistoric accounts.

Wool in seventeenth-century northern Europe was from primitive breeds of sheep that yielded hairy fleeces containing stiff bristlelike fibers called kemp, along with finer fibers. Most of the wool fragments

---

[33] Neal Salisbury, "Indians and Colonists after the Pequot Wars," and Kevin A. McBride "Archaeology of the Mashantucket Pequots," in Laurence M. Hauptman and James D. Wherry, eds., *The Pequots in Southern New England* (Norman: University of Oklahoma Press, 1990), pp. 90, 106–7.

Table 1. Archaeological Evidence for Textiles, Intersite Comparison

Cemetery	European Textiles				Native textiles
	Wool	Cotton	Linen	Silk/Metal	
West Ferry 1620–60	–	–	–	×	×
Whitford mid 1650s	×	–	–	–	×
RI-1000 1650–70	×	×	–	–	×
Burr's Hill 1650–75	×	–	×	×	×
Long Pond 1670–1720	×	–	–	–	×

Sources: William Scranton Simmons, *Cautantowwit's House* (Providence: Brown University Press, 1970), pp. 45–46, 81, 87, 97, 101, 110; William A. Turnbaugh to Linda Welters, April 2, 1985; Susan G. Gibson, ed., *Burr's Hill: A Seventeenth-Century Wampanoag Burial Ground in Warren, Rhode Island* (Providence: Brown University and Haffenreffer Museum of Anthropology, 1980), pp. 140–44, 150–56.

at both New England sites exhibited characteristics of hairy fleeces. Even fabrics made of fine wool fibers had coarse fibers mixed in. The presence of these hairy wools in the cemeteries reveals that the goods traded to the Indians were typical of the coarser woolens of the time. According to Eric Kerridge, English manufacturers sometimes used low-quality noils, flocks, and tail wools for coarse cloths such as baize, bearskin, blankets, duffels, and kersey. Plot, in his 1677 description of the woolen manufacture at Witney, wrote that "duffields" were made from "ordinary and middle wool" mixed with "the coarser Locks of Fleece-wool."[34]

Through microscopic analysis, wool fibers can be characterized by the presence and size of a central canal (medulla), scales on the outer surface, and fiber diameter. The Pequot wool fibers had large medullas, unlike merino and merino cross-bred wools that provided fiber for fine wool fabrics. A few breeds extant today, such as the Scottish black-face sheep, still have fibers with large medullas like the

[34]Kerridge, *Textile Manufactures*, pp. 5, 17, 23, 106, 147; Plot, *Natural History of Oxfordshire*; Montgomery, *Textiles in America*, p. 375.

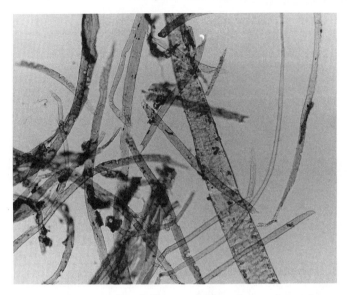

Fig. 5. Kemp mixed with fine wool fibers from a hairy fleece, Long Pond cemetery, Ledyard, Conn., cat. no. 8-2-18. (Photo, Margaret Ordoñez.)

Pequot fibers. Scale patterns vary as the diameter of the fiber varies so that fibers can be classified as fine, coarse, outercoat, and kemp. Unfortunately, most of the scales on the Pequot wool fibers had been eaten away by soil microbes and acid. Some typical patches of scales on kemp fibers remained, and with the large diameters, the scales confirmed that kemps were present in the wool. Some coarser fibers with up to eighty micron diameters also were present, but most fibers were fine (fig. 5).

Fiber diameters of seventeenth-century archaeological wool fibers have been used to determine the type of fleece from which fabrics were made, but breed of sheep is not identifiable because several breeds produce the same type of fleece. The fleece of seventeenth-century sheep typically consisted of a mixture of different fiber diameters rather than a uniform fiber diameter. The deciding factor in determining fleece type from fiber diameters is the upper limit of the range. Assuming that fibers from fabrics were representative of a specific type of

Table 2. Fiber Diameters of Early Swedish Wools

Fleece type	Source	Overall mean (microns)	Overall fiber diameter range (microns)
Hairy	Wasa	36.7	12–114
	Goth*	41.4	14–170
Hairy medium	Viking	32.4	18–80
	Medieval	37.0	16–110
	Wasa	31.3	12–120
	Goth	39.7	14–170
Generalized medium	Viking	32.1	14–60
	Medieval	29.2	12–54
	Wasa	26.9	10–64
Medium	Wasa	33.1	12–140
Short-wool	Wasa	27.1	12–52
Fine	Viking	23.0	12–38
	Wasa	22.2	12–40

* Goth samples are from current primitive Swedish Goth breed.
Source: M. L. Ryder, "Wools from Textiles in the Wasa, a Seventeenth-Century Swedish Warship," Journal of Archaeological Science 10 (1983): 259–60.

fleece, not blended fleeces, M. L. Ryder used fiber diameter measurements from historic fabrics to characterize fleece types (table 2). Ryder's divisions were hairy, hairy medium, generalized medium, medium, short-wool, and fine fleeces. He found examples of all these types in fabrics excavated from the Wasa, a seventeenth-century Swedish warship. Ryder's divisions helped to classify the Pequot textiles, which had a skewed fiber distribution with mostly fine fibers mixed with medullated large diameter fibers (80 microns) and kemp hairs (greater than 100 microns).[35] This indicated that the fabrics in the Pequot burials were made with hairy fleeces like the coarsest Wasa textiles. Such coarse, scratchy fabrics were typical of those manufactured for the mass market in the seventeenth century.

The woven wool fabrics from the RI-1000 and Long Pond sites were of many varieties, ranging from a few fragments of fine worsteds appropriate for tailored coats or cloaks to numerous examples of coarse

[35] M. L. Ryder, "Wools from Textiles in the Wasa, a Seventeenth-Century Swedish Warship," Journal of Archaeological Science 10 (1983): 259–63.

plain and twill weaves representing the low end of England's export market. Merchants' records of the time called these latter fabrics by various names, which might have been nearly synonymous judging by contemporary descriptions. Plot's description of the products of Witney's woolen manufacture as "Duffields, so called from a Town in Brabant, where the trade of them first began . . . otherwise called shags, and by the Merchants, trucking cloth" is a case in point. Making distinctions among the so-called new draperies made from long staple wool apparently also was problematic during the seventeenth century: "A buffyn, a catalowne, and the pearl of beauty, are all one cloth; a peropus and a paragon all one; a saye and piramides all one; the same cloths bearing other names in times past."[36]

Sorting out the similarities and differences in seventeenth-century fabric names for application to these archaeological textiles is a daunting task. However, by comparing the surviving textiles to fabric names that appear in documentary sources and then to descriptions of such fabrics, some possible fabric names might be suggested for the archaeological textiles from RI-1000 and Long Pond.

Most of the woolen textiles at both RI-1000 and Long Pond were woven in a plain weave structure (fig. 6). Although yarn twist and thread count varied among fragments, Z-spun yarns and thread counts of 8 warps by 8 wefts per square centimeter were typical. According to descriptions of seventeenth-century plain weave fabrics, these fragments might have been called *broadcloth, blanket, dozens, flannel, pennystone, pukes,* or *trucking cloth.* Woolens were called *broadcloth* when woven on wide looms, *dozens* when sold in twelve-yard lengths, and *pennystones* when manufactured in the town of the same name in the West Riding of Yorkshire. In the seventeenth century the term *blanket* was applied to "pukes," an older name for plain weave woolens. *Trucking cloth* could be any number of woolen fabrics "trucked" or "traded" to the Indians.[37] Because of the small size of the surviving fragments in the burials, we cannot be more specific about fabric names based on physical characteristics alone.

[36] Plot, *Natural History of Oxfordshire; Oxford English Dictionary,* 2d ed., s.v. "Duffel"; Montgomery, *Textiles in America,* p. 309.

[37] Montgomery, *Textiles in America,* pp. 177–78, 224, 320; Kerridge, *Textile Manufactures,* pp. 4, 35.

Fig. 6. Plain weave woolen, Long Pond cemetery, Ledyard, Conn., cat. no. 6–2–80D. (Photo, Margaret Ordoñez.)

Only when the documentary sources are consulted does the field of possibilities narrow. William Wood mentioned the Indian preference for "blanket" and "broadcloth," which could be used as a coat by day and a bedcover by night; John Josselyn stated that the Indians purchased from the English "a sort of Cloth called trading cloth" of which they made articles of clothing; Gookin called the fabric traded to the Indians "duffils, or trucking cloth . . . made of coarse wool." Does this mean that duffel and trucking cloth were identical or that duffel was only one of many types of cloth traded to the Indians? Was the wool fabric called *shag cotton* different from duffel and trucking cloth? According to Kerridge, duffel was a 2/2 twill (weave type where each warp yarn goes over two weft yarns, then under two weft yarns in stepwise progression). Pynchon distinguished "duffields" from "trading cloth" in his account books despite the cost being the same for both fabrics (ranging from 7 shillings 6 pence to 8 shillings per yard). Thus the fundamental difference between duffel and trading cloth must have been the weave (for example, twill versus plain) since the weight was the same. Shag cotton might have been much lighter in weight as the price per yard ranged from 3 shillings to 3 shillings 10 pence per yard, about half the cost of "duffields" and "trading cloth."[38]

Between 1652 and 1663 Pynchon delivered 3,908 yards of "shag cotton" and 2,915 yards of "trading cloth" to his subtraders, making these two fabrics his best sellers. The twill "Duffields" was a weak third, with only 1,191 yards sold.[39] Both RI-1000 and Long Pond yielded many more fragments of plain weave textiles of various weights than twills.

Some plain weave woolen textiles from RI-1000 and Long Pond displayed matted, fuzzy, or heavily napped surfaces. Although regular woolens generally were fulled after weaving, these fabrics had a more pronounced finish. The Narragansetts identified such fabrics as "Wollie on both sides" as opposed to those "Bare without Wool." The English might have called these fabrics any number of names including *baize* (also termed *bays, beys, bayes, baies, bease,* or *bayz*), *bearskin, cotton, frieze,* or *shag.* These fabrics were woven with loosely spun weft yarns so that the wool fibers could be brushed to achieve different surface textures. The terms *shag* or *napped* implied a cloth having a long nap on one or both sides. When the fibers were raised in small curls, the process was called "frizzing" or "cottoning," and the product was "frieze" or "cotton." In seventeenth-century England, the term *cotton* meant a napped woolen cloth rather than a fabric made from cotton fiber.[40]

Several lighter-weight plain weave wool fragments from RI-1000 had large diameter wefts with a shaggy surface (fig. 7). One fragment even displayed curly tufts on the surface. Might these fragments be baize, napped cotton, frieze, or shag cotton, so popular with Pynchon's customers? Such fabrics were heavy and warm, well suited to use in winter gowns and outer coats among the English. Kerridge describes baize as a plain weave wool fabric with a weft about four times as large as the warp. New types of baize were continually invented.

[38]Wood, *New England's Prospect,* p. 84; Lindholdt, *John Josselyn,* p. 93; Gookin, *Historical Collections,* p. 17; Kerridge, *Textile Manufactures,* p. 35; Thomas, "In the Maelstrom of Change," p. 461.

[39]Thomas, "In the Maelstrom of Change," p. 459.

[40]Williams, *Key into the Language,* p. 160; *Oxford English Dictionary,* 2d ed., s.v. "Baize"; Montgomery, *Textiles in America,* pp. 160, 206, 243, 346; Kerridge, *Textile Manufactures,* pp. 18–19, 29.

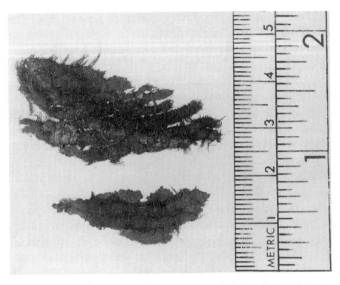

Fig. 7. Wool with large wefts and a napped surface, possibly shag baize or shag cotton, RI-1000, N. Kingstown, R.I., cat. no. 36–10. (Photo, Linda Welters.)

Examples include *shag baize*, a term known in 1634, and *burying baize*, a winding cloth of the cheapest and worst wools manufactured in response to an English statute requiring that the dead be buried in woolen cloth. Pynchon's records indicate that he sold "beys" to subtraders.[41]

The few woolen twills that appeared in the burials could have been duffel, kersey, serge, flannel, or blanket. Long Pond yielded two heavy green twills, which could very well be duffel. RI-1000 contained only one similar fabric. Curiously, duffel is mentioned often in ethnohistorical accounts in association with southern New England's Indians but turns up infrequently in these two sites. The Pynchon records show that during the period 1652–63 "duffields" represented just fifteen

---

[41] Kerridge, *Textile Manufactures*, pp. 10–11, 19, 106; Thomas, "In the Maelstrom of Change," p. 457.

percent of the total sales of his three best-selling fabrics. He sold only minor amounts of other twill fabrics identified in the ledgers as kersey, serge, flannel, and blanketing.[42]

Kersey often is mentioned in relationship to the Indian trade. True kersey, according to Kerridge, was a warp-backed twill woven on a four-harness loom with a kersey sley. Heavy warp yarns in a 2/2 twill alternated with thinner warp yarns in a 1/3 twill, yielding a cloth with a highly prominent twill line.[43] Later a variety of twill woven cloths were known by the name *kersey*. If Kerridge's description of true kersey is applied to the twill woven textiles from RI-1000 and Long Pond, no textiles from these burials were identified as kerseys.

The term *blanket* is problematic. Some archaeologists have lumped all coarse woolen fabrics under the name *blanket*, whereas textile historians are more specific about the characteristics of seventeenth-century blankets made for the Indian market. Either plain or twill woven, the ends of blankets usually were striped. A 1714 letter from James Logan of Pennsylvania to Edward Hackett specified the exact colors and stripes preferred by the Indians: "blankets that are white like other blankets," only near the ends "2 red and 2 blue or black" stripes.[44] If we adhere to this description, only the Burr's Hill striped fragments might be called true blankets. No striped blankets were found at either RI-1000 or Long Pond.

Both sites contained examples of fine wools in weaves with much higher thread counts than the fragments of trucking cloth, shag, or duffel. Several fragments of a fine twill weave were recovered from the grave of an adult male in the RI-1000 site (fig. 8). A cast of an even finer plain weave cloth from Long Pond had a thread count of 34 warps by 28 wefts per square centimeter (fig. 9). The wool fabric was coated with ferrous oxide before the fibers disintegrated creating the textile cast. These archaeological fragments approximate the high-quality worsted fabrics in the cloak of Richard Smith, Jr., at the Rhode Island Historical Society (see fig. 4). RI-1000's worsted twill might be prunella, say, stammel, or stammet. The Long Pond textile cast could be camlet or any other of the new draperies. Pynchon's records show that

[42] Thomas, "In the Maelstrom of Change," pp. 457, 459, 461.

[43] Dillon, "Trade Fabrics," p. 101; Kerridge, *Textile Manufactures*, p. 5.

[44] Montgomery, *Textiles in America*, p. 170.

Fig. 8. Fine, worsted wool twill, RI-1000, N. Kingstown, R.I., cat. no. 50–8. (Photo, Linda Welters.)

he sold small amounts of some new draperies fabrics, namely "sey," tammy, stammels, stuff, and "pagon" (paragon).[45]

The RI-1000 wool fabrics exhibited a color range of red, orange, brown, blue, and black. Williams stated that the Narragansetts preferred "sad" colors "without any whitish haires."[46] The term *sad* meant dull colors (for example, russet red) rather than dark colors (for example, black). Red and green predominated in the Long Pond samples. In burial 19, a thin red wool fabric was layered next to a heavy green twill, perhaps red shag cotton and green duffel.

Documentary evidence shows a preference for red and blue in some Indian markets. Plot stated that the Witney woolens were dyed "red or blue, which are the colours that best please the Indians of Virginia and New England." Thomas Bannister of Boston wrote to his

[45] Montgomery, *Textiles in America*, p. 351; Kerridge, *Textile Manufactures*, p. 56; Thomas, "In the Maelstrom of Change," p. 457.
[46] Williams, *Key into the Language*, p. 160.

Fig. 9. Iron cast of a fine, plain weave, worsted wool textile, possibly camlet, Long Pond cemetery, Ledyard, Conn., cat. no. 18–2-72. (Photo, Margaret Ordoñez.)

London factors in 1704 inquiring about bays of "a sort fit for the Indian trade," but if sent "they must be all blews. . . . Next the blews the red sells best and next the Red the purple." Later he added, "please leave out the purple. Those no body Chuses to buy." Gookin also mentioned the popularity of the colors blue, red, and purple, followed by white.[47] The presence of green textiles in the Long Pond cemetery is somewhat surprising since the ethnohistorical accounts emphasize a preference for blue and red.

Thomas, in his analysis of Pynchon's account books, observed that the heavier woolens such as trading cloth and duffields were primarily blue, while the lighter fabrics like shag cotton were usually red. Stroud cloths, dyed red or blue in the piece, also were mentioned in relation to the Indian trade. Writers regularly commented on the

[47] Montgomery, *Textiles in America*, pp. 228, 159; Gookin, *Historical Collections*, p. 17.

Fig. 10. Plain weave cotton, probably calico, RI-1000, N. Kingstown, R.I., cat. no. 82–148. (Photo, Linda Welters.)

superiority of stroud cloths, colored scarlet with cochineal dyed on a tin mordant. Apparently some English duffels were poorly dyed for a while but were improved when merchants complained that they were losing credibility with their Indian customers.[48] Some fragments of red-dyed cloth from these burial sites appear to have been dyed in the piece with poor dye penetration.

Three cotton fragments survived in the RI-1000 site (fig. 10). As yet few other cotton fragments have been recovered from New England archaeological sites. These fragments, neither dyed nor printed, might be calico, which was imported to New England at this time according to merchants' records. Most cotton trade goods originated in India, since England was not yet producing cotton fabrics for

[48] Thomas, "In the Maelstrom of Change," p. 304; Montgomery, *Textiles in America*, p. 353; Trent, "Blanket Fragment," p. 74.

export.[49] Also, the fine quality of the yarn and fabric points to an Asian origin.

Several fragments from the Long Pond site were knitted structures. Since knits were not sold by the yard in the seventeenth century, we must assume that the Pequot Indians acquired knitted apparel items, most likely stockings or caps, from the colonists. Records show that large numbers of knitted caps and stockings were imported to New England throughout the seventeenth century. Pynchon delivered a total of 87 caps and 198 pairs of stockings to his subtraders from 1652 to 1663. Perhaps these caps were the common Monmouth caps worn by the colonists throughout the seventeenth and eighteenth centuries. Between 1662 and 1663, 43,428 Monmouth caps were exported to the colonies from London.[50] Descriptions of the woolen yarns and the stitch gauge of extant Monmouth caps match the small fragments found at Long Pond. One knitted fragment in burial 19 was located under the head at the back of the cranium. Because there were three layers of woven woolen textiles between the cranium and the knit fragment, we know that if this fragment was a cap, it was not placed on the body's head. Rather, the knitted textile could have been used as a pillow. This illustrates that Native Americans did not necessarily use European trade goods in the manner intended by manufacturers or traders. Such evidence is not available in the documentary records, offering refinements to knowledge accessible only from the archaeological record.

Microscopic examination of many of the wool fabrics in the Long Pond site revealed the presence of insects, which an entomologist identified as fly maggots. They were most abundant on wool located near the heads of the skeletal remains. The ethnohistoric accounts do not provide detailed information on how long a body was displayed before burial. Williams wrote of wrapping the dead in "winding sheets," meaning either native-made mats or woven cloth like that located between the cranium and the knit cap in Long Pond's burial 19, but he did not specify whether this was done before or after "they lay the dead

[49] Baumgarten, "Textile Trade," p. 249; Thomas, "In the Maelstrom of Change," p. 457; Montgomery, *Textiles in America*, p. 185; Kerridge, *Textile Manufactures*, p. 125.

[50] Thomas, "In the Maelstrom of Change," p. 458; Kirstie Buckland, "The Monmouth Cap," *Costume* 13 (1979): 33.

by the Grave's mouth, and then all sit downe and lament." James Axtell described a basic pattern for aboriginal funeral customs in northeastern North America in which the corpse was publicly displayed for mourning and lamentation then buried within a certain number of days.[51] The presence of fly maggots on wool fabrics facing toward the body at the Long Pond site provides evidence for the laying out of the deceased before wrapping it in cloth for interment.

From the fragments we also can gain information about how Indians used European textiles in burials. Although the fragments were very small, the location within the graves tells us that coarse textiles were used in conjunction with mats and wooden strips to inter the body. In RI-1000, sometimes animal skins were present. Both sites yielded numerous examples of woolen textiles adhering to the remains of wood or native-made mats.

The general practice among late-prehistoric Woodland Indians in northeastern North America, according to Axtell, was to prepare the corpse for burial "by dressing him in his finest clothing, painting his face to advantage, laying him in a flexed position, knees drawn to the chest, and wrapping him in a great fur robe." The body was then placed in an oval pit lined with fur, bark, or woven mats. Favorite possessions of the deceased were sometimes thrown in. The grave was filled only after the body had been covered with branches, bark, or mats to prevent dirt from touching it. Other sources mention that the corpse was sewn into mats. William Scranton Simmons found evidence at the West Ferry site for use of mats to line graves, to wrap the body, and to bundle grave goods.[52]

After the Indians began exchanging furs for woven cloth and other trade goods, European textiles made their way into the burials as a replacement for furs. By the middle of the seventeenth century, the southern New England area had been overtrapped, reducing the number of skins available for both native clothing and burials. Woolen cloth, especially blanketing, was a likely substitute for the older fur or

---

[51]The entomologist is Kirwin E. Hylund, professor of zoology, University of Rhode Island; Williams, *Key into the Language*, p. 203; James Axtell, *The European and the Indian* (New York: Oxford University Press, 1981), p. 113.

[52]Axtell, *European and the Indian*, p. 113; Simmons, *Cautantowwit's House*, pp. 56, 63, 102, 134, 146.

mat shrouds. How the body was wrapped in the textiles is unknown. Williams translated the Narragansett word *Wesquáubenan* as "To wrap up, in winding mats or coats, as we say, winding sheets."[53] In RI-1000, two coarse woolen fragments show regular holes spaced one to two centimeters apart, which possibly were stitch marks. Stitching spaced this far apart supports the conclusion that these two fragments were parts of shrouds rather than clothing.

Textiles of various types were found adhering to pots, spoons, and other metal artifacts, indicating that they might have been used to wrap grave goods. G. Mourt observed that when the Pilgrims disturbed an Indian-style grave in 1620, they found a knife, a packneedle, and two or three iron items "bound up in a sailor's canvas cassock, and a pair of cloth breeches."[54] Field notes for RI-1000 reported that textiles appeared to be covering certain objects like metal boxes, mirrors, and rings.

European textiles also were used as part of medicine bundles. A small medicine bag of homespun cloth with strands of human hair attached was recovered from a Montauk site at Easthampton, Long Island. This site was contemporary to the Long Pond site.[55] At Long Pond, the fine wool textile illustrated in figure 9 was wrapped around a bear claw and a folded page from an English Bible. An iron ladle was then placed over the bundle, causing the fabric to transform into a textile cast. After the layer of textile was pulled away, fragmentary lines of print from the page (italicized below) were visible (fig. 11). This was just enough for consultant Hugh Amory to identify the text as the first six lines of Psalm 98.

> O Sing unto the LORD a n*ew song*,
> for he hath done marvell*ous things*:
> his right hand, and his holy *arm hath*
> gotten him the victorie.
> 2 The LORD hath made k*nown his sal-*
> vation; his righteousnesse hath *he openly*
> shewed in the sight of the heathen.
> 3 He hath remembred his mercie and

[53] Williams, *Key into the Language*, p. 203.
[54] Mourt, *Journal of the Pilgrims*, p. 27.
[55] Foster H. Saville, *A Montauk Cemetery at Easthampton, Long Island* (New York: Museum of the American Indian, 1920), p. 95.

Fig. 11. Page fragment from an English Bible covered with textile illustrated in fig. 9, Long Pond cemetery, Ledyard, Conn., cat. no. 18–2-72. (Photo, Linda Welters.)

his truth toward the house of Israel; all
the ends of the earth have seen the salvation of our God.
4 Make a joyfull noise unto the LORD,
all the earth; make a loud noise, and re-
joyce, and sing praise.
5 Sing unto the LORD with the harp;
with the harp, and the voice of a psalme.
6 With trumpers and sound of cornet;
make a joyfull noise before the LORD,
the King.
7 Let the sea roar, and the fulnesse there-
of; the world, & they that dwell therein.
8 Let the clouds clap their hands; let
the hills be joyfull together.
9 Before the LORD; for he cometh to
judge the earth; with righteousnesse shall
he judge the world, and the people with
equity.

Amory has determined that the page was taken from a duodecimo "London" edition, probably printed in Amsterdam in 1680 for English consumption. Such piratical editions were once common in the colonies, but only a single copy of this one seems to survive today, in the Pennsylvania State University Library. The date on the general title page was probably printed "1680," but an earlier owner has altered it with ink and erasures to read "1669," in conformity with the date on the title page. The Bible's characteristic two-column format, rarely used for printing other seventeenth-century texts, ensured that Indians could readily identify it, even though they could not read it. Such small-format Bibles were showpieces rather than well-read books because of the minuscule type.[56]

This Bible was the King James version (1611), whose title page informed the faithful that it was: "Newly translated out of the Originail Greek: and with the former translations diligently compared and verified by his Majesties Speciall Commandement." The King James translation used the terms *heathen* and *pagan* to denote those people who were Gentiles (that is, not part of God's chosen family at birth). The earlier Greeks septuagint version uses the term *ethnoi* in Psalm 98, translated as "nations" instead of "heathens."[57] This division of the world's peoples into categories suggesting religious differences instead of territorial differences, as expressed in the new King James Bible, helped to define how the English viewed their presence among the Indians in the New World.

How did a page from a small-format English Bible find its way into a Pequot grave? Although the Bible had been translated into Algonkian in 1661 by John Eliot, a missionary to the Indians in the Massachusetts colony, English Bibles were used by missionaries also. In the 1640s Thomas Mayhew, Jr., began preaching among the Indians on Martha's Vineyard, eventually converting them to Christianity. Mayhew was offered the post of missionary to the Pequot, Connecticut, settlement in 1646, and again in 1648, where he was promised the

[56] Hugh Amory, senior rare book cataloguer, Houghton Library, Harvard University to Linda Welters, September 2, 1991, January 27, 1992, and September 8, 1992; Hugh Amory, "The Trout and the Milk: An Essay in Ethnobibliography" (Paper delivered at Houghton Library, Cambridge, December 12, 1991).

[57] Trent C. Butler, ed., *Holman Bible Dictionary* (Nashville: Holman Bible Publishers, 1991), p. 542, Ps 98, 2.

opportunity of "preaching to many more Indians than are at martins viney'd."[58] Although Mayhew turned down the offer, the presence of the English Bible fragment in the Pequot grave indicates that some missionary was at work among the Pequots after the massacre of 1637.

Psalm 98, with its message of the English God's righteousness in judging all peoples of the world with equity, might have been read to the Pequots in an attempt to convert them to Christianity. Perhaps the corner of the page was folded down, or marked somehow, before the Bible was closed and left with the tribe. Probably the eleven-year-old child with whom Psalm 98 was buried could not read it. However, some tribal member understood enough of its meaning to tear the page out of the Bible (an English person would never have mutilated a Bible), fold it up with a bear claw, cover it with the finest cloth available, and bury it with the well-loved child.

The presence of this particular piece of paper in a Pequot burial indicates the potency that Indians assigned to the printed word during the second half of the seventeenth century. The first Indian reaction to the printed Bible was recorded by Thomas Harriot in 1585 among the natives of North Carolina. They could not perceive that the doctrine contained in the book was more important than the book itself, and they reacted by touching, embracing, and kissing the Bible, holding it to their breasts and heads, and stroking their bodies with it. Similar Indian encounters with European printed books occurred in New England in the seventeenth century. The Indians admired the technology of thin paper, uniform typeface, illustrations, and lettered leather bindings. The real power of print, however, lay in its ability to help the English learn the mind of someone far away, which "duplicated a spiritual feat that only the greatest shamans could perform."[59] The Mashantucket Pequots believed in the power of Psalm 98, thus burying it in material form as a type of talisman in a conscious appropriation of the colonists' most powerful "medicine."

Some European textiles in these burials might have been "English clothes" as indicated by the location of layered or seamed fragments

---

[58] Arthur R. Railton, "The Indians and the English on Martha's Vineyard," *Dukes County Intelligencer* 32, no. 2 (November 1990): 44.

[59] James Axtell, *After Columbus* (New York: Oxford University Press, 1988), pp. 89–93.

next to skeletal remains. The ethnohistoric accounts contain references to Indian acquisition of many different articles of European-style clothing as well as complete suits of clothes.[60] Although coats, particularly red and blue ones, are mentioned frequently in the historical records as gifts or exchanges with Native Americans, no conclusive evidence exists for coats in either of these archaeological sites.

At least one archaeologist has assigned the meaning of status-signaling to textile fragments that she mistakenly believes to be from coats. Her research, based on cemetery data from seventeenth-century New England sites rather than the artifacts themselves, divided grave goods into aboriginal goods and imported goods. For each grave, certain goods were interpreted as having high value, including all fragments of European cloth, regardless of whether the fragments were listed as blanket fragments or fine cloth. Assuming the textile fragments to be parts of European clothing, she interpreted their presence in the more elaborately furnished graves as a sign of status.[61] This interpretation is doubly flawed. First, since no archaeological evidence exists to confirm that any of the fragments were coats, they might just as well have been lengths of plain woolen cloth (shrouds or grave linings, for example). Second, the more elaborately furnished graves included metal grave goods, which preserved the textiles. Sparsely furnished graves probably included European textiles also, but without metal grave goods next to the cloth to preserve it, the fragments degraded.

What would constitute conclusive evidence of a coat for a textile historian? A wool textile in a sewn construction with a row of buttons, buttonholes located near the trunk of the body, or both would be hard to refute. Such coats have resurfaced through archaeological finds. A late seventeenth-century coat in excellent condition was found in a bog burial in Gunnister, Shetland Islands. Knitted Monmouth caps, woolen jackets, knee breeches, and stockings were recovered from the

---

[60] Linda Welters, "From Moccasins to Frock Coats and Back Again: Ethnic Identity and Native American Dress in Southern New England," in Patricia A. Cunningham and Susan Voso Lab, eds., *Dress and American Culture* (Bowling Green, Ohio: Bowling Green State University Popular Press, 1993), pp. 6–41.

[61] Elise M. Brenner, "Sociopolitical Implications of Mortuary Ritual Remains in Seventeenth-Century Native Southern New England," in Mark P. Leone and Parker B. Potter, Jr., eds., *The Recovery of Meaning: Historical Archaeology in the Eastern United States* (Washington, D.C.: Smithsonian Institution Press, 1988), pp. 172–73.

remains of individuals interred at a seventeenth-century Dutch whaling station in the Arctic. A Pawnee cemetery in Nebraska yielded a woolen twill fragment with buttonholes spaced six centimeters apart.[62]

Both RI-1000 and Long Pond yielded woolen fragments that possibly were European-style clothing. The fine worsted twill illustrated in figure 6 came from the grave of an adult male. Field notes indicated the presence of layers of this fabric around the skull, fibula, and tibia. Might it have been a cloak with a collar similar to Richard Smith's cloak (see fig. 4)? The high quality of the cloth and the layering of the fragments support the conclusion that these particular textiles were once part of clothing rather than a burial shroud. Long Pond provided examples of a sewn pleat, selvage, and seams with the seam allowances turned toward the body in burial 8, that of a three-year-old child. Although this sewn construction might have been part of a coat or jacket, it might have been a remnant of a wool shirt or waistcoat as well. The lack of buttons or buttonholes weakens the argument for its being a coat.

In conclusion, the in-depth analysis of European textiles from seventeenth-century Indian cemeteries provides evidence for the role that trade cloth played in both textile history and the transformation of Indian culture. Probate records, journals, and merchants' records attest to the importance of cloth to the North American Indian trade. The written record informs us that both piece goods and ready-made clothing were acquired by Indians, yet the archaeological record on European textiles is almost nonexistent in comparison to other less perishable goods such as metals, beads, and bone. This bias in the archaeological record makes the careful study of the few surviving fragments from sites like RI-1000 and Long Pond even more important for the information they can provide on trade patterns, physical characteristics of trade cloth, and the use of cloth in burial practices.

[62] Margaret Spufford, *The Great Reclothing of Rural England* (London: Hambledon Press, 1984), p. 131; Sandra Vons-Comis, "Seventeenth-Century Garments from Grave 579, Zeeuwse Uitkijk, Spitsbergen," in Penelope Walton and John-Peter Wild, eds., *Textiles in Northern Archaeology* (London: Archetype Publications, 1990), pp. 175–86; Jenna Tedrick Kutruff, "Repatriation and the Analysis of Museum Textile Collections" (Paper presented at the Annual Meeting of the International Textile and Apparel Association, Columbus, Ohio, October 23, 1992), p. 9. Kutruff analyzed both aboriginal and European textiles from Pawnee sites dating from the seventeenth to the nineteenth centuries. Approximately 70 percent of the 57 textiles were European.

The textile fragments inform us that many varieties of textiles, especially woven wools, were acquired by the Narragansett and Pequot Indians in the second half of the seventeenth century. These textiles represent the types manufactured in England according to written sources and in some cases might be the only surviving artifactual examples of textiles made for the colonial market. Each fragment represents a complex trade network beginning with fiber producers, who sold raw materials to merchants, who supervised manufacture of cloth and its subsequent shipment to New England's ports for distribution to colonial merchants, who sent them via land routes to reach Indian consumers. The Native American market was significant for England's wool industry judging by the large number and variety of wool fabrics in the burials. A few fabrics of other fibers, such as cotton calico from India, point to the distant origins of textiles available to Native Americans.

Analysis of the physical properties of the fragments allowed their placement into broad categories of fabrics. Most of the medium-weight plain weave fragments might have been called trucking cloth (or trading cloth) in their day, or if their surface had a long nap, shag cotton. Most fabrics were coarse rather than fine. Such fabrics, with their stiff, hairy fibers, must have been scratchy and uncomfortable next to the skin for Indians and colonists alike. Few twill fabrics appeared in these graves, suggesting that duffel and kersey were not common among the Narragansetts and the Mashantucket Pequots. Several examples of fine woven wool textiles, cotton calico, and knitted wools were present in the graves as well. The findings from RI-1000 and Long Pond confirm, fine-tune, and correct what we already knew from other contemporary sites such as Burr's Hill. Eventually, when data on textiles from other sites are analyzed, a more complete picture of textile usage will emerge. Archaeologists should exercise caution in interpreting data from textiles without fully understanding the implications of their physical characteristics.

The archaeological record shows that Indian consumers used trade cloth in ways not apparent in the written record. With few exceptions European cloth replaced animal skins in traditional burials as shrouds, grave linings, clothing, and wrappers for grave goods and as components of medicine bundles. A knitted cap might have been used as a pillow rather than a head covering. Fine textiles, although infrequently preserved in burials, seem to have been recognized as having greater value than other fabrics. Little conclusive evidence for tailored clothing existed in these cemeteries, especially the renowned red or blue coats assigned "status" by other scholars.

The manner in which European textiles were used in New England Indian burials in the last half of the seventeenth century supports William Cronon's observations that the ecological consequences of the European invasion of North America must be considered with the cultural consequences.[63] The decrease in deer and fur-bearing animal populations necessitated substituting European textiles for the furs and skins traditionally used for native clothing and burials. The Mashantucket Pequots already were living on the reservation when the Long Pond cemetery was in use, reducing access to hunting grounds. Yet some objects of native manufacture, such as mats, wampum headbands, and a few skins, appeared in these burials despite the availability of European-made products. The mix of textiles and native-made objects in these burials revealed that Native Americans in southern New England adhered to traditional lifeways even though the ecological and cultural odds were against them.

[63]William Cronon, *Changes in the Land* (New York: Hill and Wang, 1983), p. 102.

Artifacts, Networks, and Plantations

Toward a Further Understanding of the Social Aspects of Material Culture

Charles E. Orser, Jr.

In one way or another, archaeologists have always focused their attention on artifacts, those tangible things created in the past by conscious human effort. As early as 1734, Nicholas Mahudel, using the ideas of earlier antiquarians, proposed the Three Age System as a chronological way of using stone, bronze, and iron artifacts to mark what he envisioned as the three great stages of human development.[1] Since Mahudel presented this idea, numerous archaeologists have refined the study of

The author wishes to thank the Henry Francis du Pont Winterthur Museum for asking him to participate in the 1991 conference. He was honored to be included in this session, and the warmth he was shown while at the conference made the event particularly meaningful. He thanks the conference organizers, Lu Ann De Cunzo and Bernard L. Herman for their willingness to include him and for their kind suggestions about this paper. Their thoughtful comments forced him to rethink much of this presentation and to strengthen it. He is also grateful to all those people at the conference who offered their suggestions about the paper, particularly Paul Shackel, Barbara Little, Paul Mullins, and Marley Brown; Mark Groover also offered valuable suggestions. As always, Janice Orser provided insights and ideas on ways to improve this essay.

[1]Bruce G. Trigger, A *History of Archaeological Theory* (Cambridge, Eng.: Cambridge University Press, 1989), p. 60.

artifacts, and artifacts continue to constitute much of the raw material of archaeological research even though modern archaeologists obtain information from diverse sources.

The importance of artifacts is no less significant in historical archaeology. Historical archaeologists—defined here as archaeologists involved in the anthropological and historical study of the modern world from its earliest beginnings in the late Middle Ages to the present—use all kinds of artifacts in their research, including portable objects, manuscripts and maps, photographs, standing buildings, relict landscapes, and orally transmitted information. Some historical archaeologists have provided innovative ideas about the archaeological application of information sources traditionally considered to be within the purview of historians. Overall the careful use of "historical" materials—maps, documents, photographs—in conjunction with "archaeological" materials—portable objects, landscape features, botanical remains—is an important hallmark of historical archaeology. Nonetheless, portable items, those objects typically considered to be "artifacts"—ceramics, buttons, glassware, nails—justly continue to attract serious attention in historical archaeology.[2]

My purpose in this essay is to explore issues related to the analysis of portable items—termed *artifacts* for convenience—in historical archaeology, leaving aside the related issues of interpreting all those other sources of information used by historical archaeologists. I take as my primary proposition that historical archaeologists must approach the study of artifacts in a way that stresses relations over attributes. This requirement stems from the complex nature of the societies studied in historical archaeology. To illustrate my perspective, I use data obtained from three antebellum plantations in southern Georgia.

[2]For an overview of some recent works using historical sources, see Mary C. Beaudry, ed., *Documentary Archaeology in the New World* (Cambridge, Eng.: Cambridge University Press, 1988); Barbara J. Little, ed., *Text-Aided Archaeology* (Boca Raton, Fla.: CRC Press, 1992). A classic statement regarding historical materials appears in James Deetz, *In Small Things Forgotten: The Archaeology of Early American Life* (Garden City, N.Y.: Anchor/Doubleday, 1977), p. 7. Recent examples of artifacts that receive attention appear in George L. Miller, Olive R. Jones, Lester A. Ross, and Teresita Majewski, comps., *Approaches to Material Culture Research for Historical Archaeology* (California, Pa.: Society for Historical Archaeology, 1991).

Attributes versus Relations

Two broad ways exist to examine and to classify people, objects, and events: by their attributes, or physical characteristics, and by the relations between two or more such people, objects, or events. Although these kinds of analyses are sometimes described as antithetical, they usually are complementary.[3] Attributes can be divided into at least two subcategories: physical attributes and social attributes. The physical attributes of a person may be that person's height, weight, and hair color, whereas the physical attributes of a portable artifact may be its size, shape, and composition. The social attributes of a person may be his or her position in a hierarchy, esteem within a community, or prestige among peers; the social attributes of an artifact relate to its value, usefulness, and desirability.

Archaeologists are well acquainted with studying the physical attributes of artifacts. After all, Mahudel's Three Age System is based on a physical attribute (material of manufacture), and much of the culture-historical syntheses of archaeology's culture-historical past were overtly concerned with physical attributes. Ivor Nöel Hume's researches into ceramics stand as clear examples of detailed studies of physical attributes in historical archaeology.[4]

The archaeological study of the social attributes of artifacts is more difficult to characterize. The idea that artifacts can be imbued with social meaning is embodied in Lewis Binford's famous term "sociotechnic," a now archaic-sounding word used to refer to an artifact's function within a social context. Since Binford proposed this idea, most anthropological archaeologists have been interested in the social characteristics of artifacts, and archaeological research in this area has taken many

---

[3]David Knoke and James H. Kuklinski, *Network Analysis* (Newbury Park, Calif.: Sage Publications, 1982), p. 10.

[4]Examples of studies focusing on physical attributes abound in archaeology, but for an overview see Gordon R. Willey, *An Introduction to American Archaeology* (Englewood Cliffs, N.J.: Prentice-Hall, 1966); a specific study is James R. Sackett, "Quantitative Analysis of Upper Paleolithic Stone Tools," *American Anthropologist* 68 (1966): 356–92. Ivor Nöel Hume, "Rhenish Gray Stonewares in Colonial America," *Antiques* 92, no. 3 (September 1967): 349–53; Ivor Nöel Hume, *A Guide to Colonial Artifacts of Colonial America* (New York: Alfred A. Knopf, 1972), pp. 98–145; Ivor Nöel Hume, "Creamware to Pearlware: A Williamsburg Perspective," in Ian M. G. Quimby, ed., *Ceramics in America* (Charlottesville: University Press of Virginia, 1973), pp. 217–54.

forms. In historical archaeology, these kinds of analyses range from
Stanley South's efforts to discover socially relevant patterns within artifact collections to Anne Yentsch's sophisticated contextual analysis of
Chesapeake pottery. Such archaeological studies, many of which are
inspired by material culture specialists outside archaeology, have led to
the view that artifacts are "actively involved in the social world."[5]

It may seem incongruous to consider social attributes in the same
way as physical attributes because of the inherent relational qualities
of social attributes. A woman can have prestige among her peers only
in relation to someone else; to have a place in a hierarchy, others also
must be situated within the same hierarchy; one cannot have esteem
useless someone else bestows it. These statements are true, but in archaeology the study of the social characteristics of objects *as if* they
were attributes and not relations is common. George Miller's widely
cited study of the economics of nineteenth-century ceramics provides
an excellent example.[6] Miller focuses on the price of refined ceramics
and from this devises an index measure to indicate the economic value
of the ceramics found at archaeological sites. He then uses his index
to extrapolate the ability of ceramics to satisfy human needs and desires.
In Miller's scheme, both economic and social aspects of past life are
understood through the ceramics that people used. His index—really
an economic measure—can be affected by the use to which certain

[5] Lewis R. Binford, "Archaeology as Anthropology," *American Antiquity* 28 (1962):
217–25. Other studies are far too numerous to cite, but notable examples are James N.
Hill, *Broken K Pueblo: Prehistoric Social Organization in the American Southwest* (Tucson: University of Arizona Press, 1970); Ian Hodder, ed., *Symbolic and Structural Ar-
chaeology* (Cambridge, Eng.: Cambridge University Press, 1982); William A. Longacre,
"Some Aspects of Prehistoric Society in East-Central Arizona," in Sally R. Binford and
Lewis R. Binford, eds., *New Perspectives in Archaeology* (Chicago: Aldine Publishing
Co., 1968), pp. 89–102; Michael B. Schiffer, *Behavioral Archaeology* (New York: Aca-
demic Press, 1976). Stanley South, *Method and Theory in Historical Archaeology* (New
York: Academic Press, 1977); Anne Yentsch, "Chesapeake Artefacts and Their Cultural
Context: Pottery and the Food Domain," *Post-Medieval Archaeology* 25 (1991): 25–72.
Michael Shanks and Christopher Tilley, *Social Theory and Archaeology* (Albuquerque:
University of New Mexico Press, 1988), p. 117.

[6] George L. Miller, "Classification and Economic Scaling of Nineteenth-Century
Ceramics," *Historical Archaeology* 14 (1980): 1–40. For an interesting refinement of
Miller, see Suzanne M. Spencer-Wood, "Miller's Indices and Consumer-Choice Profiles: Status-Related Behaviors and White Ceramics," in Suzanne M. Spencer-Wood,
ed., *Consumer Choice in Historical Archaeology* (New York: Plenum Press, 1977), pp.
321–58.

ceramic objects were put. Everyday ceramics will outnumber fancy ceramics in archaeological deposits solely because the highly used items were more likely to be broken. In this way, the index is skewed toward utilitarian dishes. Miller comes close to studying the social attributes of ceramics and implies that the attributes are inherently relational. Still, the relations are not Miller's primary focus.

Miller's study, however, presents at least two important implications. First, as South also demonstrates by using Nöel Hume's ceramics information in developing his mean ceramics dating formula, Miller's study indicates that particularistic attribute analyses have an important place in historical archaeology. The sociological issues of concern to anthropological historical archaeologists cannot be examined in any detail until the physical attributes of historic artifacts are known. This has long been a major tenet of historical archaeology, and Miller's analysis serves to demonstrate a sophisticated and thoughtful way in which to use such information.[7] Second, and even though he does not dwell on it, Miller hints at one of the most important aspects of historic artifacts: their role as commodities. In seeing artifacts as commodities, archaeologists have the potential to pursue relational analyses.

Artifacts as Commodities in Networks

Commodities are simply things created for exchange. Commodities can exist in many forms, including portable objects, services, narratives, landscape, recipes, and even people. Commodities do not always involve economics, but because they are commonly associated with economic exchange, this is the sense of the word used here. An understanding of commodities is important because historical archaeologists study a period in world history during which commodities began to assert a powerful influence on human life.

Starting with the beginning of the modern world—typically set by

---

[7] Stanley South, "Evolution and Horizon as Revealed in Ceramic Analysis in Historical Archaeology," *Conference on Historic Site Archaeology Papers* 6 (1972):71–116. For example, the serious study of historic artifacts was a motive behind the creation of the Conference on Historic Site Archaeology in 1960; see Stanley South, "Preface," *Florida Anthropologist* 17, no. 2 (1964): 34.

historians at A.D. 1415 when the Portuguese captured Ceuta in northern Africa, though a much earlier date is also possible—greater numbers of men and women obtained access to objects that were once scarce and available only to the nobility. No longer did commoners have to wait for an inheritance to acquire material possessions. After 1415 many medieval patterns of commercial thought and activity were transformed as the rise of an expanding global economy acted like a shock wave, forever changing the social, economic, and political complexion of the world.[8] The influence of this economy has developed to the point that some daily contact with commodities today is unavoidable for most people.

Theoretically, the presence of a commodity in any social setting involves at least two individuals: someone willing to dispose of the commodity and someone willing to obtain it. This dyadic relationship indicates that a commodity can have at least two distinct but often highly related values (or attributes): an *exchange value*, often conceptualized as "price," and a *use value*. For two hypothetical actors, the exchange value is something on which they must agree to make the exchange. This exchange value also must be expressed in a recognized medium of exchange, such as money, shells, or animal hides. Use value is more problematic because a strong likelihood exists that the two actors may not agree on the "ability" of the commodity to be useful. For the offerer, the commodity has use as something that helps to establish his or her well-being (of whatever kind) by obtaining something in exchange. For the consumer, the commodity can have a myriad of uses, some of which may not even be known to him or her at the time of acquiring the commodity. When the consumer and the offerer are from different cultures, the other's use for the commodity may not be understood clearly. In fact, the use of the commodity may

[8] Janet L. Abu-Lughod, *Before European Hegemony: The World System, A.D. 1250–1350* (New York: Oxford University Press, 1989), p. 12; G. V. Scammell, *The World Encompassed: The First European Maritime Empires, ca. 800–1650* (London: Methuen, 1981). Grant McCracken, *Culture and Consumption: New Approaches to the Symbolic Character of Consumer Goods and Activities* (Bloomington: Indiana University Press, 1988), p. 14; Neil McKendrick, "Commercialization and the Economy," in Neil McKendrick, John Brewer, and J. H. Plumb, eds., *The Birth of a Consumer Society: The Commoditization of Eighteenth-Century England* (Bloomington: Indiana University Press, 1982), pp. 9–13. Lewis Mumford, *The Condition of Man* (New York: Harcourt, Brace, Jovanovich, 1973), pp. 159–63.

be viewed as an appropriate reason for revulsion and prejudice on the part of one of the actors.

Even this brief exposition on the complexities inherent in the theoretical nature of commodities gives credence to Marx's view of the commodity as "a very queer thing, abounding in metaphysical subtleties and theological niceties." At a minimum, such reflection should indicate that a commodity is a complex, multifaceted economic and social entity.[9]

Commodities played a major role in the inception, development, and spread of the so-called modern world system studied by historians, economists, environmentalists, geographers, political economists, sociologists, and cultural anthropologists. An underlying precept of the world-system perspective is that the social world is composed of a "totality of interconnected processes" that can be substantively understood only by making inquiries that are sensitive to this totality.[10]

[9] Karl Marx, *Capital: A Critique of Political Economy*, vol. 1 (New York: International Publishers, 1967), p. 71. The "social lives" of commodities are explored in Arjun Appadurai, "Commodities and the Politics of Value," in Arjun Appadurai, ed., *The Social Life of Things: Commodities in Cultural Perspective* (Cambridge, Eng.: Cambridge University Press, 1986), pp. 3–13.

[10] Eric R. Wolf, *Europe and the People without History* (Berkeley: University of California Press, 1982), p. 3. Historians who studied the system are Abu-Lughod, *Before European Hegemony*; Fernand Braudel, *Capitalism and Material Life, 1400–1800* (New York: Harper and Row, 1973); Peter Chaunu, *European Expansion in the Later Middle Ages*, trans. Katherine Bertram (Amsterdam: North-Holland, 1979); Philip D. Curtin, *Cross-Cultural Trade in World History* (Cambridge, Eng.: Cambridge University Press, 1984); G. J. Marcus, *The Conquest of the North Atlantic* (Suffolk, Eng.: Boydell Press, 1980); J. R. S. Phillips, *The Medieval Expansion of Europe* (Oxford: Oxford University Press, 1988); Scammell, *World Encompassed*; William Woodruff, *Impact of Western Man: A Study of Europe's Role in the World-Economy, 1750–1960* (New York: St. Michael's Press, 1967); William Woodruff, *The Struggle for World Power, 1500–1980* (New York: St. Michael's Press, 1981). Economists are: Rondo Cameron, *A Concise Economic History of the World* (New York: Oxford University Press, 1989); Howard F. Didsbury, Jr., *The Global Economy: Today, Tomorrow, and the Transition* (Bethesda, Md.: World Future Society, 1985); Andre Gunder Frank, *World Accumulation, 1492–1789* (New York: Monthly Review Press, 1978); A. M. Abdul Huq, *The Global Economy: An Information Sourcebook* (New York: Oryx Press, 1988); B. J. McCormick, *The World Economy: Patterns of Growth and Change* (Totowa, N.J.: Barnes and Noble, 1988); Iain Wallace, *The Global Economic System* (London: Unwin Hyman, 1990). An environmentalist study is Kirkpatrick Sale, *The Conquest of Paradise: Christopher Columbus and the Columbian Legacy* (New York: Penguin Books, 1990). For geographers' studies see Eugene D. Genovese and Leonard Hochberg, eds., *Geographic Perspectives in History* (Oxford: Oxford University Press, 1989); Peter Haggett, *The Geographer's Art* (Oxford: Basil Blackwell, 1990). For political economists studies, see Stuart A. Bremer, eds., *The*

One way to conceptualize the idea of an interconnected totality is by reference to a "network." Networks are interconnected systems of material and nonmaterial elements tied together in some fashion. Networks and their properties have been studied in biology, computer science, electronics, and management science, but my understanding of network analysis is informed by research conducted largely in the social sciences. Alexander Lesser uses the image of social relations being composed of "weblike, netlike connections," and this image neatly summarizes the idea that individuals and groups are linked together in complex ways that can be expressed in many culturally distinct manners, including kinship, power relations, class loyalties, and economic strategies.[11]

Globus Model: Computer Simulation of Worldwide Political and Economic Developments (Boulder, Colo.: Westview, 1987); Walter L. Goldfrank, ed., *The World-System of Capitalism: Past and Present* (Beverly Hills: Sage Publications, 1979); William G. Martin, ed., *Semiperipheral States in the World Economy* (New York: Greenwood Press, 1990). Sociologists' studies are Anthony D. King, *The Bungalow: The Production of a Global Culture* (London: Routledge, 1984); Anthony D. King, *Urbanism, Colonialism, and the World-Economy: Cultural and Spatial Foundations of the World Urban System* (London: Routledge, 1989); Anthony D. King, *Global Cities: Post-Imperialism and the Internationalisation of London* (London: Routledge, 1990); Immanuel Wallerstein, *The Modern World-System: Capitalist Agriculture and the Origins of the European World-Economy in the Sixteenth Century* (New York: Academic Press, 1974); Immanuel Wallerstein, *The Capitalist World-Economy* (Cambridge, Eng.: Cambridge University Press, 1979); Immanuel Wallerstein, *The Modern World-System II: Mercantilism and the Consolidation of the European World-Economy, 1600–1750* (New York: Academic Press, 1980). For cultural anthropologists' studies, see Sidney W. Mintz, *Sweetness and Power: The Place of Sugar in Modern History* (New York: Penguin Books, 1986); and Wolf, *Europe and the People*.

[11] Alexander Lesser, "Social Fields and the Evolution of Society," *Southwestern Journal of Anthropology* 17 (1961): 42. Lesser's concept is also used in Wolf, *Europe and the People*. For studies in biology, see John Casti and Anders Karlqvist, eds., *Newton to Aristotle: Toward a Theory of Models for Living Systems* (Boston: Birkhaüser, 1989); in computer science, see Edward D. Lazowska, *Quantitative System Performance: Computer System Analysis Using Queuing Network Models* (Englewood Cliffs, N.J.: Prentice-Hall, 1984); in electronics, see J. B. Murdock, *Network Theory* (New York: McGraw-Hill, 1970); and in management science, see Albert Battersby, *Network Analysis for Planning and Scheduling* (3d ed.; New York: John Wiley and Sons, 1970). In the social sciences, see Knoke and Kuklinski, *Network Analysis*; Ronald S. Burt, *Toward a Structural Theory of Action: Network Models of Social Structure, Perception, and Action* (New York: Academic Press, 1982); Ronald S. Burt and Michael J. Minor, eds., *Applied Network Analysis: A Methodological Introduction* (Beverly Hills, Calif.: Sage Publications, 1983); Samuel Leinhardt, *Social Networks: A Developing Paradigm* (New York: Academic Press, 1977).

In a relational analysis, the connections assume as much, or perhaps even more, importance than the attributes of the linked nodes themselves. It should be clear, though, that a successful relational analysis cannot be completed without first knowing something about the attributes of the things that stand in relation to one another.

When considering relationships, it becomes obvious that numerous kinds of relationships can exist and that the interconnected web formed by them can extend across both space and time. Concomitantly, the analyses can range from a simple consideration of a dyadic relation between two interacting elements of the network to the examination of the entire network. When viewed in the broadest terms, setting a network's boundaries is a particularly difficult problem.[12]

The establishment of network parameters is particularly acute in archaeology. As Robert Schuyler notes, and as every field archaeologist knows, archaeologists "do not excavate on a global level." On the contrary, archaeologists excavate individual sites or, in the best cases, a group of associated sites. To address the practical problem of the limitations of excavation, Schuyler proposes that archaeologists should not try to excavate globally but rather should confine themselves to the preparation of thoroughly researched "historic ethnographies" centered on discrete, manageable communities.[13] For Schuyler, archaeologists can make contributions to scholarship with this approach while also not exceeding the realistic limits of their knowledge. In this way, the accumulated information about a site—archaeological, historical, and otherwise—should set the boundaries of the community.

In one respect, Schuyler is absolutely correct. No archaeologist, no matter how talented or well funded, could ever expect to excavate enough of a world system to understand it in its entirety. As geographer Peter Haggett observes, anyone wishing to study global issues quickly

---

[12] Edward O. Laumann, Peter V. Marsden, and David Presky, "The Boundary Specification Problem in Network Analysis," in Burt and Minor, *Applied Network Analysis*, pp. 18–24.

[13] Robert L. Schuyler, "Archaeological Remains, Documents, and Anthropology: A Call for a New Culture History," *Historical Archaeology* 22, no. 1 (1988): 41. A similar call for community analyses in historical archaeology appears in William H. Adams, "Silcott, Washington: Ethnoarchaeology of a Rural American Community," *Reports of Investigations* 54 (Pullman: Laboratory of Anthropology, Washington State University, 1977), pp. 15–31.

discovers that "the earth's surface is so staggeringly large."[14] The reality is that archaeologists excavate sites with seemingly clear spatial and temporal limits.

In another important respect, however, Schuyler's perspective seems shortsighted. In asserting that the world system is vast, Schuyler ignores the historical reality that no world system was ever completely dominant and all-pervasive throughout every portion of the globe at the same time.[15] On the contrary, the individual elements of any large-scale network (nations, city-states, principalities) appeared and disappeared as national fortunes, goals, and advantages changed.

Many examples of this process can be identified in world history. One easily cited example is the Dutch empire of the seventeenth and eighteenth centuries. At its height, the Dutch network stretched from Java to northeastern Brazil. Within this web of activity, however, the Dutch controlled only individual ports-of-call. The Dutch never controlled the world, or even all the regions wherein they maintained outposts. Their influence was extensive but fluid. In Brazil, for instance, the Dutch controlled a small portion of the northeastern coast, building forts, conquering Portuguese forts, and then losing them.[16] This process was repeated by the Dutch—and all other European colonial powers—elsewhere around the globe throughout modern history.

At first glance, the modern world system, as it has been conceived, appears Eurocentric. The history of scholarship about the New World is replete with studies focusing on the European presence in the non-European world, with indigenous behavior frequently portrayed as reactionary. In archaeology, investigations of these contacts have often taken the form of acculturation studies. The artifacts excavated at Native American villages are seen as objects made in Europe, taken to the New World, and then accepted or modified by indigenous peoples. Recent studies show that the colonial process of cultural interaction was actually much more complex, as both Europeans and non-Europeans created new cultures forged from the new "fields of relationships" that

[14] Haggett, *Geographer's Art*, p. 28.

[15] For comments, see Abu-Lughod, *Before European Hegemony*, p. 32.

[16] C. R. Boxer, *The Dutch Seaborne Empire, 1600–1800* (London: Penguin Books, 1988); José Luiz Mota Menezes e Maria do Rosário Rosa Rodrigues, *Fortificações Portuguesas no Nordeste do Brasil: Séculos XVI, XVII, e XVIII* (Recife, Braz.: Pool Editorial, 1986).

were formed by interaction. These "mutual entanglements" created "shared histories," and, in this sense, both Europe and the various "non-Europes" built the modern world together.[17]

The importance of these "shared histories" in shaping the modern world and giving it its multicultural character cannot be understated. It can be assumed that material culture played important, albeit diverse and changing, roles in creating and enveloping these histories. From this perspective, it follows that historical archaeologists, rather than restricting themselves only to the preparation of historic ethnographies—site reports—would do well to consider the role they may play in providing an archaeological understanding of the rise, development, and maintenance of the modern world system.[18] The important question, of course, is how to do this. How can archaeologists hope to

---

[17] Eric R. Wolf, "Culture: Panacea or Problem?" *American Antiquity* 49 (1984): 397; Nicholas Thomas, *Entangled Objects: Exchange, Material Culture, and Colonialism in the Pacific* (Cambridge: Harvard University Press, 1991), p. 3. See also Talal Asad, "Are There Histories of Peoples without Europe? A Review Article," *Comparative Studies in Society and History* 29 (1987): 594–607; Ann Laura Stoler, "Rethinking Colonial Categories: European Communities and the Boundaries of Rule," *Comparative Studies in Society and History* 31 (1989): 134–61; Nicholas B. Dirks, ed., *Colonialism and Culture* (Ann Arbor: University of Michigan Press, 1992). Acculturation studies abound in archaeology, but a good example is George Irving Quimby, *Indian Culture and European Trade Goods: The Archaeology of the Historic Period in the Western Great Lakes Region* (Madison: University of Wisconsin Press, 1966). For an important critique, see Patricia E. Rubertone, "Archaeology, Colonialism, and Seventeenth-Century Native America: Towards an Alternative Interpretation," in Robert Layton, ed., *Conflict in the Archaeology of Living Traditions* (London: Unwin Hyman, 1989), pp. 32–45. The term *non-Europe* is used in Braudel, *Perspective of the World*, p. 386. One problem with this term is that it tends to make Europe the reference point for all those cultures with which Europeans came into contact. Abundant ethnographic fieldwork clearly shows that these cultures operated quite well without European interference. As a result, I use the term "non-Europes" reluctantly and only for the sake of convenience.

[18] For similar comments about the role of historical archaeology in studying global issues, see Kathleen Deagan, "Historical Archaeology's Contribution to Our Understanding of Early America," in Lisa Falk, ed., *Historical Archaeology in Global Perspective* (Washington, D.C.: Smithsonian Institution Press, 1991), p. 97; Kathleen Deagan, "Neither History nor Prehistory: The Questions That Count in Historical Archaeology," *Historical Archaeology* 22, no. 1 (1988): 7–12; James Deetz, "Archaeological Evidence of Sixteenth- and Seventeenth-Century Encounters," in Falk, *Historical Archaeology in Global Perspective*, pp. 1–9; Stanley South, "Whither Pattern?" *Historical Archaeology* 22, no. 1 (1988): 25; Robert L. Schuyler, "Historical Archaeology and Historic Sites Archaeology as Anthropology: Basic Definitions and Relationships," *Historical Archaeology* 4 (1970): 84.

contribute anything to understanding culture, society, and history beyond the site level?

Unfortunately, I cannot now offer a definitive and final answer to
this difficult question; the investigation of the complexities involved in
such study will take years. I can neither present a neat formula that
other archaeologists may adopt to discover the social networks within
which moved the inhabitants of their sites nor provide a definitive and
all-encompassing statement about the place of artifacts in these networks. The approach I advocate is directly antithetical to such formulations; the complexities and varieties of the shared histories, played out
at so many diverse sites in so many distinct landscapes, defies easy
categorization. Nonetheless, I can present ideas, using the findings of
other archaeologists, to demonstrate how a network approach can shed
light on the complexities of past life and how this approach can help
to further theoretical thought in historical archaeology regarding the
meaning of material culture.

I use as an example research conducted under the direction of
William H. Adams at three antebellum plantations located in extreme
southern Georgia. I use this example because slave plantations represent an excellent laboratory for studying the relations between material
culture and people.[19] The inhabitants of antebellum plantations were
distinguished socially, politically, economically, and racially, and interactions between them—of various sorts and complexities—occurred
daily.

I specifically use the three sites investigated by Adams because he
and his co-authors provide a thorough study of these plantations and
present data that can be readily used.[20] Adams and his co-authors have
done an admirable job of analyzing and interpreting the plantation
remains, and my use of their work should not be construed as condem-

[19] I also have made this claim in Charles E. Orser, Jr., "The Archaeological Analysis
of Plantation Society: Replacing Status and Caste with Economics and Power," *American
Antiquity* 53 (1988): 735–51; and Charles E. Orser, Jr., "Beneath the Material Surface
of Things: Commodities, Artifacts, and Slave Plantations," *Historical Archaeology* 26,
no. 3 (1992): 95–104.

[20] William Hampton Adams, ed., "Historical Archaeology of Plantations at King's
Bay, Camden County, Georgia," in *Reports of Investigations*, vol. 5 (Gainesville: Depart-
ment of Anthropology, University of Florida, 1987); William Hampton Adams and Sarah
Jane Boling, "Status and Ceramics for Planters and Slaves on Three Georgia Coastal
Plantations," *Historical Archaeology* 23, no. 1 (1989): 69–96.

natory. On the contrary, the thoroughness of their research makes it possible to use their work to explore the ᵣorts of ideas I am proposing here.

Plantation Networks, Relations, and Artifacts

Under contract with the United States Navy, Adams and others made a detailed archaeological and historical study of three antebellum plantations located along the southern Georgia coast: Kings Bay (1791–ca. 1850), Cherry Point (1791–1823), and Harmony Hall (1793–ca. 1832). Although the historical and archaeological material presented by Adams and his co-authors is extensive, what interests me here are the interpretations offered by Adams and Sarah Boling regarding plantation status and its relation to material culture, specifically to ceramics, the material culture on which they concentrate.

The data set is extensive enough to allow Adams and Boling to compare and contrast economic status (as measured by purchasing power) both within each plantation and between plantations. They compare, for example, the presence of different ceramic wares in contexts associated with a sawyer; with small, medium, and large planters; and with slaves. They conclude that little difference can be observed between small- and medium-size planters or between the slave samples. Their analysis of vessel forms suggests only that slave assemblages contain more bowls than flatware pieces, a conclusion reached by John Otto in the 1970s and now something of a platitude in plantation archaeology.[21]

Adams and Boling use Miller's ceramics index to address the question of how ceramics can help to illuminate status. Their use of the index makes sense because they are explicitly interested in *economic* status. As a result, their focus is on ceramics as commodities, objects bought and sold by conscious actors, with purchasing power serving as a surrogate measure of economic position in society. In this sense,

---

[21] Adams and Boling, "Status and Ceramics," pp. 76, 80; John Soloman Otto, "Artifacts and Status Differences—A Comparison of Ceramics from Planter, Overseer, and Slave Sites on an Antebellum Plantation," in Stanley South, ed., *Research Strategies in Historical Archaeology* (New York: Academic Press, 1977), pp. 91–118.

Adams and Boling examine the ceramics from the perspective of exchange value (price) and use this measure to extrapolate social meaning. As might be expected when considering such a complex issue, their results are neither unambiguous nor straightforward. For example, as far as fine pieces are concerned, slaves are found to have used more expensive cups and platters than did planters.[22] This conclusion contradicts the logic of master-slave relations, and it alone indicates that the archaeological deposits at the three sites are difficult to interpret.

The ambiguity of the results obtained by Adams and Boling are more interesting than their simple conclusions.[23] Their conclusions may be absolutely correct, but the problem inherent in their interpretation is that they attempt to use the physical attributes of ceramics (vessel wares and forms) to extrapolate the social attributes of people (economic status) while actually tending to think relationally. Their reasoning is based on relations, but their analysis is rooted in attributes.

The clue that a relational analysis is actually sought by Adams and Boling, but not pursued, appears in their statement, "One important question not answered by this analysis was where the slaves acquired their ceramics and other material culture." Having posed this question, they argue that many slaves, particularly those laboring in a task system, had access to material objects through the wealth they accumulated on their own. According to Adams and Boling, these slaves were not wholly dependent on masters for their material culture but participated in a market economy as "peasants or serfs."[24]

Leaving aside the controversial question of whether plantation inhabitants can be considered "peasants"—an issue debated since at least the 1930s—the significance of Adams and Boling's comment is that they attempt to extend their analysis by focusing on the dyadic relationship between a slave—as ceramics consumer—and a merchant—as ceramics supplier. In essence, what they propose is to use this extraplantation dyad to replace the intraplantation master-slave dyad.[25] In other

[22] Adams and Boling, "Status and Ceramics," p. 87.
[23] Adams and Boling, "Status and Ceramics," p. 94.
[24] Adams and Boling, "Status and Ceramics," p. 94.
[25] Wayne Gard, "The American Peasant," *Current History* 46 (1937): 47–52; Sidney W. Mintz, "Was the Plantation Slave a Proletarian?" *Review* 2 (1978): 81–98. It is perhaps pertinent to point out here that Adams and Boling, in "Status and Ceramics" (p. 94), misrepresent my statement about how slaves acquired material culture in Charles

words, Adams and Boling maintain that slaves obtained their ceramics through purchases, as true commodities, rather than as castoffs or gifts from their masters. This significant shift in focus is important because only through such a change in perspective can they learn something about the larger networks within which the three plantations operated. If market participation by slaves was indeed considerable, as Adams and Boling claim, then they must seek to demonstrate it because the customer-merchant dyad is fundamentally different from the slave-master dyad. The problem is that they do not directly address how such a focus may be framed. In attempting to examine "status," as indicated through buying power, they overshadow the relational properties of the three plantations. Further complexity is added when we realize that all the dyadic relations operate at the same time in different ways.

From the information that Adams and his co-authors present in their site report, it can be assumed that the nearby town of St. Marys, established in 1787, was the main urban center available to the inhabitants of the three plantations. This market was an important place where commodities were readily available. Even though planters undoubtedly obtained exotic items from special agents who shipped directly from Europe, they also must have obtained goods directly from St. Marys. Slaves reportedly visited St. Marys to purchase "finery & necessaries." These statements suggest, at least on one level, that masters and slaves were members of the same commercial network because both could purchase objects in town. This commercial model, however, does not exhaust the possible network connections. Other networks may have included an international economic network that tied planters to Europe and elsewhere, a social and kin network that tied together elite planter families, a network within the slave community, a network between slave communities on separate plantations, and a clandestine network that extended from the slave quarters to the maroon communities of Florida. Any of these subnetworks within the larger network of

---

E. Orser, Jr., "Plantation Status and Consumer Choice: A Materialist Framework for Historical Archaeology," in Suzannne M. Spencer-Wood, ed., *Consumer Choice in Historical Archaeology*, p. 127. My statement is, "plantation slaves did not have free access to consumer goods, but rather only received them on special occasions, *during infrequent trips to towns*, or directly from the planter or overseer as gifts or by theft" (emphasis added). I stand by this statement because slaves did not serve their masters, even in task gangs, by choice.

the New World plantation complex could have been the source of commodities.[26]

The complex interweaving of these subnetworks provides a good reason for expecting differences in archaeological collections that may have nothing to do with economic status. Commodities could enter a plantation from many sources, some of which may have been decidedly noneconomic in character. While the objects exchanged were clearly intended to be commodities and were originally transferred from factory to agent to consumer as commodities, the relations enacted during their exchange may have involved kin obligations, ritualized gift-giving, or some other noneconomical relation.

The similarities and differences in artifact collections at archaeological sites can have many explanations, and archaeologists are distinctly disadvantaged in never knowing the "truth" of why certain artifacts appear at certain sites. Archaeological explanations are notoriously incomplete and tentative. I choose to assume here that the similarity in artifact samples can be explained using many different variables and that one significant and heretofore neglected factor was the networks within which the artifact acquisitions were made, recognizing that personal choice had much to do with artifact selection. No historical actors chose material culture based solely on the tacit dictates of their class, ethnic group, or sex. In no way do I seek to discount other explanations. In all likelihood, many factors that caused certain artifacts to be bought and used as networks were modified to fit historical circumstances. My point is that the relational networks within which historical actors operated can no longer be ignored by historical archaeologists.

To show something of the complexity inherent in network analysis, I use the ceramic samples recovered by Adams and others and focused on by Adams and Boling. A measure, V, calculated by subtracting the percentage of artifacts in one category from one site from those of the same category of another site, is useful for this analysis.

---

[26]William Hampton Adams, Jeanne A. Ward, and Carolyn Rock, "Historical Background of the Kings Bay Locality," in Adams, "Historical Archaeology," pp. 23–44. Supporting comments about the plantation complex are in Philip D. Curtin, *The Rise and Fall of the Plantation Complex: Essays in Atlantic History* (Cambridge, Eng.: Cambridge University Press, 1990).

The absolute value that is produced is added to the other values from the site, and a mean is calculated. The subtraction of the two means produces a measure of the overall difference between the two samples. A mean of 0.0 indicates that the samples are exactly the same, while a mean of 50.0 indicates that the samples are completely dissimilar.[27] The underlying idea is that within a commercial environment of x kinds of ceramics, a historical actor will choose y pieces. Two actors within the same economic, educational, ideological, or similar subnetworks will have available to them the same sets of y ceramics. This idea is purposefully somewhat vague because of the complexity inherent in the subnetworks that operated. A rigid design would defeat the purpose of the analysis by constraining the interpretation.

Using the ceramicware-type information presented by Adams and Boling, I calculated the V values and V means for all possible combinations of site contexts (table 1).[28] These calculated means are ranked from lowest value (that is, most similar samples) to highest value (most dissimilar samples) (table 2).

This ranked listing of V means contains interesting information. First, all the comparisons from the site contexts, ranging from those of planters to slaves, show that all the samples are relatively similar. The greatest dissimilarity—between sawyer John King and the Harmony Hall slaves—provides a relatively low number of only 7.5. This low number may support the idea that all the plantation inhabitants, regardless of social station or ethnic affiliation, operated within the same general economic network, originating, at least locally, at the town of St. Marys. Second, the most similar comparisons are among the three planter contexts. This finding indicates that the three planter families used the same sorts of ceramic wares. Conversely, one of the slave comparisons (Harmony Hall: Kings Bay) yielded the second highest mean value. This co-occurrence may suggest that, while all the planters operated within the same subnetwork, the slaves on at least two of the plantations operated in different networks. In other words, these slaves may have been more oriented to their plantations' subnetworks than Adams and Boling suggest. For whatever reason, their ceramic collections are distinct, at least in ware types. Finally,

[27] See also Orser, "Archaeological Analysis," pp. 743–45.
[28] Adams and Boling, "Status and Ceramics," p. 75, table 2.

Table 1. V Values for Ceramic Wares at Sites

Comparisons	Y	R,C	S,C	O	R,R	S,R	P	D/M	C	PW	W	Mean
JK:JKP(E)	3.7	2.8	6.4	0.0	3.7	2.8	1.8	0.0	20.0	11.8	0.0	4.8
JK:JKP(W)	1.3	2.6	1.3	0.0	1.3	1.3	0.9	0.0	29.9	24.0	0.0	5.7
JK:HHP	1.6	2.1	4.2	0.5	1.6	1.0	6.2	0.0	24.6	15.8	0.0	5.2
JK:KBP	1.4	1.7	4.3	0.3	1.1	0.3	2.5	0.6	26.8	22.8	0.6	5.7
JK:JKS	2.9	5.9	1.5	0.0	0.0	2.9	0.0	0.0	26.3	13.0	0.0	4.8
JK:HHS	0.0	1.7	3.1	0.0	0.8	0.0	4.2	1.7	38.0	32.7	0.0	7.5
JK:KBS	8.5	7.8	0.8	0.0	2.0	0.0	3.9	0.7	23.6	1.5	0.0	4.4
JKP(E):JKP(W)	2.4	0.2	5.1	0.0	2.4	1.5	0.9	0.0	9.9	12.2	0.0	3.1
JKP(E):HHP	2.1	0.7	2.2	0.5	2.1	1.8	4.4	0.0	4.6	4.0	0.0	3.9
JKP(E):KBP	2.3	1.1	2.1	0.3	2.6	2.5	0.7	0.6	6.8	11.0	0.6	2.8
JKP(E):JKS	0.8	3.1	7.9	0.0	3.7	0.1	1.8	0.0	6.8	1.2	0.0	2.3
JKP(E):HHS	3.7	1.1	3.3	0.0	2.9	2.8	2.4	1.7	18.0	20.9	0.0	5.2
JKP(E):KBS	4.8	5.0	5.6	0.0	1.7	2.8	2.1	0.7	3.6	10.3	0.0	3.3
JKP(W):HHP	0.3	0.5	2.9	0.5	0.3	0.3	5.3	0.0	5.3	8.2	0.0	2.1
JKP(W):KBP	0.1	0.9	3.0	0.3	0.2	1.0	1.6	0.6	3.1	1.2	0.6	1.1
JKP(W):JKS	1.6	3.3	2.8	0.0	1.3	1.6	0.9	0.0	3.6	11.0	0.0	2.4
JKP(W):HHS	1.3	0.9	1.8	0.0	0.5	1.3	3.3	1.7	8.1	8.7	0.0	2.5
JKP(W):KBS	7.2	5.2	0.5	0.0	0.7	1.3	3.0	0.7	6.3	22.5	0.0	4.3
HHP:KBP	0.2	0.4	0.1	0.2	0.5	0.7	3.7	0.6	2.2	7.0	0.6	1.5
HHP:JKS	1.3	3.8	5.7	0.5	1.6	1.9	6.2	0.0	1.7	2.8	0.0	2.3
HHP:HHS	1.6	0.4	1.1	0.5	0.8	1.0	2.0	1.7	13.4	16.9	0.0	3.6
HHP:KBS	6.9	5.7	3.4	0.5	0.4	1.0	2.3	0.7	1.0	14.3	0.0	3.3
KBP:JKS	1.5	4.2	5.8	0.3	1.1	2.6	2.5	0.6	0.5	9.8	0.6	2.7
KBP:HHS	1.4	0.0	1.2	0.3	0.3	0.3	1.7	1.1	11.2	9.9	0.6	2.5
KBP:KBS	7.1	6.1	3.5	0.3	0.9	0.3	1.4	0.1	3.2	21.3	0.6	4.1
JKS:HHS	2.9	4.2	4.6	0.0	0.8	2.9	4.2	1.7	11.7	19.7	0.0	4.8
JKS:KBS	5.6	1.9	2.3	0.0	2.0	2.9	3.9	0.7	2.7	11.5	0.0	3.0
HHS:KBS	8.5	6.1	2.3	0.0	1.2	0.0	0.3	1.0	14.4	31.2	0.0	5.9

Key: Y = Yellowware; R,C = Redware, course; S,C = Stoneware, course; O = Other; R,R = Redware, refined; S,R = Stoneware, refined; P = Porcelain; D/M = Delft/majolica; C = Creamware; PW = Pearlware; W = Whiteware. JK = John King Sawyer; JKP(E) = James King Planter (East); JKP(W) = James King Planter (West); HHP = Harmony Hall Planter; KBP = Kings Bay Planter; JKS = James King Slave; HHS = Harmony Hall Slave; KBS = Kings Bay Slave.

Table 2. Ranking of V Means for Ceramic Wares

Site inhabitant pairs	Mean$\Sigma|V|$
James King Planter(W):Kings Bay Planter	1.1
Harmony Hall Planter:Kings Bay Planter	1.5
James King Planter(W):Harmony Hall Planter	2.1
James King Planter(E):James King Slave	2.3
Harmony Hall Planter:James King Slave	2.3
James King Planter(W):James King Slave	2.4
James King Planter(W):Harmony Hall Slave	2.5
Kings Bay Planter:Harmony Hall Slave	2.5
Kings Bay Planter:James King Slave	2.7
James King Planter(E):Kings Bay Planter	2.8
James King Slave:Kings Bay Slave	3.0
James King Planter(E):James King Planter(W)	3.1
James King Planter(E):Kings Bay Slave	3.3
Harmony Hall Planter:Kings Bay Slave	3.3
Harmony Hall Planter:Harmony Hall Slave	3.6
James King Planter(E):Harmony Hall Planter	3.9
Kings Bay Planter:Kings Bay Slave	4.1
James King Planter(W):Kings Bay Slave	4.3
John King Sawyer:Kings Bay Slave	4.4
John King Sawyer:James King Planter(E)	4.8
John King Sawyer:James King Slave	4.8
James King Slave:Harmony Hall Slave	4.8
James King Planter(E):Harmony Hall Slave	5.2
John King Sawyer:Harmony Hall Planter	5.2
John King Sawyer:Kings Bay Planter	5.7
John King Sawyer:James King Planter(W)	5.7
Harmony Hall Slave:Kings Bay Slave	5.9
John King Sawyer:Harmony Hall Slave	7.5

the relatively high values for the sawyer imply that this middle-class laborer operated within a subnetwork that may not have been tied strictly to the plantation. He may have maintained economic contacts unlike those of either slaves or planters, a situation not difficult to imagine.

The same computations were made for ceramic vessel forms, another ceramic variable focused on by Adams and Boling (table 3). The ranking of these V means provides further interesting information (table 4). First, the means indicate less variability in the differences among

Table 3. V Values for Ceramic Vessel Forms at Sites

Comparisons	Cup	Teapot	Misc.	Plate	Saucer	Platter	Bowl (l.)	Bowl (s.)	Mean
JK:JKP(E)	2.0	1.0	2.0	4.3	0.0	3.8	9.7	11.9	4.3
JK:JKP(W)	1.3	3.4	6.0	1.7	7.5	6.5	6.6	5.0	4.8
JK:HHP	9.4	4.2	1.1	3.1	6.3	5.5	7.9	2.6	5.0
JK:KBP	2.7	1.0	0.5	11.3	0.1	3.7	6.6	1.1	3.4
JK:JKS	4.7	0.0	6.1	2.3	2.5	7.9	12.2	21.7	7.2
JK:HHS	2.2	1.8	8.6	1.5	9.7	4.2	8.5	13.3	6.2
JK:KBS	2.6	0.9	3.2	14.4	6.5	6.9	7.1	4.9	5.8
JKP(E):JKP(W)	3.3	2.4	4.0	2.6	7.5	2.7	3.1	6.9	4.1
JKP(E):HHP	11.4	3.2	0.9	7.4	6.3	1.7	1.8	14.5	5.9
JKP(E):KBP	0.7	0.0	1.5	7.0	0.1	0.1	3.1	10.8	2.9
JKP(E):JKS	6.7	1.0	4.1	2.0	2.5	4.1	2.5	9.8	4.1
JKP(E):HHS	0.2	0.8	6.6	5.8	9.7	0.4	1.2	1.4	3.3
JKP(E):KBS	0.6	0.1	5.2	9.8	6.5	3.1	2.6	7.0	4.4
JKP(W):HHP	8.1	0.8	4.9	4.8	1.2	1.0	1.3	7.6	3.7
JKP(W):KBP	4.0	2.4	5.5	9.6	7.6	2.8	0.0	3.9	4.5
JKP(W):JKS	3.4	3.4	0.1	0.6	10.0	1.4	5.6	16.7	5.2
JKP(W):HHS	3.5	1.6	2.6	3.2	2.2	2.3	1.9	8.3	3.2
JKP(W):KBS	3.9	2.5	9.2	12.4	14.0	0.4	0.5	0.1	5.4
HHP:KBP	12.1	3.2	0.6	14.4	6.4	1.8	1.3	3.7	5.4
HHP:JKS	4.7	4.2	5.0	5.4	8.8	2.4	4.3	24.3	7.4
HHP:HHS	11.6	2.4	7.5	1.6	3.4	1.3	0.6	15.9	5.5
HHP:KBS	12.0	3.3	4.3	17.2	12.8	1.4	0.8	7.5	7.4
KBP:JKS	7.4	1.0	5.6	9.0	2.4	4.2	5.6	20.6	7.0
KBP:HHS	0.5	0.8	8.1	12.8	9.8	0.5	1.9	12.2	5.8
KBP:KBS	0.1	0.1	3.7	2.8	6.4	3.2	0.5	3.8	2.6
JKS:HHS	6.9	1.8	2.5	3.8	12.2	3.7	3.7	8.4	5.4
JKS:KBS	7.3	0.9	9.3	11.8	4.0	1.0	5.1	16.8	7.0
HHS:KBS	0.4	0.9	11.8	15.6	16.2	2.7	1.4	8.4	7.2

Key: JK = John King Sawyer; JKP(E) = James King Planter (East); JKP(W) = James King Planter (West); HHP = Harmony Hall Planter; KBP = Kings Bay Planter; JKS = James King Slave; HHS = Harmony Hall Slave; KBS = Kings Bay Slave.

the samples (from 2.6 to 7.4), suggesting that the plantation samples of ceramic vessels were fairly similar. Second, the greatest similarity occurs within the Kings Bay Plantation contexts. Kings Bay was the largest plantation included in the Adams study, and my findings may imply commodity exchange within the plantation network; in other words, that the inhabitants were part of a network of exchange that involved ceramic vessels. Third, the greatest dissimilarity occurs be-

Table 4. Ranking of V Means for Ceramic Vessel
Forms at Sites

Site inhabitant pairs	Mean$\Sigma|V|$
Kings Bay Planter:Kings Bay Slave	2.6
James King Planter(E):Kings Bay Planter	2.9
James King Planter(W):Harmony Hall Slave	3.2
James King Planter(E):Harmony Hall Slave	3.3
John King Sawyer:Kings Bay Planter	3.4
James King Planter(W):Harmony Hall Planter	3.7
James King Planter(E):James King Planter(W)	4.1
James King Planter(E):James King Slave	4.1
John King Sawyer:James King Planter(E)	4.3
James King Planter(E):Kings Bay Slave	4.4
James King Planter (W):Kings Bay Planter	4.5
John King Sawyer:James King Planter(W)	4.8
John King Sawyer:Harmony Hall Planter	5.0
James King Planter(W):James King Slave	5.2
James King Planter(W):Kings Bay Slave	5.4
Harmony Hall Planter:Kings Bay Planter	5.4
James King Slave:Harmony Hall Slave	5.4
Harmony Hall Planter:Harmony Hall Slave	5.5
John King Sawyer:Kings Bay Slave	5.8
Kings Bay Planter:Harmony Hall Slave	5.8
James King Planter(E):Harmony Hall Planter	5.9
John King Sawyer:Harmony Hall Slave	6.2
Kings Bay Planter:James King Slave	7.0
John King Slave:Kings Bay Slave	7.0
John King Sawyer:James King Slave	7.2
Harmony Hall Slave:Kings Bay Slave	7.2
Harmony Hall Planter:James King Slave	7.4
Harmony Hall Planter:Kings Bay Slave	7.4

tween the Harmony Hall planter context and the Kings Bay and James King slave contexts. This finding again may imply a substantial difference in how each plantation was involved in the various commercial networks that emanated from St. Marys. Finally, the samples associated with the middle-class sawyer are distributed throughout the ranking of V mean values, suggesting only a similarity to some samples and a dissimilarity to others. For vessels, the sawyer sample is not as distinct as it is for ceramic wares.

These findings allow the presentation of two important suggestions. First, the plantation samples used by Adams and Boling can be shown to exhibit similarities and dissimilarities that may be the result of either internal or external influences on the plantation. The relatively high values, of both ceramic wares and vessels, between the sawyer context and those of the Harmony Hall slaves (see tables 2, 4)—which indicate that these are the most dissimilar collections at the three plantations—may be related to the different relations that the sawyer and the slaves each had with the source of ceramic dishes. These differences may relate to the way in which each kind of person operated within the economic and social networks that existed in southern Georgia in the first half of the nineteenth century. Second, the different results obtained by separately examining the ceramic wares and the ceramic vessels should not be ignored. It should not cause concern, for example, that the V means for the James King Planter (West) and the Kings Bay Planter were 1.1 for ceramic wares and 4.5 for vessels. These different results merely indicate the complexity of the networks that operated in the past. This disparity shows that more than one subnetwork existed within the plantation system and that members of various communities occupied various positions within them. For this reason, this kind of research must be conceptualized as multiscalar.[29] In true multiscalar analysis, the results obtained on one level may seem to contradict those obtained at another. Rather than being a matter for consternation, such a discrepancy is a healthy sign that life is complex and that archaeology often provides only a partial glimpse of this complexity.

[29]Comments on multiscalar analysis in archaeology appear in Kenneth M. Ames, "The Archaeology of the *Longue Duree*: Temporal and Spatial Scale in the Evolution of Social Complexity on the Southern Northwest Coast," *Antiquity* 65 (1991): 935–45; Barbara J. Little and Paul A. Schackel, "Scales of Historical Anthropology: An Archaeology of Colonial Anglo-America," *Antiquity* 63 (1989): 495–509; William H. Marquardt, "Complexity and Scale in the Study of Fisher-Gatherer-Hunters: An Example from the Eastern United States," in T. Douglas Price and James A. Brown, eds., *Prehistoric Hunter-Gatherers: The Emergence of Cultural Complexity* (Orlando, Fla.: Academic Press, 1985), pp. 59–98; William H. Marquardt and Carole L. Crumley, "Theoretical Issues in the Analysis of Spatial Patterning," in Carol L. Crumley and William H. Marquardt, eds., *Regional Dynamics: Burgundian Landscapes in Historical Perspective* (San Diego: Academic Press, 1987), pp. 1–18; Charles E. Orser, Jr., *A Historical Archaeology of the Modern World* (New York: Plenum, 1996).

Conclusion

The goal of this paper is to explore the role of commodities in historical archaeology. Commodities are by nature difficult to understand. The reasons why people may have a certain kind of commodity in their possession defies easy explanation because of the many variables that can be assumed to have played a part in the choice of commodities by individual men and women. The problems in interpreting such complexities, of course, are compounded in archaeology because only partial information is ever available about why certain artifacts are found in some contexts and not in others. The issue of commodity distribution is of deep importance to historical archaeologists because most of the objects found at historic sites were commodities. As a result, historical archaeologists should try to devise ways in which to understand artifacts as commodities.

Many methods and approaches may be proposed for the study of commodities in historical archaeology, but an excellent framework within which to conceptualize these objects is the network. Networks are useful because they portray the complexity of human social relations, the relations between objects and humans, and the interconnections between individuals and groups. Obviously, however, some ambiguity and contradiction is to be expected in archaeological network analysis. In historical archaeology the simplest explanation is not necessarily the best one.[30] Network analysis provides an excellent avenue of study for historical archaeologists interested in the relations between people and things. My example, drawn from three plantations in Georgia, demonstrates the complexities and promise inherent in this kind of analysis.

My goal in this paper is not to reanalyze Adams and Boling's results or to call into question the research of Adams and others. I had nothing to do with the excavation of the three plantations, and I would be presuming too much to imagine myself any kind of expert on the sites. Adams and his co-workers held the artifacts and brushed the dirt from them; they pored through faded manuscripts and talked with local residents. The plantation men and women whom they studied—both

---

[30]James Deetz, "Archaeological Evidence of Sixteenth- and Seventeenth-Century Encounters," in Falk, *Historical Archaeology in Global Perspective*, p. 8.

slaves, masters, and those in between—created and recreated a number of complex, interwoven relationships. That I cannot shed additional light on these fluid relationships only reflects my lack of familiarity with the hard evidence Adams and his team collected. This does not distress me. On the contrary, my goal is only to suggest, in an exceedingly preliminary way, that historical archaeologists examine their artifacts in a fresh light and view their information from a different angle. I am hoping that historical archaeologists will breathe life into the silent materials they study by considering the relationships that allowed men and women to produce artifacts, to move them around in society, and ultimately to bestow meanings on them.

Cynics may say that this paper proves nothing, that any advance I have made, or may think I have made, is merely a baby step. The severest critics may argue that I have simply used new terms in an old analysis and that I am guilty of some kind of subtle trick of archaeological sleight of hand. They may believe that I should be making giant leaps forward rather than carefully and hesitatingly picking my way through the mine field of archaeological research. Admittedly, I have not shed much new light on the three Georgia plantations Adams and his colleagues excavated. I really did not think that I would, and that was not my intention. Instead, I have indicated a direction that historical archaeologists can take, a road they can travel should they wish to do so. If this paper inspires someone to take my ideas further, even to the point of showing that I am completely mistaken, then my true goal will have been attained.

I believe that the future of archaeological interpretation lies in our ability to understand the complex relationships that men and women created in the past. That some of these relationships involved people while others linked people with inanimate things should not surprise or trouble us. The same kinds of relationships swirl around us every day, and we play a willing role in many of them. The webbed nature of these relationships—with their many intersections, tangles, and turns—helps us to understand the difficulty of archaeological research. Interpretations of the past are often so difficult to formulate that we are sometimes tempted to opt for easy answers. A conscious understanding of networks should keep us from taking the simple way out, as we are constantly reminded that life, in all times and places, is complex.

"In the Active Voice": Remaking the American Landscape

Pollen Analysis in Urban Historical Landscape Research

Gerald K. Kelso

The members of human societies modify their environment in ways that are characteristic of their particular lifestyles. Plants are a part of these human environments, even those of the inner cities. Each kind of plant has unique life-support requirements—kind and amount of nutrients, light intensity, relative moisture, and many other factors. Few plants are specifically adapted to particular human-created envi-

This work is dedicated to the memory of the author's friend and colleague Kurt Faust. The pollen studies at the Boott Mills boardinghouse and Kirk Street agents' house would not have been possible without the cooperation and assistance of everyone who participated in the project. The ideas of Gregory K. Clancey, Kathleen H. Bond, David H. Dutton, Lauren J. Cook, David B. Landon, Edward L. Bell, and Grace H. Ziesing were especially critical to the interpretation of the pollen data. Discussions with Steven A. Mrozowski and Mary C. Beaudry were both continuous and spirited.

The Boott Mills boardinghouse and Kirk Street projects were funded by the National Park Service (NPS), the Lowell Historical Preservation Commission, and the City of Lowell School System. Francis P. McManamon and Dwight Pitcaithley of NPS made the original pollen studies possible. Myra F. Harrison, chief of the North Atlantic Cultural Resources Center, and Linda Towle, manager of the Archaeology Branch, encouraged an expanded role for palynology in the most recent Boott Mills research and supported this synthesis. The cooperation and assistance of officer Mark Vargas and librarian Edward Harley, Lowell National Historic Park, in undertaking special sampling and procuring significant reference material were greatly appreciated. Drafting support was provided by Sara Smith of NPS. In some cases she adapted previous work by Kurt Faust, Leslie A. Mead, and Daniel Finamore. Mary C. Beaudry provided all photographs and maps. Grace H. Ziesing provided great service in editing the paper. Alan Synenki and Linda Towle generously arranged funding for illustrations. Technical equipment for palynology was provided by the National Science Foundation under Grant No. BNS-7924470.

ronments, but people do, consciously or unconsciously, control the living conditions of the plants around them. Raising or tearing down a building or a fence will change the light conditions on a particular spot. An increase or decrease in foot or vehicle traffic will affect soil compaction and, consequently, water penetration. Even the kind of refuse discarded at a given spot will affect the fertility of the soil. Plants respond very sensitively to such human-caused changes in their living conditions, and different kinds of human activities produce characteristic kinds and densities of plant communities. The nature of these plant communities is recorded in the pollen deposited and preserved in the soils of human living sites. When this pollen is recovered and analyzed, the plant communities previously occupying a plot can be described, and this knowledge of past vegetation patterns can be used with archaeological data and documentary sources, where available, to reconstruct past human behavior and people's self-images and their attitudes toward the people with whom they interact in their societies.

Most pollen analyses (arid-lands archaeological sites excepted) employ tree pollen from lake and marsh deposits to study prehistoric climatic change and plant migration patterns in broad regions (New England, Great Plains, Prairie Peninsula, for example) over long periods (Quaternary, Holocene, Hypsithermal, for example) by reconstructing vegetation at the formation level (tundra, boreal forest, prairie).[1] The vegetation patterns defined in these investigations are of little value in historical landscape studies because they represent averages and are too generalized to be considered representative of the flora of any particular plot.

To produce an accurate historical landscape study, the analyst must investigate the pollen records of the specific landscape, rather than that of some distant lake or marsh. This is done by analyzing a series (profile) of pollen samples taken down through the soil deposits directly under the landscape. An example of such a soil profile from the late seventeenth- to mid eighteenth-century William Pepperell site

[1] Margaret B. Davis, "Phytogeography and Palynology of the Eastern United States," in H. E. Wright, Jr., and David G. Frey, eds., *The Quaternary of the United States* (Princeton: Princeton University Press, 1965), pp. 377–402; Marjorie G. Winkler, "A 12,000-Year History of Vegetation and Climate for Cape Cod, Massachusetts," *Quaternary Research* 23 (1985): 301–12; Sara L. Webb, "Beech Range Extension and Vegetation History: Pollen Stratigraphy of Two Wisconsin Lakes," *Ecology* 68 (1987): 1993–2005.

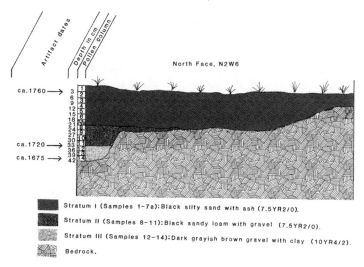

Fig. 1. Archaeological soil profile, with pollen sample locations from the William Pepperill Site, Appledore Island, off the New Hampshire coast. (Drawing, Gerald K. Kelso.)

on Appledore Island off the New Hampshire coast is presented in figure 1.[2] Archaeological experience indicates that both the oldest cultural materials and the oldest pollen should be at the bottom of an undisturbed archaeological site, and the youngest should be at the top. In historical period sites, the ages of the deposits are determined from the ages of the artifacts found in them. The Pepperell site dates are indicated to the right of the soil profile drawing. To make sure pollen dispositions reflect cultural patterns, sampling should, if possible, start below the deposits with the earliest evidence of human occupation at the locality. The profile should extend to the modern surface, and samples should be contiguous (no interval between them). The location of such pollen samples in our historical period dwelling is recorded at the left edge of the soil profile drawing in figure 1. It may, occasionally, be possible to isolate pollen evidence for local ornamental trees from

[2]Gerald K. Kelso and Faith Harrington, "Pollen Record Formation Processes and Historical Land Use at the Isles of Shoals," *Northeast Historical Archaeology* 18 (1992): 70–84.

the tree-dominated regional background pollen rain in soil profiles, but herb (nonarboreal) pollen will provide the most precise records of local groundcover and land use.

The pollen analyst studying herb pollen in historical landscapes must take into account that different kinds of plants produce different amounts of pollen and that they disperse it in different ways. The analyst also must consider the possibility that the pollen record may have been changed by natural and cultural factors after it was deposited on the ground. Herb pollen starts out closer to the ground, where wind velocities are relatively low and where the chance of pollen loss through impact with vegetation is relatively high. It does not blow nearly as far as tree pollen and, therefore, reflects the vegetation of a relatively circumscribed area.[3] It is not enough, however, to be able to tell what kind of plants contributed pollen to the deposit being investigated. Some plants produce much more pollen and disperse it more widely than others. There is no one-to-one correlation between the amount of a particular kind of pollen that fell on a given spot and the numbers of the plants producing that pollen type in the vegetation.

Three kinds of pollen transport and production must be considered. The first of these is wind pollination. Wind-pollinated (anaemophilous) plants produce large quantities of pollen and disperse it widely. Their reproductive strategy is to hit the stigma of another plant of the same species shotgun style. This dispersal mode does not preclude using wind-transported herb pollen in landscape studies because the pollen of even the most notorious hay-fever herbs travels much shorter distances than wind-transported tree pollen. The majority of ragweed pollen grains, for instance, come to earth within three meters of a one-meter high plant, and ninety-five percent of such pollen is lost from the air within nine meters. Wind-pollinated herbs are used to define general land-use patterns across the local landscape. Continuous soil disturbance destroys the roots and rhizomes of perennial grasses, while ragweeds can tolerate the harsh moisture and temperature regimen of bare ground better than even most other weeds.[4] If ragweed

[3]C. R. Janssen, "Local and Regional Pollen Deposition," in H. B. J. Birks and R. G. West, eds., *Quaternary Plant Ecology* (London: Blackwell Scientific, 1973), p. 37.

[4]Gilbert S. Raynor, Eugene C. Ogden, and Janet V. Hayes, "Dispersal of Pollens from Low-Level, Crosswind Line Sources," *Agricultural Metrology* 11 (1973): fig. 7;

pollen goes up in proportion to grass, for instance, we can say that local soils are being disturbed, while an increase in grass pollen relative to that of ragweed can be interpreted as evidence for soil stabilization and a decline in the intensity of human activity.

Insect- or animal-pollinated (zoogamous) plants need to produce much less pollen than wind-pollinated taxa because the pollen is carried directly to other flowers by the transporting creature. The pollen is securely held in the flower by the same sticky oils and resins by which it is transferred to the insect or animal vector, and any pollen not carried away falls to the ground with the flower in the immediate vicinity of the parent plant. Zoogamous pollen in the soil indicates that the source plant was growing close by and is a primary source of very local environmental data.[5] Because zoogamous pollen is deposited in such small quantities relative to that of the wind-pollinated taxa, patterns will not be visible among the counts unless the pollen analyst makes much larger counts (400 + grains) than are normal in paleoecological studies.

The pollen of self-fertilized plants (autogamous) also is significant in the interpretation of historical landscapes, but the patterns recovered by this kind of pollen are more likely to reflect human activity than groundcover. The only autogamous pollen regularly encountered in cultural sites is that of three Eurasian domesticated cereals—wheat (*Triticum*), oats (*Avena*), and barley (*Hordeum*). The pollen grains of these plants are hard to tell apart and are normally lumped under the term *Cerealia*. In these cereals the seed head incorporating both the anther and the stigma does not open until the grain is threshed, and even then much of the pollen is securely bound to the seed by entwining pollen tubes. Such pollen travels with the grain and even survives baking in bread. It is more likely to be found where grain is lost or garbage is disposed of than where the grain was grown. In inner urban sites, two to five percent Cerealia pollen are normally recovered, but

---

Karl-Ernst Behre, "The Interpretation of Anthropogenic Indicators in Pollen Diagrams," *Pollen et Spores* 23 (1981): 229; F. A. Bazzaz, "Ecophysiology of *Ambrosia artemisiifolia*: A Successional Dominant," *Ecology* 55 (1974): 112–19.

[5] K. Faegri and L. van der Pijl, *Principles of Pollination Ecology* (New York: Pergamon Press, 1971), p. 63; Gerald K. Kelso and Mary C. Beaudry, "Pollen Analysis and Urban Land Use: The Environs of Scottow's Dock in Seventeenth-, Eighteenth-, and Early Nineteenth-Century Boston," *Historical Archaeology* 24, no. 1 (1990): 61–81.

larger quantities are found in commercial sites where grain or grain products were processed, stored, or transshipped. Such pollen has proved useful in distinguishing such mercantile landscapes from those around habitations.[6]

Pollen data are customarily presented in pollen diagrams that provide a graphic representation of the quantity and relative age of the pollen recovered from an archaeological excavation. Relative age is represented by the vertical axis of each histogram. The oldest pollen is at the bottom; the youngest is at the top. Quantities of pollen are represented by the horizontal axis. These quantities are percentages, and the longer the bar to the right of the vertical line for each pollen type, the greater the percentage of that kind of pollen at the particular depth. Two kinds of percentages are presented. The solid black portion of each histogram reflects percentages calculated from the total pollen sum of each sample, and the hollow-line portion of each histogram reflects percentages calculated from only arboreal or nonarboreal pollen counts, as appropriate. Separate arboreal and nonarboreal percentages clarify land-use history by eliminating distortion of the groundcover record by the pollen contributions of ornamental trees and the pollen contributed by trees in the region around the sampling site.

When pollen is used to reconstruct historical landscapes, it also is necessary to take into account postdepositional changes in the pollen record. The pollen that is deposited annually on the surface of the ground is carried down into the soil profile by percolating rainwater, where it is moved both up and down by earthworms. These movements produce a pattern in which most of the oldest pollen is at the bottom, but some is at the top. The majority of the intermediate-age pollen grains are in the middle of the profile, but some are at the top and bottom. Most of the recent pollen grains are near the soil surface, but a few have moved to the bottom of the profile. A schematic diagram of this distribution is presented at the top of figure 2.[7]

As pollen moves downward it is attacked and progressively de-

[6]Behre, "Interpretation of Anthropogenic Indicators," p. 227; Irmeli Vuorela, "Relative Pollen Rain around Cultivated Fields," *Acta Botanica Fennica* 102, no. 27 (1973): 1–27; Kelso and Beaudry, "Pollen Analysis," p. 74.

[7]Geoffrey W. Dimbleby, *The Palynology of Archaeological Sites* (New York: Academic Press, 1985), p. 5; K. M. Walsh, J. R. Rowley, and N. J. Norton, "Displacement of Pollen Grains by Earthworms," *Pollen et Spores* 12 (1970): 39–44.

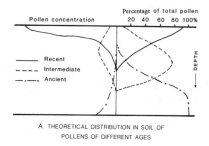

A. THEORETICAL DISTRIBUTION IN SOIL OF
POLLENS OF DIFFERENT AGES

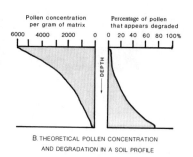

B. THEORETICAL POLLEN CONCENTRATION
AND DEGRADATION IN A SOIL PROFILE

Fig. 2. Theoretical pollen concentration, degradation, and differential age distribution patterns in soils. From Geoffrey W. Dimbleby, *The Palynology of Archaeological Sites* (New York: Academic Press, 1985), p. 5. (Redrawn and adapted by Kurt Faust.)

stroyed by free oxygen in the percolating groundwater and by aerobic fungi.[8] This produces patterns of pollen degradation and concentration in which the largest proportion of pollen grains that are too degraded to recognize are situated near the bottom of the profile, while the

[8] R. H. Tschudy, "Relationship of Palynomorphs to Sedimentation," in R. H. Tschudy and R. S. Scott, eds., *Aspects of Palynology* (New York: John Wiley and Sons, 1969), p. 79; S. Goldstein, "Degradation of Pollen by Phycomycetes," *Ecology* 41 (1960): 543–45.

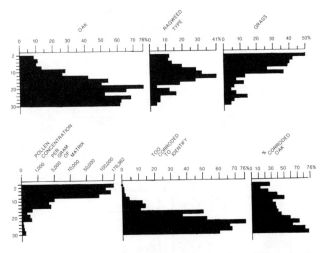

Fig. 3. Pollen percentages from core 2 at Fort Necessity in Great Meadows, Pa. (Graph, Gerald K. Kelso.) Percentages are based on combined arboreal and nonarboreal pollen sums.

highest concentrations of pollen are located near the surface. A schematic of this sequence is presented at the bottom of figure 2.

The pollen concentration and pollen degradation patterns produced by percolation have been recognized in a variety of prehistoric European and historical North American sites. An empirical example from Great Meadows, Pennsylvania, is presented in figure 3. At this site a land-use sequence from primordial forest (pre-1856) to plowed crop land (1856–1926) to regularly mowed grassland (1926–88) produced a pollen sequence in which the bottom of the profile is dominated by oak pollen, the center of the sequence is dominated by ragweed pollen, and the top of the sequence is dominated by grass pollen. This exactly matches the theoretical distribution of ancient, intermediate, and recent pollen at the top of figure 2.[9] At the same time, the

[9] Dimbleby, *Palynology*, figs. 1–35; Gerald K. Kelso, "Preliminary Pollen Analysis for Phase II Archaeological Investigations of the Central Artery/Third Harbor Tunnel Project," in Ricardo J. Elia, ed., *Phase II Archaeological Investigations of the Central Artery/Third Harbor Tunnel Project in Boston, Massachusetts, Volume One: Text and*

distribution of pollen concentrations, pollen that is too corroded to identify, and the percentages of corroded oak pollen in the Great Meadows profile replicate the theoretical pollen concentration and pollen degradation distributions that our model of soil pollen percolation and fungal/oxygen processes predicted for such soils (see fig. 2 bottom). These data clearly indicate that pollen is systematically moved and destroyed by natural processes in soil profiles.

These pollen concentration and degradation dispositions are important to the study of historical landscapes because they are the normal patterns under natural pollen deposition conditions. Soil deposit formation processes in archaeological sites may be evaluated by comparison with them. The possibilities for variation in formation processes are as diverse as culture itself, but three basic patterns have been recognized. First, when the natural pattern appears in an archaeological profile, the deposit has not been disrupted. Pollen percolation has not been impeded by sediment compression caused by intensive human activity, and cultural deposition has been slow enough for natural processes to work. Second, in places where there was more human activity, soil

Illustrations (Boston: Boston University Office of Public Archaeology, 1989), fig. B-4; Gerald K. Kelso, "The Kirk Street Agents' House, Lowell, Massachusetts: Interdisciplinary Analysis of the Historic Landscape" (Technical Report, Lowell National Historical Park, Lowell, 1990), fig. 10; Gerald K. Kelso, "Exploratory Pollen Analysis of Two Cores from the British Old Woods, Saratoga National Historical Park" (Technical Report, National Park Service, Regional Office, Boston, 1990), figs. 1, 2; Gerald K. Kelso, "Exploratory Pollen Analysis in Cedar Swamp, Pequot Reservation, Ledyard, Connecticut" (Technical Report, National Park Service, Boston, 1990), fig. 1; Gerald K. Kelso, Stephen A. Mrozowski, William F. Fisher, and Karl J. Reinhard "Contextual Archaeology at the Kirk Street Agents' House Site," in Mary C. Beaudry and Stephen A. Mrozowski, eds., *Interdisciplinary Investigations of the Boott Mills, Lowell, Massachusetts, Volume II: The Kirk Street Agents' House* (Boston: National Park Service, 1987), figs. 6-2, 6-3, 6-5; Gerald K. Kelso, Rodger Stone, and John F. Karish, "Pollen Analysis in Historical Landscape Studies at Fort Necessity National Battlefield," *Park Science* 10, no. 2 (January 1990): 10–11; Gerald K. Kelso, Stephen A. Mrozowski, William F. Fisher, and Karl J. Reinhard, "Contextual Archeology at the Boott Mills Boardinghouse Backlots," in Mary C. Beaudry and Stephen A. Mrozowski, eds., *Interdisciplinary Investigations of the Boott Mills, Lowell, Massachusetts, Volume III: The Lowell Boarding House System as a Way of Life* (Boston: National Park Service, 1989), fig. 12–9; Kelso and Harrington, "Pollen Record Formation Processes," pp. 76–77; Gerald K. Kelso and William F. Fisher, "The Botanical Context at the David Fiske Homestead," in Alan T. Synenki, ed., *Archeological Investigations of Minute Man National Historical Park, Volume I: Farmers and Artisans of the Historical Period* (Boston: National Park Service, 1990), figs. 11–5, 11–6; Dimbleby, *Palynology*, fig. 3.

compression and faster sediment deposition preclude pollen percolation. These factors produce shifts in the plant pollen-type spectra that correlate with stratigraphic levels, and the spectra reflect the groundcover associated with the human activity that produced the stratigraphic deposit. Pollen degradation patterns are irregular in deposits rapidly produced by intensive human activity. Pollen concentrations in such deposits correlate with shifts in pollen types and register the relative density of the vegetation. Third, when the natural pollen concentration and degradation patterns are reversed or when pollen concentration figures shift abruptly without clear stratigraphic boundaries in the soil, it is probable that the deposit consists of episodic fill or disturbed soil.[10]

When the members of societies modify their environment, the resulting landscape reflects their attitudes toward their surroundings and may register divisions within the society. Each of the previously described basic pollen-record formation patterns records such environmental modification. In the following section, an example of each of these patterns will be presented with conventional pollen counts, documentary evidence, plant macrofossils, archaeological artifacts, and phytoliths (plant silica deposits) in an interdisciplinary study of social structure recorded in the nature and intensity of residential land use by mill workers living in the Boott Mills boardinghouses and mill managers occupying the Kirk Street agents' house in the nineteenth-century planned industrial city of Lowell, Massachusetts (fig. 4).

The Boott Mills boardinghouses were located along the Eastern Canal in Lowell, Massachusetts. The plot was part of a circa 1821 farmstead and was successively occupied by the mansion of industrialist Kirk Boott (ca. 1825–35) and two of the eight Boott Mills boardinghouses (1835–1942). The backlot between the boardinghouses was the focus of an archaeological investigation (fig. 5). The central sections of the boardinghouses were initially occupied by typical "mill girls" (single, New England–born women) with families of male supervisors in separate tenements at the end of each structure. A corporation policy of maintaining an image of order and propriety carried over into the residences and the external appearances of the structures. The leisure-

---

[10] Kelso et al., "Contextual Archaeology," p. 258.

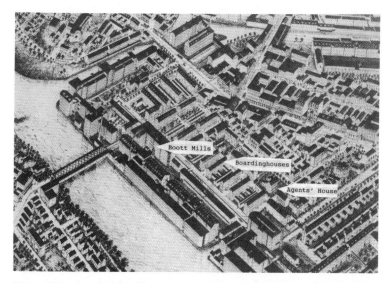

Fig. 4. Detail, 1876 bird's-eye view of Lowell showing the area of Boott Corporation mills and housing. From Mary C. Beaudry and Stephen A. Mrozowski, eds., *Interdisciplinary Investigations of the Boott Mills, Lowell, Massachusetts, Volume I: Life at the Boarding Houses* (Boston: National Park Service, 1987), p. 21, fig. 4–4.

time behavior of the boardinghouse occupants was strictly controlled, and late nineteenth-century photographs of the boardinghouses show tree-lined streets, vine-covered walls, and what appear to be rather barren utilitarian backlots.[11]

The demography of the boardinghouses changed during the latter half of the nineteenth century. More families and unmarried males moved into the boardinghouses during the 1850s and 1860s, although female occupants continued to outnumber males substantially, and the families appear to have been largely American born. The proportion

[11] Kathleen H. Bond, " 'That We May Purify Our Corporation by Discharging the Offenders': The Documentary Record of Social Control at the Boott Mills," in Beaudry and Mrozowski, *Interdisciplinary Investigations . . . Volume III*, p. 24; Mary C. Beaudry, "The Lowell Boott Mills Complex and Its Housing: Material Expressions of Corporate Ideology," *Historical Archaeology* 23, no. 1 (1989): 19–32, figs. 7, 8.

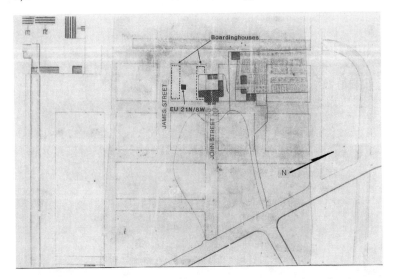

Fig. 5. Layout, Kirk Boott's estate and the subsequent boardinghouses over "A Plan of the Land and Building Belonging to the Merrimack Manufacturing Company" by Geo. R. Baldwin, 1825. (Lowell National Historical Park; overlay drawing, Kurt Faust.) The black square labeled EU 21N/8W is the 2-by-2 meter archaeological excavation unit from which the pollen profiles were taken.

of foreign workers in the mills increased markedly during this era, but the immigrants were not living in the boardinghouses. This changed after 1880, and by 1900 the majority of the boarders were both male and immigrant. Both living conditions and corporate control of the labor force deteriorated markedly during this immigrant interval. Mill managers criticized boardinghouse keepers more frequently for conditions around the boardinghouses, and employees were censured more often for their off-duty behavior. Three-fourths of the reprimanded employees had Irish surnames, and two-thirds of the extant rebukes were concerned with alcohol abuse.[12]

[12] Kathleen H. Bond, "A Preliminary Report on the Demography of the Boott Mills Housing Units #33–48, 1838–1942," in Mary C. Beaudry and Stephen A. Mrozowski, eds., *Interdisciplinary Investigations . . . Volume I*, pp. 50–53; Bond, " 'That We May Purify Our Corporation,' " pp. 27–29.

The archaeological record of the boardinghouse backlot agrees closely with the documents. Where the backlot soil deposits were undisturbed, three stratigraphic/cultural levels were evident in the archaeological record. At the bottom of the sequence was an artifact-sterile, inorganic, glacial sand (level 1; pollen samples 1–4). Level 2 (pollen samples 5–11) was the major occupation layer and encompassed the last three-fourths of the nineteenth century. Few artifacts and faunal remains were recovered from the deepest three-fourths of level 2, and weed seeds were rare compared to later deposits. All the food-plant seeds and phytoliths (plant silica bodies) found in this level came from features. The archaeological data from level 2 appear to record a well-maintained backlot with few weeds and little trash or organic waste.[13]

Most of the artifacts in level 2 were found in the upper few centimeters of the deposit. The majority of these items postdate 1890. Some of this trash—housewares, for instance—was originally the property of the boardinghouse keepers, but items such as pipe fragments marked with Irish slogans probably belonged to male immigrant boarders. Of the seventy-two alcoholic beverage bottles found in the backlot, seventy came from this post-1890 portion of level 2.[14]

Level 3 (pollen samples 12–13), at the top of the profile, was dominated by artifacts dating to the first quarter of the twentieth century. It postdates the use of the buildings as residences.[15] The boarding-

[13] Mary C. Beaudry and Stephen A. Mrozowski, "Archeology in the Backlots of Boott Units 45 and 48: Household Archeology with a Difference," in Beaudry and Mrozowski, *Interdisciplinary Investigations . . . Volume III*, pp. 27–29; David B. Landon, "Zoological Analysis," in Beaudry and Mrozowski, *Interdisciplinary Investigations . . . Volume II*, table 7–1; David B. Landon, "Faunal Remains from the Boott Mills Boardinghouses," in Beaudry and Mrozowski, *Interdisciplinary Investigations . . . Volume III*, table 9–2; Stephen A. Mrozowski, "Plant Macrofossil Analysis," in Beaudry and Mrozowski, *Interdisciplinary Investigations . . . Volume I*, p. 149; Stephen A. Mrozowski, "Macrofossil Analysis," in Beaudry and Mrozowski, *Interdisciplinary Investigations . . . Volume III*, pp. 273–75; William F. Fisher, "An Analysis of Phytoliths from the Boott Mills Boardinghouse Excavations," in Beaudry and Mrozowski, *Interdisciplinary Investigations . . . Volume III*, p. 265.

[14] David H. Dutton, "Thrasher's China or Colored Porcelain: Ceramics from a Boott Mills Boardinghouse and Tenement," in Beaudry and Mrozowski, *Interdisciplinary Investigations . . . Volume III*, p. 86; Lauren J. Cook, "Tobacco-Related Material Culture and the Working Class," in Beaudry and Mrozowski, *Interdisciplinary Investigations . . . Volume III*, p. 227; Kathleen H. Bond, "The Medicine, Alcohol, and Soda Vessels from the Boott Mills Boardinghouses," in Beaudry and Mrozowski, *Interdisciplinary Investigations . . . Volume III*, p. 138.

[15] Bond, "Medicine, Alcohol, and Soda Vessels," pp. 137–39; Cook, "Tobacco-Related Material Culture," p. 207; Dutton, "Thrasher's China," pp. 117–19.

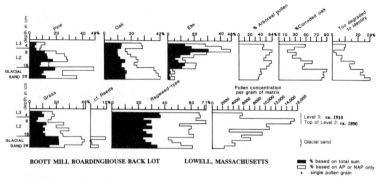

Fig. 6. Natural pollen-percolation profile. Pollen percentages of critical types in excavation unit 21N/8W, northwestern corner profile. (Graph, Kurt Faust.)

house cultural sequence was capped with a thin, relatively continuous layer of broken window glass from the 1934–42 dismantling of the boardinghouses.

A pollen sequence demonstrating natural pollen-percolation in an archaeological site was found in an undisturbed soil profile taken at the northwestern corner of excavation unit 21N/8W.[16] This pollen sequence covers the entire 1820s to 1930s Boott mansion and boarding-house occupation period. Pollen concentrations generally decline from the top to the bottom of this profile, while measures of pollen corrosion are progressively larger in the deeper fill (fig. 6). This conforms to the natural site-formation process pattern presented in figures 1 and 2. It indicates that the profile is undisturbed.

The sand of level 1 at the base of the boardinghouse stratigraphic sequence is glacial outwash. It contained no artifacts, and no plants grew on it while it was being formed. Level 1 should contain no pollen. Contrary to expectations, pollen spectra reflecting several distinct plant populations were recovered from the glacial sand. These must have percolated down into the sediment from a succession of groundcovers. Sedge (Cyperaceae) pollen and grass pollen resembling that of reeds (*Phragmites*) were present only in the level 1 glacial sand (see fig. 6, samples 1–4). These record wet conditions and reflect the poor drainage

[16]Kelso et al., "Contextual Archaeology," p. 234, fig. 12–2.

of the terrace above the river before construction on the site. Ragweeds (*Ambrosia* spp.) are the premier pioneer on disturbed soil in eastern North America because they tolerate the harsh temperature and moisture regimen of cleared ground better than most other weedy taxa.[17] The ragweed-type pollen dominating sample 1 reflects either the agricultural fields of the farm originally occupying the site or the circa 1825 construction of the Boott mansion.

Grass (Gramineae) pollen frequencies increase abruptly, replacing ragweed-type as the dominant herb in sample 2 (level 1), and decline with equal suddenness in sample 5 (level 2). Grass pollen percentages rise slowly on developed pastures or stabilizing ground but rise suddenly when a lawn is created with sod. Boott had a well-maintained grass lawn, and the sudden changes in samples 2 and 5 can only reflect the sodding and destruction of that lawn.[18]

Ragweed frequencies are higher and grass pollen counts are lower in samples 5–9 of level 2 (see fig. 6). Artifacts indicate that these samples span the 1836–90 boardinghouse occupation, and this abrupt shift in the pollen spectra reflects the sudden, planned change in land use from formal lawn to inner-urban backlot. During this period both grass and ragweed frequencies are relatively uniform, reflecting a relatively stable groundcover. During the main boardinghouse occupation, the backlot was weedier than Boott's lawn but less weedy than the subsequent, post-1890, interval. Few grains of European cereal pollen were deposited during this interval, compared with other urban dwelling backlots. This suggests that little organic garbage was being spread around. Rising chestnut (*Castanea*) and elm (*Ulmus*) frequencies in level 2 record the maturation of the trees still visible along the adjacent

---

[17] United States Army Corps of Engineers, "Geologic and Hydrologic Investigations," in *Merrimack Wastewater Management: Key to a Clean River* (Waltham, Mass.: By the Corps, 1974), p. 16; Bazzaz, "Ecophysiology," p. 112.

[18] Karl-Ernst Behre, "The Interpretation of Anthropogenic Indicators in Pollen Diagrams," *Pollen et Spores* 23, no. 2 (1983): fig. 2; Kelso, Stone, and Karish, "Pollen Analysis," p. 10; Gerald K. Kelso and Johanna Schoss, "Exploratory Pollen Analysis of the Bostonian Hotel Site Sediments," in James W. Bradley, ed., *Archaeology of the Bostonian Hotel Site* (Boston: Massachusetts Historical Commission, 1983), p. 73; Kelso et al., "Contextual Archaeology," fig. 6–2; Kelso and Beaudry, "Pollen Analysis," p. 68; Kelso, "Kirk Street Agents' House," p. 29; Mary C. Beaudry, "Archaeological Testing at the Proposed Lowell Boarding House Park Site," in Beaudry and Mrozowski, *Interdisciplinary Investigations . . . Volume I*, p. 73.

streets. Increasing vine family (Vitaceae) counts indicate the spread of Boston ivy (*Parthenocissus*, a member of the vine family), which is evident growing on the rear walls of the boardinghouses in several nineteenth-century photographs. The pollen contribution of a dense local groundcover probably would mask the pollen contribution of the trees and vines at the edge of the lot, suggesting that the soil was relatively bare as well as stable.[19] The pollen spectra agree with the documents and archaeological data in describing the backlot as a well-maintained island of utilitarian space in a landscape that was managed to project a desirable corporate image.

Ragweed pollen frequencies increase in samples 10 and 11 at the top of level 2, while those of grass pollen decline further, indicating a much weedier backlot. These samples were deposited during the immigrant labor occupation of the boardinghouses after 1890. The majority of the artifacts—liquor bottles as well as housewares—were recovered from the top of level 2. Both boardinghouse keepers and residents contributed to the mess, and mill administrators apparently were unable or unwilling to halt the decline in landscape maintenance indicated by pollen as well as archaeology and documents.

In early twentieth-century level 3, pollen concentrations decline abruptly from nearly sixteen thousand to less than six thousand grains per gram, and the percentage of corroded oaks and pollen too corroded to identify increases abruptly. The kinds of plants in the backlot did not change, but there were fewer of them. One of the boardinghouses was frequently vacant during this interval while the other served as mill storage. There was unquestionably more vehicular and foot traffic across the backlot. This suppressed the existing flora and churned the upper portion of the soil, exposing the extant pollen to corrosive agents and further depressing concentrations. Compression of the soil under the churned layer reduced soil permeability and diverted destructive oxygen and aerobic fungi from the high pollen concentrations in the top of level 2.

[19] Kelso et al., "Contextual Archaeology," figs. 6–2, 6–3, 6–4; Kelso and Beaudry, "Pollen Analysis," fig. 7; Beaudry, "Lowell Boott Mills Complex," figs. 7, 8; Paul S. Martin, "Geochronology of Pluvial Lake Cochise, Southern Arizona II, Pollen Analysis of a 42 Meter Core," *Ecology* 44 (1963): fig. 2; Henrik Tauber, *Differential Pollen Dispersion and the Interpretation of Pollen Diagrams* (Copenhagen: Geological Survey of Denmark, 1965), ser. 2, no. 89, p. 33.

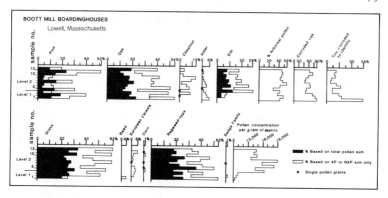

Fig. 7. Soil-disturbance pollen profile. Pollen percentages of critical types in excavation unit 21N/8W, northeastern corner profile. (Graph, Kurt Faust.)

A pollen sequence recording soil disturbance was found in another profile, taken at the northeastern corner of excavation unit 21N/8W.[20] The twentieth-century deposit, level 3, was not present in this profile, and the nineteenth-century level 2 matrix appears to have been homogenized. The archaeologists considered this locus to be a feature. The naturally percolated pollen concentration and pollen corrosion patterns are evident only in the level 1 glacial sand at the bottom of this profile (fig. 7). Reed grass and sedge pollen were most prominent in the sand, as they were in the previously discussed natural pollen-percolation profile. The pollen spectrum of level 1 is the truncated remnant of a preboardinghouse pollen spectrum that had percolated down into the sand.

In level 2 the pollen spectra of individual plant taxa are irregular, and pollen concentrations are notably higher in samples 4–8 than they are in samples 9–12. These do not appear to be natural patterns. The contrast in pollen concentrations between these two profile segments suggests two different matrix sources or two separate matrix manipulation episodes. Thirteen squash or pumpkin (*Cucurbita* spp.) phytoliths were found in sample 12, and nine phytoliths of this type were recovered from sample 11. Unusual phytoliths very similar to those of ba-

[20] Kelso et al., "Contextual Archaeology," p. 234, fig. 12–2.

nanas (*Protium panamense*) were found in samples 7, 8, and 9. The aberrant pollen concentrations' mean soil disturbance and the phytolith data indicate that the soil disturbance was associated with plants that were probably not growing in the backlot. These data suggest that this profile records two separate episodes of garbage burial during the circa 1836–90 boardinghouse-occupation period archaeologically registered in level 2. Burying garbage, rather than simply tossing it in the backlot, is consistent with the strict corporate housekeeping code of this period.

Different land-use patterns are recorded in the agents' house backlot. This structure is a two-and-one-half-story brick duplex at 63–67 Kirk Street (see fig. 3). It housed the top local agents (that is, managers) of the Massachusetts and Boott Mills corporations from 1847 through 1905. The imposing interior and formal landscape of the front and side yards of the structure reflected the high status of the occupants in the corporate hierarchy. The agents' house was sold in 1906 and was used as a boardinghouse and lodging house until 1911. The vacant property was purchased by the city of Lowell in 1914, and a boiler plant for the school system was erected on the Boott Mills half in 1922 (fig. 8).[21]

Seven stratigraphic levels were recognized in the agents' house backlot. Level 1, at the top of the sequence, consisted of modern parking-lot blacktop and concrete. Level 2 was mixed, early twentieth-century (pre-1925) fill that is probably a by-product of boiler plant construction and modifications in the 1920s. Level 3 consisted of silty sand containing late nineteenth-century ceramics, with a few possibly early twentieth-century pieces. During deposition of level 3, the house was occupied by childless, middle-aged couples. The dates of artifacts suggest that level 4, a uniform, humic-appearing deposit, dates to the middle of the nineteenth century, when the house was occupied by Homer Bartlett and his family (1846–1860/61). Level 4 incorporated large quantities of fish bones and scales and domestic animal bones.

[21] Edward L. Bell, " 'So Much Like Home': The Historical Context of the Kirk Street Agents' House," in Beaudry and Mrozowski, *Interdisciplinary Investigations . . . Volume II*, p. 8; Maureen K. Phillips, *Kirk Street Agents' House Historic Structures Report* (Boston: National Park Service, 1990): figs. 12–19; Kelso, "Kirk Street Agents' House," p. 17; Mary C. Beaudry, "The Archeological Record at the Kirk Street Agents' House, Lowell, Massachusetts. Part I: The Systematic Excavations," in Beaudry and Mrozowski, *Interdisciplinary Investigations . . . Volume II*, pp. 2, 44, 50; Bell, " 'So Much Like Home,' " p. 9.

These imply that butchering occurred in the backlot. The high phyto-lith counts of level 4 indicate that large quantities of vegetal matter were deposited in the backlot during development of the layer. This level was only six to ten centimeters thick, and there was no evidence of mixing with level 5 below. It was probably not a garden, as originally hypothesized. Level 4 seems to indicate that the occupants of the agents' house were disposing of large quantities of food waste on the surface of their backyard. This contrasts sharply with housekeeping at the Boott Mills boardinghouses. Large quantities of dishes also were recovered from level 4. These dishes (deposited after circa 1850 but probably before 1870) had suffered considerable wear in active use, but there was little evidence of postdeposition damage. The excavators suggest that the ceramics deposited in the backlot were either the result of increased breakage in the large household that occupied the structure in the late 1850s, child's play refuse associated with the younger members of that household, or refuse from the departure of that family in 1860 or 1861.[22]

Layer 5 below was both darker and thinner than level 4, and it contained no artifacts. The color of this deposit, pollen subsequently indicated, resulted from naturally deposited humic matter from weeds on waste ground at the rear of the backlot. Level 5 predates the 1850s intensive use of the backlot, but postdates, as will be seen, the late 1840s construction of the house. Patches of mortar in a sand and gravel mix were noted on the interface of level 5, and it peeled away cleanly from level 6. Level 6 was a brown sand mixed with clastic gravel, cobbles, and fine silt. Lenses of mortar in level 6 date it to the 1845–47 construction of the agents' house. Level 7 consisted of glacial sand that had been culturally disturbed. Quantities of artifacts increased steadily from level 7 through level 5, reflecting increasing human presence on the plot.

The Kirk Street agents' house backlot provides a good example of the sort of pollen profile that develops in an intense land-use situation.

[22] Beaudry, "Archeological Record," pp. 54–55; Bell, " 'So Much Like Home,' " pp. 19–20; Michael B. Schiffer, *Formation Processes of the Archaeological Record* (Albuquerque: University of New Mexico, 1987), p. 75; Mary C. Beaudry and Stephen A. Mrozowski, "Summary and Conclusions," in Beaudry and Mrozowski, *Interdisciplinary Investigations . . . Volume II*, p. 144.

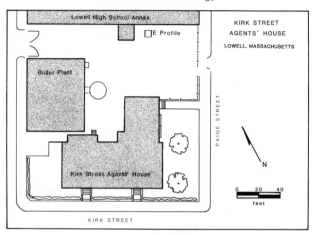

Fig. 8. Plan view of the Kirk Street agents' house in 1987.
(Drawing, Kurt Faust.)

Five of the seven archaeological levels analyzed for pollen in the back-lot were found in square E (see fig. 8). Level 7, at the bottom of the deposit, is dominated by grass pollen that may reflect former pasture (fig. 9). This is replaced by ragweed, reflecting the soil disturbance of the 1845–47 construction period in mortar-laden level 6. Pollen concentrations are highest toward the top of the layer, and a greater proportion of the pollen is degraded toward the bottom, indicating that much of this pollen is leached down into the deposit from the surface before and during the construction of the agents' house. The ragweeds apparently gave way to insect-pollinated ruderal-ground taxa (*Aster*-type) across the rear of the backlot, indicating that level 5 was deposited during the brief interval of reduced soil disturbance between the end of construction and the beginning of inhabitant activity in the backlot. The goosefoot family (*Chenopodiaceae*) pollen contribution rose abruptly during deposition of organically enriched, trash-loaded level 4. These plants favor fertile soils, and large counts of goosefoot family pollen are found only in level 4. Goosefoot frequencies rise abruptly at the lower boundary of level 4, when the inhabitants of the agents' house began to deposit food waste in the backlot, and goosefoot counts decline abruptly at the upper boundary of the level, when fertility

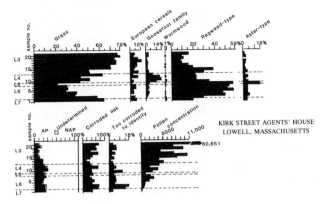

Fig. 9. Intense land-use profile. Pollen percentages of critical types in Square E, Kirk Street agents' house. (Graph, Kurt Faust.) Histograms are based on combined arboreal and nonarboreal pollen sums.

decreased because garbage was no longer being deposited in the area. These goosefoot counts, and the *Aster-type* peak in level 5 below, attest to the sensitivity with which weedy taxa respond to changes in human activities. Grass pollen percentages increase steadily at the expense of ragweed-type up through the late nineteenth-century level 3 deposit, and pollen concentrations rise parallel to grass percentages. Ragweed proliferates on disturbed soils but is replaced by perennial grasses as soil stabilizes. This has been recorded in declining ragweed pollen counts and increasing grass pollen frequencies at several historical-era sites.[23] Few artifacts and no food remains were found in level 3, and the decrease in the ragweed pollen contribution and increase in grass pollen percentages as pollen concentrations rise up through level 3 means that the grass cover in the backlot was thickening as the soil was stabilizing.

The activities of the Bartlett household indicate that the mill agents who occupied the house during the late nineteenth century could have done as they pleased in the backlot. They chose to do

[23] Kelso et al., "Contextual Archeology," p. 109; Behre, "Interpretation of Anthropogenic Indicators," p. 236; Kelso and Schoss, "Exploratory Pollen Analysis," pp. 67–76; Kelso, Stone, and Karish, "Pollen Analysis," p. 11.

nothing. The backlot was little used and disturbed not at all. It had become as neat and well kept as the formal front and side yards.[24] With no children in residence and few servants compared with the Bartlett household, these middle-aged men and their wives apparently felt no need to butcher meat or to do other things regularly that required external utility space.

The landscapes of the Boott Mills boardinghouses and the Kirk Street agents' house clearly reflect the freedom of people in management positions in the nineteenth-century industrial city of Lowell, Massachusetts, to use their living space as they pleased and the absence of such options among laborers at the other end of the social hierarchy. The men in charge of the Boott Mills Corporation were concerned with appearances. The high social status of financier Kirk Boott and the prominent position of the mill agents in the local hierarchy were publicly expressed in the imposing facades of their dwellings and in the formal lawns that the pollen spectra and the archival sources indicate surrounded their respective homes.[25] This concern with appearances carried over to the boardinghouses. An image of orderly, well-kept living conditions was projected by the vines and elms photographically and palynologically recorded on the boardinghouse walls and along the streets. No trash accumulated in the backlot before circa 1890, and pollen, phytolith, and plant macrofossil data indicate that any organic garbage deposited behind the boardinghouse was deliberately buried. Grass pollen frequencies were low compared with Boott's preceding lawn, but there were fewer weeds than during the subsequent immigrant period. The relatively low, stable grass and weed pollen counts over the circa 1836–90 period suggest that a rather barren backlot was the product of an intentional maintenance program. The pollen recovered probably reflects a few plants in inaccessible spaces. A slow to nonexistent accumulation of matrix over this interval of approximately fifty years is suggested by the natural pollen-record formation patterns characteristic of the pollen concentration and preservation measures. Such slow deposition and stable vegetation imply that the backlot was little used as well as regularly maintained.

[24] Kelso, "Kirk Street Agents' House," p. 29.
[25] Bell, " 'So Much Like Home,' " pp. 7–10; Kelso, "Kirk Street Agents' House," p. 17; Kelso et al., "Contextual Archeology," p. 245.

The mill workers occupying the boardinghouses had little influence on the pollen record of land use because they did not spend much time in the backlot. The corporation and its operatives were concerned with the backlot, but the workers were not, and it is probable that the concerns of the labor force with the boardinghouses as "home" were focused on interior spaces.[26]

After circa 1890, maintenance declined and discarded personal items made the mill workers archaeologically visible in the backlot. Weeds sprouted among the trash, while proliferating management complaints to boardinghouse keepers about the condition of the property went both unheeded and unenforced. Neither corporate managers nor boardinghouse keepers appear to have had much concern for the welfare of foreign workers, and a general deterioration of mill-worker living conditions ensued during the immigrant labor period in the boardinghouses. The liquor bottles discarded among the weeds in the backlot, in turn, record the workers' attitudes toward both their employer and the environment provided for them. The occupants of the boardinghouses cared little for the places, and their defiance of the frequently reiterated corporation rule against drinking on the premises registers their efforts to exercise some control over their lives.

A different land-use regimen is recorded in the backlot of the agents' house. The pollen spectra of individual stratigraphic layers are distinctive, while pollen preservation measures are irregular in most layers. This indicates relatively intensive human activity resulting in rapid accumulation of the deposits. The pollen types themselves reflect a local, rather weedy flora that was adapting rapidly to the way backlot use changed with the occupation history and demography of the agents' house. The ragweeds recording the soil disturbance of the construction period were superseded by insect-pollinated relatives—probably sunflowers, goldenrod, or asters—on unused ground at the rear of the lot during a brief "settling in" period at the beginning of the occupation. Goosefoot populations expanded during the subsequent interval, circa 1847–61, and this goosefoot reflects soil enriched by home-butchering

---

[26]Richard P. Horowitz, "Architecture and Culture: The Meaning of the Lowell Boarding House," *American Quarterly* 25, no. 1 (March 1973): 64–82; Stephen A. Mrozowski and Mary C. Beaudry, "Discussion and Conclusions," in Beaudry and Mrozowski, *Interdisciplinary Investigations . . . Volume III*, p. 291.

waste and organic garbage broadcast deposited by members of the household in a backlot where the grandchildren of mill agent Bartlett played with, and abandoned, old housewares. The older married couples who occupied the agents' house after 1861 could have used the backlot in a similar way. They chose not to. No trash or food waste was deposited in the backlot, and rising grass pollen contributions correlated with increasing pollen concentrations and declining weed pollen percentages reflect a thickening grass cover on progressively more stable soils through the latter decades of the nineteenth century. It would appear that with no children and fewer servants, the mill agents who succeeded the Bartletts had no need of an exterior utility space for extensive home food preparation or garbage disposal. After the Bartletts, the resident agents apparently used the backlot little and disturbed it not at all. The mill managers occupying the agents' house, unlike the mill workers in their boardinghouses, controlled the backlot of their dwelling, and they used it in ways that would not have been tolerated at the boardinghouses. The backlot groundcover reflects the attitudes of the residents as these changed through time rather than company policy, and the agents very likely included their exterior as well as interior environment in their definition of "home."

The Boott Mills boardinghouse and Kirk Street agents' house pollen investigations indicate that an interdisciplinary approach integrating archival resources, archaeological data, and paleobotanical sediment analysis is more productive than independent studies of these kinds in historical landscape reconstruction. The way in which these disciplines were applied in this study differs from the way such data sources are normally used in landscape research. In a typical landscape analysis, documents are searched for references to plantings and formal landscape features.[27] Here the target of the literature search was the compo-

---

[27] Lauren Meier and Nora Mitchell, "Principles for Preserving Historic Plant Material," *CRM Bulletin* 13, no. 6 (1990): 17–22; J. Clarke and G. F. Finnegan, "Colonial Survey Records and the Vegetation of Essex County, Ontario," *Journal of Historical Geography* 10, no. 2 (1984): 119–38; Gordon G. Whitney and William C. Davis, "Thoreau and the Forest History of Concord, Massachusetts," *Journal of Forest History* 30, no. 2 (1986): 70–81; J. Timothy Keller and Genevieve P. Keller, *How to Evaluate and Nominate Designed Historic Landscapes* (Washington, D.C.: National Park Service, 1989); Linda F. McClelland, J. Timothy Keller, Genevieve P. Keller, and Robert Z. Melnick, *How to Identify, Evaluate, and Register Rural Historic Landscapes* (Washington, D.C.: National Park Service, 1992).

sition of social units and the attitudes of people toward their living conditions and toward each other. Landscape archaeologists normally seek evidence of planting beds, paths, and other structural elements. In the Lowell study, trash and weeds—or the absence of them—were the most productive lines of evidence. It told the excavators a great deal about the forces of social control and how people felt about their surroundings. Palynologists investigating landscapes customarily seek pollen evidence for the groundcover composition. Here pollen spectra reflecting the vegetation were used with palynological evidence for soil deposit formation processes to provide information about the nature and intensity of human activity on given plots. When these three data sources—documents, material culture, and paleobiological data (pollen, phytoliths, macrofossils, and faunal remains)—are integrated, it is possible to draw inferences about sociocultural patterns and ideology beyond the capability of any single discipline.

The Urban Landscape, the Work Yard, and Archaeological Site Formation Processes in Charleston, South Carolina

Martha Zierden

The popular image of the historic city of Charleston, South Carolina, is embodied in the titles of two early publications: *Charleston: Historic and Romantic* and *Charleston: A Gracious Heritage.*[1] This bustling seaport was home to merchants and planters who earned tremendous wealth through trade in plantation staples; they influenced the political

Archaeological research in Charleston has been interdisciplinary, and many of the interpretations presented here have resulted from collaborations with colleagues: historian Jeanne Calhoun, ethnobotanist Michael Trinkley, palynologist Karl Reinhard, and especially zooarchaeologist Elizabeth Reitz and architectural historian Bernard Herman. The urban archaeology program is sponsored by Charleston Museum under the direction of Dr. John Brumgardt. Funding for excavation projects also has been provided by the City of Charleston, the South Carolina Department of Archives and History, Historic Charleston Foundation, and private property owners. This paper benefited greatly from the comments of Anne Yentsch, Bernard Herman, and Lu Ann De Cunzo.

[1] Harriette Kershaw Leiding, *Charleston: Historic and Romantic* (Philadelphia: J. B. Lippincott, 1931); Robert Molloy, *Charleston: A Gracious Heritage* (New York: D. Appleton-Century Co., 1947).

and economic systems of the new nation as the colonies won their independence from Britain, and they built a city full of stately public and private dwellings. They purchased a range of material items that reflected their secure hold on the new land and on the human chattel who wrested wealth from it. When changes in economic systems and transportation routes and the loss of a war with northern states led to economic devastation, the descendants of colonial power brokers lived in genteel poverty, shared their decaying town houses with boarders, and developed a version of history bordering on the mythical. A late twentieth-century economic resurgence, bolstered by military bases, a vital port, and a dynamic tourism industry, has revitalized the historic city and its architecture. New coats of paint, sympathetic new buildings, and generously located flower gardens visually enhance the version of Charleston as historic and romantic.

Current scholarship—archaeological, documentary, and architectural—is providing a more complex picture of Charleston's heritage by focusing on the not-so-grand buildings and the not-so-glamorous aspects of daily life. Archaeological research, in particular, has focused on the evolution of the urban landscape from the mid eighteenth through the mid nineteenth centuries. These excavations have revealed material culture that reflects the purchasing power of Charleston's elite, which was the greatest of any colonial American city. Simultaneously, data from the urban sites underscore the difficulties of daily life during this period: problems with overcrowding, health and sanitation, refuse disposal, and the segregation of noxious chores. Archaeological data also reflect the tremendous labor required from a primarily slave population to maintain the white minority in a state of luxury and maintain their presence in the urban compounds of their masters. Archaeological evidence for gracious living will be discussed here only indirectly as it relates to changes in the landscape; this essay will focus on the details of the landscape of daily life. To do this, the student of Charleston's past must move beyond the imposing residences to the outbuildings and work yards behind them.

Data from excavations in the work yards of Charleston houses, particularly the complex layers of soil and the discrete features they contain, form the basis for discussion of the evolving urban landscape. A decade of archaeological research in Charleston has produced a controlled database from eighteen urban sites and supporting information from many others. Data from these sites have been used to investigate various facets of the creation of an urban terrain and an urban society. This approach in Charleston embraces the idea of a cultural landscape, the modification of land according to a set of cultural plans, embodying often inseparable technological, social, and ideological dimensions. People used these created and used landscapes in a planned and orderly manner for everything from food production to formal design to explicit statements about their position in the world.[2]

Archaeological evidence for evolution of the landscape may generally be divided into three categories: material culture, stratigraphy (the layered deposition of earth and trash), and plant and animal remains. Of the first two categories, it is the former that most often comes to the mind of the public, yet it is the latter that is the most informative for landscape evolution; in fact, the recovered artifacts assume their importance from their position in the stratigraphy and their role in determining the source of those soil deposits. The third category of data, plant and animal remains, includes seeds, pollen, and bone fragments. These have provided information essential to the landscape studies. Archaeological research has been interdisciplinary, and archaeologists have worked closely with zooarchaeologists, ethnobotanists, palynologists, geographers, historians, and architects. The contributions of these scholars have been integral to ongoing research. Their work is discussed in detail in various site reports; interpretations, particularly those based on the architectural fabric of the city, are summa-

---

[2]Two volumes summarize general documentary research on Charleston and propose a variety of research questions. These topics have guided archaeological research at each of the sites discussed here. See Martha Zierden and Jeanne Calhoun, "An Archaeological Preservation Plan for Charleston, South Carolina," *Charleston Museum Archaeological Contributions* 8 (1984): 97–113; and Dale Rosengarten et al., "Between the Tracks: Charleston's East Side during the Nineteenth Century," *Charleston Museum Archaeological Contributions* 17 (1987): 157–64. For a detailed and eloquent summary of his goals of landscape archaeology, see James Deetz, "Prologue: Landscapes as Cultural Statements," in William Kelso and Rachel Most, eds., *Earth Patterns: Essays in Landscape Archaeology* (Charlottesville: University Press of Virginia, 1990), pp. 2–3; Martha Zierden and Bernard Herman, "Charleston Townhouses: Archaeology, Architecture, and the Urban Landscape, 1750–1850," in Rebecca Yamin and Karen B. Metheny, eds., *Landscape Archaeology: Studies in Reading and Interpreting the American Historical Landscape* (Knoxville: University of Tennessee Press, forthcoming 1996); Marwyn Samuels, "The Biography of Landscape: Cause and Culpability," in D. W. Meinig, ed., *The Interpretation of Ordinary Landscapes: Geographical Essays* (New York: Oxford University Press, 1979).

rized in a paper by Martha Zierden and Bernard Herman.[3] The present study focuses specifically on archaeological data relative to the daily activities in the work yard and their impact on public interpretation.

The eighteen archaeological sites considered here differ in many respects but can be grouped into two categories: residential only and dual residential-commercial (fig. 1). These sites in the latter category are in that portion of the city that has been used intensely from at least the early eighteenth century through the present. The dual residential-commercial sites include retail, craft, and service enterprises (Charleston Place, First Trident, Lodge Alley, 38 State Street, Visitor's Center, McCrady's Longroom and Tavern); public sites that contain some residential debris include the Beef Market and two waterfront dumps (Exchange building, Atlantic Wharf).[4]

---

[3] Elizabeth Reitz, "Urban/Rural Contrasts in Vertebrate Fauna from the Southern Coastal Plain," *Historical Archaeology* 20, no. 2 (1986): 47–58; Elizabeth Reitz and Martha Zierden, "Cattle Bones and Status from Charleston, South Carolina," in Bonnie Styles, James Purdue, and Walter Klippell, eds., *Essays in Honor of P. W. Parmalee* (Springfield: Illinois State University Publications, 1991), pp. 395–403; Michael Trinkley, Martha Zierden, Jeanne Calhoun, and Debi Hacker-Norton, "Not by Meat Alone: The Use of Plant Foods among the Antebellum Carolinians" (Paper presented at the 18th annual Society for Historical Archaeology Conference, Boston, 1985); Barbara Ruff, "Socioeconomic Subsistence Strategies in Aiken-Rhett and Gibbes House, Charleston, South Carolina" (Paper presented at the 44th annual Southeastern Archaeological Conference, Charleston, 1987); Karl Reinhard, "Pollen Analysis of the Miles Brewton House" (Charleston Museum, 1990, typescript); Zierden and Herman, "Charleston Townhouses."

[4] Nicholas Honerkamp, R. Bruce Council, and M. Elizabeth Will, "An Archaeological Investigation of the Charleston Center Site, Charleston, South Carolina" (National Park Service, Atlanta, 1982, typescript); Martha Zierden and Debi Hacker, "Charleston Place: Archaeological Investigations of the Commercial Landscape," *Charleston Museum Archaeological Contributions* 16 (1986); Martha Zierden, Jeanne Calhoun, and Elizabeth Pinckney, "An Archaeological Study of the First Trident Site," *Charleston Museum Archaeological Contributions* 6 (1983); Martha Zierden, Jeanne Calhoun, and Elizabeth Paysinger, "Archaeological Investigations at Lodge Alley," *Charleston Museum Archaeological Contributions* 5 (1983); Kimberly Grimes and Martha Zierden, "A Hub of Human Activity: Archaeological Investigations at the Visitor's Reception and Transportation Center Site," *Charleston Museum Archaeological Contributions* 19 (1988); Martha Zierden, Elizabeth Reitz, Michael Trinkley, and Elizabeth Paysinger, "Archaeological Excavations at McCrady's Longroom," *Charleston Museum Archaeological Contributions* 3 (1982); Jeanne Calhoun, Elizabeth Reitz, Michael Trinkley, and Martha Zierden, "Meat in Due Season: Preliminary Investigations of Marketing Practices in Colonial Charleston," *Charleston Museum Archaeological Contributions* 9 (1984); Elaine Herold, "Archaeological Research at the Exchange Building, Charleston, 1979–1980" (Charleston Museum, 1981, typescript); Martha Zierden and Debi Hacker, "Examination of Construction Sequence at the Exchange Building," *Charleston Museum Archaeological Contributions* 14 (1986); Martha Zierden, "Archaeological Investigations of Charleston's Waterfront" (Charleston Museum, 1983, typescript).

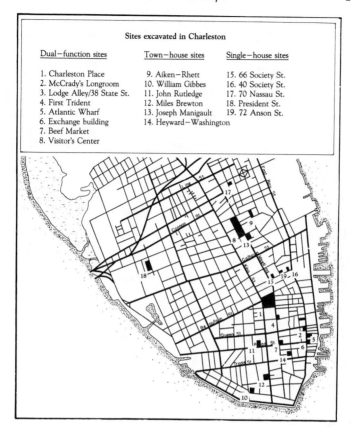

Sites excavated in Charleston

Dual—function sites	Town—house sites	Single—house sites
1. Charleston Place	9. Aiken—Rhett	15. 66 Society St.
2. McCrady's Longroom	10. William Gibbes	16. 40 Society St.
3. Lodge Alley/38 State St.	11. John Rutledge	17. 70 Nassau St.
4. First Trident	12. Miles Brewton	18. President St.
5. Atlantic Wharf	13. Joseph Manigault	19. 72 Anson St.
6. Exchange building	14. Heyward—Washington	
7. Beef Market		
8. Visitor's Center		

Fig. 1. Map of Charleston, showing the location of sites excavated. (Map, Martha Zierden.)

The nine residential sites are, with two exceptions, located in what were suburban areas in the late eighteenth or early nineteenth century and contain standing structures dating to those periods. Their continuous use as residential property to the present facilitates study of the domestic evolution of the property. All properties retain their residential landscape characteristics; six were the homes of elite, three the homes of middle-class residents. David Smith has argued that a heavy dependence on trade with Britain and on slaves for every kind of labor from domestic servitude to fine carpentry led to a lack of growth of a sturdy middle class. The few successful small proprietors employed slaves and invested their earnings into their own land and slaves; most merchants were also planters. Charleston's elite were the richest in colonial America; Peter Coclanis has suggested that in 1774 Charleston's wealth per (free) capita was 416.0, compared with 38.2 for New England and 45.2 for the Middle Atlantic colonies. Among the present sample, those property owners classified as "wealthy" and "elite" owned their town houses and at least one plantation. They maintained at least eight slaves in the city and a larger number on their plantation(s), and they held public office at some point in their adult life. Physically, the elite are those with houses in excess of 7,000 square feet and urban lots larger than 18,000 square feet. The middle-class houses averaged 4,600 square feet on lots of 6,000 square feet. These men often rented these properties and earned a living elsewhere in the city.[5]

Homes of the urban gentry that were built in the eighteenth- and nineteenth-century suburbs include those of William Gibbes (1772), Joseph Manigault (1803), Miles Brewton (1769), John Rutledge (1763),

[5]Martha Zierden et al., "Georgian Opulence: Archaeological Investigation of the Gibbes House," *Charleston Museum Archaeological Contributions* 12 (1987); Martha Zierden, "Archaeology at the Miles Brewton House" (Charleston Museum, 1989, notes); Martha Zierden and Kimberly Grimes, "Investigating Elite Lifeways through Archaeology: The John Rutledge House," *Charleston Museum Archaeological Contributions* 21 (1989); Elaine Herold, "Preliminary Report on the Research at the Heyward-Washington House" (Charleston Museum, 1978, typescript); Martha Zierden, "Archaeological Testing and Mitigation at the Stable Building, Heyward-Washington House," *Charleston Museum Archaeological Contributions* 23 (1993); Martha Zierden and Debi Hacker, "Investigation of the Northern Entrance of the Manigault House," *Charleston Museum Archaeological Contributions* 15 (1986); Martha Zierden, "The Front Yard and the Work Yard: Archaeology and Public Interpretation at the Joseph Manigault House," *Charleston Museum Archaeological Contributions* 22 (1992); Martha Zierden, Jeanne Calhoun, and Debi Hacker, "Outside of Town: Preliminary Investigation of the Aiken-Rhett House," *Charleston Museum Archaeological Contributions* 11 (1986); Martha Zierden et al., "Charleston's First Suburb: Excavations at 66 Society Street," *Charleston Museum Archaeological Contributions* 20 (1988); Martha Zierden, "Management Summary: Excavations at 40 Society Street" (Charleston Museum, 1990, typescript); Martha Zierden, "Investigations at 70 Nassau Street" (Charleston Museum, 1990, notes). All data summarized in this essay are described in detail in the above site reports. David Smith, "Dependent Urbanization in Colonial America: The Case of Charleston, South Carolina," *Social Forces* 66, no. 1 (September 1987): 1–28; Alice Hanson Jones, *Wealth of a Nation to Be: The American Colonies on the Eve of the Revolution* (New York: Columbia University Press, 1980); Peter A. Coclanis, *The Shadow of a Dream: Economic Life and Death in the South Carolina Low Country, 1670–1920* (New York: Oxford University Press, 1989).

Thomas Heyward (1772), and William Aiken (1817; built by John Robinson). The Rutledge and Heyward lots were occupied in the early eighteenth century before construction of the present houses. The remainder of the houses were among the first in their respective neighborhoods. The three middle-class sites include 66 and 40 Society Street, rebuilt on Ansonborough lots after the 1838 fire, and 70 Nassau Street, built in the Charleston Neck in the 1840s. More extensive and more recent archaeological work has been conducted at the residential sites, and this work has produced the core of information on the Charleston landscape; however, the commercial sites also have informed the interpretations presented here. Each of the phenomena discussed has been observed at multiple sites, although not all examples will be discussed in detail.

The most extensive research has been conducted at the Miles Brewton house. The occupational history of the property deserves consideration here, as it illustrates many of the processes that affected the urban landscape. The house passed through successive generations of ownership by the same family since its construction in 1769 by a wealthy merchant and slave trader. The most affluent generation occupied the house from 1791 until 1830; the next family saw increasing financial difficulties and ultimately ruin during the Civil War. The house was occupied by invading troops during both the Revolution and the Civil War and by extrafamilial boarders in the late nineteenth and early twentieth centuries. Three unmarried sisters maintained the house until 1960, defraying costs by providing paid tours and offering gifts and popular writings about the house for sale. The present owner has fully restored the property. Thus the property has been owned by a family whose social standing remained high but whose financial status was subject to varying levels of entrepreneurial skill and the whims of the regional economy. The 1750 to 1850 period of this study includes the financially ascendant period of site history; however, each of the eight generations made changes to the property and left their imprint on the archaeological record. Changes to the terrain at 27 King Street began with Brewton's clearing of his lot for construction and continued through Peter Manigault's renovations in 1990.

Alteration of the ground surface at the Brewton site is one example of the tremendous alteration to the terrain within the city of Charleston. The Low Country is aptly named; a local yarn suggests that you have to be a native to know where the hills are. To the twentieth-century eye, the Charleston peninsula is completely level, with perhaps a gradual rise as one moves northward. When first encountered by Europeans, the peninsula featured more relief.[6] Early European settlers chose to build a city adjacent to the Cooper River bluffs, between two large creeks, a location they found ideal for commerce.

Alteration of the terrain to better suit the economic and social needs of town residents began almost immediately. Major changes, such as the filling of creeks and marshes along the Ashley River and the creation of "made" land along the Cooper riverfront, began in the late seventeenth century and continued through the early twentieth. These changes have been documented from cartographic sources and verified archaeologically. While some scholars have debated the research value of fill deposits, others have convincingly argued that fill is in fact an artifact of the urban landscape formation process and as such is an important source of data.[7]

More subtle, however, and noted primarily through archaeology, is the filling of small strips of marsh and uneven areas to make appropriate "yards" for the Charleston houses. The Miles Brewton front yard serves as a graphic example (fig. 2). Tradition always held that a creek formerly ran north of the lot, while Legare Street, to the rear of the property, was also an expanse of marsh. Archaeology revealed that before construction the lower portion of the lot was deliberately filled with layers of soil. This created more usable high ground within the platted lot and leveled the most desirable yard area for house construction. An excavated trench across the entrance yard revealed layers of introduced fill, to a depth of more than four feet (fig. 3). Artifact content was sparse, suggesting that these soils were not generated from refuse disposal areas on site but were instead fill soils brought from

[6]James Akin, "A Plan of Charles Town from a Survey of Edward Crisp, 1704," (Charleston Museum); B. Roberts and W. H. Toms, "The Ichnography of Charles Town at High Water" (Charleston Museum, copy of facsimile of original 1739 map, presented to the City Council of Charleston, 1884).

[7]For a discussion of the relative value of fill deposits, see Mary Beaudry, "Analytical Scale and Methods for the Archaeological Study of Urban Households," and Marley Brown, "Issues of Scale Revisited," *Society for Historical Archaeology Newsletter* 20, no. 1 (March 1987): 22, 25; and Nicholas Honerkamp and Charles Fairbanks, "Definition of Site Formation Process in Urban Contexts," *American Archaeology* 4, no. 1 (January 1984): 60–66.

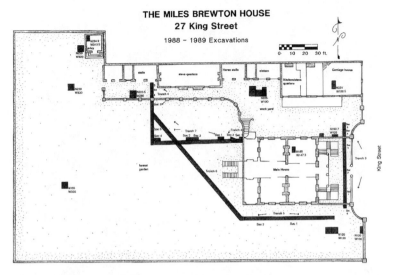

Fig. 2. Miles Brewton house site, showing the location of excavation units and standing structures. (Drawing, Martha Zierden.)

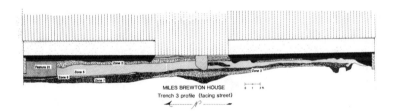

Fig. 3. Eastern profile of Trench 3, across the front yard from the Miles Brewton house (facing the street from the door). (Drawing, Martha Zierden.)

Fig. 4. Soil profile of excavation unit N225W180, in the Miles Brewton work yard. (Photo, Martha Zierden.)

other locations. For example, the heavy flint cobble content of zone 5 would suggest the waterfront ballast dump, commissioned in a 1695 statute, as a source (fig. 4). Datable artifacts contained within these fill lenses suggest that the filling occurred over a relatively short period, immediately before house construction. Subsequently, this front yard saw little alteration, except for repaving and outlining the front entrance in the nineteenth century.

Archaeological evidence for alteration of the Charleston terrain has been amplified by the seeds and pollen recovered from the layered earth. Analyses of soil samples from various sites reveal a gradual decrease in the amount of plants associated with marshes and swamps as lowlands were filled throughout the eighteenth century. These studies also have documented the dramatic deforestation of the Charleston peninsula. Land clearance for building and for firewood is revealed in the pollen spectrum, which shows a decrease in hardwoods and pine and a dramatic increase in the "weed" species that colonize disturbed habitats. The documents hint at this deforestation through a dramatic rise in firewood prices during the colonial period. In the eighteenth century, fuel became increasingly expensive in the city, as it was hauled greater distances. Use of coal by urban citizens increased proportionately with their complaints about the price of wood. Nearby forests were so depleted that British soldiers who occupied the city during the Revolution cut the protected trees lining the roads.[8]

These changes, particularly the presence of weedy species, also are seen in the few seeds that have survived archaeologically. For example, cartographic sources indicate that in the early eighteenth century the First Trident site was a narrow strip of high land along Meeting Street, while the interior of the block was marsh. By the 1780s the interior of the block had been filled. Ethnobotanical evidence mirrors this change; lower soil levels contained seeds associated with wetland habitats, while those from later zones contained seeds from weedy plants that colonize disturbed habitats on high ground.[9] Taken together, the plant and seed samples provide a tangible body of evidence for the nature and extent of vegetation changes as the peninsula was altered to suit the needs of a growing city.

These gradual changes in the urban landscape received impetus from a series of natural disasters during the study period, most notably fires and hurricanes. Specifically, the fire of 1740 and the hurricane of 1752 cleared major portions of the city for rebuilding. Simultaneously, successes with staple crop agriculture had created an urban gentry composed of planters and merchants whose new status required appropriate homes. These wealthy white men and their families participated in the cycle of conspicuous consumption, proclaiming their achieved status through diet, food customs, clothing, furnishings, and, most dramatically, architecture. Advertisements in Charleston newspapers offered a variety of luxury imports all in the "latest fashion": silks, porcelains, and lacquered furniture from the Orient; sugar from the Caribbean;

---

[8] Karl Reinhard, "Parasitological and Palynological Study of Soil Samples from the John Rutledge House," *Charleston Museum Archaeological Contributions* 21 (1989): 166; Reinhard, "Pollen Analysis"; Robert Weir, *Colonial South Carolina: A History* (Millwood, N.Y.: KTO Press, 1983), p. 44.

[9] Zierden, Calhoun, and Pinckney, "Archaeological Study," pp. 16, 88–93.

and fruits, nuts, spices, and catsups for festive tables. While many such items are not recovered from archaeological contexts, the artifacts from the town houses include a vast array of those that do not decay: porcelain table- and teaware, leaded glass, elaborate serving vessels, buttons and buckles, and faunal remains.[10]

Perhaps most graphic at these sites is evidence of building and rebuilding substantial homes and associated features. In a shift from a pan-Atlantic, more diverse style, the Charleston single and double houses emerged in the mid 1700s as local forms that dominated the city's architecture for the next 150 years. The much-discussed single house, one room wide and two deep with a central hall and a side piazza, has been interpreted in a variety of ways. Origins for this style have been attributed to England, adapted to the tropics in the West Indies, and to Africa. Most recently, Herman has suggested a new approach and has attributed this style to the pervasive ideology of Atlantic mercantilism and the plantation system, calling these "urban plantation houses."[11] The double house featured a four-square plan with central hall; Charleston's most elaborate double houses date to the late eighteenth to early nineteenth centuries.

After construction, town house owners enlarged or simply remodeled their homes to make them more fashionable. William Aiken refur-

---

[10] Jeanne Calhoun, "The Scourging Wrath of God: Early Hurricanes in Charleston, 1700–1804"(leaflet no. 29, Charleston Museum, 1983); George Rogers, *Charleston in the Age of the Pinckneys* (Columbia: University of South Carolina Press, 1980); Jeanne Calhoun, Elizabeth Paysinger, and Martha Zierden, "A Survey of Economic Activity in Charleston, 1732–1770," *Charleston Museum Archaeological Contributions* 2 (1982); Herold, "Preliminary Report."

[11] Bernard Herman, "Rethinking the Charleston Single House" (Paper presented at the Vernacular Architecture Forum, St. Louis, 1989). British antecedents are described in Kenneth Severens, *Charleston: Antebellum Architecture and Civic Destiny* (Knoxville: University of Tennessee Press, 1988); Gene Waddell, "The Charleston Single House: An Architectural Survey," *Preservation Progress* 22, no. 2 (March 1977): 4–8; Rogers, *Charleston in the Age of the Pinckneys*; Peter Coclanis, "The Sociology of Architecture in Colonial Charleston: Pattern and Process in an Eighteenth-Century Southern City," *Journal of Social History* 18, no. 2 (Summer 1985): 607–23. A West Indian origin is postulated by Warren Alleyne and Henry Fraser, *The Barbados-Carolina Connection* (London: MacMillan Caribbean, 1988), but disputed by George Rogers, "Review of *The Barbados-Carolina Connection*," *South Carolina Historical Magazine* 92, no. 1 (Spring 1991): 49–53. An African origin is cited in Genell Anderson, *The Call of the Ancestors* (Washington, D.C.: AMAR Publications, 1988).

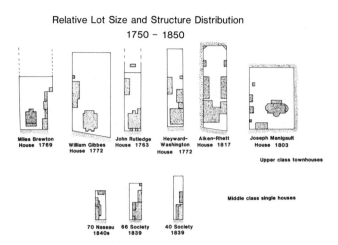

Fig. 5. Chart showing lot size and structure layout of the residential sites. (Drawing, Martha Zierden.)

bished his home in the 1830s after he inherited it from his father; another extensive renovation in the 1850s included the addition of an art gallery and changes in window treatment. William Alston made numerous changes to the Miles Brewton house in the early nineteenth century. One type of archaeological evidence for these changes is large pits filled with architectural debris such as half bricks, broken roof slates, and excess mortar.

The town house owners periodically renovated their outbuildings as well as their houses. Currently underestimated, but equally important, are the support structures and activity areas that, in conjunction with the main house, formed the urban compound. These include kitchen, slave quarters, stables, carriage house, livestock sheds, privy, well, cistern, and drainage system. The maintenance of gardens might require additional features. While variation in the size, content, construction method, arrangement, and specialization of these structures existed, they were considered essential functional components for urban life and were present in some form at all sites, not just those of the elite (fig. 5).

The town houses in the present study featured four to six separate outbuildings each. The dominant structure at these sites was a substantial two- or three-story building that housed kitchen and washing rooms on the first floor and slave quarters on the second. On each of the town house lots studied, these buildings were brick, and they dominated the work yard. Each floor was divided into a series of rooms. The first floor, for cooking and washing, was divided into two or three rooms and featured multiple fireplaces; the second-floor quarters featured two to five dwelling rooms of varying sizes. The remainder of the outbuildings were wooden on three lots and single-story brick on two others. The next largest structure often housed the carriages, horses, or both; this function was combined in a single building on two sites and segregated in separate structures on at least two others. Privies, singly or in pairs, were a feature common to all sites; most were of brick. A variety of other activities—livestock maintenance, gardening, and storage—were either incorporated into these buildings or housed in separate structures. These yards also contained, over the years, a variety of lesser-quality storage sheds, often in-filled between the better buildings.

The single-house lots featured a highly abbreviated version of this arrangement crammed into their small yards. A single substantial building often housed kitchen, horses, and carriage. Few if any slaves resided on the second floor. Privies in the rear corner might be shared with a neighbor; small in-filled sheds later occupied remaining spaces.

The support structures often were aligned along one or both walls to the rear of the house; in larger lots that could afford such spatial segregation, the work yard was separated from formal gardens. It is with these segregated layouts on large lots that archaeology has made the strongest contribution to interpretation of the landscape. Archaeology has consistently underscored the highly specialized and intensively used nature of these work yards—that area around, between, and beneath the work structures.

The work yard, surrounding the outbuildings, was the scene of intense activities, including food preparation, livestock maintenance, and cleaning and laundering. The archaeological record reflects the butchering of cattle and cleaning of fish in these areas, for example. Evidence of informal hearths, possibly for cooking and cleaning, have been encountered. Concentrations of fish bones and scales have been recovered from the silt in brick-lined drains. Sheet midden deposits contain quantities of discarded animal bone fragments; recovered skeletal elements suggest on-site butchering. The work yard also was the locus of refuse disposal, a critical problem of urban life and one most visibly reflected archaeologically. Archaeological research at Charleston town houses has consistently demonstrated that refuse deposited in the yards, either deliberately for disposal or secondarily as contained in fill dirt, was not broadcast across the entire yard but was instead concentrated in particular areas. At the Miles Brewton house, debris was concentrated in the work yard adjacent to the outbuildings from the time of initial occupation of the house in 1769. Over the next seventy-five years, two and a half feet of refuse accumulated in this area in a series of sheet deposits and small trash pits. Stratigraphy in the area of the courtyard, immediately behind the kitchen, was nearly four feet deep (see fig. 4). The lowest level was a concentration of refuse and an outdoor hearth, both dating to the mid eighteenth century. The next zone contained some domestic artifacts and large brick fragments in a matrix of mixed sand, reflecting construction of the house and outbuildings. The overlying layers of midden accumulated in a series of sheet deposits and small trash pits. This soil contained charcoal flecks, large quantities of animal bone, and domestic artifacts of all types. The faunal assemblage contained bones that were rodent or dog gnawed, suggesting that following their casual disposal they lay exposed on the ground. These soils were followed by ephemeral layers of mortar paving, then brick and slate paving laid between the 1820s and 1840s. Units excavated farther to the rear in the work yard also exhibited a dizzying array of sheet midden deposits, crosscut by large features.

Three units in this portion of the yard contained such large features as fence posts, a cistern with its builders trench, and the yard drain. Around and between these features were multiple layers of refuse-laden soil; quantities of cinders suggest that this was a favored location for fireplace sweepings. These dispersed zones and discretely dumped refuse piles also were capped with brick in the 1830s to 1840s, with four inches of topsoil and architectural debris accumulating above this in the twentieth century.

In the center of town, the John Rutledge house provides an even more graphic example. Here is an accumulation of nearly five feet of eighteenth-century refuse adjacent to the outbuildings. Near the kitchen, deep midden deposits with dense and varied refuse had accumulated. The relatively constricted Rutledge yard revealed some trash-laden soils in the center of the yard; the artifacts were basically the same type and date as those in the kitchen midden, but the stratigraphy was less than half the depth, and the soils contained fewer and smaller sherds.

Refuse also accumulated beneath the floors of kitchen buildings. The kitchen/carriage house at the Miles Brewton site featured a sus-pended wooden floor with a brick-floored crawl space four feet below. After the Civil War, soils began to accumulate in shallow zones, par-tially filling the crawl space. These deposits likely represent soils and small artifacts that sifted through the floorboards or materials trans-ported by rodents. Dense refuse deposits beneath the kitchen buildings also have been noted at the Aiken-Rhett house and the Heyward house. The area beneath the Heyward kitchen appears to have functioned as a true cellar and featured a stairway leading to this room. Evidently this cellar was five feet deep at the time of construction of the kitchen in the 1740s; refuse began to accumulate on the cellar floor after the 1790s and continued throughout the nineteenth century.[12] The data from Aiken-Rhett are less clear; excavations have been conducted be-neath the portion of the kitchen that was added in the 1850s. Many of these artifacts could have been deposited outside the original kitchen before the addition. At least some of the soils and artifacts appear to have accumulated inside the kitchen addition.

The nineteenth-century accumulation of soils and refuse in the crawl-space cellars suggests abandonment of these areas or at least de-clining attention to maintenance and efficiency. This reduced diligence corresponds temporally to the emancipation of the slave labor force, the onset of financial woes for the homeowners, and the beginning of general neglect of their town houses. A hallmark of these kitchen depos-its is great quantities of bone, suggesting that this refuse was generated from the kitchen.

Residents of the urban town house compounds generated great quantities of refuse, but the large lots provided relatively discrete and convenient spots for its disposal. The problem of trash disposal was even more critical on the smaller single-house lots such as those at 66

---

[12] Herold, "Preliminary Report."

and 40 Society Street and 70 Nassau Street. Here, lack of space precluded separation of a work yard and garden. Limited excavations in the centers of these rear yards revealed a complex and congested combination of zones and large trash pits dating to the first half of the nineteenth century.[13]

The stratigraphy of the used and reused work yards contrasts with that of the single archaeological sample from a pleasure garden. The Miles Brewton garden contained a soil horizon of 1770s artifacts, deliberately tilled into the planting beds to enrich the soil and enhance drainage.[14] Unlike the work-yard materials, these were large, with many broken in situ or in reconstructible vessels. The large quantities of animal bone also were relatively intact. Following the initial deposits of refuse to create these planting beds, only occasional sherds were cast into the garden area. This lack of refuse disposal carried into the above zone, which was associated with the early nineteenth-century redesign of the garden. Analysis of the form, content, and social intent of the Brewton garden is beyond the scope of this study; what is relevant is the contrast in stratigraphy and, as we will see later, its physical segregation from the work yard.

The deliberate placement of specialized service buildings, separation of work yards and gardens, and specific locations for refuse disposal were conscious attempts to mold an urban landscape suitable to the social values and the physical needs of urban residents. The needs and values of Charleston's citizens changed as the nineteenth century progressed. Archaeology not only has outlined the basic features of mid eighteenth-century urban compounds, it also has documented changes in these features as the ideals of a bustling colonial seaport gave way to those of an antebellum citizenry facing economic stagnation and philosophical isolation. Many of the visible changes were connected with attempts to improve sanitation and prevent disease; others were related to an increasing desire for privacy and a fear of the slave population.

Poor sanitation practices ranging from open privies to rotting carrion in the streets nurtured a wide range of diseases; these practices were

---

[13] Zierden, "Management Summary"; Zierden et al., "Charleston's First Suburb."

[14] William Kelso, archaeologist with the Thomas Jefferson Memorial Foundation, conversation with author. Dr. Kelso examined and interpreted the garden soil profiles at Miles Brewton.

battled by citizen complaints and ordinances throughout Charleston's history. As scientists and citizens began to link cause and effect in the early nineteenth century, they attempted, on both individual and municipal levels, to ameliorate the situation. These efforts coincided with and were offset by increasing population density, as lots were subdivided, additional dwellings and outbuildings were constructed, and an increasing number of wells and privies were placed in closer proximity to each other.[15]

The antebellum period (ca. 1820–60) witnessed major changes in the social, economic, and technological systems of the United States. Industrial and railroad development was a key factor, and cities were the center of these changes. This was manifested in fierce competition among cities; to capture the burgeoning commerce and industry, cities strove to be modern, clean, and attractive. Municipalities took control of such services as lighting, disease prevention, drain and street maintenance, and, ultimately, piped water and sewerage systems. In Charleston, however, fierce individuality and staunch belief in cotton monoculture by a majority of political leaders dominated attempts by others to attract railroads and new industries. Charleston's leaders remained committed to a volunteer government bolstered by a belief in public service. Jane and William Pease have suggested that this "was a conscious rejection of modernization already setting new scientific and professional standards." A city that was the home of the first railroad in 1831 was, by the 1850s, bypassed by major railroad lines. After the Civil War, poverty was the main reason for lack of modernization. Despite the pleas of the commissioner of public health, Charleston did not receive a waterborne sewerage system until the twentieth century. Municipal handling of drainage and trash disposal also lagged behind such efforts in more northern cities. Nineteenth-century Charlestonians continued their own, highly varied efforts to improve their homesites.[16]

---

[15] Honerkamp, Council, and Will, "Archaeological Investigation," pp. 158–66.

[16] Jane H. Pease and William H. Pease, "Intellectual Life in the 1830s: The Institutional Framework and the Charleston Style," in Michael O'Brien and David Moltke-Hansen, eds., *Intellectual Life in Antebellum Charleston* (Knoxville: University of Tennessee Press, 1986), p. 234. Dell Upton, "Another City: The Urban Cultural Landscape in the Early Republic," in Catherine E. Hutchins, ed., *Everyday Life in the Early Republic* (Winterthur, Del.: Henry Francis du Pont Winterthur Museum, 1994); David

Refuse disposal in the work yards, for example, reached a critical mass in the early 1800s. In the Miles Brewton courtyard, the upper zones of refuse were first covered with irregular lenses of tabby mortar and then finally paved with brick and slate (see fig. 4). Datable ceramics indicate that the mortar paving occurred after 1800 and the brick paving between 1830 and 1840. Refuse was then disposed elsewhere on the site or carted away. The total accumulation of soil in the work yard for the next 150 years amounted to less than a half foot. The postpaving soils contained primarily architectural debris with relatively little kitchen or organic refuse.

The paving of the Miles Brewton work yard was far from an isolated event. Paved work yards also have been identified at the Heyward, Rutledge, Aiken-Rhett, and Manigault houses. At the Heyward and Rutledge sites, soil deposits above the paving were similar to those at the Brewton site in age, type of deposit, and depth of stratigraphy.

Documentary sources reflect the widespread addition of paved yards; they also document such additions as cisterns, drains, and brick walls. Many nineteenth-century plats clearly label these features (fig. 6). Perhaps most revealing is a series of business ledgers preserved at the South Carolina Historical Society; the paper collections are from the business of the Horlbeck brothers, who were building contractors in Charleston from 1828 until 1869. Their ledgers detail each job daily: what they did, who they worked for, and how many laborers performed the task. The Horlbecks used primarily slave labor, listed as "hands." It is unclear if they owned these workers or hired them from others.

After 1840, the Horlbecks also hired white immigrant (German and Irish) laborers; many of these were "boys" and even "small boys." In 1834, for example, two and a half hands spent the day "digging out foundation and building a wall between house and kitchen" for Mrs. Boumillat on Meeting Street. That same year, William Guerard on Queen Street commissioned a variety of improvements. One hand bricked up a fireplace, while another took the fire grate to the blacksmith for repair. Three hands worked at the privy, two hands spent a

---

Goldfield, "Pursuing the American Dream: Cities in the Old South," in Blaine Brownell and David Goldfield, eds., *The City in Southern History* (Port Washington, N.Y.: Kennikat Press, 1977), pp. 52–90. For a discussion of primary documentation relating to these issues, see Rosengarten et al., "Between the Tracks," pp. 93–123.

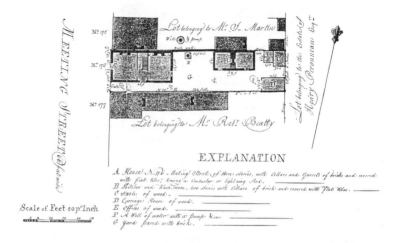

Fig. 6. Late eighteenth-century plat of 176 Meeting Street, showing a variety of features, including (G) "Yard paved with brick." (Division of Archives and Records, City of Charleston.)

half day on the vault, and one hand cleaned out the drain. Lewis Faber had two hands "taking up part and digging out cellar in kitchen," while seven hands were "cleaning brick from the celler" of the house. Two more hands were "digging out earth and wheeling same back in garden." Most of the Horlbecks' work consisted of renovation and repair, and much of it focused on outbuildings and work yards. Their laborers cleaned and repaired cisterns, wells, and privies; paved yards; and built walls; they repaired the roofs, chimneys, and windows of main dwellings. Drain repair, for both private individuals and the municipality, was a common task.[17]

Many of the sanitation efforts by individuals were evidently aimed at reducing groundwater and removing wastewater. As the nineteenth century progressed, Charlestonians became increasingly concerned with health problems that plagued the city and began to relate them to poor sanitation that resulted from diminished native resources and

[17]Horlbeck Brothers ledger books, 1828–69, South Carolina Historical Society, Charleston.

increased population pressure.[18] Cisterns built to collect rainwater and brick drains designed to remove wastewater are tangible archaeological evidence of attempts to make the yard more livable.

Cisterns were first constructed in the city in the early nineteenth century and became a standard feature by the 1850s. Many of them remained active well into the twentieth century. Their development is chronicled in the Charleston City Yearbook of 1882: "The wealthier citizens began to gather the rainwater that fell on their roofs into water-tight cisterns, mostly underground, in order to preserve it for domestic purposes. As the evil continued to increase in the wells, such cisterns came gradually into general use among the middle class and finally even among the poorest, until a cistern for rainwater became a necessary adjunct to a dwelling of any kind in Charleston." Archaeologically, cisterns were first encountered in great numbers during salvage excavations at Charleston Place. This downtown block was central to the nineteenth-century business district and served as business and residence for numerous Charleston merchants. Throughout the nineteenth century the block was increasingly improved, significantly reducing the amount of open yard area. More and more wells and privies were built and in increasingly close proximity to each other. As town residents began to recognize contaminated groundwater as a health hazard, cisterns became a necessary feature. The Charleston Place cisterns were often located under the long, narrow commercial buildings that covered the block. They collected rainwater through elaborate guttering systems that ran from the roofs to the crawl spaces beneath the first floors. These were rectangular vaults or converted wells whose openings had been narrowed and sealed with a stone slab. Either way, they were designed to be sealed and free of contamination; the archaeological signature is often a clean sand fill with no artifactual material.[19]

The town houses contain numerous examples of cisterns; most graphic is that of the Miles Brewton site, where the first set of horse stalls was altered to make a large above-ground cistern. Excavations in

---

[18] Rosengarten et al., "Between the Tracks," pp. 97–105; Honerkamp, Council, and Will, "Archaeological Investigation," pp. 163–66.

[19] Charleston City Yearbook, 1882, Charleston Library Society; Honerkamp, Council, and Will, "Archaeological Investigation," pp. 163–65; Zierden and Hacker, "Charleston Place," p. 99.

the vicinity of the rear stalls revealed an earlier cistern beneath the stalls and the foundation of the second servants quarters. The builders trench fill suggests this original cistern was constructed in the early nineteenth century. Cisterns of both types also have been encountered at the Manigault, Aiken-Rhett, and Heyward sites. The Heyward cistern is enclosed in a storage shed in-fill addition, while the Manigault vault is located beneath the piazza. The Aiken-Rhett site features at least four cisterns, including a converted well beneath the front piazza, a lead-lined tank in the attic, and a rectangular vault beneath the kitchen addition. Most impressive is a large vault beneath the art gallery addition. This feature is six feet deep and measures roughly twenty by forty feet. It appears to have been connected to the attic vault by a pump system.

Less visible to the public and revealed only by archaeology are elaborate drainage systems. Originally discovered at the Aiken-Rhett house and viewed as an innovative luxury, drains have subsequently been unearthed at most of the town house sites and appear to have been a common feature. Like cisterns, drain systems probably were first constructed by the few who could afford them; as the nineteenth century progressed, they became more common, less of a luxury and more of a necessity. Date of construction as well as physical characteristics of the system, then, may determine where a specific feature may fall in the continuum from luxury to necessity.

The drain system at the Aiken-Rhett site was constructed as part of the 1850s renovations. Built of brick and capped with slate, this elaborate feature incorporated a watering basin for animals and an entry vault that likely served as a privy for resident slaves. Data suggesting that this vault was in fact a privy were found in the nature of the fill; the soil was dark and organic, full of large artifacts such as bottles and reconstructible ceramics, and capped with a thick layer of lime. Ghosting along the stucco of the rear kitchen wall suggests that this feature was once enclosed with a small shed. The vault was connected to the drain system, which then evidently left the property and ran to an adjacent marsh. This drain may have replaced or augmented an earlier (circa 1830) system, recently discovered beneath the kitchen addition. William Aiken was recognized by his peers as an innovative and progressive thinker in other areas and owner of a "model" rice plantation. He was an outspoken proponent of the railroad and of industrial diversification. He evidently expressed his desire for sanitation and efficiency in the design and amenities of his lot: relatively spacious, yet secure slave quarters; large kitchen rooms; elaborate horse stalls and hay loft; large, separate quarters for those entrusted with care of the horses; discrete buildings for livestock; and privies far removed from the well and numerous cisterns.[20]

Aiken's antebellum accomplishments, however, diminish in comparison with the drainage systems found at the late eighteenth-century town houses. The Miles Brewton yard contained evidence of an extensive drain network built shortly after house construction. The elaborate drain featured a vaulted brick top and sides with a wooden base. The feature ran most of the length of the work yard and evidently emptied into either the street or the marsh to the rear of the property. Creamware found in the builders trench clearly date it to the 1770s–1780s. The system was expanded in the 1800s (based on pearlware in the builders trench), although this brick drain was not nearly so well constructed. The presence of yellowware and other later artifacts in association with collapsed portions of the drain top suggests that the earlier drain was repaired periodically throughout the nineteenth century. Gradual silting evidently made the system dysfunctional by the mid nineteenth century. The drain was full of small fish remains, suggesting that fresh fish were cleaned and scaled adjacent to the kitchen and the remains washed into the drain. The fill also was full of small artifacts lost rather than abandoned. These were primarily buttons, beads, marbles, and other toys, with only a few small fragments of ceramics and other kitchen refuse.

The Heyward site featured a drain of identical construction, although artifacts in the builders trench suggest that this drain was constructed in the early nineteenth century. The drain began beside the carriage house and ran down the driveway to the street. The William Gibbes site also contained a yard drain system, although less elaborate and less substantial.

Despite the buildup of soils in the past two centuries, the Miles Brewton and William Gibbes lots are relatively low; rainwater stands in the Brewton garden after a thunderstorm. The Heyward and Aiken

---

[20]Zierden, Calhoun, and Hacker, "Outside of Town," p. 12; Richard C. Wade, *Slavery in the Cities: The South, 1820–1860* (New York: Oxford University Press, 1964).

yards, in contrast, are high and require no drainage. This, plus the contents of the silt in the various drains—fish scales and small bones— suggest that they were built primarily to handle wastewater from the work yards rather than excess rainwater.

Analysis of the faunal remains recovered from drain fill, trash pits, and other work yard midden proveniences also has provided information on urban sanitation. Zooarchaeologist Elizabeth Reitz has determined that such animals as rats, mice, toads, cats, and dogs comprise 4.3 percent of rural faunal assemblages and 10.6 percent of urban ones, suggesting that vermin were more closely associated with human activity in the city. The urban elite sites contain a lower percentage of vermin, 7.7 percent, possibly indicating some success in sanitizing the urban environment.[21]

The urban town house sites evidently needed special cleanup efforts, as the faunal record also indicates that maintenance and butchering of cattle was common on these properties. This is seen in the distribution of carcass elements recovered at the residential sites when compared with those at the market. Further, the data suggest that on-site butchery was more common on elite sites than on those of the middle class. Documentary sources suggest that the maintenance of livestock, particularly cattle, by Charleston residents persisted into the twentieth century.[22] The maintenance of cattle and poultry is documented at the Aiken and Brewton sites, and Aiken even constructed elaborate brick sheds for these urban residents. These animals were in addition to the repertoire of horses that were housed on large urban lots.

Finally, archaeological evidence points to the increasing segmentation and enclosure of urban lots with brick walls. This process accelerated throughout the antebellum period as ideas about individualism and privacy changed. In Charleston, prevailing thought and the institu-

---

[21] Reitz, "Urban/Rural Contrasts," p. 53.

[22] Reitz and Zierden, "Cattle Bones and Status"; for this study, Elizabeth Reitz divided Charleston sites into public establishments, dumps, and residential sites and compared cattle element distribution at each. Reitz believes that this reflects some on-site butchery and some market purchases. See Elizabeth Reitz, "Vertebrate Fauna from Brewton House, Charleston, South Carolina" (Charleston Museum, 1990, typescript). Rosengarten et al., "Between the Tracks," p. 105; Pease and Pease, "Intellectual Life," p. 235.

tional framework were designed to keep an otherwise diverse white community united and to avoid divisive issues. While Charlestonians were proud of their differences from northerners, they also suffered from self-doubt. Simultaneously, Charleston became increasingly defensive of the institution of slavery; the rise of abolitionism in the North and heightened sectional strife ultimately led to secession of the southern states and then the Civil War. Even as the South defended slavery, Charlestonians became more and more fearful of both the enslaved and the free African American population. After 1820 increasingly harsh restrictions were applied to black Carolinians, but these laws did nothing to assuage white Charlestonians' fear of arson, poisoning, and insurrection. Social pressure from without as well as within, coupled with a floundering economy, encouraged an attitude of withdrawal manifested in changes to the landscape. This is reflected archaeologically and architecturally in forms of urban enclosure.[23] Domestic space in the city became more segmented and partitioned into discrete areas. Open walls and fences were rebuilt in brick, yards were subdivided into discrete areas with walls and fences, and exterior windows in second-floor slave quarters were sealed.

The Miles Brewton house embodies a highly developed example of this urban enclosure (fig. 7; see also fig. 2). The front of the house, elevated on an aboveground basement, is separated from the street by eight-foot brick walls and a wrought-iron gate. The chevaux-de-frise were added to the original wrought-iron fence and walls after the Denmark Vesey slave insurrection of 1822. Visitors coming to the house may advance only as far as the front portico, where they are visible from the house, yard, and street, for the front entrance is separated from the side yards by equally imposing brick walls. Excavations of builders trenches reveal that these walls were added in the 1820s–1830s.

The front wall separating the house from the street along the south side yard evolved from boundary to barricade as well. Discovery of a well-defined postmold beneath the brick wall suggests that this boundary was originally delineated by an informal wooden post-and-rail fence. Variations in the brickwork suggest that the post-and-rail

---

[23] Rosengarten et al., "Between the Tracks," pp. 59–62. Zierden and Herman, "Charleston Townhouses."

Fig. 7. Front elevation of the Miles Brewton house. (Photo, Terry Richardson; courtesy, Charleston Museum.)

fence was then replaced with a low brick wall topped with either wrought iron or wood. The builders trench for the bricks contained no firmly datable material, but the stratigraphy generally indicates a 1770s–1780s construction date. Sometime later the wooden or wrought-iron portion was replaced with solid brick to a height of eight feet. With a stuccoed exterior, the wall is physically as well as visually intimidating.

Likewise, internal segregation of the urban compound appears to have been a gradual process. The line of outbuildings is separated from the formal garden by a low brick wall surmounted by a wooden picket fence, segregating but not totally screening one from the other (see fig. 2). Ceramics contained in the builders trench suggest an 1820s construction date. Further, the two excavation units in this vicinity each revealed a well-defined posthole stain beneath the brick founda-

Fig. 8. Excavation unit adjacent to the garden wall at the Miles Brewton house, showing the excavated posthole beneath it. (Photo, Martha Zierden.)

tion. Creamware within these features date them to the 1770s. These features suggest that the present wall replaced a less formal and less restricting post-and-rail fence.

Excavation showed the somewhat unusual juxtaposition of these two features (fig. 8). The posthole initiates beneath the brick wall, but the soils of the postmold also fill a "gap" in the portion of the brick wall located beneath present grade but above the top of the posthole. This indicates that the brick wall originally incorporated the lower portion of the wooden posts. When the post remnants later rotted in place, repair to the brick wall was necessary.[24] Such features as post-

[24] A similar evolution of garden features was noted by Larry McKee at The Hermitage. His excavations clearly show wooden post remnants incorporated into later brick walls. See Kevin E. Smith and Larry McKee, "The Archaeology of Rachel's Garden at the Hermitage" (Paper presented at the annual Society for Historical Archaeology Conference, Tucson, Ariz., 1990).

Fig. 9. Charles Fraser, "View from Mr. Fraser's City Residence, 1796." From Alice R. Huger Smith, *A Charleston Sketchbook, 1796–1806: Forty Watercolor Drawings of the City and Surrounding Country, by Charles Fraser* (Charleston: Carolina Art Association, 1959). (Photo, Gibbes Museum of Art, Charleston.)

and-rail fences are no longer extant, but their existence and the more open nature of the urbanscape is captured in Charles Fraser's watercolors of the early nineteenth century (fig. 9).

The archaeological and documentary evidence from the Miles Brewton project were essential in interpreting the very fragmentary evidence for segmentation of the yard at the Charleston Museum's Joseph Manigault house. All the yard features had been destroyed by construction in the early twentieth century. An 1852 plat provides the best evidence for the arrangement of outbuildings and yard features (fig. 10); this map reveals an unusual (for Charleston) and seemingly inefficient arrangement of service structures. The main house faced John Street but had a small front yard. The brick kitchen building fronted directly on John Street beside the main house. Aligned along the side yard behind this kitchen were a privy,

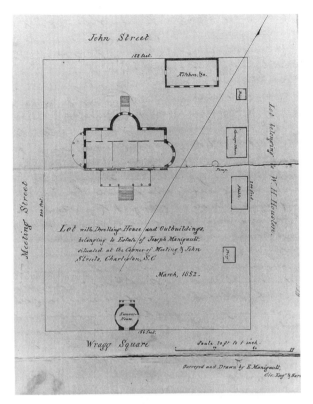

Fig. 10. Plate of the Joseph Manigault property, 1852. (Courtesy, Charleston Museum.)

carriage house, stable, and second privy, with many of the outbuildings placed in what would be the side yard. Considering this configuration vis-à-vis previous research, it seemed certain that the formal entrance was segregated in some way from the kitchen/slave quarters, privy, and carriage house.

Manigault had commissioned his brother and respected local architect Gabriel Manigault to design an imposing town house in the latest Adam style. The house interior contains features designed for "proper" entertainment of peers: a sweeping circular staircase and an

elaborately decorated dining room. A first-floor music room and adjoining parlor and a second floor ballroom each opened onto a semicircular
piazza. The front entrance was equally imposing; a "handsome flight
of stone stairs" led to a doorway surmounted by a carved stone cherub.
An 1830 painting by Charlotte Drayton Manigault shows the southern
(rear) yard filled with a formal garden.

The work yard is crammed somewhat uncomfortably into the front
and side yards, between the dining-room windows and the street front.
The physical conditions of the antebellum work yard—an area crowded
with debris, livestock, horses, and domestic slaves (as many as twenty
in 1840)—as well as the *mentalité* of antebellum Charlestonians (fear
of the very slave population on which they depended) suggest that this
work yard would have been screened from the formal front entrance.
By the 1820s none of these features would have been considered fit for
public viewing, particularly by arriving guests. Further, the human
occupants of this area needed to be locked in and other dangerous
elements locked out.

Charlotte Manigault's painting of the backyard shows a modest
picket fence separating the formal garden from the work yard. Archaeological excavations were conducted in the small undisturbed portions
of the yard to document the connection among the house, front yard,
and work yard.

Archaeology in the remaining fifteen feet of undisturbed grade
revealed a paved brick walkway leading from a basement door. All other
edges of the walk were truncated by construction of a twentieth-century
cleaners' building and the laying of modern pipes, so original dimensions were impossible to determine, as was eventual destination. Likewise, an unmistakable postmold and posthole had later pierced this
walkway. Based on recovered artifacts, it dated to the 1830s. Within
the narrow, undisturbed limits of the excavation area, only one postmold was noted; therefore, no trajectory could be determined. Yet these
fragmentary remains clearly signal first connection via a paved walk
and then segmentation via a fence between the main house and the
work yard.

Some of the changes to the Charleston landscape, such as brick
walls, sealed windows, and paved courtyards, leave lasting visible evidence. Others do not. The archaeological evidence for land filling,
trash disposal, and wastewater drainage is revealed only as it is exca-

vated; it is then destroyed or at best reburied. The concept of land-scape is a visual phenomenon; *landscape* has been defined as "the portion of land that the eye can comprehend in a single view."[25] What we comprehend in a single view today certainly clouds our vision of past landscapes, in both a physical and an academic sense. In Charleston's exploration of her past, changes made only a generation ago have become "fact" that now stretches back two hundred years; features that were subsequently abandoned, altered, or covered tend to be forgotten.

Archaeology has become a vital tool for altering public interpreta-tion of the landscape, attempting to dispel myths and uncertainties, and providing a more complete picture of the past landscape. In many cases the outbuildings are gone or, in remodeling, have become mere shells. Likewise, yard areas no longer necessary for the affairs of daily life have been given over to gardens; Charleston yards, especially the smaller ones, are now infinitely "nicer" than they once were. A casual stroll through the city, coupled with visits to historic house museums, leaves tourists with the impression that they have seen Charleston as it was in the eighteenth and nineteenth centuries. Archaeology can help to redress some of these distortions by increasing the emphasis on outbuildings in all their form and variety and on the difficulties of daily life as evidenced by features in the work yard, with a propor-tional deemphasis on main houses and gardens. In the case of the Charleston Museum's historic house properties, this has resulted in physical changes in some cases and different interpretive approaches in others.

At the Heyward-Washington house, all the outbuildings are extant and open to the public, and the yard has been tended by the Charleston Garden Club since the 1940s. While the beautiful garden creates a tranquil respite for tourists, small flower beds adjacent to the stable building and kitchen cannot be accurate; instead, this area was full of refuse and the scene of intense human and animal traffic. Likewise, the presence of a gate in the rear wall, opening onto Meeting Street via Ropemakers Lane, suggests that horse, if not carriage, traffic regu-

---

[25] John R. Stilgoe, *Common Landscape of America, 1580–1845* (New Haven: Yale University Press, 1982), p. 3.

larly crossed the yard area now crosscut by English-style garden beds.[26]
The small beds around the outbuildings are slated for removal, and a
well and an entrance to a drain system will be left uncovered for viewing. The formal garden is now interpreted as "representative of colonial
gardens" and not that specifically of Thomas Heyward.

The Manigault house embodies another graphic example. The
gardens were reconstructed from the 1830 painting. Left with no trace
of the outbuildings or the separating picket fence, the Garden Club
extended the tranquil flowered space beyond the backyard to include
the area beneath the windows of the formal dining room. Yet Manigault's guests actually looked down on, and shared malodorous breezes
with, the stable building and the work yard in general. The garden
now has been removed, and the outbuildings delineated. Based on a
lack of architectural evidence, these have been outlined in brick; the
remainder of the work yard has been sodded. While this method is
certainly commendable by current preservation standards, it recreates
only the physical parameters and not the ambience.

Just as there are more gardens in modern Charleston than there
were in the historic city, so too are there more trees. The contrast in
aerial photographs suggests that the replanting of urban trees began
with the City Beautiful Movement of the late nineteenth century and
accelerated with the urban renewal efforts of the 1960s. The current
vista masks the century-long deforestation of the city suggested by archaeological and photographic evidence. Likewise, the livestock are
gone, with the exception of the horse-drawn carriages that pull tourists
about the city streets.

Equally difficult to comprehend by viewing historic properties is
the evolving nature of their appearance. Changes made to eighteenth-
century properties throughout the nineteenth and twentieth centuries
are compressed into a seemingly static moment, and properties are
inevitably portrayed as "frozen in time." Archaeology can help to separate these events, although portrayal of these evolving changes will
require innovative interpretive techniques.

The underground complexities of the urban landscape—drains,

---

[26] No evidence of the garden remained when the house was acquired, and its restora-
tion was based on general styles of the period. In the ensuing years, the accuracy of the
garden as Heyward's was implied through interpretation, or lack of it.

cisterns, privy vaults, wells—are invisible yet were integral to daily life in the city. Archaeology is the only means of accessing this information. In the case of fence building, tree planting, and livestock maintenance, archaeological discoveries have provided the impetus for additional documentary and photographic research. Archaeological research has made the physical and social accomplishments of Charleston's elite all the more remarkable by calling attention to the rigorous requirements of daily life in a historic city.

Mind Reading the Urban Landscape
An Approach to the History of American Cities

Eric Sandweiss

This project began with a basic question, How do we begin to understand the history of the urban landscape? I think that anyone with an
interest in material culture would agree that the answer to that question
cannot be determined from written records alone. Yet a look at the
city itself is equally unlikely to supply a satisfactory answer. Cities are
messy places; they rarely present us with neat historical pictures that
we can comprehend at a glance. The urban landscape is instead a
collage of physical forms—some of them changed through time, some
standing as they first appeared, others barely visible, waiting to be
pulled out from long shadows of neglect.

The landscape is made more confusing still in that even when we
have discovered all its physical forms, we still will not have understood
it. Deeper in the recesses of its shadows of neglect, there are other

The author acknowledges the University of California, Berkeley; the American Historical Association; and the Temple Hoyne Buell Center for the Study of American
Architecture, Columbia University for their support during various stages of the research
and writing of this paper. The attendants and organizers of the 1991 Winterthur Conference: Historical Archaeology and the Study of American Culture also offered helpful
comments on the version presented there.

forms: the forms of people. They are the people who built the place, who were there to watch it go up or to tear it down, to seek warmth in its shelters or to be cast out in its streets. In fact, the place would not have existed but for them, and we could not understand what we found there but for the records they kept. The urban landscape, then, is more than a collection of inert pieces. It is, as well, the state of mind that gives those pieces meaning.

"State of mind" is the term on which sociologist Robert Park settled as he struggled to develop a systematic explanation for the relation between urban space and the life led within it.[1] Park understood that the salient, distinguishing fact of the city rests not just in the cold stones of its streets and buildings nor in the comings and goings of the people clustered so tightly within them but in the continuous, if barely distinguishable, seam where the two meet. As the spaces of the city take on a visible form, they also give a kind of form to the lives led within them. In turn, those "social forms" inevitably imprint themselves on the urban landscape. It is only from within the urban state of mind that we can see either the spatial dimension of social form or the intrinsically social form of space.

Unfortunately, Park left no explicit instructions for actually *reading* that state of mind in a given time or place. The problem is not trivial, for there are truly as many ways to experience the city as there are people to experience it. Cities are intermeshed, dynamic networks of forms and functions, appearances and intentions. In itself, unused and unseen, each element of the landscape is meaningless. A street has no identity separate from where it comes from and where it leads to; a house, like any shelter, derives its function not just from what it encloses but from what it leaves outside; a neighborhood is unrecognizable as such unless it offers some observable contrast to other neighborhoods around it. What is observable, of course, depends on the position of the observer.

One way of handling this seeming overflow of forms, images, and ideas is built into the unique, corporate character of cities. It is the

<hr>

[1] Robert E. Park, "The City: Suggestions for the Investigation of Human Behavior in the Urban Environment," in Robert E. Park, Ernest W. Burgess, and Roderick D. McKenzie, eds., *The City* (1925; reprint, Chicago: University of Chicago Press, 1967), p. 1.

function of the city to bring all its pieces together into a more or less coherent system that gives sense to each of them. The urban landscape forms a whole greater than the sum of its parts; it comprises the countless layers of urban space—from a single room to the entire streetscape—but their conceptual and legal union within a singular, socially and legally defined entity in turn gives to those components an added dimension of meaning, an added purpose, that each lacks on its own. Neither the detailed examination of highly localized communities nor the broad study of change in the citywide landscape can in itself suffice to capture that unique relationship.[2]

The discipline of historical archaeology is especially well fitted to the task of following the invisible seam that joins the city's physical and social forms into a single, recognizable pattern. This essay suggests one way of integrating the precepts of that field into the study of American history in a manner that might aid and alter our understanding of the urban landscape. It draws on a study of one city, St. Louis, which grew from an obscure trading post in the eighteenth century to America's fourth largest city by the beginning of the twentieth. Historians of the city have in recent years approached the study of places like St. Louis armed with a growing variety of research methods and questions. I believe there is still room for a greater awareness of the kinds of issues already faced by historical archaeologists. This awareness can help the historian to focus on the urban landscape as an artifact and to study the cyclical process that forever enmeshes it with the city's evolving social forms. Viewed as artifact, the landscape could then be treated, in Henry Glassie's words, as "an expression of cognitive pattern rather than a reflection of behavioral pattern."[3]

---

[2] For an overview of the legal basis of the American city, see Gerald Frug, "The City as a Legal Concept," *Harvard Law Review* 93 (1980): 1057–1154. For an admirable assessment of how that legal identity relates to broader historical conceptions of the city, see Hendrik Hartog, *Public Property and Private Power: The Corporation of the City of New York in American Law, 1730–1870* (Chapel Hill: University of North Carolina Press, 1983), which provides a valuable perspective on many of the recurring issues in this study.

[3] Eric Sandweiss, "Construction and Community in South St. Louis" (Ph.D. diss., University of California, Berkeley, 1991); Henry Glassie, "Archeology and Folklore: Common Anxieties, Common Hopes," in Leland Ferguson, ed., *Historical Archaeology and the Importance of Material Things* (Lansing, Mich.: Society for Historical Archaeology, 1977) p. 27.

Key to this cognitive pattern as I wish to describe it is a contrast between what I will provisionally call "looseness" and "tightness," labels that will apply to the forms of the city as well as to the nature of their relation to one another. Those labels are meant to describe a phenomenon almost so common as to go unnoticed: a continued need among city dwellers to define compatible physical and conceptual boundaries around themselves. There appears in the activities of not only the city government or powerful developers but also ordinary citizens a desire to confine that which is predictable and to set it apart from that which is not—a need to set explicit rules governing those things that are poorly understood in the landscape and to leave free those things that are well understood. This simple tendency is one constant that transcends the vicissitudes of urban change; its persistence should serve as a signal that perhaps the American city has not changed so much through the last two centuries as we have been led to believe. The historical archaeologist's interest in material culture as pattern, like Park's focus on the urban state of mind, gives us a useful tool for discerning the common threads woven into centuries of apparent change.

How has the story of the urban landscape been told in the past? For a place like St. Louis, it might sound like this: a colonial village is created in the image of a society that values collective stability over individual initiative. This prescribed order eventually proves too limiting for the inhabitants of the privatized American city that comes in its place. Through generations of laissez-faire urban policy and increasingly fragmented individual interests, the original unity and order of the city falls apart, leaving an ever-more poorly served and disorderly landscape in its wake. Finally, a generation of reform-minded politicians and citizens, most of them from the city's upper-class elite, steps in to promote an "urban vision," a "new urban landscape"—first, through aesthetic improvement and, later, through practical political reform. Thanks to their efforts, the form of the city is again tied together clearly and logically.[4]

---

[4]These suppositions underlie some of the essential historical surveys of the urban landscape in the 1800s, including Thomas Bender, *Toward an Urban Vision: Ideas and Institutions in Nineteenth-Century America* (Lexington: University of Kentucky Press, 1975); and David Schuyler, *The New Urban Landscape: The Redefinition of City Form in Nineteenth-Century America* (Baltimore: Johns Hopkins University

The trouble with that familiar story is not so much that it is wrong as that it is incomplete. It is incomplete for our purposes because it downplays the persistence of the small spaces that refuse to fit into any apparent larger pattern of intentionally created formal order. Rooted in the work of progressive-era social critics like Lincoln Steffens, this story has long depended on the documentary record left by civic leaders, legislators, social reformers, designers, planners, and even cartographers, who led the way in working to establish what they considered a clearly delineated urban form.[5] In the terms of that narrative, the American city has been a battleground on which was fought a struggle by the forces of order and unity against the forces of disorder and disunity. But to begin to add to the narrative a closer look at the landscape itself (beyond that portion intentionally shaped and designed with larger ideals in mind), is to discover anew that change, variety, and instability are constant in all stages of urban growth and that their presence is in itself a hallmark of the urban landscape.

Given the bewildering variety of activity that takes place within it, the basic question of how to understand the history of an urban landscape like St. Louis's should, then, be recast in more detail. How do we develop a historical narrative rich enough to capture the essential continuity between the big and small spatial levels of the city and between the social and physical forms lodged within it? Can we use the relation of historical events and spatial change to account for the

---

Press, 1986). Much American urban history is essentially the history of city planning. In this case the subject has itself demanded a similar linear view of urban change. For years, the most complete account of this important phenomenon was Mel Scott, *American City Planning since 1890: A History Commemorating the Fiftieth Anniversary of the American Institute of Planners* (Berkeley: University of California Press, 1969). More recently, Scott's largely uncritical tone was taken to task by other writers who, in refuting his benevolent interpretation of the movement, have taken for granted his assessment of its central importance. See M. Christine Boyer, *Dreaming the Rational City: The Myth of American City Planning* (Cambridge: MIT Press, 1983); Richard E. Fogelsong, *Planning the Capitalist City: The Colonial Era to the 1920s* (Princeton: Princeton University Press, 1986); Giorgio Ciucci, Francesco DalCo, and Mario Manieri-Elia, *The American City: From the Civil War to the New Deal* (Cambridge: MIT Press, 1979).

[5] Lincoln Steffens, *The Shame of the Cities* (1905; reprint, New York: Sagamore Press, 1957), remains fascinating reading, both for what it reveals about early twentieth-century American politics and, more particularly, for its extensive treatment of the political situation in St. Louis.

systematic continuity suggested by Park's formulation of the urban state of mind?

We are by no means alone in the search for answers to such questions. Urban historians, who in the last generation developed increasingly sophisticated means for understanding the variegated dimension of social mobility in this nation's cities, have at last begun to look at the actual setting in which that mobility takes place. The efforts of such scholars as Olivier Zunz and Theodore Hershberg add a historical dimension to a chain of scholarship that runs loosely from the early, pioneering work of the Chicago sociologists like Park, through a variety of contemporary urbanists who, like Gerald Suttles, have been inclined to treat "locality as a proper element of social structure." Others, without espousing an approach that is strictly historical or sociological, have likewise begun to identify the spatial and social levels of the landscape as elements of a single system. Mark Gottdiener, whose "production of space perspective" on the city draws from the work of the social theorist Henri Lefebvre, treats space as "both the geographical site of action and the social possibility for engaging in action" and sees in this duality the crux of the story of urban life. By considering space less as a palpable end result of human activity than as a dialectical process of place and action, a "commodity" that "has the property of being materialized by a specific social process to act back upon itself and that process," Gottdiener's theory has the advantage of tying together the vast urban landscape with the sum of the countless actions, accidents, and ideals that make it look as it does.[6]

[6]Gerald Suttles, *The Social Construction of Communities* (Chicago: University of Chicago Press, 1972), p. 7. See also Olivier Zunz, *The Changing Face of Inequality: Urbanization, Industrial Development, and Immigrants in Detroit, 1880–1920* (Chicago: University of Chicago Press, 1982), p. 9; Theodore Hershberg, ed., *Philadelphia: Work, Space, Family, and Group Experience in the Nineteenth Century* (New York: Oxford University Press, 1981), p. 123. Mark Gottdiener, *The Social Production of Urban Space* (Austin: University of Texas Press, 1985), pp. 123, 129, 127, 126, 128. For examples of the diverse historical applications of the presumption of the key importance of developing and inhabiting urban space, see Elizabeth Blackmar, *Manhattan for Rent, 1780–1850* (Ithaca, N.Y.: Cornell University Press, 1989); Donna R. Gabaccia, *From Sicily to Elizabeth Street: Housing and Social Change among Italian Immigrants, 1880–1930* (Albany: State University of New York Press, 1984); Anne Vernez Moudon, *Built for Change: Neighborhood Architecture in San Francisco* (Cambridge: MIT Press, 1986). Classic examples of urban sociological studies focusing on the importance of locality to social structure include Harvey Warren Zorbaugh, *The Gold Coast and the Slum: A*

These ideas will be familiar to students of archaeology and material culture. The contention that urban space is something more than a passive reflection of social structure recalls Ian Hodder's exposition of the "active" qualities of artifacts and symbols. The concern for treating the landscape as both a collection of parts and an entity in its own right echoes both Roy Dickens's suggestion that we consider "the city itself, in its entirety . . . as the 'site' under investigation," and Pamela Cressey and John Stephens's formulation of the city's "nested levels of spatial satisfaction"; taken both in its broadest definition—as a basic concern for "behavior and its productions"—and in its specific capacity for examining the material evidence of everyday life, archaeology, as it has been defined by James F. Deetz and others, is uniquely fitted to the task of rectifying some of the biases of urban planning, history, and sociology.[7]

These, then, are the related principles that might aid us as we look back to our case study, the landscape of St. Louis: close attention to both small and large spaces and to the connections that link them to one another; an awareness of the "active" quality of the material

---

Sociological Study of Chicago's Near North Side (1929; reprint, Chicago: University of Chicago Press, 1944); and Louis Wirth, *The Ghetto* (1928; reprint, Chicago: University of Chicago Press, Phoenix Press, 1962). The spirit of their work lives on, in different forms, in such subsequent classic studies as William Foote Whyte, *Street Corner Society: The Social Structure of an Italian Slum* (1943; 2d ed., Chicago: University of Chicago Press, 1966); and Jane Jacobs, *The Death and Life of Great American Cities* (New York: Vintage Books, 1961).

[7] Ian Hodder, *Symbols in Action: Ethnoarchaeological Studies of Material Culture* (Cambridge, Eng.: Cambridge University Press, 1982), p. 12; Roy S. Dickens, Jr., ed., *Archaeology of Urban America: The Search for Pattern and Process* (New York: Academic Press, 1982), p. xiv; Pamela J. Cressey and John F. Stephens, "The City-Site Approach to Urban Archaeology," in Dickens, ed., *Archaeology of Urban America*, pp. 52–53; James F. Deetz, "Archaeology as a Social Science," in Mark P. Leone, ed., *Contemporary Archaeology: A Guide to Theory and Contributions* (Carbondale: Southern Illinois University Press), p. 110. Exemplary recent studies of American urban archaeology include Nan A. Rothschild, *New York City Neighborhoods: The Eighteenth Century* (San Diego, Calif.: Academic Press, 1990); the essays in Dickens, *Archaeology of Urban America*; Mark P. Leone and Parker B. Potter, Jr., "The Archeology of Industrial Capitalism and Modern America," in Mark P. Leone and Parker B. Potter, Jr., eds., *The Recovery of Meaning: Historical Archaeology in the Eastern United States* (Washington, D.C.: Smithsonian Institution Press, 1988); and Lu Ann De Cunzo, "Adapting to Factory and City: Illustrations from the Industrialization and Urbanization of Paterson, New Jersey," in Suzanne M. Spencer-Wood, ed., *Consumer Choice in Historical Archaeology* (New York: Plenum Press, 1987).

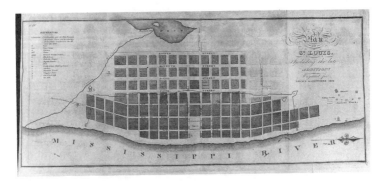

Fig. 1. *Plan of St. Louis, Including the Late Additions.* From Lewis Caleb Beck, *A Gazetteer of the States of Illinois and Missouri* (Albany: Charles R. and George Webster, 1823). (Rare Book and Manuscript Library, Columbia University.)

world and of the importance of locality on social structure; an interest in the city itself—and not simply its component parts—as an essential element of our study. Considered in these terms the story becomes at once simpler and more complex. The persistence of an internally consistent system by which big and small things, and social and physical forms, were connected is as striking as the more evident changes in the particular makeup of that system from one year to the next. Yet the complexity of smaller-scale social and physical interaction taking place within that system would seem to exceed the scope of the historian who wishes to paint a broad panorama of urban change. Let us tell the story of St. Louis's landscape, first in a broad manner that illustrates the structural dynamic taking place between space and people into the late nineteenth century, then by linking that broad pattern to the distinct layers of urban space that coexisted at the end of that period. Together, those layers form a changing tapestry of social and spatial forms that can, I think, lead us closer to the urban state of mind.

In the French and Spanish village of St. Louis, founded in 1764, social forms were imprinted on the land itself (fig. 1). The original blocks laid out beside the Mississippi River shore diagrammed a deliberate, comprehensive social hierarchy: at the center of the grid, facing the river, sat the marketplace; to the west of it was a block reserved for the use of the trading company that had established the settlement; west of that, the site of the cathedral. The original names of the village's three principal streets—the Rue Royale, Rue de l'Eglise, and Rue des Granges—reflected an intentional union and mutual dependence of crown, church, and husbandman at the edge of a pagan and uncultivated wilderness.

The welfare of this contained community was tied to and determined by the welfare of those elite few who were entrusted with its maintenance. Again, their decisions were manifest in the landscape. For a time, government officials distributed property in accordance with existing wealth, and they struggled to maintain an unchanging landscape of town lots, farm lots, and common lands that reflected the hierarchical stability of a closed, corporate society. To maintain one's lot, to till one's field, to mend the common fence—these were at once the private prerogatives and the public duties of each town dweller.

The material evidence of this idealized balance of public control and private interest, as seen in the basic division of property in and around the town, remained for years. Spatial divisions, once made, persisted long after their original purpose was forgotten. Even before the arrival of American rule in 1803, however, the original balance had begun to tilt precariously under the weight of a diversified population and an imperfectly controlled economy. By the 1770s the town's Spanish overseers were forced to offer extra incentives to keep the local population from scattering far from the village. Their efforts to mandate a stable crop supply were repeatedly resisted by a population that favored hunting and trading over farming; the fence around the town common was allowed to fall to pieces; and land grants, once an index of social status, "were now made to all who chose to apply for them, without condition, to any extent, and of course, without regard to the means of the applicant."[8]

---

[8]Wilson Primm, "History of St. Louis" (1832), in John F. McDermott, ed., *The Early Histories of St. Louis* (St. Louis: St. Louis Historical Documents Fndn., 1952), p. 115. On the Spanish administration's efforts to retain the local population, see Louis Houck, *The Spanish Regime in Missouri*, 2 vols. (Chicago: R. R. Donnelly, 1909), 1:156; on the aversion of local settlers to agriculture, see Amos Stoddard, *Sketches, Historical and Descriptive, of Louisiana* (Philadelphia: Matthew Carey, 1812), p. 254; on the common fence, see Charles E. Peterson, *Colonial St Louis: Building a Creole Capital* (St. Louis: Missouri Historical Society, 1952), pp. 11–12.

Thanks to pressures arising from changes in the population of the settlement, then, land had ceased to reflect social hierarchy prior to the American takeover. It had instead acquired a more "active" character as a means for asserting independence from the arbiters of social order and a basis for accumulating wealth. Once it acquired this character, in turn, the disposition of property around St. Louis encouraged the operations of subsequent developers whose interest lay more in individual speculation than in the formation of a cohesive and controlled townscape.

This combined spatial and social transition continued into the period that followed. Increasingly, the population that negotiated St. Louis's muddy and crooked streets in the early American period was, as residents noted, "much diversified, and [had] no general fixed character."[9] The explosive growth of the years that followed ensured that the city was soon filled with people who did not know one another or even necessarily speak the same language. The new municipal government, which lacked both the ability and the inclination to improve the town's streets and public spaces, instead used its legislative power to place the burdens (and the potential benefits) of improvement on private citizens who, acting in their own interest, would presumably straighten, pave, and extend the city's streets at their own expense. They did not. Instead, those with the money to make serious investments in urban land tended to do so along the shores of the Mississippi River, outside the city limits, where they were unburdened by city taxes and laws.

Despite the town's limited size, urban space was by the 1820s divided in numerous ways: by the presence of physical barriers in the landscape, by the uncertainties of conflicting title dating back to colonial land grants, and by the lack of a coordinated, public system for overseeing and improving city lands. Visitors to the town found few of the "rectilinear avenues" that they had been led to expect there, and a

---

[9]John A. Paxton, "Notes on St. Louis," in McDermott, *Early Histories*, p. 71. Such comments about the population were relatively common among travelers during this period. Among other examples cited in the historical literature are Timothy Flint (1828), quoted in James Neal Primm, *Lion of the Valley* (Boulder, Colo.: Pruett Publishing Co., 1981), p. 137; and Caleb Atwater (1829), quoted in Hattie M. Anderson, "Missouri, 1804–1828: Peopling a Frontier State," *Missouri Historical Review* 31 (1937): 180.

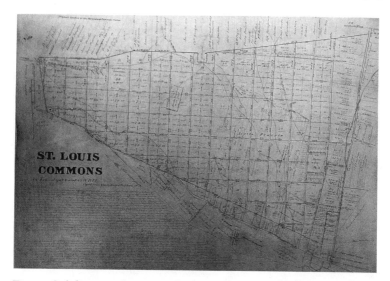

ST. LOUIS
COMMONS

Fig. 2. Subdivision plan, St. Louis Commons, 1836. (Courtesy, Pitz-man's Company of Surveyors, St. Louis.)

government survey commission found so many obstacles in the way of the supposed public streets that it was deemed "impracticable . . . to make the city conform to the plat made of same."[10] The city government's halfhearted reorganizing efforts notwithstanding, the landscape of St. Louis was as discretely and clearly delineated in 1830 as it had been in 1770. In the capitalist American city, however, those divisions reflected the dispersal, rather than the centralization, of control over space.

Little remains of the jumbled landscape of 1830. Slightly more visible are the remnants of the experiment that followed: the subdivision of the two thousand–acre town common in 1836 (fig. 2). Driving west along the streets of the city's south side, today's motorist traces the gentle angle where blocks formed from colonial land divisions give way to an even grid of forty-acre squares laid across the land. Yet the altered

[10] Edmund Flagg, *The Far West; or, A Tour beyond the Mountains*, 2 vols. (New York: Harper, 1838), 1:117; *Missouri Republican*, July 16, 1823.

street pattern suggests little of the ambitions that underlay this assertion of civic order—and still less of its unexpected consequences.

The parceling out of the common represented a reassertion of civic government's right to shape the land. Not surprisingly, it also coincided with a time when local subdividers, already a narrow and identifiable cross-section of the community, were becoming increasingly instrumental in the formulation of local law: a striking proportion of them held public office at around the time that they dedicated their subdivisions. Municipal legislation like the 1836 common sale represented an ambitious expansion of public power, but it also helped to ensure that developers' personal interest and the legally defined public interest were never far apart. Indeed, the minimum size and cost mandates of the common sales effectively limited potential purchasers to the same small group that had already taken advantage of the land market.[11]

Once again, however, spatial forms and social forms intersected in surprising ways. The large unimproved common lots, far from the city center, were impossible for most buyers to pay for in those straitened years, despite the generous terms offered by the city. By 1842 the Common Commission had foreclosed on more than one hundred purchases; the list of failed buyers included many of the city's wealthiest and most influential citizens.[12] Faced with the default of the entire

[11] The committee charged with clearing the common for survey and sale had declared, "Whatever show of claim may be exhibited by any person to a portion of said Commons, that of the inhabitants of St. Louis is at any rate the eldest and most meritorious"; rhetorically, this benign statement aligned the broad public interest (of the "inhabitants of St. Louis") with the limited cross-section of inhabitants that could afford these large tracts of land. See "An Act to Authorize the Sale of the St. Louis Commons," in *The Ordinances of the City of St Louis* (St. Louis: George Knapp, 1856), pp. 69–72. My generalizations about land developers are based on an examination of subdivider's occupations as they appear in city directories for the years in which they dedicated their lands. See Sandweiss, "Construction and Community," pp. 32–33. Among the early laws that favored private landowners were 2 key provisions in the 1835 city charter. One gave owners the power to petition the city for street openings; the other made the city liable for the entire cost of the land taken in the process of such openings. (Previously, landowners had been subject to an offsetting benefits assessment based on the increased value that might accrue to their property after the improvement.) See "Act to Incorporate," pp. 66–67.

[12] Records of the names of those purchasers who defaulted on their payments (as most of the early buyers did) show them to have been among the city's commercial and political elite, including a former mayor and several assemblymen. See "St. Louis

scheme, the commission at last changed its tack in 1853. This time, the
city subdivided the large common lots into single, twenty-five-foot-wide
house lots, much like those offered by private developers elsewhere in
the city. Suddenly, the tenor of the land sales changed. The government was selling not to wealthy developers but to individual families,
whom it attracted with announcements of free omnibus rides from
nearby working-class neighborhoods to the auction site. It offered not
large parcels for owners to develop, subdivide, or sell according to their
wishes but specific, ready-made lots, fit by their size primarily for the
construction of small-scale residential buildings.

In the rhetoric of the original common sales, the subdivision and
sale of this public land had been carried out for the good of all "the
inhabitants of St. Louis." Literally by default, that rhetoric began to
prove true in the 1850s, when at last common land became available
for a large portion of those inhabitants. The success of the revised
common sales indicated to some that the time had come for every
citizen "to have a spot, no matter how small, which one may call his
own," and government policy seemed committed to ensuring that this
social demand be met. In the common and elsewhere throughout the
city, the social profile of property developers began to change. It included a far smaller percentage of attorneys, professionals, and city
office holders than in previous decades and a far greater percentage of
people who actually lived on the property that they dedicated, rather
than in the wealthier sections of downtown.[13]

The artifactual evidence of this dispersal of the development process remains clear today: it shows up in the variety of building patterns
evident in a single neighborhood, or even a single block, of the city.
Here, one finds four houses with shallow front yards; beside them,
three duplexes of later vintage set back thirty feet from the sidewalk;
down the street, a block of apartments built up to the lot line. In each
case, a single landowner has created a tiny subdivision subject to its
own regulations and restrictions. The transition from the vague, undif-

---

Commons Claims Book," January 7, 1837, n.p., Manuscripts Collection, Missouri
Historical Society, St. Louis; and city ordinances nos. 719 (February 6, 1841) and 1077
(September 5, 1842).
   [13] John Hogan, "Thoughts about the City of St. Louis," *Missouri Republican* (ca.
1854), in *Glimpses of the Past* (Missouri Historical Society) (1936): 176; Sandweiss,
"Construction and Community," p. 64.

ferentiated grid of the first common subdivision to this architectural mélange signaled the end of the city government's efforts to impose a uniform order comparable to that of the idealized colonial landscape. Yet, uneven patterns of subdivision and development did more than reflect increasing social complexity. They were tangible, active agents in the ongoing stratification of the city's residents.

Well into the 1890s, city policy with regard to landscape-related problems like street improvement remained reactive, and the upkeep of urban space became increasingly tied to existing financial or geographic inequities. Municipal law, which might have regulated or reversed those inequities, was more closely pinned to fiscal expediency than to any compelling, idealized vision of a planned, equal-opportunity landscape. The occasional attempts of the mayor or the assembly to levy citywide assessments for street-improvement costs or to impose a consistent street plan not just in the common but also over all newly opened lands were gradually abandoned for their impracticality.[14] Because of the city's reliance on scattered, individual improvement assessments and because of the chronic unavailability of funds for large-scale public improvements (thanks in part to a strict constitutional limit on the city's bonded indebtedness), property in remote or poor neighborhoods was served and maintained much less adequately than land in more convenient or better-heeled neighborhoods. As development in areas like South St. Louis went from the sole purview of a handful of powerful men to a larger and more diversified group of people with a wider range of means and less of a clear identification with the shapers of public policy, spatial variations in the landscape magnified. Boundaries between one subdivision and another became increasingly obvious, if not always in the shapes of blocks or the direction of streets than

[14] For instance, the city charter of 1876 ordered the municipal assembly to "establish a general plan for the location and graduation of streets within the city," to which all subsequent subdivisions would be required to conform. Not only did the city fail to enforce the resultant street plan, but within 2 years legislators, faced with an avalanche of subdivision dedications awaiting approval, openly sought legal support to subvert it. Thereafter, they accepted each individual subdivision, in whatever form it was laid out, as "a part of the general plan of the city." See *Scheme for the Separation of and Reorganization of the Governments of St. Louis City and County and Charter for the City of St. Louis* (St. Louis: Woodward, Tiernan, and Hale, 1877), p. 89; "Report of the Board of Public Improvements," in *Mayor's Message, with Accompanying Documents, to the City Council of the City of St. Louis* (St. Louis, 1878), p. 199.

in the sudden absence of street pavement or the unmistakable aroma of sewage in the gutter.

This history of St. Louis's landscape has been focused thus far through a wide-angle historical lens to emphasize a broad pattern of changes in urban space up to the late 1800s. The order of the idealized colonial landscape was specific, thoroughly planned, and shaped to reflect an equally specific and regulated social order. As we saw, however, those same land divisions—once the population of the village changed—could serve to promote the breakdown of that closely regulated social order. A dispersed landscape—of distinctly shaped land parcels, ill connected through citywide improvements—actually fit the "much diversified" population of the American town quite well. Once a certain, identifiable portion of that population began to dominate both the process of developing land and the process of making the laws that affected that development, however, they worked to create a different landscape: they expanded the city limits to include hitherto-outlying developments and drew up the loosely defined and vaguely prescribed plan for the first subdivision of the town common. The manner in which the common land was to be used was as ill defined as the social profile of its eligible purchasers was well defined. When this new "fit" of social and physical space broke down after the unsuccessful conduct of the early land sales, the city experimented with a new kind of spatial order: the more carefully crafted common subdivisions of the 1850s. These new sales, which were for practical purposes made to a much wider segment of the city's "inhabitants," helped to spur a period in which the subdivision and development of land in the city was spread among a greater number and variety of people than ever before. Rather than signaling an increased governmental commitment to provide for all the city's residents, however, this trend accommodated and encouraged the continuing diversification of the city's population, as well as the increasing affiliation of social and spatial difference. The disposition of space and property, then, was never fully controlled and designed by St. Louis's more powerful citizens, nor was it ever entirely independent of their desires. Instead, social and physical forms seem to have worked back and forth in relation to one another, in a manner that was neither accidental nor entirely predictable.

One way of thinking of those forms as they evolved during this period is as a woven tapestry, held together either loosely or tightly, but nevertheless always forming a single piece of fabric—a piece that I would equate with that elusive urban state of mind. *Loose forms*, as I wish to define the term, contained recognizable communities within a minimum of explicit, defining structures and regulations. *Tight forms* offered highly structured, visibly organized settings for regulating and separating a variety of communities from one another.[15]

In spatial terms, *looseness*, as used here, applies to the quality of simplicity, of minimal definition, of permeability and malleability, that we saw in the first subdivision of the common. *Tightness*, in contrast, applies to those areas easily distinguishable from one another and more apt than loose spaces to separate the people or uses on either side of their boundaries. Both the original colonial village and the eventual fragmented city of the late nineteenth century could in this sense be seen as tight landscapes, even though one was the product of careful design while the other highlighted the absence of the same.

These definitions would be meaningless without the presumption of a necessary social component to space. And, indeed, a kind of social looseness and tightness also appears to have operated within the city-building process. Considered in this less tangible sense, the terms might refer to the residents of a neighborhood (*tight* if they share a great

[15]The basic idea behind this construction (which is meant to be suggestive rather than prescriptive in its use) underlies much of traditional sociological literature, at least as far back as Emile Durckheim's distinction between "mechanical" and "organic" forms of solidarity. While it is beyond the scope of this paper to explore deeply that paradigm, it would nevertheless be appropriate to note that it is implicit in much of the discussion that follows. Essentially, I am assuming (1) that there is a predictable and constant desire among people to create some form of community through which they in turn develop a stronger sense of personal identity, and (2) that that urge is met either through forms of primary connection that are simply felt (Durckheim's "mechanical" solidarity) or, in the absence of such connections, by others that are created through the rules, boundaries, and visible markers that help to define contemporary society ("organic" solidarity). These notions have come into the study of material culture and the urban landscape in a hundred ways. Suttles's *Social Construction of Communities*, with its notion of "contrived communities"—that is, communities defined by "formal procedures of social control" rather than by "primary relations" among human beings (pp. 30–31)—offers one compelling model for translating this social and psychological construction into the study of particular urban locations. Within the literature of historical archaeology, Glassie has convincingly tied transformations in architectural space to "extensive" and "intensive" social patterns rooted in historical change; see Henry Glassie, *Folk Housing in Middle Virginia: A Structural Analysis of Historic Artifacts* (Knoxville: University of Tennessee Press, 1975). Most relevant to the study described in these pages is the comparable model posed in Cressey and Stephens, "City-Site Approach."

number of common traits, *loose* if they seem to have little in common), to the professional organization of the practice of building construction (*tight* if controlled by a small and highly regulated group, *loose* if left in the hands of many individuals), or to a body of laws (*tight* if they closely regulated many particular activities, *loose* if they were less comprehensive or tended to leave more room for interpretation).[16] The colonial village was controlled by a tight group—readily identifiable and carefully limited. The group of people shaping land in the early American town, on the other hand, was loose: it included a variety of new arrivals who came to break up the old domination of a small, influential group of Creoles. The social profile of land developers tightened somewhat with the rise of a new group of powerful and wealthy men, including most of the failed purchasers of the first common subdivisions; then it loosened again, as the common sales and the general growth of the city at midcentury placed land in the hands of a far larger group.

What shows up in this definition of the loose-tight system is a basic dichotomy between the social profile of the men and women most responsible for shaping space (through their role in development or in legislation) on the one hand and the nature of that space on the other. After an initial, unsuccessful period in which a tightly defined group sought to maintain a tightly defined landscape, social and physical forms tended to complement one another: loosely defined social groups created (or thrived in) tight, or scattered, landscapes, while tight groups created loose, or vaguely defined, landscapes. Yet the relationship never froze in place: it was consistently redefined and restructured

---

[16]There are numerous comparable cases of the changing social structure of the city-building process in North America that chart changes similar to those to which I wish to apply the loose-tight metaphor here. On the evolving social context of land development in another fast-growing nineteenth-century city, see Barbara Sanford, "The Political Economy of Land Development in Nineteenth-Century Toronto," *Urban History Review* 16 (1987): 17–33. The changing social makeup of a key component of the process—the building trades—is treated in many useful works, including Thomas J. Surbuhr, "The Economic Transformation of Carpentry in Late Nineteenth-Century Chicago," *Illinois Historical Journal* 81 (1988): 109–24; and Catherine W. Bishir et al., *Architects and Builders in North Carolina: A History of the Practice of Building* (Chapel Hill: University of North Carolina Press, 1990), esp. pp. 264–72. For a broader perspective on occupation that plays into the issue of the increasing stratification of building and development practices in St. Louis, see Magali Sarfatti Larson, *The Rise of Professionalism: A Sociological Analysis* (Berkeley: University of California Press, 1977).

by events, accidents, and circumstances originating in both the social and the physical realm. Like unstable molecules, the momentary balances of social and physical form held together only for as long as a stronger attraction elsewhere did not pull them apart and force them to recombine again.

So far, the model is relatively straightforward. But there were not one, but several discrete, interlocking levels of shaped space constituting the overall landscape at any given time, and we have focused only on the largest and most obvious. In fact, the relation between space and the life led within it is most dynamic and most consciously felt at the level of small spaces and everyday activities: a family sitting down to the table, a father walking to work. By what means were changes in this intimate spatial level linked to the larger patterns that I have just discussed? How do we place the particular artifacts of the home, the street, the neighborhood within the larger artifact of the landscape itself?

By way of beginning to understand this process, I want to offer a pair of vignettes gathered from the study of particular neighborhoods. Each represents a particular manner of assembling big and small things into the physical and conceptual entirety of the landscape. Each entails the dynamic relation of social and spatial forms that I posited at the outset, but each shows the range of contexts in which that relation may be set.

Thomas Allen was typical of the tightly defined group responsible for shaping land around the time of the first common subdivision. Allen, a Massachusetts-born attorney, married the daughter of one of St. Louis's first Anglo-American settlers and, in the process, inherited the large piece of land on the south side of the city that surrounded her family estate. When he began to subdivide his properties in the 1840s, Allen was on the brink of a political career that would take him through various city and state offices and land him in the United States Senate. Unlike earlier local developers who incorporated their properties separately from the city to avoid the inefficiencies and ineptitude of a conservative public appropriations system, Allen lobbied successfully to expand the city limits to include his lands and then worked to make public improvement laws that supported his development interests. The ideal landscape of which his additions formed a part was, to return to our terminology, loose (fig. 3). The

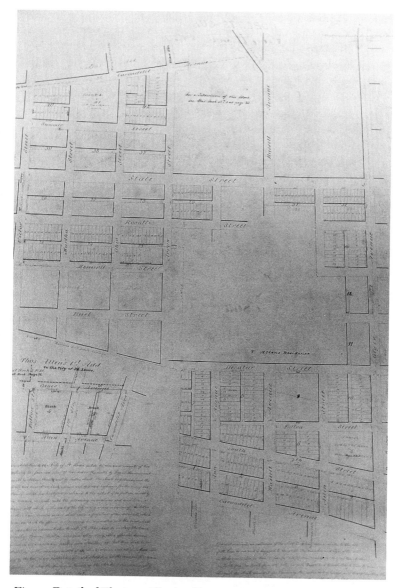

Fig. 3. Detail of Thomas Allen's additions, St. Louis, ca. 1851. (Courtesy, Pitzman's Company of Surveyors, St. Louis.)

blocks that he surveyed were both physically and politically continuous with the landscape of the older city to the north. The layout of these blocks, like the older blocks of downtown, was unspecific: two rows of identically sized lots extend to the edges of the block from a central, north-south alleyway. In contrast, the social character of the group responsible for spatial decisions at this level was, as we have seen, tight: in their occupations, their investments, and their ties to local government, they represented a highly select cross-section of the city's population.[17]

This, then, is one intersection of the city's "nested levels" of form: the relation between one subdivision and those surrounding it. At the next downward level of contrast between the city's connected forms—the relation of individual buildings to the subdivision in which they stood—a different social-spatial relationship prevailed. The houses in Allen's additions, built between the 1850s and the 1880s, were constructed one or two at a time, normally by a family that planned to move into them rather than as speculative investments. These families, most of whom already lived nearby, usually entered into renewable, ten-year ground leases with Allen, and then financed (and owned) the improvements that they erected. The financing process, like the construction process, was dispersed among a variety of familiar agents; mortgage money typically came from area merchants, relatives, or neighborhood building-and-loan companies rather than from downtown-based banks.

Despite the loosely organized decisionmaking that went into the construction of the area's buildings, however, those buildings were tightly separated from one another and from the public street (fig. 4). Each was pushed to the front edge of its lot; most butted up against their neighbors to either side or stood a narrow passageway's width apart. Access from the realm of the street to the private, family realm within was offered not, by and large, through a door fronting the street but from the side of the house, along the passageway. In some cases, that passage was visible from the street, but just as often it was hidden behind a door that appeared to lead instead into an interior hallway.

[17]Based on a comparison of names listed in the plat books of Pitzman's Company of Surveyors, St. Louis, with contemporary city directories. See Sandweiss, "Construction and Community," pp. 32–33.

Fig. 4. Two-family dwellings, 2109–2113 Menard St., St. Louis, built ca. 1875. (Photo, Eric Sandweiss.)

Outside these tightly enclosed facades, the social world of Allen's additions was loose. With few restrictions on land use aside from the developer's boilerplate restrictions against noxious industries like slaughterhouses and glue factories, these blocks were home to all sorts of businesses and to all sorts of people. The streets were noisy with the pounding of horseshoes upon rock and the cries of a motley succession of vendors: "book-agents, itinerant tintype photographers and grinders of scissors and hand-organs," as one South St. Louisan recalled them years later. Through the alleys, as the same diarist remembered, moved a different class of merchant: "ice-men, coal-men, ash-men, rag-men and the fellow with the animal wagon who gathered up dead cats and dogs." If the world outside the home was the setting for a steady flow of human traffic, it also was the site of potential danger, a fact brought home to the Fath family in the Allen additions on Menard Street when their son Bernard was struck by a passing streetcar in the confusion that followed a minor street fracas. To the Faths and their neighbors, the street was a place where their lives intersected in unpredictable ways with those of others whom they might or might not know.[18]

At the most intimate intersections of spatial and social organization—intersections of rooms within individual dwellings and of dwellings within single buildings—the tight, defined, spatial insularity of the streetscape was reversed again, for here loose spatial forms contained tight, well-defined social forms. Limited in size by the narrow width of Allen's lots (and the added expense of an additional bearing wall that would have been required for a wider structure) and lacking an interior stair hall, buildings in the area featured the most basic floor plans: two undifferentiated rooms of the same size, generally 14 to 16 feet in either direction, one in the front of the house, one in the rear (fig. 5). These interior plans—in themselves and in their relation to other units in the same building—reflected and encouraged certain basic patterns in the relative organization of private, family, and communal living among area residents. No separate space was explicitly made for interior circulation between rooms, let alone for cooking, eating, or defecating. No protected corners or light-filled bays punctuated the simple linear structure of the rooms or dictated the placement of particular household functions in one spot rather than another. Ironically, like the crowded streets through which area residents passed on their way to school, to church, to market, or to work (and from which their buildings symbolically separated them), the interior spaces of these homes were simple and open, easily traversable from one to another. Their shape dictated little intrinsic ordering to the life lived within, but demanded instead that the structures of everyday life (perhaps a wardrobe or dining table within, a corner grocery or peddler's cart without) be superimposed upon—and in the process lend added meaning to—otherwise undifferentiated space.

Also loosely arranged (and likewise tightly protected from the street) were the common spaces shared by the families living in each building. Backyards, paved with stone or brick, were crowded with alley-facing buildings, with communal privy vaults, with workshops and tool sheds, and in places—at least until water was piped into these

---

[18] Arthur Proetz, *I Remember You, St. Louis* (1916; reprint, St. Louis: Zimmerman-Petty Co., 1963), pp. 56–57; *Fath v. Tower Grove and Lafayette Railway*, 16S.W.913 and 105 Mo. 537 (1891).

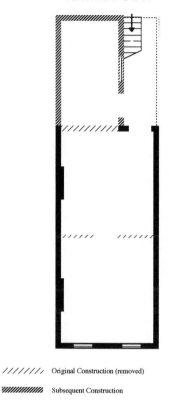

/ / / / / / /   Original Construction (removed)

///////////   Subsequent Construction

Fig. 5. First-floor plan, 2113 Menard St.,
ca. 1875. (Photo, Eric Sandweiss.)

blocks in 1878—with wells for drinking water (fig. 6). Washing was
usually done at "slop sinks," located on the side porches, which drained
into the yard through pipes tied to the porch posts. Given the crowded
condition of both interiors and yards, it is not surprising that, as one
slum investigator later discovered, "for six or seven months of the year
[the porch was] the best living room of the apartment," and that cooking

Fig. 6. Detail, interior of south St. Louis block, 1875. From Richard J. Compton, *Pictorial St. Louis: The Great Metropolis of the Mississippi Valley* (St. Louis: Compton, 1876), pl. 28. (Missouri Historical Society.)

moved from the back room onto the porch during spring and summer.[19] At such times, the shared experience of families within single buildings was further expanded from the already considerable interaction encouraged by open porches and shared yard facilities. On those porches and in those yards, separate paths and individual lives inevitably overlapped. Here, screened from the relatively uncontrolled sociability of the street, where anyone might pass and anything might happen, families shared a social experience that was more limited, more controllable, and more predictable.

The apparent social tightness that would seem to be prescribed by

[19] Charlotte Rumbold, *Housing Conditions in St. Louis* (St. Louis: Civic League of St. Louis, 1908), p. 48. Rumbold was describing an area of the near-north side that was developed at approximately the same time as Allen's additions.

the arrangement of interior spaces is confirmed by directory information and manuscript census records from 1880. Of those tenants who had resided in St. Louis ten years earlier, by far the majority had lived in the immediate vicinity—usually, within the immediate vicinity of one another, as well. When the evening whistle sounded, the residents of Allen's additions returned home to buildings full of people much like themselves. Families of common ethnicity were likely to share quarters in the same buildings (with ethnic minorities like the neighborhood's Bohemian population tending to cluster on particular block fronts), and the members of extended households sometimes occupied separate apartments in the same buildings. Within the loose space of a single apartment, social ties were tighter still: the area's households were, overwhelmingly, nuclear families. Virtually no one took in boarders or lived with relatives beyond the members of their immediate families.[20] While conditions in the area were crowded, then, families remained, within themselves, compact and well defined. That residents accepted a lack of private or differentiated space within each apartment reflected a sense of security (or, at worst, a willing resignation to the paucity of other affordable options) in regard to the others with whom they shared their living quarters.

In summary, then, the Allen additions were developed tightly or at close range: most of the property was controlled by a man who had lived on the site; its residents arrived there from adjacent city blocks; and they borrowed money from or rented apartments to others from the nearby area—others they might have known or lived beside at a previous address. This familiarity among the various actors in the settlement of the area was reflected in the loose arrangement of two spatial levels: of domestic spaces, both internally and between one unit and another, and of the additions or subdivisions themselves in relation to adjacent portions of the city. Differentiation, or the drawing of tangible lines between spaces that were shared with others and spaces that were reserved from others, took place between the domestic world and the street, where spaces were less within the control of the area's residents. Residents' chance to assert a delimited, uniquely private space came not at the level of a well-controlled streetscape

---

[20] These statistics are explicated in greater detail in Sandweiss, "Construction and Community," pp. 99–100.

(this level was beyond their power to control), but in the creation of the individual building. The world that they shaped in this close, domestic space was a world shared with family, friends, and close neighbors.

The task that awaited the reformers and planners who at the turn of the century turned a critical eye toward crowded, aging areas like Allen's additions was not to reverse the differences between such neighborhoods and other more affluent areas but to ensure that they remained predictable and clearly defined. In this sense, they took as a given the dispersed, variegated landscape first sanctioned in the second common subdivision rather than attempting to recreate the kind of uniform, preordained framework for growth represented in the short-lived first common subdivision. Where progressive-era reformers broke new ground was in looking to the innovations pioneered by private real estate developers for an answer to the question of how best to maintain the complex landscape. It was in the work of a new breed of these developers and builders that public officials found an accessible model on which to base their ambitions.

Tower Grove Heights, a mile west of the Allen additions, was a prime example of the consolidation and centralization that characterized the building industry by the end of the 1800s. The personalized cast of building in Allen's additions—where the developer had dwelt within his subdivision and where construction and financing were carried out by familiar people who likewise lived nearby—gave way here as elsewhere to city building at a new scale. The subdivision's blocks were divided in rows of spacious, forty-foot-wide house lots; a long list of deed restrictions ensured the construction of two-story homes, set back uniformly from the street. The development was financed by Connecticut Realty Company, a subsidiary of Connecticut Mutual Life Insurance Company organized specifically for the purpose of "platting, laying off, subdividing, grading, . . . improving, developing, and building on" land. In this and other local developments, the company carefully restricted land use and building placement; it laid utility and sewer lines and paved streets, all at its own expense, in advance of land sales. In addition, it provided financing to potential buyers, allowing them to purchase for the relatively low down payment of twenty percent and annual interest of five percent, a point below the common rate in St. Louis at the time. This kind of operation required access to large

Fig. 7. Two-family dwellings, 3441–3445 Pestalozzi St., St. Louis, built ca. 1905. (Photo, Eric Sandweiss.)

sources of capital—in the case of Tower Grove Heights, a half million dollars borrowed from the Mercantile Trust Company just before the developer began auctioning lots in 1905. Purchasers of this property often were professional builders who resided elsewhere in the city. They bought multiple lots, hired architects, and then sold the developed properties piece by piece.[21]

Thanks to changes in taste, law, and technology, the new street-scape of Tower Grove Heights was noticeably different from that of older South St. Louis neighborhoods (fig. 7). The area's wider lots and uniform building setbacks allowed for a less dense, more spacious scale of development than in the blocks of Allen's additions. New roofing materials allowed builders to frame simpler, flat roofs rather than the pitched gables typical of earlier periods. And precast decorative brick pieces, marketed in the catalogues of such giant local brickmaking firms as St. Louis Hydraulic-Press Brick Company, permitted them to adorn

[21] Missouri Corporate Records, nos. 28–78 and Deed no. 1523–42 (June 2, 1899), both in file no. 37,489 of the archives of First American Title Company, St. Louis.

their facades cheaply and easily. New building codes (developed in conjunction with representatives of the city's powerful trade unions) mandated indoor plumbing facilities and outlined minimum window exposures and maximum lot coverage.

The common building type that responded to and resulted from these exigencies—a two-unit flat—reflected as well as shaped the relations among tenants within the same building and between all tenants and the public world of the street. Residents of buildings in the older Allen additions had shared common space outside their apartment doors and in their backyards, all of it carefully screened (often at extra expense and labor) from the public world of the sidewalk, where women waited for streetcars, men loitered outside saloons, vendors hawked their wares, and children played ball. There, the street had enforced a different sort of sociability from that which inevitably occurred within the outlines of the building lot. Buildings in Tower Grove Heights, in contrast, opened wide onto a street that had already been cleared of nondomestic uses, a street that itself already served as a mediate zone between private and public space. Their front doors and porches emphasized the accessibility of interior from exterior space, as though to minimize the difference between household and streetscape. Yet this seeming openness was qualified—even made possible—by a sequence of factors, both visible (the small front lawns) and invisible (deed restrictions), that removed the sights, sounds, and smells of the city from within reach of the domestic world. In relation to the city as a whole, then, the loose streetscape of areas like Tower Grove Heights was tightly bounded by distinctive patterns of architectural design and massing, by private regulation, and at times by physical barriers.[22]

Moving inward from the street, the spatial-social dynamic again reversed. The families who moved to Tower Grove Heights spent their

---

[22]The tight landscape of middle- and upper middle-class development at the turn of the century was nowhere clearer than in the city's private places, where homeowners paid for their own improvement and maintenance services and erected elaborate gates at the entrances to their streets. See Charles C. Savage, *Architecture of the Private Streets of St Louis: The Architects and the Houses They Designed* (Columbia: University of Missouri Press, 1987); and David T. Beito and Bruce Smith, "The Formation of Urban Infrastructure through Nongovernmental Planning: The Private Places of St. Louis," *Journal of Urban History* 16 (1990): 263–303. For a geographical discussion of the relation of yards to streets, see Paul Groth, "Lot, Yard, and Garden: American Distinctions," *Landscape* 30, no. 3 (1990): 29–35.

time at home moving through tight interior spaces that screened sleeping, eating, and social functions from one another as clearly as their streets outside were screened from the commercial life of the city. Buildings featured highly specialized floor plans distinct from the basic linear progression from front to rear that characterized earlier, cheaper buildings in South St. Louis: their organization was not evident at first glance, and familiarity with the interior of the house depended on one's entry through a series of screened spaces. In one building typical of those constructed during the first decade of the 1900s, the visitor enters through an entry into a vestigial hall that is only minimally distinguished from the front parlor to its left (fig. 8). As he looks into the house from this open and accessible front area, the dimensions of the house seem to contract; further passage is limited by the back wall of the parlor and by the sliding doors that terminate what remains of the hall. In other words, rather than having the option of proceeding straight through to the rear of the house along either a side corridor or a path through the primary rooms, the visitor is screened from all but the front portion of the interior of the house. This public area is simultaneously made more open and accommodating by its organization as a single, wide space that allows for greeting, acclimation to the interior (a coat closet stands at one side of the room), and sitting.

A second tier of rooms, behind the entry-reception area, serves more private functions. Through the sliding doors lies a living room—dining area, which, with its wood-burning fireplace (a luxury rather than a necessity in this house fitted for steam heat) and its symmetrically aligned windows, represents the most formal room in the house. Adjoining it to one side is a master bedroom, which, thanks to the increased width of the lot, is lit through windows along the side wall of the house. Rather than being one of several undifferentiated rooms, the bedroom is now completely separated from the circulation pattern that commences in the entry of the house. The living room also stands by itself, distinct from the rest of the house. In the far corner of each of these middle rooms, doorways open onto a rear hallway, which gives access to the bathroom and storage spaces and finally to the kitchen. The rear stairs leading from the upper unit to the backyard are pushed into a projecting ell. This addition leaves space in both upper and lower units for an extra bedroom beside the kitchen and, further, reduces the amount of space shared by household members within each unit.

Fig. 8. First-floor plan, 3326 Halliday St., St. Louis, 1906. (Photo, Eric Sandweiss.)

In their careful, hierarchical separation of room uses, in the opacity of their plans, in their tendency to push neighborly interaction to the front of the house, toward the street rather than away from it, Tower Grove Heights buildings represented a thorough inversion of the spatial organization of older Allen addition buildings. That inversion extended beyond the house as well. If the transition between street and home, gently modulated by open yards and inviting porches, was unusually open, residents could at least feel secure that their private interiors opened outward onto a "good neighborhood," for their loose streetscape was tightly distinguished from the surrounding city. The distinction was rooted in part in the effect of the minimum housing costs specified in the deed restrictions and in part in the social makeup of the area's residents. They represented a far more Americanized, middle-class population than that which still characterized the older neighborhoods of the south side, and they shared a sharply increased tendency to dwell in extended family groups. A third of the households included relatives beyond the nuclear family, and one in four housed boarders. The idea of the apartment as a source of rent and not simply the refuge of one nuclear family was of course encouraged by the greater size and room separation of the units of the flats. But it also reflected the weakening of a highly predictable cultural link to home ownership. In contrast to older south side neighborhoods at the same time, where owners were far likelier than renters to be older, first-generation German or Bohemian immigrants, the property-owning population of Tower Grove Heights differed from renters only in the category most purely tied to wealth: occupation. To own a home implied little about one's ethnic background or age but much about how one made a living. If home owning was a cultural symbol, that culture was now defined by paychecks and bank accounts rather than by language, religion, or memories of the old country.[23]

---

[23] Information on the demographic characteristics of the neighborhood's residents is drawn from the manuscript enumeration tables of the *Thirteenth Census of the United States* (1910), Sutro Library Microfilm Collection, San Francisco. The practice of taking in boarders was, of course, far more common and widely accepted as of 1910 than it has since become; inferring the significance of that practice from our contemporary perspective is, therefore, fraught with difficulties. Without excluding other interpretations, I consider one vital function of taking in boarders in the Halliday area to have been the financial assistance that it offered homeowners working to pay their mortgage. For a fuller discussion of the phenomenon and its significance in American domestic

In this overview of the landscape of two distinct subdivisions, I touched on a series of interconnected spaces—rooms, dwelling units, buildings, block fronts, subdivisions, and the citywide streetscape—as well as on a corresponding series of producers and consumers of these spaces: individual families, builders and lenders, neighbors, developers. All these people were tied by their "behavior," to borrow again from Deetz, to the "productions" of urban space. All were tied, as well, by dividing or encompassing boundaries into a social and physical system that constituted the city's landscape.

If we consider levels of spatial organization within and beyond the neighborhood, we can see a two-way, complementary alternation of loose and tight structures between them, an alternation that suggested the limits of community through interlocking social and spatial boundaries. One complementary relation, which I will call "horizontal," held between spaces and the people who inhabited them. This is the relation we noticed in our overview of St. Louis's nineteenth-century landscape; it applies equally to the smaller scale of city life being considered here. If the relation of rooms within a dwelling unit, units within a building, or subdivisions within a city was loose—that is, if spaces overlapped and if the functions that they served were only minimally defined—then the social profile of the people who shared those spaces was tight: they shared common social traits or close blood ties that predisposed them to accept (or to create) open, unspecific dwelling spaces. Conversely, where interior spaces were tight—well separated, more strongly suggestive of particular functions—the households that occupied them tended to be looser: they more often included extended relatives or boarders. Similarly, where units within a particular building were carefully separated from one another, neighbors were likelier to come from different ethnic or occupational backgrounds.

The second complementary relation was vertical: it took place within either the spatial or the social axis, between one level of organization and the next. Loose domestic spaces were typically marked off by tight boundaries separating the home from the street; the street was

---

life, see John Modell and Tamara K. Hareven, "Urbanization and the Malleable Household: An Examination of Boarding and Lodging in American Families," in Tamara K. Hareven, ed., *Family and Kin in Urban Communities*, 1700–1930 (New York: New Viewpoints, 1977), pp. 164–86.

in turn loosely related to the surrounding city. Tight domestic spaces tended to open onto looser streetscapes characterized by clear, modulated transitions between street and home and between one home and another. At the next level of spatial connection, between street, or subdivision, and city at large, the connection was again tight, as distinctive building patterns and deed restrictions gave the neighborhood a particular, predetermined character that set it apart from others around it. These interrelated levels of social space can be summarized by means of the simple table below. The left-hand column describes the relation between one level of spatial organization and the next, from the individual room up to the urban landscape. In the middle are listed the users, or social groups, connected with each such level; these groups broaden from the household at one extreme to the citizenry at the opposite. The column on the right, finally, ties the experience of neighborhood space into the city-building process by describing the people responsible for the production of space at each level. These individuals (whose functions sometimes overlap from one level to the next) vary from home builders and residents whose efforts are concentrated on a single dwelling unit to subdividers working at the level of the neighborhood in relation to the rest of the city.

Spatial divisions	Users	Providers
rooms within unit	household	residents/builders
units within building	immediate neighbors	residents/builders
buildings within streets	general neighbors	builders/developers
streets within city	citizens	subdividers/politicos

If we inserted the terms *loose* and *tight* into the appropriate square for a given neighborhood at a given time, we would see a checkerboard of alternating squares, as loose social and spatial units were defined by their tight separation from one another. The exact layout of the checkerboard would depend on the different circumstances that attended each neighborhood's creation and subsequent development.

This grid offers one kind of idealized framework for describing the production of urban space, a framework that diverges from the traditional perspectives of urban history by its dependence on the mutual transformations of large and small social groupings and by its presumption of the "active" functions of space in contributing to those transformations. Rather than treating space as an index of autonomous social and political circumstances, an index that might register more or less order at one moment than at another, this suggestive framework rests on a different premise. It presumes that relations within a single neighborhood, or between neighborhood and city, were at all times complex phenomena born in the social intersections formed around the acts of producing and experiencing space and nurtured by the ongoing power of places to relocate and redefine those intersections into the future. Spatial boundaries—small and large—expressed and then redefined the boundaries by which individuals united to form communities.

In concluding, I will suggest how this abstract analysis, rooted in the study of landscape as an "expression of cognitive [and social] pattern," might bring the two subdivision examples to bear upon the way we describe American urban history. In the years that followed the first subdivision of the common, the social world framed by the production of urban space was atomized yet highly personal. The evidence of the built landscape in areas like Thomas Allen's additions suggests that community was defined at one extreme by the level of the household and the individual building and at the other by an unfettered connection between the neighborhood and the city at large. The character of space at each of those levels was the product of personalized and relatively informal procedures for claiming, developing, and dwelling upon urban land. Through the forge of the city-building process, immigrant barrelmakers and seamstresses shared an identity with a wealthy United States senator, and the smallest private world of the porch or the yard was tied to the larger public world of a citywide landscape. The idea of an intermediate level of the shared "neighborhood" was as yet relatively weak.

By the turn of the century, the formula was essentially reversed. The social landscape of areas like Tower Grove Heights was marked by a looseness that joined together communities at a level between that of the household and that of the city. These communities, which brought into contact a greater variety and range of people than had previously been typical, were regulated by a formality and a planned, intentional visual character that served to join diverse individuals in a new common interest. If the class disparity between developer (representative of the large landscape) and the home buyer or tenant (keeper of the small, domestic landscape) was not so great as it had been, neither was the opportunity to define a private level of community on the one hand or to participate in a broader, citywide level on the other.

These two models of the urban tapestry of interwoven social and spatial forms may seem equally unlikely sources of either the grand landscape visions or the wrenching political and social conflicts that marked American cities at the turn of the century. But the contrast between them—simple, concrete, rooted in the everyday perceptions of all St. Louisans as they sat down to the table or waited for the streetcar—also may suggest a path to those destinations that differs from the historical narrative that is rooted in the period. Rather than the fundamental reordering of urban space and society that supporters and detractors have claimed for it, the progressive planning movement of the early 1900s might, as I suggested earlier, be understood as an effort to justify and make predictable the existing, tightened landscape system of the time, with all its inequities and its contrasts.[24] Put in terms of the table above, the planning movement's supporters sought to rearrange the checkerboard. In the reform vision of the early twentieth century, the larger city landscape was tight and full of small, well-defined units. The group vested with control of this landscape would be tight as well: their consolidated powers, sanctioned by charter reform, federal land-use law, and gentlemen's agreements, would turn the city's many pieces from evidence of division to proof of a new kind of civic unity.

For years government officials had tried to consolidate their authority to loosen, or make less disparate, the landscape. Their efforts had gone, almost without exception, unrewarded. By the turn of the century the people who identified themselves with the forces of "good

---

[24]The historiography of early twentieth-century urban reform is a subject in itself. For 2 reviews of the literature, see Terrence J. McDonald, *The Parameters of Urban Fiscal Policy* (Berkeley and Los Angeles: University of California Press, 1986), chap. 1; and John M. Allswang, *Bosses, Machines, and Voters* (rev. ed.; Baltimore: Johns Hopkins University Press, 1986), p. 6. For recent work that reconsiders the social and political framework in which progressive-era urban conflict took place, this essay leans on the perspective presented in John Teaford, *The Unheralded Triumph: City Government in America, 1870–1900* (Baltimore: Johns Hopkins University Press, 1984). Teaford recasts that conflict away from its traditional attributed roots in class or ethnic difference, seeing in it instead the fundamental incompatibility of "a network of accommodation and compromise" and an "age . . . of cultural absolutes" (p. 9). My interest here is in identifying that conflict in terms of its articulation in opposing notions about the shaping of the urban landscape.

government" in St. Louis had turned away from traditional governmental solutions like mandating a uniform street plan and turned instead
toward the example set by the private building industry in places like
Tower Grove Heights. Thanks to the voluntary efforts of a reform
group known as the Civic Improvement League, founded in 1902, the
circumstances that shaped such areas were now adopted by a government newly empowered to assume some of the same roles that had hith-
erto been abrogated to private developers. Zoning, long discussed but not
finally enacted until 1917, allowed the city's new plan commission to
preserve such areas as had already been made in this mold, and new development plans—including a set of small "civic centers" scattered through
the city's poorer neighborhoods—were meant to promote a new "neighborhood feeling" in those parts of town that had not benefited from the
same coordinated, neighborhood-scale development.[25] Like the new
breed of developers, reformers focused on opening the space between the
household and the city at large. The "neighborhood unit," as it came to
be called in professional jargon, would be the level at which members of
a single group defined their commonalties and distinguished themselves
from others in adjoining neighborhoods.

Older areas like the Allen additions were by this time full of neighborhood feeling, although not necessarily the type of feeling that Civic
Improvement League members might have wished to promote. It was
instead a feeling born of the historical inadequacy of public services
and an increasingly visible class segregation. At the turn of the century,
residents of older south side neighborhoods began to identify collectively with their area in a way that they had not before, and that
identification often took the form of protest over the condition of their
streets and public spaces.[26]

In their efforts to reverse the accumulated effects of years of selectively allocated public services, ethnic neighborhood bosses like South
St. Louisan Henry Ziegenhein actually advocated the return of the
kind of landscape implicitly promised in the first common subdivision

---

[25] Civic League of St. Louis, A *City Plan for St. Louis* (St. Louis, 1907), p. 37.

[26] Members of the newly chartered Socialist Labor Party, for instance, felt compelled
to demand in their 1893 party platform that "in the matter of public services and improvements, the municipal government shall give the same attention to the districts inhabited
by the working men and small businessmen [essentially the city's south and north sides]
as to the grand west end boulevard districts inhabited by the 'better class' " (*Labor*, April
29, 1893).

and carried through to some extent by men like Thomas Allen—in our terms, a loose urban landscape, but one now controlled by a loose group. The kinds of sweeping changes that they advocated were in a sense more idealistic and less closely based on the existing social-spatial order of the city than was the reform vision that they opposed. Ziegenhein won the mayoral election of 1897 on his basic promises to constituencies in poorer areas of the city that they would together "make up for the West End" (the city's wealthiest neighborhood) by acquiring the improvements needed to restore a basic uniformity to the landscape of the entire city. Yet Ziegenhein's pitch (and the general resistance that South St. Louis citizens continued to voice against the reform agenda in coming years) was dismissed by its detractors as a divisive cry from the city's "fenced-off corners," a hindrance to progress at a city-wide scale.[27]

The progressive vision of the landscape, like the colonial vision of St. Louis's French and Spanish administrators, constituted a tight landscape controlled by a tight group. The urban whole described in their plans was formed by constructing a new kind of fence (built of strengthened public control over the shaping of the landscape) around the entire city, a fence that comprehended all the city's diverse pieces and was maintained by the enlightened "paternalism" of a select group of experts and public-spirited citizens. Zoning, transportation planning, and neighborhood redevelopment planning all locked in the character of discretely built areas like Tower Grove Heights, while they worked to alter the relationship of spaces in areas like the Allen additions in such a way as to make them conform to the new status quo (fig. 9).[28]

For all their talk about "eliminating the terms North and South St. Louis," for all the freedom of movement through space that they strove to achieve with parkways and expressways that sliced across the city, planners also sought to freeze in time, more strongly than ever before, the character of each quarter of the city.[29] That character, in

[27]*St. Louis Post-Dispatch*, November 6, 1898; *Missouri Republican*, January 27, 1911.

[28]The call for paternalistic control of the new urban order comes from an unidentified note by St. Louis reform activist John Gundlach (n.d.), in John Gundlach papers, Missouri Historical Society Archives, St. Louis.

[29]George Kessler, "Annual Report of the Park Commissioner," in *The Mayor's Message, with Accompanying Documents, to the City Council of the City of St. Louis* (St. Louis, 1913), p. 13.

Fig. 9. *Site Plan, Preliminary Study, Soulard Neighborhood District.*
From City Plan Commission of St. Louis (Harland Bartholomew,
Eng.), *Comprehensive City Plan, St Louis, Missouri* (St. Louis, 1947).
(Courtesy, Missouri Historical Society, St. Louis.)

turn, was described as being at last the product of deliberate decisions made far from the level of the yard, the home, or the block. Yet we would be mistaken if we accepted this description without a grain of salt. Each of the landscape-related decisions made by planners and politicians in the twentieth century made sense only insofar as it represented a way of reconciling high ideals and lofty principles to the everyday experience of the urban landscape—an experience that was just as strongly felt by lawyers, planners, and engineers as it was by factory workers and domestic servants. What citizens, politicians, dreamers, and planners fought over was not the question of whether their landscape would possess a greater or lesser degree of order but rather where the boundaries between "my" landscape and "yours," between tight and loose places, might fall. Like the multilayered urban landscape itself, the urban state of mind was never either entirely united—as reformers hoped to make it—or completely fractured, as they feared it was. Planners and reformers could pick at the urban tapestry, but they could not remove themselves from it. Their vision was inevitably more limited than they wished to believe.

To understand the history of the urban landscape is to find a constancy to the city's forms that is in many ways more pronounced than their obvious transformations. When we focus on the intersection of people and place, we see a need to define spatial and social form through boundaries that encompassed some of those forms and excluded others. It is a need that persisted throughout the seemingly complete transition from village to metropolis. Even if we shift our emphasis to the analysis of this urban state of mind, however, we will find that the same limits that hampered those who have tried to shape the city apply as well to those of us who try to understand it. Urban historians and historical archaeologists, too, are systematizers. Why? Perhaps the seeming logic that we so readily apply to the evolution of the urban landscape would be more easily understood if each person exploring the murky avenues of the urban past reached back still further, past the forgotten spaces and forgotten people, and pulled out the last form that lingered there, untouched and unseen: the form of his own reflection.

Remaking the Barnyard

The Archaeology of Farm Outbuildings in the Connecticut River Valley of Massachusetts, 1770–1870

J. Ritchie Garrison

We know too little about the process by which progressive farmers changed rural landscapes in the late eighteenth and early nineteenth centuries. And some of the best evidence—barns and outbuildings—is quietly rotting to oblivion. Scholars have acknowledged the importance of studying rural landscapes and outbuildings, but they sometimes have charted a genealogy of agricultural custom that emphasized tradition, simplicity, and household independence over complexity, change, and markets. In calling for an archaeology of farm outbuildings, this study urges that scholars of material life use a combination of aboveground and below-ground historical evidence to study how environmental, so-

The author acknowledges the collaborative efforts of a team of archaeologists and historians, Robert Paynter, Rita Reinke, Ed Hood, Amelia F. Miller, Susan McGowan, Kevin M. Sweeney, and Ken Hafertepe, who have pursued archaeological research in Deerfield, Mass., under the sponsorship of Historic Deerfield, Inc. Some portions of this essay were published in J. Ritchie Garrison, *Landscape and Material Life in Franklin County, Massachusetts, 1770–1860* (Knoxville: University of Tennessee Press, 1991). The author gratefully acknowledges the University of Tennessee Press for permission to publish information contained in the book. Thanks also to Kevin M. Sweeney, Bernard L. Herman, and Lu Ann De Cunzo for providing helpful comments during the preparation of various versions of this essay.

cial, and economic factors shaped systems of learned behavior and that they seek not only the patterns of culture but also the inflection of human agency.[1]

This case study of barnyards in the Massachusetts Connecticut River valley is an effort to work through the implications of what Ian Hodder has called "Contextual Archaeology." It attempts to get at what he called the "inside" of history—the decisions individuals or families made within a range of choices bounded by general, but usually ambiguous, cultural rules. The following picture of Connecticut River valley barnyards emerged only after linking evidence that fit into three general categories: archaeological, architectural, and archival. This process of linking and cross-checking one kind of source with another helps to "identify a reconstruction that makes sense, in terms of the archaeologist's picture of the world . . . , and in terms of the internal coherence of the argument."[2] The fieldwork and documentary research on barn-

---

[1] Much of the research on barns and farmsteads is the result of scholarship by geographers and folklorists. On barns, see Henry Glassie, *Pattern in the Material Folk Culture of the Eastern United States* (Philadelphia: University of Pennsylvania Press, 1968), pp. 133–41, 158–62, 185–87; Henry Glassie, "The Variation of Concepts within Tradition: Barn Building in Otsego County, New York," *Geoscience and Man* 5 (June 1974): 177–255; Robert Blair St. George, "The Stanley-Lake Barn in Topsfield, Massachusetts: Some Comments on Agricultural Buildings in Early New England," in Camille Wells, ed., *Perspectives in Vernacular Architecture* (Annapolis, Md.: Vernacular Architecture Forum, 1982), pp. 7–23; Robert Blair St. George, " 'Set Thine House in Order': The Domestication of the Yeomanry in Seventeenth-Century New England," in Jonathan L. Fairbanks and Robert F. Trent, eds., *New England Begins*, 3 vols. (Boston: Museum of Fine Arts, 1982), 2:159–88. For a history of New England agriculture that emphasizes a household interpretation of the New England economy, see Percy W. Bidwell, "Rural Economy in New England at the Beginning of the Nineteenth Century," *Connecticut Academy of Arts and Sciences Transactions* 20 (1916): 241–399; Percy W. Bidwell, "The Agricultural Revolution in New England," *American Historical Review* 26 (1921): 683–702; Percy W. Bidwell and John I. Falconer, *History of Agriculture in the Northern United States, 1620–1860* (Washington, D.C.: Carnegie Institute, 1925), pp. 122, 129–31; James Henretta, "Families and Farms: *Mentalité* in Pre-Industrial America," *William and Mary Quarterly*, 3d ser., 35 (January 1978): 3–32; Michael Merrill, "Cash Is Good to Eat: Self-Sufficiency and Exchange in the Rural Economy of the United States," *Radical History Review* 3 (1977): 42–71. For a contrasting view, see Howard S. Russell, *A Long Deep Furrow: Three Centuries of Farming in New England* (Hanover, N.H.: University Press of New England, 1976); Winnefred B. Rothenberg, "The Emergence of Farm Labor Markets and the Transformation of the Rural Economy: Massachusetts, 1750–1855," *Journal of Economic History* 48 (September 1988): 537–66; Winnefred B. Rothenberg, "The Market and Massachusetts Farmers," *Journal of Economic History* 41 (June 1981): 300–312; Allan Kulikoff, "The Transition to Capitalism in Rural America," *William and Mary Quarterly*, 3d ser., 46 (January 1989): 120–44.

[2] Ian Hodder, *Reading the Past: Current Approaches to Interpretation in Archaeology* (1986; 2d ed., Cambridge, Eng.: Cambridge University Press, 1991), pp. 99–100. This

yards and outbuildings proceeded from the assumption that all evidence and interpretations contain some elements of bias. For example, the superficial similarity of barn exteriors tempts us to assume that most people behaved alike. In fact there were variations in the form and distribution of the valley's barns over space and time. We can best understand these variations by studying what people did and what rationale they used in making decisions about their landscape.

The three-bay English barn and its two-bay relative seem to have been the commonest outbuilding forms in the valley during the eighteenth and early nineteenth centuries. Some of these were built as mixed-purpose barns; some were only for storing hay. Farm families in the upper two deciles of tax ratables were more likely to own the full complement of outbuildings, including barns, cowhouses, corn barns, hovels, and sheds, than those in the third or fourth (or lower) deciles of tax ratables, but household patterns differed according to occupation, age, and other factors that we must reconstruct before we can interpret. English-type barns persisted throughout the period we are concerned with, but toward the end of the eighteenth century the valley's most progressive livestock farmers began to build larger barns that integrated under one roof the specialized functions once located in separate outbuildings. Similarly, when many farmers reduced their emphasis on livestock husbandry in the 1850s, they hired carpenters to erect tobacco barns, a much different form of barn than the older English type. The point is that the early landscape in the Connecticut River valley became more complex over time as agricultural markets changed. New outbuildings constructed in response to new economic opportunities were placed next to or attached to older ones.[3]

---

study has also benefited from the insights of James Deetz, *In Small Things Forgotten: The Archaeology of Early American Life* (Garden City, N.Y.: Anchor Press/Doubleday, 1977), p. 4; and Henrietta Moore, "Paul Ricoeur: Action, Meaning and Text," in Christopher Tilley, ed., *Reading Material Culture* (Cambridge, Eng.: Basil Blackwell, 1990), pp. 85–120.
    [3]Much of the literature on barns fails to say much about outbuildings in either an economic or a social context. See, for example, Eric Ross Arthur, *The Barn: A Vanishing Landmark in North America* (Greenwich: New York Graphics Society, 1972); Charles Klamkin, *Barns: Their History, Preservation, and Restoration* (New York: Hawthorn Books, 1973); Eric Sloan, *Age of Barns* (New York: Funk and Wagnalls, 1966); Eric Sloan, *American Barns and Covered Bridges* (New York: W. Funk, 1954). For examples of how scholars have connected the history of outbuildings and agriculture, see Glassie, "Variation of Concepts," pp. 177–255; St. George, "Stanley-Lake Barn," pp. 7–23; St. George, " 'Set Thine House in Order,' " 2:159–88; Thomas C. Hubka, *Big House, Little*

Studying this process is arduous. Outbuildings are difficult to date with certainty, they often leave little subsurface archaeological information, and they sometimes seem immune to the stylistic and construction topologies that architectural historians and historical geographers have laboriously recorded for houses. Moreover, because yards and outbuildings reflected shifts in a family's life course and economic conditions, behavioral patterns that were once meaningful are now opaque or difficult to comprehend. All late eighteenth- and early nineteenth-century outbuildings and yards in the Connecticut River valley of Massachusetts have been modified, usually extensively. We can comprehend the archaeology of barnyards only by comparing stratigraphic evidence with existing structures. And we can grasp the original purposes and forms of these existing outbuildings only through an educated reading of esoteric evidence such as mortises, nail types, and framing details.[4] Even these comparisons are subject to uncertainty because so many outbuildings have disappeared. Documentary study is essential for grasping the historical stratigraphy of standing structures and yards, but even documentary information has limits. Few farm families systematically recorded information on their outbuildings, and public records were seldom more specific than terms like *barn, stable,* or *outbuildings thereon.*

Past archaeological study has many lacunae. Professional archaeologists have conducted little systematic below-ground research on barnyards and outbuildings anywhere in the Connecticut River valley. Most of the cultural resource management (CRM) research in the area has been limited to first-stage reconnaissance walkovers during which the archaeologist in charge has seldom done more than note the pres-

---

House, Back House, Barn: The Connected Farm Buildings of New England (Hanover, N.H.: University Press of New England, 1984); John Fitchen, *The New World Dutch Barn: A Study of Its Characteristics, Its Structural System, and Its Probable Erectional Procedures* (Syracuse, N.Y.: Syracuse University Press, 1968); Daniel A. Fink, *Barns of the Genesee Country, 1790–1915: Including an Account of Settlement and Agricultural Practices* (Geneseo, N.Y.: J. Brunner, 1987); Joseph W. Glass, *The Pennsylvania Cultural Region: A View from the Barn* (Ann Arbor, Mich.: UMI Research Press, 1986).

[4] Scholars such as Henry Glassie have recommended that we study barn bents as a diagnostic tool, but neither he nor other scholars are very specific about linking types of bents with dates of construction; see Glassie, "Variation of Concepts," pp. 177–255. The fieldwork on barns undertaken for this study indicates that it is important to examine the entire frame, not just the bents.

ence of foundations of farm outbuildings. Much of this information remains in the "gray" literature of CRM reports. Several factors have contributed to this paucity of archaeological reports. Given the fertility of the valley lowlands, many farmers have continued agricultural production in the area, and state and federal highway projects generally have made efforts to bypass village and farmstead landscapes where the most important archaeological information on barnyards remains. The most revealing archaeological work thus far has occurred in Deerfield, Massachusetts, where Historic Deerfield and the University of Massachusetts have cooperated to recover both documentary and subsurface information systematically. Since field crews have excavated relatively small areas of the historic landscape, this subsurface research is suggestive but inconclusive. In general, field crews have recovered several interesting soil layers and features, but the barnyards of Deerfield, and by extension much of the rest of the valley lowlands, seem to have limited artifactual remains to help date soil layers.[5] Successful interpretation of even this limited subsurface evidence depends on reconstructing the agricultural history of the area. Only after we reassemble a picture of the agricultural practices that farm families developed in the Connecticut River valley of Massachusetts can we begin to see the people and culture behind the landscape (fig. 1).

Dudley Woodbridge sketched the earliest view of a barn in the Connecticut River valley in 1727 when he visited Deerfield with a college classmate. We will never know if his sketch represented a barn he saw or if it was merely a schematic reference to barns he knew about. Nevertheless, with a few pen strokes he rendered a three-bay English-type barn among a number of houses. We know that these barns were widely built in East Anglia, the region from which New England's early settlers came in large numbers; that they were built throughout New England and the rest of the country during the seventeenth, eighteenth, and nineteenth centuries; and that they were used

---

[5]Telephone communication from Robert Paynter and Mitchell Mulholland, Department of Anthropology, University of Massachusetts, to J. Ritchie Garrison, November 1992. This research is based on several summers of excavation by the Summer Field School in Historic Archaeology, University of Massachusetts, 1984, 1985, 1987, 1990, and 1991 and by excavations and research conducted under a grant from the National Endowment for the Humanities and the L. J. and Mary C. Skaggs Foundation in 1985 and 1986.

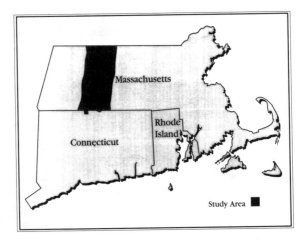

Fig. 1. Map of southern New England showing Connecticut River valley study area. (Drawing, J. Ritchie Garrison.)

by rich and middling farmers to house livestock, hay, and crops. These barns used a tripartite system of bays in which a runway passed through the barn on the structure's long side. Typically, the runway was off center to allow one of the bays flanking the runway to be larger. This larger bay and loft over the runway generally was used for hay storage; the smaller one often housed the stock with a haymow above. Such structures conform to the picture of mixed-household–based farming that historians and folklorists have constructed for seventeenth- and eighteenth-century New England material life, but are our assumptions about English-style barns and the agriculture they sustained accurate? Who owned these buildings, under what circumstances did they own them, and what were the alternatives?[6]

[6] Dudley Woodbridge, journal of a trip from Cambridge to Deerfield, Massachusetts Historical Society (photocopy, Pocumtuck Valley Memorial Association); Nigel Harvey, *A History of Farm Buildings in England and Wales* (Newton Abbott, Eng.: David and Charles, 1970), pp. 48–110; Glassie, *Pattern in Material Folk Culture*, pp. 55–62, 89–92, 146–50, 153–61; Glassie, "Variation of Concepts," pp. 177–235; St. George, "Stanley-Lake Barn," pp. 7–23.

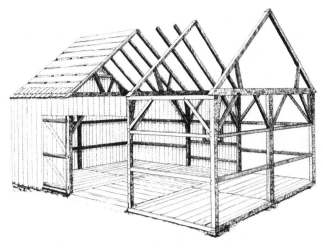

Fig. 2. Mattoon barn, Northfield, Mass., 1750–1800. (Measurements and drawing, J. Ritchie Garrison.)

Finding answers in surviving farm buildings is problematic. Few English-type three-bay barns survive in the Connecticut River valley, and even fewer seem to date to the eighteenth century. Most are in the lowlands where settlers first established permanent communities and where agriculture has continued. These surviving barns generally are large or were extensively modified to meet modern requirements, and many were *not* used according to modern scholarly notions of what traditional mixed farming was like. The Mattoon barn in Northfield, Massachusetts, for example, was probably built in the second half of the eighteenth century (fig. 2). It follows general construction practices of the period, modified to reduce the costs of framing. The Mattoon barn has shouldered posts and a common rafter system like other eighteenth-century domestic structures in the area. It was not designed to shelter livestock. There are no mortises on the inner bents that flank the runway, no evidence that there originally were any stanchions for animals, and no intermediary supporting posts for the massive girts that span the entire 32-foot width of the barn. Despite the size of the posts and girts, most of the framing is rather light. Only ten posts carry the entire weight of the building. By later standards, the bracing is minimal;

the roof has 5-inch square-hewn rafters, lap jointed and pegged at their peak, and the walls are simply nailed onto the sills and plates and to two intermediary 3-by-5-inch rails. Only the braces that connect the plates and the posts have prevented this building from racking under the pressure of high winds, but the construction was sufficient for a hay barn. The Mattoons piled hay and fodder on either side of the runway and evidently kept their animals elsewhere, probably in a cowhouse.[7]

Other structures and documentary evidence suggest that in the Connecticut River valley lowlands this light, inexpensively framed barn was once common. On a hill to the east of the Mattoon barn, the Janes family built a similar outbuilding a few years later. This barn has the same system of framing as the Mattoon barn except that the Janes barn uses a pentagonally shaped ridge pole with peeled poles for common rafters. This type of roof framing was common to valley dwelling houses during the late eighteenth and early nineteenth centuries. These framing details suggest that scholars can safely assign approximate construction dates based on local framing chronologies developed for more easily dated houses. The parallels between houses and outbuildings are most noticeable in the way carpenters shaped posts, constructed roofs, and used bracing; other outbuilding framing details differed from houses because the function of dwellings and barns differed and because most families appear to have restrained the costs associated with farm buildings. On the basis of the evidence for dwellings, the Janes barn was probably built a few years later than the Mattoon barn.[8]

Like the Mattoons, the Janes used the barn for storing hay and fodder and put their livestock in a cowhouse. The Janes cowhouse stands next to the barn (fig. 3). Three of the cowhouse's four bays were open to the air; the eastern bay was enclosed and may have been used for horses or young stock. Although the barn and cowhouses were not joined, the cowhouse was situated to take maximum advantage of southern exposure and worked with the barn to form a kind of courtyard, blocking cold northern and western winds from the animals.

[7] Fieldwork on Northfield outbuildings and the carpentry of Calvin and George Stearns was made possible in part by financial assistance from two General University Research grants, University of Delaware, 1986 and 1988.

[8] J. Ritchie Garrison, *Landscape and Material Life in Franklin County, Massachusetts, 1770–1860* (Knoxville: University of Tennessee Press, 1991), pp. 65–79, 122–44.

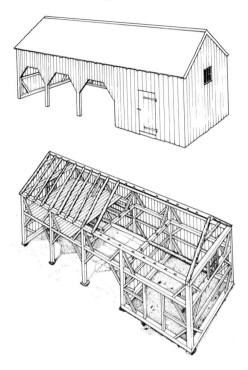

Fig. 3. Janes cowhouse, Northfield, Mass., 1815–40. (Measurements and drawing, J. Ritchie Garrison.)

Above the stock was a loft. This area probably was used for storing straw and provender and was floored over by laying loose boards atop joists made of peeled poles.

Despite the substantial construction of the Janes cowhouse, the foundation was much lighter than the foundations for either the adjacent barn or the Mattoon barn in the village below. The barns were built atop fieldstones neatly laid on top of the ground or set into a shallow trench. Both of these barns have a discernible archaeological footprint. By contrast, the cowhouse consisted of a few fieldstones set directly on the ground beneath the main supporting posts, leaving almost no stratigraphic or remote sensing anomalies for future archaeologists to find after the building is gone. If these stones for the cowhouse are removed and salvaged for other building projects (as they often were in the stone-free lowlands), there may be virtually no subsurface trace of these types of buildings except for high phosphate residues from animal wastes. We still do not know whether the foundation stones for the Janes cowhouse were typical because not many of these buildings have survived, but the implications are troubling. Unless an archaeologist was specifically looking for a cowhouse and had opened up a substantial amount of ground (an expensive and laborious proposition for state highway department administrators concerned with cultural resource management budgets), the subsurface traces of this type of building might never appear. Yet consider the possibilities for interpretive error if the cowhouse information is omitted. The evidence for the barn foundations coupled with "organic soil layers" might easily lead to the assumption that the barn was of the traditional three-bay type, which housed a mixed form of agricultural production common to much of the eastern seaboard and farther inland.

The documentary record of the region's agricultural history narrates a different, more richly textured story. Like many farm households in New England and elsewhere, families that concentrated on growing foodstuffs for local use, with provision for some marketable surpluses, could subsist with a three-bay English-style barn. Large, specialized hay barns and separate cowhouses reflected the lowland valley farmer's substantial involvement with marketing grain-fattened beef. Centered in Deerfield, Hatfield, and Hadley, but extending to other lowland towns by at least the mid eighteenth century, the valley's cattlemen fattened steers on provender and drove their "fatt cattle" overland to the Brighton market outside Boston. Lowland farmers purchased starter stock from uplanders in November and December, fed the stock through the winter, and marketed them in spring. Compared with the hay-fed cattle that normally entered the Brighton market between February and May, grain-fattened valley oxen achieved a reputation for superior meat. That reputation was earned through careful husbandry and through the construction of large barns for storing grain and fodder, feeding sheds, and cowhouses where the steers were kept.[9]

[9] J. Ritchie Garrison, "Farm Dynamics and Regional Exchange: The Connecticut Valley Beef Trade, 1670–1850," *Agricultural History* 61 (August 1987): 1–17; Garrison, *Landscape and Material Life*, pp. 65–79.

The fat-cattle system was the product of a complex interaction of natural and human resources in a dynamic process that changed through the year. Outbuildings and yards necessarily supported these seasonal changes as cattle entered the feed lots, gained weight, and were sold. In spring, many farmers put their remaining animals into upland pastures for the summer until the autumn harvest signaled the time to bring them back to the lowland home lots. Farmyards were busy spaces as cattle settled in for the feeding season, for many animals acquired from upland farms had to adjust to confinement after a life-time of comparative freedom. A Deerfield man recalled turning one homesick team of oxen purchased from a Vermont farmer into his well-fenced yard. Soon after, he "happened to see one of the strangers, with a spring as light as a deer, clear the top bar at a bound. The mate did not feel equal to this feat, but he proposed to show that some things can be done as well as others; so after giving one look around for a vulnerable point, he walked up to the bars, bent his head deliberately down, adjusted his head carefully to the rails and lifted both posts bodily out of the ground, quietly laid the whole down flat without misplacing a bar and walked out over the prostrate structure." After recapturing them in a lane leading to the highway, he returned them to the yard, secured them, and fed them lavishly until they became docile. Thus, the feeding routine was a strategy both for making money and for controlling very powerful animals.[10]

Feeding "fatt cattle" was a demanding business. During a trip to the valley in 1771, John Adams learned, "it is the whole Business of one Man to take care of em-to feed, Water, and curry them. They give an Ox but little Provender at first, but increase the Quantity till an Ox will eat a peck at a time, twice a day." Judging from Adams's description, farmers in the valley would have needed approximately two bushels of grain a week per animal to fatten the animals for market—about eight to eleven bushels of provender per week for farmers with four to six oxen. These quantities of fodder required substantial storage space to protect the fodder and hay that the animals would consume through a winter, and it imposed self-discipline on the families who were involved with the business. Beef cattle are curious animals; fattening

[10] George Sheldon, " 'Tis Sixty Years Since': The Passing of the Stall Fed Ox and the Farm Boy," *History and Proceedings of the Pocumtuck Valley Memorial Association, 1890–1898* 3 (1901): 472–90.

them efficiently required routine feeding with minimal change in the daily regimen. Feeding began at daybreak with provender, a mixture of peas and oats and corn ground at a mill. After the animals consumed their rations, the stockmen or their hired help took hay from the mow and fed it by hand to each animal until they could or would eat no more. He then led them to a trough, two at a time, to drink from freshly drawn water, after which the oxen bedded down in a cowhouse or an open shed to rest.[11]

A well-run feeding operation was both a matter of pride and a measure of good business sense. According to nineteenth-century reminiscences, cattlemen were competitive about maintaining clean yards and barns. George Sheldon recalled: "A slovenly barn was held to be a disgrace to the profession, and clear evidence of an unthrifty farmer; waste in small matters inevitably leading to carelessness in the general management of the farm." Whatever excess hay and provender the fat cattle did not eat went to the ordinary cattle. After watering the stock and getting them settled in the cowhouse, farmers or their sons swept mangers clean and collected manure for dressing the fields on which they grew crops. Afternoon feeding began punctually at two o'clock, and even funeral processions were insufficient reason to draw cattlemen away from their duties. After David Dickinson of Deerfield died, his three surviving brothers and many other mourners abandoned the procession on its way to the graveyard after the two o'clock feeding time passed. The emphasis on routine, on controlling the animals' feeding schedule and landscape, conditioned family behavior even when there were human rituals that intervened. The elite cattlemen learned work discipline before the coming of industrial production in the 1820s further reshaped the region's landscape.[12]

Cattle and their wastes represented assets with monetary value. They also were large beasts that were potentially dangerous. Most cattle raisers apparently encouraged women and young children to stay away, especially during periods of rest, because few feeders wanted to risk injury to family members or to encourage the animals to move around

---

[11] Garrison, "Farm Dynamics," pp. 1–17; John Adams, *Diary and Autobiography of John Adams*, ed. L. H. Butterfield, vol. 2 (Cambridge: Harvard University Press, Belknap Press, 1962), p. 17.

[12] Sheldon, " 'Tis Sixty Years Since,' " pp. 472–90.

while investigating unnecessary diversions. These factors have archaeo-logical implications for the ways in which yards functioned. The yards associated with these feeding operations had to have strong fences to control powerful and potentially unruly animals in close proximity to domestic dwellings. Most of these animals were purchased from other farms, and their temperaments and characteristics were initially un-known to their new owners. In addition, most owners in the stall-feeding business apparently preferred to confine their animals to rela-tively small barnyards where the animals might be controlled more easily, where manure could be scraped up and saved for later use, and where the fattening steers would not have too much room for exercising off the weight they were gaining. These farmers seem to have parti-tioned their homelots and barnyards with fences into several task-specific areas: gardens, wood yards, feed lots, laundry yards, and per-haps other areas. Although the posts of these fences and associated farm lanes would leave subsurface traces, there currently is insufficient information from excavations to confirm historical records indicating the existence or sizes of different yards.[13]

Despite the growth of a commercially scaled livestock economy, older patterns of mixed agriculture and neighborliness persisted. Pro-duction for household use continued throughout the nineteenth cen-tury on the region's family farms. Much of the fat-cattle trade was dominated by families in the top two deciles of the region's ratable polls, but even these families generally practiced mixed strategies to protect themselves from the vagaries of markets and weather. The orga-nization of the landscape reflected these mixed strategies, for the great majority of outbuildings recorded in the area's tax valuations were barns, most of which were probably of the three-bay English type. The 1798 Federal Direct Tax Census for South Hadley, Massachusetts, gives some clue about the number and types of barns. It listed ninety barns (table 1). The smallest was a 20-by-18-foot structure, and the

[13] Sheldon, " 'Tis Sixty Years Since,' " pp. 472–90; Levi Stockbridge, a Hadley farmer, wrote in his journal on July 31, 1845, that Linius Green "takes great pains to make manure by conveying dirt into his yard and mixing it with vegetable matter, the dung of the stable and lime, puts it on without stint and works land well" (quoted in Margaret Richards Pabst, "Agricultural Trends in the Connecticut Valley Region of Massachusetts, 1800–1900," *Smith College Studies in History* [October 2, 1940–July 1941]: 29).

Table 1. Number of Barns, by Square Foot,
South Hadley, Mass., 1798

Size	No.	Size	No.	Size	No.
20′ × 18′	1	38′ × 25′	1	40′ × 38′	1
22′ × 18′	1	50′ × 20′	1	56′ × 28′	1
20′ × 20′	1	36′ × 28′	5	52′ × 31′	1
30′ × 18′	1	38′ × 28′	6	45′ × 36′	1
30′ × 20′	1	40′ × 28′	5	50′ × 34′	1
40′ × 16′	1	38′ × 30′	2	45′ × 38′	1
26′ × 26′	1	41′ × 28′	1	46′ × 38′	2
28′ × 24′	1	39′ × 30′	1	62′ × 29′	1
30′ × 24′	3	40′ × 30′	12	60′ × 30′	1
40′ × 20′	1	44′ × 28′	1	73′ × 26′	1
32′ × 26′	1	42′ × 31′	1	66′ × 30′	1
30′ × 28′	3	44′ × 30′	1	56′ × 36′	1
34′ × 26′	1	45′ × 30′	2	70′ × 30′	1
42′ × 22′	1	45′ × 32′	1	70′ × 40′	1
36′ × 26′	3	50′ × 30′	4	70′ × 54′	2

Source: U.S. Secretary of the Treasury, Direct Tax Census,
1798, New England Historic Genealogical Society (Microfilm,
Henry N. Flynt Library, Deerfield, Mass.).

largest was 54-by-70 feet. The mean square footage of South Hadley's
barns was 1,137 square feet, about the size of a 30-by-38-foot barn.
The median-size barn (there were twelve of them) was 30 by 40 feet.
Of these ninety barns, 30 percent (27) were larger than the 30-by-40-
foot barn type; a larger number were smaller but not much smaller.
The list also included several long narrow buildings, which may have
been cowhouses that were enclosed on all sides.[14]

The documentary evidence for South Hadley is similar to the data
for Colrain, Massachusetts. Of the barns in Colrain, fifty-four were 30
by 40 feet (table 2). In short, if there was a barn that approximated a
"typical" outbuilding in the late eighteenth-century Connecticut River
valley, it was within a few feet of these 30-by-40-foot dimensions—
roughly the same dimensions as the Mattoon and Janes barns in North-

[14]U.S. Secretary of the Treasury, Direct Tax Census, 1798, Massachusetts Historical
and Genealogical Society (microfilm, Henry N. Flynt Library, Deerfield, Mass.). For a
comparative perspective, see Arthur C. Lord, "Barns of Lancaster County: 1798," *Lancaster County Historical Society Journal* 77 (March 1973): 26–40.

Table 2. Barn Sizes, Colrain, Mass., 1798

Size	No.	Size	No.	Size	No.
18' × 20'	1	30' × 35'	1	30' × 43'	1
22' × 26'	1	28' × 38'	1	30' × 45'	2
20' × 30'	1	30' × 36'	1	30' × 50'	7
25' × 30'	1	30' × 37'	1	30' × 60'	5
26' × 30'	1	28' × 40'	1	30' × 65'	1
30' × 30'	1	30' × 38'	1		
26' × 36'	1	30' × 40'	39		

Source: U.S. Secretary of the Treasury, Direct Tax Census, 1798, New England Historic Genealogical Society (Microfilm, Henry N. Flynt Library, Deerfield, Mass.).

field. Yet "typical" is a misleading term. As a rare 1798 list of outbuildings on David Hoyt's Deerfield property makes plain, well-established farmers on the valley's lowland "intervale" lands owned a variety of farm structures (table 3). These farmsteads generally included cowhouses, stables, corn houses, hovels, and sheds. In addition, many elite farmers like Hoyt owned two barns, one of which was often smaller and presumably dedicated to different functions.[15]

While documents like the 1798 Federal Direct Tax Census suggest that most barns in the Massachusetts portion of the Connecticut River valley at the end of the eighteenth century were English-type three-bay forms (which might have housed stock), they also recorded other barns that were smaller two-bay forms—designs that did not easily permit the sheltering of livestock and fodder under one roof. A few two-bay barns have survived in upland and lowland towns. Nathaniel Stearns was a stonemason who lived in Warwick, Massachusetts, an upland community to the east of Northfield. His barn originally was a bay-runway form, 30 feet 8 inches square. Like the Mattoon and Janes

[15] "List of Houses, Out Houses &c. own'd by D. Hoit, Feby 8th 1799," Pocumtuck Valley Memorial Association, Deerfield, Mass. (hereafter PVMA); Rosa Johnston of Northfield, Mass., notified me about the barn at Nathaniel Stearns's homestead; Joseph Barnard's barn was demolished by Deerfield Academy in 1976 to make way for a new dormitory. Information on Barnard is from Massachusetts General Court, Committees, Valuations. "A List of the Pols and Estates, Real and Personal, of the Several Proprietors and Inhabitants of the Town, 1771" (microfilm, Henry N. Flynt Library, Deerfield, Mass.); Joseph Barnard daybook, 1738–85, PVMA.

Table 3. David Hoyt's Buildings, Deerfield, Mass.,
1798

Building	Type	Size
Dwelling house*		
	House (2 story)	42' × 21'
	Bedroom (1 story)	15' × 14'
	Kitchen (1 story)	42' × 13½'
Outbuildings		
	Horse house	25' × 11'
	Cowhouse	64' × 12'
	Saddle house	10' × 9'
	Corn house	18' × 16'
	Barn	62' × 32'
	Barn	24' × 18'
	Stable at end of barn	24' × 9½'

 * These measurements represent one dwelling: a two-story central-chimney house, a one-story kitchen attached to the rear, and a one-story bedroom ell.

 Source: Papers of David Hoyt, Hoyt family papers, Pocumtuck Valley Memorial Association, Deerfield, Mass.

barns, it was probably used only for hay storage; animals were kept elsewhere—possibly in a cowhouse, stable, or hovel. Similarly, Joseph Barnard, one of Deerfield's wealthiest eighteenth-century landowners, had a two-bay barn behind his house. These smaller barns were not necessarily precise markers of class and social status but reflected the agricultural needs of their owners. The valley's agricultural elite, men like Hoyt and Barnard, usually had more than one barn and could assign specialized tasks to different outbuildings.[16]

 Besides barns, cowhouses and hovels were the commonest agricul-

[16] During fieldwork in the summer of 1986, it became clear that the Nathaniel Stearns barn was moved and turned 90 degrees from its original location. Carpenters simply nailed the original runway doors shut before the building was moved to a new foundation. They are still there with original hinges more than 6 feet above current grade level and completely inaccessible except by ladder. Carpenters cut through the old gable end, moved a post several feet to the right, and framed in a new door. From the road the barn looks like a mid nineteenth-century asymmetrical-type. From inside it is clear that it is much earlier, probably dating to the last quarter of the eighteenth century when carpenters still framed barns in the region with shouldered posts. Joseph Barnard's tax status was derived from "A List of the Pols and Estates . . . 1771." His genealogy is available in George Sheldon, *A History of Deerfield, Massachusetts*, 2 vols. (Greenfield, Mass.: Press of E. A. Hall, 1895–96), 2:68.

Table 4. Cowhouse Sizes, South Hadley, Mass., 1798

Size	No.	Size	No.	Size	No.
16′ × 12′	1	30′ × 12′	3	40′ × 14′	1
18′ × 12′	1	30′ × 14′	1	40′ × 15′	1
20′ × 11′	1	36′ × 12′	1	32′ × 20′	1
20′ × 12′	2	30′ × 15′	1	40′ × 20′	2
25′ × 12′	1	40′ × 12′	1	45′ × 22′	1
30′ × 11′	1	30′ × 16′	1		

Source: U.S. Secretary of the Treasury, Direct Tax Census, 1798, New England Historic Genealogical Society (Microfilm, Henry N. Flynt Library, Deerfield, Mass.).

tural structures in lowland barnyards. South Hadley farmers owned twenty-one cowhouses, roughly one cowhouse for every four barns. The smallest cowhouse was 16 by 12 feet; the largest was 45 by 22 feet. Three cowhouses reached the median size of 30 by 12 feet, but the dimensions of the cowhouses were more variable than the barns (table 4). Hovels were built to similar dimensions as the cowhouses. The distinctions between the two types of structures are not entirely clear, but one period reference indicates that hovels were inexpensive, possibly earthfast structures, built on posts set into the ground. On November 22, 1810, Cephas Hoyt, a wealthy Deerfield farmer, hired a carpenter to frame a new cowhouse to replace the "Old slab hovel" that he and a hired hand had demolished the day before. If hovels were earthfast structures there should be subsurface evidence of their existence. Because they were less common than cowhouses, however, and seem to have been impermanent, no hovels are known to survive, and no archaeologist has recovered evidence that might represent a hovel. Like two-bay barns, hovels were not a clear reflection of class (table 5). The

Table 5. Hovel Sizes, South Hadley, Mass., 1798

Size	No.	Size	No.
20′ × 15′	1	40′ × 15′	1
28′ × 12′	1	40′ × 20′	1
20′ × 18′	1	38′ × 28′	1

Source: U.S. Secretary of the Treasury, Direct Tax Census, 1798, New England Historic Genealogical Society (Microfilm, Henry N. Flynt Library, Deerfield, Mass.).

largest hovel in the 1798 Direct Tax Census for South Hadley was owned by the town's wealthiest merchant and top taxpayer, Ruggles Woodbridge. Judging from the Direct Tax Census, it seems that wealthier farmers were more likely to own hovels than poorer men, but not all hovels were held by rich men. Presumably, either middling or gentry farmers could acquire the lumber and labor to construct temporary buildings when needed.[17]

What is clear from this comparison of agricultural history with extant structures is that there was a greater variety of outbuildings on the past landscape than is currently visible. These buildings supported English traditions of mixed husbandry, more specialized, market-oriented livestock husbandry, or both. By 1800 many prosperous farmers in the valley lowlands organized their outbuildings in somewhat specialized ways, built more types of outbuildings of varied dimensions than fieldwork on surviving examples indicates, and framed their outbuildings lightly to reduce labor and material costs. In short, preindustrial farmers organized their buildings and landscapes according to changing family needs and economic opportunities.[18]

It is as important to recover how people used their barns as it is to find out what kinds they had. B. B. Murdock housed his stock on either side of the runway in his 1840 Northfield barn, but only on the eastern half of each bay (fig. 4). Horses were located on the northern side of the barn; cows were on the southern side. Above the stables and in the western half of each bay was hay storage. A low 28-inch-high knee wall kept hay stored in the bays from shifting into the runway. Doors on the front and rear of the barn's runway provided access to the front drive and the field out back. The stock entered through doors on the front of the barn in either corner or, in the case of the cattle, through a door on the southern wall that probably led to a fenced yard. Only the cattle stable had stanchions with a manger that was 2 feet wide. The manger was simple. It was built with two 14-inch-wide boards on the runway side of the manger—the same height as the knee

---

[17]Jonathan Hoyt diary, November 22–27, 1810, PVMA; U.S. Secretary of the Treasury, Direct Tax Census, 1798.

[18]Garrison, *Landscape and Material Life*, chap. 6. See also Christopher Clark, *The Roots of Rural Capitalism: Western Massachusetts, 1780–1860* (Ithaca, N.Y.: Cornell University Press, 1990), pp. 59–117.

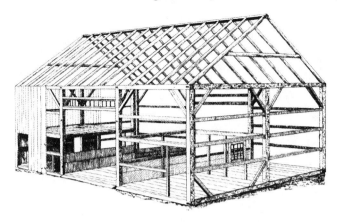

Fig. 4. B. B. Murdock barn, Northfield, Mass., ca. 1840–45. (Measurements and drawing, J. Ritchie Garrison.)

wall on the hay portion of the bay to the west. There were no shutters originally to close this area to the elements. Only after the Civil War did farmers begin to install hinged shutters that folded up and latched to cover these manger areas. The Murdock barn also had a basement. Reformers had recommended barn basements to New Englanders for years, but few of the region's farmers adopted basements before the 1830s unless their farmsteads were located on hillsides. By the 1850s barn basements were commoner in new barn construction, and a few farmers raised their barns to place basements underneath.[19]

These barns met the needs of middling farm families who had limited resources, but the form was not restricted to farmers. The Murdock barn was owned by a merchant who seems to have done little serious farming and who had modest needs for a barn. Similarly, a Northfield carpenter, Samuel Stearns, who built a like structure in 1825, used his barn to store lumber, horses, and fodder. By the 1840s, many families like the Stearnses and the Murdocks who put up English-type barns were only marginally involved with husbandry. Their barns might ally these families visually to the larger world of local agriculture,

---

[19]Calvin Stearns daybook, 1799–1850, Northfield Historical Society, Northfield, Mass.

but these families did not depend on the land for a living. Why, then, did these nonfarming families not adopt a different style of outbuilding? Stearns and Murdock could have erected different structures, but English-style barns were well understood by local carpenters, smaller examples were relatively inexpensive to build, and they were convenient for a variety of storage needs. Thus, by the 1810s, English barns might serve the needs of farmers *or* nonfarmers. Increasingly, however, progressive farmers who focused on livestock markets were building larger, more efficient buildings. [20]

Barn size and form would become one of the region's most recognizable signs of agricultural wealth and family competition. In an 1810 letter to his brother-in-law Elihu Hoyt, Justin Hitchcock of Deerfield passed on the news: "Last Thursday we raised Mr. E. H. Williams' barn. It is an enormous sized barn and covers more ground I believe than any building in town." Williams was an important cattle raiser and the son of wealthy landowners in Roxbury, Massachusetts. The scale of the lowland cattle-fattening business required storage of large quantities of hay and grains, and Williams's 40-by-90-foot barn (three times the area's "average" at the end of the eighteenth century) was built with that purpose in mind. Clearly it was big enough to merit Hitchcock's special attention, but it would not remain the largest barn in town. By the mid nineteenth century, farmers like Rowland Stebbins of Deerfield erected barns that were even larger. In May 1848 the Deerfield correspondent in the Greenfield newspaper reported, "Rowland Stebbins has raised the largest barn in town." Stebbins had his carpenters construct a 40-by-100-foot double English-type barn with two runways in a bay-runway-bay-bay-runway-bay configuration. While Stebbins's barn indicated that local people understood how to expand English-barn types along a longitudinal axis, most progressive farmers preferred to build a form that architectural historians have labeled "New England–type" barns. Unlike the English-type barns in which the runway entered the barn through the long side of the structure, New England–type barns were designed so that the runway ran through the gable end. As we shall see, the development of this barn

---

[20]J. H. Temple and George Sheldon, *A History of Northfield, Massachusetts* (Albany, N.Y.: Joel Munsell, 1875).

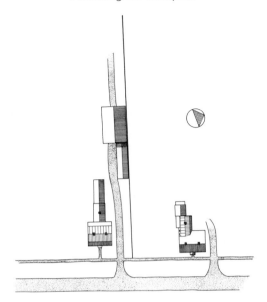

Fig. 5. Plan of Joseph Stebbins house and barnyard, Deerfield, Mass., ca. 1790–1819. (Drawing from a photogrammetric map, Historic
Deerfield, Inc., J. Ritchie Garrison.)

form is an important element of progressive farmers' attempts to increase productivity in the Connecticut River valley.[21]

The Joseph Stebbins barn was one of the earliest New England–
type examples in Deerfield. A prosperous "fatt cattle" raiser, Stebbins
constructed his large, 42-by-60-foot barn northwest of his house, separated from human space by a little more than one hundred feet (fig. 5).
There was nothing particularly odd about the position of the building;
eighteenth-century farmers in lowland villages of the Connecticut River
had followed similar patterns of land use. Nearly all these lowland
villages were platted in the seventeenth century as nucleated villages
with surrounding common fields. The villages were typically laid out

[21] Justin Hitchcock to Elihu Hoyt, June 4, 1804, PVMA; Sheldon, *History of Deerfield*, 1:454, 2:381–84; *Greenfield Gazette and Courier*, May 22, 1848; Hubka, *Big
House, Little House*, pp. 52–61.

on a long linear street, most of which followed a rough north/south axis. Street frontage was generally limited, and homelots stretched out to the east and west. The relatively small street frontage encouraged farmers to place outbuildings and barnyards to the rear of the dwelling house, and both houses and outbuildings tended to be positioned to the northern side of the lot, leaving a larger yard south of the house and barn for gardens or stockyards. A lane or drive generally ran north of the dwelling to the barnyard behind. Nearly all families on the western side of these lowland villages seem to have positioned their barns or outbuildings to the west or northwest of the house, apparently to shield the dwelling from the northwesterly winds common to the region. Families on the eastern sides of these village streets tended to place their buildings in approximately the same orientation to the house, except that in their case the rear of the dwelling would have put the barn to the northeast or to the east.[22]

Barn form and the number of outbuildings might vary, but the location of the structures on the land maximized the warmth of the winter sun and sheltered humans and animals from winter drafts. Although eighteenth- and nineteenth-century dwellings in the valley tended to project an impression of bilateral architectural symmetry, the layout of farmsteads and the barnyard was decidedly asymmetrical and was tied to experience with the New England climate, patterns of family life that centered on the household for a source of labor, and the kinds of market production common to the area. Conditions in the uplands on either side of the valley might be very different, but the Connecticut River valley lowland farmsteads represented New England's greatest concentration of prosperous farms in the eighteenth and early nineteenth centuries. Remaking the barnyard in these villages was a process of steadily refining the use and productive capacity of confined and controlled spaces.[23]

Stebbins's barnyard is one of the few homelots in the valley in which archaeologists have undertaken systematic testing of features discovered by remote sensing devices. To the south of the Stebbins barn

---

[22] Garrison, *Landscape and Material Life*, pp. 19–26; Timothy Dwight, *Travels in New England and New York*, vol. 2 (1821–22; reprint, Cambridge: Harvard University Press, 1969), p. 231.

[23] Garrison, *Landscape and Material Life*, pp. 26–35, 251–56.

in the former stockyard, archaeologists recovered the outlines of the well that was once used to water Stebbins's fat cattle. Newspaper real estate advertisements and other documents indicated that this was a relatively common feature on other barnyards raising livestock. The area around the well was excavated to sterile soil; the well itself was not fully explored. There was little sheet refuse in this yard, and what fieldworkers recovered was small—too small to harm curious animals being led out from the stall to drink water after feeding. At first the small quantity of objects and their small size in the well area seemed surprising, yet the agricultural history of the area helped to explain why there were so few artifacts. The animal wastes that accumulated in these barnyards were not merely detritus to be discarded. One cattleman later recalled, if the market for meat was down, "and the season had been an unprofitable one for feeders, the Hatfield farmer declared: 'Well! all I have to show for my year's work is a swearing pile of manure!' Now, whatever the feeders got or failed to get, they always got that—a barnyard knee deep with droppings and litter, and solid pyramids of excremental matter under the stable windows which were the prime requisites for raising Indian corn and peas-and-oats. These were the deposits upon which the farmers drew for future operations and these grains, peas-and-oats mixed half and half and called provender, were the staple feed for fattening oxen." Considering that barnyard wastes were collected for dressing tillage fields, the paucity of artifacts in the Stebbins yard corresponds to evidence in the documentary records. Moreover, the efforts of farmers to put yard wastes to good use may actually confuse archaeological stratigraphy.[24]

Reconstructing a clearer image of the Stebbins barnyard requires consideration of standing structures, archaeological features, photographs, and documents for both the Stebbinses and other families in the region. These sources suggest an intensification of market production of beef in the late eighteenth and early nineteenth centuries. By centering the fattening of beef cattle in one very large structure rather than several smaller outbuildings, the Stebbinses and others like them should have been able to increase their size without expanding labor inputs; yet to demonstrate this interpretation we must examine buildings, not just

[24] Sheldon, " 'Tis Sixty Years Since,' " pp. 472–90.

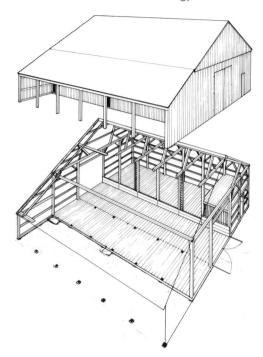

Fig. 6. Walter Field barn, Northfield, Mass.,
1795–1810. (Measurements and drawing, J.
Ritchie Garrison.)

foundation footprints. Stebbins's barn collapsed more than ten years
ago under a heavy snow load, and only the drywall foundations and
photographs survive to indicate its size and orientation. To determine
how these barns were used between 1790 and 1820, we need to locate
a similar example that dates to roughly the same period.

Like the Stebbins barn, the Field barn was carefully designed to
integrate the functions of storing fodder, sheltering stock, and fattening
cattle for market. Probably built between 1795 and 1807 for Walter
Field of Northfield, Massachusetts, it was originally the same size as
the Stebbins barn (fig. 6). Although the Field barn was thoroughly
remodeled to accommodate twentieth-century dairy codes, enough evidence survives to redraw some elements of the structure's early appear-

ance. The barn was oriented roughly east–west, with the runway off center toward the southern side, a typical pattern for the valley's early New England-type barns. The hay bay was 17 feet wide and extended the length of the structure, except for a horse stall in the northeastern corner of the barn. Ladders attached to two of the posts afforded access to the loft over the runway. A 31-inch-high knee wall helped to keep hay from falling into the runway. On the southern side was the stable for the cattle with additional hay or fodder storage above. The cattle bay was large enough to hold more than two dozen animals, far more than a family needed for household food supplies. By placing the huge mass of hay on the northern side of the barn, the Fields and other farmers like them used fodder to help to shield animals from northerly winds. Moreover, the hay or fodder was either directly over the animal stalls or across the runway within easy reach for a labor force that in early nineteenth-century New England consisted mostly of family members and local youths hired as needed. During a period when family size was decreasing and many sons were seeking alternatives to farming, the effort to ease the physical labor of forking hay and fodder into cattle mangers allowed one worker to accomplish more and may have encouraged some sons to stay on the farm. By contrast, eighteenth-century farmers with multiple outbuildings had to bring the hay to the animals, and few mixed-use English three-bay barns then in the valley could conveniently accommodate as many animals or as much food in a single building.[25]

Considering regional standards, the Field barn was as sophisticated a scheme for fattening and sheltering livestock as existed in late eighteenth- or early nineteenth-century New England. These buildings were initially rare and were owned by elites. The 1798 Federal Direct Tax Census for South Hadley listed only three barns in that community that were larger than the Field barn and only nine that were large enough to represent New England-type barns. By 1836 the Field family apparently decided the building might be improved further by adding a cattle shed. They contracted with Samuel Stearns to erect a southern-facing shed that ran the entire length of the barn

---

[25] For a fuller treatment of family members as a source of labor, see Stephen Innes, "Introduction, John Smith's Vision" in *Work and Labor in Early America* (Chapel Hill: University of North Carolina Press, 1988), pp. 21–22, 31–47.

to protect the cattle from the elements. When feeding time came, the Fields let stock into the feeding stalls through the two doors opening into the shed. The arrangement would have allowed the family to care for steer and common stock simultaneously if they wished. By setting up fencing in the appropriate area, partitioning the feeding stalls into two sections with boards temporarily nailed in place, and admitting the common stock to one side of the barn's stalls and the fat cattle to the other, the Field family could manage different kinds of animals in adjacent spaces. Thus, the large bays delineated by the structure's framing were intentionally flexible. With a hammer, a saw, nails, and boards, Field could, within limits, reconfigure the interior space of the barn to meet changing production strategies or market demand. There were constraints on this flexibility, of course. Nailing up a few temporary partition boards was a fairly simple task. Moving or adding a main supporting post was not. The Fields or any other farm family had to evaluate their desires to modify the barn against the cost of materials, the source and amount of labor that went into rebuilding, and the perceived benefits.[26]

Although initially only a few of the valley's elite cattle farmers, men in the top decile of tax ratables, built New England-type barns, the form became common by the 1840s among families who made their livings mainly from agriculture and especially from livestock husbandry. Thereafter, relatively few of the area's full-time farmers continued to build English-style barns. The framing patterns of these barns evolved over time and can serve as a dating device for the region's standing structures. Post-1850 barns usually look like their predecessors on the outside, but inside it is clear that carpenters modified the framing used earlier in the century. Some changes reflected new milling technology: most of the posts, braces, and girts have circular-saw marks, and only the sections of the frame that were too long for the local sawmill—generally the plates and the purlins—were hand hewn. Other changes involved the framing itself as carpenters learned to base their construction and design decisions on experience with anticipated load factors and economic needs. The most prominent change took

---

[26]Calvin Stearns daybook, 1836; Garrison, *Landscape and Material Life*, pp. 135–38; U.S. Secretary of the Treasury, Direct Tax Census, 1798.

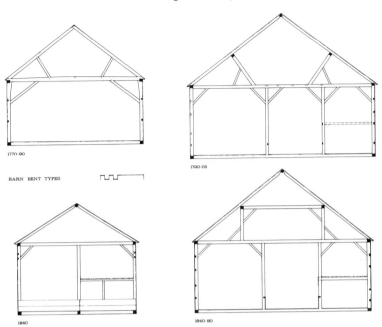

Fig. 7. Barn bent types, Connecticut River valley of Massachusetts, 1770–1880. (Drawing, J. Ritchie Garrison.)

place as they replaced the practice of angling the purlin-posts with a secondary boxed frame that rested atop the building's main girts (fig. 7). Since everything except the bracing was sawn to right angles, this secondary frame was easier to join than the angled purlin-posts. Builders had used this secondary frame system in the eighteenth and early nineteenth centuries on dwellings that had long rafters and roof slopes; the experience with gambrel-roof and double-pile mansion houses subsequently translated easily to cattle and tobacco barns. Yet framing practices for dwellings and barns increasingly diverged after the 1850s. While carpenters began to build dwellings with balloon framing in the 1840s and 1850s, they continued to employ braced timber framing in barns. This construction tradition persisted because the braced frame could hold tremendous loads in open and flexible volumes of space with minimal amounts of framing. In barns, the braced frame remained a sensible alternative to balloon framing.[27]

At the same time that they were making subtle modifications to barn framing, carpenters developed alternatives to the standard New England-type barn. Asymmetrical barns used a two-bay–wide bent system in which the barn's runway extended from one side of the gable end to the rear. Usually this runway was oriented to the southern or warmer side of the barn, but there were exceptions. On many of these asymmetrical-type barns, farmers added a lean-to to expand the barn to a bay-runway-bay form, a practice that created a three-bay asymmetrical-type barn with the roof ridge distinctively off center. The origins of these asymmetrical-type barns are difficult to trace. These buildings probably had multiple sources. Some farmers converted their two-bay–deep–by–three-bay-wide English barns; they closed in the three-bay side with the doors and opened a bay on the two-bay gable end for new doors. Both of these modifications should show some archaeological evidence. Others were inspired by examples that progressive farmers built in the 1830s to 1850s—men like Elisha Wells of Deerfield.[28]

By the mid 1850s Wells's farmstead included an asymmetrical barn built atop a low basement (fig. 8). To reach the runway on the northern side of the barn, Wells drove up an earthen ramp. The southern side of the barn was split into two levels, the lower portion for housing stock and the upper section for storing hay. Over the runway, there was a haymow. The stable was open to the south, and there was a penned yard where animals could move about and where Wells could collect their manure. This asymmetrical, split-level structure facilitated convenient livestock husbandry and maintained the three-part division used in both English- and New England–type barns—fodder storage,

[27] This observation is based on fieldwork in the Connecticut River valley with particular emphasis on buildings that are precisely dated by documentary sources; very few scholars have written much about changing patterns of barn framing or the relationships of barn frames to house frames. For exceptions, see Hubka, *Big House, Little House*, pp. 52–61; Fink, *Barns of the Genesee Country*; Richard Rawson, *Old Barn Plans* (New York: Main Street Press, 1979).

[28] Information on this barn type was gathered from a barn survey conducted in the 1970s by Frank White and John Mott for the Department of Research, Old Sturbridge Village, Sturbridge, Mass. I am grateful to them for their willingness to share this research with me. The form was known in other parts of the United States, particularly in northern New England. Hubka, *Big House, Little House*, pp. 59–60.

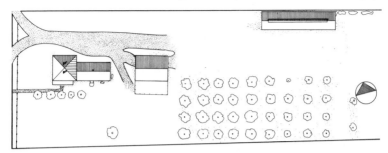

Fig. 8. Plan of Elisha Wells homelot and barnyard, Deerfield, Mass., ca. 1852–68. (Drawing, J. Ritchie Garrison.)

stable, and service runway—but in this case the barn was further reorganized to facilitate storage and feeding in a two-bay rather than a three-bay system. Wells or his hired help could simply drop hay or provender to the stock below, letting gravity ease the labor of humans. This design was related to the traditional approach of storing hay and fodder over the stables of English and New England barns, and it paralleled developments in progressive barns in other parts of the country, particularly Pennsylvania-type bank barns.[29]

The progressive features of Wells's barn and its reduced size reflected the decline of the formerly lucrative cattle-feeding business and the rise of tobacco farming. The medium-size asymmetrical barn he built was sufficient to manage a herd, but beef was no longer central to the farm's profits; his yearly cash income depended on tobacco, a crop that Connecticut River valley farmers began planting in marketable quantities about 1845, first in nearby Whately, a town on Deerfield's southern border, and gradually in the other lowland towns

[29] Elisha Wells's biography and an illustration of his farmstead is in Louis H. Everts, *History of the Connecticut Valley in Massachusetts with Illustrations and Biographical Sketches* (Philadelphia: L. H. Everts, Press of J. B. Lippincott, 1879). The farmstead was photographed in 1868 from a hill to the east. Fig. 8 is based on both this photograph (PVMA Library) and on a precise map of the village that was created for Historic Deerfield in summer 1986 as part of the National Endowment for the Humanities grant to conduct archaeological research (Henry N. Flynt Library, Deerfield, Mass.). For the most recent information on Pennsylvania bank barns, see Robert F. Ensminger, *The Pennsylvania Barn: Its Origin, Evolution, and Distribution in North America* (Baltimore: Johns Hopkins University Press, 1992).

nearby. Prices for "Connecticut Seed Leaf" tobacco were particularly good in 1850 and 1852. Sylvester Judd noted in the late 1850s: "Tobacco for the first few years was a real bonanza. The profits were large and people thought they were going to get rich in a year or two." For farmers like Wells, tobacco was a profitable crop, but the unpredictability of prices caused many families to abandon their efforts to raise it until another cycle of higher prices between 1855 and 1857 prompted more farmers to try again.[30]

By 1860 Massachusetts farmers were raising more than a million pounds of leaf per year, much of which was grown as wrappers and filler for cigars. The problem for these farmers was that the market for tobacco was very volatile, based on shifting aesthetic tastes for lighter or darker leaf. It took experience to learn what types of soil and what particular combinations of manure, potash, and seed influenced the color, texture, and taste of the leaf. It also took time to construct setting beds with glass covers for starting seedlings and tobacco barns for drying the crop. Although some farmers tried to convert their old cattle barns to tobacco barns in subsequent decades, the majority of families erected new buildings in which to dry the crop. J. M. Smith of Sunderland noted: "A building made especially for the purpose should be provided for curing tobacco, with hanging doors on each side for airing, and with sufficient means of ventilation at the top and bottom of the building. Unless one can provide such a building, with good sawn poles for hanging the crop, the raising of the crop had better not be attempted." He added that the crop cured better in narrow buildings that were about 26 feet wide and that the building should not be more than three tiers high with each tier 5 feet apart. The best quality of tobacco was cured on the tier closest to the ground. Wells's tobacco barn corresponds to the criteria that Smith set forth.[31]

Wells situated his tobacco barn toward the back of his homelot on the northern lot line (fig. 9). Framed between 1852 and 1868, it

[30] Quoted in Clark, *Roots of Rural Capitalism*, p. 295.
[31] Clark, *Roots of Rural Capitalism*, pp. 294–97; J. M. Smith, "Tobacco and Its Culture in the Connecticut River Valley," in *Thirteenth Annual Report of the Secretary of the Massachusetts Board of Agriculture, with Returns of the Finances of the Agricultural Societies, for 1882* (Boston, 1883), pp. 136–71; Elizabeth Ramsey, "The History of Tobacco Production on the Connecticut River Valley," *Smith College Studies in History* 15, nos. 3/4 (1929–30): 143.

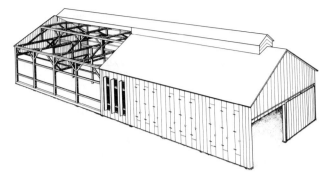

Fig. 9. Tobacco barn, Elisha Wells farm, Deerfield, Mass., ca. 1852–68. (Measurements, J. Ritchie Garrison and Robert Paynter; drawing, J. Ritchie Garrison.)

was designed only for drying tobacco. On the northern and southern elevations, hinged doors made of 16-inch-wide boards opened outward to allow air to circulate amid the tobacco hung up inside to dry. A louvered ventilator extended nearly the entire length of the roof. Near the peak of the roof, the roof boards were blackened with soot, testimony to the small fires built on the barn floor to keep the tobacco drying in damp weather. Unlike later barns, which had two hinged doors at each gable end, the Wells barn had only one door on the gable ends, suspended from a track that enabled Wells to slide it to one side. These sliding doors were known in the valley as early as the late 1830s, but most farmers seemed to have continued to use hinged doors for their barns.

Wells's decision to use a sliding door ultimately made it harder for him to load the barn because one of the two bays was accessible only from the side. Mortises on interior posts suggest how Wells originally loaded the barn. After the tobacco plants were harvested, they were tied to thin poles with twine and then were set atop the barn's girts. Smith also suggested that farmers could split the plant's stalk and stick the lath through the hole. Smith strongly preferred the tied approach, arguing that the split stalks hastened the drying process and lowered the quality of the cured leaf. Regardless of how he hung his plants, Wells could have hung three tiers of lath between the ground level and the plates of his barn, but if the crop was big, a smaller tier could be hung off the purlins under the roof. The northern side of the barn was loaded first since the southern side between the doors served as a runway. When these northern bays were full, Wells apparently filled up the southern bays, setting removable, temporary horizontal beams in place at a height of 4 feet above the dirt floor and working his way out to the door as the space filled up behind him. Wells's use of sliding doors was unusual. Other tobacco farmers who built during this period and later would employ hinged doors on both sets of bays. This plan made it easier to load the barn.[32]

The archaeological evidence for tobacco growing follows patterns established for earlier outbuilding forms, and, as in earlier examples, the experience to date is humbling. Most of the posts that supported these buildings simply were set on stones. Sometimes the long side walls of these buildings are supported by neatly laid drywall foundations; the gable ends with their doors generally were not. Because tobacco was raised in the valley until the 1970s, many of these tobacco barns have survived, although some of the earliest examples were destroyed by a hurricane that swept up the valley in 1938. The persistence of these barns to the present tempts us to think that we will find them relatively easily in future research projects. It was therefore frustrating to learn that field walkovers, magnetometer, and soil resistivity field surveys in Deerfield during 1985 and 1986 failed to detect the footprints of one of these buildings in the back section of a homelot, although photographs documented its existence as late as the 1930s. Without documentary sources, then, it is unclear whether anything short of widespread and massive excavation efforts would have allowed archaeologists to locate or prove the existence of this barn.[33]

The expansion of tobacco growing and the decline of the old beef trade altered the landscape of the Connecticut River valley profoundly. Tobacco did not grow well in some portions of the valley because it

[32] Smith, "Tobacco and Its Culture," pp. 148–49. For additional information on tobacco barns, see E. Babcock, *A Practical Treatise on Growing Tobacco in Northern States* (New York: Syracuse University Press, 1854); and J. Hart and E. Mather, "The Character of Tobacco Barns," *Annals of the Association of American Geographers* 51 (September 1961): 274–93.

[33] Telephone communication from Paynter, Department of Anthropology, University of Massachusetts, to J. Ritchie Garrison, November 1992, regarding Historic Deerfield's remote sensing results.

required rich, well-drained soils, intensive preparation, and fertilizing. Since tobacco depleted the land of nutrients, farmers had to fertilize fields carefully to maintain yields, but the traditional source of fertilizer, livestock manure, was insufficient to fulfill the demand as the number of cattle declined in the region. By the mid 1850s some valley farmers were buying imported guano and commercial chemical fertilizers; others composted organic materials and rotated crops in an effort to keep production and field quality up. Most farmers continued to mix productive strategies to guard against the failure of a single crop, but more of them were becoming wedded to the production of one or more cash crops, of which tobacco was the most important in the towns where it grew well—Deerfield, Whately, Hatfield, Sunderland, Amherst, Hadley, Northampton, and some towns farther south. The crop also altered labor patterns because it required much time-consuming hand labor, the only cheap source of which came from immigrant groups. The number of Irish workers on valley farms grew steadily from the 1850s to 1870s despite ethnic prejudice from Yankee farm owners.[34]

Since tobacco barns were expensive capital projects that were used only for one type of crop and since tobacco demanded substantial amounts of labor, middling and marginal farmers, generally in the third or fourth or lower deciles of tax lists, found it difficult to participate in tobacco growing. Although a few of these middling families converted old livestock barns for tobacco drying by putting hinges on the sides of their small New England–type barns, the majority of these farmers persisted in following agricultural practices already identified—raising livestock, dairy, grain, vegetable, fruit, and forest products for growing urban populations that, by the mid 1840s, were accessible via the railroad. The barnyards of these families and many of their wealthier neighbors continued to reflect mixed agricultural strategies. The first farmers to build tobacco barns were usually in the top two deciles of taxable wealth, and all of them were either gentleman or full-time farmers. Unlike livestock barns, where family members had to journey several times daily, winter and summer, to tend the animals, tobacco

[34] Smith, "Tobacco and Its Culture," pp. 136–71; Garrison, *Landscape and Material Life*, pp. 90–93; Elijah Fuller diary, May 13, August 4, August 5, September 17, October 8, October 10, 1851, PVMA.

barns were important only in certain seasons of the year and did not command the same level of attention except when the crop was drying.[35]

Like Wells, most families either built their tobacco barns well back in their homelots or erected them in the fields where the tobacco was grown. Often these structures were placed along or adjacent to lot lines because of their length, which could exceed 120 feet. Out in the fields, these barns still mark the direction of lot lines, for much of the region's most valuable meadowland was too expensive to consolidate until the Civil War and agricultural depression in the 1870s drove many families out of business and reduced land values. These narrow meadow lots generally forced farmers to build parallel to the boundaries, regardless of orientation to the prevailing winds or southern exposure. After two hundred years of homelot use that was focused on yards and outbuildings seldom located more than 150 feet from the dwelling house, tobacco production in the 1850s shifted to satellite buildings, some of which were still on the homelot and some of which were out in the fields a mile or so from home. Where once the unimpeded northwesterlies rippled waving fields of grain, broom corn, and hay on the acres of crop land that surrounded the lowland nucleated village plans, there were now long buildings to demarcate lot lines and serve as processing centers.

Remaking the Connecticut River valley barnyard in the postrevolutionary era was an active process in which families adapted or razed earlier landscape features and built anew. Change *and* continuity was normal for this landscape. In 1770 the barnyards of the valley's lowland villages were already organized in patterns that persist to the present: narrow homelots in which a dwelling was located near a public street, barns and outbuildings to the rear, and, if there was still room, orchards and fields behind the buildings. Although agricultural historians have

---

[35] This conclusion was based on a comparison of standing tobacco barns with known owners in Deerfield and with information from the agricultural census of 1860 for the towns of Whately, Deerfield, and Sunderland. Higher tobacco production corresponded positively with greater value of the farm. Although the agricultural census does not provide a picture of the wealth of the *nonfarming* population, the three towns sampled were largely farming communities, and the decile rankings of taxable wealth are roughly equivalent to the value of the farm in the census reports. U.S. Bureau of Census, Agricultural Census of 1860 (microfilm, Henry N. Flynt Library, Deerfield, Mass.).

generally emphasized a mixed system of production in New England with limited markets, the artifactual and documentary evidence for the valley indicates considerable specialization and excess productive capacity by the 1770s, especially on the farms owned by the region's top 20 percent of tax ratables.[36] Many of the outbuildings that these eighteenth-century farmers erected to support this production, particularly English three-bay barns and cowhouses, remained in use for a century or more after 1770.

There were changes, most of which were caused directly or indirectly by shifting market opportunities. Farmers expanded production of grain-fattened cattle by increasing the number of outbuildings, by adding sheds to existing structures, or by constructing new and larger barns that integrated production under one roof. These larger barns were built in several forms—English three-bay or double English barns and New England-type barns and asymmetrical barns. Rare in the 1790s, the New England barn would emerge by the late 1830s as the type most commonly built new by full-time farmers. Later, in the 1850s, the region's more prosperous agriculturalists began tobacco production and constructed specialized tobacco drying barns behind their livestock barns or out in their tillage fields.

It is difficult or impossible to identify all these developments from archaeological evidence. Typically, only barns were constructed on substantial foundations of dry wall, and sometimes even these foundations were removed or reused. While excavation can recover fence lines, barn basements, wells, walls, postmolds, and other features, the footprints of many outbuildings may prove too subtle to recover easily through archaeology, especially if the digging is limited to trenches or small pits. In addition, it seems unlikely that archaeologists will recover large shards or quantities of objects in these intensively used barnyards to help much with dating soil stratigraphy. The livestock lodged there represented too much of an investment to risk injury on broken glass or crockery, the value of the manure as fertilizer encouraged farmers to recycle yard dirt and wastes, the competition with neighbors for showing husbandry skills through clean barnyards was too strong, and

[36] Bettye Hobbs Pruitt, "Self-Sufficiency and the Agricultural Economy of Eighteenth-Century Massachusetts," *William and Mary Quarterly*, 3d ser., 41 (July 1984): 333–64.

the emphasis on controlled use was too great to permit casual discard of trash.

In building a contextual archaeology of Connecticut River valley barnyards, in striving to get at what Hodder called the "inside" of the past, we must excavate more than dirt and rely on more than theoretical models for an accurate understanding of the past. Although this study began with archaeological research in Deerfield, the gaps in the archaeological and architectural records prompted comparison with documentary data, structures, and landscapes in other communities in the Connecticut River valley. Architectural fieldwork and careful linkage with documentary evidence helped to explain what outbuildings looked like, how they functioned, how they were constructed, and how they changed over time. Recovering this architectural evidence and many aspects of the area's agricultural history was essential for interpreting the history of barnyards, for it helped to predict and make sense of the information retrieved from the soil. The combined evidence demonstrated valley farm families' early involvement with markets (although not necessarily a market worldview in the modern sense), their efforts to improve convenience and work discipline, and their understanding of economies of scale. For long before factories harnessed New England's waterpower and entrepreneurs established industrial capitalism, New England farm families were busy working out a disciplined approach to productivity in their barnyards.

Working Toward
Meaning:
The Scope of Historical
Archaeology

Feminist Historical Archaeology and the Transformation of American Culture by Domestic Reform Movements, 1840–1925

Suzanne M. Spencer-Wood

This paper addresses the question, What is feminist historical archaeology? The purpose of feminist historical archaeology is to critique and correct sexism in androcentric, or male-focused, constructions of the historic past. By exposing and eliminating androcentrism, feminist theoretical approaches create less biased constructions of the past. Feminists have made anthropologists and historians aware that it is essential not only to address gender but also to correct pasts that were inaccurately constructed in the shape of gender stereotypes.

In this essay, I first briefly expose and critique some fundamental and widespread androcentric biases in history and archaeology. I summarize early feminist research in historical archaeology that critiques and corrects sexism in historic documents or constructions of the past.

The author thanks Lu Ann De Cunzo and Bernard L. Herman for their extremely helpful suggestions for improving this essay; the Schlesinger Library of Women's History, Radcliffe College, Cambridge; the Wellesley College Library; and the MIT archives for providing many essential sources for this research.

Then I outline a feminist theoretical approach to correct sexist biases. Finally, most of this paper discusses examples from my research on domestic reform to illustrate new historical insights gained due to both a feminist and an archaeological approach to material culture research.

A fundamental bias critiqued and corrected by feminists is the widespread failure to analyze historic gender systems. In anthropological models of culture, including systems theory, gender is not even included as a cultural variable or subsystem. As a result, gender either is not considered at all or is subsumed within other subsystems. Thus, archaeological systems theory assumes that gender and ethnicity are small-scale internal cultural variables determined by large-scale cultural norms and institutions. Gender is not considered a distinct cultural system that requires research because it is usually reduced to purportedly biological universal stereotypes such as the "sexual" division of labor that considers only women's domestic roles and men's public roles rather than analyzing the complexity of entire gender systems.[1]

Cultural models that exclude gender are supported at a deeper linguistic level by the widespread construction of nongendered pasts, using ungendered discourse that purportedly makes valid culture-wide generalizations. An objective sounding third-person passive voice often masks the use of men's experiences and viewpoints to represent the whole society, thus excluding women from history. For instance, the overgeneralization that the American household was transformed from production to consumption when wage labor developed outside the home represents the experience and viewpoint of urban middle- and upper-class men as that of the whole society. Excluded from history are women and men in the working classes and rural middle class who continued to produce a wide variety of consumer goods in the home,

---

[1] This section draws from Suzanne M. Spencer-Wood, "Toward a Feminist Historical Archaeology of the Construction of Gender," in Dale Walde and Noreen D. Willows, eds., *The Archaeology of Gender: Proceedings of the 22nd Annual Chacmool Conference* (Calgary, Alba.: University of Calgary Archaeological Association, 1991), pp. 234–44. Lewis R. Binford, *Working at Archaeology* (New York: Academic Press, 1983), pp. 221–23. See also Grahame Clark, *Archaeology and Society* (New York: Barnes and Noble, 1957), p. 175; David L. Clarke, *Analytical Archaeology* (London: Methuen Press, 1968), pp. 103–22, 241–43. Binford is critiqued in Alison Wylie, "Gender Theory and the Archaeological Record: Why Is There No Archaeology of Gender?" in Joan Gero and Margaret W. Conkey, eds., *Engendering Archaeology: Women and Prehistory* (Oxford: Basil Blackwell, 1991), pp. 35–38, 40.

both through unpaid housework and by wage labor, such as domestic service and taking in boarders and laundry, and by outwork, such as hand sewing, making straw hats, and cigar rolling.[2] Instead, some men's ideologies and activities are portrayed as the ungendered cultural norm. Gender is equated only with women, whose domestic labor is denigrated as unproductive and outside of (men's public) history.

While it is possible to research gender by simply adding women and men to ungendered texts, this is not feminist because it reinforces androcentric constructions of the past. In the above example the urban middle-class male viewpoint is only perpetuated by overtly stating that women's role was transformed from household production to consumption when men started working at public wage labor. Feminists have critiqued this approach to engendering male-centered histories as "add women and stir." Recognizing that men and children have gender as much as women, feminists research the actual diversity and complexity in the operation of gender systems. In this case a feminist approach would produce the more accurate statement that in the nineteenth century increasing numbers of men and to a lesser extent women worked outside the home, especially in urban areas. At the same time most women produced labor (which Marxists term *reproduction*), and housework, which produces consumer goods such as food from raw foodstuffs and clean clothes from what would otherwise become trash. Feminists have critiqued the sexist devaluation of housework as an unproductive adjunct to men's paid public production.[3]

[2] Donna J. Haraway, "In the Beginning Was the Word: The Genesis of Biological Theory," *Signs* 6, no. 3 (Spring 1981): 469–81; Ian Hodder, "Writing Archaeology: Site Reports in Context," *Antiquity* 3, no. 239 (June 1989): 268–74; Margaret Conkey and Janet Spector, "Archaeology and the Study of Gender," *Advances in Archaeological Method and Theory* 7 (1984): 1–38. See also Diana di Zerega Wall and Arnold Pickman, "The Beginnings of the Family Consumer Economy," *American Archaeology* 5, no. 3 (1985): 190; Diana di Zerega Wall, "The Separation of the Home and Workplace in Early Nineteenth-Century New York City," *Archaeology* 5, no. 3 (1985): 185. The cultural model mentioned here is critiqued in Ruth Schwartz Cowan, "A Case Study of Technological and Social Change: The Washing Machine and the Working Wife," in Mary Hartman and Lois W. Banner, eds., *Clio's Consciousness Raised: New Perspectives on the History of Women* (New York: Harper and Row, 1974), pp. 245–53.

[3] Charlotte Bunch, *Passionate Politics, Essays, 1968–1986: Feminist Theory in Action* (New York: St. Martin's Press, 1987), p. 140; Margaret W. Conkey and Joan Gero, "Building a Feminist Archaeology" (Paper presented at the 53rd Annual Meeting of the Society for American Archaeology, Phoenix, Arizona, April 29, 1988); Andrea Nye, *Feminist Theory and the Philosophies of Man* (New York: Routledge, 1988), pp. 55–57.

Perhaps the most fundamental underlying sexist bias, expressed in a variety of forms, is that men's experiences and viewpoints are more important than women's. This bias supports the representation of men as culturally normative, while making women invisible by excluding domestic work from history and by subsuming women in male-defined categories such as households and classes. For instance, women are completely invisible in James A. Henretta's construction of male economic and social groups, including families, in colonial Boston. In historical archaeology, James F. Deetz, in his classic construction of eighteenth-century American lifeways, presented the male view of cows and dairying ceramics as the yeoman's property used in "the yeoman's dairy," which was central to yeoman foodways. He did not mention that dairying was usually women's work, nor did he describe this work.[4]

Historic women's work both inside and outside the home has been devalued by constructing the past in the shape of gender stereotypes. Historic data often have been interpreted to conform to a variety of idealistic sexist models that construct men versus women in monolithic structural oppositions, such as dominant versus subordinate, active versus passive, public versus private, culture versus nature, and rational versus emotional. While such Victorian separate-spheres gender ideology was espoused by some men and women, this ideology too often has been portrayed as historical reality. Thus, in historical archaeology, ungendered text frequently uses code words such as "domestic" or "kitchen artifact group" for what are assumed to be women's artifacts. The stereotypic assumption that household artifacts were used only by women is further reified by being made explicit in gender research. Women's public roles often are considered as unimportant exceptions that did not affect the vast majority of women who were domestic. Because historical archaeologists traditionally have unproblematically

---

[4]James A. Henretta, "Economic Development and Social Structure in Colonial Boston," in R. W. Fogel and S. W. Engerman, eds., *The Reinterpretation of American Economic History* (New York: Harper and Row, 1971), pp. 54–63; James F. Deetz, *In Small Things Forgotten* (Garden City, N.Y.: Anchor Press/Doubleday, 1977), pp. 52–53. See also Joan M. Jensen, "Butter Making and Economic Development in Mid-Atlantic America from 1750 to 1850," *Signs* 13, no. 4 (Summer 1988): 813–29; Sally McMurray, "Women and the Expansion of Dairying: The Cheesemaking Industry in Oneida County, New York, 1830–1860" (Paper presented at the 1987 Berkshire History Conference).

assumed gender stereotypes, until recently gender was seldom researched aside from situations of culture contact, when gender roles and artifacts were changing. As recently as 1988 in a published conference session, "Questions That Count in Historical Archaeology," gender was only mentioned as a key variable in one of five papers attempting to give direction to the field.[5]

A Feminist Theoretical Approach

This section briefly outlines the feminist theoretical approach used in my research and the sources of this approach, although there is not space to describe in detail how my approach differs from the wide variety of other feminist approaches. First, I agree with Alison Wylie and Sandra Harding that gender cannot be reduced to any other variable but is a fundamental cultural system that structures the behavior of all members of society. Thus, cultural analyses that do not consider gender are fundamentally incomplete.[6] Further, gender cannot be re-

[5] Judith A. McGaw, "No Passive Victims, No Separate Spheres: A Feminist Perspective on Technology's History," in S. H. Cutcliffe and R. C. Post, eds., *In Context: History and the History of Technology: Essays in Honor of Melvin Kranzberg* (Bethlehem, Pa.: Lehigh University Press, 1989), pp. 172–91. For code words, see Stanley South, *Method and Theory in Historical Archaeology* (New York: Academic Press, 1977). The paper that mentioned gender as a variable is Stephen A. Mrozowski, "Historical Archaeology as Anthropology," *Historical Archaeology* 22, no. 1 (1988): 18–24. In historical archaeology, Victorian separate spheres ideology has been confused with historical reality, despite a disclaimer, in Robert Jameson, "Purity and Power at the Victorian Dinner Party," in Ian Hodder, ed., *The Archaeology of Contextual Meanings* (Cambridge, Eng.: Cambridge University Press, 1987), esp. p. 65. Henrietta L. Moore, *Feminism and Anthropology* (Minneapolis: University of Minnesota Press, 1988), p. 22. Women's public roles are dismissed as unimportant exceptions in Deetz, *In Small Things Forgotten*; Anne E. Yentsch, "Access and Space: Symbolic and Material, in Historical Archaeology," in Walde and Willows, *Archaeology of Gender*, p. 258. For research on changing gender roles during cultural contact, see Kathleen A. Deagan, *Spanish St. Augustine: The Archaeology of a Colonial Creole Community* (New York: Academic Press, 1983); James F. Deetz, "Archaeological Investigations at La Purisima Mission," in *UCLA Archaeological Survey Annual Report*, 1962–1963 (Los Angeles: University of California, 1963), pp. 163–208.
    [6] My feminist theoretical approach and sources from which it developed are outlined in Suzanne M. Spencer-Wood, "Feminist Empiricism: A More Holistic Theoretical Approach" (Paper presented at the Conference on Historical and Underwater Archaeology, Richmond, 1991); Suzanne M. Spencer-Wood, "A Feminist Program for Nonsexist Archaeology," in LuAnn Wandsnider, ed., *Quandaries and Quests: Visions of Archaeology's Future* (Carbondale: Southern Illinois University Center for Archaeological Investi-

duced to biological sex differences but is a cultural construct that does not necessarily follow from biological differences. While there are two biological sexes (not including hermaphrodites), cultures construct gender categories that are not biological, as often claimed, but instead specify ideal cultural behaviors for women, men, and sometimes gay or lesbian categories. Each gender is defined in relationship to other genders, even in single-sex groups. Further, subculture groups, such as women in different classes, ethnic groups, or marital or working statuses, often espouse different gender ideals that also may differ from the gender ideals of men in such cultural subcategories.

While culturally constructed gender ideals are usually stated in monolithic terms (for example, "real men don't eat quiche"), actual behavior often varies from ideals and therefore needs to be distinguished from, and contrasted with, ideals. Thus, I agree with feminists who reject opposed, essentialist gender stereotypes that devalue the importance of women, such as passive domestic women versus active public men. Instead, I view both women and men as active important social agents who are essential to the operation and maintenance of every society.

This feminist perspective is egalitarian and centrist, rejecting the replacement of an androcentric view with a gynocentric, or female-centered, view because both are biased at opposite extremes. Thus, I have critiqued Terry H. Klein's gynocentric overgeneralization that nineteenth-century historic women were the ones who selected their household ceramics because it is as monolithically inaccurate as the opposite androcentric overgeneralization by Anne Yentsch that eighteenth-century historic men were the ones who selected their prestigious dinnerwares. While in many cases the husband bought household ceramics because he controlled household finances, women often had independent sources of money from dairying, gardening, or raising chickens, so they also could buy ceramics. Who chose the type(s) of ceramics bought by a household is seldom documented, was undoubt-

gations, 1992), pp. 98–114. Alison Wylie, "Feminist Critiques and Archaeological Challenges," in Walde and Willows, *Archaeology of Gender*, pp. 17–23; Sandra Harding, "Why Has the Sex/Gender System Become Visible Only Now?" in Sandra Harding and Merril B. Hintikka, eds., *Discovering Reality: Feminist Perspectives on Epistemology, Metaphysics, Methodology, and Philosophy of Science* (Boston: D. Reidel, 1983), pp. 311–24.

edly varied, and in some cases probably was negotiated between wife and husband.[7]

Thus, an inclusive feminist perspective considers the possible diversity, complexity, and flexibility in gender relationships. No fixed singular universal role is assumed either for men or for women. Instead, feminists research the evidence in different situations to understand historic gender relationships rather than simply labeling a culture "male dominated." Contextually specific research is needed to assess both women's and men's sources of power and how they negotiated some balance of power in relationships. In each situation we can ask: to what extent were women's and men's roles interdependent? What aspects of their gender relationships did men or women control? How did women resist male domination? Further, which women adopted culturally dominant male-defined gender ideals, identities, and roles, and which women constructed their own different gender ideologies, identities, and roles? What were these, and how did they do this? Rejecting monolithic gender stereotypes, I instead ask about the ways that diverse individuals of all genders, classes, and ethnic groups sought to empower themselves by contesting domination and negotiating a variety of gender ideals, identities, behaviors, roles, and relationships.[8]

[7]Suzanne M. Spencer-Wood, "Toward the Further Development of Feminist Historical Archaeology," *World Archaeological Bulletin* 7, (1995); Terry H. Klein, "Nineteenth-Century Ceramics and Models of Consumer Behavior," *Historical Archaeology* 25, no. 2 (1991): 79; Anne Yentsch, "The Symbolic Divisions of Pottery: Sex-related Attributes of English and Anglo-American Household Pots," in Randall H. McGuire and Robert Paynter, eds., *The Archaeology of Inequality* (Oxford: Basil Blackwell, 1991), p. 206. For a critique of projecting Victorian essentialism onto other cultures, see Michelle Z. Rosaldo, "The Use and Abuse of Anthropology: Reflections on Feminism and Cross-Cultural Understanding," *Signs* 5, no. 3 (Spring 1980): 389–417.

[8]For diversity in women's ideologies, see Spencer-Wood, "Toward a Feminist Historical Archaeology," p. 240; Mary R. Beard, *Woman's Work in Municipalities* (New York: D. Appleton, 1915); Lee Virginia Chambers-Schiller, *Liberty a Better Husband: Single Women in America, the Generations of 1780–1840* (New Haven: Yale University Press, 1984); Frances B. Cogan, *All-American Girl: The Ideal of Real Womanhood in Mid-Nineteenth-Century America* (Athens: University of Georgia Press, 1989); Dolores Hayden, *The Grand Domestic Revolution: A History of Feminist Designs for American Homes, Neighborhoods, and Cities* (Cambridge: MIT Press, 1981); Joan W. Scott, *Gender and the Politics of History* (New York: Columbia University Press, 1988); Christine Stansell, *City of Women: Sex and Class in New York, 1789–1860* (New York: Alfred A. Knopf, 1986); Ruth Rosen, *The Lost Sisterhood: Prostitution in America, 1900–1918* (Baltimore: Johns Hopkins University Press, 1982). On women contesting male domination, see Sarah Deutsch, "Learning to Talk More Like a Man: Women's Cross-Class

This feminist approach is concerned with the variation in the actual operation of gender systems in conjunction with relationships between nondominant and dominant groups. Individuals in nondominant groups, such as domestic reformers and working women, created ideologies to develop self-empowering viewpoints, identities, and behaviors in relationships with others. However, women's diversity of ideologies, classes, or ethnicity does not negate women's frequently similar experiences of oppression that can serve as a basis for unity across diversity. I agree with Sandra Harding and Nancy Hartstock that individuals in nondominant groups report their own experiences more accurately than the dominant group can describe them. Thus, women have more cultural knowledge about sexism than do men because, while everyone is taught to accept the dominant sexist cultural ideology, men do not have experiences that contradict this ideology, as do women's experiences of discrimination and oppression that often make them aware of the sexism in their culture.[9]

While this feminist perspective is polyvocal, I agree with Frances Mascia-Lees, Patricia Sharpe, and Colleen Cohen's critique of the post-processual view that androcentric constructions of the past are as accurate as feminist ones. Feminism is a more comprehensive paradigm because it must encompass and surpass androcentric constructions of the past to analyze and correct their biases. Feminists must first research sexist history and archaeology to analyze their biases. Critical analyses of historic documents, histories, and archaeologies are crucial to get beyond reifying the sexist cultural ideals that shape many of them. Feminist questions reveal overlooked data that expose and correct androcentric biases. Thus, feminist theory changes the meanings interpreted from both historic documents and material culture

---

Organizations in Boston, 1870–1950," *American Historical Review* 97, no. 2 (April 1992); Suzanne M. Spencer-Wood, "Diversity and Nineteenth-Century Domestic Reform: Relationships among Classes and Ethnic Groups," in Elizabeth M. Scott, ed., *Those of Little Note: Gender, Race, and Class in Historical Archaeology* (Tuscon: University of Arizona Press, 1994), pp. 175–208.

[9] Sandra Harding, "The Instability of the Analytical Categories of Feminist Theory," in Sandra Harding and Jean F. O'Barr, eds., *Sex and Scientific Inquiry* (Chicago: University of Chicago Press, 1987), p. 293; Nancy C. M. Hartstock, "The Feminist Standpoint: Developing the Ground for a Specifically Feminist Historical Materialism," in Sandra Harding, ed., *Feminism and Methodology* (Bloomington: Indiana University Press, 1987), p. 159.

by replacing stereotypic constructions of gender with more holistic accounts of the actual variety and flexibility in historic gender relationships.[10]

Historians, anthropologists, archaeologists, and most recently historical archaeologists have used feminist theoretical approaches to critique sexist biases in histories, ethnographies, archaeologies, and historic documents. Starting in the late 1980s, especially in some papers in the first two conference sessions on gender in American historical archaeology, which I organized, feminist historical archaeologists have critiqued and corrected androcentric constructions of the past, often due to the uncritical use of male-biased histories and documents. Several historical archaeologists have corrected the portrayal of historic women solely in domestic roles and historic men solely in public roles by researching women's and men's roles in both spheres ranging from situations of culture contact to twentieth-century southern farmsteads. Some feminists have researched women's domestic roles as sources of power, thus correcting the androcentric view of domestic women as passive and powerless.[11]

[10] Frances E. Mascia-Lees, Patricia Sharpe, and Colleen Ballerino Cohen, "The Postmodernist Turn in Anthropology: Cautions from a Feminist Perspective," *Signs* 15, no. 1 (Autumn 1989): 7–33; Sandra Harding, "Conclusion: Epistemological Questions," in Harding, *Feminism and Methodology*, pp. 182–84.

[11] For early critiques, see Berenice A. Carroll, ed., *Liberating Women's History: Theoretical and Critical Essays* (Urbana: University of Illinois Press, 1976); Joan Kelly, *Women, History and Theory: The Essays of Joan Kelly* (Chicago: University of Chicago Press, 1984); Scott, *Gender and the Politics of History*; Rayna R. Reiter, ed., *Toward an Anthropology of Women* (New York: Monthly Review Press, 1975); Conkey and Spector, "Archaeology and the Study of Gender"; Suzanne M. Spencer-Wood, "A Survey of Domestic Reform Movement Sites in Boston and Cambridge, ca. 1865–1905," *Historical Archaeology* 21, no. 2 (Fall 1987): 7–36; and "Gender in Historical Archaeology" section in Walde and Willows, *Archaeology of Gender*. For women and men as powerful actors in both domestic and public spheres, see Sheli O. Smith, "Women and Seafaring" in Walde and Willows, *Archaeology of Gender*; Linda France Stine, "Early Twentieth-Century Gender Roles: Perceptions from the Farm," in Walde and Willows, *Archaeology of Gender*, pp. 496–501; Carmen A. Weber, "The Genius of the Orangery: Women and Eighteenth-Century Chesapeake Gardens," in Walde and Willows, *Archaeology of Gender*, pp. 263–69; and the following papers presented at the Annual Meeting of the Society for Historical Archaeology, Baltimore, 1989: Elizabeth M. Scott, "Gender Roles and Historical Archaeology: A Look at the Eighteenth-Century Fur Trade Frontier of Northern Michigan"; Suzanne M. Spencer-Wood, "Feminist Archaeology and the Proactive Roles of Women in Transforming Gender Concepts, Roles, and Relationships in Nineteenth-Century America"; Diana di Zerega Wall, "The Ritualization of Family

Male-biased historic documents and resulting sexist histories have been critiqued and corrected by feminist historical archaeological research. For instance, Linda Derry has critiqued androcentric histories that researched only men's surnames to conclude incorrectly that kinship linkages were not significant in antebellum Cahawba, Alabama. This male-biased research was corrected when Derry analyzed women's kinship linkages, which she found to be significant factors not only in the locations of residences on the town landscape but also in the spatial locations of their husbands' businesses. In researching a mining town's gender landscape, Donald L. Hardesty critically compared business directories and newspapers against historic census data to find that the censuses overreported women in the stereotypic role of keeping house and underreported women's jobs and businesses outside the home. Carol Devens, Lee Fratt, and I, in separate analyses, found that contact period histories, ethnographies, and/or archaeologies of different Indian cultures were biased by European men's accounts that overemphasized women's domestic roles and men's public roles and overlooked or minimally mentioned women's public roles and men's domestic roles. Each of us critically read the sexist historic documents to tease out such evidence, permitting more complete construction of gender roles in different Indian cultures. These case studies in history and historical archaeology exemplify how feminists critique male-focused theory, practices, and constructions of the past and correct these by demonstrating how feminist theory and research brings essential new insight into historic cultures and processes of change.[12]

Dinner in New York City"; Ellen-Rose Savulis, "Alternative Visions: Shaker Gender Ideology and the Built Environment."

[12]Linda Derry, "Daughters and Sons-in-Law of King Cotton: Asymmetry in the Social Structure and Material Culture of Cahawba, an Antebellum Alabama Town," in Walde and Willows, *Archaeology of Gender*, pp. 270–79; Donald L. Hardesty, "Gender Roles on the American Mining Frontier: Documentary Models and Archaeological Strategies" in Walde and Willows, *Archaeology of Gender*; Carol Devens, "Gender and Colonization in Native Canadian Communities: Examining the Historical Record," in Walde and Willows, *Archaeology of Gender*, pp. 510–15; Lee Fratt, "Gender Bias in the Spanish Colonial Documents of the American Southwest," in Walde and Willows, *Archaeology of Gender*, pp. 245–51; Suzanne M. Spencer-Wood, "A Feminist Critique of Eggan's 'Social Organization of Western Pueblos' " (author's collection, 1971, typescript).

A *Feminist Historical Archaeology of Domestic Reform*

In historical archaeology my theoretical approach is material feminist. This means that I do not view material culture simply as a product or reflection of cultural behavior or ideology. Instead, I view material culture as an active social agent that shapes behavior. Further, this feminist archaeological approach involves contextually dependent interpretations of the meanings of material culture rather than any fixed identification of artifacts or features with women or men in different social groups. Domestic reform exemplifies how the meaning of material culture can change in different subcultural contexts. Domestic reform is particularly appropriate for this archaeological perspective because both innovative and ordinary material culture were consciously given new meanings to symbolize and implement cultural transformations in the construction of gender ideology, roles, and relationships. These meanings of material culture can be ascertained only through the integrated contextual interpretation of documents and material culture, which is the essence of historical archaeology. [13]

It is important to research domestic reform because these movements were essential to the transformation of women's lives and status from the nineteenth into the twentieth century, including female suffrage. In creating a feminist archaeology of domestic reform, I have used feminist histories, women's prescriptive domestic reform literature, writings about domestic reform organizations, drawings and photographs of domestic reform institutions and artifacts, historic business directories, maps and cityscape drawings, surviving architecture, archived artifacts, and results of excavations. [14] These types of data all fall within the interdisciplinary province of historical archaeology, and only excavated remains usually are *not* used in the field of material culture studies. However, analysis of excavated data is *not* what makes my research archaeological.

This research is archaeological because it is conducted within a theoretical framework that views material culture not simply as adding historical details but as contributing essential new information about

[13] Suzanne M. Spencer-Wood, "Toward an Historical Archaeology of Materialistic Domestic Reform" in McGuire and Paynter, *Archaeology of Inequality.*

[14] Spencer-Wood, "Toward an Historical Archaeology of Domestic Reform."

what actually happened in the past. With this theoretical perspective, domestic reform ideals are compared and contrasted with their material implementation on the ground.

This research has been theoretically inspired by many feminist anthropologists, starting in the 1970s, and contextually informed by feminist historians who began in the late 1970s to correct historians' emphasis on male reformers by writing about women's involvement in social reform—including the variety of the movements that I have grouped together in the category of domestic reform. Few feminist historians researching domestic reform have dealt with material culture. Dolores Hayden's extensive 1981 architectural history of what she calls material feminism deals with ideal material culture and in many cases with class and ethnic differences in implementation, although differences between ideal and actual material culture were not the focus of her book. Lizbeth A. Cohen has researched the reasons that domestic material culture advocated by reformers was seldom used in working-class homes or apartments, addressing the issue of implementation for one kind of domestic reform. Sarah Deutsch and Gail Dubrow have each researched a few Boston domestic reform sites with more depth but less breadth than my survey of 120 domestic reform sites in Boston.[15] My

[15] Hayden, *Grand Domestic Revolution*; Lizabeth A. Cohen, "Embellishing a Life of Labor: An Interpretation of the Material Culture of American Working-Class Homes, 1885–1915," *Journal of American Culture* 3, no. 4 (Winter 1980): 752–75; Deutsch, "Learning to Talk"; Gail L. Dubrow, "Preserving Her Heritage: American Landmarks of Women's History" (Ph.D. diss., University of California, Los Angeles, 1991), chap. 5. My work has been theoretically informed by many books and articles including those in note 11 above and especially Wylie, "Feminist Critiques," pp. 17–23; Margaret Conkey, "Does It Make a Difference? Feminist Thinking and Archaeologies of Gender," in Walde and Willows, *Archaeology of Gender*, pp. 24–34; Wylie, "Gender Theory," pp. 31–56; Margaret W. Conkey and Joan M. Gero, "Tensions, Pluralities, and Engendering Archaeology: An Introduction to Women and Prehistory," in Gero and Conkey, *Engendering Archaeology*, pp. 3–30; Linda Gordon, "What's New in Women's History," in Teresa de Lauretis, ed., *Feminist Studies/Critical Studies* (Bloomington: Indiana University Press, 1986), pp. 20–31. For domestic reform movements, see Barbara J. Berg, *The Remembered Gate* (Oxford: Oxford University Press, 1978); Catherine Clinton, *The Other Civil War: American Women in the Nineteenth Century* (New York: Hill and Wang, 1984); Laura Shapiro, *Perfection Salad: Women and Cooking at the Turn of the Century* (New York: Farrar, Straus, and Giroux, 1986); Agnes Snyder, *Dauntless Women in Childhood Education, 1856–1931* (Washington, D.C.: Association for Childhood Education International, 1972); Susan Strasser, *Never Done: A History of American Housework* (New York: Pantheon Books, 1982).

research complements these studies with a feminist historical archaeology approach concerned with (1) domestic reform meanings of both innovative and ordinary material culture; (2) comparisons of ideal material culture that actually used to implement a variety of domestic reforms; (3) the transformations of urban landscapes by domestic reform; and (4) the material negotiations of reforms among women and their families in different classes and ethnic groups that participated in domestic reform programs.

Because this research is informed by feminist theory, it corrects androcentric histories and historical archaeologies that either (1) exclude women; (2) consider women's historic roles unimportant; (3) hold women as passive victims of male-controlled cultural processes; or (4) assess women only in their domestic roles. Using a feminist theoretical approach, this research looks instead for evidence of women's powerful actions as important historical social agents and how women of different classes and ethnic groups negotiated with each other to empower themselves through domestic reform.[16]

The Historical Significance of Domestic Reform

The assessment of historical significance depends on the context and the question on which the assessment is based. From our modern context and point of view the effectiveness and importance of domestic reform organizations and programs is amply demonstrated by their rapid growth in numbers and membership, their spread across the United States, their longevity (many still exist and provide needed social services), and their legacy of cultural transformation resulting from changes in gender ideologies, roles, and relationships.[17]

---

[16] Spencer-Wood, "Survey of Domestic Reform Movement Sites," pp. 7–36; Spencer-Wood, "Toward a Feminist Historical Archaeology," pp. 234–44; Spencer-Wood, "Feminist Archaeology and the Pro-active Roles"; Spencer-Wood, "Toward an Historical Archaeology of Materialistic Domestic Reform"; Spencer-Wood, "Diversity and Nineteenth-Century Domestic Reform."

[17] Spencer-Wood, "Toward an Historical Archaeology of Materialistic Domestic Reform," pp. 239–41; Karen J. Blair, *The Clubwoman as Feminist: True Womanhood Redefined, 1868–1914* (New York: Holmes and Meier, 1980); Paula Giddings, *When and Where I Entered: The Impact of Black Women on Race and Sex in America* (New York: Bantam Books, 1985); Ann F. Scott, *Natural Allies: Women's Associations in American History* (Urbana: University of Illinois Press, 1991); Beard, *Woman's Work*.

Many historians have argued that men's and women's voluntary organizations constructed class distinctions and were aimed at social control of the working classes by the upper classes, who imposed their values through mechanisms such as Americanization of immigrants. The social control school claims to look at the actual function of reform organizations from an etic perspective. Reformers' emic statements of their goals are disregarded as irrelevant. In this dominant ideology thesis, the working classes passively accepted the control of the upper classes.[18]

The social control thesis is fundamentally flawed both in argument and fact. First, it was not possible for the mostly middle-class reformers to impose their values on the working classes because participation in reform programs was voluntary. Second, there is abundant evidence that the mostly working-class participants usually were not passive but instead shaped reform programs both through words and actions. By extending a feminist perspective to the working class, I critically analyzed historic documents to reveal previously overlooked evidence that participants in reform programs were social agents who negotiated with reformers for useful programs. Some feminist historians, especially Ruth H. Crocker, have found that the leftist perspective of "social welfare as social control" is not useful because it stresses manipulation and coercion by the dominant class, thereby overlooking the ability of the lower classes to resist and turn "controlling institutions to their own ends." Crocker, Deutsch, Stansell, and I have each

---

[18] Stuart Blumin, *The Emergence of the Middle Class: Social Experience in the American City, 1760–1900* (Cambridge, Eng.: Cambridge University Press, 1989); Howard Karger, *The Sentinels of Order: A Study of Social Control and the Minneapolis Settlement House Movement, 1915–1950* (Lanham, Md.: University Press of America, 1987); Frances Fox Piven and Richard A. Cloward, *Regulating the Poor: The Functions of Public Welfare* (New York: Pantheon Books, 1971); Walter I. Trattner, ed., *Social Welfare or Social Control? Some Historical Reflections on "Regulating the Poor"* (Knoxville: University of Tennessee Press, 1983); John A. Alexander, *Render Them Submissive: Responses to Poverty in Philadelphia, 1760–1800* (Amherst: University of Massachusetts Press, 1980); Marvin E. Gettleman, "Charity and Social Classes in the United States, 1874–1900," pts. 1 and 2, *American Journal of Economics and Sociology* 22, no. 2 (April 1963): 313–28; no. 3 (July 1963): 417–26. On Americanization, see Rivka Lissak, *Pluralism and Progressives: Hull House and the New Immigrants, 1890–1919* (Chicago: University of Chicago Press, 1989); and Paul McBride, *Culture Clash: Immigrants and Reformers, 1880–1930* (San Francisco: R and E Research Associates, 1975).

independently found that greater historical understanding is gained by considering how nondominant groups resist or contest dominant group actions. Further, my research found that many reformers did not seek to dominate but rather to help working women and their families.[19]

In contrast to the social control school, my feminist perspective revealed etic evidence that reform organizations functioned in ways that were congruent with most reformers' stated emic aims. Reformers modified their programs in response to participants' requests not simply because this was necessary to attract voluntary participation but because they wanted to assist working women and their families. My research found that many Boston organizations had religious goals to uplift the lower classes by sharing middle-class privileges. Assessed from an emic contextual perspective, most women's reform organizations sought *not* to maintain social distinctions but aimed at "breaking down barriers which for so long had interposed themselves between women." This explicitly stated goal of Boston's Women's Educational and Industrial Union (WEIU) shows that class and racial distinctions already existed and were not constructed by reformers, who often sought to unify women across social divisions. Further, my research has not yet found domestic reformers using the term *social control*. Expressed concerns for social order mostly were in contexts such as kindergartens and playgrounds and involved maintaining individual discipline as teachers must in classrooms.[20]

[19] Ruth H. Crocker, *Social Work and Social Order: The Settlement Movement in Two Industrial Cities, 1889–1930* (Urbana: University of Illinois Press, 1992), p. 309; Deutsch, "Learning to Talk"; Stansell, *City of Women*; Spencer-Wood, "Diversity and Nineteenth-Century Domestic Reform."

[20] The WEIU goal statement is from "History of the WEIU: Origin of the WEIU," extract from Harriet Clisby, "Reminiscences," handwritten ms., p. 130, Women's Educational and Industrial Union records, 1877–, Schlesinger Library of Women's History, Radcliffe College, Cambridge (hereafter SLWH). In Boston the goal of sharing middle-class privileges was expressed—for Hecht House, the Jewish settlement—in Maida Herman Solomon, "Oral Memoir," 3 vols., 1977, 2:7–366, William E. Weiner Oral History Library of the American Jewish Committee, SLWH; and in *Seventeenth Annual Report of the Young Women's Christian Association, Boston* (Boston: Frank Wood, 1883), pp. 20–22, Boston YWCA records, SLWH. *The Reminder*, May 1902, p. 5, YWCA Cambridge, Mass., records, SLWH; "Settlements: Sixty Years, 1887–1947" (United Settlements of Greater Boston), p. 7, SLWH; Denison House, the Boston College Settlement, pp. 1–2, box 6, folder 39, Denison House Records, 1891–1961, SLWH; *Report of the North-End Industrial Home, 39 North Bennet Street, January*

Reformers were not a monolithic group, and they sometimes maintained class and racial boundaries in their activities. However, my research supports the conclusions of feminist historians that the motives for reform were too varied and complex to be captured by the simplistic social control explanation. As a feminist I am concerned with the diversity among reformers. Reformers sometimes had mixed agendas, such as improving the conditions of domestic service and, the elitist goal, getting better trained servants. However, I think we cannot understand the importance of these reformers unless we evaluate them with an emic perspective from within their cultural context. It does not add to our understanding of the historical cultural transformation to dismiss the importance of reformers as a whole because some were as elitist and racist as the rest of their culture. More may be learned by researching how many of these organizations worked to diminish distinctions of class and race. The WEIU perhaps most clearly stated how barriers among women were to be broken down "from the fact that they [women] would begin to understand one another through these needs of the body, the heart, and the mind." Though sometimes hindered by elitism and racism, reformers increased women's communication and understanding of one another across social boundaries. As a result, they contributed more to decrease rather than increase social divisions.[21]

My research also found that Americanization did not have a singular meaning. While some reformers made statements about teaching immigrants and the working classes "proper" middle-class standards of housekeeping, most women reformers defined American-

1880 to April 1881 (Boston: Frank Wood, 1881), pp. 23, 16, 21–22; The Work of the North Bennet Street Industrial School from 1888 to 1889 (Boston: Industrial School Press, 1889), p. 22, both in North Bennet Street Industrial School (Boston) records, SLWH. Scott, Natural Allies, p. 147. Stephanie J. Shaw, "Black Club Women and the Creation of the National Association of Colored Women," Journal of Women's History 3, no. 2 (Fall 1991): 19.
[21] Scott, Natural Allies, pp. 4, 183; Crocker, Social Work. For an example of complexity in stated goals, see the Annual Reports of the North Bennet Street Industrial School, SLWH. Clisby, "History of the WEIU," p. 130. Useful assessments of social control theory are William A. Musaskin, "The Social Control Theory in American History: A Critique," Journal of Social History 9, no. 4 (Summer 1976): 559–69; David Rochefort, "Progressive and Social Control Perspectives on Social Welfare," Social Service Review 55, no. 4 (December 1981): 568–91.

ization as education for citizenship, economic independence, and full participation in democracy. Further, Scott, Crocker, and I all independently found that women's organizations promoted social order and Americanization not for social control or to keep people in their place but to assist those in the lower classes who sought upward mobility.[22]

From an emic, feminist contextual perspective my research asks different questions about the historical effects and significance of women's organizations than have been asked from an etic perspective. My question is, in what ways did reformers change nineteenth-century American culture? To address this question I have sought evidence of the stated goals of domestic reformers, how the elitism and racism of the age affected those goals, and, despite these hindrances, why some reform programs were useful in improving the conditions of women's lives while others were not. Considering people as powerful social actors shaping their own lives, I have sought evidence of ways that participants negotiated with reformers for programs that would empower them in improving their lives. Finally, I have examined how reform transformed American culture by changing gender ideology, roles, and relationships.

Development of Domestic Reform Ideologies

Domestic reform movements were a polythetic set of individuals and organizations with both diversity and some overlap in their ideological roots. Some reformers used Enlightenment egalitarianism to argue for equality in the status of women's and men's roles. Religious millenialism motivated many reformers with the goal of perfecting society for the second coming of Christ. Combined religious and Enlightenment beliefs in the perfectibility of "man" and society supported the development and use of scientific technology and methods to rationalize house-

---

[22] Goals of Americanization and upholding high standards were expressed in *The Work of the North Bennet Street Industrial School: Its First Quarter-Century, 1881–1906*, Annual Report, 1904/5, p. 4, North Bennet Street Industrial School (Boston) records, 1881–, SLWH. Scott, *Natural Allies*, pp. 4, 105; Crocker, *Social Work*, pp. 61, 155; Spencer-Wood, "Diversity and Nineteenth-Century Domestic Reform."

work. Utopian communitarian socialism contributed cooperative ideology, methods, and efficient technologies.[23]

Domestic reform developed out of women's earlier prayer groups, cultural self-improvement clubs, and benevolent organizations, including auxiliaries to men's Evangelical missions. Women founded a variety of organizations in nearly every town and city across the United States, starting in the late eighteenth and early nineteenth centuries. In the second half of the nineteenth century, women's organizations and clubs organized on a national scale, which some reformers had learned from nationwide organizing to supply and nurse the union troops during the Civil War. The founding of benevolent societies by women was culturally acceptable because according to Evangelical beliefs women were better suited to save souls than men. Women were supposedly naturally more pious and moral in their domestic sphere, untainted by usury and other "sinful" capitalistic practices of men in their public sphere.[24]

Domestic reform organizations differed in philosophy and in goals from earlier women's benevolent and reform organizations, although some domestic reform organizations continued to dispense charity, usually to a more limited extent. Domestic reform institutions were directed toward creating culturally acceptable female "professions" to improve the status and conditions of women's domestic and public work. Some domestic reform institutions, particularly charitable homes for indigent women, continued the earlier poorhouse practice in which residents paid for their room and board through domestic production such as sewing or washing laundry. However, domestic reform institutions also assisted women in finding remunerative employment and frequently offered some training for professions ranging from women's traditional occupations of domestic service and sewing trades to milli-

[23] Spencer-Wood, "Toward an Historical Archaeology of Materialistic Domestic Reform," pp. 237–39.

[24] Scott, *Natural Allies*, pp. 3, 15, 17; Nancy F. Cott, *The Bonds of Womanhood: "Woman's Sphere" in New England, 1780–1835* (New Haven: Yale University Press, 1977); Barbara L. Epstein, *The Politics of Domesticity: Women, Evangelism, and Temperance in Nineteenth Century America* (Middletown, Mass.: Wesleyan University Press, 1981), pp. 26–31, 67, 81, 84–85. Hayden, *Grand Domestic Revolution*, pp. 115–25; Barbara Welter, "The Cult of True Womanhood, 1820–1860" *American Quarterly*, 18, no. 2 (Summer 1966): 151–74.

nery, typing, sales, or teaching kindergarten or domestic science. Further, domestic reform ideology rejected the Puritan predestination belief that poverty was the result of original sinfulness that had to be reformed punitively. Instead, most reformers took the Evangelical view that the poor and criminals were the victims of physically and morally corrupted male-public environments and could be "saved" with a healthy physical environment shaped by women's superior domestic-moral values.[25]

Domestic reformers were mostly middle-class women who were raised with the dominant Victorian cultural ideology of separate spheres. They were taught that the public sphere belonged exclusively to men, while women were relegated to the devalued domestic sphere of the home, which was also controlled by men. These gender ideals denied the actual existence of women's public roles, such as producing and marketing goods, operating businesses, and publicly displaying their social status. During the nineteenth century increasing numbers of middle- and upper-class women rejected the ideology justifying male dominance. Suffragists directly confronted male public sphere dominance with Enlightenment-based arguments for women's political equality. However, this direct approach was not as successful as domestic reform ideologies in raising women's status and making it acceptable within the dominant ideology for women to have public professions and citizenship. The reform argument that men's corrupt government needed women's superior moral influence was instrumental in obtaining women's suffrage.

The reformers were powerful social agents who transformed the dominant separate spheres ideology from within, arguing that women should control the domestic sphere, which should be equal to men's public sphere. Further, the reformers transformed women's domesticity from a source of oppression to a source of power, generating the ideology that women's innately superior domestic skills made them best suited for both domestic and public work that was labeled "domestic."

[25] Spencer-Wood, "Survey of Domestic Reform Movement Sites," pp. 7–36; Blair, *Clubwoman as Feminist*, pp. 73–115; Scott, *Natural Allies*, pp. 141–58; Beard, *Woman's Work*; John P. McDowell, *The Social Gospel in the South: The Woman's Home Mission Movement in the Methodist Episcopal Church, South, 1886–1939* (Baton Rouge: Louisiana State University Press, 1982).

Reformers gave the whole world new domestic meanings by considering the community as a public household and by recreating domestic tasks as female public professions. They improved the status of women and their work in both spheres by blurring the shifting the ideal boundary between domestic and public.

Domestic reformers materially redefined and combined the separate spheres (1) by bringing (male) public status to women's housework through scientific rationalization and mechanization, starting circa 1840; and (2) by expanding the domestic sphere to include parts of the public sphere that they argued were really domestic, thus making it acceptable within the dominant ideology for women to work in the public sphere.[26]

Women's public work was supported by two alternative gender ideologies. Starting in 1780, the "Cult of Single Blessedness" ideologically supported a relatively large number of women in remaining unmarried and economically independent through public sphere professions. In the second half of the nineteenth century, the less radical "Cult of Real Womanhood" advocated that women be educated, marry carefully, be able to support themselves or their family if needed, and maintain physical health through exercise and healthy diet.[27]

The reformers successfully argued for female dominance in many previously male-dominated public professions, including elementary schoolteaching as early as the 1820s, and retail sales, typesetting, typing, and secretarial work in the late nineteenth and early twentieth centuries. Further, in the second half of the nineteenth century, reformers transformed many domestic tasks into female public professions, including nursing, counseling in diet and nutrition, teaching kindergarten, and social work. Among these many new female professions this research has focused on those in female-run public housekeeping enterprises. In these enterprises, reformers materially transformed the "Cult of Domesticity" into cooperative housekeeping

---

[26] Spencer-Wood, "Toward a Feminist Historical Archaeology"; Spencer-Wood, "Feminist Historical Archaeology and the Pro-active Roles"; Spencer-Wood, "Toward an Historical Archaeology of Materialistic Domestic Reform."

[27] Spencer-Wood, "Toward a Feminist Historical Archaeology of Domestic Reform," p. 240; Chambers-Schiller, *Liberty a Better Husband*; Cogan, *All-American Girl*.

and municipal housekeeping movements that socialized household tasks in the public sphere.[28]

Domestic Reform of the Home

My research on domestic reform in the home applies feminist theory to correct andocentric histories that focus on men's innovations in domestic architecture and material culture and portray women as passively manipulated into domestic consumers by men whose factory products replaced household products. Even some feminist histories have continued to assume that women were only consumers, albeit active ones, of men's household inventions. A few feminists have sought and found evidence of women's innovations in domestic architecture and material culture. Women were actively involved in professionalizing housework with scientific methods and special equipment. To this end, many women invented household equipment, and factory production of their inventions provided self-supporting royalties, as in the case of Elizabeth Hawks's stove patent in 1867, Margaret Colvin's washing machine patent in 1871, and patents for a variety of different sewing devices by Helen A. Blanchard and by Harriet Tracy, both in the 1860s.[29] Finally, domestic reformers and their ideology were

[28] Spencer-Wood, "Feminist Archaeology and the Pro-active Roles"; Spencer-Wood, "Toward an Historical Archaeology of Materialistic Domestic Reform" pp. 234–5.

[29] Scholarship that focuses on men's roles in inventing and producing household conveniences consumed by supposedly passive women include Early Lifshey, *The Housewares Story: A History of the American Housewares Industry* (Chicago: National Housewares Manufacturers Assoc., 1973); Siegfried Giedion, *Mechanization Takes Command: A Contribution to Anonymous History* (New York: Oxford University Press, 1948); James H. Collins, *The Story of Canned Foods* (New York: E. P. Dutton, 1924); and Lawrence Wright, *Home Fires Burning: The History of Domestic Heating and Cooking* (London: Routledge and Kegan Paul, 1964). For an assumption that women were merely consumers, albeit active ones, see Ruth Schwartz Cowan, *More Work for Mother: The Ironies of Household Technology from the Open Hearth to the Microwave* (New York: Basic Books, 1983). For women's active contributions see Anne L. Macdonald, *Feminine Ingenuity: Women and Invention in America* (New York: Ballantine Books, 1992), pp. 38–47, 60–63, 196, 385–86, 393; Hayden, *Grand Domestic Revolution*. Women's domestic innovations are addressed to a lesser extent in Strasser, *Never Done*; Gwendolyn Wright, *Moralism and the Model Home: Domestic Architecture and Cultural Conflict in Chicago, 1873–1913* (Chicago: University of Chicago Press, 1980); Sally Ann McMurry, *Families and Farmhouses in Nineteenth Century America: Vernacular Design and Social Change* (New York: Oxford University Press, 1988).

instrumental in mechanizing the home. In advice manuals to housewives, reformers presented detailed drawings of their innovative equipment and furnishings for increasing the efficiency of housework and for promoting healthiness in both middle-class and working-class homes.

Research by feminist historians also has corrected androcentric histories that did not consider women's domestic advice literature historically important. Feminist research found that women's domestic manuals were important texts because they both verbally and materially transformed gender ideology and relationships.[30]

The earliest domestic reform ideology appeared in the most popular mid nineteenth-century domestic manuals by Catharine E. Beecher and her famous sister, Harriet Beecher Stowe. These manuals encouraged women to replace traditional housekeeping methods with scientific methods and the latest technology to symbolize that housework was an industrial profession equivalent to men's professions. Domestic reform meaning was given to both ordinary and innovative furniture and equipment by arranging them for the efficient performance of household tasks.

In *A Treatise on Domestic Economy*, Catharine Beecher stated that Enlightenment egalitarianism and democratic and religious principles together supported the equality of women's domestic professions with men's public professions, although men were the final household authority. In *The American Woman's Home*, Beecher and Stowe further developed a view of housework as a religious ministry in which status was gained through self-sacrifice for the common good of the family. This resolved the contradiction between Beecher's earlier arguments both for equality and for submission to husbands. Beecher's change to a more religious domestic ideology was materially symbolized in a shift from advocating square house designs as most efficient in *A Treatise on Domestic Economy* to advocating a "Christian" cruciform-shape house with crosses at each gable in *The American Woman's Home*. Beecher and Stowe advocated women building houses by quoting scripture: "The wise woman buildeth her house." Woman's

---

[30]Hayden, *Grand Domestic Revolution*, pp. 55–63; Strasser, *Never Done*, pp. 181–95.

role as minister of the home church, supported by the widespread cult of home religion, was materially symbolized in a Gothic house design, including Gothic doorways, corner niches with religious statues, and a Gothic dressing table. A Gothic-arched central recess in the entrance hall held the small round table that with a Bible was the normative symbol for family communion in the church of the home. Beecher and Stowe's glorification of the dominant ideology connecting women, domesticity, nature, and morality was symbolized with a vase of flowers on this table and both romantic rural and religious pictures on the wall. The house's public entry space was filled with symbols of the preeminence of woman's role as minister of the home church. Beecher and Stowe also designed a bow-windowed conservatory in each of the two ground-floor parlors, where they recommended that women and children grow houseplants, bringing nature into the home (fig. 1).

Archaeologists often find material culture that is usually unrecognized as symbolizing the cult of home religion. These include broken flowerpots from houseplants that symbolize women's closeness to nature and God and, especially, ceramics with Gothic-paneled forms or decorated ceramics with raised or transfer-printed Gothic arches, church ruins, or other religious symbols. The cult of home religion gives more explicitly documented meaning to the connection between Gothic-paneled teaware and religious domestic ideology archaeologically inferred by Diana Wall. She also inferred that the gilt floral tea set from another house site indicated a more secular ideology. While this may be correct, both Gothic and floral designs were widely viewed in the dominant ideology as symbols of women's greater piety and morality due to their closeness to nature and God in a domestic sphere separated from men's capitalistic public sphere that was considered corrupted by usury. In fact, Wall found material evidence of the symbolic connection among religion, nature, and women in a child's paneled tea set with floral designs. When women served tea using ceramics with Gothic or floral designs they could be symbolizing their powerful role as ministers of the cult of home religion. The widespread popularity of Beecher and Stowe's domestic manual suggests this could often have been the meaning of such ceramics, although it is also possible that the teaware preferences of these households were based on the aesthetic appeal of different styles, differences in cost, or desire to dis-

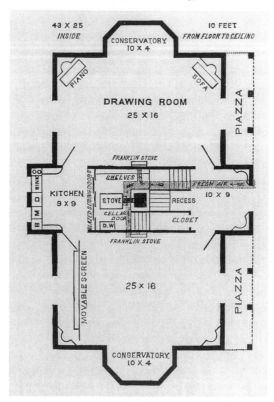

Fig. 1. First-floor plan, "Christian" house. From Catharine Beecher and Harriet Beecher Stowe, *The American Woman's Home; or, Principles of Domestic Science* (1869; reprint, Hartford, Conn.: Stowe-Day Fndn., 1985), p. 26.

play wealth, which was clearly greater for the gilt tea set than the paneled one.[31]

---

[31]Catharine Beecher, *A Treatise on Domestic Economy* (1841; reprint, New York: Schocken Books, 1977), pp. 1–14, 268–90; Catharine Beecher and Harriet Beecher Stowe, *The American Woman's Home; or, Principles of Domestic Science* (1869; reprint, Hartford, Conn.: Stowe-Day Fndn., 1985), pp. 19, 23. The American home religion movement, led by Horace Bushnell, and materially symbolized by the small round family

Beecher and Stowe's aim to "elevate both the honor and remuneration" of women's household tasks to professions "as much desired and respected as are the most honored professions of men" was materially symbolized and implemented by raising the kitchen from its frequent location in the basement to the ground floor, near the rooms opened to the public. In *The American Woman's Home* the centrality of woman's role in the home was symbolized by locating the kitchen in the center of both house and tenement designs (see fig. 1). This also expressed a conception of food preparation as central to woman's ministry of home religion, an analogy to the importance of communion in Christian churches. Kitchen doors for shutting in cooking smells could be opened at other times, expressing the interconnectedness of the domestic sphere that woman could thus survey and control as the "sovereign of her empire," who cooperatively organized her children in household tasks. The rational arrangement of furniture and equipment for efficient performance of household tasks also was supposed to express the harmony and order in "divine nature" (fig. 2).[32]

Beecher and Stowe designed this house as a suburban home for one or two families. They envisioned a cooperative colony of such houses on a rail line with a "central church and schoolroom, library, hall for sports, and a common laundry (taking the most trying part of domestic labor from each house)." They also created an early design for a "Christian neighborhood" cooperative operated by women and adopted children both as their home and as a neighborhood school and church. Beecher and Stowe felt they were following Christian teachings in connecting the individual households into a cooperative community that socialized housework. This exemplifies a religious ideology that supported cooperative housekeeping.[33]

The above interpretation represents my material feminist approach

---

communion table with a Bible in a parlor with religious pictures on the wall, is described in David P. Handlin, *The American Home: Architecture and Society, 1815–1925* (Boston: Little, Brown, 1979), pp. 4–19. Diana di Zerega Wall, "Sacred Dinners and Secular Teas: Constructing Domesticity in Mid Nineteenth-Century New York," *Historical Archaeology* 25, no. 4 (1991): 69–81.

[32] Beecher, *Treatise on Domestic Economy*, pp. 268–90, see esp. p. 270 for problems with basement kitchens in rural and urban homes and for house designs with ground-floor kitchens. Beecher and Stowe, *American Woman's Home*, pp. 17–36, 222, 442–45.

[33] Beecher and Stowe, *American Woman's Home*, pp. 42, 453–59.

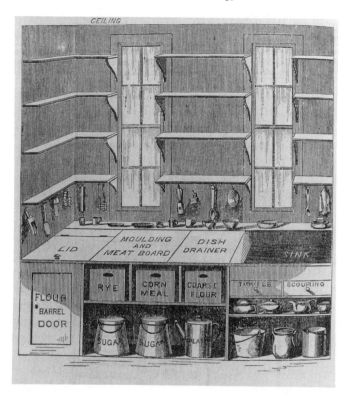

Fig. 2. View of one side of Beecher and Stowe's kitchen, with
rational arrangements of utensils, working surfaces, with shelf-
boxes for supplies below and shelves above for tableware. From
Catharine Beecher and Harriet Beecher Stowe, *The American
Woman's Home; or, Principles of Domestic Science* (1869; reprint, Hartford, Conn.: Stowe-Day Fndn., 1985), p. 34.

in analyzing how material culture was used actively to implement
change toward more egalitarian gender ideology, roles, and relationships. Archaeologists may be able to help answer the important question: to what extent were domestic reform designs for the home actually
used and by whom? This may be indicated in historic documents,
photos, or aboveground material culture. The preserved historic house
of Harriet Beecher Stowe includes some kitchen furniture similar to

Fig. 3. Small kitchen designed for efficient sequence of tasks, from food storage and preparation on the left, to cooking on the right. From Christine Frederick, *Household Engineering: Scientific Management in the Home* (5th ed.; Chicago: American School of Home Economics, 1923), p. 64. Furniture and equipment, *left to right:* an icebox on a dumbwaiter that could be raised from the cellar for use in the kitchen, a kitchen cabinet combining pantry cupboards and a table, an oil stove with an oven on top, and a fireless cooker that slid under the table when not in use.

that recommended in *The American Woman's Home* (see fig. 2). The further development of efficient arrangements of domestic furniture and equipment by Christine Frederick in her early twentieth-century manual, *Household Engineering*, includes photographs of the designs she and some friends implemented in their houses (fig. 3). The extent to which domestic reformers' designs were adopted in other households is seldom documented. However, Cohen found documented working-class cultural resistance to reformers' suggestions on domestic furnishings because they did not conform to ethnic and working-class ideas of high-status furnishings. Ellen H. Swallow Richards, in her manual on the cost of housing, illustrated a working-class apartment kitchen remodelled to include some of her suggestions to facilitate sanitation, such as sheet lignolith floor laid up the wall a few inches, glass shelves, and a glass table. However, aside from hanging pots under the glass table and a cooking range with overhead shelves and boiler, this kitchen did not implement reformers' designs for arranging furniture and equipment to efficiently perform kitchen tasks.[34]

Due to the lack of rural services for removing broken equipment, excavations on the property of rural middle- and upper-class homes might yield parts of innovative domestic equipment advocated by reformers, such as stoves, fireless cookers (insulated boxes that slowly cooked food in buckets placed over heated soapstones), steamers, washing machines, dishwashers, and vacuum cleaners. In urban areas it is much less likely that such equipment would be discarded in small household yards. Archaeologists might find remains of such equipment in community dumps, which could give some indication of degree of adoption by a community, especially if compared with assemblages from other towns or cities. However, archaeologists may be unable to identify parts of equipment unless they are relatively large and distinctive. Looking at the assemblage as a whole may be useful. The likelihood that a woman implemented domestic reform material culture innovations in her home could be suggested from historical photos, diaries, and inclusion on membership lists of local domestic reform organizations, although membership does not guarantee that a woman would implement domestic reforms at home.

A major problem for archaeologists is that many of the domestic reformers' efficient designs would not leave archaeological remains that could be distinguished from ordinary household equipment. Using functionalist theory, archaeologists most often have asked about the uses of such domestic equipment in food storage and preparation. Thus, the possibility that ordinary household equipment could have domestic reform meaning was not considered until feminist history and my research brought domestic reform to the attention of archaeologists.

---

[34]Christine Frederick, *Household Engineering: Scientific Management in the Home* (5th ed.; Chicago: American School of Home Economics, 1923); Hayden, *Grand Domestic Revolution*, pp. 55–60, 157, 285–89; Ellen H. Richards, *The Cost of Shelter* (New York: John Wiley and Sons, 1905), pp. 70–72; Strasser, *Never Done*, p. 188; Cohen, "Embellishing a Life of Labor." See also designs in Beecher, *Treatise on Domestic Economy*; Beecher and Stowe, *American Woman's Home*.

While ordinary household equipment used in domestic reform might be discarded on the sites of rural houses or in poor urban neighborhoods that lacked municipal trash-collection services, archaeologists could not identify ordinary household equipment as being used for domestic reform without documentation. Thus, it is important to conduct documentary research to identify cooperative housekeeping enterprises, especially those with high archaeological potential. Such sites, which have yards where discard might occur, are located in poor, urban neighborhoods or alongside institutions for day care or childhood domestic education, where children playing in yards might lose specially designed kindergarten toys or older girls might discard broken scientific glassware from domestic science classes.[35]

Domestic Reform and Boston's Landscape

My survey of about 120 Boston domestic reform sites corrects androcentric histories that have focused on men's voluntary organizations for social reform and largely overlooked women's voluntary organizations because they were assumed to be concerned with historically insignificant private matters. Feminist historians recently have researched the historical importance of an immense number and variety of women's voluntary organizations, including those for domestic reform.[36]

My survey focuses on women's reform organizations involved in transforming women's household tasks into public professions, especially in women's cooperative housekeeping enterprises. Here women

[35] Spencer-Wood, "Survey of Domestic Reform Movement Sites," pp. 7–36. Spencer-Wood, "Toward a Feminist Historical Archaeology," pp. 234–44. More detail on the archaeological potential of different kinds of domestic reforms sites is in Spencer-Wood, "Toward an Historical Archaeology of Materialistic Domestic Reform," pp. 248–74.

[36] Histories that focus on men's voluntary organizations include Don Harrison Doyle, *The Social Order of a Frontier Community: Jacksonville, Ill., 1825–1870* (Champaign: University of Illinois Press, 1961); Charles I. Foster, *Errand of Mercy: The Evangelical United Front, 1790–1837* (Chapel Hill: University of North Carolina Press, 1960); and Clifford S. Griffin, *Their Brothers' Keepers: Moral Stewardship in the United States, 1800–1865* (New Brunswick, N.J.: Rutgers University Press, 1960). These were critiqued and corrected with the wealth of information on women's organizations in Scott, *Natural Allies*; Giddings, *When and Where I Entered*; and Blair, *Clubwoman as Feminist*.

worked together to perform housework tasks that they previously performed individually at home, such as cooking, laundering, or child
care. Public housekeeping enterprises included neighborhood cooperatives, working women's cooperative homes, social settlements, day care
centers, and public kitchens, which provided nutritious food at low
prices. The professionalization of household tasks was symbolized
and implemented with scientific methods and equipment that were
taught and used in college home economics departments as well as
in schools and in classes on domestic science, kindergarten teaching,
cooking, and housekeeping.

In some cooperatives, particularly social settlements, reformers
lived together cooperatively in poor, often immigrant, communities for
which they provided social services. In general, settlements were more
secular in orientation than the Young Women's Christian Association
(YWCA), founded in 1866, or the WEIU, founded in 1877, both of
which developed in Boston out of women's religious clubs. In the late
nineteenth century, women's settlements and many clubs developed
municipal housekeeping in which women extended their domestic roles
as mothers and housekeepers into the community as they became aware
that the health and welfare of their families depended not only on clean
homes but also on clean public water, streets, sewers, and on pure,
commercially marketed foods. As the moral mothers of the community,
reformers established cooperatives to provide services such as day care,
health care, baths, pure water, and nutritious food to working women
and their families.[37]

As an archaeologist, I have been concerned with the importance
of material culture in domestic reform, including the use of architectural spaces and public landscapes to physically change gender ideology, roles, and relationships. Using feminist histories, guides to selected
women's historic sites, historic city guidebooks, domestic reform organization records, historic business directories, and historic maps, I

[37]Gladys G. Calkins, *The Negro in the Young Women's Christian Association: A
Study of the Development of the YWCA Interracial Policies and Practices in Their Historic
Setting* (Master's thesis, Department of Religion, Columbian College of George Washington University, 1960). The origin and ideology of the WEIU is from Blair, *Clubwoman as Feminist*, p. 75. Crocker, *Social Work*, pp. 18–19; Scott, *Natural Allies*,
chap. 6; Nancy Woloch, *Women and the American Experience* (New York: Alfred A.
Knopf, 1984), p. 287.

mapped the geographical distributions of many different kinds of domestic reform institutions. From a feminist materialist perspective, I have researched how the presence of domestic reform institutions on the urban landscape changed gender ideology by physically moving public gender geography toward greater equality. Domestic reformers merged public and domestic built environments and dramatically increased the number of women and women's institutions on public landscapes.

The integration of domestic and public spheres in domestic reform ideology was materially expressed by the establishment of some public cooperative housekeeping enterprises in residential-type structures and others in public-scale institutions in both residential and public landscapes. In residential areas, domestic reform institutions made housekeeping a public matter, and public urban areas were domesticated with a wide variety of female-dominated and female-controlled places. Domestic reformers changed the gender geography of Boston by increasing the physical presence of women engaged in culturally acceptable "domestic" roles and professions in housekeeping institutions on the public landscape. The increasing number and variety of domestic reform institutions changed the meaning of public landscapes from male-dominated space to greater gender equality. Women increasingly contested male dominance of the public built environment as most domestic reform institutions grew from small, rented quarters to owned, and sometimes specially constructed, larger public structures (fig. 4, Appendix A: sites 37, 42, 43, 52, 53, 56, 61, 62, 63). Further, domestic reform institutions dominated many geographical areas because they were large structures, numerous, or both (see fig. 4, Appendix A: sites 29, 43, 49, 62–64, 16, 38a, 38d, 41, 56, 1, 19c, 25a, 27a, 33b, 33c, 8, 11, 30b, 44a, 59a, 59c, 45).

The survey reveals how the geographic distribution of different types of domestic reform institutions varied according to their purpose and the location of people using the institutions. Kindergartens, day nurseries, and housekeeping cooperatives were located in the neighborhoods they served, whether working-class Italian Catholic or middle-class Anglo Protestant. In contrast, women's classes and schools of cooking, housekeeping, salesmanship, millinery, and kindergarten teaching were centrally located in downtown Boston or the Back Bay, close to the many South End working women's homes and easily acces-

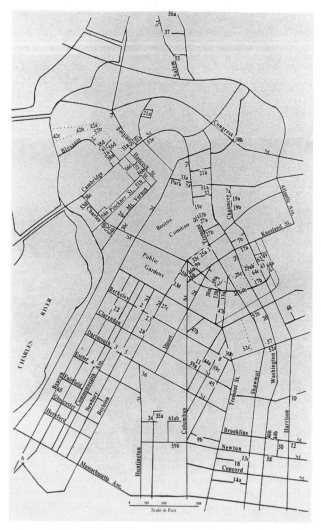

Fig. 4. Boston proper domestic reform sites. After *Arrow Metropolitan Boston Map and Street Guide* (Canton, Mass.: Arrow Publishing, 1974). See Appendix A.

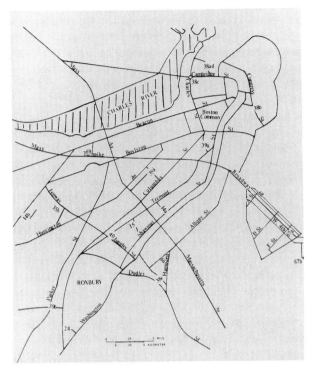

Fig. 5. Greater Boston domestic reform sites. After *Arrow Metropolitan Boston Map and Street Guide* (Canton, Mass.: Arrow Publishing, 1974). See Appendix B.

sible via public transportation (see fig. 4, Appendix A: sites 7–13, 25, 27, 34, 35, 46, 64, 65, 59). The Boston YWCA was explicitly concerned with purchasing, and later constructing, their cooperative working women's homes in central locations near the business district, where many women worked (see fig. 4, Appendix A: sites 7, 8). Domestic reform organizations, classes, and schools run by and for women in the middle classes were located in the fashionable Back Bay where many of these women lived, often in "cooperative hotels" of kitchenless apartments where servants were elevated to wage day-laborers who cooperatively performed housework, cooked, and served meals (see fig. 4, Appendix A: sites 1–6, 22, 23, 28, 34, 35, 36, 60; fig. 5, Appendix

B: site 69). Some types of domestic reform institutions included both centralized and neighborhood geographic distributions. For instance, the main New England Public Kitchen was centrally located to distribute school lunches throughout Boston, but branches were located in the neighborhoods of the immigrant groups they served (see fig. 4, Appendix A: site 30).[38]

The locations of domestic reform institutions were affected by the class and ethnic relationships between reformers and the women and communities they served. For instance, employment bureaus, classes, and schools run by middle-class reformers for working women were mostly located near the interface of the Back Bay and the downtown business district, easily accessible to both reformers and many working women. Cooperative homes for working women, often founded by elitist women's religious orders, were predominantly located in Boston's South End, where many single, working women lived (see fig. 4, Appendix A: sites 10, 12). Religious separatism led different orders of Catholic nuns to establish homes for working women. Homes founded by religious groups often had elitist, restrictive rules for residents because they were founded *for* but not *by* working women. Some settlements, industrial schools for girls, and day care sites founded by middle- and upper-class, usually Anglo, women remained in one location and served the neighborhood as its ethnic mix changed over time (see fig. 4, Appendix A: sites 37, 42, 43). Other institutions were founded by and for women of an ethnic group, particularly African Americans and Jews in Boston, and moved across the landscape with that group (see fig. 4, Appendix A: sites 38, 39, 53, 61; see fig. 5, Appendix B: sites 38, 39).

Because of my feminist perspective, I sought and found evidence that minority women were not passive victims of the racism, ethnocentrism, elitism, or anti-Semitism of Anglo or Christian domestic reform institutions. Instead, minority women empowered themselves by organizing parallel institutions in the landscapes of their communities. This demonstrates that domestic reform services were valuable to, and

---

[38] *Second Annual Report of the Young Women's Christian Association, Boston* (Boston: J. M. Hewes, 1868), p. 12; *Seventeenth Annual Report of the Young Women's Christian Association, Boston* (Boston: Frank Wood, 1883), p. 20; Boston YWCA records, SLWH; Spencer-Wood, "Survey of Domestic Reform Movement Sites."

desired by, minority communities. Further, beyond resisting exclusion by Anglos, minority women also founded their own organizations out of their separate identity as a social group with different needs. In Boston, one example of parallelism was the French YWCA established in 1902 in a residential-type row house around the corner from a large institutional structure of the Anglo YWCA (see fig. 4, Appendix A: sites 8, 59). In another instance, an African American women's club was founded by Josephine St. Pierre Ruffin in 1894. In 1904 six middle-class African American women founded Boston's Harriet Tubman House to meet the particular needs of single African American women who migrated from the South to work in the city (see fig. 4, Appendix A: sites 54, 61). After 1910 the Harriet Tubman House was organized as a settlement. Many settlements excluded African Americans, such as South End House, founded by Robert Woods in 1892. Jewish women, reacting to exclusion from the elite Protestant Boston Sewing Circle, founded their own sewing circle. They also founded a Jewish industrial school for girls, which became a settlement house that was originally for Jews exclusively (see fig. 4, Appendix A: site 53). In the 1920s, Hecht House, on the back side of Beacon Hill, was opened to non-Jews partly because the Protestant Elizabeth Peabody House, in the West End, was open to Jews. However, Hecht House was never completely open to African Americans. Although segregation and integration were underdocumented, this survey found a few records identifying several of the domestic reform institutions that were integrated by class and ethnicity, including settlements, industrial schools, day cares, classes, and clubs (see fig. 4, Appendix A: sites 37, 42, 43, 48, 52, 53, 55, 56, 57, 62, 63, 64; see fig. 5, Appendix B: sites 40, 66, 68).

Most domestic reform institutions for working women from a variety of ethnic groups were run by Anglo middle-class women. Thus, most documents about domestic reform organizations were written by middle- or upper-class reformers and not by the working-class women who often were the recipients of domestic reform. In this research, documents by elite reformers have been read critically to tease out the viewpoints of nonelite participants. Elite reformers' records of their activities sometimes include information about the reactions of the participants. The evidence corrects histories that have portrayed non elite women and their families as passive recipients of reform, instead indicating that they actively worked to empower themselves through domestic reform.[39] Working-class recipients negotiated with elite reformers for programs to meet their varying needs thus altering the construction or use of space in domestic reform institutions on the public landscape.

Women's social settlements were prime examples of sites where reformers negotiated with neighborhood residents to provide services that would meet the needs of the local community. Reformers initially offered programs to address community needs that they perceived for child care, manual education, and work or housing for single working-class women. The response of neighborhood residents to these programs and their requests for other programs led the reformers to modify and/or expand the services they provided. Reformers negotiated with the community over the use of space and the equipment needed for different programs.

For instance, although the North Bennet Street Industrial School, founded in 1881 by wealthy immigrant Pauline Agassiz Shaw in Boston's North End, was originally for girls, it rapidly expanded its programs to meet the needs of local boys, young men, and women. The neighborhood initially was mostly Irish, with Jews and Italians subsequently becoming predominant. The goal of the school was to make

[39] Robert Stein, "Girls' Cooperative Boarding Homes," *The Arena*, March 1898, pp. 397–417; Adelaide Cromwell Hill, "Josephine St. Pierre Ruffin," in Edward T. James, Janet W. James, and Paul S. Boyer, eds., *Notable American Women, 1607–1950: A Biographical Dictionary* (Cambridge: Harvard University Press, Belknap Press 1971), p. 207; Frieda Garcia, "Harriet Tubman and the Harriet Tubman House of United South End Settlements in Boston, Massachusetts," pamphlet, nd.; "South End House 1910: Democracy Domesticated," SLWH, pp. 1–2, 4, 26–27. On Hecht House, see Solomon, "Oral Memoir" 2: 336–38, 346, 381–83, 390, 425–26; *Thirteenth Annual Report of the Elizabeth Peabody House: Report for the Year 1908* (Boston: Thomas Todd Co., 1909), p. 15. On integrated settlements, see *Denison House: The College Settlement in Boston. Annual Report for the Year Ending October 1, 1914*, p. 13; Robert A. Woods, ed., *The City Wilderness: A Settlement Study by Residents and Associates of the South End House* (1898: reprint, New York: Garrett Press, 1970), pp. 176–77; Lincoln House Annual Reports, 1902–1912, Widener Library, Harvard University, Cambridge; *Frances E. Willard Settlement* (Boston, 1912), pp. 10, 16; Lillian V. Robinson, *Children's House: A History of the Hawthorne Club* (Boston: Marshall Jones Co., 1937), pp. 11–13; Geoffrey Blodgett, "Pauline Agassiz Shaw," in James, James, and Boyer, *Notable American Women*, p. 278; Robert A. Woods and Albert J. Kennedy, eds., *Handbook of Settlements* (New York: Charities Publications Committee, 1911), pp. 106–35. Participants in reform are considered passive in Lori D. Ginzberg, *Women and the Work of Benevolence: Morality, Politics and Class in the Nineteenth-Century United States* (New Haven: Yale University Press, 1990), p. 1.

neighborhood residents employable through manual training. Reports also express the goals of Americanization, uplifting the poor, and assisting poor women with regard to their employment and health, which were stressed in the Cult of Real Womanhood. Some of the services offered were well subscribed, such as a cooperative laundry, child care, millinery classes for mothers, gymnasium classes, and baths for girls and young women. The reformers discontinued or reduced the following services in response to declining subscription by neighborhood residents: (1) military drill for boys; (2) carpentry classes for older girls; (3) cooking classes (because teachers and parents discouraged manual training for girls); (4) baths for boys in the summer (especially after city baths and a swimming pool were established nearby).

The reformers also established new programs at the request of neighborhood residents, including carpentry classes requested by boys, which changed the use of school spaces and added special equipment. The equipment was at first set up in the basement, but when the boys demonstrated good behavior, they were allowed, at their request, to create a workshop on the upper floor so they could have sunshine and good air. Thus, neighborhood residents negotiated to use school spaces for programs they wanted, including acquiring requisite equipment. The reformers discontinued some of their earliest services for their own reasons, including charitable giving of coal, groceries, and shoes to the "deserving" poor; an unsuccessful domestic service employment agency; and the cooperative laundry because although it was meant to be educational, it became a workplace.[40]

Diversity in domestic reform institutions, including settlements, provides other examples of negotiation between middle-class Anglo reformers and working-class program participants. For instance, Denison House, which was founded as a women's workroom and supported

[40] *Report of the North-End Industrial Home*, p. 10, 14, 16–19; *Work of the North Bennet Street Industrial School: Its First Quarter Century, 1881–1906*, pp. 3–16; *Work of the North Bennet Street Industrial School from 1888 to 1889*, p. 21; *North Bennet Street Industrial School Annual Report*, 1908/9 (Worcester, Mass.: Davis Press, 1909), pp. 19–20; *Annual Report of the North Bennet Street Industrial School*, 1905/6 (Boston, 1906), p. 12; Reports of the North Bennet Street Industrial School, 1888–96, handwritten, June 7, December 5, 1889, March 7, 1890, March 3, 1892; *The Work of the North Bennet Street Industrial School from 1881–1887* (Boston: Rand Avery Co., 1887), pp. 3–6, North Bennet Street Industrial School (Boston) records, SLWH.

women's trade unions, responded to immigrant women's protests that production and sales of their folk handicrafts "ought not to be charity work" by putting it "on a strictly business basis" in 1919. Earlier in the century, public kitchens in several northeastern cities, and at the Hull House settlement in Chicago, had to change their Yankee menu and offer ethnic dishes in order to be patronized by working people who otherwise would take only hot water and broth. In municipal dumps or possibly site yards in poor neighborhoods, archaeologists might find remains of special equipment used in public kitchens and cooked-food delivery services (see fig. 4, Appendix A: sites 29, 30, 31, 32), including Aladdin ovens, metal-insulated food transportation containers, scientific glassware, metal tables with gas jets, and scales and weights, as well as ordinary bowls, plates, cups, glasses, and bottles (fig. 6).[41]

Similarity in the needs of many communities and the spread of ideas among reformers led to similarity in the wide range of domestic reform programs for women and their families. These included day nurseries, kindergartens, kitchen gardens, clubs and classes segregated by sex and age, libraries or reading rooms, social rooms, gymnasiums, health clinics for mothers and children, playgrounds, and vacation schools or camps. Many Boston settlements developed from day nurseries, kindergartens, or clubs (see fig. 4, Appendix A: sites 42, 48, 52, 56, 57; see fig. 5, Appendix B: sites 40, 66, 67, 68). The North Bennet Street Industrial School and the Hebrew Industrial School also developed into settlements. At these and other Boston domestic reform institutions, such as the WEIU, YWCA, public kitchens, and domestic schools and classes, reformers negotiated among themselves and with participants concerning the content of programs, the use of space and equipment, and who could participate.[42]

---

[41] "Settlements: Sixty Years, 1887–1947," p. 6; *Denison House: The College Settlement in Boston, Annual Report for the Year Ending October 1, 1919*, SLWH, p. 17. For working-class comments on Yankee menus of public kitchens, see Jane Addams, *Twenty Years at Hull-House* (1910; reprint, New York: New American Library, 1960), p. 102; Caroline L. Hunt, *The Life of Ellen H. Richards* (Boston: Whitcomb and Barrows, 1912), p. 220.

[42] "Settlements: Sixty Years, 1887–1947." In the paper that I presented at the 1991 Winterthur Conference, I briefly outlined many other examples of negotiation among women in different classes and ethnic groups participating in domestic reform and differences between ideals and their material implementation of domestic reform. See Spencer-Wood, "Diversity and Nineteenth-Century Domestic Reform," pp. 188–208.

Fig. 6. Interior, New England Public Kitchen, 142 Pleasant St., est. by Ellen H. Swallow Richards, 1890. From Ellen H. Richards, ed., *Plain Words about Food: The Rumford Kitchen Leaflets*, 1899 (Boston: Home Science Publishing Co., 1899), p. 134.

Conclusion

In contrast to the social control school, an emic contextual feminist perspective has revealed that because reformers aimed to improve the lives and status of working women, they modified and created programs to meet needs expressed by participants. Reformers not only responded because participation in reform programs was voluntary but because they wanted to help working families become full participants in the American dream, both economically and politically. Many domestic reformers rejected the dominant male definition of Americanization that involved suppressing immigrant cultures. Instead, most reformers promoted pride in ethnic cultures through clubs, folk dances, plays, pageants, lectures in foreign languages, and ethnic fairs. At the same time, they taught English, civics, hygiene, and patriotic songs to improve public health, raise the standard of living, and increase democratic participation. These reformers were on the cutting edge of the American melting pot, helping immigrants to maintain their own cultural identity while learning to become successful in their new country. Immigrants were not monolithically opposed as a whole to Americanization that assisted them in becoming economically independent citizens. For instance, in 1902, the Elizabeth Peabody House found that there were so many upwardly mobile immigrants "eager to fit themselves for American life" that evening classes in English, mathematics, and American history had to be moved to the larger Hebrew Industrial School.[43]

The clearest statements that redefined the meanings of the terms "Americanization" and "social order" were by women reformers at Denison House:

While we interpret the glory of America to these newcomers, let us not fail to interpret their aspirations and endowments to the native born, that the word *Americanization* may cease to mean to the majority of men the impossible task of shaping alien minds and hearts to the old colonial pattern. Let us not rob America of some of the best gifts these foreign-born citizens have to offer her, in our blind efforts to make them over into something too much like ourselves! . . . only by the united wisdom of all sorts and conditions of men can we attain to the better social order.[44]

This feminist research has corrected androcentric histories focused only on men, especially male reformers, and their definitions of social control and Americanization. The sexist view of women as passive recipients of men's technological innovations has been replaced with evidence that reformers created innovations in material culture, in the use of architectural spaces, and in the use of public landscapes. Further, reformers transformed the Victorian ideal of separate gender spheres into new ideologies that increased women's power. They physically subverted the Victorian gender ideals by combining domestic and

[43] *Fourteenth Annual Report of the Elizabeth Peabody House. Report for the Year 1902* (Boston: Thomas Todd, 1903), p. 7.

[44] *Denison House: The College Settlement in Boston. Annual Report for the Year Ending October 1, 1916*, pp. 11–12, 18; *Denison House: The College Settlement in Boston. Annual Report for the Year Ending October 1, 1912*, pp. 4, 12–14. See also *Nineteenth Annual Report of the Elizabeth Peabody House. Report for the Year 1914* (Boston: Thomas Todd, 1914), pp. 3–5, 13, 15.

public built environments and material culture in new ways. The reformers changed some professions from male dominated to female dominated and created a large number of new female-dominated professions and institutions that increased the public presence of women, thus physically contesting male dominance in public landscapes by moving public gender geography toward equality.

This material feminist research has brought to archaeologists' attention many new types of domestic reform sites that developed in the nineteenth century as well as the domestic reform meanings of both ordinary and innovative material culture that might be found both at domestic and public sites. Theory drives the questions we ask, the evidence we seek, the meanings interpreted from evidence, and, thus, the conclusions we draw. It is impossible to find or understand the meaning of evidence that we are not even seeking. Theory is the deepest context shaping research. Without feminist theory and questions, we would probably still know little of the historical significance of the many nation-wide domestic reform movements that transformed American culture.

Appendix A
Boston Proper Domestic Reform Sites

No.	Site	Location	Date(s)	Status
1	Hotel Pelham	Tremont and Boylston sts.	1857–99	D
2	Hotel Kempton	Berkeley and Newbury sts.	1873–1910	D
3	Hotel Vendome	Commonwealth and Dartmouth sts.	1872	E
4	Hotel Agassiz	Commonwealth and Exeter sts.	1872	E
5	Hotel Victoria	Dartmouth and New-bury sts.	1886	E
6	Charlesgate Hall	Beacon St. and Charlesgate East	1891	E
7a	Boston YWCA	23 Chauncey St.	1867	D
7b		25–27 Beech St.	1868–75	D
7c		68 Warrenton St.	1873/74	D
8	Boston YWCA	40 Berkeley St.	1885–1965	D
9a	New England Helping Hand Home	12 Carver St.	1889	D
9b		124 Pembroke St.	1895	E
10	Gray Nuns or St. Helena's Working Girls' Home	89 Union Park St.	1895– ca. 1940s	E
11	Brook House Home for Working Girls	79 Chandler St.	1901	E
12	St. Joseph's Home for Females	41–45 E. Brookline St.	1885–1901	D
13a	Temporary Home for Working Women	327 Tremont St., cor-ner of Jefferson St.	1879	D
13b		126 Pleasant St., corner of Melrose St.	1885	D
13c		453 Shawmut St., cor-ner of Rutland St.	1889–1904	E
14	Massachusetts Home for Intemperate Women	41 Worcester St.	1875	E
16	Home for Friendless and Unfortunate Women	2 Russell Pl.	1901	D
17a	New England Moral Re-form Society (organized 1836)	21 Kneeland St.	1867	D

Appendix A (Continued)

No.	Site	Location	Date(s)	Status
17b		6 Oak Pl.	1875	D
18	Penitent Females' Refuge and Bethesda Society Home (organized 1818)	32 Rutland St.	1867	E
19a	Needlewoman's Friend Society (organized 1847)	40 Chauncey St.	1869	D
19b		86 Chauncey St.	1873	D
19c		149A Tremont St.	1876	D
20	Ladies Aid Society	1031 Washington St.	1885–89	D
21a	Ladies' City Relief Assoc.	Charity Building on Chardon St.	1885	D
21b		Weslyan Hall at 36 Bromfield St.	1901	D
22	WEA Botany Course	76 Marlborough St.	1890	E
23	WEA courses	Boston Society of Natural History, Berkeley and Boylston sts.	1891	E
25a	Woman's Education Association School of Decorative Needlework	48 Boylston St.	1879	D
25b	Boston Society of Decorative Art (formerly WEA School of Decorative Needlework)	222 Boylston St.	1901	D
26a	Industrial Committee of the WEA	91 Mt. Vernon St.	1879	E
26b		11 Park Sq.	1879	D
27a	Boston Cooking School (founded by WEA)[1]	158 Tremont St.	1879	D
		158½ Tremont St.	1881, 1883	D
		159 Tremont St.	1882	D
27b		174 Tremont St.	1885	D
27c		372 Boylston St.	1898–1903	D
28	Massachusetts Institute of Technology Walker Lab[2]	Boylston St., adjacent to #23	1877–1900	D
29a	WEA South End Diet Kitchen (organized 1874)	19 Bennet St.	1880	D
29b		37 Bennet St.	1885	D
29c		21 Common St.	1901	D
30a	New England Public Kitchen (est. 1890)	142 Pleasant St.	1890	D
30b		Tremont St.	1898	D

Appendix A (Continued)

No.	Site	Location	Date(s)	Status
30c		39–45 Charles St.	ca. 1905–30	E
30d		108–112 Pleasant St.[3]	1916	D
31a	North End Diet Kitchen	34 Lynde St.	1880	D
31b		8 Staniford Pl.	1889	D
32	Women's Educational and Industrial Union (WEIU) Laboratory Kitchen and Food Supply Co.	50 Temple Pl.	1903	D
33a	WEIU (founded 1877)	4 Park St.	1877	D
33b		157 Tremont St.	1880	D
33c		72–74 Boylston St.	1883	D
33d		97–98 Boylston St. (renumbered 264 Boylston St. ca. 1892–1917)	1890	D
34	WEIU School of Housekeeping	45 and 47 Botolph St.	1897	D
35	Simmon's College[4]	Botolph St.	1902, 1903	D
36	Huntington Chambers[5]	30 Huntington Ave.	1902–50	D
37	North Bennet Street Industrial School (est. 1881)[6]	37–39 N. Bennet St.	1881–present	E
		53 Tileston St.	1908	E
38a	Sunnyside Day Nursery	35 Blossom St.	1887	D
38b		87 Milk St.	1897	D
38c		165 Charles St.	1901	D
38d		41 Blossom St.	1904	D
39	South End (Jamaica Plain) Day Nursery	82 Carver St.	1880	D
41	West End Day Nursery and Children's Hospital	37 Blossom St.	1882–1901	D
42a	Elizabeth Peabody House	156 Chambers St.	1896	D
42b		87–89 Poplar St.	1901–11,	D
		91 Poplar St.	1909–10	D
42c		357 Charles St.	1910	D
		Chambers St.	1958	D
43	Denison House[7]	93 Tyler St.	1892	D
		91 Tyler St.	1896	D
		95 Tyler St.	1898	D
		89 Tyler St.	1910	D
		97 Tyler St.	1910	D

Appendix A (Continued)

No.	Site	Location	Date(s)	Status
44a	Dorothea Dix House	72 Chandler St.	1898	E
44b		14 E. Brookline	1901	D
45	Door of Hope for Girls	67 Warren Ave., corner of Clarendon	1898	D
46a	Domestic Training Schools	17 Carver St.	1898	D
46b		2–8 E. Brookline	1898	D
47a	Boylston Working Women's Club	Fayette St.	1898	E
47b		28 Isabella St.	1901	E
48a	Louisa Alcott Club	9 Rochester St.	1895	D
48b		17 Oswego St.	1898	D
48c		15 Oswego St.	1911	D
49	Tyler Street Day Nursery	Tyler and Harvard sts.	1898	E
50	Marenholz House	E. Brookline St.	1898	D
51a	First American English-speaking Kindergarten[8]	24½ Winter St.	1862	D
51b		15 Pinckney St.	1863–6	D
52a	Lincoln House settlement[9]	1129 Washington at Dover St.	1888	D
52b		116–22 Shawmut Ave. at Castle St.	1893	D
52c		70–80 Emerald St.	1904–47	D
		68 Emerald St.[10]	1911	D
53a	Hebrew Industrial School[11]	N. Bennet St. (in North Bennet Street Industrial School)	1889	E
53b		17 Allen St.	1899–1905	D
53c		80 Charles St.	1906–8	E
53d		154 Charles St.	1909–21	D
53e	Hecht Neighborhood House (formerly Hebrew Industrial School for Girls)	22 Bowdoin St.	1922	D
		160 American Legion Highway, Dorchester	1936–ca. 1960	
54a	Woman's Era Club (for African American women)[12]	103 Charles St.	1894–1903	D
54b		Charles Street A.M.E. Church[13]	1895	E
55	North End Union	20 Parmenter St.	1892	E
		32 Parmenter St.[14]	1892	D

Appendix A (Continued)

No.	Site	Location	Date(s)	Status
56a	Frances E. Willard Settlement (founded 1897)	24 S. Russell St.	1901–9	D
56b		38–44 Chambers St.	1908–51	D
57	Hawthorn Club (founded 1900)	3 Garland St.	1900	D
		3–4 Garland St.	1913–37	D
58	Franklin Square House[15]	27 E. Newton	1904	D
		11 E. Newton	1908–11	D
		11–27 E. Newton	1912	E
		11 E. Newton	1931–61	E
59a	French YWCA (founded 1902)	65 Clarendon	1902–5	E
59b		212 W. Newton	1906–11	D
59c		28 Appleton	1912–36	E
60	Household Aid Co.[16]	88 Charles St.	1903–5	E
61a	Harriet Tubman House (founded 1904)	37 Holyoke St.	1907	E
61b		25 Holyoke St.	1910–72	E
		27 Holyoke St.	1920–72	E
62	Denison House Co-operative Home for Young Women	100 Tyler St.	1906–43	E
63	Denison House Gymnasium	65 Tyler St. (Old Colony Chapel bldg.)	1900–1943	D
64a	Hemenway House[17]	98 Tyler St.	1912–19	E
64b		14 Warrenton St.	1916–19	D
64c		11 Nassau	1923–51	D
65	YWCA Home for Business Girls	371–72 Beacon St.	1918	E

Key: E = extant building, D = destroyed

[1] Boston Cooking School was absorbed by Simmon's College in 1903.

[2] Massachusetts Institute of Technology Walker Lab was financed by WEA for Richards to teach women sanitary chemistry.

[3] The public kitchen at 108–112 Pleasant St. became School Lunch Dept. by 1916.

[4] Simmon's College absorbed the WEIU School of Housekeeping in 1902 and the Boston Cooking School in 1903.

[5] In 1902, Simmon's College rented rooms at 30 Huntington Ave. Fannie M. Farmer's School of Cookery was founded in Rm. 624; it moved to 40 Hereford in 1950.

[6] In 1905 North Bennet Industrial School absorbed adjoining Social Service House (est. 1902 at 37 Bennet St.) before expanding to the adjoining building at 53 Tileston St. The school still operates in its 1881 large institutional structure.

[7] Denison House moved to Dorchester in 1943.

[8] The kindergarten was founded by Elizabeth Peabody in 1860. Although 15 Pinckney St. was destroyed in 1892, 17 Pinckney St. is extant and is a mirror image of it.

[9] Founded by Josephine Allen and Louise Williams in 1887.

Appendix A (Continued)

[10] This location was a women's residence.

[11] The school was founded for girls by Lina (Mrs. Jacob H.) Hecht in 1889. It was initially next to the North Bennet Street Industrial School.

[12] Founded by Josephine St. Pierre Ruffin, the club met in her house 1894–1903.

[13] The extant building is today the Charles Street Meeting House.

[14] In 1886 St. Mary's Chapel yard at this site became Boston's first public playground, a sand garden founded by women.

[15] This hotel for self-supporting women was founded in 1901. The extant building is an old-age home called "The Franklin."

[16] E. S. Richards founded this WEA-sponsored cooperative home for training college women in live-out by-day domestic service.

[17] This self-supporting working women's cooperative home was founded in 1906.

Sources: Boston directories for 1860–1941, 1949–61; Boston atlases printed by G. W. Bromley, Philadelphia, for 1883, 1884, 1890, 1895, 1898, 1902, 1906, 1910, 1912, 1922, 1928; Insurance map(s) of Boston by D. A. Sanborn or Sanborn Map Co., N.Y., for 1867, 1909, 1914, 1923. For sites 1–50, see Suzanne M. Spencer-Wood, "A Survey of Domestic Reform Movement Sites in Boston and Cambridge, ca. 1865–1905," *Historical Archaeology* 21, no. 2 (1987): 7–36. For settlements, see Robert A. Woods and Albert J. Kennedy, eds., *Handbook of Settlements* (New York: Charities Publications Committee, 1911), pp. 106–35; *The Boston Social Union: A Federation of Twenty-Two Settlements and Other Neighborhood Centres in Greater Boston. Annual Report. Nov. 1913*, box 2, folder 22; and "Elizabeth Peabody House Chronology," box 2, folder 8, both in Eva Whiting White Papers, Schlesinger Library of Women's History, Radcliffe College, Cambridge (hereafter SLWH); *Lincoln House Bulletin 1899* and *Lincoln House Report for 1902*, Lincoln House Records, Widener Library, Harvard University, Cambridge; Polly Welts Kaufman, Patricia C. Morris, and Joyce Stevens, *Boston Women's Heritage Trail* (Lexington, Mass.: n.p., 1991), pp. 28, 13; Lilian V. Robinson, *Children's House: A History of the Hawthorne Club* (Boston: Marshall Jones Co., 1937), pp. 1, 7, 116. For Denison House, see SLWH documents: Denison House Records, 1891–1961; Introduction, Denison House Records; "Denison House: The Boston College Settlement," box 6, folder 39; excerpts from Report of College Settlement Assoc., October 1899–September 1900, box 2, folder 6, p. 26; excerpts from minutes of Executive Committee, June 1905, box 2, folder 7; list of Denison House activities and years they were begun, 1892–1907, box 1, folder 3; excerpts from minutes of Executive Committee, September 17, December 12, 1910, box 2, folder 7; *Denison House: The College Settlement in Boston. Annual Report for the Year Ending October 1, 1916*, pp. 10–11. For working women's homes, see Lucile Eaves, *The Food of Working Women in Boston: An Investigation by the Department of Research of the Women's Educational and Industrial Union, Boston, in Cooperation with the State Department of Health* (Boston: Wright and Potter, 1917), pp. 107–8. Annual reports of YWCA, Boston, for 1867, 1868, 1873, 1874, 1883, 1885; brief chronology (to 1931), Boston YWCA Records, SLWH; Frieda Garcia, *Harriet Tubman and the Harriet Tubman House of United South End Settlements in Boston, Massachusetts*, pamphlet. For site 75, see Kenneth L. Mark, *Delayed by Fire: Being the Early History of Simmons College* (Concord, N.H.: Privately published, 1945), p. 36. For site 60, see Household Aid Co., *House Beautiful* 14, no. 4 (September 1903): vii; "Servant Girls with a BA," *The Sunday Post*, both from the Col. Miriam E. Perry Goll Archives, Simmons College, Boston. For site 30d, see *Report of the Women's Educational and Industrial Union, 264 Boylston, Boston, Massachusetts, for the Year Ending May 1, 1906* (Boston: WEIU), pp. 29–34; *Report of the Women's Educational and Industrial Union, 264 Boylston, Boston, Massachusetts, for the Year Ending May*

Appendix A (Continued)

1, 1916; for site 33, see *Report . . . for the Year Ending May 1*, 1917, WEIU Records, SLWH. For sites 30c and 54a, see Gail Lee Dubrow, *Preserving Her Heritage: American Landmarks of Women's History* (Ph.D. diss., University of California, Los Angeles, 1991), pp. 548, 551, 375; for site 51, see Alex McVoy McIntyre, *Beacon Hill: A Walking Tour* (Boston: Little, Brown, 1975), pp. 81–82; Agnes Snyder, *Dauntless Women in Childhood Education, 1856–1931* (Washington, D.C.: Childhood Education International, 1972), p. 41. For the playground movement, see Suzanne M. Spencer-Wood, "Turn of the Century Women's Organizations, Urban Design, and the Origin of the American Playground Movement," *Landscape Journal* 13, no. 2 (Fall 1994): 125–38.

Appendix B

Greater Boston Domestic Reform Sites

No.	Site	Location	Date(s)	Status
14a	Massachusetts Home for Intemperate Women	41 Worcester St.	1875	E
14b		Binney and Smyrna sts.	1888–1901	D
15	New England Home for Intemperate Women	112 Kendall St.	1879	D
24	First nurses training school in the U.S. at New England Hospital for Women and Children[1]	Codman St., Roxbury	1873	E
35a	Simmon's College	Botolph St.	1902	D
35b		300 Fenway	1904–present	E
38a	Sunnyside Day Nursery	35 Blossom St.	1887	D
38b		87 Milk St.	1897	D
38c		165 Charles St.	1901	D
38d		41 Blossom St.	1904	D
38e		320 Dudley St.	1957–present	E
39a	South End (Jamaica Plain) Day Nursery	82 Carver St.	1880	D
39b		962 Parker St.	1956–present	E
40a	Ruggles St. Day Nursery[2] (later became Ruggles St. Neighborhood House)	147 Ruggles St.	1879–1952	D
		155 Ruggles St.	1914–52	D

Appendix B (Continued)

No.	Site	Location	Date(s)	Status
40b		38 St. Alphonsus St.	1952–present	E
66	Roxbury Neighborhood House[3]	Albany St.	1878	D
		858 Albany St.	1914–47	D
		854 Albany St.	1895–1947	D
67a	South Boston Day Nursery[4]	418 W. 4th St., South Boston	1901	E
67b		521 E. 7th St., on south side of street between I and K sts.	1907–present	D
68	The Little House	73 A St., South Boston	1906–47	E
69	Beal's Nurse's Home and Registry, Inc.[5]	20 Charlesgate West	1914–ca. 1920	E

Key: E = extant building, D = destroyed

[1] Founded by the WEA, 1873.

[2] Founded by the WEA, 1879.

[3] Founded in 1878 as a day nursery and kindergarten. The 854 Albany address was a housekeeping flat.

[4] In 1912 the day nursery became South Boston Neighborhood House, which was founded by Olivia B. James in a frame house replaced in 1923 by a brick building where it still operates.

[5] Founded in 1907. No longer listed in Boston Directory after 1921.

Sources: Boston directories for 1860–41, 1949–61; Boston atlases printed by G. W. Bromley, Philadelphia, for 1883, 1884, 1890, 1895, 1898, 1902, 1906, 1910, 1912, 1922, 1928; Insurance map(s) of Boston by D. A. Sanborn or Sanborn Map Co., N.Y., for 1867, 1909, 1914, 1923. For sites 1–50, see Suzanne M. Spencer-Wood, "A Survey of Domestic Reform Movement Sites in Boston and Cambridge, ca. 1865–1905," *Historical Archaeology* 21, no. 2 (1987): 7–36. For settlements, see Robert A. Woods and Albert J. Kennedy, eds., *Handbook of Settlements* (New York: Charities Publications Committee, 1911), pp. 106–35; *The Boston Social Union: A Federation of Twenty-Two Settlements and Other Neighborhood Centres in Greater Boston. Annual Report. November 1913*, SLWH; Eva Whiting White Papers, SLWH, box 2, folder 22; Sister Ann Fox, personal communications with author, about South Boston Neighborhood House, 1992. For working women's homes, see Lucile Eaves, *The Food of Working Women in Boston: An Investigation by the Department of Research of the Women's Educational and Industrial Union, Boston, in Cooperation with the State Department of Health* (Boston: Wright and Potter, 1917), pp. 107–8.

Nature, Society, and Culture
Theoretical Considerations in Historical Archaeology

Stephen A. Mrozowski

The purpose of the 1991 Winterthur Conference and its subsequent report has been to examine the role of historical archaeology in the study of American culture. I will explore a different but no less important issue, the influence of American culture on the development of historical archaeology. All of us working in the historical disciplines are influenced by the world in which we live. Although some degree of objectivity may be possible, it would be a mistake to ignore the role that culture plays in shaping our lives and our work. I pursue this issue to further an interdisciplinary, interpretive agenda for historical

The author would like to thank the following for their help in preparing this article: Lu Ann De Cunzo, Bernie Herman, Susan Randolph, and Patricia Anne Rice for their editorial assistance, patience, and insights; Denise Wall, Shayna Klinger, and Thomas Buckley for their guidance in sorting out the knowers from the known; Nanepashemet, Kathleen Bragdon, Brona Simon, Kevin McBride, and Barbara Luedtke for sharing their knowledge of Native American society and material culture; and all those at Winterthur who made the conference a most interesting and enjoyable time. The author also thanks Fayette S. Scheuch, Gosnold Trust of America, Public Archaeology Laboratory Inc., and University of Massachusetts, Boston, for their generous funding of the Sandy's Point Project; Ron Michael, editor of *Historical Archaeology*, for permission to reprint one of the graphics; and the University of Massachusetts, Boston, Graphics Laboratory, and in particular Fred J. Calef III for preparing the graphics of the corn field from Cape Cod. I would also like to thank Michael Davis, Melody Henkel, and Christina Adinolfi for photo and graphic production. Thanks also go to Anne Lang who hopes she never hears the words *nature* and *culture* again.

archaeology that moves beyond our cultural tendencies to categorize the world into binary opposites. This predilection to see the world in a dichotomous manner is a product of Western thought and a part of American culture. It also is a central tenet of the structuralist paradigm that has been so influential in historical archaeology.[1] Despite this influence, structuralism has limited the interdisciplinary growth of historical archaeology. By accepting the distinction between nature and society, for example, as a methodological tool, if not a cultural reality, emphasis has been placed squarely on the mind as the prime mover in human history. With its emphasis on the search for universal order and broad cultural patterns, structuralism has left little room for contextual factors such as class, gender, the economy, or the environment to play a role in the development of cultural consciousness. Furthermore, by viewing cultural cognition in terms of oppositions, we reinforce the perception that nature and society are unconnected, thereby justifying the transformation of nature into a commodity. This nurtures an attitude that sees undeveloped land as unproductive unless it generates food, metals, or tax revenues to support human society. It also is at work when humans bury hazardous wastes and presume they are being placed out of harm's way.

The cultural perceptions that reinforce the distinction between nature and society are the same as those that have shaped the epistemological underpinnings of structuralism. To provide a constructive critique of structuralism, however, it is important to recognize the dialectical character of the process. In archaeology, for example, the emergence of postprocessual archaeology has been predicated on its rejection of the processual school that held sway for the previous generation. This is normal for most disciplines. There is, however, a risk in constructing one's discourse in this manner. The risk is building a

[1] See James Deetz, *In Small Things Forgotten: The Archaeology of Early American Life* (Garden City, N.Y.: Anchor Press, 1977); James Deetz, "Material Culture and Worldview in Colonial Anglo-America," in Mark P. Leone and Parker B. Potter, Jr., eds., *The Recovery of Meaning: Historical Archaeology in the Eastern United States* (Washington, D.C.: Smithsonian Institution Press, 1988), pp. 219–33; Henry Glassie, *Folk Housing in Middle Virginia* (Knoxville: University of Tennessee Press, 1975). For critique, see Martin Hall, "Small Things and the Mobile Conflicted Fusion of Power, Fear, and Desire," in Anne E. Yentsch and Mary C. Beaudry, eds., *The Art and Mystery of Historical Archaeology: Essays in Honor of James Deetz* (Boca Raton, Fla.: CRC Press, 1992), pp. 373–99.

program of inquiry that is little more than the antithesis of a competing school of thought. An alternative approach is to avoid rigidly defined paths of inquiry and to accept the ambiguity inherent in any kind of intellectual pursuit. In her critique of feminist epistemology, Mary Hawkesworth warns against just such a dilemma by noting that we must accept the tension that comes with any debate concerning the pursuit of knowledge. For those seeking unqualified validation of their position, there is a tendency to close off the dialogue, thereby closing the door to other possibilities. This is one of the problems that structuralism presents.[2]

Structuralism in Historical Archaeology

I think few would argue with the assertion that James Deetz has been one of the most important, if not *the* most influential figure in the development of historical archaeology. This is due in large measure to his innovative use of structural analysis in the study of material culture. The structuralist paradigm employed by Deetz draws heavily on the work of French anthropologist Claude Lévi-Strauss. At the core of Lévi-Strauss's program is a belief that language and culture are fundamentally ordered by the binary structure of the human brain. Just as language is ordered by a deep structure, a grammar, so too is culture ordered by deep structures of meaning. Because of the brain's binary structure, cultural categories are generated as sets of oppositions such as culture/nature, male/female, or pure/impure.[3] In this case culture is to nature as male is to female as pure is to impure. The assumption

---

[2] See Thomas Kuhn, *The Structure of Scientific Revolutions* (Chicago: University of Chicago Press, 1970); Stephen A. Mrozowski, "The Dialectics of Historical Archaeology in a Post-Processual World," in *Historical Archaeology* 27, no. 2 (1993): 106–11; Mary Hawkesworth, "Knowers, Knowing, Known: Feminist Theory and Claims of Truth," *Signs: Journal of Women in Culture and Society* 14, no. 3 (1989): 533–77.

[3] Deetz, *In Small Things Forgotten*, pp. 28–61; Deetz, "Material Culture and World View," pp. 222–24. Lévi-Strauss outlines and develops his structuralist arguments in a series of works, including Claude Lévi-Strauss, *Structural Anthropology* (New York: Doubleday, 1963); Claude Lévi-Strauss, *The Savage Mind* (Chicago: University of Chicago Press, 1966); Claude Lévi-Strauss, *The Elementary Structures of Kinship* (Boston: Beacon Press, 1969); Claude Lévi-Strauss, *The Raw and the Cooked* (New York: Harper and Row, 1969).

is that women are viewed as closer to nature because of their biological role as the producer of offspring.

The goal of a structuralist analysis is to uncloak the deep structures that order myth, kinship, and culture itself. Although the content of myth may change over time, its underlying structure will remain as an unconscious blueprint for mediating social relations. These structural oppositions are not viewed as being independent of culture. They are instead cultural creations that are structured in the unconscious.

Despite its allure there are several questions surrounding structural analysis. Not the least of these concerns is explaining change. If the binary structure of the brain has remained constant, then how do we account for change? It is in reference to this question that structuralism has come under some of its sharpest criticism.[4] At the center of the controversy is the issue of binarism. Can the genesis of culture be traced to the mind and its binary structure? Are oppositions such as good/evil and raw/cooked cultural universals shared by all societies? Or are they the product of structural analysis itself?

In his initial attempts at structural analysis, Lévi-Strauss struggled with the issue of binarism by suggesting that oppositions such as nature and culture be seen primarily as methodological tools:

If this general distinction is relatively easy to establish, a two fold difficulty emerges with it that has to be analyzed. An attempt might be made to establish a biological or social cause for every attitude, and a search made for the mechanism whereby attitudes, which are cultural in origin, can be grafted upon and successfully integrated with forms of behavior which are themselves biological in nature. To deny or underestimate this opposition is to preclude all understanding of social phenomena, but by giving it its full methodological significance there is a danger that the problem of the transition from the biological to the social may become insoluble. Where does nature end and culture begin?

---

[4]For useful critiques, see Mary Douglas, "The Meaning of Myth," in Edmund R. Leach, ed., *The Structural Study of Myth and Totemism* (London: Tavistock, 1967), pp. 49–70; Maurice Bloch and Jean H. Bloch, "Women and the Dialectics of Nature in Eighteenth-Century French Thought," in Carol MacCormack and Marilyn Strathern, eds., *Nature, Culture, and Gender* (New York: Cambridge University Press, 1986), pp. 25–41; Carol P. MacCormack, "Nature, Culture and Gender: A Critique," in MacCormack and Strathern, *Nature, Culture, and Gender*, pp. 1–24; Christopher Tilley, "Claude Lévi-Strauss: Structuralism and Beyond," in Christopher Tilley, ed., *Reading Material Culture* (Oxford: Basil Blackwell, 1990), pp. 3–81.

Several ways can be suggested for answering this dual question, but so far all have proved singularly disappointing.[5]

These early questions faded, however, as Lévi-Strauss moved from seeing structural oppositions as tools to seeing them as a form of underlying logic that structured myths. He answered critics who questioned his decontextualized examination of myths by moving the focus from the conscious to the unconscious:

And, as I have already suggested, it would perhaps be better to go still further and, disregarding the thinking subject completely, proceed as if the thinking process were taking place in the myths, in their reflection upon themselves and their interrelation. For what I am concerned to clarify is not so much what there is *in* myths (without, incidentally, being in man's consciousness) as the systems of axioms and postulates defining the best possible code, capable of conferring a common significance on unconscious formulations which are the work of minds, societies, and civilizations chosen from among the most remote from each other.

It is this objectification of his subject matter that has come under such sharp criticism. This is especially true in light of later works, such as *Tristes Tropiques*, in which Lévi-Strauss bemoans the destruction of the Brazilian rain forest by Western forces. He also celebrates the virtues of the natural world by associating culture with violence toward both the environment and small-scale societies.[6]

Despite these concerns for the plight of the natural world, there is much at the core of Lévi-Strauss's structuralism that reinforces the cultural constructs that justify the agencies of that plight. Underlying this problem is an epistemology that fails to consider the role of the observer in the knowledge being generated. Lévi-Strauss tends to view himself as a detached scientist. The result is "structural anthropology,

---

[5]Claude Lévi-Strauss, *Elementary Structures*, p. 4. Binarism refers to the belief that human thought is structured into opposites. This structure of thought is produced by the neurophysiological structure of the brain's opposite spheres. Although cultural differences result in different views of the world, that world is, nevertheless, always perceived in terms of opposites such as good and evil and nature and culture.

[6]Lévi-Strauss, *Raw and Cooked*, p. 12; Claude Lévi-Strauss, *Tristes Tropiques* (London: Jonathan Cape, 1973), pp. 113–17; see also Christopher Tilley, "Claude Lévi-Strauss," pp. 48–50; Jacques Derrida, *Grammatology* (Baltimore: Johns Hopkins University Press, 1976); Paul Ricoeur, *Hermeneutics and Human Sciences* (Cambridge, Eng.: Cambridge University Press, 1981).

posing as a universal and comparative science" when in fact it is "an ethnocentric ideology rationalizing the Other in its own terms and ignoring itself as a form of reductionist and essentialist Western academic imperialism." The structure of meaning that Lévi-Strauss so adeptly has identified is his.[7]

The issue of reductionism is particularly significant because despite its purported goal of searching for meaning, structuralism decontextualizes myth to the point where cultural meaning is washed out. This is one reason that so much emphasis is placed on the unconscious. By sidestepping consciousness, structuralism removes itself from the complex arena of human interaction that gives rise to culture and cultural change. As elegant and compelling as some structural analyses may appear, they inevitably reduce the complexity of social discourses to a series of binary oppositions.[8]

The brand of structuralism that Deetz has adopted is different in some important respects from that practiced by Lévi-Strauss. Deetz is interested in historical context and does not aspire to be an objective scientist. His common ground with Lévi-Strauss is epistemology. A clear expression of this is Deetz's views concerning the environment, its influence (or lack of influence) in the growth of American culture, and the manner in which historical archaeology should be conducted. Although he acknowledges that "the study of plant and animal remains, of soils, or of past climates" has a place in historical archaeology, Deetz notes that the field's reliance on the natural sciences is less than that of prehistory because "this lessened dependency on the natural sciences is but a reflection of the role played by the natural world in the history of human development. The earlier in time one goes, the more directly and intimately tied to their environment . . . As culture became more complex, our removal from the natural world increased. Since historical archaeology treats only the past few hundred years of our multimillion year history, it follows that this last, brief time would find us at our greatest remove."[9]

---

[7]Tilley, "Claude Lévi-Strauss," p. 57; see also Stanley Diamond, "The Myth of Structuralism," in Ino Rossi, ed., *The Unconscious in Culture: The Structuralism of Claude Lévi-Strauss in Perspective* (New York: E. P. Dutton, 1974), p. 304.

[8]Douglas, "Meaning of Myth," pp. 49–69; K. O. L. Burridge, "Lévi-Strauss and Myth," in Leach, *Structural Study*, pp. 91–115.

[9]Deetz, *In Small Things Forgotten*, p. 22.

It is hard to accept a society like that of seventeenth-century New England, so dependent upon agriculture and imbued with conservative, agrarian values, as being far removed from the environment. Far too much scholarly work by British social and agricultural historians has linked regional cultures in Britain to different agricultural regimes to support such a contention. By adopting a structuralist methodology, Deetz is accepting culture and nature as two analytically separate spheres and arguing the value of one over that of the other. By accepting a structuralist epistemology he is placing a priori limits on what should be accepted as significant knowledge in historical archaeology.[10]

Deetz's observations reflect a structuralism that fails to account for the influence of a wide range of contextual factors in the growth of cultural consciousness. That context comprises many voices that bring different perspectives and different histories to the discourse. Collectively, they contribute to the production and reproduction of cultural consciousness through practice and mediation. History enters the equation as ideology, as the signification of the past to be evoked in the mediation of conflict. From this perspective, culture is not seen as the static product of mental constructs but rather as a set of fluid perceptions and expectations subject to both change and continuity.[11]

The meaning embedded in these perceptions and expectations is profoundly influenced by a spectrum of forces that constitute the cultural historical context in which people live. It is a context with no distinction between nature and society beyond that artificially created by culture. The richness of this context (both its social and its biological components) can be deciphered only through an interdisciplinary agenda. The primary advantage of such an approach is that it recog-

[10] Joan Thirsk, ed., *1640–1750, Regional Farming Systems*, vol. 5 of *The Agrarian History of England and Wales* (Cambridge, Eng.: Cambridge University Press, 1985); Keith Wrightson, *English Society, 1500–1680* (Cambridge, Eng.: Cambridge University Press, 1982).

[11] For a fuller discussion of the diological character of culture and the role of practice in the production and reproduction of cultural consciousness, see James Clifford and G. E. Marcus, *Writing Culture: The Poetics and Politics of Ethnography* (Berkeley: University of California Press, 1986); Pierre Bourdieu, *Outline of a Theory of Practice* (Cambridge, Eng.: Cambridge University Press, 1977). This important point concerning the role of history in ideology is discussed in Henrietta Moore, *Space, Text, and Gender: An Anthropological Study of the Marakwet of Kenya* (Cambridge, Eng.: Cambridge University Press, 1986), pp. 86–88.

nizes the relationship that social and biological forces share in contributing to the formation of cultural identity and class consciousness. It
is not just that pollen analysis or the analysis of parasite ova provide
lines of evidence to construct past landscapes or patterns of disease, it
is that they help us to link past conditions with the reality of class
structures. This information can serve several ends. It can be used to
examine pathologies of social inequality and the biological ramifications of class differences that might be manifest in overcrowding, poor
sanitation, or the presence of disease-carrying rodents or hazardous
substances such as lead. Or, it can reveal changes over time in the
overall conditions where people worked and where they lived. When
combined with more traditional concerns for documentary and material
culture analysis, this fully integrated contextual approach takes full
advantage of historical archaeology's interdisciplinary potential to conduct sophisticated social inquiry into the events and forces that have
shaped the past and continue to shape the present.

To illustrate this point I will present some case studies that suggest
the potential that interdisciplinary research offers. These studies also
demonstrate why it is essential to look at issues such as disease and the
biological ramifications of social inequality. I will begin with a discussion of the Queen Anne Square project that focused on a portion of
what had been the commercial center of Newport, Rhode Island, in
the eighteenth century.

Eighteenth-Century Newport

In Newport the interdisciplinary examination of eighteenth-century
merchant and artisan households delineated landscape differences and
patterns of disease linked to occupational and class distinctions. These
households were located in the heart of the city's commercial district
and separated by only a few hundred feet (fig. 1). The extensive collection of eighteenth-century commercial records housed at the Newport
Historical Society provided the corpus from which a rich context for
our interdisciplinary investigations was constructed. Through a review
of numerous account, day, and receipt books of prominent Newport
merchant John Bannister, it was possible to rediscover important social
and economic links between the household of Mary and William Tate

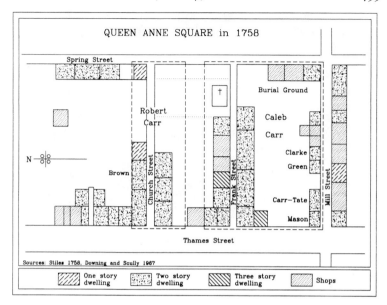

Fig. 1. Queen Anne Square, 1758, showing Brown and Carr-Tate properties. (Society for Historical Archaeology.) The Tates purchased the Carr house.

and that of merchant and militia captain James Brown. William Tate worked as a blacksmith, relying upon Bannister for his coals and bar iron as well as finding in Bannister an outlet for his finished products. The large deposits of cinder and bloom residue in the yard of the Tate household also attests to the use of this area for work-related activities.

Mary Tate appears to have worked as a seamstress. This assumption is based on a combination of documentary and material evidence. She appears often in Bannister's accounts, sometimes receiving cash, but primarily for purchases of numerous yards of cloth and related items such as buttons. In June 1748, for example, the Tate account is debited for 70 yards of linen. In another entry in November of the same year "5 yds Kersey, 7½ yds. Shallon, 4 yds Bays, 5½ yds. Kersey, 1 bag buttons" are noted. These fabrics generally are used to make bed linens and blankets, although clothing and even furniture coverings are other possible uses. It would not have been unusual for Mary Tate

Fig. 2. Fazackerly-ware punch bowl recovered from Tate privy. (Photo, University of Massachusetts, Boston.)

to have been producing clothing for Bannister. Sarah Arnold (another Newport resident) appears in Bannister's receipt book in 1748 as receiving "Irish Linen" and "8¼ yds check" besides cash in return for having made "87 shirts."[12] The large number of pins recovered from the yard and privy as well as a brass thimble and an ornately decorated pair of scissors lend support to the interpretation that Tate worked as a seamstress.

With no children indicated in tax records or the will of William Tate, it appears that the Tates lived alone. There is, however, both material and documentary evidence that suggests that they kept boarders. This evidence consists of an entry in one of Bannister's account books in which Tate's account is credited for two persons' board.[13] The remains of at least sixteen white, salt-glazed plates, a Fazackerly-ware punch bowl (fig. 2), and more than twenty glass tumblers indicate that

[12] John Bannister account book, June 15, November 14, 1748, Newport Historical Society, Newport, R.I.; Linda R. Baumgarten, "The Textile Trade in Boston, 1650–1700," in Ian M. G. Quimby, ed., *Arts of the Anglo-American Community in the Seventeenth Century* (Charlottesville: University Press of Virginia, 1975), pp. 219–73; *The Compact Edition of the Oxford English Dictionary* (Oxford: Oxford University Press, 1979), s.v. "Kersey." John Bannister receipt book, September 17, 1748, Newport Historical Society.

[13] Bannister account book, December 18, 1747, Newport Historical Society.

the Tates possessed the accoutrements to entertain or serve a household that included boarders, apprentices, or possibly slaves. This last observation is based solely on the presence of five sherds of colonoware in the lower depths of the privy.

Bannister's records also indicate that Tate had some commercial dealings with James Brown. In one instance Bannister debits Tate's account for money he paid to Brown. Both the Tate and Brown households were also members of Trinity Church, Newport's Anglican church. Archaeological evidence also indicates that both households possessed goods that would have been classified as contraband by the English government during the eighteenth century. French painted earthenwares, which were prohibited from being imported into the colonies, were recovered from the Tate privy. Bottles from Dutch gin and French brandy (also outlawed) were recovered from the Brown privy.[14] This is not to suggest that there were no material differences between the two households however. Many of the ceramic and glass vessels recovered from the Brown privy were for entertainment purposes. Among the most notable is a large tin-enameled punch bowl (fig. 3). In addition to the punch bowl several examples of stemmed glasses were found in the privy.

The contrast between the delft punch bowl and stemmed glassware in the Brown privy with that of the Fazackerly-ware punch bowl and tumblers in the Tate privy may mark a subtle but no less real class distinction. Taken alone, however, this comparison of material culture seems weak in light of other evidence that points to social and economic commonalities between these two eighteenth-century households. How is such an anomaly to be resolved? The answer is to broaden the analytical scope to include other forms of information.

A combination of archaeological and botanical evidence from the two households indicates that gardening was taking place at the Tate household. This is evident from physical remains of a garden found in

[14]John Bannister ledger book, December 12, 1747, Newport Historical Society; George Mason, *The Annals of Trinity Church* (Newport, R.I.: By the author, 1890). This privately published work details much of the early history of the church. Copies can be found at the Newport Historical Society and at Trinity Church, Newport. Peter R. Schmidt and Stephen A. Mrozowski, "Documentary Insights into the Archaeology of Smuggling," in Mary C. Beaudry, ed., *Documentary Archaeology in the New World* (Cambridge, Eng.: Cambridge University Press, 1988), p. 32–34.

Fig. 3. Tin enameled punch bowl recovered from Brown privy. Probably produced in Bristol between 1730 and 1750. (Photo, University of Massachusetts, Boston.)

the Tate yard and the palynological evidence of corn. Botanical remains of summer squash (*Cucurbita pepo*) and the common herb Agrimony (*Agramonia striata*), also suggest gardening. The Brown privy contained little in the way of garden crops but did contain jimsonweed (*Datura stramonium*) and poison hemlock (*Conium maculatum*). Both species colonized disturbed soils found in many urban areas and were well known in the eighteenth century for their medicinal and narcotic effects.[15]

[15] Botanical analysis involves the study of plant macrofossils, large fruits and seeds of plants that are visible, and plant pollen. The study of plant pollen, called palynology, involves the identification of pollen that is used to reconstruct regional vegetation and, in some instances, more localized plant communities. Although pollen is subject to decay in the soil, its use in historical archaeology is enhanced by better preservation in more recent deposits; see Gerald K. Kelso, "Pollen Analysis in Urban Historical Landscape Research," elsewhere in this volume. Karl J. Reinhard to author, 1990; Stephen A. Mrozowski, "Examining the Urban Environment through the Analysis of Floral Remains," *Newsletter of the Conference on New England Archaeology* 3, no. 2 (1983): 31–50.

Additional differences in the character of the two households comes from landscape information. As noted earlier, the Tate yard contained remains of a garden as well as extensive residue of smithing. The Brown yard, by contrast, appears to have been well maintained, with little evidence of widespread sheet refuse. In an interesting example of the value of pollen analysis, evidence seems to suggest the presence of a structure over the Brown privy. This is based on the low percentages of windblown arboreal pollen. Normally, arboreal pollen, which comes primarily from trees, constitutes the largest percentage of that recovered from the soil. In this instance the lower than normal percentages of arboreal pollen in the Brown privy have been interpreted as being caused by the presence of a structure while the privy was in use.[16] Normal percentages of arboreal pollen were recovered from the Tate privy soils. This suggests that a less substantial structure, or no structure, covered the privy.

These contrasts in sanitary conditions also are reflected in the results of the parasitological analysis that illustrate differences in the level of infection between households.[17] The artisan privy contained thousands of parasite eggs in comparison to a few hundred in the privy of the merchant household. The presence of thousands of *Ascaris lumbricoides* (round worm) eggs in the Tate privy may indicate the presence of children (a possibility apparently discounted by the lack of documentary support unless it represents young apprentices), the presence of pigs, the use of pig feces for fertilizer in the garden, or the use of infected human feces for the same purpose. Parasites also were a part of life in the merchant's household but not to the same degree as that evidenced in the privy of the artisan's household. There is a markedly

---

[16] Karl J. Reinhard, Stephen A. Mrozowski, and Kathleen Orloski, "Privies, Pollen, Parasites, and Seeds: A Biological Nexus in Historical Archaeology," *MASCA Journal* 4 (1986): 31–36.

[17] Parasitological analysis involves the identification and analysis of parasite ova, or eggs. These eggs, which can survive in anaerobic (oxygen-free) environments such as filled-in privies or drains, often are recovered from fecal material. The presence of parasite ova signals the presence of different species within human or animal populations and can be used for microenvironmental analysis. The different species of parasites require very specific environmental conditions in which to complete their reproductive cycle. Part of this cycle includes a period outside the host, the individual person, or animal. During this stage, the eggs require very specific conditions in which to survive. Therefore, their presence suggests that those conditions were present.

lower number of ascaris ova in the Brown privy. Because the eggs are large enough to be visible in the feces (most human parasites were so small that their presence was evidenced only in either intestinal pain or bronchial infection), those with the means could turn to medicines to combat the symptoms. The lower number of ascaris eggs in the Brown privy may reflect such attempts. Another explanation is a lack of sunlight needed to maintain temperatures high enough to allow the parasite to move through its reproductive cycle. The presence of a structure over the privy or heavy shade trees is a possible explanation suggested by the pollen analysis.

The discovery of hookworm (*Necator americanus*) ova in the Brown privy provides one further indication of possible differences between the two households. This parasite, indigenous to West Africa, was transported to the New World with slaves. Therefore its presence in the Brown privy may point to the presence of slaves.[18]

The combined results of the various analyses suggest that in eighteenth-century Newport, artisans such as the Tates, who used their yards for work space, to keep livestock, and to cultivate gardens may have created environments that bred disease. Although merchants such as James Brown may not have used their yard space as intensively, they too faced the problems posed by parasites. The difference would have been one of degree as evidenced by the thousands of parasite eggs in the Tate privy as compared with hundreds in the Brown feature. Together with the material culture recovered from the features associated with the two households and what can be gleaned from documentary sources, a picture can be constructed that speaks to subtle, but clear differences. Brown and his family may have lived close to the Tates. He may have been involved in commercial relations with the Tates, and he and his family even may have sat in the same church with the Tates. Yet as the combined evidence attests, the two households lived different lives. What the biological dimension adds is the knowledge that these differences were felt every day in the pits of the stomachs and in the lungs of the likes of William Tate, who died in 1758, and Mary Tate, who lived until 1780. It is difficult to say whether these differences were more meaningful than the distinctions evident from a comparison of material culture. In an ironic twist, the democratic

[18] Karl J. Reinhard, "Parasitology in Archaeology," *American Antiquity* 57, no. 2 (1992): 241.

character of disease may have been a leveling force in eighteenth-century society, a condition lessened only by spirits or drugs. It may well be that the material differences, the more elaborate or finer accoutrements of entertaining, were more culturally charged because of their ability to mask a reality in which the social and biological arenas were one.

In eighteenth-century Newport, class differences were manifest in a variety of ways. Whether it was measured in the power of a single merchant to control access to both goods and markets or in the ability to afford stemmed glassware, class distinctions were a part of everyday life. Disease also was a part of everyday life. Its noteworthiness as a yardstick of social inequality is no less significant. In the nineteenth century the growth of mechanized industry and corporate paternalism would put a new face on class divisions. The emergence of a "middle class" only helped to accentuate social distinctions that once again defied the barriers of society and nature.

Nineteenth-Century Lowell

Even in the first planned industrial city in the United States, mill workers were not removed from the natural world. Although the urban landscape of Lowell, Massachusetts, was the material expression of ideas and aspirations, it was constructed of brick and soil. In this instance the power of an interdisciplinary approach is perhaps best illustrated through a comparison of the life histories of the Boott Cotton Mill boardinghouses and the company-owned agents' house. Through a combination of pollen, opal phytolith, plant macrofossil, soils and parasitological analysis, a picture emerges of changes over time that mark a shift in company policy concerning its commitment to the welfare of its workers. This combined evidence indicates that company promises to maintain the boardinghouses were honored for the first forty years of operation. There is little to suggest that garbage was being disposed of in the yards, for example. Evidence suggests that some small fruit trees, such as elderberry bushes, were present in a grassy yard with little evidence of weeds.[19]

---

[19]The Lowell Archaeological Survey was a 5-year collaborative effort between the Division of Cultural Resources of the North Atlantic Regional Office of the National Park Service and the Center for Archaeological Studies at Boston University. Mary C.

During this time, however, some boardinghouse keepers made cost-cutting decisions that seem to have contributed to a deterioration of sanitary conditions. By purchasing many items, including meats, in large quantities, keepers found that they needed to store the foodstuffs in areas such as the boardinghouse cellars. The meats and produce attracted rats. The presence of these rodents is evidenced by skeletal remains, rodent-gnawed bone, and parasite ova. The hazard to health posed by these rodents was probably less than that perceived by a boardinghouse population raised during a time in history when the association between rats and disease was a powerful image of the ills of urban life.[20]

Company efforts to maintain the boardinghouses also may have contributed to unsanitary conditions. Dangerously high lead levels were detected when soils collected from the boardinghouse yards were analyzed. The source of this lead is most likely chipped paint or a result

---

Beaudry and I served as co-directors of the project. Opal phytoliths are produced by many plants. They are microscopic rocks that form as hydrated silicon dioxide, commonly found in ground water, that precipitates out into the intercellular spaces along cell walls. The fossil-like casts survive well in soils and are useful in the identification of plant communities or individual species. They are especially useful in the identification of grasses that produce an abundance of phytoliths. See Irwin Rovner, "Plant Opal Phytolith Analysis: Major Advances in Archaeobotanical Research," in Michael Schiffer, ed., *Advances in Archaeological Method and Theory, Volume 6* (New York: Academic Press, 1983), p. 226. Mark Robinson and Vanessa Straker, "Silica Skeletons of Macroscopic Plant Remains from Ash," in Jane Renfrew, ed., *New Light on Early Farming* (Edinburgh: Edinburgh University Press, 1991), pp. 3–13. Soil analysis can reveal the presence of various elements and metals. In some cases these metals can signal the presence of hazardous materials in the environment. A case in point is lead, which can cause lead poisoning. Stephen A. Mrozowski and Gerald K. Kelso, "Palynology and Archaeobotany of the Proposed Lowell Boarding House Park Site," in Mary C. Beaudry and Stephen A. Mrozowski, eds., *Interdisciplinary Investigations of the Boott Cotton Mills, Lowell, Massachusetts, Vol. 1: Life at the Boardinghouses, A Preliminary Report* (Boston: North Atlantic Regional Office, National Park Service, 1987): 134–52. Gerald K. Kelso, William Fisher, Stephen A. Mrozowski, and Karl J. Reinhard, "Contextual Archaeology at the Boott Mill Boarding House," in Mary C. Beaudry and Stephen A. Mrozowski, eds., *Interdisciplinary Investigations of the Boott Cotton Mills, Lowell, Massachusetts, Vol. 3: The Boarding House System as a Way of Life* (Boston: North Atlantic Regional Office, National Park Service, 1989): 231–78.

[20] Kelso et al., "Contextual Archaeology," pp. 271–72; Stephen A. Mrozowski, Edward L. Bell, Mary C. Beaudry, David B. Landon, and Gerald K. Kelso, "Living on the Boott: Health and Well Being in a Boardinghouse Population," *World Archaeology* 21, no. 2 (1989): 298–319; Howard Zinner, *Rats, Lice, and History* (New York: Bantam Books, 1967).

of scraping and repainting episodes. The lead levels found in the board-inghouse soils are high enough by modern standards to be linked to learning disabilities among children.[21]

This same interdisciplinary analysis was successful in identifying a trend toward increasingly less sanitary conditions in the boardinghouse yards. This trend coincides with company decisions in the 1870s to divest themselves of their responsibility to their workers by selling the boardinghouses. Profits were beginning to drop and the company shifted to the use of immigrant labor. The selling of the boardinghouses in the late nineteenth century has left a clear signature in the archaeo-logical record in the form of refuse disposal in the yards and the coloni-zation of the area by weeds.

One can only speculate on the effects that a combination of preju-dice and deteriorating living conditions may have had on the self-esteem of the immigrant families who continued to live in the boarding-houses. They would not have known that lead in the soils posed a health hazard to their children or themselves. Still they may have associated health problems caused by lead with other factors such as the presence of rats or increasingly unsanitary conditions.

During this same period company officials moved forward with plans to update factory machinery, a step they had debated for some time. Although the Boott Mill remained profitable, other companies were investing in new technologies that furnished the means to produce a much wider of assortment of textiles. These changes led some in the company's hierarchy to call for increased investment while more conservative voices argued against the move because it would mean decreased profits. With the decision made, steps also were taken to upgrade the company's agents' residence. A combination of documen-tary, architectural, and archaeological evidence indicates that improve-ments in domestic technology included running water and gas lighting. These were all part of the company's stated goals to provide a dwelling for its operations manager that befit his status in society.[22]

---

[21] Kelso et al., "Contextual Archaeology," pp. 266–72; Mrozowski et al., "Living on the Boott," p. 311.

[22] Laurence Gross, *The Course of Industrial Decline: The Boott Cotton Mills of Lowell, Massachusetts, 1835–1955* (Baltimore: Johns Hopkins University Press, 1992); Mary C. Beaudry and Stephen A. Mrozowski, "Summary and Conclusions," in Mary C. Beaudry and Stephen A. Mrozowski, eds., *Interdisciplinary Investigations of the Boott*

A public expression of this policy was the use of ornamental space to surround the front of the agents' house. The house was elevated above street level by using loam in the front and side yards of the dwelling. This difference was symbolic but far from trivial in the minds of Lowell's social architects. It was done expressly to differentiate worker from manager by elevating the latter to reflect his higher position in the social hierarchy.

The sanitary conditions of the agents' house can only be inferred from indirect evidence. No evidence of rats was recovered, and soil analysis found the lead levels safe even by modern standards. No privies were found on the property, and none are indicated on maps or plans, yet they may have been present in ancillary structures such as the stable. Within a generation of the house's construction in 1845, however, there is documentary evidence that indoor plumbing was installed in the agents' house.

Although it appears that members of the agent's household and mill workers shared a similar diet, differences were apparent in the manner of eating. The plain, white ironstone plates and cups that were common in boardinghouse assemblages stand in contrast to the large, matched sets of various colored, transfer-printed whitewares recovered from the agents' house yard deposits. Yet this difference may say as much about class consciousness as it does about buying power. The plain whitewares of the boardinghouse tables may have met the expectations of the mill workers but not the agent and his family. Like the dwelling in which they lived and the ornamental space that was an extension of its facade, the finer wares that graced their table were an expression of their middle-class cultural values.

The middle class were a highly influential sector of nineteenth-century society, but they were not the only voice. Mill workers, boardinghouse keepers, mill company agents, and mill owners all contributed to the cultural discourse that enlivened nineteenth-century New England. Each group saw the world differently depending upon their class, their gender, or their ethnicity. The conditions in which they lived differed as well. Some experienced lives shaped by the structures of inequality while others saw these inequalities as part of the natural

Cotton Mills, Lowell, Massachusetts, Vol. 2, The Kirk Street Agents' House (Boston: North Atlantic Regional Office, National Park Service, 1987), pp. 143–51.

order of things. For the latter, a world of order expressed in manicured landscapes and formal table settings was a world in which nature was controlled by culture. Nature was, in effect, reinvented as part of culture, assuring it's proper place in the order of things. Social hierarchy was merely the product of natural law.[23]

Formal landscapes and fine tablewares were not new to the nineteenth century. They were present in the urban centers of eighteenth-century British colonial America as well and can be linked to a deeper historical movement. Although the ultimate source, or sources, of the attitudes and cultural values that are a part of this movement remain unclear, it seems that concerns for order and formality are linked in a discursive manner to a belief in the division of society and nature.[24]

The Origins of Nature in Culture

What are the origins of these attitudes concerning order in the universe and the character of nature? Can they be traced to Rousseau as Lévi-Strauss suggests, to the idea that the savage side of humankind, its natural side, needs to be subdued by the more advanced, cultured side of human consciousness so that humankind survives? Keith Thomas is one scholar who has attempted to answer this question for English society. He provides an exhaustive study of the subject in *Man in the Natural World*. In this work Thomas attempts to reconcile the English love of the countryside and their antiurbanism with the fact that Britain has been the most urbanized nation for most of the last two centuries. Thomas argues that a shift in perceptions evolved in English culture between 1500 and 1800, accompanying the rise of urbanism and industrialization. The love of gardens, pets, and the trappings of status afforded the rural gentry were all part of a cause and effect relationship in which the ever-growing domination of nature fostered a new appreci-

[23] This idea is more fully developed in Roy Wagner, *The Invention of Culture* (Englewood Cliffs, N.J.: Prentice Hall, 1975).

[24] Stephen Mrozowski, "For Gentlemen of Capacity and Leisure: The Archaeology of Colonial Newspapers," in Mary C. Beaudry, ed., *Documentary Archaeology in the New World* (Cambridge, Eng.: Cambridge University Press, 1988), pp. 184–91; Stephen Mrozowski, "Landscapes of Inequality," in Randall H. McGuire and Robert R. Paynter, eds., *The Archaeology of Inequality* (Oxford: Basil Blackwell, 1991), pp. 79–101.

ation for rural values: "In 1500 . . . Man stood to animal as did heaven to earth, soul to body, culture to nature."[25] The perceived distance between nature and culture expanded as urbanism and industrialization came to dominate portions of the English landscape, leading some to develop an emotional attachment to nature.

The crux of Thomas's argument is that the transformation of nature that accompanied the industrialization of Britain led to a new appreciation for what was being lost. This feeling was most widely shared among the rural gentry, a group actively involved in the growing commercialization of agriculture during the late sixteenth century. Although this expansion was connected to the growth of towns and the stirring of industrial development, the full weight of the latter would not be felt for almost two centuries. Therefore, Thomas suggests that one could expect the concern for nature to intensify among those, like the rural gentry, who were less involved in the urban industries and the progress this typified.

In his lengthy analysis of Thomas's work, Alan Macfarlane argues that the English celebration of nature is an element of the culture of capitalism: "It would seem that the very early development of money relations, markets and capitalistic relations of production in England not only helped to provide the wealth and security which was a necessary precondition for the disinterested appreciation of nature, but also those curious ambivalences that make capitalist societies simultaneously the most exploitative and the most protective towards nature."[26]

Macfarlane's portrait is much less sympathetic toward capitalism than that painted by Thomas. By focusing on the dynamics of culture, Macfarlane stresses its role in the commodification of nature, a cornerstone of capitalist ideology. Equally intriguing is his suggestion that the culture of capitalism in Britain can be traced to Anglo-Saxon society, an argument that complements that made by Richard Hodges concerning the origins of the world economy discussed by the likes of Fernand Braudel and Immanuel Wallerstein. If, as Hodges suggests, its origins can be traced to a Roman world dominated by cultural values born of

[25] Keith Thomas, *Man and the Natural World* (London: Allen Lane, 1983), p. 70.
[26] Alan Macfarlane, *The Culture of Capitalism* (Oxford: Basil Blackwell, 1987), p. 94.

the *civitas*, then the ultimate genesis of the distinction between nature and society may be linked to the evolution of urban society on a global scale.[27]

The arguments outlined by both Thomas and MacFarlane indicate that nature was recast as a by-product of industrialization, the emergence of capitalism, and possibly the evolution of urban society. Once nature was brought under control, it was reinvented as a part of culture. With nature conveniently controlled and reproduced in formal gardens and managed estates, capitalism was unleashed to consume what remained, and this included the "wild savages" of the New World.

Nature and Culture in the New World

Many of the Europeans who migrated to the New World probably shared cultural values that saw Native Americans as the products of nature and less than human. Men such as John Smith left testimony of his attitudes and the context in which they were cultivated: "The Warres in Europe, Asia and Africa taught me how to subdue the wild savages in Virginia and New England."[28] This statement reveals not only Smith, but also the world in which he lived. The colonial experience had introduced many Europeans to new lands and new people. All were thirsting for cultivation. The religious doctrine of the day provided all the justification necessary to subjugate the land and the people of the New World. Native Americans were viewed as children of nature in need of enlightenment but also dangerous. Their subjugation would be their salvation, an important victory for light over darkness, good over evil, culture over nature.

This dichotomous view of the world was a major force in shaping

---

[27] Richard Hodges, "Anglo-Saxon England and the Origins of the Modern World Economy," in Della Hooke, ed., *Anglo-Saxon Settlements* (Oxford: Basil Blackwell, 1988), pp. 211–304; Fernand Braudel, *The Perspective of the World: Civilization and Capitalism, Fifteenth–Eighteenth Century*, Vol. 3 (New York: Harper and Row, 1984); Immanuel Wallerstein, *The Modern World System I* (New York: Academic Press, 1974); Immanuel Wallerstein, *The Modern World System II: Mercantilism and the Consolidation of the European World Economy, 1600–1750* (New York: Academic Press, 1981).

[28] Quoted in Neil Salisbury, *Manitou and Providence: Indians, Europeans, and the Making of New England, 1500–1643* (Oxford: Oxford University Press, 1982), p. 99.

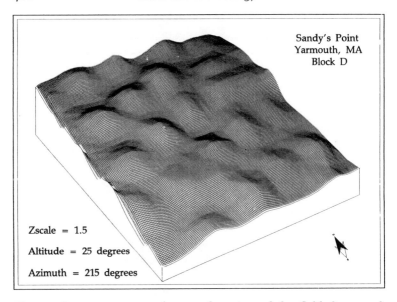

Fig. 4. Computer-generated map of portion of the field discovered during the 1991 season, Cape Cod, Mass. (University of Massachusetts, Boston, Graphics Laboratory.)

European cultural attitudes concerning Native American society. Embodied in structuralism, it may be equally as biased and inappropriate for evaluating Native American culture and its material expression. Native American landscapes are no less laden with meaning than those constructed by Europeans. They are, however, less formal in a European sense and less linear. Their meaning comes from a different perspective that cannot necessarily be decoded through a structuralist approach.

One illustration of this difference is manifest in the late prehistoric/early historic field remains that were recently discovered on Cape Cod, Massachusetts (fig. 4). The field is associated with a Native American settlement that appears to have been briefly occupied several times during the late sixteenth and early seventeenth centuries. It may have been last occupied just before King Philip's War in 1675–76. Besides being the only example of a Native American field to be uncovered archaeologically in the northeastern United States, it provides some insight into the cultural concerns that shaped its construction.[29]

To begin with, there is no evidence of fencing around the field. There also is little formality evident in its spatial configuration. There does not appear to be a rigidly defined division between the field and occupation areas. The field is oriented northeast/southwest in the direction of Cautantowwit's House, the great realm to which all spirits would travel. The sacredness of the southwest also is evident in the positioning of burials in several seventeenth- and eighteenth-century Native American cemeteries in southern New England. All these cemeteries date to the period when Native American beliefs were being shaken by the onslaught of English society. There is, however, compelling archaeological evidence of cultural persistence from the late prehistoric period to the beginnings of the eighteenth century. A dramatic example of this comes from several Christian Indian cemeteries that recently have been discovered in Massachusetts. In her analysis of the seventeenth- and early eighteenth-century Ponkapoag cemetery, Brona G. Simon, Massachusetts state archaeologist, notes that despite the presence of coffins (a distinctly European practice), burials were still oriented to the southwest and grave goods were present. This appears as irrefutable proof that Native American society maintained a strong level of cultural coherence.[30]

The analysis of the material culture from the Ponkapoag cemetery indicates that it was still in use during the second decade of the eighteenth century. This suggests that cultural persistence continued despite decades of forced acculturation by the English. The material culture that was recovered from the graves present an interesting combination

---

[29] Stephen A. Mrozowski, "The Discovery of a Native American Cornfield on Cape Cod," in *The Archaeology of Eastern North America* 22 (1994): 47–62.

[30] William Simmons, *Cautantowwit's House: An Indian Burial Ground on the Island of Conanicut in Narragansett Bay* (Providence: Brown University Press, 1970); Paul Robinson, Marc A. Kelly, and Patricia E. Rubertone, "Preliminary Biocultural Interpretations from a Seventeenth-Century Narragansett Indian Cemetery in Rhode Island," in William Fitzhugh, ed., *Cultures in Contact: The European Impact on Native Cultural Institutions in Eastern North America, A.D. 1000–1800* (Washington, D.C.: Smithsonian Institution Press, 1985), pp. 107–29; John Tuma, "Contact Period Burials in Southeast New England" (Master's thesis, University of Massachusetts, Boston, 1985); Brona G. Simon, "Native American Culture Change and Persistence in Contact Period New England: Analysis of Mortuary Data from a Praying Indian Burial Ground in Massachusetts" (Paper presented at the 55th annual meeting of the Society for American Archaeology, Las Vegas, Nev., 1990).

of European and Native American goods. One grave contained a metal pot that appears to have held the remains of a snake. Snakes are mentioned in Native American folklore attributed to the Gay Head group of Martha's Vineyard.[31] Although the tales date to the early twentieth century, the pot suggests that snakes had a place in the cosmology of the local Native American groups during the seventeenth and eighteenth centuries as well.

The presence of the snake within the European pot in a grave dating to the late seventeenth or early eighteenth century is intriguing. It not only illustrates the persistence of Native American cultural practices but also reflects a spirituality centered on a world in which nature and society were one. Unlike the monotheism of Western society in which male figures in human form dominate the cosmos, Native Americans in New England incorporated both human and animal figures into their beliefs. This distinction reveals a fundamental difference in the way nature was perceived. The fact that these contrasts continued into the eighteenth century suggests that Native American beliefs did indeed survive.

This example is one of several recent studies that point to the adaptive character of Native American society.[32] Whether it was in the persistence of language or burial practices, Native American society did not passively accept cultural domination. Even in the adoption of European technology, new classes of material culture were given meaning within traditional Native American culture.

This resiliency on the part of Native American society is an example of the dialogical character of cultural dynamics. Native Americans did not accept Western culture entirely; they negotiated a path of their own. This process of mediation continues today as evidenced by the

[31] The Ponkapoag Cemetery Project was a collaborative effort between the office of the State Archaeologist of the Massachusetts Historical Commission and the Department of Anthropology at the University of Massachusetts, Boston. William Simmons, *Spirit of the New England Tribes: Indian History and Folklore, 1620–1984* (Hanover, N.H.: University Press of New England, 1986), p. 284.

[32] See Kathleen Bragdon, " 'Another Tongue Brought In': An Ethnohistorical Study of Native Writings in Massachusetts" (Ph.D. diss., Brown University, 1981); Kathleen Bragdon, "The Material Culture of the Christian Indians of New England, 1650–1775," in Beaudry, *Documentary Archaeology in the New World*, pp. 126–31; Constance Crosby, "From Myth to History; or Why King Philip's Ghost Walks Abroad," in Leone and Potter, *Recovery of Meaning*, pp. 183–209; Simmons, *Spirit of the New England Tribes*.

recent resurgence in Native American political and economic power. The agricultural landscapes and mortuary practices of the past now reveal a culture that was markedly different from that of the English who sought to alter the destiny of Native American society. Less formal and linear in design, they reflect the meaning embedded in the cultural consciousness of the Native Americans who produced them.[33]

I believe this lack of formality and linearity is a subtle but important difference that distinguishes Native American landscapes from many of those constructed by Europeans. Native American culture appears to have seen no boundary between nature and their society, and this is reflected in the lack of rigid boundaries or formal design in their landscapes. Their agricultural and mortuary landscapes were textured into nature not set apart from it.

Conclusion

The different permutations of the nineteenth-century landscape discussed in other essays in this volume speak to a process of transformation that was distinctly European in character. Nevertheless, these are landscapes that stand at the nexus of social and ecological forces. Although ordered by human hands, ecological processes continued. The planned urban landscape of Lowell, the standardization and mass production of material goods, and the crafted "white" landscapes of New England village communities, all evoke a world in which nature (both water power and slave power) was being reordered as part of culture. Formal gardens, place settings, ornamental yards, and architecture served to reinforce the celebration of a cultured world in which nature was controlled. Having reordered society to accommodate Native Americans and African slaves as part of nature, New World society took on some of the trappings of Europe; a society in which many viewed social inequality as the result of natural law.

These are the material expressions of the same society that gave rise to ethnocentric programs of inquiry such as structuralism. Historical archaeology has benefited from structuralism's focus on meaning,

---

[33] I thank Brona G. Simon who suggested the use of the term *linear* as opposed to *symmetry* for describing Native American and European landscapes.

but its epistemology has proved limiting. Meaning is not universal; it is the product of historical processes that are complex in nature and that change in response to a wide variety of contextual factors. For historical archaeologists to address this complexity, they require an approach that places no boundaries between the social and biological realms. To do so is to cut the discipline off from a rich perspective that offers a path beyond the suffocating epistemology of structuralism.

Historical archaeology has an important role to play in the study of American culture. That role should be predicated on an understanding of the influence our culture has on the way we view the world and the manner in which we conduct our research. It should not, however, result in a paralysis of hyperrelativisim. If we are to have any real impact on our own society and its future cultural development, the image of the past we construct should be as rich as life itself. American society is a mosaic of cultures that reflect different histories. In the same manner that historical archaeology cannot afford to limit itself to one perspective, neither can American society curtail the dialogue between cultural groups. There is too much to learn from the dialogue. The same is true of historical archaeology. Its practitioners should strive to incorporate different approaches that can help to broaden our view of the past rather than limit it. [34]

The tendencies in Western culture to define the nature of inquiry rigidly are the same tendencies that reduce the world's complexity to binary opposites. This view of the world results in its division rather than an understanding of its binding forces. To elevate the importance of culture and its influence above that of nature is to succumb to the same conceit that has led to an American history without women, without Africans, without Asians, and without class conflict. To assume that the order we see in the universe, real or imagined, can be extended to all people and all societies is to deny the variable character of historical process. Our task is to rediscover the past and interpret its meaning in light of a present that it continues to shape.

---

[34] This includes building on the contributions that both Deetz and Glassie have made to historical archaeology. They are to be applauded for their search for meaning in material culture. Our goal should be to construct a historical archaeology that incorporates this concern for meaning into an emically sensitive interpretive approach that embraces the kind of flexible epistemology required to foster interdisciplinary collaboration. See Mrozowski, "Dialectics"; Hall, "Small Things."

Reinventing Historical Archaeology

Mary C. Beaudry

In seeking a way to frame a discussion of changes in the field of historical archaeology over the past two decades, I have chosen to paraphrase
the title of a book first published in 1969—*Reinventing Anthropology*,
edited by Dell Hymes. My purpose is to make the point that historical
archaeologists influenced by critical anthropology have been rethinking
and reinventing their field for some time now, rejecting the notion that
archaeology, especially historical archaeology, falls within the realm
of natural sciences. Claiming status for historical archaeology as an
interpretive, human science is a process that began before proponents
of the "New Archaeology" developed by prehistorians in the 1960s
inspired historical archaeologists to turn to "archaeological science"—
characterized by positivism and pattern recognition—throughout the
1970s and early 1980s. It was a quiet process whose practitioners were
in the minority, but it was under way long before anyone began to
hear the perhaps not-so-siren calls from the radical left wing of our
discipline ("critical archaeologists") from their vantage on the shores of
hyperrelativism and political correctness.[1]

---

[1] Dell Hymes, ed., *Reinventing Anthropology* (2d ed.; New York: Pantheon Books,
1972). The essays in the Hymes reader, first published in 1969, heralded the advent of
radical critique in anthropology; the authors' concerns about the uses of anthropology
and the responsibility of the ethnographer to his or her subject (the "Other"), issues of
power and domination, and the need for reflexivity began to penetrate archaeological
discourse in one form or another by the early 1980s. Examples include Joan M. Gero,
David M. Lacy, and Michael L. Blakey, eds., "The Sociopolitics of Archaeology,"
Department of Anthropology Research Report No. 23 (Amherst: University of Massachu-

As a result, there are in historical archaeology alternatives that offer safe passage between the Scylla of Southian pattern recognition and the Charybdis of critical theory at its most extreme. All along there has been a counter-paradigm to the cultural materialist/cultural ecological approach that characterizes much of historical archaeology; its practitioners have not sought to dominate the theoretical scene. It is epitomized by James Deetz's structuralist analyses and by the contextual, interpretive work of a number of others, some of whom trained with Deetz. In the 1970s some United States historical archaeologists were content to let the New Archaeology bandwagon roll on without them; they began working in an experimental, interpretive mode and drew from areas of anthropology and other fields that stress context and meaning and the communicative aspects of culture. The penetration of such concepts into the wider realm of prehistoric archaeology is exemplified by "contextual" or "postprocessual" archaeology as developed in England by Ian Hodder, and interest in ideology has become even greater with the growing acceptance of a wider range of alternative theoretical approaches. [2]

---

setts, 1983); Alison Wylie, "Putting Shakertown Back Together: Critical Theory in Archaeology," *Journal of Anthropological Archaeology* 4 (1985): 133–47; Valerie Pinsky and Alison Wylie, eds., *Critical Traditions in Contemporary Archaeology: Essays in the Philosophy, History, and Socio-Politics of Archaeology* (Cambridge, Eng.: Cambridge University Press, 1990); Mark P. Leone, Parker B. Potter, Jr., and Paul A. Shackel, "Toward a Critical Archaeology," *Current Anthropology* 28, no. 3 (1987): 283–302. Stanley South remains the most influential proponent of the "processualist" approach in historical archaeology, set forth in Stanley South, *Method and Theory in Historical Archaeology* (New York: Academic Press, 1977). Grounded in positivist epistemology and cultural materialism (a focus on the material basis of human existence: technology, subsistence, economy, ecology), the processualist approach stresses use of the scientific method (especially hypothesis testing) for statistical delineation of broad-based cross-cultural regularities (pattern recognition) and the search for universal laws of human behavior. For a discussion of how the postmodern critique of positivism has been interpreted by some as justification for an "extreme relativism" and how, in a sort of "philosophical nihilism," some propose to use archaeological data as propaganda to promote political or social causes, see Bruce G. Trigger, A *History of Archaeological Thought* (Cambridge, Eng.: Cambridge University Press, 1989), pp. 379–82. Some have taken this further and advise that the archaeologist should suppress data so that it cannot be used by others in ways not intended or approved by the investigator.

[2] James Deetz, *In Small Things Forgotten: The Archaeology of Everyday Life in Early America* (Garden City, N.Y.: Doubleday, Anchor Books, 1977); Henry Glassie, *Folk Housing in Middle Virginia: A Structural Study of Historic Artifacts* (Knoxville: University of Tennessee Press, 1976). See also the essays by Deetz, Glassie, and Mark Leone in Leland Ferguson, ed., *Historical Archaeology and the Importance of Material Things*

This collection of essays based on papers presented at the 1991 Winterthur Conference offers examples of several recent trends in our field, not the least of which is the turn away from the positivist, empiricist notion of archaeological data as fundamental and perhaps the sole "reliable" primary source for our inquiry. The essays in this volume share a concern for constructing context, and most if not all find that while our "primary" archaeological data may generate research questions, such questions likely will never occur to us unless we have a clear understanding of cultural and historical as well as archaeological context. That context must be constructed from a truly interdisciplinary merging of diverse intellectual and analytical frameworks is increasingly clear, and most historical archaeologists no longer maintain the self-

---

(Tucson: Society for Historical Archaeology, 1977). Anne E. Yentsch, "Expressions of Cultural Diversity and Social Reality in Seventeenth-Century New England" (Ph.D. diss., Brown University, 1980), combines demographic and symbolic analysis in a case study in comparative historical ethnography. Mary C. Beaudry, " 'Or What Else You Please to Call It': Folk Semantic Domains in Early Virginia Probate Inventories" (Ph.D. diss., Brown University, 1980), employs ethnomethodology in an analysis of terms for vessels and livestock. Ian Hodder, "Postprocessualism," in *Advances in Archaeological Method and Theory*, vol. 8, ed. Michael B. Schiffer (Orlando, Fla.: Academic Press, 1985), pp. 1–26. Contextualism is discussed in Ian Hodder, *Reading the Past: Current Approaches to Theory in Archaeology* (2d ed.; Cambridge, Eng.: Cambridge University Press, 1991), pp. 121–55. Its application is demonstrated through case studies in Ian Hodder, ed., *The Archaeology of Contextual Meanings* (Cambridge, Eng.: Cambridge University Press, 1988). Hodder for the most part rejects anthropological approaches and claims archaeology's affinity with history, and, given his background, this is understandable. He may be throwing the baby out with the bathwater, however, by rejecting all of anthropology with what the New Archaeologists touted as anthropological science— cultural materialism. Much recent work in historical archaeology draws on variants of Marxism; see Mark P. Leone and Parker B. Potter, Jr., eds., *The Recovery of Meaning: Historical Archaeology in the Eastern United States* (Washington, D.C.: Smithsonian Institution Press, 1989). Structuralism was developed by French cultural anthropologist Claude Lévi-Strauss, who was influenced by the principles of structural linguistics to conceive of culture as a mental phenomenon that was universally constructed on the basis of paired oppositions (nature versus culture, good versus evil). Structuralists subscribe to the notion that the basic "structure" of the human mind is the same at all times and in all places (that there is such a thing as a "universal human psyche") and that the goal of cultural analysis is to strip away the idiosyncrasies of local cultural expressions to reveal this underlying structure. Like cultural materialism, structuralism focuses on regularities and universals; both perspectives perceive of culture as a sort of mechanism that imposes and codifies beliefs and behavior over which members of a given culture have little or no influence or control. See Stephen A. Mrozowski's critique of the structuralist approach in historical archaeology, "Nature, Society, and Culture: Theoretical Considerations in Historical Archaeology," elsewhere in this volume.

absorption of archaeological positivism, which justified its isolation with an insistence that archaeology turn its back on the humanities, reject much of social science, and emulate the natural sciences.[3]

To the contrary. More and more historical archaeologists have come to acknowledge that, ideally, historical archaeology combines many elements of the human sciences in an anthropologically informed dialogue with the past.[4] The impact of a new empiricism and the interpenetration of anthropology, history, literary theory, cultural geography, material culture studies, and other fields, combined with the influences of radical theoretical perspectives (such as feminism and Marxism), provide the impetus for a reinvention of historical archaeology as a creative discipline whose aim is the holistic study and interpretation of cultures with archival and oral histories.

Increasingly, historical archaeologists are combining sophisticated ethnographic analysis of documentary and oral historical data with their anthropologically sensitive excavation and material culture research to produce highly contextualized and nuanced studies of historical sites, neighborhoods, and communities.[5] Embracing documents and devel-

[3] For a discussion of American archaeologists' continuing resistance to the use of nonarchaeological data, see Bruce G. Trigger, "History and Contemporary American Archaeology: A Critical Analysis," in C. C. Lamberg-Karlofsky, ed., *Archaeological Thought in America* (Cambridge, Eng.: Cambridge University Press, 1989), pp. 30–31. Margaret W. Conkey, "The Structural Analysis of Paleolithic Art," in Trigger, *History of Archaeological Thought*, p. 140. Conkey elaborates on the ways in which the "New Archaeology" restricted its purview by grounding its claims for legitimacy in anthropology but ignoring all but a small part of the field of anthropology. Note Binford's restatements of his position in Lewis R. Binford, "The 'New Archaeology,' Then and Now," in Trigger, *History of Archaeological Thought*, pp. 50–62; Lewis R. Binford, "Data, Relativism, and Archaeological Science," *Man*, n.s., no. 3 (September 1987): 391–404. For a cogent discussion of Binford's position, see Alison Wylie, "Gender Theory and the Archaeological Record: Why Is There No Archaeology of Gender?" in Joan M. Gero and Margaret W. Conkey, eds., *Engendering Archaeology: Women and Prehistory* (Oxford: Basil Blackwell, 1990), p. 46.

[4] More than one historical archaeologist voiced objection to the attempts of the New Archaeologists to turn archaeology into a hard science, among them William H. Adams, "Historical Archaeology: Science and Humanism," *North American Archaeologist* 1, no. 1 (1979–80): 85–96; and James Deetz, "Scientific Humanism and Humanistic Science: A Plea for Paradigmatic Pluralism in Historical Archaeology," *Geoscience and Man* 22 (1983): 27–34.

[5] See Anne Elizabeth Yentsch and Mary C. Beaudry, eds., *The Art and Mystery of Historical Archaeology: Essays in Honor of James Deetz* (Boca Raton, Fla.: CRC Press, 1992); Mary C. Beaudry, Lauren J. Cook, and Stephen A. Mrozowski, "Artifacts and Active Voices: Material Culture as Social Discourse," in Randall H. McGuire and Robert

oping sophisticated approaches to their analysis without abandoning the legacy of "dirt archaeology" will form the basis for reinventing historical archaeology as a discipline in its own right, one that no longer relies on either history or prehistoric archaeology for validation or for definition of appropriate or "significant" research goals.

"That's Not Archaeology"

Rethinking and reinvention in historical archaeology stem largely from newly forged approaches to documentary and material culture analysis. Garry Wheeler Stone in 1977 observed that "artifacts are not enough," and since then many of us have realized that, when dealing with historical culture, *archaeology* is not enough.[6] For many, the construction of context so necessary to interpreting historical sites and their settings as well as the artifacts and features we observe or recover from them involves the painstaking sort of material culture research for which institutions such as Winterthur are so highly regarded along with their innovative approaches to the written and pictorial record.

No longer do historical archaeologists find the old definition of "historical research" acceptable; for many, training in anthropology included training in the methods of ethnographic research. An ethnographic approach to documents draws on analytical methods developed by British social anthropologists such as Mary Douglas and interpretive cultural anthropologists such as Clifford Geertz. Douglas called for an "active voice theoretical approach" that shifted focus from mechanical, physical factors as governing human culture to a concern for human agency, diverse cultural goals, and different intentions within and be-

---

Paynter, eds., *The Archaeology of Inequality* (Oxford: Basil Blackwell, 1991); David V. Burley, "Function, Meaning, and Context: Ambiguities in Ceramic Use by the *Hivernant* Métis of the Northwestern Plains," *Historical Archaeology* 23, no. 1 (1989): 97–106; Adrian Praetzellis, Mary Praetzellis, and Marley R. Brown III, "Artifacts as Symbols of Identity: An Example from Sacramento's Gold Rush Era Chinatown Community," in Edward Staski, ed., *Living in Cities: Current Research in Urban Archaeology* (Tucson: Society for Historical Archaeology, 1987), pp. 38–47; Anne Yentsch, "Chesapeake Artefacts and Their Cultural Context: Pottery and the Food Domain," *Post-Medieval Archaeology* 25 (1991): 25–72.

[6] Garry Wheeler Stone, "Artifacts Are Not Enough," *Conference on Historic Sites Archaeology Papers 1976* 11 (1972): 43–63.

tween cultures; the method "consists in setting people's beliefs back into the social context of their lives, by careful, intensive field research."[7]

A fine illustration of a historian's use of ethnographic method is Rhys Isaac's analysis of Landon Carter's diary, which delved beneath the diarist's narrative of his dealings with his slaves to reveal the active strategies that Carter's slaves employed to negotiate and even to manipulate aspects of their relationship with their master. Similar methods have been applied to historical records by archaeologists who created ways of eliciting ethnographic data from both promising and unlikely sources—censuses, tax lists, probate inventories, military orderly books, farmers' accounts, letters, diaries, obituaries—that complement and augment their archaeological data. In some measure this trend parallels (and, one hopes, is enriched by) developments in historical circles, where anthropologically inspired histories such as Natalie Zemon Davis's *Return of Martin Guerre* or Robert Darnton's *Great Cat Massacre* have been in the vanguard of the "new cultural history."[8]

---

[7] Mary Douglas, "Passive Voice Theories in Religious Sociology," in Mary Douglas, ed., *In the Active Voice* (London: Routledge and Kegan Paul, 1982), p. 9 (Originally published in *Review of Religious Research* 21, no. 2 (1979): 51–61). See also Mary Douglas, *Purity and Danger: An Analysis of Concepts of Pollution and Taboo* (London: Routledge and Kegan Paul, 1966); Mary Douglas, *Natural Symbols: Explorations in Cosmology* (New York: Vintage Books, 1973); Mary Douglas, ed., *Rules and Meanings: The Anthropology of Everyday Knowledge* (Harmondsworth, Eng.: Penguin Books, 1973); Mary Douglas and Baron Isherwood, *The World of Goods: Toward an Anthropology of Consumption* (New York: W. W. Norton, 1979). The work of Pierre Bourdieu also has influenced the development of contextual approaches; see Pierre Bourdieu, *Outline of a Theory of Practice* (Cambridge, Eng.: Cambridge University Press, 1977); Pierre Bourdieu, *Distinction: A Social Critique of the Judgment of Taste*, trans. Richard Nice (Cambridge: Harvard University Press, 1984).

[8] Rhys Isaac, "Ethographic Method in History: An Action Approach," *Historical Methods* 13, no. 1 (1980): 43–61 (Reprinted in Robert B. St. George, ed., *Material Life in America, 1600–1860* [Boston: Northeastern University Press, 1988], pp. 39–61). Mary C. Beaudry, ed., *Documentary Archaeology in the New World* (Cambridge, Eng.: Cambridge University Press, 1983); Natalie Zemon Davis, *Return of Martin Guerre* (Cambridge: Harvard University Press, 1984); Robert Darnton, *The Great Cat Massacre and Other Episodes in French Cultural History* (New York: Basic Books, 1984). See also Lynn Hunt, ed., *The New Cultural History* (Berkeley: University of California Press, 1989). My use of the phrase "dialogue with the past" is based on the theme of a conference held in Davis's honor at Boston University in 1990. Folklorist Henry Glassie's sensitivity to the nuances of culture and scrupulous attention to ethnographic context in material culture analysis also have been influential; see especially Henry Glassie, *Passing the Time in Ballymenone: Culture and History in an Ulster Community* (Philadelphia: University of Pennyslvania Press, 1982).

But there is always opposition to the blurring of genres. In his discussion of how persons within fields such as anthropology act out of self-interest to preserve disciplinary boundaries against perceived encroachment, Dell Hymes called attention to the tendency to apply ideological and institutional—as opposed to intellectual—criteria of relevance to the work of those who charge the barriers (or, in current parlance, attempt to "expand the envelope"). While "productive scholars know that problems lead where they will and that relevance commonly leads across disciplinary boundaries," those who feel threatened by the ground shifting under their feet, who sense that the openness and expansiveness of creative scholarship threatens their niche as they have defined it, hasten to apply the label "that's not anthropology"—or, in our case, "that's not archaeology."[9]

Historical archaeologists who have challenged the accepted wisdom by becoming truly interdisciplinary in the intellectual as well as technical sense will find this negative sentiment all too familiar. Many have been ridiculed by old-guard positivists (practitioners of what was once the "New Archaeology" and is now more commonly known as "processual archaeology"), who remain unhappily suspicious of documents and anything that can be labeled "mentalist" (that is, studies concerned with symbolism, ritual in daily life, sentiment, or any other seemingly humanistic topic—the stock in trade, by the way, of much sociocultural anthropology!). It is heartening to note that most members of the new generation of historical archaeologists who pursue an interdisciplinary course remain uncowed by the fatal curse on their work—how many of us have heard it too many times?—"That's not archaeology!" or, even more frustrating, "That's not archaeological enough!"

Would the papers in this volume similarly fall victim to the kiss-of-death syndrome? Are they or are they not historical archaeology?

---

[9]Dell Hymes, "The Use of Anthropology: Critical, Political, Personal," in Hymes, *Reinventing Anthropology*, p. 44. Corollary to defining a field based on restrictions on practice is the insistence that disciplinary boundaries must be preserved to demarcate or to appropriate territory for the sole use of "licensed practitioners"; Kellner (in asking "Who owns history?") notes that the boundaries of academic disciplines "are all the more bitterly defended when criss-crossing becomes prevalent" (Hans Kellner, *Language and Historical Representation: Getting the Story Crooked* [Madison: University of Wisconsin Press, 1989], pp. x–xi). I am grateful to Lauren J. Cook for bringing this source to my attention.

Does use of documents and material culture to construct context or to elucidate the archaeological record mean that you are doing something other than archaeology? Is archaeology only dirt, only excavation? To rephrase the question, is it a specific technique or practice that makes what we do archaeology, or is it a shared intellectual process and a shared goal? The title of the 1991 conference, Historical Archaeology and the Study of American Culture, provides a clue to what I think the answer should be. Our goal is to study culture, American culture writ large, the culture of slaves and free blacks, of immigrants and working people, of colonial elites and industrial capitalists. Archaeology is an approach to this study, and we all know that an archaeological approach can be applied as readily to documents, landscapes, and aboveground material culture as it can to things buried in the ground.

As Suzanne Spencer-Wood notes, analysis of excavated data is not necessarily what makes our work archaeological. Or, as Lewis Binford put it, archaeology is not so much a process of discovery as it is one of interpretation. The papers in this volume demonstrate that there are many lines of investigation, multiple scales of analysis, and manifold sources of data.[10]

Definitions of Culture

A common theme in recent scholarship in historical archaeology is a rejection of the strictly materialist notion of culture embodied in the New Archaeology's definition of culture as "man's extra-somatic means of adaptation." A different definition of culture has prevailed; it views culture as grounded in systems of meaning for which material culture serves as expression, medium, sign, or symbol. Culture is seen as "the shared meanings, practices, and symbols that constitute the human

---

[10] Lewis R. Binford, *In Pursuit of the Past: Decoding the Archaeological Record* (London: Thames and Hudson, 1988), p. 1. I suspect that Binford would not wholly approve of my using this statement to support this point, but I think it argues persuasively in its favor. See also Robert W. Preucel, ed., "Processual and Post-Processual Archaeologies: Multiple Ways of Knowing the Past," *Center for Archaeological Studies, Occasional Paper No. 10* (Carbondale: Southern Illinois University Press, 1991).

world."[11] Meaning is negotiated through human interaction, and hence culture is not static, not a mental template or an expression of universal human psyche or universal adaptive pattern. Culture is seen as active, as something people invent and reinvent in daily life.

This active view of culture is to be found throughout the papers that appear in this volume. Some of the authors have been explicit about it, others have not. The focus on human actors, on humans as active agents in shaping their world and in negotiating meaning through the shared yet multivalent communicative medium of material culture, has several implications for the direction of our research.

The first of these has been a reorientation of documentary research away from treatment of the historical record as received wisdom, as the dry tool for constructing site-specific histories. It is probably shocking for historians to learn that archaeologists could ever have held such little regard for written sources, but they did, and, what is worse, some still do. Bruce Trigger's analysis of how this came about helps to clarify the matter. He notes that in the late 1950s and early 1960s, American archaeologists attempted to dissociate themselves from their predecessors, whose efforts had been aimed largely at constructing culture histories of particular geographic regions. The New Archaeologists wanted to do science, which, in a series of highly polemical position statements, they contrasted with earlier anthropologists' cultural historical work. "As a result of such arguments, a growing number of archaeologists identified scientific studies with generalizations, evolutionism, and ecology, while history was equated with a mechanical interest in chronologies and with attributing changes to historical accidents. Hence history came to be viewed as the opposite of science; and as descriptive rather than explanatory."[12] This suggests that the New Archaeologists derived their definition of history from what they saw of its practice among anthropologists; it was not based on history as defined and practiced by historians. Sadly, the perpetuation of this misperception, this artificial dichotomy, stunted the growth of historical archaeology by

---

[11] Lewis R. Binford, "Archaeology as Anthropology," *American Antiquity* 28 (1962): 217–25; Paul Rabinow and William M. Sullivan, "The Interpretive Turn: A Second Look," in Paul Rabinow and William M. Sullivan, eds., *Interpretive Social Science: A Second Look* (Berkeley: University of California Press, 1987), pp. 7–8.

[12] Trigger, "History and Contemporary American Archaeology," p. 22.

encouraging many of its practitioners to devalue and at times to reject their most valuable asset—the historical record.

What we have seen happening as historical archaeology matures is prompted in part by the development of interest in history on the part of anthropologists and a concomitant interest in culture, if not in anthropology, on the part of historians. To this end, archaeologists have taken an ethnographic approach to documents, seeking to address cultural questions in conjunction with historical ones and, using a variety of analytical techniques drawn from linguistics, literary theory, semiotics, demography, and so forth, have looked at documents as texts to be read critically for what they reveal inadvertently as much as for what they say openly.

A similarly ethnographic approach to sites and artifacts is an outgrowth of historical archaeologists' new attitude toward documents. This finds expression in concern for how artifacts were used and how sites were formed. Once again it is human action and the negotiation of cultural meaning in social contexts that is central.

Reinvention Embodied

The essays in this volume exemplify the reinvention of historical archaeology in many ways. Primary among these is a conscious expansion, a deliberate blurring of genres with the aim of redefining historical archaeology as an interdisciplinary field in its own right. Anthropologist Clifford Geertz argues that blurred genres have become the natural condition of things, leading to significant realignments in scholarly affinities, especially in who borrows what from whom. Such blurring has altered our view of what counts as science; hence, it is not just theory or method or subject matter that alters but the whole point of the enterprise. I see this as an apt characterization of what is taking place in historical archaeology; as more and more practitioners turn to interpretive, contextual approaches, a shift in goals is inevitable. Richly detailed case studies will no longer be seen as particularistic and unscientific; the debate over whether historical archaeology is history, anthropology, science, or humanity will fade into embarrassing irrelevance as we acknowledge that our field is all of the above, all at once, and that its power and vitality arises out of its inclusiveness.[13]

A splendid illustration of this is John Worrell, Myron Stachiw, and David Simmons's exhortation for us to broaden our definition of historical archaeology, as well as our investigative process, using all the direct and indirect means at our disposal. Making powerful statements about the past is possible through a synergistic approach that combines and integrates converging lines of evidence; the majority of authors in this volume—especially Stephen A. Mrozowski, Gerald K. Kelso, and Martha Zierden—affirm the richness and vitality afforded by the interdisciplinary approach that almost by definition historical archaeology requires.

The details of human life are as important as the broader generalities, and placing human actors in the social and historical context adds "drama to the flatly generic narrative." The Old Sturbridge Village approach and case study of the Emerson Bixby site provide us with a richly textured and highly nuanced account of a family, a neighborhood, a community. The threads of the narrative were not woven simply from the raw fibers of documents, dirt, artifacts, houses, plant remains, animal bones, and secondary histories. The scale and scope of investigation that resulted in the sophisticated, compelling, and dense weave of the narrative we read was possible through team effort and long-term institutional support. The Bixby case study serves as prima facie evidence that the effort expended striving for local knowledge, in telling particular stories not by making them up but by piecing them together, rewards us well beyond the specific and proves "there is nothing about a localized history that dooms it to parochialism."[14]

[13] Clifford Geertz, *Local Knowledge: Further Essays in Interpretive Anthropology* (New York: Basic Books, 1983), p. 8. This long-winded and tendentious debate found its most recent incarnation in a plenary session at the 1987 annual meetings of the Society for Historical Archaeology. See Nicholas Honerkamp, ed., "Questions That Count in Historical Archaeology: Plenary Session, 1987 Meeting of the Society for Historical Archaeology Conference on Historical and Underwater Archaeology, Savannah, Georgia," *Historical Archaeology* 22, no. 1 (1988): 5–42.

[14] Jan Davidson, "Blacksmithing in Western North Carolina: A Folklore and History Project at an Appalachian Museum" (Ph.D. diss., Boston University, 1992), p. 37. By "local knowledge" Geertz refers to the internal logic, or common sense, of a particular culture—he feels this is the key subject of anthropological inquiry: "the interpretive study of culture represents an attempt to come to terms with the diversity of the ways human beings construct their lives in the act of leading them" (Geertz, *Local Knowledge*, p. 16).

Scholars working on their own with limited funding lack the advantages of the Old Sturbridge Village team, but their work nevertheless contributes along several dimensions of our multistranded effort. Paul R. Mullins's study of mechanisms of change among potters in Rockingham County, Virginia, offers an example of how textual analysis can help to establish a context for subsequent interpretation of sites and artifacts. His study is valuable because, in taking a Marxist perspective, Mullins makes issues of class a focus of his analysis. He does so without recourse to the notion of dominant ideologies but instead seeks to examine the organization of labor from the perspective of nondominants. In so doing, he shows that workers adopted a diverse range of social identities and played an active role in constructing these identities within the broader confines of industrial capitalism.

Spencer-Wood recognizes that contemporary feminist theory is an outgrowth of interpretive social science.[15] It is an especially valuable perspective because it constitutes an active critique not just of bias in scholarship and its practice but also of prevalent modes of scholarly discourse. It shares with interpretive theories a concern for multiple meanings and multiple voices. Feminist theory critiques social theory, and it also critiques itself to reveal how the cultural construction of gender permeates the way we conceptualize the past every bit as much as it does the way we go about studying it. Of special interest in Spencer-Wood's study of domestic reform is the clear exposition of the ways in which domestic reformers self-consciously employed the enculturative and didactic qualities of artifacts as agents of the reform process. Here is a compelling instance of "artifacts in action," of at

---

In an interesting permutation of Geertz's formulation, French archaeologist Jean-Claude Gardin has used this conceptual framework to characterize "ways of knowing" and processes of inference in archaeology (that is, "universal" orders of knowledge "go without saying"—they are "natural" and "self-evident,"—while "local" orders of knowledge are relative, context-bound, and open to question, thereby requiring evidentiary justification); see Jean-Claude Gardin, "The Rôle of 'Local Knowledge' in Archaeological Interpretation," in Stephen Shennan, ed., *Archaeological Approaches to Cultural Identity* (London: Unwin Hyman, 1989), pp. 110–22.

[15] See, for example, Michelle Z. Rosaldo, "Moral/Analytic Dilemmas Posed by the Intersection of Feminism and Social Science," in Rabinow and Sullivan, *Interpretive Social Science*, pp. 280–301. Note that I am making a distinction between *feminism* and its manifestations since the nineteenth century and its incarnation as *feminist theory* in contemporary social science theory.

least a belief in the power of material culture to influence and perhaps even to control social action.

A similar theme emerges in Ann Smart Martin's discussion of teawares as social props and cues designed to elicit appropriate responses and behaviors within a highly charged meaning system embodied by an almost universal domestic social ritual—tea drinking.[16] Her chief concern, however, is *acquisition:* how do people find out about what to purchase? How do they go about making choices as consumers? What do such choices tell us about the social contexts in which objects functioned?

Consumption: Expressing "What Happened Afterwards in the Active Voice"

Such questions are addressed in one way or another by several of the essays in this volume, and this is far from surprising; consumption and consumer choice are areas of material culture analysis that are of major import for many historical archaeologists. Anthropologist Mary Douglas has written extensively of goods as a system of communication; she notes:

goods, money and food are . . . all media in which people make statements about their life. Sometimes they know what they want to say and the statement comes out clear, in the active voice. Sometimes they want to say two things at once or to maintain two contradictory attitudes. Then the statements are oblique or confused. Then we have more problem in interpreting them. A helpful procedure is to look for a way in which to express what happened afterwards in the active voice. Not that they were excluded, not that they were misunderstood, neglected or misread; the exercise is to ask whether style and

---

[16] As Martin rightly notes, tea drinking and use of teawares have thus been a focus of interest among material culture researchers and historical archaeologists, including some of my early efforts. See Mary C. Beaudry, "A Study of Ceramics in York County, Virginia, Inventories, 1730–1750" (Master's thesis, Brown University, 1975); Mary C. Beaudry, "A Preliminary Study of Ceramics in York County, Virginia, Inventories, 1730–1750: The Tea Service," *Conference on Historic Site Archaeology Papers 1977* 12 (1978): 201–10.

message did not combine to give exactly the effect that was intended and received.[17]

Douglas's approach to commodities, which she terms *active voice* analysis, emphasizes communication, negotiation, and manipulation; it coalesces nicely with more recent formulations of material culture as manifestations of discourse. Discourse analysis in archaeology selectively adopts strategies from various theories of literary criticism by considering artifacts and the archaeological record as "texts" to be read critically to examine outright intended messages as well as ambiguous meanings for users as well as producers; it incorporates elements of performance theory and in some cases feminist theory (particularly its call for integration of multiple voices and differing perspectives), and it places emphasis on multiple meanings of material culture, on the nuances that only highly contextualized studies can provide.[18]

The issue of how vessels functioned in their cultural context is

---

[17] Mary Douglas, "Preface," in *In the Active Voice*, p. x. See also Douglas and Isherwood, *World of Goods*; Suzanne Spencer-Wood, ed., *Consumer Choice in Historical Archaeology* (New York: Plenum Press, 1987); Terry H. Klein and Charles H. LeeDecker, eds., "Models for the Study of Consumer Behavior," *Historical Archaeology* 25, no. 2 (1991): 1–91. The studies in these edited collections emphasize the effects that factors such as wealth, status, and ethnicity have on consumer choice, touching very little, if at all, on the intended and actual uses to which goods are put, practically or symbolically, by those who acquire them. Examples of alternative approaches are offered in *Historical Archaeology* 26, no. 3, Meanings and Uses of Material Culture, ed. Barbara J. Little and Paul A. Shackel (1992). The majority of essays in this volume employ a variant of Euro-Marxist critical theory, dominant ideology thesis, presenting instances of how ideologically charged artifacts may be said to "act back" (through a quality referred to as *recursivity*) on their users not just to give form to but, literally, to control human social life. Dominant ideology theory thus offers a narrow view of the transformative properties of material culture; other perspectives (for example, those offered in this volume) fall more within the realm of interpretive social science and give greater attention to negotiation, mediation, and discourse.

[18] Among the scholars who have been influential in this regard are literary theorist Paul Ricoeur and social theorist Anthony Giddens. See Paul Ricoeur, *Time and Narrative*, 3 vols. (Chicago: University of Chicago Press, 1984–87); J. Thompson, ed., *Paul Ricoeur: Hermeneutics and the Human Sciences* (Cambridge, Eng.: Cambridge University Press, 1982); Anthony Giddens, *A Contemporary Critique of Historical Materialism*, vol. 1, *Power, Property, and the State* (1981; reprint, Berkeley: University of California Press, 1987). Examples of discourse analysis in historical archaeology include Beaudry, Cook, and Mrozowski, "Artifacts and Active Voices"; Martin Hall, "High and Low in the Townscapes of Dutch South America and South Africa: The Dialectics of Material Culture," *Social Dynamics* 17, no. 2 (1991): 41–75; Yvonne Brink, "Places of Discourse and Dialogue: A Study in the Material Culture of the Cape during the Rule of the Dutch East India Company, 1652–1795" (Ph.D. diss., University of Cape Town, S. Afr., 1992).

taken up by Martin in her analysis of teawares in Bedford County, Virginia, probate inventories. She merges interest in patterns of consumer choice with a semiotic analysis of the meaning of material culture. What Martin attempts to capture is very much "a way in which to express what happened afterwards in the active voice," to provide a context for interpreting material culture. The approach provides a way of comprehending how the meanings, implicit or explicit, of artifacts within the contexts of behavior and cultural communication—what she alludes to as the writing, rewriting, and performance of social scripts—affected the acquisition of goods.

At a more specific level, Jane Perkins Claney's survey of the use of Rockingham ware is an example of a contextual study focusing on functional analysis of vessel form that reveals the very specialized nature of the use of this ware. The occurrence of Rockingham ware on archaeological sites shows that consumer preference affected production and that cost was not the major concern affecting the decision to purchase Rockingham teapots, spittoons, and so forth. Claney's study provides a cautionary tale for those who would evaluate ceramics on archaeological sites solely economically. It is as important to know what people did with things as it is to know what they paid for them.

Linda Welters, Margaret Ordoñez, Kathryn Tarleton, and Joyce Smith examine a category of material culture rarely excavated from archaeological sites—textiles. They draw attention to what we do not find and emphasize that items such as textiles were highly important as aspects of cultural systems even though they almost never appear in archaeological context (thereby following Stone's lead). In examining European textiles from Native American graves, the authors demonstrate compellingly how the application of specialized technical analysis permits a close reading of the archaeological evidence, revealing the cultural significance of textiles as substitutes for furs (noting the irony of the situation in which exchange of peltry for trade goods rendered furs increasingly scarce in the indigenous culture, thereby exacerbating the need to replace them with European textiles), as wrappings for a variety of goods, and as items of clothing, bedding, and so forth. Furthermore, the presence of fly larvae trapped within the woven fibers can be interpreted as indirect evidence of burial ritual.[19]

---

[19]The need to consider artifacts that do not survive in the ground, especially pewter, is discussed by Mary C. Beaudry et al., "The Potomac Typological System: A Vessel

With its emphasis on the active role that Native Americans played as consumers exercising choice and selectivity in their acquisition of European goods, this study underscores what so often gets overlooked in economic studies of consumption, especially when the fur trade is involved: that consumer choice inevitably originates from *intention*, from the cultural actors' awareness of the active ways that goods will convey meaning to those around them. Mrozowski elaborates on this in his essay, making the point that the "resiliency" of Native American culture was not based solely in modes of reacting and adapting to European culture but was actively generated out of deliberate choices, through native mediation and negotiation of European ideas and goods with their own, through accommodation, and through selective adoption and incorporation of elements of the so-called dominant culture into the traditional structure of Native American culture.[20]

At times our studies do not achieve the biographical immediacy of the Bixby project described by Worrell, Stachiw, and Simmons because that degree of detail and even intimacy with the past is denied

---

Typology for Ceramics from Seventeenth-Century Virginia," *Historical Archaeology* 17, no. 1 (1983): 24–25. This theme is expanded in Ann Smart Martin, "The Role of Pewter as Missing Artifact," *Historical Archaeology* 23, no. 2 (1989): 1–27. Apparently in this instance species identification was not possible; since certain fly species appear in the corpse almost immediately after death, the presence of fly maggots may not in all cases represent a passage of time indicative of a lengthy "laying out" period before burial. Data on fly species and growth stage also are used by forensic experts to determine season of death; such evidence from an archaeological context might serve as corroboration for similar lines of evidence for season of interment derived, for example, from palynological data. See also William M. Bass, "Time Interval since Death," in Ted A. Rathbun and Jane E. Buikstra, *Human Identification: Case Studies in Forensic Anthropology* (Springfield, Ill.: C. C. Thomas, 1984), pp. 136–47.

[20]The mechanisms at work in episodes of cultural interaction whereby transformation is effected through incorporation of nontraditional elements into the existing structure of indigenous culture has been extensively explored in the work of Marshall Sahlins. See Marshall Sahlins, "Historical Metaphors and Mythical Realities: Structure in the Early History of the Sandwich Islands Kingdom," in *Association for Social Anthropology in Oceania Special Publications No.* 1 (Ann Arbor: University of Michigan Press, 1981); Marshall Sahlins, *Islands of History* (Chicago: University of Chicago Press, 1985); Patrick V. Kirch and Marshall Sahlins, *Anahulu: The Anthropology of History in the Kingdom of Hawaii*, 2 vols. (Chicago: University of Chicago Press, 1992). Sahlins expressed many of the same dissatisfactions with structuralism outlined by Mrozowski in this volume and rejected its ahistorical and decontextualized approach. The result is an intriguing and provocative amalgam—poststructuralist historical anthropology grounded in historical *and* cultural materialism.

us. Such, perhaps, is often the case in the study of the lives of enslaved African Americans. Here (to borrow from Worrell, Stachiw, and Simmons) we confront issues of cultural distance that are especially difficult to transcend. Yet we should not hesitate to make the effort, for sometimes it is the seemingly most ephemeral details that allow us truly to bridge cultural time and distance to "lend drama to the flatly generic narrative." The archaeological evidence of the lives of slaves is compelling and immediate; it complements the work of scholars such as Herbert Gutman and Charles Joyner in making vivid the everyday struggles and possibilities of African Americans who created their worlds separate from, yet enmeshed with, the dominant culture. Artifacts of conjury and evidence of economic possibilities as part of slave life do not constitute an apology for slavery, nor do they alter reality in any way. Understanding these objects in cultural context, however, perhaps helps to remedy certain cultural biases implicit in a strictly materialist conceptualization of culture. An active view of culture allows nondominant members of society a role in creating their culture and in negotiating meaning through mechanisms other than passivity or simple resistance. The power of makers and users of objects to invest material items with multiple and at times subversive meanings must be taken into consideration.[21] It is clear that the archaeology of slavery has sociopolitical implications beyond the confines of archaeology, but the contributions of our work to correcting notions that slavery as a condition somehow restricted or curtailed African American "culture" are among the best our field has to offer.

The efforts of Charles E. Orser, Jr., to situate the interpretation of artifacts recovered from sites of enslaved Africans within a world systems perspective through network analysis embroils him in the thorny issue of how slaves acquired goods (as rations, as hand-me-

---

[21] Herbert G. Gutman, *The Black Family in Slavery and Freedom, 1750–1925* (New York: Vintage Books, 1977); Charles W. Joyner, *Down by the Riverside: A South Carolina Slave Community* (Urbana: University of Illinois Press, 1984); Mechal Sobal, *The World They Made Together: Black and White Values in Eighteenth-Century Virginia* (Princeton: Princeton University Press, 1987); Edward D. C. Campbell, Jr., with Kym S. Rice, eds., *Before Freedom Came: African-American Life in the Antebellum South* (Richmond and Charlottesville: Museum of the Confederacy and the University Press of Virginia, 1991). See also Martin Hall, "Small Things and the 'Mobile, Conflictual Fusion of Fear, Power, and Desire,'" in Yentsch and Beaudry, *Art and Mystery*, pp. 373–99.

downs, through barter, or through purchase). His concern for relations over attributes is clearly one shared by others, including Martin and Claney in this volume, neither of whom fall into the trap of conflating the social characteristics of commodities with their attributes. Orser's sense of dissatisfaction about his inability to pinpoint the nodes in the acquisition network seems to arise from problems in the comparative method he adopts. The chief shortcoming of decontextualized statistical or even simple numerical comparison is that it forces the investigator to argue back toward context (for example, "maybe we can explain these differences/similarities by going back and looking at what's going on at our site"). This could be overcome by closer attention to context at the outset. What is more, the impasse imposed by our inability to define precisely how slaves acquired commodities might be circumvented by paying more attention to *using* rather than getting (the approach taken by Martin and Claney). While network analysis is an important component of the study of commodities, our understanding of slave life is vastly enriched only when we apply ourselves to a close reading of how commodities were transformed into meaningful as well as useful items in everyday life.[22]

It is clear that "freedom" to participate, albeit in a severely limited sense, in capitalist exchange relations did nothing at all to alter the

----

[22] Paying closer attention to context is how I interpret Robert Schuyler's recommendation that we take care to understand local contexts through constructing historical ethnographies; my understanding of Schuyler's piece is not that we should eschew a global perspective nor that the approach he recommends precludes consideration of global systems. Rather, as Orser notes, we profit more from *contextualized* global comparisons such as those offered in the work of Martin Hall than we do from decontextualized comparison of attributes of world systems such as those proposed by Deetz. See Robert L. Schuyler, "Archaeological Remains, Documents, and Anthropology: A Call for a New Culture History," *Historical Archaeology* 22, no. 1 (1988): 36–42. Hall, "High and Low"; James Deetz, "Archaeological Evidence of Sixteenth- and Seventeenth-Century Encounters," in Lisa Falk, ed., *Historical Archaeology in Global Perspective* (Washington, D.C.: Smithsonian Institution Press, 1991); Mary C. Beaudry, "Historical Archaeology: Local Contexts, Global Perspectives" (Keynote address delivered to the Australian Society for Historical Archaeology 12th annual meetings, Sydney, November 9, 1992). Many historical archaeologists have taken their analyses in this direction; see Leland Ferguson, "Medicine, Meaning, and Tension on South Carolina Plantations" (Paper presented at the 80th annual meetings of the American Anthropological Association, San Francisco, December 6, 1992); and Larry McKee, "The Ideals and Realities behind the Design and Use of Nineteenth-Century Virginia Slave Cabins," in Yentsch and Beaudry, *Art and Mystery*, pp. 195–214.

social and physical realities of slavery. Nevertheless, the cultural implications of the evidence emerging from the archaeological and documentary study of slave sites are manifold. The evidence explodes all the old assumptions about acculturation, assimilation, and cultural disintegration; archaeologists for too long have restricted themselves to the material basis of culture in examining processes of culture contact and interaction, too often concluding that failure to detect continuities in material culture indicates greater or lesser degrees of acculturation or assimilation, or even the death, destruction, or disappearance of a culture. Anthropologists now realize that culture dies only when all members of a culture are exterminated; under conditions of servitude and imposed degradation in varied colonial contexts, African Americans continued as cultural actors, adapting to new environments and situations while drawing on remembered customs and beliefs, inventing new cultures (or many subcultures) through creative recombination and manipulation of elements from diverse African backgrounds.

The Biggest Artifact of All

Landscape archaeology is another domain of our research that has benefited from a dynamic approach to cultural analysis. No longer seen as static and slow to change, landscapes, both urban and rural, are seen as shifting and as having multiple meanings for their makers and users. Also of increasing interest has been attention to inadvertent as well as intentional landscape change; "landscape archaeology" thus encompasses the study of human use, misuse, or neglect of the landscape (including environmental history) and the study of the built environment, as well as the examination and interpretation of intentional, formalized landscaping efforts (the archaeology of formal gardens). As Anne Yentsch so rightly notes, landscape archaeology is a gloss for "close attention to place" that is an inevitable result of the interpretive, contextual turn in historical archaeology.[23]

[23] Anne Elizabeth Yentsch, "Close Attention to Place: Landscape Studies by Historical Archaeologists," in Rebecca Yamin and Karen B. Metheny, eds., *Landscape Archaeology: Studies in Reading and Interpreting the American Historical Landscape* (Knoxville: University of Tennessee Press, forthcoming 1996).

Archaeologists' ability to interpret landscapes in these ways stems from perceptual as well as technical shifts. We no longer tend to accept that landscape is static or that it should be interpreted from the perspective of dominant ideologies whereby attention narrows to meaning assigned to landscapes only by elites (with the assumption that nonelites received this meaning passively). Social use of landscape, as the essays by Kelso, Eric Sandweiss, J. Ritchie Garrison, and Zierden illustrate, is complex, layered with multiple meanings and every bit as amenable to "action" or discourse analysis as are artifacts and documents.

Kelso's brilliant use of pollen analysis exemplifies the best of what archaeologists term *middle-range theory*—linking the statics of the archaeological record to natural and cultural factors that shaped it. Middle-range research was developed to bridge the gap between the unremitting particulars of the archaeological record (potsherds, pollen grains, soil chemistry, seeds, bones) and the broader generalizations most archaeologists seek by providing a means of delineating and modeling the effects of specific past human behaviors as well as specific past and current natural processes that operate in combination to produce the archaeological record that we excavate in the present.[24] Kelso achieves the transition from pollen grains to human agency through an integrative, interdisciplinary approach akin to the synergistic approach outlined by Worrell, Stachiw, and Simmons.

Sandweiss formulates a conceptual model of the urban landscape analysis that is essentially binary in form, readily acknowledging the influence of Deetz and Glassie's structuralist approach. Few historical archaeologists embrace the structuralist program quite so wholeheartedly (see, for instance, Mrozowski's essay in this volume)—not even any of the contributors to a recent Festschrift for Deetz—but Sandweiss's scheme is not rigid and does allow for human agency.

Sandweiss notes that "change, variety, and instability are constant in all stages of urban growth," claiming their presence is a "hallmark of the urban landscape." This is incontrovertibly true, as the essays by Sandweiss, Kelso, Mrozowski, and Zierden amply demonstrate, but reading the contributions by Garrison and by Worrell, Stachiw, and Simmons strengthens my conviction that change, variety, and instabil-

----

[24] Michael B. Schiffer, *Formation Processes of the Archaeological Record* (Albuquerque: University of New Mexico Press, 1987).

ity comprise the hallmark of rural landscapes as much as they do that of cities.[25] Human and land relationships at any level of complexity are dynamic; transformation and change occur within the framework of tradition, and incremental change occurs within stasis or equilibrium, which in turn is interrupted or punctuated at unpredictable intervals. Perhaps what intrigues me most in reflecting on Sandweiss's attempt to find a way to examine the urban landscape as a state of mind, as an entity whose visible or tangible form gives form to human lives, is that the ideology of change and variability penetrates the ethos of urban dwellers while the ethos of country dwellers, equally as busy altering their landscape, is more often imbued with and espouses values of tradition and stability.

We carry this dichotomy of urban versus rural into our scholarly practice, often using such distinctions to justify applying different archaeological methods to the study of rural and urban sites. Yet the Old Sturbridge Village study of the rural neighborhood of Barre Four Corners, Massachusetts, and Zierden's synthesis of archaeological data from Charleston, South Carolina, show that urban and rural sites are subject to similar actions—site preparation, landfilling, utility installation, and so forth—intended to meet the practical and social needs of their owners. Zierden's treatment of Charleston's urban landscape demonstrates the richness of a transdisciplinary historical archaeology that goes beyond looking at artifacts in feature fill to address the multiple factors at work in urban site formation processes. Zierden's ability to link grand and subtle landscape change to the households whose actions these reflect is elegant proof that the integrated, synergistic approach described by Worrell, Stachiw, and Simmons is readily applicable to urban sites.[26] When urban archaeology is performed in a con-

---

[25] My research at the Spencer-Pierce-Little Farm in Newbury, Mass. (in progress), shows this to be the case; papers presented at a symposium, "Unnatural Acts: Deciphering Historical Alteration of the Natural Environment," organized by Martha Lance at the Society for Historical Archaeology meetings, Kansas City, Mo. (January 9, 1993) confirm and expand on this observation.

[26] Zierden notes, however, that urban dwellers are often compelled to comply with the dictates of municipal ordinances and improvement campaigns, strictures that seldom confront country dwellers. For discussion of the archaeological impact of city ordinances, see Nicholas Honerkamp and Charles H. Fairbanks, "Definition of Site Formation Processes in Urban Contexts," *American Archaeology* 4, no. 1 (1985): 60–66; Mary Praetzellis, Adrian Praetzellis, and Marley R. Brown III, "What Happened to the Silent

textual framework, the reward—a greater understanding of people as cultural actors—is more gratifying and far more engaging than decontextualized comparisons of artifact counts.

Whose Traditions? Shaking Up Myths

Garrison's essay and, to a certain extent, Zierden's, share a point in common that I see in several other essays in this volume and throughout much of historical archaeology today. This is the role of historical archaeology in constructing as well as confronting and debunking myths and mythic history. Garrison approaches this in the realm of agricultural landscapes, noting that barnyards were action-oriented spaces requiring frequent remodeling in response to the concerns and interest of farmers and farm families. Our notions of agricultural conservatism and of stable, traditional agricultural landscapes are exploded by the reality of what Garrison's work brings to light—farmers acted in response to contemporary needs and readily dropped traditional ways of doing things if old ways did not serve.

Zierden likewise addresses the issue of myth, of ideals versus reality. The walking city of the late twentieth-century yuppie is a far cry from the cityscape of the colonial era in sights, sounds, smells, and spaces. Yet contemporary notions, including those embedded in preservation philosophy, perceive the twentieth-century vision as a crystallization or recapturing of a past as we know it, or at least think we know it. There is, of course, nothing really wrong with twentieth-century urban dwellers reshaping the past with their environment to serve contemporary needs, but it brings the archaeologist as myth-buster into confrontation with a whole series of problems. Most garden clubs,

---

Majority? Research Strategies for Studying Dominant Group Material Culture in Late Nineteenth-Century California," in Beaudry, *Documentary Archaeology*, pp. 201–2. Country and city dwellers alike are subject to the vicissitudes of natural and other disasters—the results of which, with cleanup, prevention, and rebuilding efforts, leave distinctive archaeological traces; see Adrian Praetzellis and Mary Praetzellis, "Faces and Facades: Victorian Ideology in Early Sacramento," in Yentsch and Beaudry, *Art and Mystery*, pp. 75–99; Geneviève Duguay, "Illustrated Retrospective: The History of the Terrace," in *Under the Boardwalk in Québec City: Archaeology in the Courtyard and Gardens of the Château Saint-Louis*, under the direction of Pierre Beaudet (Sillery, Québec: Editions du Septentrion, 1990), pp. 185–86.

historical societies or house museums, or even government agencies, cherish a view of the past that they are loathe to abandon merely because the archaeologist offers evidence to the contrary.[27]

Similarly, the Old Sturbridge Village research into tradition and transformation in rural New England, discussed by Worrell, Stachiw, and Simmons, reveals how rural people incorporated change into traditional agrarian lifeways by adapting their income strategies, by incorporation of selected elements of industrial production, and by selective purchase of industrial goods.[28] What is more, the Barre Four Corners study further illustrates how variable the character of rural agrarian life could be even without the pressure of the transformative influences of the industrial revolution.

Considerable recent scholarship has been devoted to exposing the easy fallacies of assumptions about the nature of historical culture, specifically the tendency for historians and archaeologists to characterize aspects of culture, as well as cultural actors, in fixed dichotomies such as rural versus urban, traditional versus progressive, dominant versus passive, and so forth. Spencer-Wood's feminist rejection of stereotypical formulations of gender roles in archaeological research exposes yet another false dichotomy: the Victorian ideology of separate spheres for men and women that slipped into scholarly discourse virtually unchallenged to emerge as a historical truism. Historical archaeologists are far from alone in their uncritical adherence to what British historian Amanda Vickery characterizes as "this crippling model of domesticated femininity" based on the initial key concepts of recent women's history ("domesticity," "public and private," "separate spheres") that focused on the lives of middle-class women in the industrializing West.[29] A shift in focus from totalizing generalizations to

---

[27] See Dell Upton, "The City as Material Culture," in Yentsch and Beaudry, *Art and Mystery*, pp. 51–74; Anne Yentsch, "Legends, Houses, Families, and Myths: Relationships between Material Culture and American Ideology," in Beaudry, *Documentary Archaeology*, pp. 5–19.

[28] See also Leslie C. Stewart-Abernathy, "Industrial Goods in the Service of Tradition: Consumption and Cognition on an Ozark Farmstead before the Great War," in Yentsch and Beaudry, *Art and Mystery*, pp. 101–26.

[29] Amanda Vickery, "Shaking the Separate Spheres: Did Women Really Descend into Graceful Indolence?" *Times Literary Supplement* (London), March 12, 1993. See also Judith A. Megaw, "No Passive Victims, No Separate Spheres: A Feminist Perspective on Technology's History," in S. H. Cutcliff and R. C. Post, eds., *In Context: History*

contextual analysis emphasizes what people were actually doing in their lives and readily offers a challenge to the mythic constructions that even scholars are capable of accepting calmly and without question.

Conclusion

While historical archaeology as we practice it today does have the potential to bring to light heretofore unknown—or, more properly, unseen or misperceived—facets of the historical past, its greatest potential does not lie in its ability to contribute in a major and meaningful way to what are referred to as "important issues in history"—unless it is cultural, ethnographic history we are talking about—or to our understanding of sweeping and amorphous cultural processes. Rather, it lies in its ability to inform us of the intimate and unheralded details of day-to-day life through the minute inspection of written clues as well as grains of dirt, artifacts, and features of all shapes, sizes, and descriptions to help us bring to light and to understand the life history of one site and its inhabitants, and then of another, and another, such that we gradually construct a more and more complex mosaic by putting together our many individual cases. It is then that we can do what we do best. As novelists and poets know, it is in the very particularity of individual experience that a broader understanding of the human experience is to be found.

Reinvention of historical archaeology has permitted us to shift our attention from totalizing frameworks and to focus on cultural actors. A reinvented historical archaeology moves freely across disciplinary boundaries, but it does not reject the old positivist, cultural materialist approach in its entirety; in fact, the emphasis placed on *context* in all its manifestations necessarily fosters a grounded empiricism and an openness to scientific procedures and technical analyses. An interpretive, contextual archaeology is not reductionist or formulaic but rather inclusive, open-ended, and self-critical. Historical archaeology in this

---

and the History of Technology: Essays in Honor of Melvin Kranzberg (Bethlehem, Pa.: Lehigh University Press, 1989), pp. 172–91; Linda K. Kerber, "Separate Spheres, Female Worlds, Woman's Place: The Rhetoric of Women's History," *Journal of American History* 75, no. 1 (1988): 9–39.

mode stresses internal cultural logic through "active voice"—indeed, multiple voice—interpretation of artifacts, features, sites, and landscapes; is attentive to nuance, ambiguity, and variability; and acknowledges and welcomes complexity—cultural complexity as well as complexity in the archaeological record.

A definition of culture as active, as constituted in meaning and expressed in words and actions as well as in things, encourages and makes this possible; for, by its very nature it requires us to acknowledge multiple meanings and readings and to seek them out. Hence an admittedly positivist and empiricist attention to the minutiae of potsherds, pollen grains, seeds, and site sediments is far from incompatible with theoretical perspectives that address symbols and ideology in everyday custom and practice. An interpretive approach impels us toward the multifaceted consideration of all aspects of our sites and their contexts—historical, cultural, and environmental—so that we can arrive at a point where the lines of evidence begin to coalesce and point toward meaning. We have it in our power to obtain intimate understanding not just of what happened in the dirt but of the everyday context of human life. It is in this regard that historical archaeologists may be seen as working together and with their colleagues in allied fields toward redefining and reinventing historical archaeology.